19th Edition

How to File for
Chapter 7
Bankruptcy

Attorney Stephen Elias & Albin Renauer, J.D.

Updated by Attorney Cara O'Neill

NINETEENTH EDITION	OCTOBER 2015
Editor	KATHLEEN MICHON
Production	COLLEEN CAIN
Proofreading	IRENE BARNARD
Index	THÉRÈSE SHERE
Printing	BANG PRINTING

ISSN: 2330-3298 (print)
ISSN: 2167-5791 (online)
ISBN: 978-1-4133-2194-4 (pbk)
ISBN: 978-1-4133-2195-1 (epub ebook)

This book covers only United States law, unless it specifically states otherwise.

Please note

We believe accurate, plain-English legal information should help you solve many of your own legal problems. But this text is not a substitute for personalized advice from a knowledgeable lawyer. If you want the help of a trained professional—and we'll always point out situations in which we think that's a good idea—consult an attorney licensed to practice in your state.

Dedications

To Mom and Dad, who gave me what money can't buy, and to whom I'm forever indebted.

—A.R.

To everyone who uses this and other Nolo books, for their courage and for having the good sense to take the law into their own hands.

—S.R.E. and A.R.

Acknowledgments

This most recent edition would not have been possible without the knowledgeable guidance and superb editorial assistance of Kathleen Michon. Thanks for not only the vote of confidence, but also for infusing the sublime combination of positivity and efficiency into this, and every, project. Also, thank you to Mark and Chris at the law library in Auburn, California for the uncanny ability to find the right legal resources in the most obscure of circumstances, as well as a true appreciation for, and extensive collection of, all of the Nolo titles. Of course, a respectful nod must go out to the original author of this book, the late Stephen Elias, who championed the ability of everyone to take the law into their own hands. And finally, to Trenton, Jacqueline, Christian, and Mia because sometimes it's enough to simply be wonderful people.

—Cara O'Neill

About the Authors and Updater

Stephen R. Elias (1941–2011), the original author of this book, was a bankruptcy and foreclosure expert. Over the many years of his career, he provided low-cost, high-quality legal help to thousands of clients. Steve is the author of many Nolo books, including *Chapter 13 Bankruptcy*, *The Foreclosure Survival Guide*, and *The New Bankruptcy*.

Albin Renauer received his J.D. in 1985 from the University of Michigan Law School, where he served on the *Michigan Law Review*. He worked for various public interest law firms, the California Supreme Court, and Nolo before launching LegalConsumer.com, a website that helps people determine whether or not they're eligible for bankruptcy.

Cara O'Neill has been practicing law in California for over 20 years. She currently concentrates in the areas of civil litigation, family law, and bankruptcy. Before opening her law office, she served as an Administrative Law Judge mediating disputes between automotive manufacturers and franchisees; taught undergraduate and graduate courses in the areas of employment law, business law, and criminal law; and served as house counsel for a large insurance company. She earned her law degree in 1994 from the University of the Pacific, McGeorge School of Law.

Table of Contents

Glossary

Appendixes

Index

Your Chapter 7 Bankruptcy Companion

If you're considering filing for bankruptcy, you're not alone. Many Americans turn to the bankruptcy system to get out from under credit card debt, medical bills, car loans, and more, often after being derailed by one of the common life events that can lead to bankruptcy:

- job loss
- health problems (and the resulting medical expenses)
- divorce, or
- small business failures.

Of course, none of these events would necessarily require bankruptcy if the people who experience them had adequate savings to weather the storm. But most of us lack such savings. In fact, many of us are up to our eyeballs in debt, making ends meet from paycheck to paycheck. As we all know too well, when a recession hits or a factory relocates and the pink slips start flowing, many otherwise stalwart citizens find themselves turning to bankruptcy for relief.

These are the very situations bankruptcy was intended to address. Chapter 7 bankruptcy gives debtors a fresh start by wiping out some or all of their debts. If you decide that Chapter 7 bankruptcy is the right solution to your financial woes, this book will guide you through each step of the process.

The typical Chapter 7 bankruptcy requires no special courtroom or analytical skills. The typical filer will have to follow only these steps:

- Get credit counseling from an approved agency before filing for bankruptcy.
- File a packet of official forms and documents.
- Give the trustee certain supporting documents (such as a copy of his or her most recent tax return).
- Attend a five-minute meeting, usually held in the nearest federal building, with a bankruptcy official called the "trustee."
- Take a two-hour course in budget management.

- Wait a couple of months for the bankruptcy to be completed and his or her debts discharged.

Sounds simple enough, right? But understanding your options, filling out the extensive paperwork, and figuring out the best ways to protect the property you want to keep can get confusing in a hurry. This book will help you through the process, whether your bankruptcy is routine or you face a complication or two along the way.

First, we explain the alternatives and help you figure out whether Chapter 7 bankruptcy is the right choice for you. If you decide to file for Chapter 7 bankruptcy, this book provides information and step-by-step instructions to help you: figure out what property you'll be able to keep and which debts (if any) will survive your bankruptcy; decide how to handle your mortgage and other secured debts; fill out the necessary paperwork; handle routine bankruptcy procedures; eliminate as much debt as possible; and rebuild your credit after bankruptcy. If you're ready for a fresh financial start, let this book help you navigate the bankruptcy process and get back on your feet.

Don't be daunted by the size of this book: Most people won't need to read every chapter. If you have already decided to file for Chapter 7 and you understand what will happen to your property and debts, you can proceed straight to Ch. 6 for step-by-step instructions on completing the official bankruptcy forms. If you don't own a home or any other valuable property, you might want to skip Chs. 3 and 4, which explain how your property is handled in bankruptcy and when you can keep it. If none of your debts are "secured" (that is, you haven't pledged collateral or otherwise given the creditor the right to take your property if you don't pay the debt) you can certainly skip Ch. 5.

Use the chart below to figure out where to find the information you need.

Question	Where to Find the Answer
How does Chapter 7 bankruptcy work?	Ch. 1, "An Overview of Chapter 7 Bankruptcy"
Am I eligible to file for Chapter 7?	Ch. 1, "Who Cannot File for Chapter 7" and Ch. 6, "Form 22A"
Is my income low enough to qualify for Chapter 7?	Ch. 1, "Who Cannot File for Chapter 7" and Ch. 6, "Form 22A"
Does it make sense for me to use Chapter 7?	Ch. 1, "Does Chapter 7 Bankruptcy Make Economic Sense?"
Do I have options other than filing for bankruptcy?	Ch. 1, "Alternatives to Chapter 7 Bankruptcy"
Can I avoid being evicted by filing for bankruptcy?	Ch. 2, "Evictions"
Does bankruptcy stop my creditors from trying to collect what I owe them?	Ch. 2
What will happen to my car if I file?	Ch. 3 and Ch. 5
What will happen to my house if I file?	Ch. 4
What personal property might I lose if I file?	Ch. 3
Can I keep property that I've pledged as collateral for a debt?	Ch. 5
Should I sign a reaffirmation agreement promising to repay a debt even after I file for bankruptcy?	Ch. 5
Will I lose my retirement account or pension?	Ch. 3, "Property That Isn't in Your Bankruptcy Estate"
Where can I get the credit counseling required before I file for bankruptcy?	Ch. 1, "An Overview of Chapter 7 Bankruptcy"
Where can I get the budget counseling required after I file for bankruptcy?	Ch. 1, "An Overview of Chapter 7 Bankruptcy"
Can I get my student loans cancelled or reduced in bankruptcy?	Ch. 9, "Debts That Survive Chapter 7 Bankruptcy"
Is there any way I can keep valuable property when I file for Chapter 7?	Ch. 3, "Property You Can Keep"
Which debts will be wiped out after my bankruptcy?	Ch. 9, "Debts That Will Be Discharged in Bankruptcy"
Which debts will I still have to pay after my bankruptcy?	Ch. 9, "Debts That Survive Chapter 7 Bankruptcy"
Can I get my tax debts wiped out in bankruptcy?	Ch. 9, "Debts That Survive Chapter 7 Bankruptcy"
How will my bankruptcy affect someone who cosigned for one of my debts?	Ch. 1, "Does Chapter 7 Bankruptcy Make Economic Sense?"
What will happen if I forget to list a debt on my bankruptcy papers?	Ch. 8, "Newly Discovered Creditors"
Can I give property away to friends or relatives to avoid losing it in bankruptcy?	Ch. 1, "Who Cannot File for Chapter 7"

Question	Where to Find the Answer
How will bankruptcy affect my child support obligations?	Ch. 2, "When the Stay Doesn't Apply" and Ch. 9, "Debts That Survive Chapter 7 Bankruptcy"
How do I fill out the bankruptcy forms?	Ch. 6
How do I file my bankruptcy forms?	Ch. 6, "How to File Your Papers"
What happens at the 341 hearing?	Ch. 1, "An Overview of Chapter 7 Bankruptcy" and Ch. 7, "Routine Bankruptcy Procedures"
What documents do I need to bring to the 341 hearing?	Ch. 1, "An Overview of Chapter 7 Bankruptcy" and Ch. 7, "Routine Bankruptcy Procedures"
Can I change my bankruptcy papers once I file them?	Ch. 7, "Amending Your Bankruptcy Papers"
Will I need an attorney to handle my bankruptcy?	Ch. 10, "Bankruptcy Lawyers"
How can I find a bankruptcy lawyer?	Ch. 10, "Bankruptcy Lawyers"
If I can't afford a lawyer, what other types of help are available to me?	Ch. 10
Can I be fired because I filed for bankruptcy?	Ch. 8, "Postbankruptcy Discrimination"
How can I rebuild my credit after bankruptcy?	Ch. 8, "Rebuilding Credit"

Get Legal Updates and More at Nolo.com

You can find the online companion page to this book at:

www.nolo.com/back-of-book/HFB.html

There you will find important updates to the law, Nolo's Bankruptcy and Debt blog posts, and links to online articles on bankruptcy, debt, credit, and foreclosure.

Should You File for Chapter 7 Bankruptcy?

n the chapters that follow, we explain how to complete the required bankruptcy paperwork, what happens to your debts and property when you file for bankruptcy, how to get help with your bankruptcy, and how to pick up the financial pieces once your bankruptcy is final, among other things. But before you get to these important topics, you need to figure out whether you can—and should—file for Chapter 7 bankruptcy in the first place. This chapter will give you an overview of the bankruptcy process and help you decide whether Chapter 7 bankruptcy is right for you.

Bankruptcy in America: The Big Picture

Although you may not care much about the larger bankruptcy picture, understanding it will help you keep your situation in perspective. It may be reassuring to know that you're not alone, even though you may feel isolated or even like a failure.

Why People File for Bankruptcy

Studies show that the most common reasons for filing for bankruptcy are:

- job loss, followed by an inability to find work that pays nearly as well
- medical expenses that aren't reimbursed by insurance or government programs
- divorce or legal separation, and
- small business failures.

Once a financial catastrophe strikes, many of us wind up having to take on significant debt just to weather the storm. If we saved enough, maybe we'd be ready for these unexpected twists and turns. But, for a variety of reasons, many of us spend too much and save too little. Let's take a closer look at how we got so financially overextended.

Why You Shouldn't Feel Guilty About Filing for Bankruptcy

The American economy is based on consumer spending. Roughly two-thirds of the gross national product has come from consumers like us spending our hard-earned dollars on goods and services we deem essential to our lives. As Americans, we learn from an early age

that it's a good thing to buy all sorts of products and services. A highly paid army of persuaders surrounds us with thousands of seductive messages each day that all say, "buy, buy, buy."

These sophisticated advertising techniques (which can often cross the line into manipulation) work, and as a result, we buy. And for those of us who can't afford to pay as we go, credit card companies relentlessly offer credit, even to those of us deeply in debt.

Readily available credit often makes it easy to live beyond our means and difficult to resist the siren songs of the advertisers. If, because of illness, loss of work, or just plain bad planning, we can't pay for the things we need, feelings of fear and guilt are often our first responses. But, as we've also seen, the American economy has depended on our spending—the more, the better. In short, much of American economic life is built on a contradiction.

If you are grappling with guilt, remember that large creditors expect defaults and bankruptcies and treat them as a cost of doing business. Banks issue many credit cards because they are very profitable, even though some credit card debts are wiped out in bankruptcies and never repaid.

Bankruptcy is a truly worthy part of our legal system, based as it is on forgiveness rather than retribution. Certainly, it helps keep families together, frees up income and resources for children, reduces suicide rates, and keeps the ranks of the homeless from growing even larger. And, perhaps paradoxically, every successful bankruptcy returns a newly empowered person to the ranks of the "patriotic" consumer. If you suddenly find yourself without a job; socked with huge, unexpected medical bills you can't pay; or simply snowed under by an impossible debt burden, bankruptcy provides a chance for a fresh start and a renewed, positive outlook on life.

What About the Downside?

Despite its many benefits, bankruptcy also has disadvantages—economically, emotionally, and in terms of your future credit rating. The bankruptcy process can get intrusive. As part of your public filing, you are required to disclose your financial activities during the previous year or two, as well as your income, debts, and current property holdings.

Bankruptcy also carries a certain stigma. (Otherwise, why would we spend so much time talking you out of feeling bad about it?) Some people would rather struggle under a mountain of debt than accept the label of "bankrupt."

If you have a bankruptcy on your credit report, you will need to convince those who have business dealings with you that you made every effort to meet your financial obligations before resorting to bankruptcy. Whether you are renting or buying a home, purchasing or leasing a car, or seeking financing for a business, your bankruptcy will be counted against you, at least for several years (and it will stay on your credit report for ten years). And, although you may be able to get credit cards after bankruptcy, you will have a high interest rate, at least for a while.

While these facts may seem like downsides, they collectively have an upside. You may have to pay as you go for several years because it will be tough to get credit. Filing for bankruptcy can be a harsh wake-up call, one that will give you a new perspective on the credit system. A bankruptcy temporarily removes you from the credit hamster wheel and gives you some time and space to learn to live credit free (or, at least, to fashion a saner relationship to the credit industry).

Bankruptcy Law: A Work in Progress

In October 2005, Congress passed a law that changed the way bankruptcy works. One of the purposes of this law, known as the Bankruptcy Abuse Prevention and Consumer Protection Act (BAPCPA), was to cut down on Chapter 7 bankruptcies. BAPCPA was drafted by lobbyists for the credit card and banking industries, who assumed that many would-be bankruptcy filers could afford to pay back at least some of their debt, and should therefore be required to do so.

The hallmark of BAPCPA is what's known as the means test—a questionnaire that helps determine whether filers have sufficient "disposable" income to fund a Chapter 13 bankruptcy plan. In general, those with higher incomes are more likely to fail the test and be forced out of Chapter 7 bankruptcy.

As it turns out, however, very few people need to worry about this test. Contrary to what the supporters of the BAPCPA thought, the vast majority of those who use Chapter 7 have little or no income to spare. As a result, almost everyone who wants to file for Chapter 7 bankruptcy can still do so.

There were numerous additional changes in the law that make filing for Chapter 7 bankruptcy somewhat more difficult and, if you use an attorney, more expensive. But, by following our step-by-step instructions, most people will be able to handle their own cases.

This 19th edition of *How to File for Chapter 7 Bankruptcy* also incorporates the many interpretations of the law handed down by the nation's bankruptcy courts. New court decisions come out every day, from bankruptcy courts, federal district courts, bankruptcy appellate panels (B.A.P.s), federal Circuit Courts of Appeal, and even the U.S. Supreme Court. What all this means, of course, is that the day after this book hits the shelves, a new case may add some spin on a procedure or rule that you really need to know about. To make sure you have the most up-to-date information and forms, check this book's companion page on Nolo.com (See "Get Legal Updates and More at Nolo.com," in the introductory chapter, "Your Chapter 7 Bankruptcy Companion.")

An Overview of Chapter 7 Bankruptcy

This book explains how to file for Chapter 7 bankruptcy. (It's called "Chapter 7" because that's where it appears in the bankruptcy code.) Chapter 7 bankruptcy is sometimes called "liquidation" bankruptcy. It cancels most types of debt. Most people who use Chapter 7 get to keep all their property, but if you have too much, the bankruptcy trustee will liquidate (sell) your nonexempt property for the benefit of your creditors. Some states are more generous than others when it comes to how much you can keep. (You can find a list of each state's exemptions, as well as the federal exemptions, in Appendix A; Ch. 3 delves into the subject of exemptions in much more detail.)

What This Book Doesn't Cover

This book explains the procedures for filing a Chapter 7 bankruptcy if you are an individual, a married couple, or a small business owner with personal liability for your business debts. This book doesn't cover:

- **Chapter 13 bankruptcy.** Chapter 13 allows filers to keep their property and repay some or all of their debt over three to five years. For more information on Chapter 13, see "Pay Over Time With Chapter 13 Bankruptcy," below. You can get details about Chapter 13 bankruptcy in *Chapter 13 Bankruptcy*, by Stephen Elias (Nolo).
- **Bankruptcy for business partnerships.** If you're a partner in a business (with someone other than your spouse), filing for a personal bankruptcy will affect your business; we don't address that situation in this book.
- **Bankruptcy for major stockholders in privately held corporations.** If you're a major owner of a private corporation, filing for bankruptcy could affect the corporation's legal and tax status. This book doesn't cover your situation.
- **Business reorganization.** This book doesn't cover Chapter 11 of the bankruptcy laws, which allows a business to continue operating while paying off all or a portion of its debts under court supervision.
- **Farm reorganization.** A special set of bankruptcy statutes, called Chapter 12, lets family farmers continue farming while paying off their debts over time. Chapter 12 isn't addressed in this book.

Here is a brief overview of the Chapter 7 bankruptcy process, from start to finish.

What Bankruptcy Costs

The whole Chapter 7 bankruptcy process takes about three to six months, costs $335 in filing fees (unless you get a waiver), and usually requires only one brief meeting, out of court, with the bankruptcy trustee—the official appointed by the bankruptcy judge to process your bankruptcy. If you use a lawyer, you can expect to pay an additional $1,500 or more in legal fees. Of course, you can save most of this money by representing yourself with the help of this book. See Ch. 10 for information on finding lawyers.

Mandatory Credit Counseling

Before you can file for bankruptcy, you must consult a nonprofit credit counseling agency. The purpose of this consultation is to see whether there is a feasible way to handle your debt load outside of bankruptcy, without adding to what you owe. You can complete this mandatory credit counseling course online or over the phone.

To qualify for bankruptcy relief, you must show that you received credit counseling from an agency approved by the U.S. Trustee's office within the 180-day period before you file.

Once you complete the counseling, the agency will give you a certificate showing that you participated. It will also give you a copy of any repayment plan you worked out with the agency.

There are a few exceptions to this counseling requirement. You don't have to participate if you are in the military on active duty, you are incapacitated, or you have a disability that prevents you from participating. You also don't have to get counseling if there is no agency available to you. For example, one court excused a debtor's failure to get counseling because no agency could provide counseling in the debtor's Creole language, and the debtor could not afford to hire an interpreter. (*In re Petit-Louis*, 344 B.R. 696 (Bankr. S.D. Fla. 2006).)

The purpose of credit counseling is to give you an idea of whether you really need to file for bankruptcy or whether an informal repayment plan would get you back on your economic feet. Counseling is required even if it's perfectly clear that a repayment plan isn't feasible (that is, your debts are too high and your income is too low) or you have debts that you find unfair and don't want to pay. (Credit card balances inflated by high interest rates and penalties are particularly unpopular with many filers, as are emergency room bills and deficiency judgments based on auctions of repossessed cars.)

Rules Counseling Agencies Must Follow

In addition to providing services without regard to your ability to pay, counseling agencies have to meet a number of other requirements. They must:

- disclose to you their funding sources, their counselor qualifications, the possible impact of their proposed plan on your credit report, the cost of the program, if any, and how much of the costs you will have to pay
- provide counseling that includes an analysis of your current financial condition, factors that caused the condition, and how you can develop a plan to respond to the problems without adding to your debt
- use trained counselors who don't receive any commissions or bonuses based on the outcome of the counseling services (that is, the counselors may not receive kickbacks, although kickbacks to the agency may be legal), and
- maintain adequate financial resources to provide continuing support services over the life of any repayment plan. For example, if they propose a three-year payment plan, they must have adequate reserves to service your case for three years.

The law requires only that you participate—not that you go along with whatever the agency proposes. Even if a repayment plan is feasible, you aren't required to agree to it. However, if the agency does come up with a plan, you must file it along with the other required bankruptcy paperwork. See Ch. 6 for more information on the credit counseling requirement, including how to get the certificate of completion that you'll have to file with your other bankruptcy papers.

Filing Your Papers

To begin a Chapter 7 bankruptcy case, you must complete a packet of forms and file them with the bankruptcy court in your area. Many filers are shocked to see the long list of documents required in a Chapter 7 case. But don't be alarmed: Many of these forms require very little time and effort to fill in, and most filers won't have to complete them all. Just take things one step at a time, following the detailed instructions in Ch. 6, and you'll do just fine.

Once you file the papers described below, the court will send a notice of your bankruptcy filing to all of the creditors listed in your bankruptcy documents. You will get a copy as well. This notice (called a "341 notice" because it is required by Section 341 of the bankruptcy code) sets a date for the meeting of creditors (see "The Meeting of Creditors (341 Hearing)," below), provides the trustee's name, address, and telephone number, and gives creditors the deadlines for filing objections to your bankruptcy or to the discharge of particular debts.

The Voluntary Petition

You begin a Chapter 7 case by filing a Voluntary Petition, the official court form that requests a bankruptcy discharge of your debts. This form asks for some basic information, including your name, address, and the last four digits of your Social Security number; information about your creditors, debts, and property; and whether you have lived, maintained a residence or business, or had assets in the district where you are filing for most of the 180-day period before you file (this gives you the right to file in that district). You'll find line-by-line instructions for completing the Voluntary Petition in Ch. 6.

Additional Documents

You will have to submit quite a few more documents, either when you file the petition or (with a few exceptions) within 14 days after you file. These additional documents include lists of your creditors, assets, debts, income, and financial transactions prior to filing; copies of your most recent federal tax return, bank statements, and wage stubs; a list of property you are claiming as exempt (that is, property that you are entitled to keep even though you are filing for bankruptcy); information on what you plan to do with property that serves as collateral for a loan (such as a car or home); proof that you have completed your prefiling credit counseling; and, later in your bankruptcy case, proof that you have completed budget counseling.

Emergency Filing

If you need to stop creditors quickly, you can do so without filing all of the bankruptcy forms we describe in Ch. 6 (although you'll eventually have to complete the full set). In some situations, speed is essential. For example, if you face foreclosure and your house is going to be sold in a few days, or your car is about to be repossessed, filing an emergency petition will stop the repossession or foreclosure cold.

To put an end to collection efforts, you can simply file the three-page Voluntary Petition form, a form providing your Social Security number, and a document known as the Creditors' Matrix, which lists the name, address, and zip code of each of your creditors. On the petition, you'll have to either swear that you've completed credit counseling or explain why emergency circumstances prevented you from doing so. The automatic stay, which stops collection efforts and lawsuits against you, will then go into effect. (Ch. 2 covers the automatic stay in detail.) You'll have 14 days to file the rest of the forms. (Bankruptcy Rule 1007(c).)

You should file on an emergency basis only if you absolutely must. Many emergency filers fail to meet the 14-day deadline and have their petitions dismissed as a result. Because you are rushing, you are more likely to make mistakes that have to be corrected later, which just adds work and potential errors to the process. But if filing an emergency petition is the only way to stop a potentially disastrous creditor action, go for it. Just remember the deadline for filing the rest of the forms.

Perhaps the most important form requires you to compute your average gross income during the six months prior to your bankruptcy filing date and compare that to the median income for your state. If your income is more than the median, another form takes you through a series of questions (called the "means test") designed to determine whether you could file a Chapter 13 bankruptcy and pay some of your unsecured debts over time. The outcome of this test will largely determine whether you qualify for Chapter 7 bankruptcy. (See "Who Cannot File for Chapter 7," below, and Ch. 6 for detailed information about these calculations.)

After you file, you may want to amend some or all of your forms to correct mistakes you discover or to reflect agreements you reach with the trustee. Amending these forms is fairly simple; we explain how to do it in Ch. 7.

The Automatic Stay

Often, people filing for bankruptcy have faced weeks, months, or even years of harassment by creditors demanding payment and threatening lawsuits and collection actions. Bankruptcy puts a stop to all this. Filing your bankruptcy petition instantly creates a federal court order (called an "Order for Relief" and colloquially known as the "automatic stay") that requires your creditors to stop all collection efforts. So, at least temporarily, most creditors cannot call you, write dunning letters, legally grab (garnish) your wages, empty your bank account, go after your car, house, or other property, or cut off your utility service or welfare benefits. As explained in Ch. 2, the automatic stay is not absolute. Some creditors are not affected by the automatic stay, and others can get the stay lifted to collect their debts, as long as they get the judge's permission first.

CAUTION
Renters beware. The automatic stay's magic does not extend to certain eviction actions. Even if the automatic stay does kick in to temporarily halt your eviction when you file for bankruptcy, the bankruptcy court will almost always lift the stay and let the eviction proceed, upon the landlord's request. See Ch. 2 for more information on the automatic stay and eviction proceedings.

Court Control Over Your Financial Affairs

By filing for bankruptcy, you are technically placing the property you own and the debts you owe in the hands of the bankruptcy trustee (see "The Trustee," below). While your case is open, you can't sell or give away any of the property that you own when you file without the trustee's consent. However, with a few exceptions, you can do what you wish with property you acquire and income you earn after you file for bankruptcy. You are also allowed to borrow money after you file.

The U.S. Trustee

The U.S. Trustee Program is a division of the U.S. Department of Justice. Each U.S. Trustee oversees several bankruptcy courts. Individual cases within those courts are assigned to assistant U.S. Trustees, who also employ attorneys, auditors, and investigators. U.S. Trustees work closely with their Department of Justice colleagues from the FBI and other federal agencies to ferret out fraud and abuse in the bankruptcy system. The U.S. Trustees (and the assistant U.S. Trustees) also supervise the work of the panel or standing trustees, who are appointed by the courts.

You will most likely encounter the U.S. Trustee in one of the following cases:

- Your bankruptcy papers suggest that you may be engaging in fraudulent behavior.
- Your case is selected for a random audit. (Closer scrutiny of bankruptcy petitions seems to be on the rise as the total number of bankruptcy filings decreases.)
- Your bankruptcy schedules show that you don't pass the means test (explained later in this chapter).
- You use a bankruptcy petition preparer (BPP) to help you with your paperwork (see Ch. 10 for more on BPPs), and the trustee believes that the BPP has done something illegal—typically, that the BPP has not just helped you complete your papers, but has given you legal advice as well, something that only lawyers are allowed to do. In this situation, your bankruptcy won't be affected, but the U.S. Trustee may want you to act as a witness against the BPP.

The Trustee

The bankruptcy court exercises control over your property and debts by appointing an official called a "trustee" to manage your case. Your trustee's name and contact information will be in the official notice of filing you receive in the mail several days after you file your petition. The trustee (or the trustee's staff) will examine your papers to make sure they are complete and to look for property to sell for the benefit of your creditors. The trustee's primary duty is to see that your creditors are paid as much as possible. The trustee is mostly interested in what you own and what property you claim as exempt, but will also look at your financial transactions during the previous years (in some cases these can be undone to free up assets that can be distributed to your creditors). While it is tempting to believe the trustee is there to help you, that is not the case. The more assets the trustee recovers for creditors, the more the trustee is paid.

Some courts appoint full-time trustees (called "standing" trustees) to handle all cases filed in that courthouse. Other courts appoint trustees on a rotating basis from a panel of bankruptcy lawyers (called "panel" trustees). Either way, the trustees have the same responsibilities.

How Trustees Get Paid

Trustees receive a flat fee of $60 per Chapter 7 case. In addition, trustees are entitled to a percentage of the funds they disburse to the debtors' creditors: 25% of the first $5,000 disbursed, 10% of the next $45,000, and so on. Most Chapter 7 cases involve no disbursements (because typically there are no nonexempt assets), so trustees usually have to settle for the $60 fee. But these fee rules give trustees a financial incentive to look closely at bankruptcy filings, especially if debtors appear to have some valuable property. Trustees can earn a "commission" if they can actually grab some property, sell it, and distribute the proceeds to creditors.

The Meeting of Creditors (341 Hearing)

As explained above, you will receive notice of the date of your meeting of creditors (also called the 341 hearing) shortly after you file your bankruptcy papers. This meeting is typically held somewhere in the courthouse or federal building (but almost never in a courtroom). The trustee runs the meeting and, after swearing you in, may ask you questions about your bankruptcy and the documents you filed. For instance, the trustee might ask how you arrived at the value you assigned to an item of property listed in your papers, whether you have given anything away in the last year, and whether the information you put in your papers is 100% accurate. All together, this questioning usually takes about five minutes. Creditors rarely attend this meeting—but if they do, they will also have a chance to question you under oath, usually about where property that serves as collateral to a loan is located, information you gave them to obtain a loan, or the nature and location of your assets in general. In most bankruptcy cases, this will be the only personal appearance you have to make. We discuss the creditors' meeting in more detail, and explain other situations when you might have to appear in court, in Ch. 7.

When a Disgruntled Ex-Spouse Casts Suspicion on Your Petition

Most of the time, a trustee won't question the accuracy of your personal property schedules unless there is a reason to do so. So what causes a trustee to become suspicious? One source of suspicion that's hard to ignore is a disgruntled ex-spouse who shows up at the meeting of creditors claiming that you didn't list the Rolex watch she gave you for your fifth wedding anniversary or the artwork you bought on a cruise to Mexico. These types of allegations, if credible, might prompt the trustee to take a closer look at your petition and, if warranted, request an inventory of your home or storage facility. Of course, the easiest way to prevent this is to be as transparent as possible and to keep in mind that sometimes your past does indeed come back to haunt you.

What Happens to Your Property

In your bankruptcy papers, you'll be asked which items of your property you claim as exempt. Each state allows debtors to keep certain types of property or a certain amount of equity in that property. The exemptions available to you depend on where you lived prior to filing for bankruptcy. (For more information, see Ch. 3.)

If, after the creditors' meeting, the trustee determines that you have some nonexempt property, you may be required to either surrender that property or provide the trustee with its equivalent value in cash. The trustee is highly unlikely to inventory your home (though it can happen) or seize your property, but will order you to turn over property listed in your schedules or identified during your creditors' meeting or in other proceedings. If you don't turn over the property, the bankruptcy judge can order you to do it (and hold you in contempt if you don't). Plus, the court can dismiss your bankruptcy petition if you fail to cooperate with the trustee.

If your nonexempt property isn't worth very much or would be hard to sell, the trustee may "abandon" it— which means that you get to keep it, even though it's nonexempt. As it turns out, most of the property that Chapter 7 debtors own is either exempt or essentially worthless for purposes of raising money for creditors. As a result, few debtors end up losing any of their property, unless the property is collateral for a secured debt. (See "Secured Debts," below, and Ch. 5 for a detailed discussion of secured debts.)

Secured Debts

If you've pledged property as collateral for a loan, the loan is called a secured debt. The most common examples of collateral are houses and motor vehicles. If you are behind on your payments, a creditor can ask to have the automatic stay lifted so it can repossess the property or foreclose on the mortgage. However, if you are current on your payments, you can keep the property and continue making payments as before— unless you have built up enough nonexempt equity in the property to make it worthwhile for the trustee to sell it for the benefit of your unsecured creditors. (See Ch. 5 for more information on secured debts.)

If a creditor has recorded a lien against your property without your consent (for example, because the creditor obtained a money judgment against you in court), that debt is also secured. However, in some cases and with certain types of property, you may be able to wipe out the debt and keep the property free of the lien. This is called "lien avoidance," and it is also covered in Ch. 5.

Contracts and Leases

If you're a party to a contract or lease that's still in effect, the trustee may take your place as a party to the contract—known as "assuming" the contract—and enforce it for the benefit of your unsecured creditors. Alternatively, the trustee can decide not to step in as a party to the contract—called "rejecting" the contract—in which case you get to decide whether you want the contract to continue in force or not.

For example, suppose you have a five-year lease on some commercial property when you file for bankruptcy. If you've got a good lease (perhaps at a below-market rate, with a few years left on it, for property in an up-and-coming part of town), the trustee may decide to assign the lease to a third party in exchange for money to pay your unsecured creditors. In this situation, the trustee will assume the lease and assign it to the highest bidder. The trustee can do this even if the lease forbids assignments because the trustee's rights trump any transfer restrictions in the lease. However, if the trustee doesn't think selling the lease is worth the trouble (as is almost always the case), the trustee will take no action, which is the same thing as rejecting the lease. Of course, you and the landlord can renew the lease at any time.

You can assume leases on personal property (such as a car or business equipment) rather than having the trustee assume them. However, you will be allowed to do this only if you are able to cure any defaults on the lease, as required by the creditor. (Ch. 6 provides instructions for completing Schedule G, a required bankruptcy form in which you list all current contracts and leases, and the Statement of Intention, another required form in which you tell your creditors and the trustee whether you would like to assume any leases.)

Personal Financial Management Counseling

All debtors must attend a two-hour course on managing finances in order to receive a bankruptcy discharge. This is sometimes referred to as budget counseling, debtor education, or predischarge counseling. You must take this course from an agency approved by the U.S. Trustee Program. (For a list of approved agencies, go to the U.S. Trustee's website, www.usdoj.gov/ust, and click "Credit Counseling & Debtor Education.") You will be charged fees on a sliding scale, but you can't be denied services because of your inability to pay. Once you complete your counseling, you must file a certification form with the court.

The Bankruptcy Discharge

About 60 days after the 341 hearing, you will receive a Notice of Discharge from the court. This notice doesn't list which of your particular debts are discharged, but it provides some general information on the back of the form about what kinds of debts are and are not affected by the discharge order. In most cases, all debts are discharged except:

- debts that automatically survive bankruptcy (child support, most tax debts, and student loans are examples), and
- debts that the court has declared nondischargeable as a result of an action brought by a creditor, as might be the case for debts you incurred through fraudulent or willful and malicious acts.

Ch. 9 explains which debts are—and are not—discharged at the end of your bankruptcy case. See also "Who Cannot File for Chapter 7," below, which explains the circumstances in which your entire discharge—not just the discharge of a specific debt—may be denied.

What If You Change Your Mind About Chapter 7 Bankruptcy After Filing?

If you don't want to go through with your Chapter 7 bankruptcy after you file, you can ask the court to dismiss your case. A court will generally agree, as long as the dismissal won't harm your creditors' interests. For example, if you have substantial nonexempt equity in your house, the court will probably deny your dismissal request so the trustee can sell the house to make some money for your unsecured creditors. (See Ch. 4 for more on what happens to your home in bankruptcy.)

As an alternative to having your case dismissed, you may exercise your one-time "right to convert" the case to a Chapter 13 bankruptcy, as long as you really intend to propose and follow a repayment plan. This will keep your property out of the trustee's hands, because in Chapter 13 you don't have to surrender property if you complete your repayment plan. (You do, however, have to pay your unsecured creditors at least the value of your nonexempt property, as explained in "Pay Over Time With Chapter 13 Bankruptcy," below.)

After Bankruptcy

Once you receive your bankruptcy discharge, you are free to resume your economic life without reporting your activities to the bankruptcy court unless you receive (or become eligible to receive) an inheritance, insurance proceeds, or proceeds from a divorce settlement within 180 days after your filing date. In that case, you have a duty to report those assets to the trustee. If you don't, and they are discovered, the trustee (and the court, if necessary) can order you to turn over the assets and your discharge may be revoked.

After bankruptcy, you cannot be discriminated against by public or private employers solely because of the bankruptcy, although this ban on discrimination has exceptions (discussed in Ch. 8). You can start rebuilding your credit almost immediately, but it may take several years (or more) to get decent interest rates on a credit card, mortgage, or car note. You can't file a subsequent Chapter 7 bankruptcy case until eight years have passed since your last filing date. You can file for Chapter 13 bankruptcy any time, but you can't get a Chapter 13 discharge unless you file at least four years after you filed the earlier Chapter 7 case.

Who Cannot File for Chapter 7

Filing for Chapter 7 bankruptcy is one way to solve debt problems, but it isn't available to everyone. Here are some situations in which you may not be able to use Chapter 7.

You Can Afford a Chapter 13 Repayment Plan

Under the bankruptcy rules, filers with higher incomes must pay back some of their debts over time to file under Chapter 13 rather than liquidating their debts outright in Chapter 7. If the U.S. Trustee decides, based on the information about your income, debts, and expenses you provide in your required paperwork, that you can afford a Chapter 13 plan under the rules, it will file a motion to have your case dismissed. The court is likely to grant that motion and throw out your case unless you convert to a Chapter 13 bankruptcy.

To figure out whether you will be allowed to use Chapter 7, you must first:

- determine your "current monthly income" (actually, your average income in the six months before you file for bankruptcy), and
- compare that figure to the median family income in your state for the same size household.

If your current monthly income is no more than the state's median income, your Chapter 7 bankruptcy won't be presumed to be "an abuse" of the bankruptcy process. However, if your actual income (as shown in Schedule I of your bankruptcy papers, explained in Ch. 6) is significantly higher than your expenses (as listed in Schedule J, also explained in Ch. 6), you might still be forced into Chapter 13. (*In re Boule*, 415 B.R. 1 (Bankr. D.Mass. 2009), *In re Lanza*, 450 B.R. 81 (Bankr. M.D. Pa. 2011).)

If your current monthly income exceeds the state median income, you will have to do some calculations (called the means test) to determine whether you can afford to pay off at least some of your unsecured debts in a Chapter 13 plan. (If you have to take the means test, you can find step-by-step instructions in Ch. 6.)

Certain Disabled Veterans Can Skip the Math

If you are a disabled veteran, and the debts you wish to discharge were incurred primarily while you were on active duty or engaged in homeland defense activities, the court is legally required to treat you as if your income is less than the state median. This means that you'll be able to file for Chapter 7 regardless of your income or expenses.

The law doesn't clearly indicate what will happen if only some of your debts were incurred while you were on active duty. Some courts require that more than 50% of your debts be incurred while on active duty to qualify for this exception. However, other courts may have stricter requirements. If you are unsure about whether you qualify, talk to a bankruptcy attorney in your area to learn the requirements in your jurisdiction.

Determine Your Current Monthly Income

Legally, your current monthly income is your average monthly income over the six months preceding the month in which you filed for bankruptcy. You must include almost all types of income (with a few exceptions such as benefits received under the Social Security Act), taxable or not—this means, for example, that if you are including wages in your income, you must use your gross earnings, not the net income you actually take home after taxes are withheld and other deductions are made. For filers who lost jobs or other income during the six-month period before filing for bankruptcy, this current income figure may be significantly more than what they are actually earning each month by the time they file for bankruptcy.

EXAMPLE: John and Marcia are married and have two young children. They fell quickly into debt after John was forced out of his job because of a work-related injury on April 1, 2014. Three months later, on July 1, 2014, John and Marcia decide to file for bankruptcy.

To compute their current monthly income, Marcia adds up the family's income for the period from January 1, 2014 through June 30, 2014 (the six-month period before their filing date). This includes John's gross salary for the first three months (he made $8,000 a month as a software engineer), plus $1,800 in workers' compensation benefits for each of the last three months. Marcia made $1,000 during each of the first three months and had no income for the last three months. The total family income for the six-month period is $32,400. The family's current monthly income is $32,400 divided by six, or $5,400, even though the amount they actually took in during each of the three months before filing was only $1,800.

Use the Current Monthly Income Worksheet, below (and in Appendix B), to calculate your current monthly income by:

- adding up all of the income you received during the six-month period before the month in which you filed for bankruptcy, and
- dividing by six to come up with a monthly average.

You should include all of the following types of income on the form:

- wages, salary, tips, bonuses, overtime, and commissions
- gross income from operating a business, profession, or farm
- interest, dividends, and royalties
- rents and other income from real property
- pension and retirement income
- regular contributions someone else makes to your or your dependents' household expenses, including child or spousal support
- regular contributions of your spouse, if he or she isn't filing for bankruptcy with you
- unemployment compensation (in some states; in others you may not have to include state unemployment insurance benefits)

- workers' compensation insurance
- state disability insurance
- annuity payments, and
- lump-sum, windfall payments (such as lottery winnings).

Income You Don't Have to Include

Your current monthly income includes income from all sources, *except*:
- income tax refunds
- payments you receive under the Social Security Act (including Social Security retirement benefits, Social Security Disability Insurance, Supplemental Security Income, Temporary Assistance for Needy Families, and possibly state unemployment insurance)
- payments to you as a victim of war crimes or crimes against humanity, and
- payments to you as a victim of international or domestic terrorism.

Determine Your Household Size

The size of your household is also very important. The more members you have, the less likely it is that your income will exceed the state median for households of the same size, and the less likely you are to have to take the means test. For example, assume that your current monthly income is $6,000, the median income for a household of three in your state is $5,800, and the median income for a household of four is $6,500. Being able to count that additional person means you won't have to take the means test.

Unfortunately, neither Congress nor the courts have given clear guidance on how to calculate household size. Many courts adopt the census test for a household, which includes all of the people, related and unrelated, who occupy a house, apartment, group of rooms, or single room that is intended for occupancy as separate living quarters. Under this test, you can count your children or stepchildren even if they are not your dependents for tax purposes.

However, some courts allow debtors to count only the people they can claim as dependents on their tax return. Other courts use the economic unit approach to household size, which includes individuals who financially depend on or support the debtor or whose income and expenses are closely intermingled with and connected to the debtor's.

Domestic partners count as a single household. But mere roommates are not part of the same household if they have separate rooms within a house and don't act as a single economic unit by mingling their incomes and jointly paying expenses.

One vexing issue is whether children can be counted as part of a household if they are only living with the parent part time under a custody and visitation agreement. In general, the answer depends on the rules in your jurisdiction. While there is no uniform rule, the 4th Circuit Court of Appeals recently approved a fractional approach, based on how many days out of the year each child lives with the debtor, to calculate household size. (*Johnson v. Zimmer*, 686 F.3d 224 (4th Cir. 2012).) If this describes your situation, and being able to count your children as part of your household would mean you don't have to take the means test, it might make sense to talk to a local bankruptcy attorney and find out how your local court handles this issue. (See Ch. 10 for information on finding a bankruptcy lawyer.)

Compare Your Income to Your State's Family Median Income

The census bureau publishes *annual* family median income figures for all 50 states. To compare your current *monthly* income to the family median income for your state, you'll need to multiply your current monthly income by 12 (or divide the annual family median income figure by 12). Let's do it the first way. In John and Marcia's case, the family's current monthly income ($5,400) multiplied by 12 would be $64,800.

Once you've got your current monthly income and your family median income for the same time period (one month or one year), compare them to see whether your current monthly income is more or less than the median. You can find the family median

Current Monthly Income Worksheet

Use this worksheet to calculate your current monthly income; use figures for you and your spouse if you plan to file jointly.

Line 1. Calculate your total income over the last six months from wages, salary, tips, bonuses, overtime, and so on.

    A.   Month 1 $ _____

    B.   Month 2   _____

    C.   Month 3   _____

    D.   Month 4   _____

    E.   Month 5   _____

    F.   Month 6   _____

    G.   TOTAL WAGES (add lines A–F) $ _____

Line 2. Add up all other income for the last six months.

    A.   Business, profession, or farm income   _____

    B.   Interest, dividends, and royalties   _____

    C.   Rents and real property income   _____

    D.   Pension and retirement income   _____

    E.   Alimony or family support   _____

    F.   Spousal contributions (if not filing jointly)   _____

    G.   Unemployment compensation   _____

    H.   Workers' compensation   _____

    I.   State disability insurance   _____

    J.   Annuity payments   _____

    K.   Lump-sum payments   _____

    L.   Other   _____

    M.   TOTAL OTHER INCOME (add lines A–L) $ _____

Line 3. Calculate total income over the six months prior to filing.   _____

    A.   Enter total wages (Line 1G).   _____

    B.   Enter total other income (Line 2M).   _____

    C.   TOTAL INCOME OVER THE SIX MONTHS PRIOR TO FILING (add Lines A and B together) $ _____

Line 4. Average monthly income over the six months prior to filing. This is called your current monthly income.

    A.   Enter total six-month income (Line 3C).   _____

    B.   CURRENT MONTHLY INCOME (divide Line A by six) $ _____

income figures as of the writing of this edition in the Median Family Income Chart in Appendix B. You can also find up-to-date figures at the website of the U.S. Trustee at www.usdoj.gov/ust (select "Means Testing Information") or the United States Census Bureau, www.census.gov (search for "State Median Income" from the home page).

You can see from the chart in Appendix B that John and Marcia's current monthly income would be more than the family median income in most states.

State Median Income Figures Change Frequently

The figures in the Median Family Income Chart change about twice a year, so be sure you are using the most recent chart. Until 2010, you could pretty much rely on the figures going up slightly; however, the last several times the figures were updated, the median income decreased in many states.

For Larger Families

Although the U.S. Census Bureau generates median figures for families that have up to seven members, Congress does not want you to use these figures if you have a larger family. The Census figures are to be used for families that have up to four members (these are the numbers you will find in Appendix B). If there are more than four members of your family, you must add a set amount per additional person to the four-member family median income figure for your state (currently, this amount is $8,100).

What to Do Next

If, like most bankruptcy filers, your current monthly income is equal to or less than your state's median, then you will likely be allowed to file for Chapter 7 bankruptcy. As you will discover, however, your *actual* monthly income and *actual* expenses, as calculated on Schedules I and J (see Ch. 6) may also affect your eligibility to use Chapter 7. And, because of how the means test works, your actual income and expenses may be quite different than what the means test shows, primarily because the means test uses your average income over the six months before you file, which might not be the same as what you actually earn each month.

If your income exceeds the state median income, you'll need to take the full means test to figure out whether a court would presume your Chapter 7 bankruptcy case to be abusive. (If this happens, you would have to persuade the court that it's appropriate for you to file for Chapter 7, under the circumstances—see "Special Problems" in Ch. 7.) You can find the means test forms and step-by-step instructions for completing them in Ch. 6.

If you are required to take the means test and you pass it—which means you don't have enough disposable income to fund a Chapter 13 repayment plan—you've passed the first Chapter 7 eligibility hurdle. Remember, you'll also have to show that your *actual* income and expenses don't allow you to afford a Chapter 13 plan. So, even if you qualify for Chapter 7 based on the means test, you may face another hurdle down the road.

If you can't pass the means test, you might consider filing for Chapter 13 bankruptcy, with the help of Nolo's *Chapter 13 Bankruptcy*, by Stephen Elias and Kathleen Michon. You should also look at options outside of the bankruptcy system, in "Alternatives to Chapter 7 Bankruptcy," below.

You Previously Received a Bankruptcy Discharge

You cannot file for Chapter 7 bankruptcy if you obtained a discharge of your debts under Chapter 7 in a case filed within the past eight years, or under Chapter 13 in a case filed within the previous six years. (11 U.S.C. § 727.) However, if you obtained a Chapter 13 discharge in good faith after paying at least 70% of your unsecured debts, the six-year bar does not apply.

Note that these eight- and six-year periods run from the date you filed for the earlier bankruptcy, not the date you received your discharge.

EXAMPLE: Brenda files a Chapter 7 bankruptcy case on January 31, 2012. She receives a discharge on April 20, 2012. Brenda files another Chapter 7 bankruptcy on February 1, 2020. The second bankruptcy is allowed because eight years have passed since the date the earlier bankruptcy was filed (even though fewer than eight years have passed since Brenda received a discharge in the earlier case).

Converting to Chapter 7 After Filing for Chapter 13

Can you file under Chapter 13 and then convert to Chapter 7 later, even though you would have flunked the means test had you initially filed for Chapter 7? Probably not. More and more bankruptcy courts are ruling that you must take the means test in this situation.

In re Fox, 370 B.R. 639 (Bankr. D. N.J. 2007) serves as an example of the minority view. In that case, the court found that the debtor did not have to file the means test form when converting from a Chapter 13 to a Chapter 7. However, the court emphasized that the debtor must have filed the Chapter 13 in good faith and not just to avoid taking the means test. This means the debtor must have proposed a feasible (or close to feasible) Chapter 13 plan. (See "Pay Over Time With Chapter 13 Bankruptcy," below.)

But many other courts have taken the opposite stance. For example, a Rhode Island bankruptcy court held that a debtor who converted to Chapter 7 only two weeks after filing a Chapter 13 case would have to take the means test. (*In re Perfetto*, 361 B.R. 27 (D. R.I. 2007).) The 8th Circuit Bankruptcy Appellate Panel decided that the means test does apply to converted cases. (*In re Chapman*, 447 B.R. 250 (B.A.P. 8th Cir. 2011).) The 10th Circuit Court of Appeals went even further and denied the debtors' discharge altogether when they willfully disobeyed their Chapter 13 confirmation order and subsequently converted their case to a Chapter 7. (*Standiferd v. U.S. Trustee*, 641 F.3d 1209 (10th Cir. 2011).) In fact, one court recently noted that the majority of judges looking at this issue have held that you must take the means test when converting from Chapter 7 to Chapter 13. (*In re Hayes*, 2015 LEXIS 161 (Bankr. S.D. Tex. 2015.)

A Previous Bankruptcy Was Dismissed Within the Previous 180 Days

You cannot file for Chapter 7 bankruptcy if your previous Chapter 7 or Chapter 13 case was dismissed within the past 180 days because you:

- violated a court order, or
- requested the dismissal after a creditor asked for relief from the automatic stay. (11 U.S.C. § 109(g).)

You Haven't Met the Credit Counseling Requirements

To file for Chapter 7 bankruptcy, you have to satisfy all the requirements for credit counseling. This means that you must obtain the counseling within 180 days before you file, and file a certificate of completion no later than 14 days after you file, unless you fit within one of the exceptions to the counseling requirement (discussed in "Mandatory Credit Counseling," above) or you didn't obtain counseling for some other reason that is acceptable to the bankruptcy court. (See Ch. 6 for more on these requirements.)

You Defrauded Your Creditors

Bankruptcy is geared toward the honest debtor who got in too deep and needs a fresh start. A bankruptcy court will not help someone who has played fast and loose with creditors or the court. This type of behavior can lead to a denial of your bankruptcy discharge and even to criminal charges if you lie under oath.

Certain activities are red flags to the courts and trustees. If you have engaged in any of them within the past several years, do not file for bankruptcy until you consult with a bankruptcy lawyer. These no-nos are:

- unloading assets to your friends or relatives
- incurring debts for luxury items when you were clearly broke, and
- concealing property or money from your spouse during a divorce proceeding.

EXAMPLE: Joan wants to file for bankruptcy but is worried that she'll lose her house. Before filing, Joan puts the house in her mother's name on the understanding that her mother will deed it back to her after the bankruptcy is completed. Before filing, Joan learns that this is a definite no-no and can land her in serious trouble. She retransfers the house back into her own name and files a Chapter 7 bankruptcy. The trustee learns of the transactions and successfully opposes Joan's discharge on the ground that she acted fraudulently. The fact that she undid the fraud before filing doesn't help her.

Your Filing Constitutes "Abuse"

The court can dismiss your case if it finds that your filing is abusive—that is, that your actions demonstrate that you aren't entitled to the remedy offered by Chapter 7. As explained above, if you fail the means test, the court can presume that your bankruptcy filing is abusive and prevent you from using Chapter 7. However, even if you pass the means test, the court might find abuse. For example, if your actual income (as calculated in Schedule I of your bankruptcy paperwork) significantly exceeds your actual expenses (as calculated in Schedule J of your papers), the court might find that you should not be allowed to use Chapter 7, even if you pass the means test.

Even if you clearly can't afford a Chapter 13 repayment plan, the court can still deny you the benefit of Chapter 7 by refusing to discharge your debts. Here are some examples:

- The court can refuse to grant a Chapter 7 discharge if the debtor fails to explain how he or she got so deeply in debt. (*In re Tanglis*, 344 B.R. 563 (Bankr. N.D. Ill. 2006).)
- If the debtor fails to explain what happened to money received from a personal injury settlement or tax refund, the court can refuse to grant a Chapter 7 discharge. (*In re O'Donnell*, 528 B.R. 308 (Bankr. D.Mass. 2014).)
- Voluntary unemployment can be considered abusive, because the debtor could pay back some or all of the debts if employed. (*In re Richie*, 353 B.R. 569 (Bankr. E.D. Wash. 2006).)

- A debtor who couldn't account for how cash advances were spent during the previous year may be denied a Chapter 7 discharge on grounds of abuse. (*In re Yanni*, 354 B.R. 708 (Bankr. E.D. Penn. 2006).)

These types of cases are pretty rare. You can pretty much count on receiving a discharge without having to prove your virtue—even if you lack it in large degree.

The U.S. Trustee Program Actively Roots Out Fraud

The U.S. Trustee Program, a branch of the U.S. Department of Justice, is charged with rooting out bankruptcy-related fraud. Copies of all bankruptcy petitions filed in your district are passed on to the U.S. Trustee for that district. The U.S. Trustee randomly selects some cases for audit, and audits others that have red flags indicating possible fraud. In early 2013, the U.S. Trustee Program suspended its random bankruptcy audits, citing budget constraints but resumed auditing in 2014 at a reduced level. It's unknown if, and when, the audits will start again. However, your case trustee will continue to look for signs of fraud. You don't need to worry long as you are scrupulously honest in your paperwork and disclosures.

You Are Attempting to Defraud the Bankruptcy Court

Misleading the court is a terrible idea. If you lie, cheat, or attempt to hide assets, your current debt crisis may no longer be your biggest legal problem. You must sign your bankruptcy papers under "penalty of perjury," swearing that everything in them is true. You also have to verify your papers, under oath, at your creditors' meeting. If you get caught deliberately failing to disclose property, omitting material information you are asked to provide about your financial affairs during previous years, or using a false Social Security number (to hide your identity as a prior filer), you will not get any bankruptcy relief. You may even be prosecuted for perjury or fraud on the court.

Does Chapter 7 Bankruptcy Make Economic Sense?

If you are inclined to file for Chapter 7 bankruptcy, take a moment to consider whether it makes economic sense. If filing for Chapter 7 won't help you out of your current debt problems, will force you to give up property you want to keep, or is unnecessary because of your financial situation, then Chapter 7 might not be the best option.

FOR MARRIED COUPLES

If you are married, consider the debts and property of both spouses as you read this section. Married couples usually benefit from filing jointly, but not always. For example, if one spouse brings a lot of debt to the marriage, while the other spouse has clean credit, it might make more sense for the debt-ridden spouse to file alone. Filing alone might also be a good idea if the couple is separated or divorcing, one spouse is barred from filing due to a previous bankruptcy, or filing together would put valuable property at risk (for example, property owned only by the nonfiling spouse or property the couple owns as tenants by the entirety). You'll find more information on the benefits of filing jointly versus filing alone in Ch. 6.

Are You Judgment Proof?

Most unsecured creditors are required to obtain a court judgment before they can start collection procedures, such as a wage garnishment or seizure and sale of personal property. Holders of tax, child support, and student loan debts are exceptions to this general rule. If your debts are mainly of the type that requires a judgment, the next question is whether you have any income or property that is subject to seizure by your creditors if they obtain a judgment. For instance, if all of your income comes from Social Security (which can't be taken by creditors), and all of your property is exempt (see Ch. 3), there is nothing your creditors can do with their judgment. That makes you judgment proof.

While you may still wish to file for bankruptcy to get a fresh start, nothing bad will happen to you if you don't file, no matter how much you owe. For more on what it means to be judgment proof, see "Alternatives to Chapter 7 Bankruptcy," below.

Even though you may be judgment proof, you may want to file for bankruptcy to stop harassment by your creditors. In most cases, you can stop creditors from making telephone calls to your home or work by simply telling them to stop. Changing your phone number may also help, as will using caller ID and a message machine to screen the calls. If collection agencies are doing the harassment, you can also send them a letter like the one shown below, which almost always does the trick.

Sample Letter Telling Collection Agency to Stop Contacting You

Sasnak Collection Service
49 Pirate Place
Topeka, Kansas 69000

November 11, 20xx

Attn: Marc Mist

Re: Lee Anne Ito

Account No. 88-90-92

Dear Mr. Mist:

For the past three months, I have received several phone calls and letters from you concerning an overdue Rich's Department Store account.

This is my formal notice to you under 15 U.S.C. § 1692c(c) to cease all further communications with me at my home or place of employment except for the reasons specifically set forth in the federal law.

This letter is not meant in any way to be an acknowledgment that I owe this money.

Very truly yours,

Lee Anne Ito

Lee Anne Ito

If a collector continues to harass you after you have given written notice, you can sue the collector under the Fair Debt Collection Practices Act (15 U.S.C. §§ 1692–1692o) for any damage you suffer (such as medical conditions caused by the harassment) and statutory damages of up to $1,000. You can also collect attorneys' fees, which makes it easier to find an attorney who will represent you without requiring you to pay a retainer up front. Your state may have similar legal protections against harassment by a collection agency or an original creditor—and additional remedies for violations of the law. For more information on illegal debt collection practices, see *Solve Your Money Troubles*, by Robin Leonard and Margaret Reiter (Nolo).

Using Bankruptcy to Get New Credit

Even if you are judgment proof, you may want to file for bankruptcy to clear the decks for your next foray into the world of credit. It's very likely that you will be able to rebuild your credit sooner by filing for bankruptcy than by ignoring your debts. In fact, you'll likely receive offers for credit cards and car loans shortly after receiving your discharge. (For more on rebuilding your credit, see Ch. 8.)

Will Bankruptcy Discharge Enough of Your Debts?

Certain categories of debts may survive Chapter 7 bankruptcy, depending on the circumstances. It may not make much sense to file for Chapter 7 bankruptcy if your primary goal is to get rid of these nondischargeable debts.

There are three categories of nondischargeable debts:
- debts that always survive bankruptcy
- debts that survive bankruptcy unless you convince the court that a particular exception applies, and
- debts that survive bankruptcy only if a creditor mounts a successful challenge to them in bankruptcy court.

If most of your debts are the kind that automatically survive bankruptcy or that survive unless a particular exception applies, hold off on filing your Chapter 7 bankruptcy until you have at least read Ch. 9 and learned what is likely to happen to these debts in your case. In particular, you should be concerned about:
- back child support and alimony
- debts other than support that arise from a marital settlement agreement or divorce decree
- student loans
- government fines, penalties, or court-ordered restitution
- tax arrearages (including debts incurred to pay a tax—for example, if you used a credit card to pay back taxes), and
- court judgments for injuries or death resulting from your drunk driving convictions.

The following types of debts can survive bankruptcy, but only if the creditor mounts a successful challenge to them in the bankruptcy court:
- debt incurred on the basis of fraud, such as lying on a credit application or writing a bad check
- debt for luxury items that you recently bought on credit with no intention of paying for them
- debt from willful and malicious injury to another person or another's property, including assault, battery, false imprisonment, libel, and slander, and
- debt from larceny (theft), breach of trust, or embezzlement.

TIP
Chapter 13 might be a better choice. In some situations, Chapter 13 offers relief that is not available in Chapter 7. For example, if you are facing foreclosure on your home because of mortgage defaults, you have debts that you can discharge in Chapter 13 but not in Chapter 7, or you need an affordable way to pay back your nondischargeable debts, you might want to consider using Chapter 13. See "Pay Over Time With Chapter 13 Bankruptcy," below, for more information.

Sorting It All Out

If your debt load consists primarily of debts that will be discharged unless a creditor convinces the court that they shouldn't be, it may make sense to file for bankruptcy and hope that the creditor doesn't challenge the discharge. Many creditors don't—mounting a challenge to the discharge of a debt usually requires a lawyer, and lawyers don't come cheap. Also, many lawyers advise their clients to write off the debt rather than throw good money after bad in a bankruptcy court challenge.

On the other hand, if your debt load consists primarily of debts that will survive your bankruptcy unless you convince the court otherwise, you must decide whether the debts are large enough to warrant paying an attorney to argue in court that the debts should be discharged. For example, if you owe $50,000 in student loans and have a good argument that they should be discharged, it will be worth your while to file for bankruptcy and pay an attorney $1,000 to push the issue. (You could also do this yourself, although this sort of procedure is difficult to navigate without competent expert help.) If the amount in question is small and your chances of victory slim, however, you may choose to forgo bankruptcy altogether.

Will a Cosigner Be Stuck With Your Debts?

If someone else cosigned a loan or otherwise took on a joint obligation with you, that person can be held wholly responsible for the debt if you don't pay it. If you receive a Chapter 7 bankruptcy discharge, you may no longer be liable for the debt—but your cosigner will still be on the hook. Especially if your cosigner is a friend or relative, you might not want to stick him or her with your debt burden.

If you have a cosigner whom you want to protect, you'll need to use one of the alternatives to Chapter 7 bankruptcy that are outlined below. By arranging to pay the debt over time, you can keep creditors from going after your cosigner for payment. And, if you decide to file for Chapter 13, you can include the debt in your repayment plan to keep creditors off your cosigner's back, at least for the duration of your plan.

Will You Lose Valuable Property?

Chapter 7 bankruptcy essentially offers this deal: If you are willing to give up your nonexempt property (or exempt property of equivalent value) to be sold for the benefit of your creditors, the court will erase your dischargeable debts. If you can keep most of the things you care about, Chapter 7 bankruptcy can be a very effective remedy for your debt problems. But if Chapter 7 bankruptcy would force you to part with treasured property, you may want to look for another solution.

The laws that control what property you can keep in a Chapter 7 bankruptcy are called exemptions. Each state's legislature produces a set of exemptions for use by people who are sued in that state. These same exemptions are available to people who file for bankruptcy in that state and meet the residency requirements described below. In 19 states (and the District of Columbia), debtors who meet the residency requirements can choose between their state's exemptions or another set of exemptions created by Congress (known as federal bankruptcy exemptions). States that currently allow debtors this choice are Alaska, Arkansas, Connecticut, Hawaii, Kentucky, Massachusetts, Michigan, Minnesota, New Hampshire, New Jersey, New Mexico, New York, Oregon, Pennsylvania, Rhode Island, Texas, Vermont, Washington, and Wisconsin. The federal exemptions may also be available in Alaska.

As it does so often, California has adopted a unique system. Rather than using the federal exemptions, California offers two sets of state exemptions for those who meet the residency requirements described below. As in the 19 states that have the federal bankruptcy exemptions, people filing for bankruptcy in California must choose one or the other set of California's state exemptions.

Property that is not exempt can be taken from you and sold by the trustee to pay your unsecured creditors. You can avoid this result by finding some cash to pay the trustee what the property is worth or convincing the trustee to accept some exempt property of roughly equal value as a substitute.

If your nonexempt property isn't worth enough to make selling it worthwhile, the trustee may decide to let you keep it. For instance, few trustees bother to take well-used furniture or secondhand electronic gadgets or appliances. Even if your property is more valuable, the trustee may be willing to let you pay to keep it, so the trustee can avoid the trouble and cost of putting it up for sale. For example, if you have a flat-screen television that's worth about $1,500, and only $500 of it is exempt, the trustee may let you keep it if you can pay $500 or so. Even though the trustee could take the TV and sell it, that would take time and cost money. While this may seem like buying back property you already own, the trustee is entitled to that property once you file for Chapter 7 bankruptcy; in effect, you are paying the trustee to get the property back.

When Buying Back Nonexempt Property Can Take a Bite Out of Your Tax Debt

While it is no fun to buy back your own property from the bankruptcy trustee, in one situation it doesn't sting quite so much—and that's when you owe taxes. Here's how it works. It is unlikely that your tax debt will be discharged in bankruptcy (see Ch. 9). What's more, taxes are priority debts, which means that if there is money to be distributed, your taxes stand at the head of the line. (See "Schedule E—Creditors Holding Unsecured Priority Claims" in Ch. 6.) They get paid before most other debts. As a result, when you rebuy your own property, the trustee turns around and uses those same funds to pay down your tax debt—a win-win situation.

As you've no doubt figured out, the key to getting the most out of the bankruptcy process is to use exemptions to keep as much of your property as possible, while erasing as many debts as you can. To make full and proper use of your exemptions, you'll want to:

- learn which exemptions are available to you
- become familiar with the exemptions you can use, and
- use the available exemptions in the way that lets you keep more of your treasured property.

Ch. 3 gives step-by-step instructions for figuring out whether your personal property is exempt under the state laws available for use in your bankruptcy, and Ch. 4 covers exemptions for your home. Here, we provide a brief overview of exemptions.

Domicile Requirements for Using Exemptions

You may use a state's exemptions if that state has been your "domicile" for at least two years before you file for bankruptcy (called the 730-day rule). Domicile has been defined as "the place where a man has his true fixed and permanent home and principal establishment and to which whenever he is absent he has the intention of returning." This means something more than your residence, which generally means wherever you are living at any given time.

Your domicile is the place where you are living and intend to live for the indefinite future, the place where you work, vote, receive your mail, pay taxes, do your banking, own property, participate in public affairs, register your car, apply for your driver's license, and send your children to school. Your domicile might be different from the state where you are actually living. For example, members of the military, professional athletes, and corporate officers all might spend significant amounts of time working in other states or countries, but their domiciles are the states where they make their permanent homes.

If you have not been domiciled in your current state for at least two years before filing, you must use the exemptions of the state where you were living for the better part of the 180-day period ending two years before your filing date. In other words, if you file for bankruptcy on January 1, 2014, and you have not lived in your current state for two years, you will have to use the exemptions available in the state where you lived for most of the period between July 5, 2011 and December 31, 2011. These somewhat bewildering rules are explained in detail in Ch. 3. A separate rule determines whether you may claim your state's homestead exemption; that rule, which has a 40-month domicile requirement, is explained in Ch. 4.

The History Behind Convoluted Residency Requirements

Prior to 2005, if you wanted to keep more of your property, you could shop around until you found a state with better exemptions and then move there shortly before you filed for bankruptcy.

That all changed in October of 2005, however, when sweeping bankruptcy law changes went into effect. The new, two-year residency requirement prevents people from maximizing exemptions by strategically moving prior to filing.

Property That Is Typically Exempt

Certain kinds of property are exempt in almost every state, including:

- equity in your home, up to a certain value (commonly called the homestead exemption)
- equity in a motor vehicle, up to a certain value (usually between $1,000 and $5,000)
- reasonably necessary clothing (no mink coats)
- reasonably necessary household furnishings and goods (the second TV may have to go if it has any value)
- household appliances
- jewelry, to a certain value
- personal effects
- life insurance (cash or loan value, or proceeds), to a certain value
- retirement funds necessary for current support
- tools of your trade or profession, to a certain value
- a portion of unpaid but earned wages, and
- public benefits (welfare, Social Security, unemployment compensation) accumulated in a bank account.

Some states also provide a "wildcard" exemption—an exemption for a set dollar amount that you can apply to any property that would otherwise not be exempt. (See Ch. 3 for more on wildcard exemptions.) Also, if you are using the federal exemptions or the California System 2 exemptions and you don't need to protect substantial equity in a home, you can use some or all of the homestead exemption as a wildcard.

How Property Is Valued for Exemption Purposes

Under the old rules, you could value your property at roughly what you could get for it at your own garage sale. The 2005 bankruptcy law uses a different standard: You must value property at what it would cost to buy it from a retail vendor, taking the property's age and condition into account. (11 U.S.C. §§ 506 and 527(b).) For cars, this "replacement value" will be the retail amount listed in the *Kelley Blue Book* or similar price guides. For other property, you will have to use the amount for which similar property is sold on eBay or at used clothing or furniture stores, flea markets, and the like.

Although the bankruptcy code uses the "replacement value" (as discussed above) in valuing property for exemption purposes, how the trustee ultimately decides what to do with the property depends more on the property's auction value (what the trustee would get for it at auction) less costs of storage and sale.

Here's an example of how this works. Assume your state provides a $3,000 exemption for car equity, and your car's replacement value is $6,000. If the trustee sells the car at auction, the trustee would incur additional costs associated with picking up, storing, and auctioning the car, probably to the tune of $3,000. This means the trustee would net about $3,000 from the sale of the car after deducting these costs (sale price of $6,000 less $3,000 in costs), but the trustee would also have to write you a check for the amount of your car equity exemption, which is $3,000. Since the trustee won't end up with much (or perhaps nothing) to give to creditors, it's likely that the trustee would instead "abandon" the property (which means you can keep it).

Property That Is Typically Nonexempt

In most states, you will have to give up or pay the trustee if you have equity in the following types of property (in legal terms, equity in these items is "nonexempt"):

- expensive musical instruments (unless you're a professional musician)

- cameras, camcorders, and personal digital assistants
- stamp, coin, and other collections
- valuable family heirlooms
- cash, bank accounts, stocks, stock options, bonds, royalties, and other investments
- business assets and inventory
- real estate you're not living in
- boats, planes, and off-road vehicles, and
- a second or vacation home.

CAUTION

For those with nonexempt property. If it appears that you have a lot of nonexempt property, read Ch. 3 before deciding whether to file for bankruptcy. That chapter helps you determine exactly how much of your property is not exempt and suggests ways to:

- buy it from the trustee (if you really want to hold on to it)
- use exempt property to barter with the trustee, or
- retain the value of your nonexempt property by selling some of it and buying exempt property with the proceeds before you file.

If Chapter 7 Bankruptcy Won't Let You Keep Treasured Property

If it looks like Chapter 7 bankruptcy is destined to come between you and property that you really want to keep, consider filing for Chapter 13 bankruptcy (or using one of the other options discussed in "Alternatives to Chapter 7 Bankruptcy," below). Chapter 13 bankruptcy lets you keep your property regardless of its exempt status, as long as you will have sufficient income over the next three to five years to pay off all or a portion of your unsecured debts and to pay any priority debts you have (such as back child support, alimony, and taxes) in full. However, even in Chapter 13, you will be required to propose a plan that pays your unsecured creditors a total amount that is at least equal to what they would receive in a Chapter 7 bankruptcy.

EXAMPLE 1: Several years ago, John and Louise inherited a genuine Chinese jade vase, their most prized possession. It's worth $10,000. They don't want to give it up but are in desperate financial shape, with debts of more than $60,000.

If they file for Chapter 7 bankruptcy, their debts will be discharged, but they will probably lose the vase, assuming it's not exempt in their state and there's no wildcard exemption available that will cover its value. In Chapter 13 bankruptcy, however, they could keep the vase and pay their debts out of their income over the next three to five years, as long as their payments to their unsecured creditors over the life of the plan total at least what their creditors would have received from the sale of the vase in a Chapter 7 bankruptcy. This would be the amount likely received at auction, less any exemption that is available to John and Louise, less the trustee's commission, less the costs of sale; given the costs and possible exemption, the final tally would be much less than $10,000. After several anguished days, John and Louise decide to file for Chapter 7 bankruptcy and risk losing the vase.

John and Louise might be tempted to hide the vase and hope the trustee doesn't discover it. That would be a crime (perjury), for which they could be fined or jailed. It's also an abuse of the bankruptcy process that could get their petition dismissed and prevent them from filing again for six months and discharging the debts they listed in their schedules. A much safer alternative (but still risky in some courts) would be to sell the vase before they file and use the proceeds to buy necessities (document these purchases) or exempt property. (See Ch. 3 for information on when you can do this.) Or, John and Louise might offer the trustee exempt property in place of the vase.

EXAMPLE 2: Over the years, Mari has carefully constructed an expensive computer system that she uses primarily for hobbies but also as a work tool for her marginal desktop publishing business. The computer system does not qualify for a specific exemption in her state. Over a substantial period of time, Mari has also amassed a debt of $100,000, consisting primarily of credit card debts, medical bills, and department store charges.

If Mari files for Chapter 7 bankruptcy, she can discharge all of her debts, because they are unsecured and she did not incur them fraudulently. However, unless a wildcard exemption protects the computer system's value, Mari must either surrender most of the computer equipment so it can be sold for the benefit of her creditors (though she may be able to keep the pieces essential to her desktop publishing business as exempt tools of her trade) or find a way to replace them with exempt property of equivalent value. Mari decides that canceling her debts is far more important to her than hanging on to the entire system, and proceeds to file for Chapter 7 bankruptcy.

Alternatives to Chapter 7 Bankruptcy

In many situations, filing for Chapter 7 bankruptcy is the best remedy for debt problems. In others, however, another course of action makes more sense. This section outlines your main alternatives.

Do Nothing

Surprisingly, the best approach for some people who are deeply in debt is to take no action at all. If you're living simply (that is, with little income and property) and look forward to a similar life in the future, you may be judgment proof. This means that anyone who sues you and obtains a court judgment won't be able to collect—simply because you don't have anything they can legally take. (As a famous song of the 1970s said, "Freedom's just another word for nothing left to lose.") Except in highly unusual situations (for example, if you are a tax protester or willfully refuse to pay child support), you can't be thrown in jail for failing to pay your debts.

Normally, creditors cannot take your property or income without first suing you and obtaining a court judgment (except for taxing authorities and student loan collectors). Even if the creditor is armed with a court judgment, the law prevents creditors (except the IRS, of course) from taking property that is exempt under your state's general exemption laws, including food, clothing, personal effects, and furnishings. (See "Will You Lose Valuable Property?" above.) And creditors won't go after your nonexempt property unless it is worth enough to cover the creditor's costs of seizure and sale.

Before taking property, creditors usually try to go after your wages and other income. But a creditor can take only 25% of your net wages to satisfy a court judgment, unless it is for child support or alimony. Often, you can keep more than 75% of your wages if you can demonstrate that you need the extra amount to support yourself and your family. Income from a pension or another retirement benefit is usually treated like wages. Creditors cannot touch public benefits such as welfare, unemployment insurance, disability insurance, SSI, or Social Security.

To sum up, if you don't have a steady job or another source of income that a creditor can snatch, or you can live on 75% of your wages (or perhaps a little more), you needn't fear a lawsuit. Similarly, if most of your property is exempt, there is little the creditor can seize to repay the debt. In this situation, most creditors don't bother trying to collect the debt at all.

Now that you have the good news, here's some bad: Judgments usually last for five to ten years and are usually subject to renewal for similar periods of time. In this age of computers, credit reporting agencies, and massive databases that track our every activity, you may have to live with your decision to do nothing for a long, long time. And, in many cases, interest on your debt will continue to accrue, which means the $10,000 you owe today could become a $100,000 debt in the future.

Even if you are judgment proof, you may be better off dealing with your debt situation now, either through bankruptcy or through one of the other alternatives discussed below. For example, if you don't file for bankruptcy and later receive a windfall— lottery winnings or an unexpected inheritance—you may lose the windfall to your creditors. Windfalls you receive after you file for Chapter 7 bankruptcy, on the other hand, are usually yours to keep.

Negotiate With Your Creditors

If you have some income, or you have assets you're willing to sell, you may be a lot better off negotiating with your creditors than filing for bankruptcy. Through negotiation, you may be able to come up with a new payment plan that allows you to get back on your feet. Or, you may be able to settle your debt for less than you owe.

Negotiating With Creditors After the Great Recession

Back in the good old days (before the economy collapsed), if you stopped paying your bills you could easily negotiate a settlement of 50% or less as soon as six months after your default, with no questions asked—and sometimes for even far less. Things have changed, however, and most creditors now require proof that you're experiencing financial distress just to get the conversation started. This means filling out financial questionnaires and turning over documents such as paycheck stubs and bank statements. Of course, it is understandable why creditors do this. Your creditors (and debt collectors) want to get as much from you as possible. However, be aware that when you turn this information over, you're providing the creditor with information it can later use to garnish your wages and levy against your bank account.

 RESOURCE
Negotiating with creditors. How to negotiate with your creditors is covered in detail in *Solve Your Money Troubles* by Robin Leonard (Nolo).

Tax Consequences of Forgiven Debts

Deciding to ignore your debts could increase your tax burden. The IRS treats certain forgiven debts (debts for which a creditor agrees to take nothing or less than is owed) and debts written off (debts that the creditor has stopped trying to collect, declared uncollectible, and reported as a tax loss to the IRS) as taxable income to you. (26 U.S.C. § 108.) Any bank, credit union, savings and loan, or other financial institution that forgives or writes off all or part of a debt for $600 or more must send you and the IRS a Form 1099-A or 1099-C at the end of the tax year. When you file your tax return, you must report the write-off as income and pay taxes on it.

There are a number of exceptions to this rule. For example, if your mortgage was partly or wholly forgiven in 2007 through 2014 through foreclosure or loan restructuring, you may not have to report it as income. (This may be extended beyond 2014. Check "Get Legal Updates and More at Nolo.com" in the introductory chapter, "Your Chapter 7 Bankruptcy Companion.") You also don't have to report a debt if you were insolvent when the creditor agreed to waive or write it off. Generally, you are insolvent if your debts, including the debt that was forgiven or written off, exceed the value of your assets.

If you receive a Form 1099-C, you may need to complete IRS Form 982, *Reduction of Tax Attributes Due to Discharge of Indebtedness*, to show that an exception applies. (You can download the form and instructions at www.irs.gov.) Unfortunately, using this form can be complicated, especially if you're claiming the insolvency exception; you might need help from an accountant to complete it correctly.

Get Outside Help to Design a Repayment Plan

Many people have trouble negotiating with creditors, either because they don't have the skills and negotiating experience to do a good job or because they find the whole process exceedingly unpleasant. Because the ability to negotiate is an art, many people benefit from outside help.

TIP
The best time to negotiate. Your best chance of getting a good settlement is at the end of the month when collection agency employees are trying hard to meet their end-of-the-month collection goals. A good strategy involves calling a few days before the month's end and offering to make a lump sum payment within 24 hours. Cold hard cash will motivate the agent to settle for less; payment plans are not as enticing.

Avoiding Credit Counseling and Debt Repayment Plan Scams

Be careful if you plan to use credit counseling services or enter into a debt repayment plan. According to the Federal Trade Commission, scams involving debt repayment plans are rampant. According to numerous consumer complaints, some of these companies:

- fail to pay creditors on time or at all
- make promises they don't keep, like getting lower interest rates and reduced fees from creditors
- charge unreasonably high fees to consumers
- hide charges or take them out of deposits that are earmarked for creditors, and
- lie about the company's nonprofit status.

Before considering a debt repayment plan, make sure you are dealing with a legitimate nonprofit credit counseling agency, explore all of your other options first, get everything in writing, and follow up with your creditors to make sure they are getting paid on time.

Better yet, use an agency that has been approved by the U.S. Trustee for bankruptcy credit counseling. These agencies must be nonprofits and meet certain requirements and are overseen by the U.S. Trustee, which gives you some protection against fraudulent practices. You can find a list of approved agencies at the U.S. Trustee's website, at www.usdoj.gov/ust.

If you don't want to negotiate with your creditors, you can turn to a lawyer or to a credit counseling agency. These agencies come in two basic varieties: nonprofit and for profit. They all work on the same basic principle: A repayment plan is negotiated with all of your unsecured creditors. You make one monthly payment to the agency, which distributes the payment to your creditors as provided in the plan. As long as you make the payments, the creditors will not take any action against you. And, if you succeed in completing the plan, one or more of your creditors may be willing to offer you new credit on reasonable terms.

The nonprofit agencies tend to be funded primarily by the major creditors (in the form of a commission for each repayment plan they negotiate) and by moderate fees charged the user (roughly $20–$25 per plan negotiated). The for-profit agencies are funded by the same sources but tend to charge much higher fees.

The big downside to entering into one of the repayment plans is that if you fail to make a payment, the creditors may pull the plug on the deal and come after you, regardless of how faithful you've been in the past. When that happens, you may find that you would have been better off filing for bankruptcy in the first place.

Pay Over Time With Chapter 13 Bankruptcy

In Chapter 13 bankruptcy, you enter into a court-approved plan to deal with your debts over three to five years. Some debts must be paid in full (back taxes are the most common examples), while others may be paid only in part. The basic idea is that you must devote all of your disposable income to payment of your unsecured creditors. So if you experience a significant increase in income during the plan period, the Chapter 13 bankruptcy judge can increase your plan payments.

With a few exceptions, Chapter 13 doesn't require you to give up any property. However, you must pay a price if you have nonexempt property. To propose a feasible Chapter 13 plan, you are required to pay your unsecured creditors at least what they would have received from the property had you filed for Chapter 7 bankruptcy. In other words, while you don't have to give up your property, you sort of have to buy a portion of it back over three to five years, plus 10% (roughly) in trustee fees. In addition to this "buy-back" requirement, the bankruptcy code has guidelines for calculating exactly how much you must pay into your plan, based on your income:

- If your current monthly income (as defined by the bankruptcy law—see "Who Cannot File for Chapter 7" above) is more than the median family income for your state, you must commit to paying all of your "disposable income" into your plan for five years. To calculate your disposable income, you must use expenses dictated by the IRS, which could be significantly less than your actual expenses. This means that you may be obligated to pay more money into your plan than you actually have left over each month, after paying your bills and living expenses.

- If your current monthly income is less than the state median, you can propose a three-year repayment plan. You can also calculate your disposable income using your actual expenses, rather than the IRS standards.

To file for Chapter 13 bankruptcy, you fill out almost the same set of forms as in a Chapter 7 bankruptcy and file them with the bankruptcy court along with a filing fee of $310. In addition, you must file your most recent tax return for the last four years. (It's OK if you are delinquent on taxes, but you must file the returns.) You must also file a feasible repayment plan and serve a copy of the plan on each of your creditors. With the possible exception of current payments on your mortgage and car note, you make plan payments directly to the bankruptcy trustee, who in turn distributes the money to your creditors. When you complete your plan, any remaining unpaid balances on unsecured, dischargeable debts are wiped out.

Chapter 13 requires you to pay down your debts over time, but few filers pay back 100% of what they owe. Priority debts, like child support you owe your family and recent back taxes, must be paid in full. (See Ch. 6 for more on which debts qualify as priority debts.) Short-term secured debts (debts that will mature while your plan is in effect) must also be paid in full. However, the debts that bedevil most people—such as credit card debts and medical bills, which are neither priority nor secured—only have to be paid down if you have enough "disposable income" to manage the task after you've met all the other repayment requirements.

For instance, if your Chapter 13 paperwork shows that you will have only $200 left each month after paying your reasonable living expenses, and you need to put all of that money toward paying off an income tax debt or other priority debt over the life of your plan, you can propose what's known as a "zero-percent plan." In this type of plan, your unsecured, nonpriority creditors get nothing. (If you have nonexempt property, however, your plan must pay your unsecured, nonpriority creditors at least what they would have received from the property in a Chapter 7 bankruptcy, as explained above.) If your paperwork shows that you'll have income left after paying your expenses and priority debt, that money goes to your unsecured, nonpriority creditors. If you still have unpaid unsecured debt when your plan ends, it will be discharged.

Like Chapter 7 bankruptcy, Chapter 13 bankruptcy doesn't wipe out all types of debts. Alimony and child support arrearages, criminal penalties, certain tax debts, debts arising from injuries caused by your intoxicated driving, certain debts or creditors you don't list on your bankruptcy papers, and debts arising from your fraudulent conduct all may survive your bankruptcy filing, whether you file under Chapter 7 or Chapter 13. And, as in Chapter 7, student loan debts will be discharged only if you can show that repaying the loan would cause a substantial hardship. (For more on each of these types of debts, see Ch. 9.) Debts arising from a civil judgment against you for maliciously or willfully injuring or killing someone will also survive a Chapter 13 bankruptcy.

In addition to these debts, there are certain debts that are discharged only in Chapter 13—that is, these debts will survive Chapter 7 bankruptcy, but will be wiped out at the end of your repayment plan if you file under Chapter 13. These debts include:

- marital debts (other than for support) created in a divorce or settlement agreement
- debts incurred to pay a nondischargeable tax debt
- court fees
- condominium, cooperative, and homeowners' association fees

- debts for loans from a retirement plan, and
- debts that couldn't be discharged in a previous bankruptcy.

You can file for Chapter 13 bankruptcy at any time, even if you got a Chapter 7 bankruptcy discharge the day before. However, you can't get your Chapter 13 discharge if you filed your Chapter 13 case within four years after filing your Chapter 7 case. Even if you can't get a discharge, however, you can still benefit from being a Chapter 13 debtor. For instance, if you continue to owe taxes or back child support after your Chapter 7 bankruptcy, Chapter 13 will let you propose a plan under which you will pay off these arrearages over a three- to five-year period—and keep these creditors off your back in the meantime. Another benefit, according to some courts, is that the debtor may eliminate (strip off) a completely unsecured second mortgage lien even though the discharge is not available. Several courts, however, have ruled that lien stripping is not allowed absent a discharge. (*In re Gerardin*, 447 B.R. 342 (Bankr. S.D. Fla. 2011), *In re Victorio*, 454 B.R. 759 (Bankr. S.D. Cal. 2011), aff'd, 470 B.R. 545 (Bankr. S.D. Cal. 2012).

CAUTION

Check with an attorney if you want to strip off liens without a discharge. Whether you can strip off a wholly unsecured second mortgage lien in a Chapter 13 if you are not entitled to a discharge is one of the most hotly debated issues in bankruptcy. Currently, bankruptcy courts have conflicting opinions on whether debtors may eliminate an unsecured second mortgage without a discharge. As a result, if you wish to strip off a junior mortgage from your house, talk to a knowledgeable bankruptcy attorney in your area to learn the rules in your jurisdiction before filing for Chapter 7 bankruptcy.

If you start, but are not able to finish, a Chapter 13 repayment plan—for example, you lose your job six months into the plan and can't make the payments—the trustee may agree to modify your plan. The trustee may give you a grace period (if the problem seems temporary), reduce your total monthly payments, or extend the repayment period. As long as it looks like you're acting in good faith, the trustee will try to help you across rocky periods. If it's clear you won't be able to complete the plan because of circumstances beyond your control, the court might let you discharge your debts on the basis of hardship. Examples of hardship would be a sudden plant closing in a one-factory town or a debilitating illness. However, a hardship discharge lacks many of the benefits that a regular discharge gets you.

If the bankruptcy court won't let you modify your plan or give you a hardship discharge, you still have two options:

- You can convert your case to a Chapter 7 bankruptcy (unless you received a Chapter 7 discharge in a case filed within the previous eight years).
- You can ask the bankruptcy court to dismiss your Chapter 13 petition, which would leave you in the same position you were in before you filed, except you'll owe less because of the payments you made on your debts through the repayment plan. If your Chapter 13 bankruptcy is dismissed, your creditors may add any interest that was abated during your Chapter 13 case to the total amount you owe.

CAUTION

You may qualify for Chapter 13 even if you don't have sufficient disposable income to complete your plan. The bankruptcy law assumes that your monthly income during your plan will be the same as your average income during the six months before you filed for bankruptcy. If you lost a job or otherwise experienced a drop in income during those six months, your actual income could be quite a bit less than the law assumes it will be. In addition, certain higher-income filers will have to calculate their expenses using IRS standards, which are often less than their actual living expenses. This means that you may not be able, as a practical matter, to make the payments required by a Chapter 13 plan, even if you qualify to file under the figures used in the new law.

Do You Qualify for Chapter 13 Bankruptcy?

Like Chapter 7, there are several requirements you must meet in order to qualify for Chapter 13 bankruptcy:

- **You must file as an individual.** Only individuals, not business entities (such as partnerships or corporations), can file for Chapter 13. If you are the sole owner of a business entity (like a corporation) and you vote to transfer all of its assets and debts to yourself as an individual, you can effectively liquidate the business and claim all of its debts and assets as belonging to you personally in a Chapter 13 bankruptcy, however.

- **Your debt must not be too high.** Your total secured debt (debt for which you have pledged collateral or that otherwise gives the creditor the right to seize property if you don't pay) may not exceed $1,149,525, and your total unsecured debt may not exceed $383,175.

- **You must be able to propose a legally feasible repayment plan.** If you have sufficient income to pay all of your priority debts (for instance, child support and tax debts), make required monthly payments—and pay back any arrearages—on your secured debts (such as a mortgage or car note), and pay at least some money toward your unsecured debts over the next five years, you can probably propose a Chapter 13 plan that will pass legal muster.

  One way to figure out whether you can propose a feasible plan is to take the means test—an eligibility requirement for Chapter 7 that asks higher-income filers to show that they cannot propose a feasible Chapter 13 repayment plan. If the means test shows that you will have at least some money left over each month to pay toward your unsecured, nonpriority debts, you should be able to come up with a feasible Chapter 13 plan. The means test is covered in detail in Ch. 6.

RESOURCE

Resources for Chapter 13 bankruptcy. For general information on Chapter 13 bankruptcy, get a copy of *The New Bankruptcy* by Stephen Elias and Leon Bayer (Nolo). If you are interested in filing for Chapter 13 bankruptcy, see *Chapter 13 Bankruptcy* by Stephen Elias and Kathleen Michon (Nolo), which provides comprehensive information about Chapter 13 bankruptcy.

Family Farmers Should Consider Chapter 12 Bankruptcy

Chapter 12 bankruptcy, which is similar to Chapter 13 bankruptcy in many respects, is specially designed for family farmers and provides a way to keep the farm while paying off debts over time.

Only people and entities that meet the definition of family farmer may use Chapter 12. To qualify as a family farmer:

- your debts cannot exceed $4,031,575 for farming operations or $1,868,200 for commercial fishing operations

- 50% or more of your debt (80% for a family fisherman) must have arisen from the farming operation, not including a purchase money mortgage

- 50% or more of your income must have been earned from the farming or fishing operation in the year preceding the filing of the petition, and

- your income must be "sufficiently stable and regular" to enable payments under a Chapter 12 plan.

Like Chapter 13, you must file a schedule of assets and liabilities and a statement of financial affairs. Even though a trustee is appointed to supervise the plan, the farm debtor remains in possession of the farm assets and actions by creditors are automatically stayed upon filing the petition.

As in Chapter 13, you must file a plan that meets Chapter 12 requirements. The plan must provide that all unsecured debts are paid in full or, alternatively, all disposable income is used to pay down the unsecured debt over the ensuing three-year period (which can be extended to five years with court permission). Plan payments must pay unsecured creditors at least what they would have received in a Chapter 7 bankruptcy. After completion of the plan, all are discharged except debts that wouldn't be dischargeable in Chapter 7.

Chapter 12 has several advantages over Chapter 13 bankruptcy. The court has unrestricted authority to modify (cram down) secured debts, such as mortgages and car notes, so the debt matches the market value of the property. This is different from Chapter 13, where cramdowns cannot be used for mortgages on your primary residence and recent car loans. Another advantage of Chapter 12: Secured debts that extend beyond the plan period can be modified without having to pay them all off in the plan. That is, payments can extend beyond the plan until the debt is paid off in the normal course of time. And unlike Chapter 13, priority debts do not have to be paid in full so long as all disposable income over a five-year period is devoted to the plan.

If you are a farmer, we recommend that you speak with a bankruptcy attorney about Chapter 12 bankruptcy before choosing to file a Chapter 7 bankruptcy. (For information on finding a bankruptcy lawyer, see Ch. 10.)

Business Entities Might Benefit From Chapter 11 Bankruptcy

Chapter 11 bankruptcy is a procedure in which everyone who has an economic interest in a business comes together under court supervision to work out a plan under which the business can get on top of its debt and continue its operations. General Motors and Chrysler are the most recent examples of businesses using Chapter 11 to put themselves in a better economic position.

You don't have to be a huge corporation to file under Chapter 11. Even individuals qualify. You do, however, have to be prepared to pay an enormous amount of attorneys' fees. A typical Chapter 11 bankruptcy requires lots of meetings and court hearings on various disputed issues, and everyone has to appear through lawyers who are paid out of the bankrupt business's coffers. It's not at all unusual for a business to pay more

than $100,000 in attorneys' fees, often much more. Most businesses that start in Chapter 11 with the hope of staying in business end up converting to Chapter 7 (and liquidating what's left of their assets) after they run out of money to pay the lawyers.

Chapter 13 May Reduce Certain Secured Debts That Are Heavy With Interest

Chapter 13 bankruptcy allows you to break certain secured debts into two parts: the part that is secured by the fair market value of the collateral, and any part of the debt that is unsecured because it exceeds the value of the collateral. You must pay the replacement value of the collateral (the secured part) in your Chapter 13 plan, but you can discharge the unsecured portion along with your other unsecured debts. This procedure is popularly referred to as a cramdown.

For example, people often owe more on a car than the car is worth. This is because the car note includes a lot of interest, and most cars depreciate in value fairly rapidly. In some cases, Chapter 13 allows you to cram down the debt on the car to the car's replacement value (what it would cost to purchase the car from a retail vendor, considering its age and condition) and get rid of the rest of the debt over the life of your plan. You may also be able to cram down debts for other types of property, including real estate in some situations. However, there are a couple of exceptions to the cramdown rule:

- You can cram down a car contract only if you bought the car more than 30 months before filing for bankruptcy.
- You can cram down contracts on other types of property only if you bought the property more than a year before filing for bankruptcy.
- You can cram down a mortgage on a mobile home if your state law classifies mobile homes as personal property, even though the mobile home is situated on real property. (*In re Ennis*, 558 F.3d 343 (4th Cir. 2009).)
- You can cram down mortgages owed on second homes, vacation homes, and rental properties.

The Automatic Stay

One of the most powerful features of bankruptcy is the automatic stay: a court order that goes into effect as soon as you file and protects you from certain actions by your creditors. The automatic stay stops most debt collectors dead in their tracks and keeps them at bay for the rest of your case. Once you file, all collection activity (with a few exceptions, explained below) must go through the bankruptcy court. Most creditors cannot take any further action against you directly while the bankruptcy is pending.

The purpose of the automatic stay is, in the words of Congress, to give debtors a "breathing spell" from their creditors and a break from the financial pressures that drove them to file for bankruptcy. In a Chapter 7 bankruptcy, it serves another purpose as well: to preserve the status quo at the time you file. The automatic stay ensures that the trustee—not your creditors—will be responsible for ultimately deciding which property you will be able to keep, which property you will have to give up, and how the proceeds will be divided if the trustee takes and sells any of your belongings.

This chapter explains how the automatic stay applies to typical debt collection efforts, including a couple of situations in which you might not get the protection of the automatic stay. It also covers how the automatic stay works in eviction proceedings, vital information for any renter who files for bankruptcy.

TIP

You don't need bankruptcy to stop your creditors from harassing you. Many people begin thinking about bankruptcy when their creditors start phoning them at home and on the job. Federal law (and the law of many states) prohibits this activity by debt collectors once you tell the creditor, in writing, that you don't want to be called. And if you orally tell debt collectors that you refuse to pay, they cannot, by law, contact you except to send one last letter making a final demand for payment before filing a lawsuit. While just telling the creditor to stop usually works, you may have to send a written follow-up letter. (You can find a sample letter in Ch. 1.)

Actions Prohibited by the Stay

When you file for any kind of bankruptcy, the automatic stay goes into effect. It's "automatic" because you don't have to ask the court to issue the stay, and the court doesn't have to take any special action to make it effective; once you file, the stay is in place, automatically. The stay prohibits creditors and collection agencies from taking any action to collect most kinds of debts you owe them, unless the law or the bankruptcy court says they can.

In some circumstances, the creditor can file an action in court to have the stay lifted (called a Motion to Lift Stay or a Motion for Relief From Stay). In others, the creditor can simply begin collection proceedings without seeking advance permission from the court.

The good news is that the most common type of creditor collection actions are still stopped dead by the stay—harassing calls by debt collectors, threatening letters by attorneys, lawsuits to collect payment for credit card and health care bills, and actions to recover property, such as car repossessions, home foreclosures, and wage garnishments. This section explains which collection actions are stopped by the automatic stay.

Credit Card Debts, Medical Debts, and Attorneys' Fees

Anyone trying to collect credit card debts, medical debts, attorneys' fees, debts arising from breach of contract, or legal judgments against you (other than for child support and alimony) must cease all collection activities after you file your bankruptcy case. A creditor or collector cannot:

- file a lawsuit or proceed with a pending lawsuit against you
- record liens against your property
- report the debt to a credit reporting bureau, or
- seize your property or income, such as money in a bank account or your paycheck.

Warning: Stop Your Bank From Draining Your Account

You know it's a bad day when you try to use your debit card to pay for lunch only to find out that your credit card company wiped out your bank account. If your rent money is gone too, you're probably facing a truly catastrophic situation. To put it plainly, it is risky to have savings and checking accounts from a bank that also has provided you with a credit card or loan. If you do, and you fall behind on your credit card or loan payments, the bank can take your checking and savings account funds to pay your debt through a nasty collection trick called a "setoff," something you likely gave your bank permission to do when you signed your credit agreement.

Fortunately, you'll only have to worry about this before you file bankruptcy because once filed, the automatic stay prevents your creditors from surprising you with these devastating collection maneuvers. Keep in mind, though, that your bank could still "freeze" funds to cover your debts. (See "Bank Setoffs v. Account Freezing," below.)

In the meantime, there is an easy work-around for this pitfall. To prevent your bank from emptying your account, make sure the bank you get a credit card or loan from is different from the bank where you have a checking or savings account. If they aren't, switch your checking and savings accounts to another bank.

Bank Setoffs v. Account Freezing

Setoffs and the freezing of accounts are two separate banking problems. A setoff can occur *before* you file bankruptcy, but not afterwards since once filed, the automatic stay stops a creditor from taking collection actions against you. (See "Warning: Stop Your Bank From Draining Your Account," above.)

The freezing of your bank account is something that can happen *after* you file bankruptcy. Some banks—but not all—will freeze your account after receiving notice of your filing as a way of protecting money for creditors. They are allowed to do this because the bank isn't taking the money in violation of the automatic stay—only preventing you from removing the money before the trustee decides what should be done with it. If, on Schedule C, you claimed as exempt the money in the frozen account (meaning that you declared that you have the right to keep it), this situation is fairly easy to fix. Call the trustee and explain that the bank froze funds that are not a part of the bankruptcy estate and that you need the money for living expenses. In most cases, the trustee will contact the bank and instruct it to release your funds. Of course, this can take some time (usually a week or two) so you should do your best to prepare yourself in case it happens.

Public Benefits

Government entities that are seeking to collect overpayments of public benefits, such as SSI, Medicaid, or Temporary Assistance to Needy Families (welfare) benefits, cannot reduce or terminate your benefits to get that money back while your bankruptcy is pending. If, however, you become ineligible for benefits, including Medicare benefits, bankruptcy doesn't prevent the agency from denying or terminating your benefits on that ground.

Debt Associated With Criminal Proceedings

If a case against you can be broken down into criminal and debt components, only the criminal component will be allowed to continue. The debt component will be put on hold while your bankruptcy is pending. For example, if you were convicted of writing a bad check and have been sentenced to community service and ordered to pay a fine, your obligation to do community service will not be stopped by the automatic stay, but your obligation to pay the fine will.

IRS Liens and Levies

Certain tax proceedings are not affected by the automatic stay (see "When the Stay Doesn't Apply," below, for more information). The automatic stay does, however, stop the IRS from issuing a lien or seizing (levying against) your property or income.

Foreclosures

Foreclosures are initially stayed by your bankruptcy filing. However, if you filed another bankruptcy case previously and the court lifted the stay as to a specific piece of real property you own through an "in rem" order in that proceeding, the stay won't apply to that property for a period of two years after the order was entered. In other words, the law doesn't allow you to prevent a foreclosure by filing serial bankruptcies.

Even if this is your first bankruptcy, filing won't stop certain time periods associated with a state's foreclosure procedures from "running." For example, state law might give a homeowner the right to two or three months' notice before the home is sold. Once a homeowner receives advance notice of foreclosure, the home may not be sold until the notice period has ended. In these states, filing for bankruptcy won't stop the notice period from elapsing. However, the sale itself can't happen while you are in bankruptcy unless the foreclosing party gets permission from the bankruptcy judge by filing a motion to lift the stay.

If the lender moves to lift the stay and can show that even with the bankruptcy the foreclosure will ultimately occur, the court is likely to lift the stay. You may be able to successfully oppose the motion to lift the stay by challenging the lender's right to file the motion because it cannot show proof that it owns the mortgage. A lender's inability to show proof that it owns the mortgage is increasingly common in this age of robosigning, shoddy bank paperwork, and bundling mortgages together and then transferring them to various banks, trusts, and investment vehicles. But, even if you are successful in defeating the motion to lift the stay, in Chapter 7 bankruptcy, your victory will only last as long as your bankruptcy—typically only a month or two after the motion is heard.

However, in Chapter 13 cases, if you defeat the motion to lift the stay, you might be able to prevent foreclosure altogether. (See Ch. 7 to learn more about opposing a motion to lift the automatic stay.)

Utilities

Companies providing you with utilities (such as gas, heating oil, electricity, telephone service, and water) may not cut you off because you file for bankruptcy. However, they can shut off your service 20 days after you file if you don't provide them with a deposit or another means to assure future payment. They can also terminate service if you fail to pay for it after you file. (See *In re Jones*, 369 B.R. 745 (B.A.P. 1st Cir. 2007).)

One court has found that cable television isn't a utility, and service can therefore be stopped if the debtor fails to pay the bill before filing for bankruptcy. (*In re Darby*, 470 F.3d 573 (5th Cir. 2006).)

When the Stay Doesn't Apply

The stay doesn't put a stop to every type of collection action, nor does it apply in every situation. Congress has determined that certain debts or proceedings are sufficiently important to "trump" the automatic stay. In these situations (described in "Actions Not Stopped by the Stay," below), collection actions can continue just as if you had never filed for bankruptcy.

In addition to the specific types of collection actions that can continue despite the stay, there are circumstances in which you can lose the protection of the stay through your own actions. These are described below as well.

Actions Not Stopped by the Stay

The automatic stay does not prohibit the following types of actions from proceeding.

Divorce and Child Support

Almost all proceedings related to divorce or parenting continue unaffected by the automatic stay. These include actions to:

- set and collect current child support and alimony
- collect back child support and alimony from property that is not in the bankruptcy estate (see Ch. 3 for more information on what's in the bankruptcy estate)
- determine child custody and visitation
- establish paternity in a lawsuit
- modify child support and alimony
- protect a spouse or child from domestic violence
- withhold income to collect child support
- report overdue support to credit bureaus
- intercept tax refunds to pay back child support, and
- withhold, suspend, or restrict drivers' and professional licenses as leverage to collect child support.

Tax Proceedings

The IRS can continue certain actions, such as conducting a tax audit, issuing a tax deficiency notice, demanding a tax return, issuing a tax assessment, or demanding payment of an assessment.

Pension Loans

The stay doesn't prevent withholding from a debtor's income to repay a loan from an ERISA-qualified pension (this includes most job-related pensions and individual retirement plans). See Ch. 3 for more on how pensions are treated in bankruptcy.

How You Can Lose the Protection of the Stay

Even in circumstances where the stay would otherwise apply, you can lose its protection through your own actions. The stay may not protect you from collection efforts if:

- you had a bankruptcy case pending within the year before you file your current case, and the court refuses your request to allow the stay to kick in, or

- you don't meet the deadlines set out in the bankruptcy code for dealing with property that serves as collateral for a secured debt.

Prior Cases Pending

The automatic stay will last only 30 days if you had a prior bankruptcy case pending within the year before you file (unless you can get the court to extend it). (11 U.S.C. §§ 362(c)(3) and (4).) And if you had two cases pending in the last year, the automatic stay will not kick in at all (unless the court orders it).

If the automatic stay terminates because of one or two prior pending cases, the property of the bankruptcy estate—in your current bankruptcy filing—is still protected. As explained in more detail in Ch. 3, your bankruptcy estate includes most types of property that you own or are entitled to receive when you file your bankruptcy papers, but does not include money earned or most property received after filing. For example, a creditor would not be entitled to seize money that was in your bank account on the date you filed, but could levy on wages you earned after filing, which are not part of the bankruptcy estate.

One Dismissal in the Past Year

With a couple of exceptions, if you had a bankruptcy case pending and dismissed during the previous year for any reason, voluntarily or involuntarily, the court will presume that your new filing is in bad faith, and the stay will terminate after 30 days in your new case. You, the trustee, the U.S. Trustee, or the creditor can ask the court to continue the stay beyond the 30-day period, but the court will do this only if you (or whoever else makes the request) can show that your current case was not filed in bad faith.

The motion to continue the stay must be scheduled for hearing within the 30-day period after you file for bankruptcy and must give creditors adequate notice of why the stay should be extended. This means the motion must:

- be filed within several days after you file for bankruptcy, (unless you obtain an "Order Shortening Time" from the judge, a simple procedure in which you ask the judge to shorten the time between service of the motion on your creditors and the hearing on the motion)

- be served on all creditors to whom you want the stay to apply, and
- provide specific reasons why your current filing is not in bad faith and the stay should be extended.

When Is a Case Pending?

If you've had a bankruptcy case dismissed within the last couple of years, you may be wondering exactly when that case is no longer "pending" and, therefore, when the one- and two-year time periods for losing the automatic stay begin to run. This can be tough to figure out, partly because some cases remain open long after they are dismissed. The general rule is that a dismissed case is no longer pending, even if it continues to be open after that date. In other words, the one- and two-year periods start on the date a case is dismissed.

> **EXAMPLE:** Clayton's Chapter 7 bankruptcy case is dismissed by the court on January 20, 2012, because Clayton missed a deadline for filing required documents. Before the case is closed, Clayton files a motion to set aside the dismissal and be allowed to proceed with his case; the court denies his motion. The case is ultimately closed on March 20, 2012. Clayton files for bankruptcy again on January 21, 2013. Because at least one year has passed since Clayton's previous case was dismissed, he is entitled to the protection of the automatic stay.

When deciding whether to extend the stay beyond 30 days, the court will look at a number of factors to decide whether your current filing is in good faith. Here are some of the factors that will work against you:

- More than one prior bankruptcy case was filed by (or against) you in the past year.
- Your prior case was dismissed because you failed to file required documents on time (for instance, you didn't file your credit counseling certificate within 14 days or failed to amend the petition on a timely basis when required to do so). If you failed to file these documents

inadvertently or because of a careless error, that won't help you with the judge—unless you used an attorney in the prior case. Judges are more willing to give debtors the benefit of the doubt if their attorney was responsible for the mistake.

- The prior case was dismissed while a creditor's request for relief from the stay was pending.
- Your circumstances haven't changed since your previous case was dismissed.

Two Dismissals in the Past Year

If you had two or more cases pending and dismissed during the previous year, no stay will apply in your current case. You won't even get the initial 30-day stay that would apply if you had only one bankruptcy case pending within the past year. The only way to get the benefit of the stay is to convince the court, within 30 days of your filing, that your current case was not filed in bad faith and that a stay should therefore be granted. The court will look at the factors outlined above to decide whether you have overcome the presumption of bad faith.

Missing Deadlines for Handling Secured Debts

If you have property that secures a debt—that is, property that the creditor has a right to take if you don't pay the debt—you will have to file a Statement of Intention with the court and serve it on your creditors. The Statement of Intention explains what you want to do with the collateral. You have several choices:

- give the property back to the creditor and get rid of the debt (called "surrendering" the property)
- keep the property and pay the creditor what it would cost to replace it, given its age and condition, which is often less than what you still owe on the debt (called "redeeming" the property), or
- keep the property and reaffirm the contract, which means that you will continue to owe some or all of the debt after your bankruptcy (called "reaffirming" the debt).

The bankruptcy rules require you to mail this Statement of Intention to the secured creditor within 30 days after filing your bankruptcy case and to actually carry out your stated intention—by giving back the property, paying its replacement value to the creditor, or signing a reaffirmation agreement—within 30–45 days after your first creditors' meeting (because the law is contradictory on this time limit, you should take action within 30 days, to be on the safe side). If you don't meet these deadlines, the stay will no longer apply to that property (although it will continue to protect you otherwise). For example, assume you want to continue paying on your car note, but you don't serve your Statement of Intention on time. The stay will no longer protect your car or prevent the creditor from repossessing it, but your other property will still be protected. The Statement of Intention is discussed in more detail in Ch. 6; you can find lots more information on secured debts, including tips that will help you decide which of these options makes the most sense in your case, in Ch. 5.

Evictions

In the past, many people filed for Chapter 7 bankruptcy to stop the sheriff from enforcing a judgment for possession (an eviction order). While landlords could come into court and ask the judge to lift the automatic stay and let the eviction proceed, many landlords didn't know they had this right—and many others didn't have the wherewithal to hire attorneys (or the confidence to handle their own cases). In other words, filing for Chapter 7 bankruptcy often stopped court-ordered evictions from proceeding for the duration of the bankruptcy.

Today, things are a bit different. The 2005 bankruptcy law gives landlords the right to evict a tenant, despite the automatic stay, in either of the following cases:

- The landlord got a judgment for possession before the tenant filed for bankruptcy (if the judgment was for failing to pay rent, there is a possible exception to this rule, discussed below).
- The landlord is evicting the tenant for endangering the property or the illegal use of controlled substances on the property.

If the landlord does not already have a judgment when you file, and he or she wants to evict you for reasons other than endangering the property or using controlled substances (for example, the eviction is based on your failure to pay rent or violation of another lease provision), the automatic stay will prevent the landlord from beginning or continuing with eviction proceedings. However, the landlord can always ask the judge to lift the stay, and courts tend to grant these requests.

If the Landlord Already Has a Judgment

If your landlord has already obtained a judgment of possession against you when you file for bankruptcy, the automatic stay won't help you (with the possible exception described below). The landlord may proceed with the eviction just as if you never filed for bankruptcy.

If the eviction order is based on your failure to pay rent, you may be able to have the automatic stay reinstated. However, this exception applies only if your state's law allows you to stay in your rental unit and "cure" (pay back) the rent delinquency after the landlord has a judgment for possession. Here's what you'll have to do to take advantage of this exception:

Step 1: As part of your bankruptcy petition, you must file a certification (a statement under oath) stating that your state's laws allow you to cure the rent delinquency after the judgment is obtained, and to continue living in your rental unit. Very few states allow this. To find out whether yours is one of them, ask the sheriff or someone at legal aid (if you have legal aid in your area). In addition, when you file your bankruptcy petition, you must deposit with the court clerk the amount of rent that will become due during the 30-day period after you file.

Once you have filed your petition containing the certification and deposited the rent, you are protected from eviction for 30 days unless the landlord successfully objects to your initial certification before the 30-day period ends. If the landlord objects to your certification, the court must hold a hearing on the objection within ten days, so theoretically you could have less than 30 days of protection if the landlord files and serves the objection immediately.

Step 2: To keep the stay in effect longer, you must, before the 30-day period runs out, file and serve a second certification showing that you have fully cured the default in the manner provided by your state's law. However, if the landlord successfully objects to this second certification, the stay will no longer be in effect and the landlord may proceed with the eviction. As in Step 1, the court must hold a hearing within ten days if the landlord objects.

SEE AN EXPERT

If you really want to keep your rental, talk to a lawyer. As you can see, these rules are somewhat complicated. If you don't interpret your state's law properly, file the necessary paperwork on time, and successfully argue your side if the landlord objects, you could find yourself put out of your home. A good lawyer can tell you whether it's worth fighting an eviction—and, if so, how to go about it.

Endangering the Property or Illegal Use of Controlled Substances

Under the bankruptcy law, an eviction action will not be stayed by your bankruptcy filing if your landlord wants you out because you endangered the property or engaged in the "illegal use of controlled substances" on the property. And your landlord doesn't have to have a judgment in hand when you file for bankruptcy. The landlord may start an eviction action against you or continue with a pending eviction action even after your filing date if the eviction is based on property endangerment or drug use.

To evict you on these grounds after you have filed for bankruptcy, your landlord must file and serve on you a certification showing either of the following:

- The landlord has filed an eviction action against you based on property endangerment or illegal drug use on the property.
- You have endangered the property or engaged in illegal drug use on the property during the 30-day period prior to the landlord's certification.

If your landlord files this certification, he or she can proceed with the eviction 15 days later unless, within that time, you file and serve on the landlord an objection to the truth of the statements in the landlord's certification. If you do that, the court must hold a hearing on your objection within ten days. If you prove that the statements in the certification aren't true or have been remedied, you will be protected from the eviction while your bankruptcy is pending. If the court denies your objection, the eviction may proceed immediately.

As a practical matter, you will have a very difficult time proving a negative—that is, that you weren't endangering the property or using drugs. Similarly, once allegations of property endangerment or drug use are made, it's hard to see how they would be "remedied." In short, this is another area where you'll need a lawyer if you have to fight it out.

CAUTION

Landlords can always ask the court to lift the automatic stay to begin or continue an eviction on any grounds. Although the automatic stay will kick in unless one of these exceptions applies, the judge can lift the stay upon the landlord's request. And many courts are willing to do so, because most evictions will have no effect on the bankruptcy estate—that is, your tenancy isn't something that the trustee can turn into money to pay your creditors. As a general rule, bankruptcy courts are inclined to let landlords exercise their property rights regardless of the tenants' debt problems.

RESOURCE

Need help with your landlord? For more information on dealing with landlords—including landlords that are trying to evict you—see *Every Tenant's Legal Guide*, by Janet Portman and Marcia Stewart (Nolo).

When the Automatic Stay Protects Against Evictions

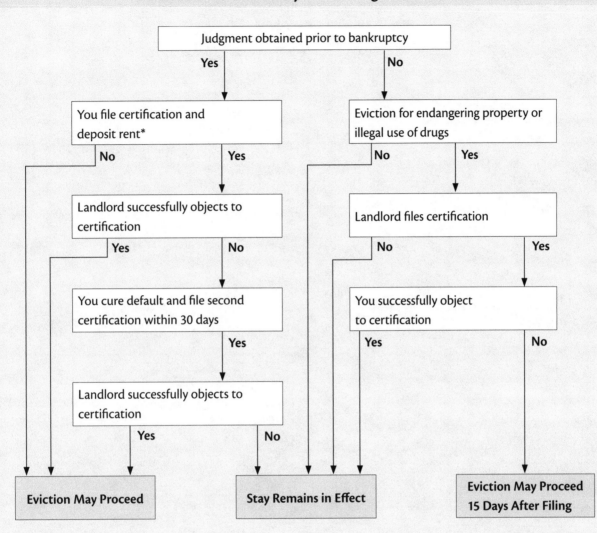

* This path only applies in the few states that allow a tenant to cure the rent delinquency after the landlord obtains a judgment for possession.

Your Property and Bankruptcy

This chapter explains what happens to your personal property when you file for Chapter 7 bankruptcy. First, we explain what property is subject to the reach of the bankruptcy court. Next, we cover exemptions: state and federal laws that determine what property you can keep when you file for bankruptcy. Happily, most people find that they can keep virtually all their personal property through the bankruptcy process.

If some of your property is not exempt, you may be able to exchange it for exempt items before you file or "buy it back" by paying the trustee a steeply discounted price. Below, we offer suggestions—and important cautions—if you want to try this.

RELATED TOPIC

More information on homes and collateral. This chapter covers personal property only, not real estate. If you own your home, Ch. 4 explains how to figure out whether you'll be able to keep it. And, if you own personal property that serves as collateral for a debt, that property is handled a bit differently. The special rules for these debts (called "secured" debts) are explained in Ch. 5.

Property in Your Bankruptcy Estate

When you file for Chapter 7 bankruptcy, almost everything you own when you file becomes subject to the bankruptcy court's authority. (The exceptions, listed in "Property That Isn't in Your Bankruptcy Estate," below, include pensions, tuition and individual education accounts, and, if you are filing alone, property you own with a spouse as tenants by the entirety.)

All property subject to the court's jurisdiction is collectively called your "bankruptcy estate." In addition to the property you own when you file, your estate also includes property you used to own but improperly transferred to someone else. Property you acquire after filing generally isn't part of your estate, although exceptions apply to certain types of property you acquire within six months after filing.

The trustee is very interested in your bankruptcy estate because he or she is entitled to a commission on any property that can be taken from your estate and sold to come up with some money to distribute to your unsecured creditors. Only property from which the trustee can realize a profit will be sold; you won't lose property that is worth very little or is protected by an exemption. (As explained in "Property You Can Keep (The Exemption System)," below, most state exemptions allow you to keep necessities, but may require you to give up one or more luxuries.)

Using the Information in This Chapter

This chapter will help you:

- **Decide whether bankruptcy is in your best interest.** Knowing what you own and how much you can get for it will help you decide whether or not to file for Chapter 7 bankruptcy. It may be easier simply to sell off some property (especially property that you would have to give up if you filed for bankruptcy) and pay creditors directly rather than to go through bankruptcy.

- **Determine what property you can keep.** You'll be able to keep some property no matter how much it is worth. However, your right to keep many types of property in bankruptcy often depends on the value of your ownership—that is, your equity. For instance, many states allow you to keep a car, but only if your equity is less than a certain amount (vehicle exemptions can range from $1,000 to $24,000 depending on the state you live in). If you own considerably more equity, you will have to turn the car over to the trustee to be sold (or "buy it back" by paying the trustee the equivalent value in cash or other exempt property). If the trustee sells the car, you'll get your exempt amount, and your creditors will get the rest.

- **Summarize information about your property before you file.** If you decide to file for bankruptcy, you'll need to fill out forms listing what property you own, how much it's worth, and what you claim as exempt. The work you do in this chapter can be transferred to those forms.

If You Convert From Chapter 13

If you originally filed for Chapter 13 bankruptcy and convert your case to Chapter 7, your Chapter 7 bankruptcy estate consists of everything you owned when you filed the Chapter 13 (as long as you still own it when you convert to Chapter 7). In one case, a trustee required debtors who converted from Chapter 13 to Chapter 7 to hand over their clothes, $3,660 worth of personal property, and their family dog, all of which were classified as "nonexempt" in their Chapter 13 paperwork. (*In re John*, 352 B.R. 895 (Bankr. N.D. Fla. 2006).) This happened because the debtors did not claim the right to exempt this property when they filed for Chapter 13. If you find yourself in this situation, consult with an attorney. He or she can ask the court to allow you to keep your property on the grounds that to relinquish it would cause you hardship.

If you convert your case in bad faith, your Chapter 7 bankruptcy estate will include all property of the estate as of the conversion date.

Property You Own and Possess

Property that you own and possess—for example, clothing, books, computers, cameras, TV, stereo system, furniture, tools, car, real estate, boat, artworks, and stock certificates—is included in your bankruptcy estate.

Property that belongs to someone else is not part of your bankruptcy estate—even if you control the property—because you don't have the right to sell it or give it away. Here are some examples.

EXAMPLE 1: A parent establishes a trust for her child and names you as trustee to manage the money in the trust until the child's 18th birthday. You possess and control the money, but it's solely for the child's benefit under the terms of the trust; you cannot use it for your own purposes. It isn't part of your bankruptcy estate.

EXAMPLE 2: Your sister has gone to Zimbabwe for an indefinite period and has loaned you her computer system while she's gone. Although you might have use of the equipment for years to come, you don't own it. It isn't part of your bankruptcy estate.

EXAMPLE 3: You are making monthly payments on a leased car. You are entitled to possess the car as long as you make the monthly payments, but you don't own it. It is not part of your bankruptcy estate (but the lease itself is).

EXAMPLE 4: Your name appears on the title (and note) to your son's car because he was underage when he bought it. Your son makes all the payments. While the two of you probably consider the car to "belong" to your son, the bankruptcy laws initially consider it to be yours, and you have to disclose it in your bankruptcy paperwork. You can explain that you have "bare legal title" and your son is the equitable owner, which means it shouldn't be considered part of your bankruptcy estate. However, the court may disagree, which means your son could lose the car unless it fits within an available exemption. Courts have gone both ways on this issue; you should definitely talk to a lawyer if valuable property is at stake.

Property in a Living Trust

A revocable living trust is a popular estate planning tool in which the grantor puts property in trust to be managed by the trustee, for the benefit of one or more beneficiaries. The trust is revocable because the grantor can change his or her mind and revoke it at any time.

If you are both the grantor and the trustee of a revocable living trust, property in the trust is considered property of your estate, even though, as a technical matter, the trust "owns" the property. However, if the trust is irrevocable (that is, you can't change your mind and dissolve the trust), property in the trust won't be considered part of your bankruptcy estate, unless the court finds that you created the trust to shelter the property from your creditors or that you improperly transferred the money or assets into the trust.

Property You Own but Don't Possess

Any property you own is part of your bankruptcy estate, even if you don't have physical possession of it. For instance, you may own a share of a vacation cabin in the mountains but never spend time there. Or you may own furniture or a car that someone else is using. Other examples include a deposit held by a stockbroker, stock options, contractual rights to a royalty or commission, or a security deposit held by your landlord or the utility company.

Property You Have Recently Given Away

People contemplating bankruptcy are often tempted to unload their property on friends and relatives or pay favorite creditors before they file. Don't bother. Property given away or paid out in anticipation of filing for bankruptcy is still part of your bankruptcy estate—and the trustee has the legal authority to take it back.

Prefiling Transfers of Property

Certain types of actions you take before filing for bankruptcy have such serious consequences that, as a practical matter, they render you ineligible to file for bankruptcy for a period of time. For example, if you sell or give away property during the two-year period immediately before you file, you will have to disclose those transactions on your bankruptcy papers. The consequences can be very severe—from losing the property to having your whole case thrown out—if the trustee decides that the transfer was fraudulent and the court agrees.

The basic problem here is that some filers are tempted to unload their assets so the trustee won't be able to take them, sell them, and distribute the proceeds to the creditors. These transactions often take the form of selling property to a friend or relative for a nominal amount (such as a dollar), with the understanding that the friend will give back the property once the bankruptcy case is closed. Other common examples include taking one's name off a joint account, deed, or vehicle title (which is really a gift of half of the property to the other joint owner).

> **EXAMPLE:** You want to file for Chapter 7 bankruptcy, but you are listed on a deed as the co-owner of property where a friend is living (which was necessary to allow the friend to buy the property because he has bad credit). After learning that the trustee could take and sell that property for the benefit of your unsecured creditors, you take yourself off the deed before you file for bankruptcy. Because you're unwilling to commit perjury, however, you have to list the transaction on your bankruptcy papers, and your entire bankruptcy case could go down the tubes.

Whatever form they take, prefiling gifts and sales of property for substantially less than the property is worth are frequently judged to be fraudulent or improper transfers. This means the property can be taken—from its new owner—and sold for the benefit of the creditors, and the bankruptcy case could be dismissed. Even if you're able to convince the trustee that your intentions were good, the trustee can still require the person to whom you gave or sold the property to give it back so it can be sold. In these situations, you usually don't have an opportunity to claim that the property is exempt, so you won't even get any of the sale proceeds.

If you learn that you made a mistake like this, you may be tempted to try to undo it by, for example, getting the property back, putting your name back on the deed or title certificate, and so on. This looks even worse to the trustee: It indicates that you are trying to deceive the court. Because of this, the best way to handle prefiling transfers is simply to wait out the two-year period. For example, if you "sold" your car to a relative for a small sum, you should wait two years before filing. The bankruptcy forms require you to list all transfers made during the previous two years, so as long as the transfer didn't fall within that period, you should be fine.

People often wonder how the trustee would find out about a particular transfer. If the transferred property has a title document (as with cars, boats, and real estate), the transfer might show up in the trustee's routine search of state and local databases (for example, at the state DMV). Also, when you attend the creditors' meeting, you must affirm, under oath, that you truthfully answered the questions in your bankruptcy papers, including questions about prefiling transfers. As explained above, trustees stand to profit directly by finding property they can take and sell, and they are very skilled at picking up on any hesitancy you may show in swearing that your papers are correct. A trustee who senses trouble can follow up by questioning you under oath in a deposition-like proceeding. Most importantly, it's a bad idea to commit perjury. Period.

Often, property that people try to transfer before filing for bankruptcy would have been exempt anyway. In other words, prefiling transfers often occur simply because the debtor doesn't understand the bankruptcy laws. Had the person just kept the property and claimed it as exempt, he or she could have held on to it and avoided a whole lot of trouble.

Paying Off a Preferred Creditor

A basic principle of bankruptcy law is that all creditors deserve to be treated fairly in comparison to each other. In many cases, fair treatment means that no one gets anything. In some cases, it means that your unsecured creditors share equally in the proceeds if the trustee takes your nonexempt property and sells it.

This principle is threatened if you pay a creditor off before you file for bankruptcy. Bankruptcy law forbids you from paying more than $600 to any creditor who's an insider—a relative, friend, or business associate, typically—during the year before you file for bankruptcy. So, if you use your tax refund to pay back an emergency loan from your sister, brother, or mother, you have preferred that creditor over your other unsecured creditors. Bluntly put, when in bankruptcy, you are required to treat your mother and Visa equally.

If the creditor is not an insider (and most of your creditors probably aren't), the court will look at your transactions for only three months before you file for bankruptcy. If you are a business debtor—that is, a majority of your debt arises from your business activities—the court will look only at transactions that exceed $6,225.

At least one court has found that transferring your balance from one credit card to another might be considered a preference. In that case, the debtor used her credit on one credit card to pay off her debt on another credit card. Because she made the transfer within three months of filing for bankruptcy, and she could have used the money for any purpose (in other words, she didn't have to use it to pay off her other card), the court ruled that the transfer constituted a preferential transfer. (*In re Dilworth*, 560 F.3d 562 (6th Cir. 2009).)

The consequences of violating the preference rules can be harsh. The trustee is authorized to take back the money and distribute it among your creditors. If you paid back a family member, this may cause some tension. Even if you paid back a creditor that isn't an insider, it could cause some problems. For example, if you paid back a credit card issuer so you could keep your card, that creditor will probably take your card back once it has to cough up the money.

There is one important exception to the preference rule. A payment to an insider won't be considered a preference if you made the payment more than 90 days prior to your filing date and you weren't insolvent at the time. For example, if you repaid a $3,000 loan from your mother nine months before you file, and you can show that the value of your assets was greater than your liabilities when you repaid her, the payment won't be considered a preference. This insolvency rule also applies to preferences to noninsiders. However, because insolvency is presumed during the 90-day period before you file for bankruptcy, you will most likely need to hire a lawyer if you made a recent preference payment.

Even though you can't pay a favorite creditor before you file, nothing prevents you from doing so after you file, as long as you do it with income earned after you file your case or property that isn't in your bankruptcy estate.

Property You Are Entitled to Receive but Don't Yet Possess When You File

Property to which you are legally entitled at the time you file for bankruptcy is included in your bankruptcy estate, even if you haven't actually received it yet. The most common examples are wages or commissions you have earned but have not yet been paid and tax refunds that are legally owed to you. Here are some other examples:

- Vacation or severance pay earned before you filed for bankruptcy.

- Property you've inherited, but not yet received, from someone who has died.
- Property you are entitled to receive from a trust. If you receive periodic payments from a trust but aren't entitled to the full amount of the trust yet, the full amount of the trust is considered property of your bankruptcy estate and should be listed on Worksheet B and your bankruptcy papers. Although the bankruptcy trustee may not be able to get the money (depending on the type of trust), you don't want to be accused of hiding it.
- Future interest in an irrevocable trust. If you are listed as a beneficiary in an irrevocable trust (that is, the terms of the trust can't be changed) you may have what's called a future interest, which is considered part of your bankruptcy estate. It's hard to assign a value to this type of interest because of potential developments between the time the trust was created and your time to receive the benefits rolls around. For instance, intervening beneficiaries are often able to use some of the principal in an irrevocable trust, and it's possible that there will be little or nothing left by the time it gets around to you. Nevertheless, the future interest should be listed in your bankruptcy papers (list the value as "undetermined" if it is unknowable).
- Proceeds of an insurance policy, if the death, injury, or other event that triggers payment has occurred. For example, if you were the beneficiary of your father's life insurance policy, and your father has died but you haven't received your money yet, that amount is part of your bankruptcy estate.
- A legal claim to monetary compensation (sometimes called a legal "cause of action"), even if the value of the claim hasn't yet been determined. For example, if you have a claim against someone for injuring you in a car accident, you must include this potential source of money in your bankruptcy papers, even if the amount you will receive (if any) has not yet been determined in a lawsuit, settlement agreement, or an insurance

claim. If you don't list a legal claim in your bankruptcy petition, you may lose the right to make it in a lawsuit after your bankruptcy. Under a legal principle known as judicial estoppel, failing to raise a legal claim in one judicial proceeding prevents you from raising it in a later proceeding. For example, if you file for bankruptcy to prevent a foreclosure sale of your home but fail to list a cause of action for predatory lending (assuming your loan was a predatory loan, which many are), you may not be allowed to sue the mortgage broker and its assignees for predatory lending after your bankruptcy is completed. (*In re Lopez*, 283 B.R. 22 (B.A.P. 9th Cir. 2002).)
- Accounts receivable (money you are owed for goods or services you've provided). Even if you don't think you'll be paid, that money is considered part of your bankruptcy estate. It's the trustee's job to go after the money; leaving it off the bankruptcy forms can get you into trouble.
- Money earned (but not yet received) from property in your bankruptcy estate. This includes, for example, rent from commercial or residential real estate, royalties from copyrights or patents, and dividends earned on stocks.

Proceeds From Property of the Bankruptcy Estate

If property in your bankruptcy estate earns income or otherwise produces money after you file for bankruptcy, this money is also part of your bankruptcy estate. For example, suppose a contract to receive royalties for a book you have written is part of your bankruptcy estate. Any royalties you earn under this contract after you file for bankruptcy are also property of the estate. The one exception to this rule is money you earn from providing personal services after filing for bankruptcy, which isn't part of your bankruptcy estate. Continuing our example, work on a new edition of the book after you file for bankruptcy would be considered personal services. The royalties you earn for that new work would not be part of your bankruptcy estate.

Another example of money that ends up in your bankruptcy estate (and therefore is not yours to keep) are proceeds from what's called a "contingent future interest." This bit of legalese refers to money that you will receive if certain things happen in the future. The mere possibility that you will receive property after filing for bankruptcy is enough to put that property in your bankruptcy estate once you do file. For example, in one case an employee had the right to participate in a profit-sharing plan, but only if he was still employed by the company at the end of the year. He filed for bankruptcy before the end of the year, but remained employed and received a hefty check, which the trustee claimed belonged to the bankruptcy estate, at least in part. The court ruled that the debtor's interest in the profit-sharing plan was a "contingent future interest" (contingent on whether the debtor remained employed), and that the check based on that interest belonged in the bankruptcy estate even though the debtor didn't receive it until after the filing date. (*In re Edmunds*, 273 B.R. 527 (Bankr. E.D. Mich. 2000).)

Certain Property Acquired Within 180 Days After You File

Most property you acquire—or become entitled to acquire—after you file for bankruptcy isn't included in your bankruptcy estate. But there are exceptions. If you acquire (or become entitled to acquire) certain items within 180 days after you file, you must report them to the bankruptcy court—and the bankruptcy trustee may take them. (11 U.S.C. § 541(a)(5).)

The 180-day rule applies to:
- property you inherit during the 180-day period (some courts have held that property that passes to you as a beneficiary of a revocable living trust is not part of your bankruptcy estate; see, for example, *In re Mattern*, 55 Collier Bankr. Cas. 2d 1677 (Bankr. D. Kan. 2006) and *In re Roth*, 289 B.R. 161 (Bankr. D. Kan. 2003))
- property (not including alimony) from a property settlement agreement or divorce decree that goes into effect during the 180-day period, and

- death benefits or life insurance policy proceeds that become owed to you during the 180-day period.

You must report these items on a supplemental form, even if your bankruptcy case is over. You can find instructions for filing the supplemental form in Ch. 8.

If you convert from Chapter 13 to Chapter 7, the 180-day period runs from the date you originally filed for Chapter 13, not from the date you converted to Chapter 7. (*In re Carter*, 260 B.R. 130 (Bankr. W.D. Tenn. 2001).)

Are Stock Options Part of Your Bankruptcy Estate?

If you own stock options, you have the right to purchase stock at the price that was assigned when the stock options were granted. Most of the time, you have to wait for a while after you get the options before being able to buy the stock (stock options "vest" when that waiting period is up). Making such a purchase is called "exercising your stock options." Whether stock options are part of your bankruptcy estate depends on when you received them and when they vest.

As a general rule, stock options that you own when you file for bankruptcy are part of your bankruptcy estate. In addition, any stock you purchase by exercising your stock options is also part of the estate, even if you exercise those options after you file for bankruptcy. Courts treat these stock purchases as proceeds earned on property of the estate.

Sometimes, your stock options do not vest (that is, you cannot exercise them) until you have been with your company for a certain period of time. In that case, depending on the rules in your jurisdiction, your bankruptcy estate may include only those stock options that have already vested on the date you file for bankruptcy. (*In re Allen*, 226 B.R. 857 (Bankr. N.D. Ill. 1998).)

To calculate the value of your stock options, multiply the number of vested stock options you own by the difference between your option price and the fair market value of the stock. (Value of options = [number of vested stock options] × [fair market value – option price].) Even if the value of your options is very uncertain, they are still part of your bankruptcy estate and the trustee will take them if they are marketable.

Your Share of Marital Property

How much of your marital property—the property you and your spouse own together—is included in your bankruptcy estate depends on two factors: (1) whether you file jointly or alone, and (2) the laws of your state regarding marital property.

If you file jointly, all marital property that fits into one of the categories listed above belongs to your bankruptcy estate.

However, if you are married and you file for bankruptcy alone, some marital property may not be part of your bankruptcy estate. Whether property is part of the estate depends on whether you live in a community property, tenancy by the entirety, or common law property state.

Community Property States

These are the community property states: Alaska (if the spouses sign a written agreement to treat the property as community property), Arizona, California, Idaho, Louisiana, Nevada, New Mexico, Texas, Washington, and Wisconsin.

In these states, the general rule is that all property either spouse earns or receives during the marriage is community property and is owned jointly by both spouses. Exceptions are gifts and inheritances received by only one spouse and property owned by one spouse before the marriage or acquired after permanent separation; these are the separate property of the spouse who acquired or received them.

If you are married, live in a community property state, and file for bankruptcy, all the community property you and your spouse own (regardless of whose name is on the title) is considered part of your bankruptcy estate, even if your spouse doesn't file. This is true even if the community property might not be divided 50-50 if you were to divorce.

> **EXAMPLE:** Paul and Sonya live in California, a community property state. Sonya contributed $20,000 of her separate property toward the purchase of their house. All the rest of the money used to pay for the house is from community funds, and the house is considered community property. If Paul and Sonya were to divorce and split the house proceeds, Sonya would be entitled to $20,000 more than Paul as reimbursement for her down payment. But they aren't divorced, and Paul files for bankruptcy without Sonya. Their house is worth $250,000. Paul must list that entire value on his bankruptcy papers—that is, he can't subtract the $20,000 Sonya would be entitled to if they divorced.

The separate property of the spouse filing for bankruptcy is also part of the bankruptcy estate. But the separate property of the spouse *not* filing for bankruptcy is not part of the bankruptcy estate.

> **EXAMPLE:** Paul owns a twin-engine Cessna as his separate property (he owned it before he married Sonya). Sonya came to the marriage owning a grand piano. Because only Paul is filing for bankruptcy, Paul's aircraft will be part of his bankruptcy estate, but Sonya's piano won't be.

You may need to do some research into your state's property laws to make sure you understand which of your property is separate and which is community. See Ch. 10 for tips on legal research.

Tenancy by the Entirety States

States that recognize some form of tenancy by the entirety for married couples are Alaska, Arkansas, Delaware, the District of Columbia, Florida, Hawaii, Illinois, Indiana, Kentucky, Maryland, Massachusetts, Michigan, Missouri, New York, North Carolina, Ohio, Oklahoma, Oregon, Pennsylvania, Rhode Island (subject to conditions), Tennessee, Vermont, Virginia, and Wyoming.

Real estate (and personal property, in some states) a couple owns as tenants by the entirety belongs to the marriage, rather than to one spouse or the other. If both spouses file for bankruptcy, property held in tenancy by the entirety is property of the bankruptcy estate. If only one spouse files for bankruptcy, this property is not part of the bankruptcy estate and is generally exempt from claims for which only one spouse is liable. Because the property belongs to the marriage, one spouse cannot give it away or encumber it with debts on his or her own. The property is not exempt from debts the couple takes on jointly, however. We discuss this, as it applies to real estate, in Ch. 4.

Common Law Property States

If your state is not listed above as a community property or tenancy by the entirety state, it is a "common law" property state. When only one spouse files for bankruptcy in a common law property state, all of that spouse's separate property plus half of the couple's jointly owned property go into the filing spouse's bankruptcy estate.

The general rules of property ownership in common law states are:

- Property that has only one spouse's name on a title certificate (such as a car, a house, or stocks), is that spouse's separate property, even if it was bought with joint funds.
- Property that was purchased or received as a gift or inheritance by both for the use of both spouses is jointly owned, unless title is held in only one spouse's name (which means it belongs to that spouse separately, even if both spouses use it).
- Property that one spouse buys with separate funds or receives as a gift or inheritance for that spouse's separate use is that spouse's separate property (unless, again, a title certificate shows differently).

CAUTION

Check your state's status. It's imperative that you check your state's status. In particular, the rules regarding tenancy by the entirety can be complicated, so it's best to double-check whether your state is a community property state, tenancy by the entirety state, or common law property state.

Domestic Partnerships and Civil Unions

Several states offer couples the option of entering into civil unions or domestic partnerships, which extend many of the rights and obligations of marriage—including those that apply to debts and property ownership. If you are not married, but registered in a civil union or domestic partnership, you cannot file a joint bankruptcy petition. However, in some situations, your domestic partnership or civil union may affect what property is in your bankruptcy estate and how the exemption laws apply to you. That's because you and your partner are subject to your state's community and common law property rules (although this can vary depending on where you live and whether yours is a same-sex union).

If you are in a domestic partnership or civil union, the interplay between bankruptcy law on the one hand and state community and common law property rules on the other, can be complicated. If you have questions about your property rights or are worried about liability for your partner's debts, you should consult with a local lawyer to learn about your state's laws and how they apply to your situation.

This uncertainty extends only to couples that have registered as domestic partners, however. If you and your partner are not registered in a state that gives partners marriage-like benefits, any property you own together will be treated like property owned with any other person: The share that you own will be part of the bankruptcy estate and will be subject to the court's jurisdiction. Your partner will be treated as a co-owner on any debts you owe jointly. But your partner will not be part of your bankruptcy case.

Property That Isn't in Your Bankruptcy Estate

Property that is not in your bankruptcy estate is not subject to the bankruptcy court's jurisdiction, which means that the bankruptcy trustee can't take it to pay your creditors under any circumstances.

The most common examples of property that doesn't fall within your bankruptcy estate are:

- property you buy or receive after your filing date (with the few exceptions described in "Certain Property Acquired Within 180 Days After You File," above)
- pensions and retirement plans
- tax-deferred education funds

- property pledged as collateral for a loan, if a licensed lender (pawnbroker) retains possession of the collateral
- property in your possession that belongs to someone else (for instance, property you are storing for someone)
- wages that are withheld, and employer contributions that are made, for employee benefit and health insurance plans, and
- child support arrearages owed to the debtor, because the parent is entitled to the funds only in his or her capacity as trustee for the child. (*In re Perry*, No. 06-50237 (Bankr. D. S.D. 2009).) However, some courts retain arrearages if they exceed the debtor's total exemption allotment. (*In re Poffenbarger*, 281 B.R. 379 (Bankr. S.D. Ala. 2002).)

TIP
Retirement accounts are exempt, no matter which exemptions you use. When it passed the new bankruptcy law in 2005, Congress created a broad exemption for all types of tax-exempt retirement accounts, including 401(k)s, 403(b)s, profit-sharing and money purchase plans, IRAs (including Roth, SEP, and SIMPLE IRAs), and defined-benefit plans. These exemptions are unlimited—that is, the entire account is exempt, regardless of how much money is in it—except in the case of traditional and Roth IRAs. For these types of IRAs only, the exemption is limited to a total value of $1,245,475 per person (this figure will be adjusted every three years for inflation). These accounts are exempt regardless of whether you use the federal or a state exemption system.

Funds placed in a qualified tuition program or Coverdell education savings account are also not part of your bankruptcy estate, as long as:
- you deposit the funds into the account at least one year before filing for bankruptcy, and
- the beneficiary of the account is your child, stepchild, grandchild, step-grandchild, or in some cases, foster child.

Funds placed in the account more than two years before you file are excluded from the bankruptcy estate without limit. However, you can exclude only $6,225 of the contributions you make between one and two years before filing. And contributions made within the year before filing are not excluded at all.

For amounts that are not excluded from the bankruptcy estate, you can use a state exemption, if one exists (assuming you are using your state's exemptions and not the federal exemptions).

Property You Can Keep (The Exemption System)

Your property includes everything you own. If you own your own home (or you have any ownership interest in land or buildings of any kind), you are the proud owner of what is called "real property." If you don't own any real estate, everything you own is considered personal property.

When filing for Chapter 7 bankruptcy, you may be able to keep your home. (See Ch. 4 for more information.) However, you will probably have to give up any other real estate in which you have equity, which will be sold for the benefit of your creditors. You will also be able to keep some or all of your personal property. How much you get to keep will depend on whether the property is considered exempt under the state exemption system available to you (or under the federal exemption statute, if the state where you file allows you to choose between the federal and state exemptions).

This section describes how exemptions work and how to figure out which exemptions you can use. Once you know which exemptions are available to you, you can start applying them to your personal property to figure out which items you'll be able to keep. To help you keep track, we've included a Personal Property Checklist, which you can use to take an inventory of your property. Then, using the Property Exemption Worksheet, you'll be able to figure out, item by item, whether you'll be able to hang on to your property.

If You Are Named on Someone Else's Bank Account

It's common for older parents to put their son or daughter's name on the parents' bank account. This allows the child to write checks and otherwise manage the account if the parent becomes unable to do so; it also means the account goes straight to the child when the parent dies, outside of probate or other inheritance procedures.

If you are named on someone else's account and file for bankruptcy, however, that account could be considered property of your bankruptcy estate, subject to being taken by the trustee for the benefit of your unsecured creditors. Of course, it's not really your money while your parent is living, but if the trustee thinks you are free to withdraw the money and use it for your own purposes (as lowdown as that would be), the trustee may consider at least some of it to be part of your bankruptcy estate.

In these situations it's important to tell the trustee, up front, that it really isn't your money to use as you wish. That would be a breach of your fiduciary duty toward the account holder, and possibly elder abuse. To make sure that the trustee understands why you are named on the account, you should declare the account on your property schedule (Schedule B) but explain that it really isn't yours. You also can explain that it would be a breach of your duty of trust (fiduciary duty) toward the main account holder for you to use the money for any purpose other than his or her welfare. You should identify the account and explain why you are named on it in Question 14 ("Property held for another person") on the Statement of Financial Affairs. Finally, you would be well advised to gather documents showing that the sources of the money in the account clearly belong to the main account owner. (See Ch. 6 for more on these paperwork requirements.)

If you are able to exempt the account on your bankruptcy Schedule C, you can just list it on Schedule B as your own property and avoid any argument over who owns it. For example, suppose your mother has put your name on her savings account, which has a balance of $4,000. If the exemption system you are using in your bankruptcy protects that amount of money, you could list the account on your personal property schedule (Schedule B) and claim the full amount as exempt on your Schedule C. You won't have to argue over who owns the money; either way, the trustee can't take it.

To avoid all this trouble, you may be tempted to remove your name from the account before you file bankruptcy. Don't do it. Removing your name makes it look like you are trying to hide the whole issue from the bankruptcy court (which you are). The trustee might well convince the court to dismiss your bankruptcy altogether, on the ground that you committed fraud on the court. You're better off leaving your name on the account and explaining the situation to the trustee. If there is significant money in the account, consider consulting with a lawyer about the best way to handle the situation in your paperwork. Incidentally, if you are thinking that the trustee won't find out about the account if you don't list it, don't go there. They have their ways.

Note: If you are listed as a custodian or a trustee of the account funds for a minor under the Uniform Transfers to Minors Act, you don't have to worry about the bankruptcy trustee taking the funds. The law is clear that those funds belong to the minor, not to you in your fiduciary capacity as a custodian or trustee.

How Exemptions Work

Figuring out exactly what property you're legally entitled to keep if you file for bankruptcy takes some work, but it's very important. It's your responsibility—and to your benefit—to claim all exemptions to which you're entitled. If you don't claim property as exempt, you could lose it unnecessarily to your creditors.

Exempt property is the property you can keep during and after bankruptcy. Nonexempt property is the property that the bankruptcy trustee is entitled to take and sell to pay your creditors. Therefore, the more you can claim as exempt, the better off you are.

Each state's legislature produces a set of exemptions for use by people who are residents of that state. Nineteen states (and the District of Columbia) allow debtors to choose between their state's exemptions or another set of exemptions created by Congress (called the federal bankruptcy exemptions). States that currently allow debtors this choice are Alaska, Arkansas, Connecticut, Hawaii, Kentucky, Massachusetts, Michigan, Minnesota, New Hampshire, New Jersey, New Mexico, New York, Oregon, Pennsylvania, Rhode Island, Texas, Vermont, Washington, and Wisconsin. You have to choose one system or the other—you can't mix and match some exemptions from one and some from the other. However, if you use one system when you first file your petition and later on decide that the other system would work better for you, you can amend Schedule C—the form where you list your exemption claims—to change systems.

California has adopted its own unique exemption system. Although California doesn't allow debtors to use the federal exemptions, California offers two sets of state exemptions. With a few important exceptions, the alternative California exemptions are the same as the federal exemptions. As in the 19 states that have the federal bankruptcy exemptions, people filing for bankruptcy in California must choose one or the other set of state exemptions.

TIP

You might be able to keep your nonexempt property. You may not have to surrender a specific item of nonexempt property if you have the cash to buy it back from the trustee, who will often accept less than its value to avoid having to collect, store, and sell the property at an auction (also for less than its full value). Instead of cash, the trustee may be willing to accept exempt property of roughly equal value instead. The trustee may also allow you to pay via a payment plan. Finally, the trustee might reject or abandon the item if it would be too costly or cumbersome to sell. In that case, you also get to keep it. So when we say that you have to give up property, remember that you still might be able to keep it, depending on the circumstances.

TIP

Buying nonexempt assets when you owe taxes can be a good idea. If you owe tax debts that you cannot discharge in your bankruptcy and you pay the trustee to buy back nonexempt property, the money you give to the trustee will likely be used to repay your taxes (tax debts usually get paid first). A win-win situation. To learn more about this tactic, see "When Buying Back Nonexempt Property Can Take a Bite Out of Your Tax Debt," in Ch. 1.)

Types of Exemptions

Both state and federal exemptions come in several basic varieties.

Exemptions to a Limited Amount

Some exemptions protect the value of your ownership in a particular item only up to a set dollar limit. For instance, the New Mexico state exemptions allow you to keep $4,000 of equity in a motor vehicle. If you were filing for Chapter 7 bankruptcy in that state and using the state exemption list, you could keep your car if it was worth $4,000 or less. You could also keep the car if selling it would not raise enough money to pay what you still owe on it and give you the full value of your $4,000 exemption. For example, if you own a car worth $20,000 but still owe $16,000 on it, selling it would raise $16,000 for the lender and $4,000 for you (thanks to the exemption). The trustee wouldn't take the car because there would be nothing left over to pay your other creditors. Instead, you would be allowed to keep it as long as you are—and remain—current on your payments.

However, if your equity in the car significantly exceeded the $4,000 exemption, the trustee might sell the car to raise money for your other creditors. To continue our example, let's say you owe only $10,000 on that $20,000 car. Selling the car would pay off the lender in full, pay your $4,000 exemption, and leave a portion of the remaining $6,000 (after the costs of sale are deducted) to be distributed to your other creditors. In this scenario, you are entitled to the full value of your exemption—$4,000—but not to the car itself.

Exemptions Without Regard to Value

Another type of exemption allows you to keep specified property items regardless of their values. For instance, the Utah state exemptions allow you to keep a refrigerator, freezer, microwave, stove, sewing machine, and carpets with no limit on their values. For comparison purposes, another Utah state exemption places a $500 limit on "sofas, chairs, and related furnishings." Go figure.

Wildcard Exemptions

Some states (and the federal exemption list) also provide a general-purpose exemption, called a wild-card exemption. This exemption gives you a dollar amount that you can apply to any type of property. If you play poker, you undoubtedly have played a game where a particular card is designated a wildcard, which means you can use it as a queen of diamonds, a two of spades, or any other card you want in order to make the most of the other cards in your hand. The same principle applies here. For example, suppose you own a $3,000 boat in a state that doesn't exempt boats but does have a wildcard of $5,000. You can take $3,000 of the wildcard and apply it to the boat, which means the boat will now be considered exempt. And if you have other nonexempt property, you can apply the remaining $2,000 from the wildcard to that property.

State "Bankruptcy-Specific" Exemptions May be Unconstitutional

Most states' exemptions can be used in bankruptcy and in other situations (for example, if a creditor is trying to collect a judgment against you, you can use the state exemption system to exempt some of your property from collection)—we'll refer to these as general state exemptions. However, a few states have particular exemptions or exemption systems that apply only in bankruptcy (often called bankruptcy-specific or bankruptcy-only exemptions.) These states are California (System 2), Colorado, Georgia, Michigan, Montana, New York, Ohio, and West Virginia.

Some trustees have challenged the constitutionality of these bankruptcy-specific exemptions. A few courts have agreed, and ruled that these types of state bankruptcy-specific exemptions are unconstitutional because they aren't authorized by the federal bankruptcy laws. However, the vast majority of courts addressing this issue have upheld the constitutionality of bankruptcy-specific exemptions and allowed bankruptcy filers to use them. (For example, see *Sheehan v. Peveich*, 574 F.3d 248 (4th Cir. 2009) and *In re Applebaum*, 422 B.R. 684 (B.A.P. 9th Cir. 2009).) Most recently, the Sixth Circuit Court of Appeals held that Michigan's bankruptcy-specific exemption statute is constitutional (*In re Schafer*, 689 F.3d 601 (6th Cir. 2012), and in 2013 the U.S. Supreme Court denied certiorari in the case.

For the most part, it's safe to use California's bankruptcy-specific exemptions (identified as System 2 in Appendix A) as well as bankruptcy-specific exemptions in other states. Just be aware that a trustee or creditor may decide to challenge your right to use the bankruptcy-specific exemptions. If that happens, you may have to amend your paperwork to use the general state exemptions. If that happens, talk to an attorney right away.

You can also use a wildcard exemption to increase an existing exemption. For example, if you have $5,000 worth of equity in your car but your state only allows you to exempt $1,500 of its value, you will likely lose the car. However, if your state has a $5,000 wildcard exemption, you could use the $1,500 motor vehicle exemption and $3,500 of the wildcard exemption to exempt your car entirely. And you'd still have $1,500 of the wildcard exemption to use on other nonexempt property.

Why State Exemptions Vary So Much

Each state's exemptions are unique. The property you can keep, therefore, varies considerably from state to state. Why the differences? State exemptions are used not only for bankruptcy purposes but also to shelter property that otherwise could be taken by creditors who have obtained court judgments. The exemptions reflect the attitudes of state legislators about how much property, and which property, a debtor should be forced to part with when a victorious creditor collects on a judgment. These attitudes are rooted in local values and concerns. But in many cases there is another reason why state exemptions differ. Some state legislatures have raised exemption levels in recent years, while other states last looked at their exemptions many decades ago. In states that don't reconsider their exemptions very often, you can expect to find lower dollar amounts.

Domicile Requirements for Using State Exemptions

Usually filers use the exemptions of the state where they reside when they file for bankruptcy. However, some filers have to use the exemptions of the state where they *used* to reside. This is to avoid people gaming the system by moving to states with generous exemptions just to file for bankruptcy.

Below are the rules that govern which state's exemptions you must use. Keep in mind that your domicile is where you make your permanent home—where you get mail, vote, pay taxes, and so on—even if you are temporarily living elsewhere due to work or military service.

- If you have made your domicile in your current state for at least two years, you can use that state's exemptions.
- If you have had your domicile in your current state for more than 91 days but less than two years, you must use the exemptions of the state where you were domiciled for the better part

of the 180-day period immediately prior to the two-year period preceding your filing.

- If you have had your domicile in your current state for less than 91 days, you can either file in the state where you lived immediately before (as long as you lived there for at least 91 days) or wait until you have logged 91 days in your new home and file in your current state. Once you figure out where you can file, you'll need to use whatever exemptions are available to you according to the rules set out above.
- If the state you are filing in offers a choice between the state and federal bankruptcy exemptions, you can use the federal exemption list regardless of how long you've been living in the state.
- If these rules deprive you of the right to use *any* state's exemptions, you can use the federal exemption list, even if it isn't otherwise available in the state where you file. For example, some states allow their exemptions to be used only by current state residents, which might leave former residents who haven't lived in their new home state for at least two years without any available state exemptions. (See, for example, *In re Underwood*, 342 B.R. 358 (Bankr. N.D. Fla. 2006); *In re Crandall*, 346 B.R. 220 (Bankr. M.D. Fla. 2006); and *In re West*, 352 B.R. 905 (Bankr. M.D. Fla. 2006).) If you have recently returned to the United States after being domiciled in another country, and no state exemption system is available to you under these rules, you are also entitled to use the federal exemptions.

A longer domicile requirement applies to homestead exemptions: If you acquired a home in your current state within the 40 months before you file for bankruptcy (and you didn't purchase it with the proceeds from selling another home in that state), your homestead exemption will be subject to a cap of $155,675, even if the state homestead exemption available to you is larger. (The principal residence of a family farmer is exempt from this rule.) For detailed information on homestead exemptions, see Ch. 4.

EXAMPLE 1: Sammie Jo lives in South Carolina from July 2010 until January 2012, when she gets lucky at a casino, moves to Texas, and buys a car for $15,000. In March 2013, Sammie Jo files for bankruptcy in Texas. Her car is now worth $14,000. Because Sammie Jo has been living in Texas for only 14 months—not two years—she can't use the Texas exemption for cars, which can be up to $30,000, depending on the value of other personal property a filer claims as exempt. Because Sammie Jo filed in March 2013, she must use the exemptions of the state where she lived for most of the six-month period (180 days) ending two years before she filed, or March 2011. Sammie Jo lived in South Carolina for the six months prior to March 2011, so she must use the South Carolina exemptions. As it turns out, the South Carolina exemption for cars is only $5,825, which means that Sammie Jo will probably lose her car if she uses the South Carolina exemptions.

However, Texas gives filers the option of using either its state exemptions or the federal bankruptcy exemptions. Under the law, the rules of the state where a person files determine whether the federal exemptions are available, even if that person has not lived in the state long enough to use its *state* exemptions. This means that Sammie Jo can use the federal exemptions instead of the South Carolina state exemptions. Under the federal exemptions, Sammie Jo is entitled to exempt a motor vehicle worth up to $3,675—still not enough to cover her car. But wait: The federal exemptions also provide a wildcard of $1,225, plus $11,500 of unused homestead exemption. Sammie Jo doesn't own her home, so she can add the entire wildcard of $12,725 to her $3,675 vehicle exemption, for a total exemption of $16,400 she can apply to her car.

EXAMPLE 2: Julia lived in North Dakota for many years, until she moved to Florida on January 15, 2013. She files for bankruptcy in Florida on November 30, 2014. Because she has lived in Florida for slightly less than two years when she files, she must use the exemptions from the state where she lived for the better part of the 180-day period that ended two years before she filed—which is North Dakota. As it turns out, Julia's most valuable possession is a prepaid medical savings account with $20,000 in it. While the account would be exempt under Florida law, North Dakota has no exemption for this type of property. Nor are the federal exemptions available in Florida. So the trustee will probably seize the medical savings account and use the money in it to pay Julia's creditors. Had Julia waited another month and a half to file, she would have been able to use Florida's exemptions and keep her medical savings account.

If You Are Married and Filing Jointly

If the federal bankruptcy exemptions are available in the state where you file and you decide to use them, you may double all of the exemptions if you are married and filing jointly. (See Ch. 6 for more on whether to file jointly.) This means that you and your spouse can each claim the full amount of each federal exemption (but joint filers must use one exemption system or the other; they can't use different systems).

If you decide to use your state's exemptions, you may be able to double some exemptions but not others. For instance, in the California exemption System 1 list, the $2,975 limit for motor vehicles may not be doubled, but the $7,625 limit on tools of the trade may be doubled in some circumstances. In order for you to double an exemption for a single piece of property, title to the property must be in both of your names. In Appendix A, we've noted whether a court or state legislature has expressly allowed or prohibited doubling. If the chart doesn't say one way or the other, it is probably safe to double. However, keep in mind that this area of the law changes rapidly—legislation or court decisions issued after the publication date of this book will not be reflected in the chart. (See Ch. 10 for information on doing your own legal research; you can find the latest exemption laws at www.legalconsumer.com.)

Applying Exemptions to Your Property

The Personal Property Checklist and Property Exemption Worksheet will help you figure out what personal property you own and whether you will get to keep it if you file for bankruptcy. You also can use this information to complete the official forms that accompany your bankruptcy petition, if you later decide to file.

Inventory Your Property

If you decide to file for bankruptcy, you will have to list all property that belongs in your bankruptcy estate. Whether or not you can hold on to that property, or at least some of the property's value in dollar terms, depends on what the property is worth and which exemptions are available to you. The best way to start figuring out what you'll be able to keep—and get a jump on your filing paperwork—is to create an inventory (list) of your property.

Use the Personal Property Checklist shown above—you can find a blank copy in Appendix B—to create an inventory of your possessions. Place a checkmark in the box next to each item you own. If you are married and filing jointly, list all property owned by you and your spouse.

Using the Property Exemption Worksheet

Now that you have a comprehensive list of your property, you can decide how to use the exemptions available to you to your best advantage. This will require you to come up with a value for each item, decide which exemption system to use (if you have a choice), then figure out how to apply those exemptions to your property.

To do this, use the Property Exemption Worksheet in Appendix B. A portion of the worksheet is set out below. As you can see, it includes four columns:

- a description of the property
- the property's replacement value
- the exemption (if any) that applies to the property, and
- the number of the statute where that exemption appears (you'll need this information when you complete your bankruptcy forms).

Complete each of these columns as follows.

Column 1: Using your completed checklist as a guide, describe each item of property and its location.

For personal property, identify the item (for example, 1994 Ford Mustang) and its location (for example, residence). For cash on hand and deposits of money, indicate the source of each, such as wages or salary, insurance policy proceeds, or the proceeds from selling an item of property. Although cash on hand is usually not exempt, you may be able to exempt all or some of it if you can show that it came from an exempt source, such as unemployment insurance.

Column 2: Enter the replacement value of each item of property in Column 1 (what you would pay a retail vendor to buy the property, given its age and condition).

It's easy to enter a dollar amount for cash, bank deposits, bonds, and most investment instruments. For items that are tougher to value, such as insurance, annuities, pensions, and business interests, you may need to get an appraisal from someone who has some financial expertise.

For your other property, estimate its replacement value—again, what you could buy it for from a retail vendor, considering its age and condition. As long as you have a reasonable basis for your estimates, the lower the value you place on property, the more of it you will probably be allowed to keep through the bankruptcy process. But be honest when assigning values. Trustees have years of experience and a pretty good sense of what property is worth. It's okay to be wrong as long as you have an arguable basis for the value you list and briefly explain any uncertainties. If you can't come up with a replacement value, leave this column blank. If you file for bankruptcy, you can simply indicate that the value is unknown. If the trustee is concerned about the value, you will be asked at your creditors' meeting to provide more detail.

Personal Property Checklist

Cash on hand (include sources)

☐ In your home

☐ In your wallet

☐ Under your mattress

Deposits of money (include sources)

☐ Bank account

☐ Brokerage account (with stockbroker)

☐ Certificates of deposit (CDs)

☐ Credit union deposit

☐ Escrow account

☐ Money market account

☐ Money in a safe deposit box

☐ Savings and loan deposit

Security deposits

☐ Electric

☐ Gas

☐ Heating oil

☐ Rental unit

☐ Prepaid rent

☐ Rented furniture or equipment

☐ Telephone

☐ Water

Household goods, supplies, and furnishings

☐ Antiques

☐ Appliances

☐ Carpentry tools

☐ Cell phones

☐ China and crystal

☐ Clocks

☐ Dishes

☐ Electronics (MP3 player, DVR, Kindle, video games)

☐ Food (total value)

☐ Furniture (list every item; go from room to room so you don't miss anything)

☐ Gardening tools

☐ Home computer (for personal use)

☐ Iron and ironing board

☐ Lamps

☐ Lawn mower or tractor

☐ Microwave oven

☐ Patio or outdoor furniture

☐ Radios

☐ Rugs

☐ Sewing machine

☐ Silverware and utensils

☐ Small appliances

☐ Snow blower

☐ Stereo system

☐ Telephone and answering machines

☐ Televisions

☐ Vacuum cleaner

☐ Video equipment (VCR, camcorder)

Books, pictures, and other art objects; stamp, coin, and other collections

☐ Art prints

☐ Bibles

☐ Books

☐ Coins

☐ Collectibles (such as political buttons, baseball cards)

☐ Family portraits

☐ Figurines

☐ Original artworks

☐ Photographs

☐ Records, CDs, audiotapes

☐ Stamps

☐ Videotapes

Apparel

☐ Clothing

☐ Furs

Jewelry

☐ Engagement and wedding rings

☐ Gems

☐ Precious metals

☐ Watches

Firearms, sports equipment, and other hobby equipment

- ☐ Board games
- ☐ Bicycle
- ☐ Camera equipment
- ☐ Electronic musical equipment
- ☐ Exercise machine
- ☐ Fishing gear
- ☐ Guns (rifles, pistols, shotguns, muskets)
- ☐ Model or remote-controlled cars or planes
- ☐ Musical instruments
- ☐ Scuba diving equipment
- ☐ Ski equipment
- ☐ Other sports equipment
- ☐ Other weapons (swords and knives)

Interests in insurance policies

- ☐ Credit insurance
- ☐ Disability insurance
- ☐ Health insurance
- ☐ Homeowners' or renters' insurance
- ☐ Term life insurance
- ☐ Whole life insurance

Annuities

Pension or profit-sharing plans

- ☐ IRA
- ☐ Keogh
- ☐ Pension or retirement plan
- ☐ 401(k) plan

Stock and interests in incorporated and unincorporated companies

Interests in partnerships

- ☐ Limited partnership interest
- ☐ General partnership interest

Government and corporate bonds and other investment instruments

- ☐ Corporate bonds
- ☐ Municipal bonds
- ☐ Promissory notes
- ☐ U.S. savings bonds

Accounts receivable

- ☐ Accounts receivable from business
- ☐ Commissions already earned

Family support

- ☐ Alimony (spousal support, maintenance) due under court order
- ☐ Child support payments due under court order
- ☐ Payments due under divorce property settlement

Other debts for which the amount owed you is known and definite

- ☐ Disability benefits due
- ☐ Disability insurance due
- ☐ Judgments obtained against third parties you haven't yet collected
- ☐ Sick pay earned
- ☐ Social Security benefits due
- ☐ Tax refund due under returns already filed
- ☐ Vacation pay earned
- ☐ Wages due
- ☐ Workers' compensation due

Any special powers that you or another person can exercise for your benefit (but not relating to real estate)

- ☐ A right to receive, at some future time, cash, stock, or other personal property placed in an irrevocable trust
- ☐ Current payments of interest or principal from a trust
- ☐ General power of appointment over personal property

An interest in property due to another person's death

- ☐ Any interest as the beneficiary of a living trust, if the trustor has died
- ☐ Expected proceeds from a life insurance policy where the insured has died
- ☐ Inheritance from an existing estate in probate (the owner has died and the court is overseeing the distribution of the property), even if the final amount is not yet known
- ☐ Inheritance under a will that is contingent on one or more events occurring, but only if the owner has died

All other contingent claims and claims where the amount owed you is not known, including tax refunds, counterclaims, and rights to setoff claims (claims you think you have against a person, government, or corporation, but you haven't yet sued on)

- ☐ Claims against a corporation, government entity, or an individual
- ☐ Potential tax refund on a return that is not yet filed

Patents, copyrights, and other intellectual property

- ☐ Copyrights
- ☐ Patents
- ☐ Trade secrets
- ☐ Trademarks
- ☐ Trade names

Licenses, franchises, and other general intangibles

- ☐ Building permits
- ☐ Cooperative association holdings
- ☐ Exclusive licenses
- ☐ Liquor licenses
- ☐ Nonexclusive licenses
- ☐ Patent licenses
- ☐ Professional licenses

Automobiles and other vehicles

- ☐ Car
- ☐ Minibike or motor scooter
- ☐ Mobile or motor home if on wheels
- ☐ Motorcycle
- ☐ Recreational vehicle (RV)
- ☐ Trailer
- ☐ Truck
- ☐ Van

Boats, motors, and accessories

- ☐ Boat (canoe, kayak, rowboat, shell, sailboat, pontoon, yacht)
- ☐ Boat radar, radio, or telephone
- ☐ Outboard motor

Aircraft and accessories

- ☐ Aircraft
- ☐ Aircraft radar, radio, and other accessories

Office equipment, furnishings, and supplies

- ☐ Artwork in your office
- ☐ Computers, software, modems, printers
- ☐ Copier
- ☐ Fax machine
- ☐ Furniture
- ☐ Rugs
- ☐ Supplies
- ☐ Telephones
- ☐ Typewriters

Machinery, fixtures, equipment, and supplies used in business

- ☐ Military uniforms and accoutrements
- ☐ Tools of your trade

Business inventory

Livestock, poultry, and other animals

- ☐ Birds
- ☐ Cats
- ☐ Dogs
- ☐ Fish and aquarium equipment
- ☐ Horses
- ☐ Other pets
- ☐ Livestock and poultry

Crops—growing or harvested

Farming equipment and implements

Farm supplies, chemicals, and feed

Other personal property of any kind not already listed

- ☐ Church pew
- ☐ Health aids (such as a wheelchair or crutches)
- ☐ Hot tub or portable spa
- ☐ Season tickets

Here are some tips for valuing specific items:

- **Cars.** Unfortunately, the replacement value requirement doesn't exactly square with the way car values are determined by the *Kelley Blue Book*, the most common source for car prices. To be absolutely safe in your estimate, use the average retail price for your car (based on its mileage) listed at the website of the National Automobile Dealers Association, www.nada.com. If your car is inoperable or in poor condition (with obvious and significant body damage or serious mechanical problems), you can reasonably list whatever you could sell it for on the open market. Because such cars are not sold by car dealers, there's no way to figure out what a retail merchant would charge for such a car.

- **Older goods.** If the items are sold in used goods stores (for example, used furniture stores, Goodwill stores, or hospice outlets), check their prices. If not, you can check the want ads in a local flea market or penny-saver newspaper. eBay is also a good source for values: You can find retail merchants selling a wide variety of used goods at www.ebay.com.

- **Life insurance.** List the current cash surrender value of your policy (call your insurance agent to find out what it is). Term life insurance has a cash surrender value of zero. Don't list the amount of benefits the policy will pay, unless you're the beneficiary of an insurance policy and the insured person has died.

- **Stocks and bonds.** Check the listing in a newspaper business section. If you can't find the listing, or the stock isn't traded publicly, call your broker and ask what it's worth. If you have a brokerage account, use the value from your last statement. For information on how to calculate the value of any stock options you own, see "Are Stock Options Part of Your Bankruptcy Estate?" above.

- **Jewelry, antiques, and other collectibles.** Any valuable jewelry or collections should be appraised.

Add up the amounts in Column 4 and enter the total in the space provided on the last page.

Property Exemption Worksheet

1 Property	2 Replacement Value	3 Exemption	4 Statute No.
1. Cash on hand			

The Trustee May Abandon Nonexempt Property

Even if you have property that's worth more than the exemption amount, the trustee may not want to deal with it. As in other areas, the bankruptcy laws in this area are sort of odd. The replacement value of property, as defined by the bankruptcy code, will almost always be higher than what the property will likely fetch at an auction held by a trustee. For example, assume you have a piano that, given its age and condition, would cost you $2,000 from a retail vendor. If the piano is not exempt, the trustee theoretically has a $2,000 asset to sell for the benefit of your creditors. Moving and storing pianos can be expensive, however, and this particular piano might only fetch $500 at an auction. If the trustee sees that little or no money will be realized from taking the asset, he or she will abandon it, which means you're free to keep it, even if it isn't technically exempt.

TIP

Ignore liens against your personal property when computing the property's value. If you owe money to a major consumer lender such as Beneficial Finance, the lender may have a lien on some or all of your personal property. You can often remove this lien in the course of your bankruptcy. Similarly, there may be a lien against your personal property if a creditor has obtained a court judgment against you. These liens, too, can frequently be removed. See Ch. 5 to find out more about personal property liens and your options for dealing with them.

Columns 3 and 4: Identify exemptions for your personal property.

You can find every state's exemptions in Appendix A. If the state exemption system you're using allows you to choose the federal exemptions instead of your state's exemptions, you can find these listed directly after Wyoming.

Think Creatively About Exemptions

"Tools of the trade" is a common exemption category. The term used to mean hand tools, but now it refers more broadly to the things you need in order to do the job you rely on for support. Here are some examples of property that could be considered tools of the trade in various fields:

- art camera, scanner (artist)
- car, truck, or van that is used for more than just commuting (sales manager, insurance adjuster, physician, firewood salesperson, traveling salesperson, real estate salesperson, mechanic)
- cream separator, dairy cows, animal feed (farmer)
- drills, saws (carpenter)
- electric motor, lathe (mechanic)
- guitar, acoustic amplifier, cornet, violin and bow, organ, speaker cabinet (musician)
- hair dye, shampoo, cash register, furniture, dryer, fan, curler, magazine rack (barber, beauty parlor operator)
- oven, mixer (baker)
- personal computer, printer (insurance salesperson, lawyer, accountant)
- photographic lens (photographer)
- power chain saw (firewood salesperson)
- sewing machine (tailor), and
- truck (logger, tire retreader, truck driver, farmer, electrician).

Review the tools of the trade exemption rules available to you carefully—you may be pleasantly surprised by what you can keep.

TIP

Focus on the property you really want to keep. If you have a lot of property and are afraid of getting bogged down in exemption jargon and dollar signs, start with the property you would feel really bad about losing. After that, if you are so inclined, you can search for exemptions that would let you keep property that is less important to you.

If You Can Only Use Your State's Exemptions

Unless you are using the exemptions for Arkansas, Connecticut, the District of Columbia, Hawaii, Kentucky, Massachusetts, Michigan, Minnesota, New Hampshire, New Jersey, New Mexico, New York, Oregon, Pennsylvania, Rhode Island, Texas, Vermont, Washington, or Wisconsin, you must use your state's exemptions (subject to the domicile rules discussed above).

Step 1: In Column 3, list the amount of the exemption or write "no limit" if the exemption is unlimited. In Column 4, list the number of the statute identified in Appendix A for the exemption that may reasonably be applied to the particular property item. If you need more information or an explanation of terms, use the notes at the beginning of Appendix A and the glossary. In evaluating whether your cash on hand and deposits are exempt, look to the source of the money, such as welfare benefits, insurance proceeds, or wages.

> **TIP**
>
> **Err on the side of exemption.** If you can think of a reason why a particular property item might be exempt, list it even if you aren't sure that the exemption applies. If you later decide to file for Chapter 7 bankruptcy, you will only be expected to do your best to fit the exemptions to your property. Of course, if you do misapply an exemption and the bankruptcy trustee or a creditor files a formal objection within the required time, you may have to scramble to keep the property that you mistakenly thought was exempt.

Step 2: If a particular exemption has no dollar limit, then apply that exemption to all property items that seem to fall into that category. If there is a limit (for instance, an exemption allows you to keep up to $1,000 worth of electronic products), total the value of all property items you wish to claim under that exemption. Then compare the total with the exemption limit. If the total is less than the limit, then there is no problem. However, if the total is more than the limit, you may have to either give the trustee enough of the property to bring your total back under the limit or apply a wildcard exemption to the extra property, if the state system you are using has one.

If You Live in California or a State That Allows You to Choose the Federal Exemptions

If the state system you're using allows you to use the federal bankruptcy exemptions or you qualify to use the California exemptions (which give you a choice between two state systems), you'll need to decide which exemption system to use. You can't use some exemptions from one system and some from the other. If you own a home in which you have equity, your choice will often be dictated by which system gives you the most protection for that equity. In California, for example, the homestead exemption in System 1 protects up to $175,000 in equity, while the System 2 list protects only $25,575 (including the $1,350 wildcard). While System 1 used to be the system of choice for California homeowners who had substantial equity in their homes, recent declines in home values have systematically wiped out home equity, and homeowners now frequently use System 2.

Unless your choice of exemption lists is dictated by your home equity, you'll be best served by going through the Property Exemption Worksheet twice. The first time through, use the state exemptions (or System 1 in California). The second time, use the federal bankruptcy exemptions (or System 2 in California).

After you apply both exemption lists to your property, compare the results and decide which exemption list will do you the most good. You may find that one set of exemptions is more generous or better protects the property you really want to keep. You may be sorely tempted to pluck some exemptions out of one list and add them to the other list. Again, this can't be done. You'll either have to use your state's exemption list or the federal bankruptcy exemptions—you can't mix and match.

EXAMPLE: Paula Willmore has lived in Albuquerque, New Mexico, for several years. Other than clothing, household furniture, and personal effects, the only property Paula owns is a vintage 1967 Chevy Camaro Rally Sport. Paula often checks out local car magazines and knows that the model she owns typically sells for about $14,000, although this price varies by several thousand dollars based on the car's condition. Paula wants to know what will happen to her car if she files for Chapter 7 bankruptcy.

Because Paula has lived in New Mexico for more than two years, she will use that state's exemption rules. Her first step is to locate the exemptions for New Mexico in Appendix A. At the bottom of the New Mexico exemption listings for personal property, Paula finds an entry for motor vehicles and sees that the exemption is $4,000. Paula begins to worry that she may lose her car, which is worth more than double the exemption limit.

Paula's next step is to search the New Mexico state exemptions for a wildcard exemption. (See above for an explanation of wildcard exemptions.) Paula discovers (at the bottom of the list) that she has a $5,500 wildcard exemption that she can apply to any property, including the Camaro. Add that to the $4,000 regular motor vehicle exemption, and Paula can now exempt $9,500. This amount still doesn't cover the Camaro's replacement value, which means the trustee would probably sell it, give Paula her $9,500 exemption, and distribute the rest of the sales proceeds to Paula's unsecured creditors.

Paula next checks to see whether New Mexico allows debtors to use the federal bankruptcy exemptions. She looks at the top of the exemption page and sees a note that the federal bankruptcy exemptions are available in her state. Hoping that the federal bankruptcy exemptions will give her a higher exemption limit for her Camaro, she turns to the end of Appendix A (right after Wyoming) and finds the federal bankruptcy exemption list. Under personal property she sees a listing for motor vehicles in the amount of $3,675—not high enough.

Paula examines the federal bankruptcy exemptions to see whether they provide a wildcard exemption. She discovers that the federal bankruptcy exemptions let you use up to $11,500 of the homestead exemption as a wildcard. Because Paula has no home equity to protect, she can apply the wildcard to the Camaro, in addition to the federal exemption for motor vehicles of $3,675. Further, Paula sees that she can get an additional wildcard exemption of $1,225 under the federal exemption system. Putting these exemptions together, Paula sees she can exempt $16,400—more than the value of her car.

Because Paula is most concerned about keeping her car, and because the federal bankruptcy exemptions let her keep her car while the state exemptions don't, Paula decides to use the federal bankruptcy exemption list.

Using Federal Nonbankruptcy Exemptions

If you are using state exemptions, you are also entitled to use a handful of exemptions called "federal nonbankruptcy exemptions." As the name suggests, these exemptions are generally used in cases other than bankruptcies, but you can also use them in a bankruptcy case. (In California, they apply only if you're using System 1.)

Skim the list at the end of Appendix A to see whether any of these exemptions would help you. If they would, you can use them in addition to the state exemptions. If they duplicate each other, though, you cannot add them together for any one category. For example, if both your state and the federal nonbankruptcy exemptions let you exempt 75% of disposable weekly earnings, you cannot combine the exemptions to keep all of your wages—75% is all you get.

Five Steps to Applying Exemptions to Your Personal Property

1. Check the exemptions you are using for specific property items that you want to keep.
2. If the state exemptions don't cover the property you want to keep (either because they don't exempt that property at all or because they exempt substantially less than your property is worth), look for a wildcard exemption in the state exemption list.
3. If the state also lets you use the federal bankruptcy exemptions (or you live in California), see whether a federal exemption (or a System 2 exemption in California) covers your property.
4. If the federal bankruptcy exemptions are available to you but don't seem to cover your property, see whether the federal bankruptcy wildcard exemption will work.
5. If you have the choice of two exemption systems, decide which exemption list you want to use. Don't mix and match. (In California, if you own your home and have considerably more than $25,000 in equity, you'll probably want to use System 1. If you don't own a home, System 2 will often be a better choice.)

Tip #1: Double your exemptions if you're married and filing jointly, unless the state exemption list in Appendix A says that doubling isn't allowed. If you're using the federal bankruptcy exemptions, you may double all exemptions.

Tip #2: While you're figuring out which of your property is exempt, write down in Column 4 the numbers of the statutes that authorize each exemption. (You can find these in Appendix A.) You will need this information when you fill out Schedule C of your bankruptcy papers.

Selling Nonexempt Property Before You File

If you want to reduce the amount of nonexempt property you own before you file for bankruptcy, you might consider selling the nonexempt property and using the proceeds to buy exempt property.

Or you might want to use the proceeds to pay certain types of debts, such as for necessities of life. But be careful: If the trustee learns that you sold the property and believes that you did so in order to defraud, hinder, delay, or shortchange a creditor, your efforts to shelter the property may fail. The court may decide to treat any exempt property you purchase as nonexempt property. And, if the court believes you acted fraudulently, your entire bankruptcy discharge may be at risk.

CAUTION

Talk to a lawyer first. Before you sell nonexempt property, consult a bankruptcy attorney. Your local bankruptcy court may automatically consider these kinds of transfers attempts to defraud a creditor. The only sure way to find out what is and isn't permissible in your area is to ask an attorney familiar with local bankruptcy court practices. A consultation on this sort of issue should not run more than $250 and is well worth the cost if it will help you hold on to the value of your nonexempt property by converting it to exempt property.

How to Proceed

Depending on your local bankruptcy court, there may be several ways to turn your nonexempt property into exempt property.

Replace Nonexempt Property With Exempt Property

You may:

- Sell a nonexempt asset and use the proceeds to buy an asset that is completely exempt. For example, you can sell a nonexempt coin collection and purchase clothing, which in most states is exempt without regard to value.
- Sell a nonexempt asset and use the proceeds to buy an asset that is exempt up to the amount received in the sale. For example, you can sell a nonexempt coin collection worth $1,200 and purchase a car that is exempt up to $1,200 in value.

- Sell an asset that is only partially exempt and use the proceeds to replace it with a similar asset of lesser value. For example, if a television is exempt up to a value of $200, you could sell your $500 television and buy a workable secondhand one for $200, putting the remaining cash into other exempt assets, such as clothing or appliances.
- Use cash (which isn't exempt in many states) to buy an exempt item, such as furniture or work tools.

Pay Nondischargeable Debts

If you choose to reduce your nonexempt property by selling it and using the proceeds to pay debts, keep the following points in mind:

- **It's usually unwise to pay off a debt that could be discharged in bankruptcy.** Many debts (such as credit card bills) can be completely discharged in bankruptcy. The only reason you should consider paying a dischargeable debt is to pay a debt for which a relative or friend is a cosigner, so that the friend or relative is not stuck paying the whole debt after your liability is discharged. Also, you might want to pay off a small credit card balance in order to keep the card out of your bankruptcy (you don't have to list it if you don't owe anything on it).
- **If you pay a creditor more than $600, you may want to wait to file for bankruptcy.** You should wait at least 90 days before you file for bankruptcy if the total payments to any one regular "arm's length" creditor during that period exceed $600. Otherwise, the payment may be considered a preference, and the trustee may be able to get the money back and add it to your bankruptcy estate. If the creditor you pay is a relative, close friend, or company in which you are an officer, you should wait at least one year before filing. The $600 limit applies only if you owe primarily consumer debts; if you owe primarily business debts or taxes, you can pay a creditor up to $6,225 during the 90-day prefiling period without it being considered a preference.

- **You can pay regular bills.** You can pay regular monthly bills right up until you file for bankruptcy. So keep paying your utilities and mortgage or rent.
- **Think twice before paying secured debts.** If you want to use the proceeds from nonexempt property to pay off a debt secured by collateral, read Ch. 5 of this book first. If the collateral for the debt isn't exempt, paying off the debt won't do you much good, because the trustee will take the collateral anyway when you file for bankruptcy. If the collateral is exempt, you may be able to keep it even if you don't pay off the debt before you file for bankruptcy.

EXAMPLE: John owes $5,000 on his 2004 Toyota truck, which is worth $4,000. John sells his nonexempt musical equipment, pays off the $5,000 note, and files for bankruptcy. It turns out that John can exempt only $1,000 in the motor vehicle. The trustee orders John to turn over the truck, which John does. The trustee sells the truck and gives John his $1,000 exemption. Not only did John lose his truck, but he also no longer has his musical equipment.

A better alternative: Because John owes more on the truck than it's worth, he could hold on to it through bankruptcy, making regular payments on the loan. The trustee would not take the truck away to sell it, because there would be no money left for unsecured creditors if the truck were sold with $5,000 in debt still hanging over it. And John might be able to hold on to the musical equipment for a small price paid to the trustee.

CAUTION

If you own your home. If you own your home and plan to claim a homestead exemption to protect your home equity (see Ch. 4), your exemption can be reduced, dollar for dollar, by the value of nonexempt property you converted if (1) the conversion took place in the ten years before you filed for bankruptcy, and (2) you converted the property to defraud, cheat, hinder, or delay your creditors. Courts haven't clarified exactly what constitutes defrauding, cheating, and so on. Because the amount of your homestead exemption often determines whether or not you can keep your home, however, you should definitely not try to convert nonexempt property without first talking to a lawyer who knows how your local bankruptcy court handles this issue.

You Can Pay Favored Creditors After You File

You may be tempted to leave certain creditors off your bankruptcy papers, perhaps because the creditor is a relative, a local provider of important services (for example, a doctor, lawyer, veterinarian, or department store), or your employer. Unfortunately, bankruptcy requires that all creditors be identified on the appropriate schedules. However, just because you got rid of a debt doesn't mean you can't pay it—as long as you wait until after you file and don't use property of the estate. For instance, if you file for bankruptcy on March 12, 2015, you can use income you earn after that date to pay the creditor, because that income is not part of your bankruptcy estate. One last point: While you are free to pay off a discharged debt, the creditor is not permitted to hound you for it.

Six Guidelines for Prebankruptcy Planning

Here are six important guidelines for staying out of trouble when you're making these kinds of prebankruptcy transactions.

1. **Don't convert nonexempt property if you have equity in your home.** As noted above, you risk losing some or all of your homestead exemption if you engage in this type of prebankruptcy planning. Our advice is not to do it until you talk to a lawyer.

2. **Accurately report all your prefiling transactions** on Form 7, the Statement of Financial Affairs. (See Ch. 6 for more on completing the official bankruptcy forms.) If the subject comes up with the trustee, creditors, or the court, freely admit that you tried to arrange your property holdings before filing for bankruptcy so that you could better get a fresh start. Courts see frankness like this as a sign of honorable intentions. If you lie or

attempt to conceal what you did or why you did it, the bankruptcy trustee or court may conclude that you had fraudulent intentions and either not allow the transaction or—even worse—deny you a bankruptcy discharge.

3. **Sell and buy for equivalent value.** If you sell a $500 nonexempt item and purchase an exempt item obviously worth $500, you shouldn't have a problem. If, however, you sell a $500 nonexempt item and purchase a $100 exempt item, be prepared to account for the $400 difference. Otherwise, the court will probably assume that you're trying to cheat your creditors and either force you to cough up the $400 (if you still have it) or, possibly, dismiss your bankruptcy case.

4. **Sell and buy property at reasonable prices.** When you sell nonexempt property in order to purchase exempt property, charge an amount as close to the item's market value as possible. This is especially true if you sell to a friend or relative. If you sell your brother a $900 stereo system for $100, a creditor or the trustee may cry foul, and the judge may agree.

   At the other end of the transaction, if you pay a friend or relative significantly more for exempt property than it is apparently worth, the court may suspect that you're just trying to transfer your assets to relatives to avoid creditors.

5. **Don't make last-minute transfers or purchases.** The longer you can wait to file for bankruptcy after making these kinds of property transfers, the less likely the judge is to disapprove. For example, judges frequently rule that a hasty transaction on the eve of filing shows an intent to cheat creditors. The open, deliberate, and advance planning of property sales and purchases, however, is usually considered evidence that you didn't intend to defraud. But even this isn't foolproof. One court ruled that the debtor's deliberate planning more than a year before filing was evidence of an intent to cheat creditors. This conflict reinforces our earlier warning: You must find out your bankruptcy court's approach before you sell nonexempt property.

6. **Don't just change the form of property ownership.** Simply changing the way property is held from a nonexempt form to an exempt form is usually considered fraudulent.

EXAMPLE: Although he's married, Jeff owns a house as his separate property. Also, Jeff incurred virtually all of his debts alone, so he plans to file for bankruptcy alone. In Jeff's state, the homestead exemption is only $7,500. Jeff's equity in his home is nearly $30,000. Jeff's state also exempts property held as tenancy by the entirety, so Jeff transfers ownership of the house to himself and his wife as tenants by the entirety. That would normally exempt the house from all debts Jeff incurred separately. But because Jeff merely changed the form of property ownership, rather than buying exempt property or paying off debts to give himself a fresh start, the bankruptcy court would probably find the transfer fraudulent and take Jeff's house. (Jeff might get $7,500 from the sale as his homestead exemption, but not necessarily.)

CAUTION

Community property warning. As mentioned earlier, if you're married and live in a community property state (Alaska, Arizona, California, Idaho, Louisiana, Nevada, New Mexico, Texas, Washington, or Wisconsin), the trustee can usually take both your share of community property and your spouse's, even if your spouse doesn't file for bankruptcy. But if you're tempted to change all or a portion of the community property into your spouse's separate property, beware: Creditors or the trustee are apt to cry fraud, and the trustee is likely to take the property anyway.

To give you an idea of what judges consider improper behavior shortly before filing for bankruptcy, here are some transactions that courts have found to be fraudulent:

- A debtor bought goods on credit but never paid for them. He then sold those goods and bought property that he tried to exempt.
- A debtor with nonexempt property was forced into involuntary bankruptcy by a creditor. The debtor convinced the creditor to drop the forced bankruptcy. Then the debtor sold the nonexempt property, purchased exempt property, and filed for Chapter 7 bankruptcy.
- A debtor sold nonexempt property that was worth enough to pay off all her debts (but didn't pay them off).
- A debtor sold nonexempt items for considerably less than they were worth.
- A debtor sold valuable property to a nonfiling spouse for one dollar.
- A debtor transferred nonexempt property the day after a creditor won a lawsuit against him, then filed for bankruptcy.
- A debtor in a state with an "unlimited" homestead exemption sold all her nonexempt property and used the proceeds to pay off a large portion of her mortgage.
- A debtor bought a piano and harpsichord and a whole life insurance policy, all exempt in his state. He didn't play either instrument, and he had no dependents who needed insurance protection.

Taking Out Loans to Pay Nondischargeable Debts

Some people are tempted to borrow money to pay off debts that aren't dischargeable—for instance, a student loan—and then list the new loan as a dischargeable unsecured debt. Be careful if you do this. A court could consider your actions fraudulent and dismiss your bankruptcy. If the court doesn't dismiss your case, the creditor may ask the court to declare the debt nondischargeable. If you take out the loan while you're broke and file for bankruptcy soon after, you probably will be penalized. And, if you borrow money or use your credit card to pay off a nondischargeable tax debt, you will not be able to discharge the loan or credit card charge in a Chapter 7 bankruptcy (although you could in a Chapter 13 bankruptcy).

Your House

f you own a home, Chapter 7 bankruptcy may not be the best strategy to deal with your debts. If you have significant nonexempt equity in your home (that is, equity that isn't protected by a homestead or another exemption), you risk losing your home if you file for Chapter 7 bankruptcy. As long as there will be equity left over after paying off what you owe, paying you the exempt amount, and covering the costs of sale, the trustee may sell your home if you use Chapter 7. (Exemptions for real estate are covered in "Will You Lose Your Home?" below.)

What's more, filing for Chapter 7 bankruptcy won't ultimately prevent a foreclosure on your home, although the automatic stay will put it on hold while your bankruptcy case is pending (unless the creditor convinces the judge to allow the foreclosure to proceed). If you want to keep your home, you must keep making your payments before, during, and after bankruptcy. If you've already missed mortgage payments, you'll have to make them up to prevent foreclosure. (If you want to keep your home, make sure your mortgage payments are current before filing. See "If You're Behind on Your Mortgage Payments," below.)

Chapter 13 bankruptcy provides many opportunities for saving a home that are unavailable to a Chapter 7 filer. For more information, see *The Foreclosure Survival Guide*, by Stephen Elias and Amy Loftsgordon (Nolo), and *Chapter 13 Bankruptcy*, by Stephen Elias and Kathleen Michon (Nolo).

This chapter explains how filing for Chapter 7 bankruptcy—or pursuing alternative strategies—affects your ability to hold on to your home. Of course, your home isn't your only consideration in deciding whether or not to file for bankruptcy, so make sure to read Ch. 1 of this book before making the decision.

How Bankruptcy Affects a Typical Homeowner

Here's an overview of how bankruptcy affects you as a homeowner. As you review this material, keep these basic principles in mind:

- You can keep your home in Chapter 7 bankruptcy unless your home equity exceeds the homestead exemption available to you by about 10% or more (to cover the costs of sale).

- If you are behind on your payments when you file for bankruptcy, your lender can ask the court for permission to proceed with a foreclosure. The court will usually grant this permission, as long as the lender can prove that it is the correct party to be making the request (that is, that it holds the required proof that it owns the mortgage). The lender or servicer trying to foreclose has the burden of proving that it has the right to ask the court to lift the automatic stay and allow the foreclosure.

- Mortgages and deeds of trust have two parts: a promissory note, by which you agree to repay the debt, and a lien on the property, which gives the lender the right to foreclose on the property to get its money back. Unless you reaffirm it (covered in Ch. 5), the promissory note is cancelled in the bankruptcy. But the lien will remain, which means you must keep making your payments or face foreclosure.

- You may not qualify for a mortgage modification after bankruptcy unless you reaffirm the mortgage; without reaffirmation, there is no promissory note to modify. (Although you may still be eligible to modify your mortgage using the federal government's Home Affordable Modification Program (HAMP).) On the other hand, reaffirming a mortgage can leave you with a huge debt that you'll be responsible for after your bankruptcy—and for that reason is generally a very bad idea. Check with your bank or HUD-approved housing counselor to see how bankruptcy may affect your mortgage modification efforts. The best approach is to hold off filing for bankruptcy until your modification efforts are completed—whether successfully or not.

- If you don't reaffirm your mortgage, your lender probably won't report your payments to the credit reporting agencies, which means your payments won't help you rebuild your credit report and score. But it's a bad idea to reaffirm a mortgage solely to rehabilitate your credit, because you'll be on the hook for the mortgage if you can't make your payments later. In fact, certain bankruptcy judges won't approve mortgage reaffirmations at all.

When You Need a Lawyer

We recommend that homeowners talk to a bankruptcy lawyer before filing if they have any concerns about being able to keep their house. The procedures and strategies discussed in this chapter can be complex. A mistake in estimating your equity or applying a homestead exemption could cost you your home. And, your state's law may offer you rights and options that aren't covered here.

You should also consult with a bankruptcy lawyer if:

- You own two homes, or you want to protect equity in a home that isn't your residence.
- You are married, own a home with your spouse, and plan on filing alone. Because the rules for how community property and "tenancy by the entirety" property are treated in bankruptcy can get complicated, it's a good idea to get some legal advice geared to your situation.

Mortgage Payments

You must keep making your mortgage payments if you want to avoid foreclosure. As you probably know all too well, you don't really "own" much of your home—a bank or another lender that has a mortgage or deed of trust on the home probably owns most of it. (Throughout this chapter, we use the term "mortgage" to include deeds of trust.)

Until the mortgage is paid off, the lender has the right to foreclose if you miss mortgage payments. Chapter 7 bankruptcy doesn't change this, although it may put the foreclosure on hold for a while.

Sometimes, a mortgage holder refuses to accept payments from a debtor who is in bankruptcy. If you make your payments but the lender rejects them, create a separate bank account in which to deposit the payments each month—and be prepared to make your account current whenever the lender agrees to start accepting payments. Why create a separate bank account? If you leave that money in your regular bank account, you may end up spending it on other necessities, and not have it available at the end of your bankruptcy. For example, if your mortgage payment is $1,500 a month, and your bankruptcy lasts four months, you may owe $6,000. That's a lot of money that you might be tempted to spend unless you lock it away in its own dedicated account.

Liens on Your House

Chapter 7 bankruptcy won't eliminate liens on your home that were created with your consent nor will it eliminate certain nonconsensual liens (such as tax liens or mechanics' liens). If you've pledged your home as security for loans other than your mortgage—for example, you took out a home equity loan or second mortgage—or a creditor such as the IRS has recorded a lien, those creditors, too, have claims against your home.

If there is a judgment lien on your home—that is, if a creditor sued you, obtained a court judgment, and recorded a lien at the land records office—you may be able to get rid of the lien entirely without paying a cent to the lienholder. And, in some states, if your home is sold in bankruptcy, you will get your homestead amount ahead of secured creditors holding judicial liens.

You can get rid of the lien created by a judgment by filing a Motion to Avoid a Judicial Lien. You may also be able to get rid of some liens by filing a separate lawsuit in bankruptcy court. Lien avoidance is explained in Ch. 5.

Keeping Your House

Even if you keep up with your mortgage payments, you may still lose your house unless a homestead exemption protects your equity (the difference between what your house is worth and what you owe the mortgage lender and all lienholders). If you were to sell your home today, without filing for bankruptcy, the money raised by the sale would go first to the mortgage lender to pay off the mortgage, then to lienholders to pay off the liens, and finally to pay off the costs of sale and any taxes due. If anything were left over, you'd get it.

If you file for bankruptcy and the trustee sells your house, the creditors will get paid in pretty much the same order, with one big difference. In a bankruptcy sale, whatever is left after the mortgages, liens, costs of sale, and taxes have been paid goes not to you, but to your unsecured creditors—unless a homestead exemption entitles you to some or all of it.

As a practical matter, the trustee won't bother to sell your house if there will be nothing left over for your unsecured creditors. Thus, the amount of your homestead exemption often determines whether or not you'll lose your home in bankruptcy.

If the bankruptcy trustee calculates that there would be leftover proceeds from a sale of your home to give to your unsecured creditors, the trustee will, almost always, take your home and sell it at auction to get that money, unless you can buy it back—that is, pay the trustee the amount that your unsecured creditors would get from the sale.

We explain how to figure out whether a homestead exemption will prevent the trustee from selling your home in "Will You Lose Your Home?" below.

How a Homestead Exemption Works: An Example

This chart applies only to those states that use dollar-amount homestead exemptions. If your state bases the homestead exemption on acreage, your lot size will determine whether or not you keep your home. (See "Will You Lose Your Home?" below.)

This example is based on a home worth $100,000, with a $35,000 homestead exemption.

If you have nonexempt equity in your home, the trustee will sell it. Here, the homeowner's total equity is $60,000 ($100,000 [value of home] − $40,000 [mortgages and liens against home]). The homeowner's nonexempt equity is $25,000 ($60,000 [total equity] − $35,000 [homestead exemption]). Because the homeowner has $25,000 in nonexempt equity, the trustee will sell the house and use the nonexempt equity to pay unsecured creditors.

If you don't have any nonexempt equity, the trustee won't sell your home. Here, the homeowner's total equity is $30,000 ($100,000 [value of home] − $70,000 [mortgages and liens against home]). The homeowner doesn't have any nonexempt equity ($30,000 [total equity] − $35,000 [homestead exemption] = less than zero).

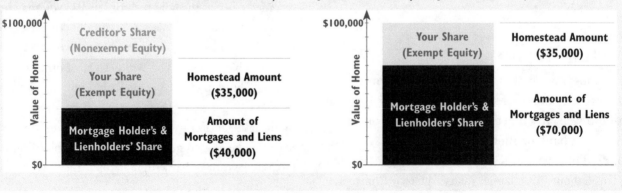

If You're Behind on Your Mortgage Payments

If you're behind on your mortgage payments but want to keep your house, your first strategy should be to negotiate with the lender and try other non-bankruptcy alternatives discussed in this section. (This section deals only with secured debts created with your consent. For a discussion of eliminating judicial liens on your home, see Ch. 5.)

Chapter 7 bankruptcy's automatic stay won't prevent foreclosure if you fall behind on your mortgage payments. At most, it will postpone foreclosure for a few months. Some lenders will just wait out your bankruptcy (a few months) and then proceed with the foreclosure. Others will file a motion to have the bankruptcy judge lift the automatic stay so that foreclosure can proceed, this will cut short the automatic stay's protection and allow the lender to process the foreclosure.

If you can come up with the money to catch up on your arrearages before the hearing on the motion to lift the stay (this usually means within about 45 days of your bankruptcy filing), you might be able to prevent the foreclosure. But you risk having the trustee question whether you are truly bankrupt if you can raise such a large sum of money post-filing. If you can get enough money to bring your mortgage current, then a better course of action is to delay filing for bankruptcy until you pay off the arrearages.

The bottom line: Usually the best course of action if you want to keep your house is to either wait to file for Chapter 7 until your mortgage payments are current, or file a Chapter 13 bankruptcy and catch up with the payments over time.

RESOURCE

What to do if foreclosure looms. If you're facing foreclosure, you'll want all the help you can get. You can start with *The Foreclosure Survival Guide*, by Stephen Elias (Nolo). If you want to try to negotiate a workout with your lender, consider seeking help from a nonprofit, HUD-approved housing counselor. (See "How to Find a HUD-Approved Housing Counselor," below.) You should also consider talking to an attorney to find out whether you have grounds to fight the foreclosure in court, and how filing for bankruptcy might affect your situation. Some lawyers specialize in foreclosure, and most bankruptcy lawyers understand foreclosure defenses. (See Ch. 10 for information on finding an attorney.)

If Your Home Is Worth Less Than You Owe

These days, many people have second or third mortgages on their homes that are no longer secured by home equity, due to the steep decline in home values.

EXAMPLE: Toni has a $175,000 first mortgage on her home, and second and third mortgages of $50,000 each. Her home is worth $300,000. Because all of the mortgages are covered by the home's value, any mortgage holder could foreclose on its lien if Toni defaulted. Her house would be sold, and all the mortgage holders would get paid pretty much what they were owed. A few years later, things are different. The value of the house has decreased by 50%, to $150,000. If the second or third mortgage holder tried to foreclose, all the money from the sale would go to the first mortgage holder and the foreclosing party would get nothing.

If your home's value has declined so much that a second or third mortgage holder no longer has any equity upon which to foreclose, and you discharge the underlying debt (the promissory note) in your bankruptcy, there will be no immediate consequence if you stop making payments on those mortgages. The mortgage holders can't personally sue you on the promissory note because it was discharged in your bankruptcy. And they won't foreclose on the lien, because they wouldn't get any money out of it.

As home values rise, however, stopping payment on your second or third mortgages could be risky. If your home regains enough equity, those liens might once more be secured by your home. At that point, you may not have the resources to bring those loans current. You'll have to work something out with those lenders or pay the lien off (plus accrued interest) when you sell the home. The bottom line: Stopping payment on your junior mortgages should be an option of last resort.

The Roller Coaster of Property Values

Before the Great Recession, some people who were relatively cash poor had significant equity in their homes, thanks to the housing bubble. Some had so much equity in their homes that they were effectively precluded from filing for Chapter 7 bankruptcy, because their equity exceeded the available homestead exemption.

After the housing bubble popped, we had the opposite problem. Home values declined significantly. (Later in this chapter we explain how this decrease in value affects your property in a bankruptcy.)

Recently home prices are no longer declining and have actually begun to appreciate. And now this question arises: Who owns appreciation in the property after you file for bankruptcy, you or the trustee? Some courts have found that the value of that appreciation technically belongs to the trustee. (See *In re Farthing*, 340 B.R. 346 (Bankr. D. Ariz. 2006); *In re Reed*, 940 F.2d 1317 (9th Cir. 1991).) Your equity may be protected by your state's homestead law when you file, but not be fully protected six months or a year after you file, if your bankruptcy court follows these cases. For example, assume the equity in your home is $100,000 and your state's homestead exemption is $100,000. In that case your entire equity is protected. But if, while your bankruptcy is still open, your home appreciates significantly in value, the trustee may be able to sell the home, give you your exemption, and pay the appreciated value to your unsecured creditors.

At the height of the housing bubble, trustees were known to keep bankruptcies open in the hope that the debtor's home would appreciate sufficiently in value to warrant a sale. To counter this, debtor's attorneys were asking courts to order their clients' cases closed as soon as possible. If you find yourself in a similar situation—that is, your home is appreciating in value—ask the court to close your case and hire an attorney if you run into problems. It will be worth it.

Negotiating With the Lender

If you've missed a few mortgage payments, most lenders will be willing to negotiate. What the lender agrees to will depend on your credit history, the reason for your missed payments, and your financial prospects.

> **EXAMPLE:** Doug misses a few house payments because he had a car accident and couldn't work for two months. It looks like he'll be back to work soon. The bank will probably work out a deal with Doug rather than immediately move to foreclose.

Mortgage Modifications

In 2009, the federal government launched an ambitious program designed to get banks to modify the repayment terms of some mortgages so that homeowners would have a better shot at avoiding foreclosure. Known as HAMP (Home Affordable Modification Program), this program encourages mortgage servicers (banks and companies who manage your mortgage for the mortgage owner) to lower your payments so that your mortgage payment is not more than 31% of your gross income, and add any arrearage on your current mortgage payments to the end of your mortgage term.

HAMP is just one of a number of programs available through the federal Making Home Affordable Program (MHA). In addition to mortgage modifications for both first and second lien loans, under MHA you may be able to refinance your mortgage, get a principal reduction, or temporarily suspend mortgage payments if you are unemployed or have been unemployed in the recent past.

Although HAMP and other MHA programs got off to a rocky start, Congress has tried to address some of the problems that previously prevented people from getting assistance by expanding some of the programs and revising the eligibility criteria for others. In addition, Congress has extended the deadlines to apply for many of the programs. You can learn more about the MHA programs in Nolo.com's Foreclosure Center or on the government's Making Home Affordable website at www.makinghomeaffordable.gov.

Beware of Scam Artists When Seeking Help With a Foreclosure or Loan Modification

As foreclosures mushroomed in 2008 and beyond, many lawyers and people associated with the real estate business starting offering advice and help on how to fight foreclosures and obtain mortgage modifications from the bank—usually for a steep up-front fee in the neighborhood of $3,000 and up. In many cases, these folks failed to deliver promised results but kept all or most of the money. While the FTC and laws of some states have made it illegal to take money up front to provide these services, most states (and the FTC) make exceptions for lawyers. Some businesses get around the laws by operating under a lawyer's umbrella.

The fact is, the help you can get from HUD-approved housing counselors is usually as good (or better) as the help you get from for-profit businesses. And the HUD-approved counseling is free. As for foreclosure prevention, you should be able to get a systematic analysis of your case from a real estate or bankruptcy lawyer for less than $1,000—much less in most cases.

If you don't qualify for a HAMP modification or your lender doesn't participate in the MHA programs, you may have other options.

- Lender/servicer modification procedures. Some of the larger mortgage servicers have their own modification procedures.
- National mortgage settlements. The settlement agreements in national lawsuits brought by 49 state attorneys general requires certain banks to provide extensive relief to distressed homeowners. If you have a mortgage serviced by Ally/GMAC, Bank of America, Citi, JPMorgan Chase, American Home Mortgage Servicing, Homeward Residential Holdings, Litton, Ocwen, SunTrust, or Wells Fargo, you might be eligible for a loan modification, refinancing, or a cash payout.
- State foreclosure prevention mediation. In response to the foreclosure crisis, some states have implemented mediation programs for those in foreclosure.

- State hardest hit funds. The Housing Finance Agency Innovation Fund for the Hardest Hit Housing Markets provided money to 18 states and the District of Columbia to assist homeowners in need. If your state is a recipient, you may be able to get mortgage payment assistance, a principal reduction, or other help.

For more on these and other options, visit Nolo.com's Foreclosure Center or get *The Foreclosure Survival Guide*, by Stephen Elias and Amy Loftsgordon (Nolo).

How to Find a HUD-Approved Housing Counselor

Here are some ways to find a housing counselor in your area:

- Visit the Making Home Affordable website, www.makinghomeaffordable.gov, and click "Get Started" to speak with a housing expert.
- The federal Department of Housing and Urban Development (HUD) has a list of approved counselors. You can find a HUD-approved counseling agency at www.hud.gov/foreclosure/index.cfm.
- The Homeownership Preservation Foundation website, www.995hope.org, offers free online counseling, among other things. Or you can call 888-995-HOPE and talk with someone.
- The National Foundation for Credit Counseling will get you to a nonprofit counselor (typically HUD certified) through its toll-free hotline, 800-388-2227.

In addition to the government-sponsored modification programs, here are some workout options your lender might agree to:

- Let you pay back missed payments over a few months. For example, if your monthly payment is $1,000 and you missed two payments ($2,000), the lender might let you pay $1,500 for four months.
- Reduce or suspend your regular payments for a specified time, then add a portion of your overdue amount to your regular payments later on.

- Extend the length of your loan and add the missed payments at the end.
- For a period of time, suspend the amount of your monthly payment that goes toward the principal, and require payment of interest, taxes, and insurance only.
- Refinance your loan to reduce future monthly payments.
- Let you sell the property for less than you owe the lender and waive the rest of the loan. This is called a "short sale." Short sales can have negative tax ramifications, so it is important to consult with an accountant before choosing this option.

Before you contact the lender about a workout, you should prepare information about your situation, including:

- an assessment of your current financial situation and a reasonable budget for the future
- a plan to deal with other essential debts, such as utility bills and car payments
- a hardship letter explaining why you fell behind on your mortgage (emphasize the most sympathetic aspects of your situation)
- information about the property and its value, and
- information about your loan and the amount of the default.

You should also find out whether your mortgage is insured by the Federal Housing Administration (FHA), the U.S. Department of Veterans Affairs (VA), or the U.S. Department of Housing and Urban Development (HUD). Borrowers with these types of mortgages have some special rights that those with "conventional" mortgages don't have.

Be advised that modifications are not for everyone—nor will lenders always agree to a modification. Be realistic about your situation before you approach the lender. If it is likely that you will lose your house because of your dire financial situation or because you have other pressing financial problems, it doesn't make sense to keep paying your mortgage even if you are able to get a modification.

If the Lender Starts to Foreclose

If your debt problems look severe or long-lasting, the lender may take steps toward foreclosure. In most states, before the lender can foreclose, it has to accelerate your loan. This means that the lender declares that you have defaulted and calls for immediate payment of the entire loan, as provided by the terms of the loan agreement.

> **EXAMPLE:** Don and Louise bought a $100,000 home by putting $20,000 down and getting an $80,000 mortgage. Their monthly house payments are $900. After making their payments consistently for several years, they miss three payments in a row. The bank accelerates the loan and demands the entire $76,284 balance left on the loan. Because Don and Louise can't come up with the money, the bank begins foreclosure proceedings.

In most states, this acceleration can be canceled if you are able to make up all the missed payments plus fees and interest; this is called "reinstating" the loan. In many cases, it's the add-ons that prevent homeowners from reinstating their loans. If the add-ons are what's standing between you and reinstatement, consider using a HUD-aproved housing counselor to help you negotiate a settlement with the lender. Different states have different time limits for reinstatement. Your counselor should know the time limit for your state; you can also find this information in *The Foreclosure Survival Guide,* by Stephen Elias and Amy Loftsgordon (Nolo).

Foreclosure can take anywhere from several weeks to several years, depending on where you live and what type of loan you have. During this time, you have several options:

- Sell your house. If you don't get any offers that will cover what you owe your lender, a short sale may be possible.
- Get another lender to give you a loan that pays off all or part of the first loan and puts you on a new schedule of monthly payments. If the original lender has accelerated the loan, you'll need to refinance the entire balance of the loan to prevent foreclosure. If the lender hasn't accelerated the loan, however, you can prevent foreclosure simply by paying the

missed payments, taxes, and insurance, plus interest. But be careful when deciding whether to refinance. In many cases, refinancing hurts more than it helps. Many lenders have figured out clever ways to hide high costs and fees in refinancing deals.

- If you are at least 62 years old and have significant equity in your home, consider getting a reverse mortgage. You can use this type of loan to pay off the lender and receive some money each month, based on your equity. (For more on reverse mortgages, see "Ways to Keep Your House," below.)

- File for Chapter 13 bankruptcy if you can't come up with the needed money in a lump sum right away but you can propose a feasible repayment plan. Chapter 13 bankruptcy allows you to "cure the default"—make up missed payments over time and make the regular payments as they come due. (See "Ways to Keep Your House," below.)

- Use Chapter 13 bankruptcy to get rid of liens. If you have a second or third mortgage that is no longer secured because of the depreciation in your property's value, filing for Chapter 13 bankruptcy allows you to remove them in many, but not all, courts. In some circumstances, it may also allow you to modify a first mortgage down to the property's actual value (for the most part, though, bankruptcy can't be used to modify residential mortgages in this manner). (See "Ways to Keep Your House," below.)

Defenses to Foreclosure

You may be able to delay or stop the foreclosure if you have defenses to paying the mortgage or if the lender has not properly followed state foreclosure procedures. If you think you might have a defense to foreclosure, contact a lawyer immediately. Some possible defenses are:

- **Interest rate that violates state or federal law.** Some states limit how much interest can be charged on a loan. Federal law prohibits lenders from making deceptive or false representations about the loan and from charging high closing costs and fees. If your interest is very high or your lender didn't tell you the truth about the terms of your loan, consult a lawyer.

- **Violations of the federal Truth in Lending law.** The federal Truth in Lending law, and an amendment known as the Home Ownership and Equity Protection Act (HOEPA), require the lender to give you certain information about your loan before you sign the papers. If the lender failed to provide this information, you may be able to cancel (rescind) the mortgage. But this doesn't apply to loans you used to purchase your home.

- **Home improvement fraud.** If you got ripped off by a home improvement contractor, you may be able to cancel a loan used to pay for that work.

- **Failure to follow foreclosure procedures.** Each state requires lenders to follow specific procedures when foreclosing on a home. If the lender doesn't follow these rules (for example, by not giving proper notice of the foreclosure or failing to inform you of certain rights), you may be able to delay the foreclosure.

- **Failure to follow new mortgage servicing rules.** The Consumer Financial Protection Bureau implemented new rules that apply to mortgage servicers, effective January 10, 2014. Those rules provide more protection to homeowners that default on mortgages or are in the foreclosure process. If a servicer fails to follow a rule, the homeowner might be able to delay, postpone, or cancel a foreclosure sale. The extra time might allow you to apply for a loan modification or explore another foreclosure alternative.

How to Raise a Foreclosure Defense

About half the states require that foreclosures go through court. The other half allow foreclosure to be brought outside of court under what's known as a "power of sale" clause in the mortgage or deed of trust. If you're facing foreclosure in a state that uses court, you can raise your defense just as you would in any other civil action. If you are in a state where the foreclosure occurs outside of court (called nonjudicial foreclosure states), you have to bring your own action in civil court to stop the foreclosure and then offer your defense.

RESOURCE
Learn about your options in foreclosure. For detailed information about your options if you are struggling to pay your mortgage or already in foreclosure, get *The Foreclosure Survival Guide*, by Stephen Elias and Amy Loftsgordon (Nolo). It covers the various federal mortgage modification options under the Making Home Affordable Program, foreclosure defenses, short sales, deeds in lieu, and more.

If Foreclosure Is Unavoidable

If you've exhausted the suggestions described above, you have equity in your home, and it looks like foreclosure is inevitable, you should know that losing your home in a bankruptcy sale will often be a better deal than losing it in a foreclosure sale, for two reasons.

First, a forced sale of your home in bankruptcy is supervised by the bankruptcy trustee, who will want to sell the house for as much as possible. In a foreclosure sale, the foreclosing creditor cares only about getting enough to cover its own debt. If you have a homestead exemption on the house, the amount you get increases as the amount your home is sold for goes up.

Benefits of Filing Bankruptcy Before the Foreclosure Sale

If you will ultimately lose your home to foreclosure, it often makes sense to file for bankruptcy before the foreclosure sale is final in order to avoid a possible tax hit. Here's why.

If you lose your home to foreclosure, you may end up owing a deficiency. The deficiency is the difference between your mortgage balance and the foreclosure sale price (minus costs and fees related to the sale). For example, if you owed $400,000 on your mortgage, your home sold for $300,000 and the servicer incurred $10,000 to sell the property, you will owe a deficiency in the amount of $90,000 ($400,000 - $300,000 - $10,000).

What happens next depends a lot on the state you live in so it is important to consult your local laws. In some states, your lender can choose whether to come after you for the deficiency or to forgive the debt. In other states, such as California, lenders cannot collect deficiencies for loans used to purchase the property, which are called "recourse" or "purchase money" loans. Because there is no deficiency to collect, so to speak, taxes do not attach. However, this is not true for junior loans used for things other than purchasing the property, such as for remodeling or paying bills. The deficiency rules apply.

Regardless of the state you live in, if, after the foreclosure sale, your lender forgives a deficiency, the government considers the forgiven debt to be taxable income, meaning that you must pay tax on this amount at the end of the year. If the amount of forgiven debt is large, you end up with a big tax debt, especially if the extra "income" pushes you into a higher tax bracket.

For the last seven years or so, most homeowners haven't had to worry about this tax hit because of the Mortgage Forgiveness Debt Relief Act, which absolved people of tax liability for forgiven mortgage debt (assuming the debt was taken out to purchase or improve a principal residence). The Act initially applied to debt that was forgiven from 2007 through 2012. The ending date has been extended a few times (the last was though 2014). It's possible Congress will extend the date again; but then again, it might not.

One of the benefits of filing for Chapter 7 bankruptcy *before* your home forecloses is that it wipes out the debt before any tax obligation attaches. By contrast, once you owe the tax, filing for bankruptcy alone won't get rid of it. There are ways you might still be able to avoid paying it (for example, you meet certain criteria for insolvency), but you'll need the help of an accountant or lawyer to handle the extra steps. Given the uncertainty, it might be better to avoid the tax problem altogether by timing your bankruptcy filing accordingly.

One final note—this stuff gets complicated. If you think you might be on the hook for a tax bill, talk to a lawyer.

Second, debtors are rarely entitled to the homestead exemption if the house is sold through foreclosure. In a bankruptcy sale, however, you are entitled to your homestead amount in cash, if there are proceeds left over after the secured creditors have been paid off.

In the end, what happens to your home will be up to the bankruptcy trustee. If there is enough equity in your home to produce some money for your unsecured creditors, the trustee will sell it, pay off the mortgage and other lienholders, give you your exemption, and distribute the rest. If there is not enough equity to generate money for your unsecured creditors, the trustee will release his or her authority over the home (called abandonment) and let the mortgage holder pursue any remedies available to it, which will most likely result in foreclosure if you owe an arrearage.

Getting Your Equity Out of Your Home

Many people who fall behind on their mortgage payments discover that the longer they can stall the foreclosure, the longer they can live in the home for free. In essence, this is a backdoor way to get a sizable chunk of equity out of your home without selling it or taking it into bankruptcy. For example, if your mortgage payment is $1,500 a month and you manage to live in the house for a year without making your payments, you've pulled the equivalent of $18,000 equity out of your home. And, if you have no equity in your home to begin with, that $18,000 is gravy.

Even if you have no equity in your home, remaining in your home without having to make any payment is a golden opportunity to save some money to help you transition into future housing. *The Foreclosure Survival Guide* (Nolo) devotes an entire chapter to strategies for remaining in your home payment-free as long as possible.

Will You Lose Your Home?

If you file for Chapter 7 bankruptcy, the fact that you've kept up on your house payments may not protect you from losing it. The trustee will still have your house sold if doing so will produce some cash to pay your unsecured creditors (and you aren't able to pay the trustee an equivalent amount). If the sale won't produce cash, the trustee will not take the house.

Whether the sale will produce cash depends on two factors:

- whether you have any equity in your home, and
- if so, whether that equity is exempt.

Use the Homeowners' Worksheet below to figure out the answers to these questions. (You'll find a copy of the worksheet in Appendix B.) Here are the instructions for filling out the form.

Part I: Do You Have Any Equity in Your Home?

Line 1: Estimated market value of your home
Estimate how much money your home could produce in a quick, as-is sale. The trustee will often use this value in deciding whether to sell the home. However, the trustee may instead use the full market value of your property. So, if there is a significant difference between the quick sale value and the full value of the home, use the latter to be on the safe side. To get a rough idea of what your home is worth in either type of sale, ask a realtor what comparable homes in your neighborhood have sold for. Or look in newspaper real estate sections. You can also generate rough home valuation estimates from websites such as www.zillow.com, www.homegain.com, or www.realtor.com. (As stated, these estimates are rough. They won't replace the opinion of a professional appraiser.)

Line 2: Costs of sale
Costs of sale vary, but they tend to be about 6%–8% of the sales price. The trustee is not required to subtract the costs of sale in determining whether to take your home, but most do. (If you want to err on the side of caution, put "0" in this blank.) When you complete your bankruptcy paperwork, you can note that you are deducting the costs of sale from the property's fair market value.

Line 3: Amount owed on mortgages and other loans
Enter the amount needed to pay off your mortgage and any other loans that are secured by the home as collateral. If you can't come up with a reasonably reliable estimate, contact each lender and ask how much is necessary to cancel the debt.

Line 4: Amount of liens

Enter the amount of all liens recorded against your home (other than liens created by mortgages and home equity loans). Liens are claims against your home that have been recorded with the land records office. The three most common types of liens are tax liens, mechanics' liens, and judgment liens. Tax liens can be recorded against your home by the county, state, or federal government for failure to pay property, income, or other taxes. People who do work on your home and claim that you didn't pay them what you owe can record mechanics' or materialmen's liens against your home. And judgment liens can be recorded by anyone who has sued you and won.

If you think there might be liens on your home, visit the county land records office. Tell the clerk you'd like to check your title for liens. The clerk should direct you to an index (often computerized) that lists all property in the county by the owner's last name. Next to your home should be a list of any liens recorded against it.

Line 5 = Line 2 + Line 3 + Line 4

Add up the total costs that would have to be paid if you were to sell your home.

Line 6 (your equity) = Line 1 – Line 5

If Line 1 is more than Line 5, subtract Line 5 from Line 1, and put the result on Line 6. For bankruptcy purposes, this is your equity in the property—that is, the amount that would be left over after all mortgages, loans, liens, and costs of sale are paid.

If the amount on Line 5 is more than the amount on Line 1, you have no equity; you can stop here. There will be no reason for the trustee to take your home in bankruptcy—once all of the liens and mortgage(s) are paid off, there would be nothing left to distribute to your unsecured creditors.

If you do have equity, go on to Part II to determine how much of it is protected by an applicable exemption.

The Trustee's Power to Eliminate Liens— And How It May Cost You Your Home

When property has liens on it for more than the property is worth, it is "oversecured." If a trustee sells oversecured property, there won't be enough money to pay off all liens, which means that one or more lienholders will be left with nothing. And there certainly won't be any money to pay unsecured creditors, who get paid only after all lienholders have been paid off.

The trustee's job is to find money to pay unsecured creditors, so the trustee usually won't bother selling an oversecured home. The picture changes, however, if the trustee can knock out enough lienholders to free up some equity. Once that happens, it might make sense to sell the home.

All states have laws specifying the procedures that must be followed to make a mortgage or another secured agreement or lien valid (called "perfecting" the lien). These typically include a proper acknowledgement signed in front of a notary public and recorded in the local land records office. While real estate practitioners usually have a firm grasp of these rules, mistakes can happen. If a lien hasn't been perfected, the trustee may seek to knock it out, turning an oversecured property into one that, when sold, will yield some cash after the remaining lienholders get their share.

Before you file for bankruptcy, check on the legal status of any liens you are relying on to save your home or other property. In particular, make sure the document creating the lien is recorded and contains a proper acknowledgement. If not, you may have more equity than you think—and the trustee may have a greater incentive to sell your home.

TIP

Legal research note. If you do legal research on equity and homestead exemptions, note that the word "equity" has multiple meanings. "Unencumbered" equity is the value of your home, minus the mortgage and the liens you can't get rid of. (That's what we mean when we say equity.) Then there's "encumbered" equity, which is the value of your home minus only the mortgage. Sometimes courts refer to encumbered equity simply as "equity."

Part II: If You Have Equity, Is It Protected by an Exemption?

We're assuming that, in Part I, you found that you have some amount of home equity. Here in Part II, we'll determine how much of that equity you can claim as exempt—that is, how much of it you're entitled to keep.

Before you can figure out how much of your equity is protected by an exemption, you must determine which set of exemptions to use. The new bankruptcy law imposes strict domicile requirements on filers seeking to use a homestead exemption. Filers who don't meet these requirements may have to use the exemptions of the state where they used to live—and will be subject to a $155,675 limit on the amount of equity they can exempt. (Because many states protect less than $155,675 in home equity, this cap won't affect the majority of filers.) The purpose of these rules is to prevent filers from moving to another state to take advantage of its better homestead protection.

Here are the rules:

- If you bought your home at least 40 months ago, you can use the homestead exemption of the state where your home is.
- If you bought your home at least two years ago, you can use the homestead exemption of the state where your home is. However, if you bought your home within the last 40 months, your homestead exemption is capped at $155,675, unless you bought the home with the proceeds from the sale of another home in the same state.
- If you bought your home within the last two years, then you must use the homestead exemption of the state where you were living for the better part of the 180-day period that ended two years before your filing date. And you are still subject to the $155,675 limit.

EXAMPLE 1: Four years ago, John and Susie retired and moved from Massachusetts to Maine, where they bought a home. If they file for bankruptcy in Maine, they can use Maine's exemptions, because they have lived there for more than 40 months. If they had moved to Maine three years ago, they would still be able to use Maine's exemptions, but their homestead exemption would be capped at $155,675. Maine's homestead allowance for joint filers who are at least 61 years old is $190,000, so John and Susie would lose just over $34,325 worth of homestead exemption ($190,000 exemption minus the $155,675 cap).

EXAMPLE 2: After moving from Vermont to Boston, Julius and his family buy a fine old Boston home for $700,000. A little more than two years later, after borrowing heavily against the home because of financial reversals, Julius files for bankruptcy. At that point, he owns $250,000 in equity. Although the Massachusetts homestead exemption of $500,000 would cover Julius's equity, he can claim only $155,675 of that exemption because he moved to Massachusetts from another state within the last 40 months.

EXAMPLE 3: Eighteen months ago, Fred moved from Florida to Nevada, where he purchased his current home with $400,000 he received from an inheritance. Fred files for bankruptcy in his current home state of Nevada. Because Fred lived in Florida for two years prior to moving to Nevada, he must use Florida's homestead exemption—and because Fred hasn't lived in Nevada for 40 months, his exemption is subject to the $155,675 cap. The cap imposes an extreme penalty on Fred. Florida offers an unlimited homestead exemption, while Nevada's homestead exemption is $550,000. Because of the cap, however, Fred can protect only $155,675 of his equity, which means that the trustee will undoubtedly sell his home, give Fred his $155,675, and use the rest to pay off his unsecured creditors.

EXAMPLE 4: Joan moves from New Jersey to Vermont, where she buys a home for $250,000, with a $225,000 mortgage. Less than two years after moving, Joan files for bankruptcy. Because Joan was living in New Jersey for years before moving to Vermont, she must use either New Jersey's state homestead allowance or the federal homestead allowance (New Jersey gives filers a choice of exemptions). New Jersey provides no homestead exemption at all, but the federal homestead exemption is approximately $22,975. It isn't hard for Joan to figure out that she should use the federal exemption system if protecting the equity in her home is her top priority. However, if Joan's personal property is more important to her, and she would be able to keep more of it using the New Jersey state exemptions, she might choose the state exemptions and let the trustee sell her home.

How Appreciation Might Affect the Homestead Cap

As explained above, your homestead exemption will be capped at $155,675 if you acquired your home within the 40 months prior to filing for bankruptcy and you did not purchase it with the proceeds from selling another home in the same state.

But what if you have owned your home for more than 40 months, and the *value* of your home has appreciated significantly within the 40 month period prior to the bankruptcy filing? Does the $155,675 cap apply to that appreciated value? Some courts have said "no." (See, for example, *In re Rasmussen*, 349 B.R. 747 (Bankr. M.D. Fla. 2006). Other courts, however, have held that the cap will be applied in this situation. (*In re Nestlen*, 441 B.R. 135 (B.A.P. 10th Cir. 2010)).

CAUTION

The cap also applies to filers who commit certain types of misconduct. No matter how long you have lived in the state where you are filing, your homestead exemption will be capped at $155,675 if you have been convicted of a felony demonstrating that your bankruptcy filing is abusive, you owe a debt arising from a securities act violation, or you have committed a crime or an intentional, willful, or reckless act that killed or caused serious personal injury to someone in the last five years. The court may decide to lift the cap if it finds that the homestead exemption is reasonably necessary for you to support yourself and your dependents.

If you are filing in a state that allows you to choose between the state and federal exemption lists, you

are always entitled to use the federal exemptions, regardless of how long you have lived in the state. The federal homestead exemption allows you to protect about $22,975 in equity, (and you can exempt an additional $1,225 by using the wildcard exemption) and married couples can double that amount.

Homes in Revocable Living Trusts

Revocable living trusts have become a popular way to pass valuable property on when people die. The property owner creates a trust document naming him- or herself as the trustee, another person as successor trustee to take over when the owner dies, and typically one or more beneficiaries to receive the property upon the owner's death. When the original property owner dies, the successor trustee steps in and distributes the property to the beneficiaries. All of this happens without going through court. (It's called a living trust because it takes effect during the property owner's life, not when he or she dies; it's revocable because the property owner can undo it any time.)

Legally, the trustee owns the property in the trust, although it's common to refer to the trust itself as the legal owner of the property. So, if John Henry creates a revocable living trust and puts his house in it, he will be the initial trustee and own his house as "trustee of the John Henry Revocable Living Trust." If John Henry files for bankruptcy, can he claim a homestead exemption for the house he owns as trustee?

Almost every court to consider this issue has allowed homestead exemptions to be claimed on homes held in typical revocable living trusts. When you create a revocable living trust, you retain actual ownership of the property even though it's titled as a trust rather than outright ownership, so it's only fair to allow you to claim an exemption. Despite this court trend, however, it's probably safest to remove the property from a living trust by executing a new deed (for yourself as trustee(s) to yourself as an individual or a married couple). After your bankruptcy, you can execute a new deed placing the property back in the trust.

Homeowners' Worksheet

Part I. Do you have any equity in your home?

1. Market value of your home ....$_____

2. Costs of sale (if unsure, put 5% of market value)......................$_____

3. Amount owed on all mortgages ....$_____

4. Amount of all liens on the property ....$_____

5. Total of Lines 2, 3, and 4...$_____

6. Your equity (Line 1 minus Line 5)..$_____

If Line 6 is zero or less, skip the rest of the worksheet. The trustee will have no interest in selling your home.

Part II. Is your property protected by an exemption?

7. Does the available homestead exemption protect your kind of dwelling?

   ☐ Yes. Go on to Line 8.

   ☐ No. Enter $0 on Line 11, then continue on to Line 12.

8. Do you have to file a "declaration of homestead" to claim the homestead exemption?

   ☐ Yes, but I have not filed it yet.

   ☐ Yes, and I have already filed it.

   ☐ No.

9. Is the homestead exemption based on lot size?

   ☐ No, it is based on equity alone. Go to Line 10.

   ☐ No, it is unlimited (true only of the exemptions for Washington, DC).

   If you are using the D.C. exemptions, you can stop here. Your home is protected.

   ☐ Yes. The exemption is limited to property of _____ acres.

   If your property is smaller than this limit, you can stop here. Your home is protected. If your property exceeds this limit, see the instructions.

   ☐ Yes, but there is an equity limit as well. The exemption is limited to property of _____ acres.

   If your property is smaller than this limit, go on to Line 10. If your property exceeds this limit, see the instructions.

10. Do you own the property with your spouse in "tenancy by the entirety"?

    ☐ Yes. *See the instructions and talk to a bankruptcy attorney to find out whether your house is fully protected.*

    ☐ No. *Go on to Line 11.*

11. Is the dollar amount of the homestead exemption limited?

    ☐ Yes. *Enter the dollar limit here:* $_____

    ☐ No dollar limit. *You can stop here. Your home is protected.*

12. Can you protect more equity with a wildcard exemption?

    ☐ Yes. *Enter the dollar amount here:* $_____

    ☐ No.

13. How much of your equity is protected?
Total of Lines 11 and 12: $_____

If the total exceeds $155,675 and you are subject to the cap on homestead exemptions, write "$155,675" on this line. See the instructions for more information.

14. Is your home fully protected?
Subtract Line 13 from Line 6: $_____

If this total is a negative number, your home is protected. If this total is a positive number, you have unprotected equity in your home, and the trustee might choose to sell your home (or allow you to keep it in exchange for cash or exempt property roughly equal in value to your unprotected equity).

Line 7: Does the available homestead exemption protect your kind of dwelling?

Only two states do not have a homestead exemption. If you are using the exemptions in one of these two states, enter $0 on Line 11.

States With No Homestead Exemption	
New Jersey	Pennsylvania

For all other states, check the table in Appendix A to see if your type of dwelling is protected. Some types of dwellings may not be covered, including:

- **Mobile homes.** Most states specifically include mobile homes in their homestead exemptions. Other states include any "real or personal property used as a residence." This would include a trailer, mobile home, or houseboat, as long as you live in it. Some states don't detail the types of property that qualify for homestead protection. If your mobile home does not qualify for a homestead exemption, it would be protected only by the exemption for a "motor vehicle."
- **Co-ops or condominiums.** Some homestead laws specifically cover co-ops or use language that says the exemption protects "any property used as a dwelling."
- **Apartments.** Most homestead statutes do not protect apartments, though a few do.

If your type of dwelling is not covered, enter $0 on Line 11.

If it is unclear whether your type of dwelling is covered by the available homestead exemption, you may need to do some legal research. (See Ch. 10 for help getting started.)

Line 8: Do you have to file a "declaration of homestead" to claim the exemption?

States That May Require a Declaration of Homestead		
Alabama	Montana	Utah
Idaho	Nevada	Virginia
Massachusetts	Texas	Washington

To claim a homestead exemption in Virginia, you must have a declaration of homestead on file with the land records office for the county where the property is located when you file for bankruptcy. The other states on this list vary in what they require and when. If you are using exemptions for one of these states, the safest approach is to file a declaration of homestead.

Requiring you to record a declaration before you can get the benefit of a homestead exemption may violate the bankruptcy laws. (*In re Leicht*, 222 B.R. 670 (B.A.P. 1st Cir. 1998).) Regardless of the legalities, however, you will be best served by filing your declaration of homestead before you file for bankruptcy.

Other states allow (but do not require) you to file a homestead declaration in certain circumstances. In Texas, for example, you may file a homestead declaration to claim protection for property you own but are not currently living in.

EXAMPLE: John and Doris live in Texas. They have retired and have decided to rent out their spacious country home and move to an apartment closer to town. They can still claim their country home as their homestead by recording a declaration of homestead with the land records office in the county where their country home is.

In some states, a "declared" homestead offers additional protection in situations other than bankruptcy. Also, if you own more than one piece of real estate, some states allow a creditor to require you to file a declaration of homestead to clarify which property you are claiming as your homestead.

Line 9: Is the homestead exemption based on lot size?
Most states place a limit on the value of property you can claim as your homestead exemption, but a few states have no such limits. Find out what kind of homestead exemption system your state uses by looking at the lists below.

Unlimited Homestead Exemption
District of Columbia

If you are lucky enough to be using the District of Columbia exemptions, congratulations: You can skip the rest of this chapter. Your home is not at risk in a Chapter 7 bankruptcy.

Homestead Exemption Based on Lot Size Only		
Arkansas	Kansas	Texas
Florida	Oklahoma	
Iowa	South Dakota	

In these states, you can easily determine whether your home is exempt. The homestead exemption is based simply on acreage. Look in Appendix A for the acreage limitation for the state. (In Oklahoma, if you use more than 25% of the property as a business, the one-acre urban homestead exemption cannot exceed $5,000.)

If your property is smaller than the maximum allowable acreage, your home is fully protected. You can skip the rest of this chapter.

If your property exceeds the maximum allowable acreage, the trustee will sell the excess acreage if you have any equity in it (unless you are able to buy it back from the trustee for a negotiated amount). Enter $0 in Line 11 of the worksheet.

Homestead Exemption Based on Lot Size and Equity		
Alabama	Michigan	Nebraska
Hawaii	Minnesota	Oregon
Louisiana	Mississippi	

These states use the size of your lot and the amount of your equity to determine whether your home is exempt. First look in Appendix A for the state acreage limitation and enter it on Line 9.

If your property exceeds the maximum allowable acreage, the trustee will want to sell the excess acreage (or get the equivalent in value from you) if you have enough equity in it.

If your lot size is within the allowed acreage, your exemption is determined by the equity amount limit. Proceed to Line 10.

Homestead Exemption Based on Equity Alone		
Federal exemptions	Maine	Ohio
Alaska	Maryland	Rhode Island
Arizona	Massachusetts	South Carolina
California	Missouri	
Colorado	Montana	Tennessee
Connecticut	Nevada	Utah
Georgia	New Hampshire	Vermont
Idaho		Virginia
Illinois	New Mexico	Washington
Indiana	New York	West Virginia
Kentucky	North Carolina	Wisconsin
	North Dakota	Wyoming

If the state homestead exemption is based on equity alone, or if you are using the federal exemptions, go to Line 10.

Line 10: Do you own the property with your spouse in "tenancy by the entirety"?

If you are married and live in the right state, you may be able to exclude your home from your bankruptcy estate—which means you can keep it, no matter how much equity you own or how large your state's homestead exemption is—if you own it with your spouse in tenancy by the entirety.

Tenancy by the entirety (TBE) is a form of property ownership available to married couples in about half of the states, some of which have laws that prohibit TBE property from being sold to pay debts that are owed by only one spouse. If this type of law applies, you can keep TBE property, regardless of its value. Some states also protect personal property owned in tenancy by the entirety, such as checking accounts.

States That Recognize TBE

These states recognize TBE home ownership (as does the District of Columbia): Alaska, Arkansas, Delaware, Florida, Hawaii, Illinois, Indiana, Kentucky, Maryland, Massachusetts, Michigan, Missouri, New Jersey, New York, North Carolina, Ohio, Oklahoma, Oregon, Pennsylvania (subject to conditions), Rhode Island, Tennessee, Vermont, Virginia, and Wyoming.

Unlike exemptions, tenancy by the entirety protection generally depends on the law of the state where your property is, not where you live. For example, if you and your spouse live in Minnesota but own a condo in Florida as tenants by the entirety, Florida law protects your condo from being seized to pay debts owed by only one spouse, even though Minnesota law offers no such protection. Recently, however, an Illinois case reached the opposite conclusion: The court found that debtors filing in Illinois could claim tenancy by the entirety protection only for property in Illinois, not for property located in Michigan—even though Michigan is a state that recognizes tenancy by the entirety. (*In re Giffune* 343 B.R. 883 (Bankr. N.D. Ill. 2006).) If you own property in another state, you should talk to a lawyer to find out whether you can protect it.

To qualify for this type of property protection, all of the following must be true:

- You are married.
- You are filing for bankruptcy alone, without your spouse. If you file jointly, your TBE property is not protected.
- All of the debts you are trying to discharge are yours alone; none are debts that you owe jointly with your spouse.
- You and your spouse own property in one of the states that recognize TBE (see above).
- You and your spouse own the home as tenants by the entirety. In some of these states, the law presumes that married people own their property as tenants by the entirety, unless they specify that they wish to own it in some other way (as joint tenants, for example).

If you meet these five criteria, this protection could be extremely valuable to you. You may want to see a bankruptcy attorney to figure out the best way to take full advantage of it.

Line 11: Is the dollar amount of the homestead exemption limited?

Most states place a dollar limit on the homestead exemption. For example, New York allows you to exempt between $75,000 and $150,000 in equity depending on which county you live in, while Massachusetts allows you to exempt up to $500,000. If the state homestead exemption you're using works this way, write down the amount of equity the exemption protects on Line 11. If your state allows you to use the federal exemptions and you plan to do so, write down the federal exemption instead. (See Appendix A for these figures.)

In some states, if you own your home with your spouse and you file jointly for bankruptcy, you can each claim the full homestead exemption amount (called "doubling"). Other states don't allow doubling. When you look at Appendix A, check to see whether doubling is prohibited. If the chart doesn't mention it, assume that you and your spouse can double.

Your Homestead Exemption May Be Reduced If You Converted Nonexempt Property in the Last Ten Years

The court can look back ten years before you filed for bankruptcy to find out whether you have converted nonexempt property to exempt property in order to defraud, hinder, cheat, or delay your creditors. If the court finds that you have converted property for one of these reasons, the value of your homestead exemption will be reduced by the value of the property you converted. (11 U.S.C. § 522(o); *In re Maronde*, 332 B.R. 593 (Bankr. D. Minn. 2005); *In re Lacounte*, 342 B.R. 809 (Bankr. D. Mont. 2005).)

EXAMPLE: In 2006, Peter sold three nonexempt vehicles for a total of $10,000, which he used to pay down the equity on his home, which in turn increased the amount of equity he could claim as exempt. In 2015, Peter files for Chapter 7 bankruptcy. Depending on his reasons for selling the cars and paying down his mortgage, Peter may lose $10,000 worth of homestead protection. If Peter sold his cars so he could keep that money (by putting it into his home) and escape a judgment pending against him, the court might rule that he did so in order to defraud, hinder, cheat, or delay his creditors. If, on the other hand, Peter sold his cars because he legitimately wanted to pay down his mortgage, and he wasn't facing any creditor collection actions at the time, the court would probably find that the conversion was legitimate and would not reduce his homestead exemption.

Our advice? If you undertook any "asset protection" activities in the last ten years and plan to claim a homestead exemption, talk to a lawyer before you file for bankruptcy.

Line 12: Can you protect more equity with a wildcard exemption?

Some states allow you to add a wildcard exemption to the amount of your homestead exemption. Although these wildcard amounts are usually small, they might be enough to tip the balance in favor of keeping your home.

Check Appendix A to see whether the state where you're filing has a wildcard exemption you can use for real estate; if so, write the amount on Line 12. If your state doesn't have a wildcard exemption that you can use for real estate, leave this line blank.

Line 13: How much of your equity is protected?

Add Lines 11 (the state homestead exemption available to you) and 12 (any wildcard exemption you can add to your homestead exemption). This is the amount of home equity you can protect in bankruptcy. If you aren't subject to the $155,675 cap (explained above), write this amount on Line 13.

If you are subject to the $155,675 cap, it might limit the amount of equity you can protect. If the total of Lines 11 and 12 doesn't exceed $155,675, it doesn't matter—the cap won't affect you, and you can write the total amount on Line 13. However, if the total is more than $155,675 and the cap applies, you can protect only $155,675 in equity. Even if your state law would otherwise allow you to take a larger exemption, you'll be limited to $155,675, and this is what you should write on Line 13.

Line 14: Is your home fully protected?

Subtract Line 13 from Line 6, and enter the total on Line 14. If you generate a negative number, all of your home equity should be protected by the applicable exemptions, if your estimates are correct. The trustee probably won't have your home sold, because there would be no proceeds left over (after your mortgage holder was paid off and you received your exempt amount of equity) to pay your unsecured creditors.

If, however, you generate a positive number, your equity exceeds the applicable exemption—in other words, you have unprotected equity in your home. If your estimates are right, the trustee can force the sale of your home to pay off your creditors, unless you can pay the trustee the value of your unprotected equity (perhaps by selling property that would otherwise be exempt). From the proceeds of the sale, your secured creditors will be paid the amounts of their mortgages, liens, and so forth; you will receive the amount of your exemption; and your unsecured creditors will get the rest.

If you have significant unprotected equity, you shouldn't file for Chapter 7 bankruptcy if you want to keep your house. The trustee will almost certainly sell your home, unless you can come up with the cash to keep it. You'll probably fare better—and hold on to your home longer—by using your equity to help pay off your debts, either directly or through a reverse mortgage, or to fund a Chapter 13 reorganization plan. Some of these strategies are discussed in "Ways to Keep Your House," below.

> ! CAUTION
> **This worksheet is for estimate purposes only.** If this worksheet shows that your equity is equal to or near the maximum amount of your state's homestead exemption, take note: The trustee can challenge the value you claim for your home and may determine that it's worth more than you think. If it looks like property values are rising, the trustee can also leave your case open and wait to see whether the amount of appreciation will produce some nonexempt property. However at least one court has tacitly disapproved of this practice: It denied the trustee's motion to reopen a case to take advantage of a speculative increase in value in inherited property. (See *In re Saunders*, 2011 WL 671765 (Bankr. M.D. Ga. 2011).)
>
> If these things happen, the trustee may seek to have your home sold. If your estimates show that you might be close to the exemption limit, get some advice from an experienced bankruptcy lawyer. Or, if it looks like the trustee is keeping your case open to capture appreciation in your home's value, ask an attorney to intervene and request a court order that the case be closed.

Ways to Keep Your House

If you have nonexempt equity in your home and would lose it if you filed for bankruptcy, you probably want to explore other options. We outline some of them here, but you should ask an experienced bankruptcy lawyer for help.

Reduce Your Equity Before Filing for Bankruptcy

If you can reduce your nonexempt equity before you file, you may be able to pay off your other debts and avoid bankruptcy. And, if you later file for bankruptcy, you may be able to save your home.

There are two ways to reduce your equity:
- Borrow against the equity.
- Sell part ownership of your house.

You can use the proceeds to buy exempt property or to pay off other debts.

> ! CAUTION
> **Consult a local bankruptcy lawyer before reducing your equity.** If you file for bankruptcy after reducing your equity, the bankruptcy court in your area might view your actions as an abuse of the bankruptcy process and dismiss your bankruptcy petition. This is more likely if you reduced your equity within two years of filing. How to stay out of trouble is covered in Ch. 3.

Borrow Against Your Equity

If you borrow against your equity, you won't reduce your overall debt burden. You may be able to lower your overall monthly bills, however, if you can get a lower interest rate or a longer-term equity loan to pay off short-term, high-interest debts. You can also fully deduct the interest you pay on home equity loans from your income taxes.

Be careful when you shop for a loan. Many lenders offer loans with very high rates to people in financial trouble. Although you may be desperate to save your home, taking out another loan with high interest rates or high costs and fees will only get you into deeper financial trouble. Also, be extra cautious about taking out a loan with a balloon payment (a large lump sum of money due at the end of the loan term). If you can't make the balloon payment when it comes due, you will lose your home. Most people can't come up with $25,000, $50,000, or $100,000 all at once. You might be able to refinance your home to pay off the balloon, but don't count on it.

CAUTION

Beware foreclosure scams. When people are close to foreclosure, they become targets for an army of con artists who have descended into their communities to give them one last kick. Unless you know the person who is offering to help you save your home—for instance, a neighborhood real estate or mortgage broker, or a community bank or credit union—we recommend that you decline all offers of foreclosure assistance unless you first consult with a HUD-approved nonprofit housing counselor (see "How to Find a HUD-Approved Housing Counselor," above). Nolo's *The Foreclosure Survival Guide* has a large section on the various scams and some dos and don'ts that will help you avoid being a victim.

Sell Some of Your Equity

Another way to protect your equity is to sell some of your house. By owning your home jointly with someone else, your equity is reduced.

Selling a portion of your equity may appeal to you; after all, what you need now is more cash, not another monthly bill. Perhaps a friend or relative would be willing to buy a half share in your home. If you pursue this strategy, you may need to wait two years after the sale before filing for bankruptcy. Otherwise, the bankruptcy trustee might void the sale, especially if it appears that you gave your friend or relative a bargain on the price.

Even two years may not be sufficient in some courts if the judge views your actions as defrauding your creditors. (See Ch. 3.) Be sure to consult a bankruptcy attorney who is aware of local practice before you try this.

Also, think long and hard about whether you want to share ownership of your home. A co-owner can sell his or her interest, force a sale of the property, die and leave it to someone else, and so on. Again, consult a bankruptcy lawyer before you sell. This strategy can be fraught with complications and traps for the uninformed.

Consider a Reverse Mortgage

If you are at least 62 years old and you own substantial equity in your home, a reverse mortgage may be just the ticket. When you get a reverse mortgage, you borrow against your home equity and receive monthly payments that you can use to fix your home, pay down your debts, or pay them off altogether. This allows you to use your equity without getting deeper into the type of debt trouble that might cause you to lose your home.

You don't have to pay a reverse mortgage loan back during your lifetime—instead, the loan is collected after your death, from your home equity. Of course, this also means that your heirs are less likely to inherit your home (it may have to be sold to pay off the reverse mortgage). For more information about reverse mortgages, visit the website of the Federal Trade Commission, at www.ftc.gov (select "Tips & Advice," "For Consumers," then "Money & Credit," then "Credit & Loans").

If You File for Bankruptcy

If you do file for Chapter 7 bankruptcy and have significant nonexempt equity, you may be able to keep the trustee from selling your house through one of the following methods:

- **Offer to substitute cash for the amount of non-exempt equity.** You may be able to convince the trustee not to sell your house if you can come up with as much cash as would be available from the proceeds to pay unsecured creditors. You may be able to raise the cash by selling exempt property or using income you earn after you file.

  EXAMPLE: The Robertsons have approximately $20,000 of nonexempt equity in their home. All of their home furnishings are exempt. After discussing the matter with the trustee, they sell three pieces of furniture and a camera for a total of $12,000 and scrape together $3,000 extra cash from income earned since they filed for bankruptcy. They offer the $15,000 cash to the trustee as a substitute for the nonexempt equity. The trustee accepts the money, because the creditors will end up with almost as much as they would have gotten if the home were sold—and the trustee will be spared the hassle and expense of selling the Robertsons' home.

- **File for (or convert to) Chapter 13 bankruptcy.** Chapter 13 bankruptcy lets you pay your debts out of your income rather than by selling your property. If you file for Chapter 13 bankruptcy, you won't have to give up your home, even if you have nonexempt equity. (However, over the life of your plan you will have to pay your unsecured creditors at least the value of what they would have received had the property been liquidated in a Chapter 7 bankruptcy.) Chapter 13 bankruptcy also permits you to spread out repayments of missed installments, taxes, and late charges on a mortgage. And, if your lender has begun foreclosure proceedings, Chapter 13 bankruptcy can halt them as long as your house hasn't yet been sold. (For more information on Chapter 13, see *Chapter 13 Bankruptcy*, by Stephen Elias and Robin Leonard (Nolo).)

  You can convert to Chapter 13 bankruptcy any time during a Chapter 7 bankruptcy proceeding. If you miss mortgage payments after you file for Chapter 7 bankruptcy, however, some courts won't let you include them in your Chapter 13 repayment plan. So try to make all payments due after you file for Chapter 7.

CAUTION
If the lender refuses your payments. As explained in "How Bankruptcy Affects a Typical Homeowner," above, mortgage lenders sometimes refuse to accept payments once you file for bankruptcy. If this happens to you, deposit the payments in a separate account solely for this purpose. This will help you make sure you have enough money to pay off what you owe once your bankruptcy ends.

Secured Debts

This chapter explains how Chapter 7 bankruptcy affects secured debts: debts that give the creditor the right to take back a particular piece of property (the collateral) if you don't pay. We tell you how to recognize a secured debt when you see one and explain your options for dealing with secured debts (and the collateral that secures them) in bankruptcy. This chapter ends with step-by-step instructions on several simple procedures for handling secured debts. (If you opt for one of the more complex procedures, we explain the basics, but you'll probably need the help of a lawyer.)

Here's a brief summary of what's likely to happen to your secured debts and the property that secures them. First, the bad news:

- If you have a mortgage on your home or a home equity loan, bankruptcy will get rid of the debt, but not the underlying lien. The same is true for other secured debts such as car notes and installment payments on business equipment.
- If the government has a lien on your home for unpaid taxes, you can't remove it even if the tax debt itself is discharged in your bankruptcy.

Now, the good news:

- If your property has a lien on it because of a judgment that someone got against you in civil court (a money judgment), you can often get the lien removed. While you can do this yourself (it's called lien avoidance), it's typically more difficult than the bankruptcy itself.
- If you want to get out from under your loan on a car, house, or other property, and return the property without any further liability, you can do it in your bankruptcy case. This is called "surrendering" the collateral.
- If you owe a lot more than the collateral is worth, you can redeem it—that is, buy the property at its replacement value (what you could buy it for, considering its age and condition). You'll need to come up with a lump-sum payment or arrange for financing; creditors rarely accept installment payments.
- If you aren't in a position to redeem the property but are current on your payments, you may be able to get rid of (discharge) the underlying debt and keep your property by staying current. This is called the "ride-through" option.
- You can always keep your car or other personal property by reaffirming the debt and remaining current on your payments. When you reaffirm a debt, you remain personally liable for the debt after the bankruptcy.

That's the big picture for the most common kinds of secured debts. Now it's time to learn the details about:

- which of your debts are secured
- which secured debts you can turn into unsecured ones (via lien avoidance), and
- how to deal with the debts that remain secured.

RELATED TOPIC

Dealing with leased cars and other property. This chapter addresses secured debts—debts secured by collateral that the borrowers are purchasing or already own. However, many people choose to lease rather than purchase their cars (and equipment and commercial space, if they are in business). You must list all leases on Schedule G, then indicate on your Statement of Intention whether you will assume the lease (meaning the lease will continue in effect as if you'd never filed for bankruptcy) or reject the lease (meaning you can walk away from all rights and obligations under the lease). In some bankruptcy courts, you'll also have to get approval from the court in a reaffirmation hearing in order to assume the lease. See below for more on reaffirmation hearings. Also, some courts require a written "assumption agreement." You can find more information on leases in bankruptcy, and how to complete these forms, in Ch. 6.

TIP

Chapter 13 may provide better protection for secured property you want to keep. As explained in Ch. 1, debtors who use Chapter 13 may "cram down" many types of secured debts. In a cramdown, the court reduces the principal owed on the debt to the property's replacement value (and often reduces the interest rate, too). Although you can't cram down mortgages on your home or newer car loans, many other types of debts are eligible. If you are significantly upside down on a secured debt and you want to keep the collateral, review the material in Ch. 1 to make sure Chapter 7 is the right bankruptcy choice.

What Are Secured Debts?

A debt is secured if it is linked to a specific item of property, called collateral, that guarantees payment of the debt. Mortgages and car loans are the most common examples of secured debts. If you don't make your payments when they come due, the creditor can repossess the collateral. Often, the collateral is the property you purchased with the debt. For example, a mortgage typically gives the lender the right to foreclose on your home if you don't pay. However, you can also pledge property you already own as collateral for a debt. For example, assume you inherit a new car from a parent, and the car is paid for in full and worth $20,000. You can use the car as collateral for a bank loan—the bank will put a lien on the car as security for repayment of the loan.

An unsecured debt, on the other hand, is not secured by any type of collateral. Credit card and medical debts are common examples of unsecured debt. Debts owed to lawyers and other professionals are also typically unsecured, as are "deficiency judgments" arising from foreclosures and car repossessions (if the lender sells the property for less than you owe, the remainder of the debt that you owe is called a deficiency judgment).

For bankruptcy purposes, there are two types of secured debts:

- those you agree to (called security interests), such as a mortgage or car note, and
- those created without your consent, such as a lien the IRS records against your property because you haven't paid your taxes.

Security Interests

Security interests are secured debts you have taken on voluntarily. If you pledge property as collateral for a loan or line of credit—that is, as a guarantee you will repay the debt—the lien on your property is a security interest. A security interest created to buy the collateral is called a purchase-money security interest. If you use property you already own as collateral (for instance, you refinance a car or pledge business assets as collateral for a loan), the debt is a non-purchase-

money security interest. These two types of security interests may be treated somewhat differently in bankruptcy, as discussed later in this chapter.

Usually, you must repay a security interest by making installment payments. If you fail to make your payments on time or to comply with other terms of an agreement (for example, a mortgage lender's requirement that you carry homeowners' insurance), the lender or seller has the right to take back the property.

Lenders Must Perfect Their Security Interests

For bankruptcy purposes, security interest agreements qualify as secured debts only if they have been perfected: recorded with the appropriate local or state records office. For instance, to create a lien on real estate, the mortgage holder (the bank or another lender) must typically record it with the recorder's office for the county where the real estate is located. To perfect security interests in cars or business assets, the holder of the security interest must typically record it with whatever statewide or local agency handles recordings under the Uniform Commercial Code (these are called "UCC recordings," and they are usually filed with the secretary of state or department of state).

Common Examples of Security Interests

Many everyday loans qualify as security interests, including:

- **Mortgages.** Called deeds of trust in some states, mortgages are loans to buy or refinance a house or other real estate. The real estate is collateral for the loan. If you fail to pay, the lender can foreclose.
- **Home equity loans or HELOCs.** You can borrow against the equity in your home to remodel your home, or pay for other things, such as college tuition or a car. No matter how you spend the money, the house is collateral for the loan. If you fail to pay, the lender can foreclose.
- **Loans for cars, boats, tractors, motorcycles, or RVs.** Here, the vehicle is the collateral. If you fail to pay, the lender can repossess it.

- **Loans for business equipment, machines, or inventory.** The lender can repossess the property you pledged as collateral if you don't repay the loan.
- **Store charges with a security agreement.** Almost all purchases on store credit cards are unsecured, as are major credit cards. Some stores, however, print on the credit card slip or other receipt that the store "retains a security interest in all hard goods (durable goods) purchased," meaning that if you don't pay the credit card bill, the store will have the right to take back the purchased items. If you didn't specifically sign a security agreement setting out repayment terms, debts like these are generally considered unsecured debts in bankruptcy. However, if the store makes you sign an actual security agreement setting out the amount financed, the interest rate, and the number of required payments (the basics required by the Truth in Lending Act for installment payments) when you use the store's credit card, the debt may be secured. For example, if you buy building supplies on credit, the store may require you to sign a security agreement in which you agree that the items purchased are collateral for your repayment. If you don't pay back the loan, the seller can repossess the property, as long as it perfects its security interest.
- **Title loans, or personal loans from banks, credit unions, or finance companies.** Often, you must pledge valuable personal property you already own, such as a paid-off motor vehicle, as collateral for this type of loan. This is a non-purchase-money secured debt, which will be treated as a secured debt in your bankruptcy as long as it has been perfected by the lender.

Nonconsensual Liens

In some circumstances, a creditor can get a lien on your property without your agreement. These are called nonconsensual liens. In theory, a nonconsensual lien gives the creditor the right to force a sale of the property in order to get paid. In practice, however, few creditors exercise this right because forcing a sale is expensive and time-consuming. Instead, they typically wait until you sell or refinance the property, at which point the lien has to be paid off with the proceeds, to give the new owner or lender clear title to the property.

For bankruptcy purposes, there are four types of nonconsensual liens:

- judgment liens
- execution liens
- statutory liens, and
- tax liens.

Judgment Liens

A judgment lien can be imposed on your property only after somebody sues you and wins a money judgment against you. In most states, the judgment creditor (the person or company who won) must then record the judgment by filing it with the county or state. In a few states, a judgment entered against you by a court automatically creates a lien on the real estate you own in that county—that is, the judgment creditor doesn't have to record the judgment to get the lien.

A judgment lien affects real estate you own in the county where the lien is recorded or the judgment is entered. In many states, a judgment lien also applies to your personal property (property other than real estate) for a period of time after the judgment, if certain judgment collection techniques are employed. However, judgment liens on personal property are generally ineffective, because most personal property has no title, and the liens are not recorded. This means that the personal property could easily be sold to a third party who has no idea that the lien existed.

A judgment creditor can also file a judgment with your state motor vehicles department to get a judgment lien on any car, truck, motorcycle, or other motor vehicle you own. You may not know about this type of lien unless you check with the motor vehicles department or the creditor files a proof of claim in your bankruptcy case, describing its interest as "secured."

Typically, judgment liens that have been recorded in your county will attach to property that you acquire later. For example, a judgment may be recorded in your county land records office even if you don't own any real estate. If you buy some real estate a few years later, you'll discover that it is now burdened by that pesky old lien that was just sitting there, waiting for you to make a move. Most real estate liens expire after a certain number of years (seven to ten in most states), though they can typically be renewed.

Execution Liens

In some states, a creditor who seeks to collect a judgment under a writ of execution automatically obtains an "execution" lien on your property. Like judicial liens, execution liens can be removed (avoided) as part of your bankruptcy case. See "How to Avoid Judicial Liens on Exempt Property," below, for more on lien avoidance.

Statutory Liens

Some liens are created by law. For example, in most states, when you hire someone to work on your house, the worker or supplier of materials is entitled to obtain a mechanic's lien (also called a materialman's lien) on the house if you don't pay. In some states, a homeowners' association has the same right if you don't pay your dues or special assessments.

Statutory liens affect only your real estate. They don't attach to your personal property, such as a car or equipment.

Tax Liens

Federal, state, and local governments have the authority to impose liens on your property if you owe delinquent taxes. If you owe money to the IRS or another taxing authority, the debt is secured only if the taxing authority has recorded a lien against your property (and you still own the property) or has issued a notice of tax lien, and the equity in your home or retirement plan is sufficient to cover the debt. For example, in these times of upside down or underwater mortgages, a debt to the IRS may be unsecured even if a lien has been imposed on your home, if you don't have enough equity to secure the debt.

If you don't pay an IRS bill, the IRS can record a Notice of Federal Tax Lien at your county land records office or your secretary of state's office. While the federal tax lien attaches to all of your property, for practical purposes a lien will be effective only if your real estate equity, your retirement account, or your bank account is sufficient to cover the debt. Similarly, your local government can attach a lien to your real estate for unpaid property taxes. And, if your state taxing authority sends you a bill and you don't contest or pay it, the state can record a tax lien against your real estate in that state.

What Happens to Secured Debts When You File for Bankruptcy

Unsecured debts and secured debts are treated differently in Chapter 7 bankruptcy. Creditors with unsecured debts may receive some money in the bankruptcy process, if the trustee is able to take and sell any of your nonexempt property. (The proceeds from a sale of your nonexempt property are divided among all of your unsecured creditors according to priorities established in the bankruptcy code.) Once your case is over, however, unsecured creditors have no rights. Most types of unsecured debts are wiped out in bankruptcy, whether or not the creditor was paid off, and the creditor has to simply take the loss and move on.

Secured debts are different in two ways: First, if the trustee takes and sells property that secures a debt, the secured creditor is entitled to be paid in full before unsecured creditors get anything. This may effectively allow you to keep the property securing the debt, because the trustee has no incentive to take the property and sell it if the secured creditor would be entitled to all of the nonexempt proceeds.

Second, even though bankruptcy wipes out your personal obligation to repay a secured debt, the creditor's lien on your property survives your bankruptcy case (unless the property is returned to the creditor). A secured debt consists of two parts:

- **Your personal liability for the debt, which obligates you to pay back the creditor.** Bankruptcy wipes out your personal liability for the debt, assuming the debt qualifies for the bankruptcy discharge. (See Ch. 9.) This means the creditor cannot later sue you to collect the debt.

- **The creditor's legal claim (lien or security interest) on the collateral for the debt.** A lien gives the creditor the right to repossess the property or force its sale if you do not pay the debt. If the collateral is unavailable, the lender can sue you for the value of the collateral. A lien sticks with the property even if you give the property to someone else. Bankruptcy, by itself, does not eliminate liens. However, during bankruptcy, you may be able to take additional steps to eliminate, or at least reduce, liens on collateral for security interests.

| Unsecured Debt | Secured Debt | Secured Debt After Bankruptcy |

EXAMPLE: Mary buys a couch on credit from a furniture store. She signs a contract agreeing to pay for the couch over the next year. The contract also states that the creditor (the store) has a security interest in the couch and can repossess it if any payment is more than 15 days late. In this type of secured debt, Mary's obligation to pay the debt is her personal liability, and the store's right to repossess the couch is the lien. Bankruptcy eliminates her obligation to pay for the couch, but the creditor retains its lien and can repossess the couch if she doesn't pay.

CAUTION

You may lose property if you have nonexempt equity. Remember, if your equity in collateral securing a debt is higher than the exemption you can claim in it, the trustee can take the collateral, sell it, pay off the secured creditor, pay you your exemption amount, and distribute the balance to your unsecured creditors. Fortunately, most filers are upside down on their secured debts—that is, they owe more than the collateral is worth, primarily because of the interest figured into their payments which is usually front-loaded (meaning, you pay most of the interest off at the beginning of the loan term) and, in the case of personal property, the depreciation

of the property's value over time. In these situations, the trustee has no interest in taking the property. The proceeds would all go to the secured creditor and nothing would be left to distribute to unsecured creditors. The filer could then use one of the options discussed in this section.

Eliminating Liens in Bankruptcy

There are several steps you can take during bankruptcy to eliminate or reduce liens. But these procedures are neither automatic nor required: You have to request them.

The most powerful of these procedures lets you eliminate (avoid) some types of liens on certain kinds of exempt property without paying anything to the creditor. (See Ch. 3 for a definition of exempt property.) With the lien eliminated, you get to keep the property free and clear without paying anything more to the creditor.

Other procedures let you eliminate a creditor's lien (and keep the property) by paying the creditor either the amount of the lien or the current replacement value of the property, whichever is less.

Finally, you can rid yourself of a lien simply by surrendering the property to the creditor.

The choice of which procedure to use for each item of secured property is up to you.

If You Don't Eliminate Liens

If you do not take steps to eliminate a lien as a part of your bankruptcy case, the lien will survive your bankruptcy intact, and the creditor will be free to take the property or force its sale if you fall behind on the payments. Fortunately, the courts are very liberal about reopening a case to allow a debtor to file a motion to avoid a lien. So if, after your bankruptcy case is over, you discover a lien that you missed while your bankruptcy case was open, don't worry. Reopening a bankruptcy is a routine procedure.

If the property is valuable and could be easily resold (an automobile, for example), the creditor will surely repossess the item at the first opportunity unless you agree to keep your payments current. (See "Options for Handling Secured Debts in Chapter 7 Bankruptcy," below.) If, however, the property is of little value and not worth the cost of repossessing (such as Mary's couch), the creditor may do nothing.

If the property is of the type with a "title" or ownership document, such as a house or car, and the creditor does nothing, the lien simply remains on the property until you sell it. At that time, the lien must be paid out of the proceeds of the sale if the buyer wants to have clear title to the property. On the other hand, if the property has no ownership title document, as would be the case with Mary's couch, a computer, or a washer and dryer set, the creditor has no practical way to enforce the lien. In some cases, if the property is declining in value and it is clear that you aren't going to take steps to keep it, the creditor might ask for the bankruptcy court's permission to take the property even before your bankruptcy case is over. For example, if you own a new photocopier subject to a security interest and the copier depreciates in value at a fairly steep rate (say, 30% a year), the creditor would want it back as soon as possible to get the highest price on resale.

Options for Handling Secured Debts in Chapter 7 Bankruptcy

As part of your Chapter 7 bankruptcy paperwork, you must list all creditors who hold secured debts. You must also tell the bankruptcy trustee and the secured creditors what you plan to do with the collateral that secures those debts: whether you plan to surrender the property or keep it. You do this in an official form called the "Statement of Intention," which you must file with the court along with your other bankruptcy papers and mail to your creditors. Then, you must carry out your stated intention within the applicable time limits. (You'll find step-by-step instructions on how to complete the forms at the end of this chapter.)

This section explains the basic options for handling secured debts in bankruptcy, including the advantages and disadvantages of each option, any restrictions that may apply, when each option makes sense, and what steps you have to take to use each option. You should review this material carefully and decide how you want to treat the collateral for each

secured debt before you file for bankruptcy. If you plan on keeping the collateral, call the lender before filing to see whether you will have to reaffirm the debt (agree to be liable for it after bankruptcy, as explained further below) or whether you can keep the collateral by simply remaining current on your payments even if your liability for the debt is discharged.

Once you've filed for bankruptcy, the automatic stay prevents secured creditors from repossessing property that serves as collateral for a secured debt, unless the court gives permission or you miss the deadline for carrying out your stated intention. It's much easier to hold on to property in the first place than to get it back after the creditor repossesses it. So, if you have some secured property that a creditor is about to take and you haven't filed for bankruptcy yet, you may want to file right away to prevent the seizure.

> **CAUTION**
> **You may lose your property if you fail to choose.** If you don't make a choice about how you intend to treat collateral, the secured creditor might have the right to repossess the collateral 30 days after you file for bankruptcy, whether or not you have kept up with your payments. Most security agreements contain what's known as an "ipso facto" clause, which says that filing for bankruptcy qualifies as a default allowing the creditor to repossess the property, even if you are current on your payments. If you don't use one of the choices provided by the bankruptcy code, the creditor may use the ipso facto clause to grab your property. However, some states don't honor these ipso facto clauses as long as you remain current on your payments.

Option 1: Surrender the Collateral

If you don't want or need to keep the property, you can surrender it. Surrendering the collateral simply means allowing the creditor to take it back or foreclose on the lien. This is the simplest option for dealing with secured property. It completely frees you from the debt: Giving back the property satisfies the terms of the lien, and the bankruptcy discharges your personal liability for the original debt (and prevents the creditor from seeking a deficiency judgment).

Advantages. A quick and easy way to completely rid yourself of a secured debt.

Disadvantages. You lose the property. Also, if you surrender the property, some bankruptcy courts won't let you use the payments that were due under the contract as deductions for purposes of the means test. (Ch. 1 explains the means test.) However, other courts let you deduct these payments, reasoning that that the means test is backward-looking (that is, it is calculated based on your past expenses) and not concerned with your future intentions.

Restrictions. None. You can surrender any kind of collateral for a secured debt.

When to use it. For property that you don't need or want or that would cost too much to keep.

How it works. On the Statement of Intention form, check the box indicating that you will surrender the property. You must file the form and send a copy to the secured creditor within 30 days after you file for bankruptcy. It's then up to the creditor to contact you and arrange a time to pick up the property. If the creditor doesn't take the property, and the trustee doesn't claim it, it's yours to keep. This might happen if the property isn't worth much. For example, it probably isn't worth the creditor's time to pick up, store, and auction off used household furniture or old computer equipment, no matter how much you still owe on it.

Option 2: Redeem the Collateral

If you want to keep certain types of property, you may "redeem" it by paying the secured creditor the property's current replacement value (what you would have to pay a retail vendor for that type of property, considering its age and condition), usually in a lump sum. Essentially, you are buying the property back from the creditor. In return, the creditor delivers title to you in the same manner as if you had followed through on your original agreement. You then own the property free and clear.

> **EXAMPLE:** Susan and Gary owe $500 on some household furniture with a replacement value of $200. They can keep the furniture and eliminate the $500 lien by paying the creditor the $200 replacement value within 45 days after the first creditors' meeting.

Advantages. Redemption is a great option if you owe significantly more than the property is worth. The creditor must accept the current replacement value of the item as payment in full. If you and the creditor don't agree on the replacement value of the property, the court will decide the issue in a proceeding called a "valuation" hearing. (Ch. 6 explains how to figure out the replacement value of various types of property.)

Disadvantages. Most debtors will have to pay the full replacement value of an item in a lump sum in order to redeem it. It may be difficult for you to come up with that much cash on short notice. You may be able to get a loan; some companies specialize in lending to people seeking to redeem their collateral in bankruptcy. (For more information about these companies, see www.legalconsumer.com.) Or, you can try to get the creditor to agree to accept installment payments, but courts cannot require creditors to make this type of deal.

Restrictions. You have the right to redeem property only if all of the following are true:

- The debt is a consumer debt: one incurred "primarily for a personal, family, or household purpose." This includes just about everything except collateral for loans and credit obtained for business purposes.
- The property is tangible personal property. Tangible property is anything you can touch. A car, furniture, a boat, a computer, and jewelry are all examples of tangible property. Stocks are intangible. The property must also be "personal property," which simply means it can't be real estate.
- The property is either:
  - claimed as exempt (exempt property is explained in Ch. 3), or
  - abandoned by the trustee. A trustee will abandon property that has little or no nonexempt value beyond the amount of the liens. The trustee may notify you of the abandonment or you may have to proactively request it. Once the property is abandoned, you can redeem it by paying the secured

creditor its replacement value. If you know you'll want to redeem property if the trustee abandons it, check the "redeem" box on the Statement of Intention. If you haven't done this and the trustee abandons the property, you may have to amend your Statement of Intention (instructions for amending a form are in Ch. 7). Call the trustee to find out.

When to use it. Redemption may be a good idea if you really want to keep personal property, but you don't want your liability for the debt to survive your bankruptcy (this is a consequence of reaffirmation, discussed below). Use redemption only if you owe more than it would cost to purchase the property and you would not be able to get rid of the lien (lien avoidance is covered below in Option 5). It often makes sense to redeem small items of household property that you want to keep, because raising money for the lump sum payment probably would not be that difficult.

Redemption can also be used for cars, which are not eligible for lien avoidance and are likely to be repossessed if a lien remains after bankruptcy and you don't agree to keep making payments. If the creditor won't agree to installment payments, however, raising the cash necessary to redeem a car may be difficult.

How it works. You and the creditor must agree on the value of the property, then draft and sign a redemption agreement. Agreeing on the replacement value may take a little negotiation. Sometimes, you can get the creditor to accept installment payments if you agree to pay a higher total amount. Whatever you agree to, put it in the redemption agreement. A sample agreement is at the end of this chapter.

Option 3: Retain and Pay (the "Ride-Through" Option)

Before the bankruptcy law changed in 2005, a majority of bankruptcy courts recognized the "ride-through" or "retain and pay" option for dealing with secured debts. Where this option was available, debtors could keep the collateral for secured debts without reaffirming the debts or redeeming the property, as long as they stayed current on their payments. Debtors who took advantage of this option wouldn't owe a deficiency

balance if they had to give the property back after receiving their bankruptcy discharge.

The ride-through option is no longer an explicit part of the bankruptcy code, and it isn't recognized in the bankruptcy courts of every state. However, some lenders (and some courts) still allow debtors to keep the collateral without reaffirming secured debts, as long as they remain current on the payments. These lenders would rather continue to receive payments from reliable borrowers than have to repossess and auction off property only to receive a fraction of what they're owed.

Advantages. The ride-through option allows you to keep property without obligating yourself to a debt that will survive your bankruptcy or having to come up with lump-sum payment. You can keep the property as long as you can keep up with your payments. If you reach a point where you can't afford the payments, you can essentially surrender the property: give it back without owing a deficiency balance.

Disadvantages. Because the ride-through option is no longer part of the bankruptcy code, your lender usually gets to decide whether to allow it or not. And, the ride-through option isn't allowed in every judicial district. Even if you are allowed to use this option, you'll have to keep making your payments if you want to keep the property. In contrast, surrendering or redeeming the property allows you to exit your bankruptcy case without ongoing payment obligations (unless your lender allows you to redeem on an installment plan).

Restrictions. Generally, your lender gets to decide whether to allow you to use the ride-through option or to require you to redeem or reaffirm the debt. Whether or not your creditor will be so accommodating depends on how close you are to paying off the debt, your history with the creditor, and the creditor's experience with the reaffirmation process.

If your lender doesn't want you to use this option, it might still be available to you if one of the following is true:

- Your state's law forbids lenders from repossessing property as long as you stay current on your payments. In this situation, if you don't redeem or surrender the property, or reaffirm the debt, the debtor can't do anything to enforce its security interest as long as you keep making those payments. (For information on researching your state's law, see Ch. 10.)

- The court rejects your reaffirmation agreement. In this situation, most courts have allowed debtors to keep their property as long as they continue making their payments. These courts have held that, as long as you sign and file a valid reaffirmation agreement in a timely manner and attend the reaffirmation hearing, you will be protected from repossession, even if the court ultimately rejects the agreement (typically, because it looks like you won't be able to make the payments required by the contract). (See *In re Chim*, 381 B.R. 191 (Bankr. Md. 2008) and *In re Moustafi*, 371 B.R. 434 (Bankr. Ariz. 2007).)

In at least one federal judicial circuit—the 11th Circuit, which covers Alabama, Florida, and Georgia—debtors may not use the ride-through option. If debtors in these states want to keep property, they must either redeem it or sign a reaffirmation agreement for the debt. (See *In re Linderman*, 435 B.R. 715 (Bankr. M.D. Fla. 2009).)

When to use it. If your lender will allow it and you think you'll be able to make your payments, the ride-through option is often the best choice for property you really want to keep. It allows you to retain the property and avoid any penalty (in the form of a deficiency judgment) if you later have to give it back.

How it works. First, you'll have to contact your lender to see whether it will allow you to "retain and pay for" the collateral rather than reaffirm. If the lender agrees, check the box on the Statement of Intention indicating that you will retain the property. Then, check the "Other" box, and write this in the space provided: "Debtor will retain collateral and continue to make regular payments."

If you default to the ride-through option because the court rejects your reaffirmation agreement, you should complete your Statement of Intention as explained in the instructions for reaffirming a debt, below.

Option 4: Reaffirm the Debt

When you reaffirm a debt, you agree that you will still owe the debt after your bankruptcy case is over. Both the creditor's lien on the collateral and your personal liability for the debt under the original promissory note survive bankruptcy intact—often, just as if you never filed for bankruptcy. For example, if you owe $25,000 on your car before you file for Chapter 7 bankruptcy, you most likely will continue to owe $25,000 on your car after you file for bankruptcy (unless you negotiate a lower amount in your reaffirmation agreement). If you can't keep up your payments and the car is repossessed, you'll owe the difference between the amount you reaffirm for and the amount the lender is able to sell the car for at auction (considerably less than you owe, in most cases). This is called a "deficiency balance." Nearly all states permit a creditor to sue for a deficiency balance for most types of property. About half of the states, however, don't allow deficiency balances on repossessed personal property if the original purchase price was less than a few thousand dollars.

Advantages. Reaffirmation provides a sure way to keep collateral as long as you abide by the terms of the reaffirmation agreement and keep up your payments. Reaffirmation also provides a setting in which you may be able to negotiate new terms to reduce your payments, your interest rate, and/or the total amount you will have to pay over time.

Disadvantages. Because reaffirmation leaves you personally liable for the debt, you can't walk away from the debt after bankruptcy. You'll still be legally bound to pay the deficiency balance even if the property is damaged or destroyed. And because you have to wait eight years before filing another Chapter 7 bankruptcy case, you'll be stuck with that debt for a long time.

For example, if you reaffirm your car note and then default on your payments after bankruptcy, the creditor can (and probably will) repossess the car, auction it off, and bill you for the difference between what you owe and what was received in the auction.

EXAMPLE: Tasha owns a computer worth $900. She owes $1,500 on it. She reaffirms the debt for the full $1,500. Two months after bankruptcy, she spills a soft drink into the disk drive and the computer is ruined. Although she has lost the computer, because she reaffirmed the debt, she still has to pay the creditor $1,500.

Restrictions. Reaffirmation can be used with any kind of property and any kind of lien, but the creditor must agree to the terms of the reaffirmation if they are different from the current agreement. You or the lender must file the agreement in court as part of your bankruptcy case. Unless an attorney is representing you in the bankruptcy or in the reaffirmation process, the bankruptcy court must review the agreement in a reaffirmation or discharge hearing. At that hearing, the judge will review your bankruptcy paperwork to see how the reaffirmation might affect your post-bankruptcy budget and whether you can afford the payments. The judge can disapprove the agreement if it is not in your best interest or would create an undue hardship for you. The judge is likely to reject the agreement if it looks like you won't be able to make the payments after paying your basic living expenses or if you owe much more on the debt than the property is worth.

When to use it. Because reaffirmation comes with the very serious disadvantage of leaving you in debt after your bankruptcy case is over, you should consider it only if:

- the creditor insists on it
- it's the only way to hang on to collateral that you really need to keep, and
- you have good reason to believe you'll be able to pay off the balance.

Reaffirmation may be the only practical way to keep some types of property, such as automobiles or your home. Also, reaffirmation can be a sensible way to keep property that is worth significantly more than what you owe on it.

If you decide to reaffirm, try to get the creditor to accept less than you owe as full payment of the debt. Don't reaffirm a debt for more than what it would cost you to replace the property.

If you need to reaffirm a debt in order to keep the collateral, make sure you keep up your payments prior to filing for bankruptcy so you can stay on the creditor's good side. If you fall behind, the creditor has the right to demand that you make your account current before agreeing to a reaffirmation contract, but you will probably have some room to negotiate. In addition, many bankruptcy judges will not approve reaffirmation agreements unless you are current on your payments at the time of the reaffirmation hearing. If the creditor rejects your payments during bankruptcy (which often happens), deposit that money into a separate account so it's available once the creditor decides to accept it. If you can't make these rejected payments when the creditor wants them, you might lose your property.

How it works. Use official bankruptcy Form 240. You can find this form on the website of the United States Courts. (See in Ch. 6, "Where to Get the Official Forms.") Most large creditors will complete the paperwork, ask you to sign it, and file it with the court. If you're dealing with a smaller creditor, you may have to file it yourself.

The reaffirmation agreement includes a number of legally required disclosures and warnings. These provisions are intended to put you on notice of how much you'll be paying overall, the interest rate, and your liability to pay the debt in full, even if something happens to the collateral. In Part D of the agreement, you must explain why you are reaffirming the debt and provide information on your income and expenses, so the court can determine whether the agreement creates an undue hardship for you. Your income and expense information should be in the same ballpark as the information you include in Schedules I and J (see Ch. 6). If these figures indicate that you can't afford the required payments, the court may reject your reaffirmation agreement. If this happens, you will probably be able to keep the property as long as you stay current on your payments under the old loan; see Option 3, above, for more information.

You can cancel a reaffirmation agreement by notifying the creditor before the later of:

- the date of your discharge, or
- 60 days after you filed the reaffirmation agreement with the bankruptcy court.

If your case is already closed, however, you will not be able to switch to the other options listed in this chapter.

If the Court Refuses to Approve Your Reaffirmation Agreement

If the judge disapproves the reaffirmation agreement, does that mean that you will have to surrender your property? Not at all. In fact, disapproval may work to your advantage. A vast majority of the bankruptcy courts that have disapproved reaffirmation agreements have also interpreted the bankruptcy code to protect people from repossession as long as they go along with the program—that is, file the reaffirmation agreement, attend a discharge hearing, and do their best to get it approved. (See *In re Chim*, 381 B.R. 191 (Bankr. Md. 2008); and *In re Moustafi*, 371 B.R. 434 (Bankr. Ariz. 2007).) In other words, by disapproving the agreement the courts are giving a green light to the ride-through option.

If a debtor doesn't cooperate in the reaffirmation process, courts have ruled that the lender is free to exercise whatever rights it has under state law once the judge disapproves the reaffirmation agreement. In some states, the laws governing commercial transactions forbid repossession as long as the borrower remains current on the debt. Even in states that don't have those laws, experience is showing that lenders would rather have money coming in, especially if the borrower has been faithfully making payments in the past, than take back the property and resell it at a discounted price. Simply put, a lender who has the right to repossess property after a judge disapproves a proposed reaffirmation agreement can pretty much be counted on not to.

Option 5: Eliminate (Avoid) Liens

Lien avoidance is a procedure by which you ask the bankruptcy court to eliminate or reduce liens on some types of exempt property. Lien avoidance is neither automatic nor required: You have to request it in a separate legal proceeding in your bankruptcy case.

One common lien avoidance procedure lets you eliminate or reduce liens on certain types of exempt personal property, depending on the value of the property and the amount of the exemption available to you. This procedure is available only for what are called "nonpossessory, non-purchase-money liens": liens on property that you already owned when you pledged it as security for a loan. It can't be used for real estate.

A different lien avoidance procedure allows you to eliminate judgment liens on personal property or real estate that falls within an exemption. By eliminating the judgment lien, you get to keep the property free and clear without paying anything more to the creditor, assuming the underlying debt can be discharged in bankruptcy (which it usually can).

Nonpossessory, Non-Purchase-Money Liens

If you have pledged some item of personal property (not real estate) that you already owned as security for a loan, and the property is completely or partially exempt, you may be able to eliminate a lien on the property. (You'll find sample forms for this remedy later in this chapter; you will need to modify them to fit your situation.)

How much of the lien can be eliminated depends on the value and type of property and the amount of the exemption. If the property (or your equity in it) is entirely exempt, the court will eliminate the entire lien, and you'll get to keep the property without paying anything. If the property (or your equity in it) is worth more than the exemption limit, the lien will be reduced to the difference between the exemption limit and either the property's value or the amount of the debt, whichever is less.

EXAMPLE: A creditor has a $500 lien on Harold's guitar, which is worth $300. In Harold's state, the guitar is exempt only to $200. He could get the lien reduced to $100. The other $400 of the lien is eliminated (avoided).

$500 lien	$300	=	value of item
	− $200	=	exemption amount
	$100	=	amount of lien remaining after lien avoidance

Advantages. This type of lien avoidance costs nothing (if you are representing yourself), involves only a moderate amount of paperwork, and often allows you to keep property without paying anything.

Disadvantages. Some paperwork is involved. Also, by trying to avoid a lien on exempt property, you may reopen the issue of whether the property really is exempt in the first place. This may happen if the property was deemed exempt by default (that is, the property is exempt because the trustee and creditors didn't challenge your claim of exemption within the applicable time limit). Some courts have allowed creditors to argue that the property is not exempt at a hearing on a motion to avoid a lien.

As a practical matter, however, motions to avoid liens are usually not contested.

Restrictions. There are several important limits on this type of lien avoidance. First, as noted above, you may avoid only nonpossessory, non-purchase-money security interests. That sounds complicated, but it makes sense when you break it down:

- Nonpossessory means the creditor does not physically keep the property you've pledged as collateral. It stays in your possession; the creditor only has a lien on it. (In contrast, if you leave your property at a pawnshop to get a loan, that is a possessory security interest—for which this lien avoidance procedure is not available.)
- Non-purchase-money means that you didn't use the money you borrowed to purchase the collateral. Instead, you used property you already owned as collateral for the loan.

- Security interest means the lien was created by voluntary agreement between you and the creditor. In other words, the lien wasn't involuntary, like a tax or judgment lien.

Second, the property you pledged as collateral must be exempt under the exemption system you are using. (Remember that domicile requirements may limit the exemptions available to you. See Ch. 3 for more information.) If the property isn't exempt, then the lien doesn't impair your exemption rights, and it can't be eliminated.

Third, only certain types of property are covered. Unfortunately, the property most commonly pledged as collateral for nonpossessory, non-purchase-money security interests doesn't qualify—homes and cars (unless the vehicle qualifies as a tool of the trade, discussed below). You may eliminate a nonpossessory, non-purchase-money security interest lien only if the collateral falls into one of these categories:

- household furnishings, household goods, clothing, appliances, books, and musical instruments or jewelry that are primarily for your personal, family, or household use
- health aids professionally prescribed for you or a dependent
- animals or crops held primarily for your personal, family, or household use (but only the first $6,225 of the lien can be avoided), or
- implements, machines, professional books, or tools used in a trade (yours or a dependent's), but only the first $6,225 of the lien can be avoided.

You can remove up to $6,225 of a lien from a vehicle that qualifies as a tool of your trade. Generally, a motor vehicle is considered a tool of the trade only if you use it as an integral part of your business—for example, if you do door-to-door sales or delivery work. It is not considered a tool of the trade if you simply use it to commute, even if you have no other means of getting to work.

What Are Household Goods?

For the purpose of avoiding a consensual lien, household goods are limited to:

- clothing
- furniture
- appliances
- one radio
- one television
- one VCR
- linens
- china
- crockery
- kitchenware
- educational equipment and materials primarily for the use of your minor dependent children
- medical equipment and supplies
- furniture exclusively for the use of your minor children or your elderly or disabled dependents
- your personal effects (including your wedding rings and the toys and hobby equipment of your minor dependent children) and those of your dependents, and
- one personal computer and related equipment.

Items in the following categories are not considered to be household goods, and you cannot avoid liens on them:

- works of art (unless they were created by you or a relative)
- electronic entertainment equipment with a fair market value of more than $650 total (not including the one television, one radio, and one VCR listed above)
- items acquired as antiques that have a fair market value of more than $650 total
- jewelry (other than wedding rings) that has a fair market value of more than $650 total, and
- a computer (excluding the personal computer and related equipment listed above), motor vehicle (including a tractor or lawn tractor), boat, motorized recreational device, conveyance vehicle, watercraft, or aircraft.

Judgment Liens

A nonconsensual judgment lien on property can be avoided if all of the following are true:

- The lien resulted from a money judgment issued by a court.
- You are entitled to claim an exemption in at least some of your equity in the property.
- The lien would result in a loss of some or all of this exempt equity if the property were sold. (That is, the exemption would be impaired.)

If these three conditions are met, you can remove judgment liens from any exempt property, including real estate and cars.

When to use it. Use lien avoidance if it's available, especially if a lien can be completely wiped out. Even if you don't need or want the property, you can avoid the lien, sell the property, and use the money for other things.

To keep things simple, you may want to avoid liens only on property that is completely exempt. The lien will be eliminated entirely and you'll own the property free and clear, without paying anything to the creditor.

Even partial lien avoidance can be beneficial, but sooner or later you'll have to pay the amount remaining on the lien if the property has a title document or is subject to repossession or foreclosure on what's left of the lien. Most often, you'll have to pay off the lien in a lump sum, but some creditors may be willing to accept installments, especially if you compromise on the value of the lien.

How it works. You request lien avoidance by checking the column "Property is claimed as exempt" on the Statement of Intention, and by typing and filing a motion. (Complete instructions for preparing and filing a motion to avoid a judgment lien on real estate are at the end of this chapter.) Although it may sound complicated, lien avoidance is often a routine procedure that can be accomplished without a lawyer.

Some bankruptcy filers don't realize they have liens on their property, or don't realize that they could eliminate those liens. Others may not be able to eliminate liens when they file for bankruptcy (typically, because they have no exempt equity in the property), but later they become eligible to do so. Fortunately, bankruptcy courts are very liberal about allowing a debtor to reopen a case in order to file a motion to avoid a lien. Reopening a bankruptcy case is a routine procedure, described in Ch. 7.

One final note. Some courts have allowed debtors to avoid judicial liens even if there is no equity in the property (and therefore no "impaired" exemption). Their reasoning is convoluted (in our humble opinion) since it would seem impossible for a lien to impair an exemption if there is no equity to exempt. Nonetheless, if a lien has been placed on your home and you have no equity or negative equity, you should still consult with a lawyer on whether that lien can be avoided in your bankruptcy court. Even if the lawyer is pricey, it may be worth your while to get the lien removed.

Eliminating Judicial Liens

To determine whether you can eliminate a judicial lien, apply this simple formula. Add the following items:
- all consensual liens on the property (for example, a mortgage and home equity loan)
- all tax liens, and
- your exemption amount.

If the total of all these items is greater than the value of the property, then you can completely eliminate judicial liens on the property. The Judicial Lien Worksheet, below, will help you do the math. Below are a few sample calculations:

One more point to remember: For the purposes of bankruptcy lien avoidance provisions, judicial liens get the lowest priority, behind consensual liens and tax liens, regardless of when the liens were placed on the property and regardless of what state law says. So, in Example C below, it would not matter if the $30,000 judgment lien was created before or after the $40,000 second mortgage: The judicial lien can be eliminated either way.

Example A

Value of property	$ 200,000
Mortgage	$ 100,000
Second mortgage	20,000
Exemption	10,000
Total	$ 130,000
Amount available for judicial liens	$ 70,000
Amount of judicial lien	$ 30,000

RESULT: Lien cannot be eliminated.

Example B

Value of property	$ 200,000
Mortgage	$ 150,000
Second mortgage	20,000
Exemption	10,000
Total	$ 180,000
Amount available for judicial liens	$ 20,000
Amount of judicial lien	$ 30,000

RESULT: $10,000 of lien can be eliminated, $20,000 of lien cannot be eliminated.

Example C

Value of property	$ 200,000
Mortgage	$ 160,000
Second mortgage	40,000
Exemption	10,000
Total	$ 210,000
Amount available for judicial liens	$ 0
Amount of judicial lien	$ 30,000

RESULT: Judicial lien can be completely eliminated.

Judicial Lien Worksheet

1. Value of your home.. $_____

2. Amount of first mortgage .... $_____

3. Amount of other mortgages and home equity loans.......................... $_____

4. Amount of tax liens.. $_____

5. Amount of mechanics' liens.. $_____

6. Total of Lines 2 through 5... $_____

    (Total of all liens that are not judicial liens)

    If Line 6 is greater than Line 1, you can stop here—you can eliminate all judicial liens. Otherwise, go on to Line 7.

7. Line 1 minus Line 6.. $_____

    This is the amount of equity you can protect with an exemption.

8. Exemption amount .... $_____

    If Line 8 is greater than Line 7 you can stop here—you can eliminate all judicial liens. Otherwise, go on to Line 9.

9. Line 7 minus Line 8.. $_____

    This is the amount of the judicial liens that you can't eliminate.

10. Amount of judicial liens... $_____

    If Line 9 is greater than Line 10, you can stop here—you cannot eliminate judicial liens from this property. Otherwise go on to Line 11.

11. Line 10 minus Line 9... $_____

    This is the portion of the judicial lien that you can eliminate. (Line 9 is the portion of judicial lien you cannot eliminate.)

Lien avoidance on real estate in the current housing market. As home values rise, more and more bankruptcy filers will be able to avoid judgment liens on their homes or other real estate. This is a change from previous years, when the economic downturn meant that many people had no equity in their homes, and therefore usually couldn't avoid judgment liens. If you don't have home equity when you file for bankruptcy, however, and that later changes, you might be able to reopen your bankruptcy case and bring a lien avoidance action.

Lien Elimination Techniques Beyond the Scope of This Book

Deep in the recesses of the bankruptcy code are other procedures for eliminating certain kinds of nonconsensual liens. Section 11 U.S.C. § 522(h) gives a debtor the power to use a wide range of lien avoidance techniques that have been made available to the bankruptcy trustee. The techniques are found in Sections 545, 547, 548, 549, 553, and 724(a) of the bankruptcy code. These liens include:

- nonjudgment liens securing the payment of penalties, fines, or punitive damages, and
- nonconsensual liens that were recorded or perfected while you were already insolvent or within the 90 days before you filed for bankruptcy.

To use these procedures, you'll need the help of a bankruptcy attorney.

You can pay off a lien in a follow-up Chapter 13 bankruptcy. Another way to handle liens is through what some bankruptcy practitioners call a "Chapter 20" bankruptcy: filing for Chapter 13 bankruptcy after completing a Chapter 7 bankruptcy. You use the Chapter 13 bankruptcy to deal with or eliminate any liens remaining after your Chapter 7 case has wiped out your personal liability. And, if a lien exceeds the value of the property, you can often get the lien fully discharged by simply paying the current replacement value of the item, rather than the full amount of the lien.

Bankruptcy law prohibits you from receiving a Chapter 13 discharge if you file within four years of the date you filed a Chapter 7 case in which you received a discharge. However, even if you can't discharge debts, you can still receive most of the other benefits associated with a Chapter 13, including a plan to pay off liens and in some cases elimination of the lien altogether. Because this book covers Chapter 7 bankruptcies only, space does not permit us to give a full explanation of how to do a successful follow-up Chapter 13 case. For more information, see *Chapter 13 Bankruptcy*, by Stephen Elias and Robin Leonard (Nolo).

Choosing the Best Options

Now it's time pick the best option for each of your secured debts. If an item has more than one lien on it, you might use a different procedure to deal with each lien. For example, you might eliminate a judicial lien on exempt property through lien avoidance and redeem the property to satisfy a consensual lien.

Don't pay too much. If the option you're considering would require you to pay significantly more than the current market value of the property you want to keep, it's a bad deal. There are frequently ways you or a lawyer can keep any item of secured property by paying no more than its current replacement value.

What Property Should You Keep?

Be realistic about how much property you will be able to afford to keep after bankruptcy. Face the fact that you may not be able to keep everything, and decide which items you can do without. These questions will help you decide whether an item is worth keeping:

- How important is the property to you?
- Will you need the property to help you make a fresh start after bankruptcy?
- How much would it cost to keep the property? (This will depend on the procedure you use.)
- Would it be more expensive to redeem the property or to replace it?

- If you're considering reaffirming the debt, are you sure you'll be able to make the payments after bankruptcy? Or, will you be making a bad investment decision (for instance agreeing to be liable for $10,000 for a car that is only worth $5,000)?

- If you're considering surrendering your property and buying a replacement item, will you need a loan to purchase it? If so, will you be able to get such a loan after bankruptcy?

Schedule D and the Statement of Intention Form

When you file for Chapter 7 bankruptcy, you must list on Schedule D all creditors who hold secured claims. (See Ch. 6.) You must also tell the bankruptcy trustee and your affected creditors your plans for the property that secures those debts. You do this by filing a form called the Statement of Intention and mailing a copy to each creditor listed on it. (If you have no secured debts, you simply have to sign the Statement of Intention and file it with the court.)

There are line-by-line instructions on how to fill out these forms in Ch. 6. To make the decisions requested on the Statement of Intention, though, you'll need the information from this chapter. Here are some timing tips:

- Try to decide what to do with each item of secured property before you file for bankruptcy.

- The Statement of Intention is due within 45 days after you file for bankruptcy but is often filed at the same time or right after you file your other papers.

- The law requires you to carry out your stated intentions within 30 days after the creditors' meeting. If you miss the deadline, your collateral will no longer be protected by the automatic stay, which leaves the creditor free to take it.

If you change your mind after you file your Statement of Intention, you can amend the form using the amendment instructions in Ch. 7.

EXAMPLE 1: Fran bought a sports car two years ago for $16,000. Now Fran is unemployed but is about to start a new job. She still owes $13,000 on the car, which is currently worth $10,000. Although she likes the car, she can't come up with the $10,000 in cash to redeem it, and she doesn't want to remain personally liable for the $13,000 debt after her bankruptcy case is over. If Fran is willing to lower her standards a little, she can surrender her car and buy a reliable used car to get her to work and back for about $3,000. However, she'll have to come up with the money to buy the car—or make sure she'll be able to borrow it—to make this plan work.

Gambling That the Court Won't Approve the Reaffirmation

Since any reaffirmation agreement you sign will have to be approved by the Court in a reaffirmation hearing, you might consider gambling that the judge will disapprove the agreement. If that happens, you can still keep the property as long as you continue to be current on your payments, but you won't be liable on the loan after your bankruptcy. A win-win situation for you. (See "If the Court Refuses to Approve Your Reaffirmation Agreement," above.)

What's the chance that the judge won't approve the reaffirmation? Let's take the example of a car note. If your car payment is high compared to your income, you have a very high interest rate, or the car is worth significantly less than the amount you are trying to reaffirm, the judge is less likely to approve the reaffirmation. And the judge definitely will not approve the reaffirmation if your expenses on Schedule J exceed your net income on Schedule I.

What happens if the judge does approve the reaffirmation? You can still bail on the reaffirmation within 60 days of filing the agreement or as long as your case remains open. For instance, if the judge approves the agreement at the hearing, you can say, "Oops, I changed my mind, I no longer want to reaffirm" and the judge should enter that in your case record. So, it's really not much of a gamble after all, although there's a risk that the creditor will repossess the property.

EXAMPLE 2: Joe owns a six-year-old Toyota with a replacement value of $2,000. It is security for a debt of $2,500. If Joe files for bankruptcy, he will probably be able to keep the car by paying the secured creditor only $2,000 (the value of the car). Joe decides it's worth paying that amount. He knows the car is reliable and will probably last another six years. He also believes it would be a hassle to find a car of comparable quality at that price, and he needs the car to get to work. Joe offers to redeem the car by making payments, but the creditor demands a lump sum (as it has a legal right to do). Joe borrows $2,000 from his parents and redeems the car.

EXAMPLE 3: Now assume that Joe makes a different decision: Instead of redeeming the debt for $2,000, he decides to discharge the $2,500 debt and continue making payments to the creditor. Joe figures that the creditor would rather receive the payments than go through the expense and hassle of repossessing a car that would sell for only $2,000. If Joe is wrong, however, he will have no recourse against the repossession.

Real Estate and Motor Vehicles

Liens on real estate and cars involve special considerations.

Your Home

Filing for bankruptcy when you own your home is discussed in Ch. 4, but here's a reminder: If you own your home and are behind on the payments, Chapter 13 bankruptcy will allow you to keep your house if your proposed repayment plan is feasible. Chapter 7 bankruptcy, on the other hand, does not offer a procedure for catching up on missed mortgage payments ("curing an arrearage"). Unless you can become current on your payments—using property or income you acquire after your filing date—the creditor can ask the court to lift the automatic stay so it can proceed with the foreclosure.

If you are current on your mortgage, however, Chapter 7 bankruptcy might help you eliminate other liens on your house. As explained in "Option 5: Eliminate (Avoid) Liens," above, you can use lien avoidance to get rid of judicial liens if they conflict with your homestead exemption. And you can do this without a lawyer's help.

With the help of a lawyer, you might be able to eliminate other types of liens, including "unrecorded" tax liens and liens for penalties, fines, or punitive damages from a lawsuit.

As for reaffirmation—most bankruptcy courts do not require you to reaffirm a mortgage, even if the bank requests it. And some bankruptcy judges won't approve mortgage reaffirmation agreements at all.

Your Car

Because repossessed motor vehicles can easily be resold, if a lien remains on your car, the creditor will probably act quickly to either repossess it or force its sale (unless you stay current on your payments and the creditor wouldn't gain much by taking and selling the car). Still, if you intend to keep your car, you should deal with liens on it during bankruptcy.

If your automobile is exempt, any judicial liens on it can be eliminated through lien avoidance, as explained above.

The purchase-money security interest held by the seller can be dealt with only through redemption or reaffirmation. Raising the lump sum amount necessary for a redemption is your best option. If that is not possible, your only realistic option is to reaffirm the debt unless you are willing to gamble that the creditor will let you keep the car as long as you make your payments.

If your automobile falls within the tools of the trade exemption, you can use lien avoidance for any non-purchase-money liens on the vehicle.

Exempt Property

There are four ways to deal with liens on exempt property:

- Give the property back (if there's no property, there's no lien).
- Get rid of the lien in a lien avoidance action.
- Redeem the property.
- Reaffirm the debt.

If you are keeping the property, you should use lien avoidance whenever possible to eliminate judicial liens and non-purchase-money security interests. Use redemption whenever the lien exceeds the replacement value of the property and you can raise the cash necessary to buy the property back.

If you can't raise the lump sum necessary for redemption, you'll have to either reaffirm the debt or attempt to pay off the lien outside of bankruptcy. The option you choose will depend on how anxious the creditor is to repossess the item. If the property is of little value, you can probably get away with informally paying off the lien. If the property is of greater value, however, you may have to sign an agreement and cooperate in the reaffirmation process. Remember never to agree to pay more than it would cost to replace the property.

Also, remember that even if you can get liens wiped out, you still may not get to keep the property if your equity in the property is worth significantly more than your exemption amount. The trustee might want to sell the property, pay you your exemption amount, and distribute the remaining portion among your unsecured creditors. (See "Nonexempt Property," below, for information on what happens to nonexempt property, including equity that exceeds the available exemption.)

In this situation, the only way to hold on to the property is to buy the equity back from the trustee. How much you will have to pay depends on several factors, but keep in mind this basic rule: The amount you offer to the trustee has to leave your unsecured creditors no worse off than they would have been had the trustee sold the property to somebody else.

> **EXAMPLE:** Mindy has a $1,000 asset on which she can claim a $500 exemption. There is a $200 judicial lien on the asset. Mindy cannot avoid the lien, because it does not "impair" her exemption. If the trustee sold the property, Mindy would get her full $500 exemption, the lienholder would get $200, and the remaining $300 would go to Mindy's unsecured creditors. If Mindy wanted to buy the property from the trustee, she'd have to offer $500: $200 for the lienholder and $300 for her unsecured creditors.

As you can see, the amount you have to offer the trustee will vary from case to case, depending on the amount of the liens, the amount of your exemption, and whether you or the trustee can eliminate the liens on the asset. You can consult with the trustee to work out the particulars.

Nonexempt Property

If you want to keep nonexempt property, your options are more limited.

- Redeem the property if the trustee abandons it. (Abandoning property means that the trustee releases it from the bankruptcy estate. A trustee may abandon property that is not valuable enough to justify selling it to raise money for the unsecured creditors.)
- Reaffirm the debt if the trustee abandons the property.
- Risk trying to pay off the lien informally, outside of bankruptcy.

Property Worth More Than the Debt

If your nonexempt property is worth significantly more than the liens on it, you probably won't have a chance to keep it—unless you pay the trustee the net amount the property would realize upon sale, after deducting whatever exemption you are entitled to, the costs of sale and the trustee's commission. Otherwise the trustee is likely to sell the property, pay off the liens, and distribute the rest of the proceeds to your unsecured creditors.

> **EXAMPLE:** Elena pledges her $4,000 car as security for a $900 loan. The $900 lien is the only lien on her car, and only $1,200 of the $4,000 is exempt. If Elena files for bankruptcy, the trustee will first allow Elena to informally bid on the property. If Elena and the trustee can't reach agreement, the trustee can take the car, sell it, pay off the $900 lien, give Elena her $1,200 exemption, and distribute the rest of the proceeds to Elena's creditors.

If the trustee does not take the property and you want to keep it, your best bet is to either remain current on your payments or begin the reaffirmation process (if your creditor requires it).

Property Worth Less Than the Debt

If the property is worth less than the liens on it, the trustee will probably abandon it.

> **EXAMPLE:** When Stan bought his $500 sofa on credit from the Reliable Furniture Co., he pledged the sofa as security. Since then, the sofa has declined in value to only $100, but he still owes $250 on it. The trustee will abandon the property, because selling it would yield no proceeds for the unsecured creditors.

The trustee might also abandon property with more than one lien on it if the total of all the liens exceeds the property's value. In this case, the creditors with the lowest-priority liens are called undersecured creditors. (State and federal law determine the priority of the liens. Most of the time, the most recent lien is the lowest-priority lien, but certain types of liens always have priority over others.)

> **EXAMPLE:** Aaron's car is currently worth $3,000. He pledged his car as collateral for the loan he used to buy it. That loan has a remaining balance of $2,200. He later pledged his car for two personal loans on which he owes $500 each. In addition, there is a judgment lien against his car for $1,000. The total balance of all liens is $4,200.
>
> In this situation, the original $2,200 purchase-money loan is fully secured, and so is the first personal loan for $500. The other $500 loan is secured only by the remaining $300 in equity, so it is an undersecured claim. And there is nothing securing the $1,000 judgment lien.

If the trustee abandons the property, you have the right to redeem it at its current replacement value. This is your best option, if you can come up with the necessary lump sum payment. Redemption eliminates all liens on the property.

If you are unable to come up with the lump sum required to purchase the property, and the creditor is unwilling to accept installment payments, you'll need to find out whether your lender will require you to reaffirm the debt or whether you can keep the car by remaining current on your payments without reaffirmation.

Reclaiming Exempt Property Repossessed Just Before Bankruptcy

If, during the 90 days before you filed for bankruptcy, a secured creditor took exempt property that would qualify for either lien avoidance or redemption, you may be able to get the property back. But you must act quickly, before the creditor resells the property. If the creditor has already resold the property, you are probably out of luck. Repossessed cars are usually resold very quickly, but used furniture may sit in a warehouse for months.

If you catch the creditor in time, the creditor must legally give back the property because the repossession is an illegal preference, which means that the property is still part of the bankruptcy estate (as explained in Ch. 3). In practice, however, the creditor won't give the property back unless the court orders it (which usually means you'll need the help of a lawyer) or unless you make a reasonable cash offer for the item.

Assuming you don't want to hire a lawyer, you probably won't be able to get an item back unless you talk the creditor into allowing you to redeem it or reaffirm the debt. The creditor might prefer to have cash in hand rather than used property sitting in a warehouse. If you plan to avoid the lien on the exempt item and not pay anything, however, the creditor probably won't turn over the property unless forced to by court order.

Whether hiring a lawyer is worth the expense to get back an exempt item so you can avoid the lien depends on how badly you need the property and what you'll save through lien avoidance. Compare what it would cost to redeem the property or buy replacement property. If those options are cheaper, or you decide you can get along without the property, don't bother with the court order.

TIP

Planning reminder. Once you've filed for bankruptcy, a creditor cannot legally take your property unless the court lifts the automatic stay or you miss the deadline for dealing with your secured debts. (One note regarding cars: If you miss the deadline, most creditors will still ask the court to lift the automatic stay before repossessing your vehicle.) It's much easier to hold on to property in the first place than to get it back after the creditor repossesses it. So, if you have some exempt property that a creditor is about to take and you haven't filed for bankruptcy yet, you may want to file right away to prevent the seizure.

Step-by-Step Instructions

Once you decide what to do with each item of secured property, you must list your intentions on your Statement of Intention, file that form, mail a copy to each secured creditor listed on the form, and then carry out the procedures you commit to on the form within 30 days after the creditors' meeting. (See Ch. 6 for instructions on completing the form.)

How to Surrender Property

If you plan to surrender any secured property, here's how to proceed:

Step 1: When you fill out your Statement of Intention, state that you are surrendering the property that secures the debt.

Step 2: The creditor must make arrangements to pick up the property. It's not your responsibility to deliver. But you can call your creditor, explain the situation, and ask if they want the property back. If they don't, great—you don't have to worry about it anymore. If they do pick it up, get a receipt. (See sample receipt below.)

Receipt for Surrender of Property

1. This receipt certifies that __[name of repossessor (print)]__ took the following item(s): _(list items)_

   _____

   _____

   _____ .

   on ___[date]___ , 20__ , because of debt owed to ___[name of creditor (print)]___ .

2. __[Name of repossessor (print)]__ is an authorized agent of ___[name of creditor (print)]___ .

   Signed: __[Your signature]_____

   Dated: _____

   Signed: __[Repossessor's signature]_____

   Dated: _____

How to Avoid Judicial Liens on Exempt Property

To avoid a judicial lien on exempt property you'll first need to claim an exemption on the property on Schedule C. In those courts that will allow you to avoid a lien even if you have no equity in the property, you should list a negative equity number in Schedule A or B and also list the negative equity number on Schedule C. For instance if you are $50,000 underwater on your mortgage, you have a negative equity number of $50,000, and minus $50,000 should be listed as your ownership amount on Schedule A and as the amount of the equity you are claiming as exempt on Schedule C. But remember, in most states you need positive equity to avoid a lien.

SEE AN EXPERT

If you miss the deadline, talk to a lawyer. You might not discover a lien until after the deadline passes for filing a motion. In fact, it's not uncommon to discover liens only after a bankruptcy case is closed. If this happens to you, you can file a motion asking the court to let you proceed even though you missed the deadline, or even to reopen the case if necessary. For sample forms to reopen a bankruptcy case, see Ch. 7.

What goes in your motion papers depends on the kind of lien you're trying to get eliminated.

Nonpossessory, Non-Purchase-Money Security Interests

You will need to fill out one complete set of forms for each affected creditor—generally, each creditor holding a lien on that property. Sample forms are shown below. Some courts have their own forms; if yours does, use them and adapt these instructions to fit.

TIP

Do you need to use pleading paper? Pleading paper is a special type of paper, used in many state and federal courts, with numbers running down the left side of the page. The federal bankruptcy rules do not require you to submit motions or other pleadings on pleading paper. However, it's possible that your local court rules do. Check with the applicable court clerk and if numbered paper is required, use the pleading paper found in Appendix B, or search for "pleading paper" on the Internet to find free, downloadable pleading paper.

Step 1: If your court publishes local rules, refer to them for time limits, format of papers, and other details of a motion proceeding.

Step 2: Type the top half of the pleading form (where you list your name, the court, the case number, and so on) following the examples shown below. This part of the form is known as the "caption." It is the same for all pleadings.

> ### Checklist of Forms for Motion to Avoid Nonpossessory, Non-Purchase-Money Security Interest
>
> ☐ Motion to Avoid Nonpossessory, Non-Purchase-Money Security Interest
> ☐ Notice of Motion to Avoid Nonpossessory, Non-Purchase-Money Security Interest
> ☐ Order to Avoid Nonpossessory, Non-Purchase-Money Security Interest
> ☐ Proof of Service by Mail

Step 3: If you're using a computer to prepare the forms, save the caption portion and reuse it for other pleadings. If you're using a typewriter to prepare the forms, stop when you've typed the caption and photocopy the page you've made so far, so you can reuse it for other pleadings.

Step 4: Using one of the copies that you just made, start typing again just below the caption and prepare a Motion to Avoid Nonpossessory, Non-Purchase-Money Security Interest, as shown in the example.

Step 5: Most courts require you only to file the motion with the court and serve the creditor and trustee with a notice explaining that the lien will be avoided by default if the creditor doesn't respond and request a hearing on your motion. (These are colorfully called "scream or die" motions—see the sample Notice of Motion and Motion to Avoid Judicial Lien on Real Estate, below, for language you can use instead of a formal notice if your district follows this procedure.) Because motions to avoid liens are usually pretty straightforward and are usually granted, many creditors don't bother to respond. If they do, however, either you or the creditor will have to schedule a hearing.

Step 6: If a hearing is required, call the court clerk and give your name and case number. Say you'd like to file a motion to avoid a lien and need to find out when and where the judge will hear arguments on your motion. Under some local rules the clerk will give you a hearing date; ask for one at least 31 days in the future, because you must mail notice of your motion to the creditor at least 30 days before the hearing (unless local rules set a different time limit). Write down the information. If the clerk won't give you the information over the phone, go to the bankruptcy court with a copy of your motion filled out. File that form and schedule the hearing. Write down the information about when and where your motion will be heard by the judge.

If there will be a hearing, prepare a Notice of Motion that lists the date, time, and location. (See the Sample Notice of Motion to Avoid Nonpossessory, Non-Purchase-Money Security Interest, below.) If you are filing in a district that requires a hearing only if the creditor requests one, use the language in the sample Notice of Motion and Motion to Avoid Judicial Lien on Real Estate, below, to give the creditor proper notice of this procedure.

Step 7: Prepare a proposed Order to Avoid Nonpossessory, Non-Purchase-Money Security Interest. This is the document the judge signs to grant your request. In the space indicated in the sample, specify exactly what property the creditor has secured. You can get this information from the security agreement you signed. Make two extra copies, and take them with you to the hearing if there is one. The court's local rules may require you to file the proposed order with the rest of your motion papers.

Step 8: Prepare at least two Proofs of Service by Mail, one for each affected creditor and one for the trustee. These forms state that a friend or relative of yours, who is at least 18 years old and not a party to the bankruptcy, mailed your papers to the creditor(s) or the trustee. Fill in the blanks as indicated. Have your friend or relative sign and date the form at the end as shown on the sample. See "How to Serve the Creditor," below, for more information.

Step 9: Make at least three extra copies of all forms.

Step 10: Keep the proofs of service. Have your friend mail one copy of the motion, notice of motion, and proposed order to each affected creditor and the trustee.

Step 11: File (in person or by mail) the original (signed) notice of motion, motion (and proposed order, if required in your area), and proof of service with the bankruptcy court.

Step 12: The trustee or creditors affected by your motion may submit a written response. However, most courts will grant your motion if the trustee or creditor doesn't file a response to the motion and you ask the court to enter a default judgment in your favor (see Step 14, below).

Step 13: If there is a hearing, attend it. The hearing usually lasts ten minutes or less. Because you filed the motion, you argue your side first. Explain briefly how your property falls within the acceptable categories of exempt property, that the lien is a nonpossessory non-purchase-money security interest, and that the lien impairs your exemption. (11 U.S.C. § 522(f)(2).) "Impairs your exemption" means that because of the lien, your ownership interest in this item of exempt property has been reduced.

The trustee or creditor (or an attorney) responds. The judge either decides the matter and signs your proposed order or takes it "under advisement" and mails you the order in a few days.

Step 14: If the creditor doesn't show up at the hearing, or if the creditor doesn't file a response to your motion when it is required to do so (see Step 12, above), file and serve a Request for Entry of Order by Default. (See the sample request with the papers for avoiding a judicial lien, below, to get an idea of what this should look like. Of course, you'll have to change the language so it refers to a nonpossessory, non-purchase-money security interest rather than a judicial lien.) This document tells the court that you followed all of the proper procedures and gave the creditor notice of your motion, but the creditor didn't respond as it was required to do. The request asks the court to grant your motion by default. You must prepare another Proof of Service and serve this request on the creditor.

How to Serve the Creditor

Here are the rules for providing notice to the creditor:

- If the creditor provided you with a contact address and a current account number within the 90 days before you filed for bankruptcy, you must use that address and include the account number and the last four digits of your Social Security or taxpayer identification number with your papers.
- If the creditor was prohibited from communicating with you during this 90-day period, you must use the address and account number contained in the two written communications you received most recently from the creditor.
- If the creditor has filed a preferred contact address with the court, you must use that address.

If your creditor is a business, you must serve a live human being who represents the creditor—you can't just send your motion to "Visa" or "First Bank," for example. Here's how to find that warm body:

- Call the creditor and ask for the name and address of the person who accepts service of process for the business.
- If you don't know how to reach the creditor, contact your state's Secretary of State office and ask for the name and address of the person who is listed as the registered agent for service of process for the company. Many states make this information available online, too.

 SEE AN EXPERT

Get an attorney, if you need one. If you are having trouble figuring out how to draft the necessary paperwork to avoid a lien, think about asking a lawyer for help—especially if the lien is substantial.

Judicial Lien

To eliminate a judicial lien, follow the steps to eliminate a nonpossessory, non-purchase-money security interest, above, but use the Sample Notice of Motion and Motion to Avoid Judicial Lien on Real Estate and Sample Order to Avoid Judicial Lien on Real Estate forms as examples.

The sample forms are for eliminating a judicial lien on your home. To eliminate a lien on personal property, you will need to change the language accordingly.

Checklist of Forms for Motion to Avoid Judicial Lien

- ☐ Motion to Avoid Judicial Lien or Motion to Avoid Judicial Lien (on Real Estate)
- ☐ Notice of Motion to Avoid Judicial Lien
- ☐ Order to Avoid Judicial Lien
- ☐ Proof of Service
- ☐ Request for Entry of Order by Default and Proof of Service by Mail (if the creditor doesn't respond)

You may have to prove the value of the property in question. Typically, when you file for bankruptcy and assign a value to your property, the only person who may check your figures is the trustee—and that doesn't happen very often. However, if a creditor opposes your motion to avoid a judicial lien, the creditor can make you prove the property's value, because the more the property is worth, the less the lien impairs the exemption. For instance, if you listed property as worth $50,000 and the exemption is $45,000, a lien exceeding $5,000 would impair the exemption and entitle you to have the lien removed.

Sample Motion to Avoid Nonpossessory, Non-Purchase-Money Security Interest

UNITED STATES BANKRUPTCY COURT

_____ DISTRICT OF _____
[name of district]   [your state]

In re _____)
[Set forth here all names including married,)
maiden, and trade names used by debtor)
within last 8 years.])
                      Debtor)
) Case No. _____
) [Special number for Avoidance of Lien motions, if any]
Address _____)
)
_____) Chapter 7
)
Last four digits of Social Security or Individual)
Taxpayer Identification No(s). (ITIN) (if any): _____)
)
Employer's Tax Identification No(s). (EIN) (if any): _____)
_____)

MOTION TO AVOID NONPOSSESSORY,
NON-PURCHASE-MONEY SECURITY INTEREST

1. Debtors _____[your name(s)]_____ , filed a voluntary petition for relief under Chapter 7 of Title 11 of the United States Code on _____[date you filed for bankruptcy]_____ .

2. This court has jurisdiction over this motion, filed pursuant to 11 U.S.C. § 522(f), to avoid a nonpossessory non-purchase-money security interest held by __[name of lienholder]__ on property held by the debtor.

3. On or about [date you incurred the debt] , debtors borrowed $ [amount of loan] from [name of creditor] . As security for the loan, [name of creditor] insisted upon, and the debtors executed, a note and security agreement granting to [name of creditor] a security interest in and on the debtor's personal property, which consisted of [items held as security as they are listed in your loan agreement] which are held primarily for the family and household use of the debtors and their dependents.

4. All such possessions of debtors have been claimed as fully exempt in their bankruptcy case.

5. The money borrowed from [name of creditor] does not represent any part of the purchase money of any of the articles covered in the security agreement executed by the debtors, and all of the articles so covered remain in the possession of the debtors.

6. The existence of [name of creditor] 's lien on debtor's household and personal goods impairs exemptions to which the debtors would be entitled under 11 U.S.C. § 522(b).

Sample Motion to Avoid Nonpossessory, Non-Purchase-Money Security Interest (cont'd)

WHEREFORE, pursuant to 11 U.S.C. § 522(f), debtors pray for an order avoiding the security interest in their personal and household goods, and for such additional or alternative relief as may be just and proper.

Date: _____ Signed by: _____
                                                                Debtor in Propria Persona

Date: _____ Signed by: _____
                                                                Debtor in Propria Persona

Sample Notice of Motion to Avoid Nonpossessory, Non-Purchase-Money Security Interest

UNITED STATES BANKRUPTCY COURT

_____ DISTRICT OF _____

In re _____)
     [Set forth here all names including married,)
     maiden, and trade names used by debtor)
     within last 8 years.])
                  Debtor) Case No. _____

) *[Special number for Avoidance of Lien motions, if any]*

Address _____)

_____) Chapter 7

)

Last four digits of Social Security or Individual)
Taxpayer Identification No(s). (ITIN) (*if any*): _____)

)

Employer's Tax Identification No(s). (EIN) (*if any*): _____)

_____)

NOTICE OF MOTION TO AVOID NONPOSSESSORY,
NON-PURCHASE-MONEY SECURITY INTEREST

Please take notice of motion set for a hearing on: _____ *[leave blank]* _____ , 20_____ , at _____

o'clock _____ .m. at _____ *[leave blank]* _____ , in courtroom _____ .

Sample Order to Avoid Nonpossessory, Non-Purchase-Money Security Interest

UNITED STATES BANKRUPTCY COURT
_____ DISTRICT OF _____

In re _____)
    [Set forth here all names including married,)
    maiden, and trade names used by debtor)
    within last 8 years.])
                       Debtor   ) Case No. _____
) [Special number for Avoidance of Lien motions, if any]
Address _____)
)
_____) Chapter 7
)
Last four digits of Social Security or Individual)
Taxpayer Identification No(s). (ITIN) (_if any_): _____)
)
Employer's Tax Identification No(s). (EIN) (_if any_): _____)
_____)

ORDER TO AVOID NONPOSSESSORY,
NON-PURCHASE-MONEY SECURITY INTEREST

The motion of the above-named debtor(s) _____ [_your name(s)_] _____ , to avoid the lien of the

respondent, _____ [_name of creditor_] _____ , is sustained.

The lien is a nonpossessory, non-purchase-money lien that impairs the debtor's exemptions in the following

property:

   [list all items held as security as listed in your loan agreement] _____

Unless debtor's bankruptcy case is dismissed, the lien of the respondent is hereby extinguished and the lien shall

not survive bankruptcy or affix to or remain enforceable against the aforementioned property of the debtor.

_____ [_name of creditor_] _____ shall take all necessary steps to remove any record of the lien from the

aforementioned property of the debtor.

Date: __[_leave blank for judge to sign_]__   Signed by: __U.S. Bankruptcy Judge [_leave blank for judge to sign_]__

Sample Proof of Service by Mail

UNITED STATES BANKRUPTCY COURT
_____ DISTRICT OF _____

In re _____)
     [Set forth here all names including married,)
     maiden, and trade names used by debtor)
     within last 8 years.])
                        Debtor) Case No. _____
) *[Special number for Avoidance of Lien motions, if any]*

Address _____)
)
_____) Chapter 7
)
Last four digits of Social Security or Individual)
Taxpayer Identification No(s). (ITIN) *(if any)*: _____)
)
Employer's Tax Identification No(s). (EIN) *(if any)*: _____)
_____)

PROOF OF SERVICE BY MAIL

I, _____ *[name of server]* _____ , declare that: I am a resident or

employed in the County of _____ *[server's county]* _____ , State of ___ *[server's state]* ___ .

My residence/business address is _____ *[server's address]* _____ .

I am over the age of eighteen years and not a party to this case.

On _____ *[date request served]* _____ , 20___ , I served the enclosed _____ *[papers served]* _____

_____

on the following parties by placing true and correct copies thereof enclosed in a sealed envelope with

postage thereon fully prepaid in the United States Mail at _____ *[city and state]* _____ ,

addressed as follows:

    [Name and address of lien owner]
    [Name and address of trustee]
    [Address of U.S. Trustee]

I declare under penalty of perjury that the foregoing is true and correct, and that this declaration was

executed on

Date: *[date Proof of Service signed]* , 20___ at ___ *[city and state]* _____

                          _____ *[Server's signature]* _____
                          Signature

But if the evidence you provide at the hearing shows that the property is worth $60,000, a lien of less than $15,000 wouldn't impair the exemption, because you would be able to take your $45,000 exemption and still pay the full lien. So be prepared to show how you determined the value of your property.

SEE AN EXPERT

Use an attorney, if necessary. If you are having trouble figuring out how to draft the necessary paperwork to avoid a lien, think about asking a lawyer for help—especially if the lien is substantial.

Tax Liens

If your federal tax debt is secured, you may have a basis for challenging the lien. Quite often, the IRS makes mistakes when it records a notice of federal tax lien.

SEE AN EXPERT

Help from a lawyer. You will need the help of a tax or bankruptcy attorney—preferably one who has experience in both areas—to challenge a tax lien.

Here are some possible grounds for asking the court to remove the lien:

- The notice of federal tax lien was never recorded, though the IRS claims it was.
- The notice of federal tax lien was recorded after the automatic stay took effect.
- The notice of federal tax lien was recorded in the wrong county: it must be recorded where you own real estate for it to attach to the real estate in that county.

Even if the notice of federal tax lien was recorded correctly, you still may have a basis to fight it if either of the following is true:

- The lien expired—liens last only ten years.
- The lien is based on an invalid tax assessment by the IRS.

How to Redeem Property

If you want to redeem exempt or abandoned property, list the property on your Statement of Intention as property to be retained and check the column that says property will be redeemed. (More instructions are in Ch. 6.) You must pay the creditor the current replacement value of the property within 45 days after the creditors' meeting.

TIP

Explore lien avoidance first. If lien avoidance is available, you may be able to get rid of a lien on exempt property without paying anything.

Agreeing on the Value of the Property

Before you can redeem property, you and the creditor must agree on what the property is worth. If you believe the creditor is setting too high a price for the property, tell the creditor why you think the property is worth less—it needs repair, it's falling apart, it's damaged or stained, or whatever. If you can't come to an agreement, you can ask the bankruptcy court to rule on the matter. But you will probably need an attorney to help you make this request, so it is not worth your while unless the property is worth more than the lawyer will cost, and you and the creditor are very far apart in your estimates of the property's value.

You and the creditor should sign a redemption agreement that sets forth the terms of your arrangement and the amount you are going to pay, in case there is a dispute later. (See the sample forms below.)

If the Creditor Won't Cooperate

The creditor may refuse to let you redeem property, because the creditor claims that it isn't one of the types of property you can redeem or because you can't agree on the value. If so, you will need to file a formal complaint in the bankruptcy court to have a judge resolve the issue. You will need an attorney to help you, so think twice about whether you really want to redeem the property. It may be better just to let the creditor have it or reaffirm if the creditor insists and you are current on your payments.

Sample Notice of Motion and Motion to Avoid Judicial Lien on Real Estate

UNITED STATES BANKRUPTCY COURT

_____ [*name of district*] _____ DISTRICT OF _____ [*your state*] _____

In re _____)
     [*Set forth here all names including married,*)
     maiden, and trade names used by debtor)
     within last 8 years.])
                 Debtor) Case No. _____
) [*Special number for Avoidance of Lien motions, if any*]
Address _____)
)
_____) Chapter 7
)
Last four digits of Social Security or Individual)
Taxpayer Identification No(s). (ITIN) (*if any*): _____)
)
Employer's Tax Identification No(s). (EIN) (*if any*): _____)
_____)

NOTICE OF MOTION AND
MOTION TO AVOID JUDICIAL LIEN ON REAL ESTATE

PLEASE TAKE NOTICE that Debtor _____ [*debtor's name*] _____ is moving the court to avoid a judicial lien held by _____ [*name of lien owner*] _____ on certain real property owned by the Debtor.

This motion is being brought under procedures prescribed by ___ [*local bankruptcy rule allowing motion to be decided without a hearing unless the creditor objects*]___ .

If you wish to object to the motion, or request a hearing on the motion, your objection and/or request must be filed and served upon Debtor within 20 days of the date this notice was mailed.

You must accompany any request you make for a hearing, or any objection to the relief sought by Debtor(s), with any declarations or memoranda of law you wish to present in support of your position.

If you do not make a timely objection to the requested relief, or a timely request for hearing, the court may enter an order granting the relief by default and either 1) set a tentative hearing date or 2) require that Debtors provide you at least 10 days' written notice of hearing (in the event an objection or request for hearing is timely made).

1. Debtor _____ [*debtor's name*] _____ commenced this case on ___ [*date of bankruptcy filing*]___ by filing a voluntary petition for relief under Chapter 7 of Title 11 of the United States Bankruptcy Code.

2. This court has jurisdiction over this motion, filed pursuant to 11 U.S.C. Sec. 522(f), to avoid and cancel a judicial lien held by ___ [*name of lien owner*]___ on real property used as the debtors' residence, under 28 U.S.C. Sec. 1334.

Sample Notice of Motion and Motion to Avoid Judicial Lien on Real Estate (cont'd)

3. On _[date of lien being recorded]_ , creditors recorded a judicial lien against the debtors' residence at

_____ [address] _____ . The said judicial lien is entered of

record as follows: _____ [describe how lien appears in public records] _____ .

4. The Debtors' interest in the property referred to in the preceding paragraph and encumbered by the lien has

been claimed as fully exempt in their bankruptcy case.

5. The existence of _____ [lien owner's name] _____ lien on Debtors' real property impairs

exemptions to which the Debtors would be entitled under 11 U.S.C. Sec. 522(b).

WHEREFORE, Debtors pray for an order against _____ [lien owner's name] _____ avoiding and

canceling the judicial lien in the above-mentioned property, and for such additional or alternative relief as may be

just and proper.

Date: _____   Signed by: _____

                                         Debtor in Propria Persona

Sample Request for Entry of Order by Default

UNITED STATES BANKRUPTCY COURT

_____ [name of district] _____ DISTRICT OF _____ [your state] _____

In re _____)
   [Set forth here all names including married,)
   maiden, and trade names used by debtor)
   within last 8 years.])
                  Debtor)
) Case No. _____
) [Special number for Avoidance of Lien motions, if any]
Address _____)
)
_____) Chapter 7
)
Last four digits of Social Security or Individual)
Taxpayer Identification No(s). (ITIN) (if any): _____)
)
Employer's Tax Identification No(s). (EIN) (if any): _____)
_____)

REQUEST FOR ENTRY OF ORDER BY DEFAULT AND PROPOSED ORDER

Now comes _____ [debtor's name] _____ who declares and says under penalty of perjury this __[date of request]__ that the following statements are true and correct:

1. On __[date notice and motion served]__ , Debtor _____ [debtor's name] _____ caused a Notice of Motion and Motion to Avoid Judicial Lien on Real Estate to be served on _____ [name of person served on behalf of lien owner] _____ .

2. A copy of the Notice of Motion and Motion and a proposed order are attached to this request. Also attached is a Proof of Service of this request on _____ [name of lien owner] _____ , the Trustee, and the U.S. Trustee.

3. The Trustee and the U.S. Trustee were also served with the Notice of Motion and Motion on __[date notice and motion served]__ .

4. A proof of service duly executed by _____ [name of person who mailed the notice] _____ as to service of the Notice of Motion and Motion is on file with the court.

5. The Notice of Motion and Motion complies in all respects with __[local bankruptcy rule allowing motion to be decided without a hearing unless the creditor objects]__ .

Sample Request for Entry of Order by Default (cont'd)

6. The Debtor has received no response from any of the served parties as of the date of this request, more than 20 days after the service of the Notice of Motion and Motion.

WHEREFORE, Debtor respectfully requests that the court enter by default the attached Order to Avoid Judicial Lien on Real Estate.

Date: _____ Signed by: _____

Debtor in Propria Persona

Sample Order to Avoid Judicial Lien on Real Estate

UNITED STATES BANKRUPTCY COURT

[name of district] _____ DISTRICT OF ___ *[your state]* _____

In re _____)
    [Set forth here all names including married,)
    maiden, and trade names used by debtor)
    within last 8 years.])
                      Debtor)
) Case No. _____
) *[Special number for Avoidance of Lien motions, if any]*

Address _____)
)
_____) Chapter 7
)

Last four digits of Social Security or Individual)
Taxpayer Identification No(s). (ITIN) *(if any):* _____)
)
Employer's Tax Identification No(s). (EIN) *(if any):* _____)
_____)

ORDER TO AVOID JUDICIAL LIEN ON REAL ESTATE

Upon request of Debtor for relief by default under Bankruptcy Local Rule *[local rule number]* , and good cause appearing therefore, the motion of the above-named debtor   *[debtor's name]*   to avoid the lien of respondent *[creditor's name]*   is sustained.

It is hereby ORDERED AND DECREED that the judicial lien held by *[creditor's name]* in and on Debtor's residential real estate at_____ *[address of real estate]* _____ recorded *[date lien recorded and description of lien as it appears in the records]* and any other amounts due under the lien be hereby canceled.

It is further ORDERED that unless Debtor's bankruptcy case is dismissed, _____ *[creditor's name]* _____ and its successors shall take all steps necessary and appropriate to release the judicial lien and remove it from the local judgment index.

Date: _____   Signed by: _____
                                            U.S. Bankruptcy Judge

Sample Proof of Service by Mail

UNITED STATES BANKRUPTCY COURT

_____ DISTRICT OF _____

In re _____)
      [Set forth here all names including married,)
      maiden, and trade names used by debtor)
      within last 8 years.])
                          Debtor) Case No. _____
) *[Special number for Avoidance of Lien motions, if any]*

Address _____)
)
_____) Chapter 7
)

Last four digits of Social Security or Individual)
Taxpayer Identification No(s). (ITIN) (*if any*): _____)
)
Employer's Tax Identification No(s). (EIN) (*if any*): _____)
_____)

PROOF OF SERVICE BY MAIL

I, _____ *[name of server]* _____ , declare that: I am a resident or employed in the County of

_____ *[server's county]* _____ , State of _____ *[server's state]* _____ .

My residence/business address is _____ *[server's address]* .

I am over the age of eighteen years and not a party to this case.

   On _____ *[date request served]* _____ , 20____ , I served the enclosed _____ *[papers served]* _____

_____

on the following parties by placing true and correct copies thereof enclosed in a sealed envelope with postage

thereon fully prepaid in the United States Mail at _____ *[city and state]* _____ ,

 addressed as follows:

     [Name and address of lien owner]
     [Name and address of trustee]
     [Address of U.S. Trustee]

I declare under penalty of perjury that the foregoing is true and correct, and that this declaration

was executed on

Date: ___ *[date Proof of Service signed]* ___ , 20____ at _____ *[city and state]* _____

_____ *[Server's signature}*
          Signature

Paying in Installments

If you can't raise enough cash to pay the creditor within 45 days after the creditors' meeting, try to get the creditor to let you pay in installments. Some creditors will agree if the installments are substantial and you agree to pay interest on them. But a creditor is not required to accept installments; it can demand the entire amount in cash.

If the creditor refuses to accept installments, you can ask the bankruptcy court to delay your deadline for making the payment for a month or two. But to do so, you will need to file a formal complaint in the bankruptcy court. Again, you will need an attorney to help you, so it may not be worth it.

Paperwork

Below are two sample redemption agreements you can use. Form 1 is for installments and Form 2 is for a lump sum payment. Type the form on pleading paper (the blank paper in Appendix B with numbers down the left side) and put your bankruptcy case number on it in case you need to file it later. You should fill out a separate form for every item of property you want to redeem. Have the creditor sign it.

There is no need to file these agreements with the trustee. Keep them with your other bankruptcy papers, in case the trustee or the judge wants to see them.

How to Reaffirm a Debt

Bankruptcy courts frown on reaffirmation agreements, because they obligate debtors to make payments after bankruptcy, which contradicts bankruptcy's purpose of providing a fresh start. Nevertheless, if you do decide to reaffirm a debt, you must say so on your Statement of Intention. Within 45 days after the 341 hearing, you must be willing to sign a reaffirmation agreement. The law provides that either you or the creditor must file the reaffirmation agreement and, if you aren't represented by an attorney, file a motion asking the court to approve it (the motion is part of the official reaffirmation form). If you are dealing with a major creditor, you can count on the creditor to provide the agreement, get your signature, and file

it with the court. After all, these creditors are familiar with reaffirmation agreements, and they want you to be legally obligated to repay the loan after your bankruptcy discharge is granted. You or the creditor can draft an agreement or you can use the one on the website of the United States Courts at www.uscourts. gov/forms/bankruptcy-forms (Form B240A/B ALT).

The reaffirmation agreement includes a motion and a request for a reaffirmation hearing. After you file the agreement, you will receive notice of the scheduled hearing in the mail. At the hearing, the judge will make sure that you understand the consequences of signing the agreement. The judge must approve the agreement unless it appears, based on the income and expenses you reported on Schedule I and Schedule J, that you won't be able to make the required payments or that reaffirmation is not in your best interests. In that case, the judge will disapprove the agreement and send you and the creditor back to the drawing board. (See "If the Court Refuses to Approve Your Reaffirmation Agreement," above.)

> **TIP**
> **Don't agree to pay too much.** If the creditor requires you to reaffirm for the full amount owed on the collateral (an amount that is greater than the current replacement value of the collateral), select another option unless you really, really want the property and won't be able to get similar property after bankruptcy. In general, you shouldn't reaffirm a debt for more than it would cost you to replace the property.

Your right to cancel a reaffirmation agreement. The bankruptcy code gives you the right to cancel a reaffirmation agreement by notifying the creditor:

- before you receive your discharge, or
- within 60 days after the reaffirmation agreement is filed with the bankruptcy court, whichever is later. (11 U.S.C. § 524(c)(2).)

Notice to the creditor of your cancellation should be by certified mail, return receipt requested. This precludes the creditor from later claiming it didn't receive notice.

Sample Agreement for Installment Redemption of Property

AGREEMENT FOR INSTALLMENT REDEMPTION OF PROPERTY

_____ (Debtor) and

_____ (Creditor) agree that:

1. Creditor owns a security interest in _____ (Collateral).

2. The replacement value of Collateral is $_____ .

3. Creditor's security interest is valid and enforceable despite the Debtor's bankruptcy case.

4. If Debtor continues to make payments of $_____ a month on Creditor's security interest, Creditor will take no action to repossess or foreclose its security.

5. Debtor's payments will continue until the amount of $_____ , plus interest (to be computed at the same annual percentage rate as in the original contract between the parties), is paid.

6. Upon being fully paid as specified in Paragraph 5, Creditor will take all steps necessary to terminate its security interest in Collateral.

7. If Debtor defaults, Creditor will have its rights under the original contract.

Dated: _____   _____
                                     Debtor in Propria Persona

Dated: _____   _____
                                     Creditor

Sample Agreement for Lump Sum Redemption of Property

1	AGREEMENT FOR LUMP SUM REDEMPTION OF PROPERTY
2	_____ (Debtor) and
3	_____ (Creditor) agree that:
4	1. Creditor owns a security interest in _____ (Collateral).
5	2. The replacement value of Collateral is $_____ .
6	3. Creditor's security interest is valid and enforceable despite the Debtor's bankruptcy case.
7	4. Debtor agrees to pay the full value of the collateral no later than _____ .
8	5. Upon receiving the payment specified in Paragraph 4, Creditor will take all steps necessary to terminate its security interest in Collateral.
9	
10	Dated: _____ _____
	Debtor in Propria Persona
11	Dated: _____ _____
12	Creditor
13	
14	
15	
16	
17	
18	
19	
20	
21	
22	
23	
24	
25	
26	
27	
28	

Canceling your reaffirmation will leave your debt in the same condition as if you had never filed the reaffirmation agreement. That is, your personal liability for the debt will be discharged (assuming the debt is dischargeable), and the creditor will be able to enforce its lien on your property by either repossessing or foreclosing on it. If your bankruptcy case is still open, you can still try other options discussed in this chapter.

Complete and File Your Bankruptcy Paperwork

This chapter shows you how to take all of the necessary steps to prepare your case for filing under Chapter 7. For the most part, the process is very simple, as long as you follow all of the instructions we provide.

> **CAUTION**
> **Chapter 7 bankruptcy can be a very straight-forward process, but only if you follow the rules.** If you make a mistake—even accidentally—your bankruptcy case might be dismissed. In most cases, you can correct errors with an amendment. But sometimes errors are not correctable and your case will be dismissed with dire consequences: Not only will you continue to owe your debts and face creditor collection actions, but you might also lose the protection of the automatic stay in any future bankruptcy case you file within the next year (see Ch. 2 for more information on the automatic stay).

Gather the Necessary Documents

Along with the official bankruptcy forms, you will also have to provide:

- certification showing that you completed a credit counseling workshop within the last 180 days
- your most recent federal tax return or a transcript of the return (this goes to the trustee, not the court), and
- your wage stubs for the last 60 days.

Before you can get your bankruptcy discharge, you must also file a certification showing that you completed counseling on personal financial management (Form 23—Debtor's Certification of Completion of Postpetition Instructional Course Concerning Personal Financial Management, covered in Ch. 7) along with a certificate of completion from the counseling agency itself. In addition, the trustee may mail you a request for other documents—or request the documents at your 341 hearing. You should do your best to comply with any request.

Follow These Rules to Stay Out of Trouble

If you keep these golden rules in mind, you'll save yourself a lot of time and trouble:

- Don't file for Chapter 7 bankruptcy unless you are sure it is the right choice (Ch. 1 explains how to make this decision).
- Don't file until you have completed all of your documents as directed in this chapter.
- Don't file until you have a certificate showing that you have completed your credit counseling workshop.
- If you can, pay your filing fee in full rather than in installments, so you don't have to worry about your case being dismissed if you miss a payment.
- Be absolutely complete and honest in filling out your paperwork.
- File all of your documents at the same time (unless you have to file an emergency petition to stop an impending foreclosure, wage garnishment, or repossession).
- Don't file your case until you have your most recent federal tax return (or a transcript) in your hands.
- Serve your tax return (or transcript) on the trustee and any creditors who request it as soon after you file as possible. If you don't serve it at least seven days before the creditors' meeting, theoretically your case could be dismissed, although that is rare.
- If you haven't filed a tax return for two or more tax years, send the trustee a written, signed note explaining when you last filed and, if relevant, why you haven't filed (for instance, your income no longer requires you to file).
- Immediately amend your paperwork if the trustee asks you to.
- Respond to the trustee's request for any supplemental documentation as quickly as possible.
- Don't forget your personal financial management counseling. You won't receive a discharge unless, within 45 days after your creditors' meeting, you file Form 23 certifying that you have completed this course along with the certificate of completion from the counseling agency itself. (Ch. 7 explains how.)

The Credit Counseling Certificate

As explained in Ch. 1, every person who files a consumer bankruptcy has to first attend credit counseling. This credit counseling must be provided by an agency approved by the United States Trustee's Office within the 180-day period before you file for bankruptcy. The counseling can be done by phone, on the Internet, or in person.

You can obtain a list of approved counselors by visiting the U.S. Trustee's Office website at www. usdoj.gov/ust (click "Credit Counseling & Debtor Education"). The agencies are listed by state, but you can use any agency in any state or region.

Once you complete your counseling, the agency should give you a certificate of completion. You must either attach this certificate to Exhibit D of your bankruptcy petition (see the instructions for completing the petition below) or file the certificate within 15 days after you file. Although you don't have to file your certificate of completion when you file your petition, you must have completed your counseling by that time (unless you fit within one of the rare exceptions discussed below).

Repayment Plans

The purpose of credit counseling is to get you to sign up for a debt repayment plan instead of filing for bankruptcy. Indeed, if the plan makes sense and you believe you can faithfully make the payments required to complete it, you might reasonably consider signing up for it. However, keep in mind that even if you make the required payments on the plan month after month, the creditors can pull out of the plan if you later fall behind—and they can go after you for the remaining debt. If you then decide to file for Chapter 7 bankruptcy, you will have paid back all that money for no good reason. This is why most bankruptcy professionals discourage their clients from signing up for a debt repayment plan.

Even if you have no intention of signing up for a plan, you are still required to cooperate with the debt counseling agency in fashioning a plan if they think one is possible. You then have to file this plan along with your certificate of completion and your other bankruptcy papers. If the U.S. Trustee suspects that you might be able to complete a Chapter 13 repayment plan, it will review the agency's plan as part of its decision-making process.

Counseling Fees

Most of these credit counseling agencies charge a modest sum ($25–$50 is common) for the counseling, coming up with a repayment plan (if it gets that far), and the certificate of completion that you'll need to file with your other bankruptcy papers. Some credit counseling agencies don't charge anything for the counseling, but require a fee of $50 or more for the certificate.

Agencies are legally required to offer their services without regard to your ability to pay. (11 U.S.C. § 111(c)(2)(B).) If an agency wants to charge more than you can afford, inform the agency of this legal requirement.

Exceptions to the Counseling Requirement

You don't have to get counseling if the U.S. Trustee certifies that there is no appropriate agency available to you in the district where you will be filing. However, counseling can be provided by telephone or online if the U.S. Trustee approves, so it is unlikely that approved debt counseling will ever be unavailable.

In one case, however, a bankruptcy court found that counseling was not "available" to a debtor who spoke Creole because none of the credit counseling agencies in his area could accommodate his language needs. (*In re Petit-Louis,* 344 B.R. 696 (Bankr. S.D. Fla. 2006).) Presumably, this same rule would apply to any debtor who doesn't speak standard English and can't obtain counseling in his or her native language (or through a translator). Since this case was decided, the U.S. Trustee has begun to approve multilingual credit counseling agencies.

You can also avoid the requirement if you move the court to grant an exception and prove that "exigent circumstances" prevented you from getting counseling. This means that both of the following are true:

- You had to file for bankruptcy immediately (perhaps to stop a creditor from levying on your paycheck or bank account).
- You were unable to obtain counseling within five days after requesting it.

CAUTION

A foreclosure may not be "exigent" enough. Several courts have found that a debtor who waits until the last minute to seek credit counseling might not qualify for an exception to the counseling requirement. For example, in *Dixon v. La Barge, Jr.*, 338 B.R. 383 (B.A.P. 8th Cir. 2006), the court found that no exigent circumstances existed when a debtor filed for bankruptcy on the day of a scheduled foreclosure sale. In that case, the debtor claimed to have learned that he could file for Chapter 7 bankruptcy—and that he would have to complete credit counseling—on the night before he filed.

If the court grants an exception, you must complete the counseling within 30 days after you file (you can ask the court to extend this deadline by 15 days).

You may also escape the credit counseling requirement if, after notice and hearing, the bankruptcy court determines that you couldn't participate because of your:

- physical disability that prevents you from attending counseling (this exception probably won't apply if the counseling is available on the Internet or over the phone)
- mental incapacity (you are unable to understand and benefit from the counseling), or
- active duty in a military combat zone.

Consequences of Failing to Get Counseling

Courts have handled a debtor's failure to get counseling in two different ways. Some courts dismiss the debtor's case. (See *In re Stuart*, 2014 Bankr. LEXIS 3035 (Bankr. N.D. Ohio 2014).) Other courts have "stricken" the debtor's case instead. (See *In re Carey*, 341 B.R. 798 (Bankr. M.D. Fla. 2006) and *In re Thompson*, 344 B.R. 899 (Bankr. S.D. Ind. 2006).) This seemingly technical difference can be very important: If your case is stricken, you may refile without any of the negative consequences of dismissal (including losing the protection of the automatic stay) explained in Ch. 2.

Your Tax Return or Transcript

Under the new bankruptcy law, you are supposed to give the trustee and the U.S. Trustee your most recent federal tax return no later than seven days before your creditors' meeting. (11 U.S.C. § 521(e)(2).) You also have to provide the return to any creditor who asks for it. To protect your privacy, you can redact (black out) your birthdate and Social Security number. If you don't provide your tax return on time, your case could be dismissed.

If you can't find a copy of your most recent tax return, you can ask the IRS to give you a transcript of the basic information in your return—and you can use the transcript as a substitute for your return. Because it can take some time to receive the transcript, you should make your request as soon as you can.

CAUTION

If you haven't filed tax returns. As mentioned earlier, if you haven't filed federal tax returns for more than two years, send the trustee a written, signed note explaining the circumstances surrounding your nonfiling. An example of wording might be "Five years ago I retired from my job and have been living on Social Security. As a result I've had no need to file taxes."

Wage Stubs

If you are employed, you receive stubs or "advisements" with your paycheck. You are required to produce these stubs for the 60-day period prior to filing. If you have already tossed your stubs, you have two options: Wait 60 days (and keep your stubs) before filing, or go ahead and file, hand over the stubs you have, and explain why you don't have 60 days' worth. This second option might not work, however: The law states that failing to provide all wage stubs for the prior 60 days will result in dismissal of the bankruptcy case. (*In re Wilkinson*, 346 B.R. 539 (Bankr. D. Utah 2006).)

Many bankruptcy courts require you to use a local form as a cover sheet for wage stubs. (See "Get Some Information From the Court," below, for more on local rules and forms.) You should be able to get a copy of this form from the court or its website. Some of these local forms require you to provide information about income that comes from other sources too, not just wages. Our advice is to get your court's local form and provide all of the information it requests.

If you are not employed, don't worry about this requirement. However, if you receive Social Security or workers' compensation, you should plan on providing proof of those payments. (*In re LaPlante*, 354 B.R. 648 (Bankr. W.D.N.Y. 2006.))

Other Documents

In addition to your tax return and pay stubs, you may have to provide the trustee with other documents prior to your 341 hearing. Check your local court rules and Chapter 7 trustee standing administration guidelines, or call the trustee's office to make sure you have all required documentation.

In general, the most commonly requested documents include your:

- bank statements
- retirement account statements
- deed of trust or mortgage payoff information
- car loan statement
- car registration
- proof of home or car insurance, and
- property valuations.

Get Some Information From the Court

Every bankruptcy court has its own requirements for filing bankruptcy papers. If your papers don't meet these local requirements, the court clerk may reject them. So, before you begin preparing your papers, find out your court rules.

Finding the Right Bankruptcy Court

Because bankruptcy is a creature of federal, not state, law, you must file for bankruptcy in a special federal court. There are federal bankruptcy courts all over the country.

The federal court system divides the country into judicial districts. Every state has at least one judicial district; most have more. You can file in any of the following districts:

- the district where you have been living for the greater part of the 180-day period before you file
- the district where you are domiciled—that is, where you maintain your home, even if you have been living elsewhere (such as on a military base) temporarily
- the district where your principal place of business is located (if you are a business debtor), or
- the district where the majority of your business assets are located.

Most readers will be using the first option—and many will probably file in the large city closest to their home. To find a bankruptcy court in your state, check the government listings in your white pages (under "United States, Courts"), call directory assistance, ask your local librarian, or use the Court Locator found on the U.S. Court's website at www.uscourts.gov. If you live in a state with more than one district, you can also call the court in the closest city and ask whether that district includes your county or zip code.

EXAMPLE: For the past two months, Tom has lived in San Luis Obispo, which is in California's Central Judicial District. Before that he lived in Santa Rosa, in California's Northern Judicial District. Because Tom spent more of the past six months in the Northern District than in the Central, he should file in the bankruptcy court in the Northern District. If it's too inconvenient to file there, he could wait another month, when he would qualify to file in the Central District court.

In urban areas especially, you may get no response to a letter or phone call. You may need to visit the court and get the information in person. Or, the information may be available on the Internet. Almost all bankruptcy courts have websites with this sort of information. To find your court's website, visit www.uscourts.gov/court_locator.aspx.

Fees

The total fee to file for Chapter 7 bankruptcy is $335. Fees change, however, so make sure you verify the amount with the court. This fee is due upon filing, unless the court waives the fee or gives you permission to pay in installments. (To make these requests, you must complete Form 3A or 3B, as explained below.)

Local Forms

In addition to the official forms that every bankruptcy court uses (they are listed below), your local bankruptcy court may require you to file one or two additional forms that it has developed. For example, different courts have different forms that you must file along with your wage stubs (as explained above). You can get all local forms from your local bankruptcy court or a local stationery store, or you can download them from your court's website. (Go to www.uscourts.gov/ court_locator.aspx for a list of links to local courts.) Of course, we can't include all local forms in this book or tell you how to fill them out. Most, however, are self-explanatory. If you need help in obtaining or understanding them, see a local bankruptcy lawyer.

Local Court Rules

Most bankruptcy courts publish local rules that govern the court's procedures. These rules mainly govern hearings conducted by the bankruptcy judge and aren't relevant in routine bankruptcy cases, which usually involve only filing papers and appearing at a 341 hearing. Still, on occasion, a rule does affect a routine Chapter 7 bankruptcy. You can get your local rules from the bankruptcy court—in person or on its website—but be prepared to comb through reams of material to find the one or two rules that might apply in your case.

Number of Copies

Before filing your papers, find out how many copies your court requires. Most ask for an original and one copy. The original will be scanned into the court's database, and your copy will be "conformed" for your records. (A conformed copy is either stamped or receives a computer-generated label, with information showing that you filed, the date of your filing, your case number, and the tentative date of your 341 hearing.) A few courts still require you to provide an original plus more than one additional copy.

Order of Papers and Other Details

Every court has a preferred order in which it wants to receive the forms in the package you submit for filing. Most courts also have rules indicating whether the forms should be hole-punched or stapled, and other details. If you mess up, most clerks will put your forms in the correct order or punch and staple your papers in the right way. Some, however, will make you do it yourself. This can be a major pain if you are filing by mail. Every court has an exhibit of the standard Chapter 7 filing with the forms arranged correctly. If you want to get it right the first time, visit the court and carefully examine the court's sample filing, taking notes on the order in which forms fall.

Below is a sample letter you can adapt to your situation and send to the court, requesting the information discussed above. Include a large, self-addressed envelope. Call and ask the court if you need to affix return postage. Again, if you live in an urban area, you'll probably have to visit the court to get this information.

For Married Filers

If you are married, you and your spouse will have to decide whether one of you should file alone or whether you should file jointly. To make this decision, you'll first have to make sure that you're married in the eyes of the federal law (a trickier issue than you might think), then consider how filing together or separately will affect your debts and property.

Sample Letter to Bankruptcy Court

Sandra Smith
432 Oak Street
Cincinnati, OH 45219
513-555-7890

July 2, 20xx

United States Bankruptcy Court
Atrium Two, Room 800
221 East Fourth Street
Cincinnati, OH 45202

Attn: COURT CLERK

TO THE COURT CLERK:

Please send me the following information:

- copies of all local forms required by this court for an individual (not corporation) filing a Chapter 7 bankruptcy and for making amendments
- the number of copies or sets required for filing
- the order in which forms should be submitted, and
- complete instructions on this court's emergency filing procedures and deadlines.

I would also appreciate answers to four questions:

1. Do you require a separate creditor mailing list (matrix)? If so, do you have specific requirements for its format?
2. Is the filing fee still $335? If not, please advise.
3. Should I two-hole punch my papers or is that done by the court?
4. Should I staple the papers or use paper clips?

I've enclosed a self-addressed envelope for your reply. Thank you.

Sincerely,

Sandra Smith

Sandra Smith

Enclosure

Are You Married?

If you were married with a valid state license, you are married for purposes of filing a joint petition, and you can skip down to "Should You File Jointly?" below. However, if you were not married with a license and ceremony, read on.

Some states allow heterosexual couples to establish common law marriages, which the states will recognize as valid marriages even though the couples do not have state marriage licenses or certificates. Contrary to popular belief, a common law marriage is not created when two people simply live together for a certain number of years. In order to have a valid common law marriage, the couple must do all of the following:

- live together for a significant period of time (not defined in any state)
- hold themselves out as a married couple—typically this means using the same last name, referring to the other as "my husband" or "my wife," and filing a joint tax return, and
- intend to be married.

Alabama, Colorado, the District of Columbia, Iowa, Kansas, Montana, New Hampshire (but only for inheritance purposes), Oklahoma, Rhode Island, South Carolina, Texas, and Utah recognize some form of common law marriage. Florida, Georgia, Idaho, Indiana, Ohio, and Pennsylvania previously allowed common law marriage; those states only recognize common law marriages created before a certain date. The rules for what constitutes a marriage differ from state to state.

If you live in one of these states and you meet your state's requirements for a common law marriage, you have the option to file jointly, if you wish.

Same-Sex Married Couples

If you married your same-sex partner in a state, country, or province that recognizes same-sex marriage, as of June 26, 2013 you may file a joint bankruptcy petition. June 26, 2013 is the date that the U.S. Supreme Court declared unconstitutional Section 3 of the Defense of Marriage Act (DOMA) which had denied federal benefits to gay couples who were legally married. *United States v. Windsor*, 133 S. Ct. 2675 (2013). This decision cleared the way for same-sex married couples to file joint bankruptcy petitions. (When the decision came down, some bankruptcy courts were already allowing same-sex married couples to file joint petitions). As of June 2015 all same-sex couples can legally marry in the United States (see *Obergefell v. Hodges*, 576 U.S. __ (2015)), which opens up the opportunity to file a joint bankruptcy to many more couples.

Should You File Jointly?

Unfortunately, there is no simple formula that will tell you whether it's better to file alone or with your spouse. In the end, it will depend on which option allows you to discharge more of your debts and keep more of your property. Here are some of the factors you should consider:

- If you are living in a community property state and most of your debts were incurred, and your property acquired, during marriage, you should probably file jointly. Even if only one spouse files, all community property is considered part of the bankruptcy estate. The same is generally true for debts—that is, all community debts are listed and discharged even though only one spouse files. Even if a creditor doesn't agree that all community debts are discharged if only one spouse files, creditors rarely, if ever, go after a nonfiling spouse for a debt unless his or her name is listed as a joint account owner. (See Ch. 3 for more on community property.)

- If you have recently married, you haven't acquired any valuable assets as a married couple, and one of you has all the debts, it may make sense for that spouse to file for bankruptcy alone (especially if the nonfiling spouse has good credit to protect).

- You may want to file alone if you and your spouse own property as tenants by the entirety (see Ch. 3), you owe most of the debts in your own name, and you live in a state that excludes property held as tenancy by the entirety from the bankruptcy estate when one spouse files.

This is a particularly important consideration if you own your home as tenants by the entirety: Filing jointly could cause you to lose your home if you have significant nonexempt equity. (See Ch. 4 for more information.)

- If the exemption system you are using allows married spouses to double their exemptions, filing jointly may help you hang on to more of your property. (See Ch. 3 for more information on exemptions, and Appendix A for state-by-state information on doubling.)

- If you are still married but separated, you may have to file alone if your spouse won't cooperate. Still, if your debts and property are joint rather than separate, a joint filing would probably be to your best advantage.

- If you are married, you and your spouse have shared finances, and your spouse's income is significantly larger than your own, be aware that filing alone won't prevent the court from considering your spouse's income. You must disclose your spouse's earnings on your bankruptcy petition, and the amount left after deducting your spouse's separate debts will be income attributed to you. (This is called the marital adjustment deduction, and is discussed in Form 22A-2, below.) If you fail to report your spouse's income, or underreport it, the court will likely dismiss your case. (See *In re Reeves*, 327 B.R. 36 (Bankr. W.D. MI 2005), in which the court considered the nonfiling spouse's income, found it to be underreported, and dismissed the filing spouse's bankruptcy case.)

 SEE AN EXPERT

If you are uncertain about how to file, see a lawyer. The decision to file jointly or alone can have significant consequences. Because the best choice will depend on your unique situation, we advise you to talk to a bankruptcy lawyer if you have any questions about which option makes more sense.

Required Forms and Documents

Bankruptcy uses official forms prescribed by the Federal Office of the Courts. In addition, you must file certain documents, as described above in "Gather the Necessary Documents." Here and in Appendix B we provide complete lists of (1) the official forms you will be completing in this chapter, and (2) the documents that you will have to file along with the official forms. We also explain how to get these forms and documents.

TIP
How the Official Forms are listed. On the United States Courts' website (www.uscourts.gov), where you find the official bankruptcy forms, you'll see that many of the forms start with the letter "B." We've dispensed with the "B" in this book.

Checklist of Required Official Bankruptcy Forms

These are the standard forms that must be filed in every Chapter 7 bankruptcy:

- ☐ Form 1—Voluntary Petition
- ☐ Form 3A (if you want to pay your filing fee in installments)
- ☐ Form 3B (if you apply for a fee waiver)
- ☐ Form 6A—Schedule A—Real Property
- ☐ Form 6B—Schedule B—Personal Property
- ☐ Form 6C—Schedule C—Property Claimed as Exempt
- ☐ Form 6D—Schedule D—Creditors Holding Secured Claims
- ☐ Form 6E—Schedule E—Creditors Holding Unsecured Priority Claims
- ☐ Form 6F—Schedule F—Creditors Holding Unsecured Nonpriority Claims
- ☐ Form 6G—Schedule G—Executory Contracts and Unexpired Leases
- ☐ Form 6H—Schedule H—Codebtors
- ☐ Form 6I—Schedule I—Current Income
- ☐ Form 6J—Schedule J—Current Expenditures
- ☐ Form 6—Summary—Summary of Schedules A through J and Statistical Summary of Certain Liabilities
- ☐ Form 6—Declaration—Declaration Concerning Debtor's Schedules
- ☐ Form 7—Statement of Financial Affairs
- ☐ Form 8—Chapter 7 Individual Debtor's Statement of Intention
- ☐ Form 21—Full Social Security Number Disclosure
- ☐ Form 22A-1—Statement of Current Monthly Income
- ☐ Form 22A-1 Supp—Statement of Exemption from Presumption of Abuse Under § 707(b)(2)
- ☐ Form 22A–2—Chapter 7 Means Test Calculation
- ☐ Form 23—Certification of Instructional Course on Financial Management
- ☐ Form 201A—Notice to Individual Consumer Debtors
- ☐ Creditor mailing list
- ☐ Required local forms, if any.

With the exception of Forms 22A-1 and 22A-2, which might require you to do a fair bit of math, the forms are very straightforward and easy to complete, as long as you take them one at a time. The forms are designed to be read and understood by the lay public—that is, by the bankruptcy filers themselves. Although you must include each and every form as part of your filing package, some of them may require very little time to complete. For instance, if you don't own real estate, you can simply check the "None" box on Schedule A and proceed to Schedule B.

All together, these forms usually are referred to as your "bankruptcy petition," although technically your petition is only Form 1. (In case you're wondering, Forms 2, 4, and 5 aren't used in voluntary Chapter 7 bankruptcy filings.)

Fee Waiver

You may ask the court to waive the fees by filing Form 3B. To qualify, you must be unable to pay in installments and your income must be below 150% of the poverty line. You will have to appear in court so the judge can ask you questions.

If the court won't grant your request to waive the fee entirely, it may allow you to pay in up to four installments. In this situation, you must be very careful. If you miss even one installment, the court may dismiss your case without giving you a chance to explain yourself. It's best to deliver your payments directly to the court and get a receipt from the clerk. A second, not-as-good alternative is to send the payments by registered mail, return receipt requested. Whether you use first class or registered mail, if the court fails to apply the payments to your account, it will be the court's word against yours. And guess who wins?

Checklist of Required Documents

As explained above, bankruptcy law requires filers to submit some additional documents along with the official forms. The documents you must file are:

- ☐ your most recent federal tax return or a transcript of the return obtained from the IRS (or, if you haven't filed for two or more years, a written, signed note explaining why)
- ☐ a certificate showing that you have completed the required credit counseling
- ☐ any repayment plan that was developed during your credit counseling
- ☐ your pay stubs for the previous 60 days (along with an accompanying form, if your local court requires one), and
- ☐ a certificate of completion for a course in personal financial management (you must attach this to Form 23).

Where to Get the Official Forms

You can find all of the bankruptcy forms on the website of the United States Courts (at www.uscourts.gov). You can complete the forms online, save, edit, and print at your convenience. To get the forms, go to www.uscourts.gov/forms/bankruptcy-forms. You'll notice that the website usually includes the letter "B" before each form number. We dispense with the "B" in this book. So, for example, if we refer to Form 7, that form will be listed as Form B 7 on the court's website.

Tips for Completing the Forms

Here are some tips that will make filling in your forms easier and the whole bankruptcy process smoother. A sample completed form accompanies each form's instructions. Refer to it while you fill in your bankruptcy papers.

Use your worksheets and credit counseling plan (if you have one). If you've completed the worksheets in Chs. 1, 3, 4, and 5, you've already done a lot of the work. These worksheets will save you lots of time when you prepare your bankruptcy forms, so keep them handy. If you skipped any of those chapters, refer to the worksheets and accompanying instructions for help in figuring out what to put in your bankruptcy forms.

Make several copies of each form. That way, you can make a draft, changing things as you go until the form is complete and correct. Prepare final forms to file with the court only after you've double-checked your drafts. If you use the PDF, fill-in-the-blanks forms available on the official U.S. Courts' website (see above), no copies are necessary.

Type your final forms. The easiest, neatest way to complete the forms is by using the fillable forms on the U.S. Courts' website. However, if you wish to print out the forms from the website or get blank forms from your local bankruptcy court, then it's best to type the information into the blanks. You are allowed to provide handwritten information, but the trustee handling your case will likely be friendlier if forms are typewritten. If you don't have access to a typewriter, many libraries have typewriters available to the public (for a small rental fee), or you can hire a bankruptcy form preparation service to prepare your forms using the information you provide. (See Ch. 10 for more on these services.)

! CAUTION
Interpret the forms literally. When completing the forms, read each one carefully, including the instructions at the top. Then follow the instructions as closely as possible. You should interpret the form and instructions literally. Don't get stumped by hidden meanings. If, for some reason, you misinterpret the literal language of the form, and you are able to explain how the misinterpretation arose, you'll be allowed to amend the form without further explanation.

Be ridiculously thorough. Always err on the side of giving too much information rather than too little. If you leave information out, the bankruptcy trustee may become suspicious of your motives. If you leave creditors off the forms, the debts you owe these creditors might not be discharged—hardly the result you would want. In reality, this rarely happens—as long as your case is a "no asset" case, your debt will likely be discharged even if you don't list it. But, if you do have assets that are distributed to your creditors, and a particular creditor doesn't get its share of the distribution because you left it off the form, the debt may well live on after your bankruptcy. In either event, it's better to take care to list everything.

It gets worse if you intentionally or carelessly fail to list all your property and debts, or fail to accurately describe your recent property transactions. The court, upon a request by the trustee, may rule that you acted with fraudulent intent. It may deny your bankruptcy discharge altogether, and you may lose some property that you could otherwise have kept. The cardinal rule is: Measure twice, cut once!

Respond to every question. Most of the forms have a box to check when your answer is "none." If a question doesn't have a "none" box and the question doesn't apply to you, type in "N/A" for "not applicable." This will let the trustee know that you didn't overlook the question. Occasionally, a question that doesn't apply to you will have a number of blanks. Put "N/A" in only the first blank if it is obvious that this applies to the other blanks as well. If it's not clear, put "N/A" in every blank.

Explain uncertainties. If you can't figure out which category on a form to use for a debt or an item of property, list the debt or item in what you think is the appropriate place and briefly note next to your entry that you're uncertain. The important thing is to disclose the information somewhere. The bankruptcy trustee will sort it out, if necessary.

Be scrupulously honest. As part of your official bankruptcy paperwork, you must complete declarations, under penalty of perjury, swearing that you've been truthful. It's important to realize that you could be prosecuted for perjury if it becomes evident that you deliberately lied.

Use continuation pages if you run out of room. The space for entering information is sometimes skimpy, especially if you're filing jointly. Most of the forms come with preformatted continuation pages that you can use if you need more room. But if there is no continuation sheet, prepare one yourself, using a piece of regular, white 8½" × 11" paper. Write "see continuation page" next to the question you're working on and enter the additional information on the continuation page. Label the continuation pages with your name and the form name and indicate "Continuation page 1," "Continuation page 2," and so on. Be sure to attach all continuation pages to their appropriate forms when you file your bankruptcy papers.

Get help if necessary. If your situation is complicated, you're unsure about how to complete a form, or you run into trouble when you go to file your papers, consult a bankruptcy attorney or do some legal research before proceeding. (See Ch. 10.)

Emergency Filing

Although people usually file all of their bankruptcy forms at once, you don't absolutely have to. If you really need to stop creditors quickly—because of a foreclosure or threatened repossession—you can simply file the Voluntary Petition (including Exhibit D, concerning credit counseling), the statement of your Social Security number (Form 21), and a form called a Matrix, which lists the name, address, and zip code of each of your creditors. The automatic stay, which stops most collection efforts against you, will then go into effect. You have 14 days to file the rest of the forms. (Bankruptcy Rule 1007(c).)

Although it's an option if you're really in a jam, we urge you to not do an emergency filing unless it's absolutely necessary. That 14-day extension goes by fast; many people blow the deadline, then have their cases dismissed. So, if at all possible, file all your paperwork at the same time.

Refer to—but don't copy—the sample forms. Throughout this chapter, we have included the completed sample forms of Carrie Anne Edwards, who lives in California. These forms are intended to be used as examples, so you can see what a completed form should look like. However, everyone's bankruptcy situation is different—you will owe different debts, own different property, have different bank accounts and Social Security numbers, and otherwise be utterly dissimilar from this fictional woman. DO NOT COPY THESE EXAMPLES VERBATIM, even if you live in California, because they won't fit your precise situation.

Form 1—Voluntary Petition

A completed sample Voluntary Petition and line-by-line instructions follow.

First Page

Court Name. At the top of the first page, fill in the name of the judicial district you're filing in, such as the "Central District of California." If your state has only one district, fill in your state's name. If your state divides its districts into divisions, enter the division after the state name, such as "Northern District of California, Santa Rosa Division."

Name of Debtor. Enter your full name (last name first), as used on your checks, driver's license, and other formal documents. If you are married and filing jointly, put one of your names as the debtor (on the left) and the other as the "joint debtor (spouse)," on the right. If you are married but filing separately, enter "N/A" in the second blank.

All Other Names. The purpose of this box is to make sure that your creditors will know who you are when they receive notice of your bankruptcy filing. If you have been known by any other name in the last eight years, list it here. If you've operated a business as a sole proprietor during the previous eight years, include your trade name (fictitious or assumed business name) preceded by "dba" for "doing business as." But don't include minor variations in spelling or form. For instance, if your name is John Lewis Odegard, you don't have to put down that you're sometimes known as J.L. But if you've used the pseudonym J.L. Smith, you should list it. If you're uncertain, list any name that you think you may have used with a creditor. Do the same for your spouse (in the box to the right) if you are filing jointly. If you're married and filing alone, type "N/A" in the box to the right (and the remaining joint debtor boxes on the form).

Last four digits of Soc. Sec. or Individual-Taxpayer I.D. Enter only the last four digits of your Social Security number or taxpayer's ID number. Do the same for your spouse (in the box to the right) if you are filing jointly. (You must provide your full Social Security number on a different form.)

Street Address of Debtor. Enter your current street address. Even if you get all of your mail at a post office box, list the address of your personal residence.

Street Address of Joint Debtor. If filing jointly, enter your spouse's current street address (even if it's the same as yours)—again, no post office boxes.

County of Residence or of the Principal Place of Business. Enter the county in which you live. (Do the same for your spouse if you're filing jointly. Otherwise, type "N/A" in the box.) If you are doing business, enter

Sample Voluntary Petition—page 1

B1 (Official Form 1)(04/13)

United States Bankruptcy Court Eastern District of California	Voluntary Petition

Name of Debtor (if individual, enter Last, First, Middle): **Edwards, Carrie Anne**	Name of Joint Debtor (Spouse) (Last, First, Middle):
All Other Names used by the Debtor in the last 8 years (include married, maiden, and trade names):	All Other Names used by the Joint Debtor in the last 8 years (include married, maiden, and trade names):
Last four digits of Soc. Sec. or Individual-Taxpayer I.D. (ITIN)/Complete EIN (if more than one, state all) **xxx-xx-6287**	Last four digits of Soc. Sec. or Individual-Taxpayer I.D. (ITIN) No./Complete EIN (if more than one, state all)
Street Address of Debtor (No. and Street, City, and State): **3045 Berwick St.** **Rocklin, CA** ZIP Code **95765**	Street Address of Joint Debtor (No. and Street, City, and State): ZIP Code
County of Residence or of the Principal Place of Business: **Placer**	County of Residence or of the Principal Place of Business:
Mailing Address of Debtor (if different from street address): **PO Box 1437** **Rocklin, CA** ZIP Code **95765**	Mailing Address of Joint Debtor (if different from street address): ZIP Code
Location of Principal Assets of Business Debtor (if different from street address above):	

Type of Debtor
(Form of Organization) (Check one box)
- ■ Individual (includes Joint Debtors)
  See Exhibit D on page 2 of this form.
- ☐ Corporation (includes LLC and LLP)
- ☐ Partnership
- ☐ Other (If debtor is not one of the above entities, check this box and state type of entity below.)

Nature of Business
(Check one box)
- ☐ Health Care Business
- ☐ Single Asset Real Estate as defined in 11 U.S.C. § 101 (51B)
- ☐ Railroad
- ☐ Stockbroker
- ☐ Commodity Broker
- ☐ Clearing Bank
- ☐ Other

Chapter of Bankruptcy Code Under Which the Petition is Filed (Check one box)
- ■ Chapter 7
- ☐ Chapter 9
- ☐ Chapter 11
- ☐ Chapter 12
- ☐ Chapter 13
- ☐ Chapter 15 Petition for Recognition of a Foreign Main Proceeding
- ☐ Chapter 15 Petition for Recognition of a Foreign Nonmain Proceeding

Chapter 15 Debtors
Country of debtor's center of main interests:

Each country in which a foreign proceeding by, regarding, or against debtor is pending:

Tax-Exempt Entity
(Check box, if applicable)
- ☐ Debtor is a tax-exempt organization under Title 26 of the United States Code (the Internal Revenue Code).

Nature of Debts
(Check one box)
- ■ Debts are primarily consumer debts, defined in 11 U.S.C. § 101(8) as "incurred by an individual primarily for a personal, family, or household purpose."
- ☐ Debts are primarily business debts.

Filing Fee (Check one box)
- ■ Full Filing Fee attached
- ☐ Filing Fee to be paid in installments (applicable to individuals only). Must attach signed application for the court's consideration certifying that the debtor is unable to pay fee except in installments. Rule 1006(b). See Official Form 3A.
- ☐ Filing Fee waiver requested (applicable to chapter 7 individuals only). Must attach signed application for the court's consideration. See Official Form 3B.

Chapter 11 Debtors
Check one box:
- ☐ Debtor is a small business debtor as defined in 11 U.S.C. § 101(51D).
- ☐ Debtor is not a small business debtor as defined in 11 U.S.C. § 101(51D).

Check if:
- ☐ Debtor's aggregate noncontingent liquidated debts (excluding debts owed to insiders or affiliates) are less than $2,490,925 *(amount subject to adjustment on 4/01/16 and every three years thereafter).*

Check all applicable boxes:
- ☐ A plan is being filed with this petition.
- ☐ Acceptances of the plan were solicited prepetition from one or more classes of creditors, in accordance with 11 U.S.C. § 1126(b).

Statistical/Administrative Information
- ☐ Debtor estimates that funds will be available for distribution to unsecured creditors.
- ■ Debtor estimates that, after any exempt property is excluded and administrative expenses paid, there will be no funds available for distribution to unsecured creditors.

THIS SPACE IS FOR COURT USE ONLY

Estimated Number of Creditors

■	☐	☐	☐	☐	☐	☐	☐	☐	☐
1-49	50-99	100-199	200-999	1,000-5,000	5,001-10,000	10,001-25,000	25,001-50,000	50,001-100,000	OVER 100,000

Estimated Assets

☐	☐	■	☐	☐	☐	☐	☐	☐	☐
$0 to $50,000	$50,001 to $100,000	$100,001 to $500,000	$500,001 to $1 million	$1,000,001 to $10 million	$10,000,001 to $50 million	$50,000,001 to $100 million	$100,000,001 to $500 million	$500,000,001 to $1 billion	More than $1 billion

Estimated Liabilities

☐	☐	■	☐	☐	☐	☐	☐	☐	☐
$0 to $50,000	$50,001 to $100,000	$100,001 to $500,000	$500,001 to $1 million	$1,000,001 to $10 million	$10,000,001 to $50 million	$50,000,001 to $100 million	$100,000,001 to $500 million	$500,000,001 to $1 billion	More than $1 billion

the county where your (or your spouse's) business assets are located, if it's different from your mailing address.

Mailing Address of Debtor. Enter your mailing address if it is different from your street address. If it isn't, put "N/A." Do the same for your spouse (in the box to the right) if you are filing jointly.

Location of Principal Assets of Business Debtor. Leave blank. This only applies to corporations and other business entities that are filing bankruptcy. Even if you are a sole proprietor, or have primarily business debts arising from your business, you are not considered a "business debtor."

Type of Debtor. Check the first box—"Individual"—even if you were self-employed or operated a sole proprietorship during the previous six years. If you are filing for bankruptcy for a corporation, partnership, or another type of business entity, you shouldn't be using this book.

Nature of Business. See a bankruptcy lawyer if any of these descriptions apply to you or your spouse. For instance, if you or your spouse own an assisted living facility (11 U.S.C. § 101 (27A)), you will need a lawyer's services, because the law has gotten quite complicated regarding how health care businesses are treated in bankruptcy.

Tax-Exempt Entity. Leave this blank. This box is for nonprofits only.

Chapter of Bankruptcy Code Under Which the Petition is Filed. Check "Chapter 7."

Nature of Debts. Check the box for consumer debts if most of your debts are owed personally, rather than by a business. If, however, the bulk of your debts are due to the operation of a business, check the business debts box. If you are in doubt, check the business debts box.

💡 **TIP**

Taxes and mortgages—are they consumer or business debt? Debts for back taxes are considered to be business debt while mortgage debt is considered to be consumer debt. Because mortgage debt usually makes up the majority of a homeowner's debts, most sole proprietors file as consumers even though the bulk of their unsecured debt arises from their businesses.

Filing Fee. If you will attach the entire fee, check the first box. If you plan to ask the court for permission to pay in installments, check the second box. (Instructions for applying to the court are in "How to File Your Papers," below.) If you wish to apply for a full waiver of the filing fee, check the third box and see "How to File Your Papers," below.

Chapter 11 Debtors. Leave this section blank.

Statistical/Administrative Information. There are a number of boxes here. The first set of boxes tells the trustee whether you think there will be assets available to be sold for the benefit of your unsecured creditors. If you did your homework in Ch. 3 and Ch. 4, you will have a good idea of whether all of your assets are exempt, or whether some will have to be surrendered to the trustee. Check the top or bottom box accordingly. If you check the bottom box, your creditors will be told that there is no point in filing a Proof of Claim unless they hear differently from the trustee. If you check the top box, your creditors will be told to file Proof of Claim forms. If you haven't a clue yet about your property and exemptions, come back to this question after you've completed Schedules A, B, and C.

Similarly, if you can provide pretty good estimates of the other information requested (estimated number of creditors, assets, and liabilities), fill in the appropriate boxes on the form. If not, come back to these questions when you've completed more of your paperwork.

Second Page

Name of Debtor(s). Enter your name, and your spouse's name if you are filing jointly.

All Prior Bankruptcy Cases Filed Within Last 8 Years. If you haven't filed a bankruptcy case within the previous eight years, type "None" or "N/A" in the first box. If you—or your spouse, if you're filing jointly—have, enter the requested information. A previous Chapter 7 bankruptcy bars you from filing another one until eight years have passed since you filed the previous case. And, if you filed a Chapter 7 bankruptcy case that was dismissed for cause within the previous 180 days, you may have to wait to file again, or you may not be able to discharge all your debts. (See Ch. 2 for more information.) If either situation applies to you, see a bankruptcy lawyer before filing.

Sample Voluntary Petition—page 2

B1 (Official Form 1)(04/13)	Page 2
Voluntary Petition *(This page must be completed and filed in every case)*	Name of Debtor(s): **Edwards, Carrie Anne**

All Prior Bankruptcy Cases Filed Within Last 8 Years (If more than two, attach additional sheet)

Location Where Filed: **- None -**	Case Number:	Date Filed:
Location Where Filed:	Case Number:	Date Filed:

Pending Bankruptcy Case Filed by any Spouse, Partner, or Affiliate of this Debtor (If more than one, attach additional sheet)

Name of Debtor: **- None -**	Case Number:	Date Filed:
District:	Relationship:	Judge:

Exhibit A	Exhibit B
(To be completed if debtor is required to file periodic reports (e.g., forms 10K and 10Q) with the Securities and Exchange Commission pursuant to Section 13 or 15(d) of the Securities Exchange Act of 1934 and is requesting relief under chapter 11.) ☐ Exhibit A is attached and made a part of this petition.	(To be completed if debtor is an individual whose debts are primarily consumer debts.) I, the attorney for the petitioner named in the foregoing petition, declare that I have informed the petitioner that [he or she] may proceed under chapter 7, 11, 12, or 13 of title 11, United States Code, and have explained the relief available under each such chapter. I further certify that I delivered to the debtor the notice required by 11 U.S.C. §342(b). **X** _____ Signature of Attorney for Debtor(s) (Date)

Exhibit C

Does the debtor own or have possession of any property that poses or is alleged to pose a threat of imminent and identifiable harm to public health or safety?

☐ Yes, and Exhibit C is attached and made a part of this petition.

■ No.

Exhibit D

(To be completed by every individual debtor. If a joint petition is filed, each spouse must complete and attach a separate Exhibit D.)

■ Exhibit D completed and signed by the debtor is attached and made a part of this petition.

If this is a joint petition:

☐ Exhibit D also completed and signed by the joint debtor is attached and made a part of this petition.

Information Regarding the Debtor - Venue
(Check any applicable box)

■ Debtor has been domiciled or has had a residence, principal place of business, or principal assets in this District for 180 days immediately preceding the date of this petition or for a longer part of such 180 days than in any other District.

☐ There is a bankruptcy case concerning debtor's affiliate, general partner, or partnership pending in this District.

☐ Debtor is a debtor in a foreign proceeding and has its principal place of business or principal assets in the United States in this District, or has no principal place of business or assets in the United States but is a defendant in an action or proceeding [in a federal or state court] in this District, or the interests of the parties will be served in regard to the relief sought in this District.

Certification by a Debtor Who Resides as a Tenant of Residential Property
(Check all applicable boxes)

☐ Landlord has a judgment against the debtor for possession of debtor's residence. (If box checked, complete the following.)

_____
(Name of landlord that obtained judgment)

_____
(Address of landlord)

☐ Debtor claims that under applicable nonbankruptcy law, there are circumstances under which the debtor would be permitted to cure the entire monetary default that gave rise to the judgment for possession, after the judgment for possession was entered, and

☐ Debtor has included with this petition the deposit with the court of any rent that would become due during the 30-day period after the filing of the petition.

☐ Debtor certifies that he/she has served the Landlord with this certification. (11 U.S.C. § 362(l)).

Sample Voluntary Petition—page 3

B1 (Official Form 1)(04/13)
Page 3

Voluntary Petition

(This page must be completed and filed in every case)

Name of Debtor(s):
Edwards, Carrie Anne

Signatures

Signature(s) of Debtor(s) (Individual/Joint)

I declare under penalty of perjury that the information provided in this petition is true and correct.
[If petitioner is an individual whose debts are primarily consumer debts and has chosen to file under chapter 7] I am aware that I may proceed under chapter 7, 11, 12, or 13 of title 11, United States Code, understand the relief available under each such chapter, and choose to proceed under chapter 7.
[If no attorney represents me and no bankruptcy petition preparer signs the petition] I have obtained and read the notice required by 11 U.S.C. §342(b).

I request relief in accordance with the chapter of title 11, United States Code, specified in this petition.

X **/s/ Carrie Anne Edwards**

Signature of Debtor **Carrie Anne Edwards**

X _____

Signature of Joint Debtor

(916) 274-1234

Telephone Number (If not represented by attorney)

_____
Date

Signature of Attorney*

X **Debtor not represented by attorney**

Signature of Attorney for Debtor(s)

_____

Printed Name of Attorney for Debtor(s)

_____

Firm Name

_____

Address

_____

Telephone Number

_____
Date

*In a case in which § 707(b)(4)(D) applies, this signature also constitutes a certification that the attorney has no knowledge after an inquiry that the information in the schedules is incorrect.

Signature of Debtor (Corporation/Partnership)

I declare under penalty of perjury that the information provided in this petition is true and correct, and that I have been authorized to file this petition on behalf of the debtor.

The debtor requests relief in accordance with the chapter of title 11, United States Code, specified in this petition.

X _____

Signature of Authorized Individual

_____

Printed Name of Authorized Individual

_____

Title of Authorized Individual

_____
Date

Signature of a Foreign Representative

I declare under penalty of perjury that the information provided in this petition is true and correct, that I am the foreign representative of a debtor in a foreign proceeding, and that I am authorized to file this petition.

(Check only one box.)

☐ I request relief in accordance with chapter 15 of title 11. United States Code. Certified copies of the documents required by 11 U.S.C. §1515 are attached.

☐ Pursuant to 11 U.S.C. §1511, I request relief in accordance with the chapter of title 11 specified in this petition. A certified copy of the order granting recognition of the foreign main proceeding is attached.

X _____

Signature of Foreign Representative

_____

Printed Name of Foreign Representative

_____

Date

Signature of Non-Attorney Bankruptcy Petition Preparer

I declare under penalty of perjury that: (1) I am a bankruptcy petition preparer as defined in 11 U.S.C. § 110; (2) I prepared this document for compensation and have provided the debtor with a copy of this document and the notices and information required under 11 U.S.C. §§ 110(b), 110(h), and 342(b); and, (3) if rules or guidelines have been promulgated pursuant to 11 U.S.C. § 110(h) setting a maximum fee for services chargeable by bankruptcy petition preparers, I have given the debtor notice of the maximum amount before preparing any document for filing for a debtor or accepting any fee from the debtor, as required in that section. Official Form 19 is attached.

_____

Printed Name and title, if any, of Bankruptcy Petition Preparer

_____

Social-Security number (If the bankrutpcy petition preparer is not an individual, state the Social Security number of the officer, principal, responsible person or partner of the bankruptcy petition preparer.)(Required by 11 U.S.C. § 110.)

_____

Address

X _____

_____

Date

Signature of bankruptcy petition preparer or officer, principal, responsible person,or partner whose Social Security number is provided above.

Names and Social-Security numbers of all other individuals who prepared or assisted in preparing this document unless the bankruptcy petition preparer is not an individual:

If more than one person prepared this document, attach additional sheets conforming to the appropriate official form for each person.

A bankruptcy petition preparer's failure to comply with the provisions of title 11 and the Federal Rules of Bankruptcy Procedure may result in fines or imprisonment or both. 11 U.S.C. §110; 18 U.S.C. §156.

Pending Bankruptcy Case Filed by any Spouse, Partner, or Affiliate of this Debtor. "Affiliate" refers to a related business under a corporate structure. "Partner" refers to a business partnership. Again, you shouldn't use this book if you're filing as a corporation, partnership, or another type of business entity. Any business entity filing bankruptcy must be represented by a lawyer. This is true even if you are the sole owner of your corporate or LLC entity. If your spouse has a bankruptcy case pending anywhere in the country, enter the requested information. Otherwise, type "None" or "N/A" in the first box.

Exhibit A. This is solely for people who are filing for Chapter 11 bankruptcy. Leave it blank.

Exhibit B. This is solely for a person who is represented by an attorney. If you are representing yourself or using a bankruptcy petition preparer, leave this section blank.

Exhibit C. If you own or have in your possession any property that might cause "imminent and identifiable" harm to public health or safety (for example, real estate that is polluted with toxic substances, or explosive devices, such as hand grenades or dynamite), check the "Yes" box, fill in Exhibit C, and attach it to this Petition. If you are unsure about whether a particular piece of property fits the bill, err on the side of inclusion.

Exhibit D. As explained above, debtors filing for Chapter 7 bankruptcy are required to participate in debt counseling sessions within 180 days of their bankruptcy filings. Exhibit D tells the court whether you've complied with this requirement. Instructions for completing Exhibit D are set out below. Check the top box in this part of the petition if you are filing individually and have completed Exhibit D; if you are filing jointly and your spouse has completed Exhibit D, also check the bottom box.

Information Regarding the Debtor—Venue. Most filers will check the top box. Check the middle box if it is appropriate (it won't be for most users of this book, which is intended for individuals and sole proprietors). Leave the bottom box blank. If it applies to you, see a lawyer.

Certification by a Debtor Who Resides as a Tenant of Residential Property. As explained in Ch. 2, certain evictions are allowed to proceed after you file for bankruptcy, despite the automatic stay. The questions in this section are intended to figure out whether your landlord has already gotten a judgment for possession (eviction order), and whether you might be able to postpone the eviction. See Ch. 2 for the information you need to complete these boxes, if they apply.

Third Page

Signature(s) of Debtor(s) (Individual/Joint). You—and your spouse, if you are filing jointly—must sign, date, and provide your telephone number where indicated. By signing, you—and your spouse, if you are filing jointly—declare that you are aware that you may file under other sections of the bankruptcy code, and that you still choose to file for Chapter 7 bankruptcy. (The other types of bankruptcy are described in Ch. 1.) If you think you want to pursue one of those options, put your Chapter 7 petition aside and either consult a lawyer or find a book that explains your proposed alternative in more detail. For example, check out *Chapter 13 Bankruptcy,* by Stephen Elias and Robin Leonard (Nolo).

Signature of Attorney. If you are representing yourself, type "debtor not represented by attorney" in the space for the attorney's signature. If you are represented by a lawyer, fill in the blanks accordingly.

Signature of Non-Attorney Bankruptcy Petition Preparer. If a bankruptcy petition preparer typed your forms, have that person complete this section.

Signature of Debtor (Corporation/Partnership). Enter "N/A" anywhere in this blank.

Exhibit D

At the top of the page, fill in the court name, your name(s) as debtor(s), and the case number (if you have it).

The warning (in bold letters) explains that you have to check one of the five statements regarding credit counseling listed in Exhibit D.

Most people will check **Box 1,** which means you obtained a certificate of completion from a credit counseling agency and can attach the certificate (and any debt repayment plan developed through the agency) to your petition.

Sample Exhibit D—page 1

B 1D (Official Form 1, Exhibit D) (12/09)

United States Bankruptcy Court
Eastern District of California

In re   **Carrie Anne Edwards**

                                     Debtor(s)

Case No. _____

Chapter   **7** _____

EXHIBIT D - INDIVIDUAL DEBTOR'S STATEMENT OF COMPLIANCE WITH CREDIT COUNSELING REQUIREMENT

Warning: You must be able to check truthfully one of the five statements regarding credit counseling listed below. If you cannot do so, you are not eligible to file a bankruptcy case, and the court can dismiss any case you do file. If that happens, you will lose whatever filing fee you paid, and your creditors will be able to resume collection activities against you. If your case is dismissed and you file another bankruptcy case later, you may be required to pay a second filing fee and you may have to take extra steps to stop creditors' collection activities.

Every individual debtor must file this Exhibit D. If a joint petition is filed, each spouse must complete and file a separate Exhibit D. Check one of the five statements below and attach any documents as directed.

■ 1. Within the 180 days **before the filing of my bankruptcy case**, I received a briefing from a credit counseling agency approved by the United States trustee or bankruptcy administrator that outlined the opportunities for available credit counseling and assisted me in performing a related budget analysis, and I have a certificate from the agency describing the services provided to me. *Attach a copy of the certificate and a copy of any debt repayment plan developed through the agency.*

☐ 2. Within the 180 days **before the filing of my bankruptcy case**, I received a briefing from a credit counseling agency approved by the United States trustee or bankruptcy administrator that outlined the opportunities for available credit counseling and assisted me in performing a related budget analysis, but I do not have a certificate from the agency describing the services provided to me. *You must file a copy of a certificate from the agency describing the services provided to you and a copy of any debt repayment plan developed through the agency no later than 14 days after your bankruptcy case is filed.*

☐ 3. I certify that I requested credit counseling services from an approved agency but was unable to obtain the services during the seven days from the time I made my request, and the following exigent circumstances merit a temporary waiver of the credit counseling requirement so I can file my bankruptcy case now. *[Summarize exigent circumstances here.]* ____

If your certification is satisfactory to the court, you must still obtain the credit counseling briefing within the first 30 days after you file your bankruptcy petition and promptly file a certificate from the agency that provided the counseling, together with a copy of any debt management plan developed through the agency. Failure to fulfill these requirements may result in dismissal of your case. Any extension of the 30-day deadline can be granted only for cause and is limited to a maximum of 15 days. Your case may also be dismissed if the court is not satisfied with your reasons for filing your bankruptcy case without first receiving a credit counseling briefing.

☐ 4. I am not required to receive a credit counseling briefing because of: *[Check the applicable statement.]* *[Must be accompanied by a motion for determination by the court.]*

Sample Exhibit D—page 2

☐ Incapacity. (Defined in 11 U.S.C. § 109(h)(4) as impaired by reason of mental illness or mental deficiency so as to be incapable of realizing and making rational decisions with respect to financial responsibilities.);

☐ Disability. (Defined in 11 U.S.C. § 109(h)(4) as physically impaired to the extent of being unable, after reasonable effort, to participate in a credit counseling briefing in person, by telephone, or through the Internet.);

☐ Active military duty in a military combat zone.

☐ 5. The United States trustee or bankruptcy administrator has determined that the credit counseling requirement of 11 U.S.C. § 109(h) does not apply in this district.

I certify under penalty of perjury that the information provided above is true and correct.

Signature of Debtor: **/s/ Carrie Anne Edwards**
                       Carrie Anne Edwards

Date: _____

If you have received counseling but haven't got your certificate yet, check **Box 2**. To remain in bankruptcy, you'll need to obtain and file your certificate (and debt repayment plan if any) within 14 days after your bankruptcy filing date.

Checking **Box 3** indicates that you have requested credit counseling but were unable to obtain the services within seven days after your request, and have not yet received counseling. If you check this box, you'll have to explain why you couldn't complete the credit counseling before your filing date. Read the bold type for additional information regarding your obligations if you wish to remain in bankruptcy.

Box 4 summarizes the exceptions to the credit counseling requirement and asks you to check the appropriate reason.

Box 5 only applies if the credit counseling requirement doesn't apply in your district. This exception is very rare.

Sign and date this document under penalty of perjury and file it with your petition.

Form 6—Schedules

Form 6 refers to a series of schedules that provides the trustee and court with a picture of your current financial situation. Most of the information needed for these schedules is included in the Personal Property Checklist, Property Exemption Worksheet, and Homeowners' Worksheet that you (hopefully) completed in Chs. 3 and 4.

CAUTION
Use the correct address for your creditors.
Many of these schedules ask you to provide addresses for the creditors you list. For a creditor who has dunned you with written requests or demands for payment, you should provide the address that the creditor listed as a contact address on at least two written communications you received from the creditor within the 90-day period prior to your anticipated filing date. If the creditor has not contacted you within that 90-day period, provide the contact address that the creditor gave in the last two communications it sent to you. If you no longer have the address of your original creditor, use the contact address of the most recent creditor (such as a collection agency or an attorney's office). If a creditor is a minor child, simply put "minor child" and the appropriate address. Don't list the child's name.

Schedule A—Real Property

Here you list all the real property you own as of the date you'll file the petition. Don't worry about whether a particular piece of property is exempt; you don't have to claim your exemptions until you get to Schedule C. If you completed the Personal Property Checklist, Property Exemption Worksheet, and Homeowners' Worksheet in Ch. 3 and Ch. 4, get them out. Much of that information goes on Schedule A.

A completed sample of Schedule A and line-by-line instructions follow. Even if you don't own any real estate, you still must complete the top of this form.

Real Property Defined

Real property—land and things permanently attached to land—includes more than just a house. It can also include unimproved land, vacation cabins, condominiums, duplexes, rental property, business property, mobile home park spaces, agricultural land, airplane hangars, and any other buildings permanently attached to land.

You may own real estate even if you can't walk on it, live on it, or get income from it. This might be true, in a case like either of the following:

- You own real estate solely because your spouse owns real estate and you live in a community property state.
- Someone else lives on property that you are entitled to receive in the future under a trust agreement.

There's a separate schedule for leases and time-shares. If you hold a time-share lease in a vacation cabin or property, lease a boat dock, lease underground portions of real estate for mineral or oil exploration, or otherwise lease or rent real estate of any description, don't list it on Schedule A. All leases and time-shares should be listed on Schedule G. (See the instructions for that schedule below.)

⚠ CAUTION

List all of your property. When you complete your paperwork, you must list all your real estate in Schedule A and all of your personal property in Schedule B. Then, to the extent possible, you claim exemptions for that property in Schedule C. In most cases, you will be able to claim all your property as exempt. However, if you fail to disclose a particular property item, you may end up losing it even though you could have claimed it as exempt had you listed it.

💡 TIP

Tab this page. You might want to put a sticky note alongside the instructions for Schedule A, because we'll keep referring back to the instructions on these pages.

In re. (This means "In the matter of.") Type your name, and the name of your spouse if you're filing jointly. "In re [your name(s)]" will be the name of your bankruptcy case.

Case No. If you made an emergency filing, fill in the case number assigned by the court. Otherwise, leave this blank.

➡ SKIP AHEAD

If you don't own any real estate in whole or in part, type "N/A" anywhere in the first column, type "0" in the total box at the bottom of the page, and move on to Schedule B.

Description and Location of Property. For each piece of real property you own, list the type of property—for example, house, farm, or undeveloped lot—and street address. You don't need to include the legal description of the property (the description on the deed).

💡 TIP

List time-shares on Schedule G. Time-shares should be listed on Schedule G rather than on Schedule A. This can be confusing because time-shares sometimes come with deeds and other documents indicating real estate ownership. If you want to keep the time-share, treat it as an "executory contract" and assert that you want to "assume" the contract on your Statement of Intention. The time-share company will probably want you to assign an "assumption" agreement, which should then be filed with the court.

Nature of Debtor's Interest in Property. In this column, you need to provide the legal definition for the interest you (or you and your spouse) have in the real estate. The most common type of interest—outright ownership—is called "fee simple." Even if you still owe money on your mortgage, as long as you have the right to sell the house, leave it to your heirs, and make alterations, your ownership is fee simple. A fee simple interest may be owned by one person or by several people jointly. Normally, when people are listed on a deed as the owners—even if they own the property as joint tenants, tenants in common, or tenants by the entirety—the ownership interest is in fee simple. Other types of real property interests include:

- **Life estate.** This is the right to possess and use property only during your lifetime. You can't sell the property, give it away, or leave it to someone when you die. Instead, when you die, the property passes to whomever was named in the instrument (trust, deed, or will) that created your life estate. This type of ownership is usually created when the sole owner of a piece of real estate wants his surviving spouse to live on the property for the rest of her life, but then have the property pass to his children. In this situation, the surviving spouse has a life estate. Surviving spouses who are beneficiaries of A-B, spousal, or marital bypass trusts have life estates.

- **Future interest.** This is your right to own property sometime in the future. A common future interest is owned by a person who—under the terms of a deed or irrevocable trust—will inherit the property when its current possessor dies. Simply being named in a will or living trust doesn't create a future interest, because the person who signed the deed or trust could amend the document to cut you out.

Sample Schedule A

B6A (Official Form 6A) (12/07)

In re   **Carrie Anne Edwards**   Case No. _____

                                    Debtor

SCHEDULE A - REAL PROPERTY

Except as directed below, list all real property in which the debtor has any legal, equitable, or future interest, including all property owned as a cotenant, community property, or in which the debtor has a life estate. Include any property in which the debtor holds rights and powers exercisable for the debtor's own benefit. If the debtor is married, state whether husband, wife, both, or the marital community own the property by placing an "H," "W," "J," or "C" in the column labeled "Husband, Wife, Joint, or Community." If the debtor holds no interest in real property, write "None" under "Description and Location of Property."

Do not include interests in executory contracts and unexpired leases on this schedule. List them in Schedule G - Executory Contracts and Unexpired Leases.

If an entity claims to have a lien or hold a secured interest in any property, state the amount of the secured claim. See Schedule D. If no entity claims to hold a secured interest in the property, write "None" in the column labeled "Amount of Secured Claim." If the debtor is an individual or if a joint petition is filed, state the amount of any exemption claimed in the property only in Schedule C - Property Claimed as Exempt.

Description and Location of Property	Nature of Debtor's Interest in Property	Husband, Wife, Joint, or Community	Current Value of Debtor's Interest in Property, without Deducting any Secured Claim or Exemption	Amount of Secured Claim
Residence **Location: 3045 Berwick St., Roseville, CA** **Residence is in foreclosure. Sale of property has been scheduled for July 19, 20xx. I am still living in the house and am hoping to modify the mortgage.**	**Fee simple**	-	**130,000.00**	**153,000.00**

Sub-Total >	**130,000.00**	(Total of this page)
Total >	**130,000.00**	

0   continuation sheets attached to the Schedule of Real Property

(Report also on Summary of Schedules)

- **Contingent interest.** This ownership interest doesn't come into existence unless one or more conditions are fulfilled. Wills sometimes leave property to people under certain conditions. If the conditions aren't met, the property passes to someone else. For instance, Emma's will leaves her house to John provided that he takes care of her until her death. If John doesn't care for Emma, the house passes to Emma's daughter Jane. Both John and Jane have contingent interests in Emma's home.
- **Lienholder.** If you are the holder of a mortgage, deed of trust, judgment lien, or mechanic's lien on real estate, you have an ownership interest in the real estate.
- **Easement holder.** If you are the holder of a right to travel on or otherwise use property owned by someone else, you have an easement.
- **Power of appointment.** If you have a legal right, given to you in a will or transfer of property, to sell a specified piece of someone's property, that's called a power of appointment and should be listed.
- **Beneficial ownership under a real estate contract.** This is the right to own property by virtue of having signed a binding real estate contract. Even though the buyer doesn't yet own the property, the buyer does have a "beneficial interest"—that is, the right to own the property once the formalities are completed. For example, property buyers have a beneficial ownership interest in property while the escrow is pending.

If you have trouble figuring out which of these definitions best fits your type of ownership interest, leave the column blank and let the trustee help you sort it out at your 341 hearing.

Husband, Wife, Joint, or Community. If you're not married, put "N/A." If you are married, indicate whether the real estate is owned:
- by the husband (H)
- by the wife (W)
- jointly by husband and wife as joint tenants, tenants in common, or tenants by the entirety (J), or
- jointly by husband and wife as community property (C).

For more information on ownership of real property by married couples, see Ch. 4.

Current Value of Debtor's Interest in Property, without Deducting any Secured Claim or Exemption. Enter the current fair market value of your real estate ownership interest. If you filled in the Homeowners' Worksheet in Ch. 4, use the value you came up with there.

Don't figure in homestead exemptions or any mortgages or other liens on the property. Just put the actual current market value as best you can calculate it. However, you can deduct the costs of sale from the market value and enter the difference, as long as you explain what you did on the schedule. (See Ch. 4 for information on valuing real estate.)

Know What Your Property is Worth Before Filing Bankruptcy

In recent years, real property values have been volatile. This can be problematic. If you don't know what your property would sell for right now (its market value), you won't know how much equity, if any, you have in your home. Filing bankruptcy without knowing what your property is worth can result in an unwelcome surprise, like the loss of your home. For example, if the real estate exemption available to you is $50,000 but you have $100,000 of equity in your home, it's likely that the trustee will sell your home in order to get the $50,000 worth of your equity that is not exempt. A word to the wise: Know what your property is worth before you file. To protect yourself, consider having your property professionally appraised before you file.

If you own the property with someone else who is not joining you in your bankruptcy, list only your ownership share in this column. For example, if you and your brother own a home as joint tenants (each owns 50%), split the property's current market value in half and list that amount here.

If your interest is intangible—for example, you are a beneficiary of real estate held in trust that won't be distributed for many years—enter an estimate provided by a real estate appraiser or put "don't know" and explain why you can't be more precise.

Total. Add the amounts in the fourth column and enter the total in the box at the bottom of the page. The form reminds you that you should also enter this total on the Summary of Schedules (see the instructions for completing the summary, below).

Mobile Home Owners

If you own a mobile home in a park, use the value of the home in its current location. Many parks are located in desirable areas, and a park itself may add value to the motor home even though you have no ownership interest in the park itself. A mobile home that might not be worth much on its own could be worth quite a bit if it's sitting in a fancy park.

Amount of Secured Claim. List mortgages and other debts secured by the property. If there is no secured claim of any type on the real estate, enter "None." If there is, enter separately the amount of each outstanding mortgage, deed of trust, home equity loan, or lien (judgment lien, mechanic's lien, materialmen's lien, tax lien, or the like) that is claimed against the property. If you don't know the balance on your mortgage, deed of trust, or home equity loan, call the lender. To find out the existence and values of liens, visit the land records office in your county and look up the parcel in the records; the clerk can show you how. Or, you can order a title search through a real estate attorney or title insurance company. If you own several pieces of real estate and there is one lien on file against all the real estate, list the full amount of the lien for each separate property item. Don't worry if, taken together, the value of the liens is higher than the value of the property; it's quite common.

How you itemize liens in this schedule won't affect how your property or the liens will be treated in bankruptcy. The idea here is to notify the trustee of all possible liens that may affect your equity in your real estate.

Schedule B—Personal Property

Here you must list and evaluate *all* of your personal property, including property that is security for a debt and property that is exempt. If you didn't fill in the Personal Property Checklist and Property Exemption Worksheet in Ch. 3, turn to that chapter for explanations and suggestions about what property you should list in each of the schedule's categories.

How to List Property That Is Subject to Foreclosure Proceedings

Even if your property is subject to foreclosure proceedings, you still own the property until the foreclosure sale is held and a new deed is recorded either in the lender's name (if the property fails to sell) or in the purchaser's name if the foreclosure auction ends in a successful bid. You should list the property in Schedule A and include all of the required information. You should also explain that the house is in foreclosure and provide the date set for the foreclosure sale (if it has gotten that far) or, if not, when you expect the property to be sold.

CAUTION

Be honest and thorough. When listing all of your stuff on a public document like Schedule B, you might feel tempted to cheat a little. Don't give in to the temptation to "forget" any of your assets. Bankruptcy law doesn't give you the right to decide that an asset isn't worth mentioning. Even if, for example, you've decided that your CD collection is worthless given the advent of the iPod, you still have to list it. You can explain on the form why you think it's worthless. If you omit something and get caught, your case can be dismissed—or your discharge revoked—leaving you with no bankruptcy relief for your current debts. Remember, you can use exemptions to keep much of your property; if no exemption is available, you may be able to buy the property back from the trustee.

A completed sample of Schedule B follows, along with instructions for certain lines that need some explanation. If you need more room, use an attached continuation page, or create a continuation page yourself.

In re and **Case No.** Follow the instructions for Schedule A.

Type of Property. The form lists general categories of personal property. Leave this column as is.

None. If you own no property that fits in a category listed in the first column, enter an "X" in the "None" column. But make sure that you really don't own anything in this category.

Description and Location of Property. List specific items that fall in each general category. If you filled out the Personal Property Checklist and Property Exemption Worksheet in Ch. 3, you already have this information. If not, be sure to go over the Personal Property Checklist, which lists types of property to include in each category. Although the categories in the checklist correspond to the categories in Schedule B, the checklist describes some of them differently (where we felt the Schedule B descriptions weren't clear).

CAUTION

Use the property's replacement value. Although some bankruptcy experts believe that you must use the property's replacement value—what it would cost to purchase the property from a retail vendor, given the property's age and condition—for your estimates on Schedule B, we are not convinced that this is required by the bankruptcy code. The only value that really matters in this context is its "fire sale" value (what the trustee would get for the property in an auction), which is less than the property's replacement value. Despite our view of this matter, we recommend that you at least start with the property's replacement value. If that value renders the property nonexempt, then consider listing the lower "fire sale" value and disclosing that fact along with the description of the property. Chances are that the trustee will choose not to take the property because there would be nothing left to pay the creditors with after you receive your exemption amount. (See Ch. 3 for more on how exemptions work.)

Separately list all items worth $50 or more. Combine small items into larger categories whenever reasonable. For example, you don't need to list every spatula, colander, garlic press, and ice cream scoop; instead, put "kitchen cookware" (unless one of these items is worth more than $50). If you list numerous items in one category (as is likely for household goods and furnishings), you may need to attach a continuation sheet.

For each category of property listed, you must describe where it is located. If your personal property is at your residence, just enter "Residence" or your home address beneath the property description. If someone else holds property for you (for example, you loaned your aunt your color TV), put that person's name and address in this column. The idea is to tell the trustee where all your property is located.

Following are further instructions for filling in some of the blanks.

If You Are Listed on Someone Else's Account

As explained in Ch. 3, if you are named on a parent's bank account (typically, to manage the parent's finances if he or she becomes incapacitated or otherwise needs help), the trustee might believe that account should be part of your bankruptcy estate. To prevent the trustee from getting a false idea about the nature of the account, the best approach is to list it under Item 2 and then describe the true facts, which usually are that the money in the account came from and belongs to the parent, that the bankruptcy filer was only added to the account as a fiduciary (a trusted assistant), and that it would be a breach of the fiduciary duty for the filer to use any of the parent's money for the filer's own purposes.

If the exemptions you are using allow you to exempt bank accounts or cash up to a certain amount, and you have enough of that exemption left over to apply to the money in your parent's account, it makes sense to claim the money in your parent's account as exempt on Schedule C (explained below). The claim of exemption is legally unnecessary, but it will prevent the trustee from trying to prove that the money should be considered part of your bankruptcy estate; even if it is, you'll be able to keep it all.

Sample Schedule B—page 1

B6B (Official Form 6B) (12/07)

In re   **Carrie Anne Edwards**   Case No. _____

                                      Debtor

SCHEDULE B - PERSONAL PROPERTY

Except as directed below, list all personal property of the debtor of whatever kind. If the debtor has no property in one or more of the categories, place an "x" in the appropriate position in the column labeled "None." If additional space is needed in any category, attach a separate sheet properly identified with the case name, case number, and the number of the category. If the debtor is married, state whether husband, wife, both, or the marital community own the property by placing an "H," "W," "J," or "C" in the column labeled "Husband, Wife, Joint, or Community." If the debtor is an individual or a joint petition is filed, state the amount of any exemptions claimed only in Schedule C - Property Claimed as Exempt.

Do not list interests in executory contracts and unexpired leases on this schedule. List them in Schedule G - Executory Contracts and Unexpired Leases.

If the property is being held for the debtor by someone else, state that person's name and address under "Description and Location of Property." If the property is being held for a minor child, simply state the child's initials and the name and address of the child's parent or guardian, such as "A.B., a minor child, by John Doe, guardian." Do not disclose the child's name. See, 11 U.S.C. §112 and Fed. R. Bankr. P. 1007(m).

Type of Property	N O N E	Description and Location of Property	Husband, Wife, Joint, or Community	Current Value of Debtor's Interest in Property, without Deducting any Secured Claim or Exemption
1. Cash on hand		**Cash in wallet**	-	50.00
2. Checking, savings or other financial accounts, certificates of deposit, or shares in banks, savings and loan, thrift, building and loan, and homestead associations, or credit unions, brokerage houses, or cooperatives.		**Bank of America Checking Account Rocklin, California**	-	150.00
		WestAmerica Bank Savings Account Rocklin, California	-	300.00
3. Security deposits with public utilities, telephone companies, landlords, and others.	X			
4. Household goods and furnishings, including audio, video, and computer equipment.		**All items at replacement value**	-	2,450.00
		Stereo system ($300), washer dryer set (200), refrigerator (400), electric stove (250), misc. furniture (couch, 2 chairs) (450), minor appliances (blender, toaster, mixer) (125), vacuum (50), 20 inch TV (75), lawnmower (200), swing set and children's toys (240), snowblower (160) Location: 3045 Berwick St., Rocklin, CA		
		End table (700), rolltop desk (700), bed and bedding (800), oriental rug (2500) Location: 3045 Berwick St., Rocklin, CA	-	4,700.00
5. Books, pictures and other art objects, antiques, stamp, coin, record, tape, compact disc, and other collections or collectibles.		**First edition encyclopedia at rare book store price Location: 3045 Berwick St., Rocklin, CA**	-	1,250.00
6. Wearing apparel.		**Normal clothing at used clothing store prices Location: 3045 Berwick St., Rocklin, CA**	-	800.00
7. Furs and jewelry.		**Diamond necklace at used jewelry store price (800), watch at flea market price (75) Location: 3045 Berwick St., Rocklin, CA**	-	875.00

                                                 Sub-Total >   **10,575.00**

                                                 (Total of this page)

3   continuation sheets attached to the Schedule of Personal Property

Sample Schedule B—page 2

B6B (Official Form 6B) (12/07) - Cont.

In re   **Carrie Anne Edwards**   ,   Case No. _____

                                          Debtor

SCHEDULE B - PERSONAL PROPERTY
(Continuation Sheet)

Type of Property	N O N E	Description and Location of Property	Husband, Wife, Joint, or Community	Current Value of Debtor's Interest in Property, without Deducting any Secured Claim or Exemption
8. Firearms and sports, photographic, and other hobby equipment.		**Mountain bike at used bicycle store price (250), Digital camera priced at eBay (200), sword collection priced at antique store (800) Location: 3045 Berwick St., Rocklin, CA**	-	1,250.00
9. Interests in insurance policies. Name insurance company of each policy and itemize surrender or refund value of each.	X			
10. Annuities. Itemize and name each issuer.	X			
11. Interests in an education IRA as defined in 26 U.S.C. § 530(b)(1) or under a qualified State tuition plan as defined in 26 U.S.C. § 529(b)(1). Give particulars. (File separately the record(s) of any such interest(s). 11 U.S.C. § 521(c).)	X			
12. Interests in IRA, ERISA, Keogh, or other pension or profit sharing plans. Give particulars.		**TIAA/CREF (ERISA Qualified Pension), not in bankruptcy estate**	-	Unknown
		IRA, Bank of America, Rocklin, CA (25,000), not in bankrupcy estate	-	0.00
13. Stock and interests in incorporated and unincorporated businesses. Itemize.		**5,000 shares in BLP Bankruptcy Services, Inc., a close corporation Location of certificates: 3045 Berwick St., Rocklin, CA (valued at $.10 a share)**	-	500.00
14. Interests in partnerships or joint ventures. Itemize.	X			
15. Government and corporate bonds and other negotiable and nonnegotiable instruments.		**Negotiable promissory note from Jonathan Edwards, Carrie's brother, dated 11/3/xx Location: 3045 Berwick St., Rocklin, CA**	-	500.00
16. Accounts receivable.	X			
17. Alimony, maintenance, support, and property settlements to which the debtor is or may be entitled. Give particulars.	X			
18. Other liquidated debts owed to debtor including tax refunds. Give particulars.		**Refund for 2015 taxes (expected but not yet received)**	-	600.00

                                                  Sub-Total >   **2,850.00**
                                           (Total of this page)

Sheet __1__ of __3__ continuation sheets attached
to the Schedule of Personal Property

Sample Schedule B—page 3

B6B (Official Form 6B) (12/07) - Cont.

In re   **Carrie Anne Edwards**   Case No. _____
,
                Debtor

SCHEDULE B - PERSONAL PROPERTY
(Continuation Sheet)

Type of Property	NONE	Description and Location of Property	Husband, Wife, Joint, or Community	Current Value of Debtor's Interest in Property, without Deducting any Secured Claim or Exemption
19. Equitable or future interests, life estates, and rights or powers exercisable for the benefit of the debtor other than those listed in Schedule A - Real Property.	X			
20. Contingent and noncontingent interests in estate of a decedent, death benefit plan, life insurance policy, or trust.	X			
21. Other contingent and unliquidated claims of every nature, including tax refunds, counterclaims of the debtor, and rights to setoff claims. Give estimated value of each.	X			
22. Patents, copyrights, and other intellectual property. Give particulars.		Copyright in book published by Nolo Press (Independent Paralegal's Handbook)	-	1,000.00
23. Licenses, franchises, and other general intangibles. Give particulars.	X			
24. Customer lists or other compilations containing personally identifiable information (as defined in 11 U.S.C. § 101(41A)) provided to the debtor by individuals in connection with obtaining a product or service from the debtor primarily for personal, family, or household purposes.	X			
25. Automobiles, trucks, trailers, and other vehicles and accessories.		2003 23 foot Travel Trailer Location: 3045 Berwick St., Rocklin, CA	-	11,000.00
		2009 Buick LaCrosse (45,000 miles) fully loaded, good condition (replacement value - nada.com) Location: 3045 Berwick St., Rocklin, CA	-	8,000.00
26. Boats, motors, and accessories.	X			
27. Aircraft and accessories.	X			
28. Office equipment, furnishings, and supplies.		Used computer valued at eBay price, used in business	-	800.00
		Copier (used Xerox), used in business	-	300.00
		Sub-Total > (Total of this page)		21,100.00

Sheet __2__ of __3__ continuation sheets attached to the Schedule of Personal Property

Software Copyright (c) 1996-2014 - Best Case, LLC - www.bestcase.com   Best Case Bankruptcy

Sample Schedule B—page 4

B6B (Official Form 6B) (12/07) - Cont.

In re   **Carrie Anne Edwards** _____,   Case No. _____
                                          Debtor

SCHEDULE B - PERSONAL PROPERTY
(Continuation Sheet)

Type of Property	N O N E	Description and Location of Property	Husband, Wife, Joint, or Community	Current Value of Debtor's Interest in Property, without Deducting any Secured Claim or Exemption
29. Machinery, fixtures, equipment, and supplies used in business.	X			
30. Inventory.	X			
31. Animals.	X			
32. Crops - growing or harvested. Give particulars.	X			
33. Farming equipment and implements.	X			
34. Farm supplies, chemicals, and feed.	X			
35. Other personal property of any kind not already listed. Itemize.	X			

Sub-Total >   0.00
(Total of this page)
Total >   34,525.00

Sheet __3__ of __3__ continuation sheets attached
to the Schedule of Personal Property

(Report also on Summary of Schedules)

Items 1 and 2: Explain the source of any cash on hand or money in financial accounts—for example, from wages, Social Security payments, or child support. This will help you (and the trustee) decide later whether any of this money qualifies as exempt property. You must list the amount in your account on the day you file for bankruptcy, even if you have written checks on the account that haven't yet cleared. All money in your accounts on the day you file is property of your bankruptcy estate, and the trustee can take that money unless it's exempt (even if that means you bounce a check or two). (*In re Ruiz*, 455 B.R. 745 (B.A.P. 10th Cir. 2011).)

Item 11: Although an education IRA and a qualified state tuition plan may technically not be part of the bankruptcy estate, list them here anyway. Also, you are required to file any records you have of these interests as attachments to Schedule B.

Item 12: Although ERISA-qualified pension plans, 401(k)s, IRAs, and Keoghs may not be part of your bankruptcy estate, list them here anyway and describe each plan in detail. In the Current Value column, enter the value of the pension, if known. Otherwise, list the value as "undetermined."

Item 13: Include stock options.

Item 16: If you are a sole proprietor or an independent contractor, you likely are owed money by one or more of your customers. Specify each such debt by customer name, the reason for the debt, and the date the debt was incurred. These debts belong to your bankruptcy estate and may be collected by the trustee unless you are able to claim them as exempt.

Item 17: List all child support or alimony arrears—that is, money that should have been paid to you but hasn't been. Specify the dates the payments were due and missed, such as "$250 monthly child support payments for June, July, August, and September 20xx." Also list any debts owed you from a property settlement incurred in a divorce or dissolution.

Item 18: List all money owed to you and not yet paid, other than child support, alimony, and property settlements. If you've obtained a judgment against someone, but haven't been paid, list it here. State the defendant's name, the date of the judgment, the court

that issued the judgment, the amount of the judgment, and the kind of case (such as "car accident"). If you are filing your tax return early in the year and think you'll get a refund, list it here even though you haven't received it yet. If you don't know how much you'll get, provide an estimate if possible. Otherwise, write "undetermined." If your state's exemption system allows you to exempt cash, you can exempt the tax refund on Schedule C (explained below). Incidentally, some people like to use their tax refund to pay off loans from family members. Don't do it. The trustee may be able to demand the money back from the relative on the grounds it was a preference (preferring your relative over your other creditors).

Item 19: An "equitable or future interest" means that sooner or later you will get property that is currently owned by someone else. Your expectation is legally recognized and valuable. For instance, if your parents' trust gives them the right to live in the family home, that's a "life estate." If the trust gives you the home when they die, you have an "equitable interest" in the home while they're alive. "Powers exercisable for the benefit of the debtor" means that a person has been given the power to route property to you, but it hasn't happened by the time you file your bankruptcy petition. In sum, if it looks like property is coming your way eventually, and that property hasn't been listed in Schedule A, list it here.

Item 20: You have a contingent interest in property if, for example, you are named the remainder beneficiary of an irrevocable trust (a trust that can't be undone by the person who created it). It's contingent because you may or may not get anything from the trust—it all depends on whether there's anything left by the time it gets to you. A noncontingent interest means you will get the property sooner or later, for example, under the terms of an insurance policy. Also list here any wills or revocable living trusts on which you are named as a beneficiary. Even though you don't have any right to inherit under these documents (they can be changed at any time prior to the person's death), the trustee wants to know this information because the inheritance becomes part of your bankruptcy estate if the person dies within the six-month period following your bankruptcy filing date.

Item 21: List all claims that you have against others that might end up in a lawsuit. For instance, if you were recently rear-ended in an automobile accident and are struggling with whiplash, you may have a cause of action against the other driver (and that driver's insurer). Failure to list this type of claim here can result in your inability to pursue it after bankruptcy.

Item 22: This question asks about assets commonly known as intellectual property. State what the patent, copyright, trademark, or similar right is for. Give the number assigned by the issuing agency and length of time the patent, copyright, trademark, or other right will last. Keep in mind that both copyright and trademark rights may exist without going through a government agency. If you claim trademark rights through usage, or copyright through the fact that you created the item and reduced it to tangible form, describe them here.

Item 23: List all licenses and franchises, what they cover, the length of time remaining, who they are with, and whether you can transfer them to someone else.

Item 24: Describe customer lists or other compilations containing personally identifiable information that you obtained from people as part of providing them with consumer goods or services.

Items 25–27: Include the make, model, and year of each item.

Item 32: For your crops, list whether they've been harvested, whether they've been sold (and, if so, to whom and for how much), whether you've taken out any loan against them, and whether they are insured.

Husband, Wife, Joint, or Community. If you're not married, put "N/A" at the top of the column.

If you are married and live in a community property state, then property acquired during the marriage is community property and you should put "C" in this column. Gifts and inheritances received by one spouse are separate property, as is property a spouse owned prior to marriage or after separation. Identify this property with an "H" (for husband) or "W" (for wife), as appropriate.

If you live in any state that is not a community property state, write "J" if you own the property jointly with a spouse, and "H" or "W" if a spouse owns that property as an individual.

Current Value of Debtor's Interest in Property, without Deducting any Secured Claim or Exemption. You can take the information requested here from the Property Exemption Worksheet in Ch. 3. List the replacement value of the property, without regard to any secured interests or exemptions. For example, if you own a car with a replacement value of $6,000, you still owe $4,000 on the car note, and your state's motor vehicle exemption is $1,200, put down $6,000 for the market value of the car.

Bankruptcy law technically requires that you use the replacement value of property, which is defined as what it would cost to purchase equivalent property from a retail vendor given its age and condition. Since many types of property can't be purchased from retail vendors (banged up cars and ripped furniture are examples) it's common to value such property at its market value, whatever that is. The fact is, the only value that counts in the end is what the trustee can sell it for, since you will usually be allowed to keep the property unless the trustee could realize enough of a profit to justify its sale.

TIP
List exempt property on Schedule C. If you have property that is exempt, list it on Schedule C as well. If you are unsure about the value of the property, see "How to Exempt Property of Undetermined Value," below.

Total. Add the amounts in this column and put the total in the box at the bottom of the last page. If you used any continuation pages in addition to the preprinted form, remember to attach those pages and include the amounts from those pages in this total.

Schedule C—Property Claimed as Exempt

On this form, you claim all property you think is legally exempt from being sold to pay your unsecured creditors. In the overwhelming majority of Chapter 7 bankruptcies filed by individuals, all—or virtually all—of the debtor's property is exempt.

CAUTION

If you own a home. Be sure to read Ch. 4 before completing Schedule C.

When you work on this form, you'll need to refer frequently to several other documents. Have in front of you:

- the worksheets from Ch. 3 and Ch. 4
- your drafts of Schedules A and B
- the list of state or federal bankruptcy exemptions you'll be using, provided in Appendix A, and
- if you're using a state's exemptions, the additional nonbankruptcy federal exemptions, provided in Appendix A.

Set out below is a sample completed Schedule C and line-by-line instructions.

Looking at the sample Schedule C exemptions, you might notice that a particular exemption can apply to more than one category of personal property from Schedule B. That's because the exemption categories are set up by each state, but the property categories are determined by the feds, who also wrote Schedule B. As a result, the property and exemption categories don't necessarily match up neatly. For example, the California "tools of the trade" exemption (see Appendix A) could apply to a number of the property categories, including Category 28 (Office equipment, furnishings, and supplies), Category 33 (Farming equipment and implements), Category 25 (Automobiles, trucks, trailers and other vehicles, and accessories), and Category 5 (Books, etc.).

In re and **Case No.** Follow the instructions for Schedule A.

Debtor claims the exemptions to which the debtor is entitled under: If you're using the federal exemptions, check the top box. Everybody else, check the second box. See Ch. 3 for information on residency requirements for using a state's exemptions and tips on how to choose between the federal and state exemption systems. As we point out in Ch. 3, if you are living in a state that offers the federal exemption system, but you haven't been there long enough to meet the two-year residency requirement, you can choose the federal system (and check the top box on Schedule C).

Also, if you don't qualify to use any state's exemption system, you can use the federal exemptions, even if the state you're filing in doesn't otherwise allow them. (Ch. 3 explains the situation when this might happen.)

Give Yourself the Benefit of the Doubt

When you claim exemptions, give yourself the benefit of the doubt. If an exemption seems to cover an item of property, claim it. You may find that you're legally entitled to keep much of the property you're deeply attached to, such as your home, car, and family heirlooms.

Your exemption claims will be examined by the trustee and possibly a creditor or two, although historically few creditors monitor bankruptcy proceedings. In close cases, bankruptcy laws require the trustee to honor rather than dishonor your exemption claims. In other words, you're entitled to the benefit of the doubt.

If the trustee or a creditor successfully objects to an exemption claim, you've lost nothing by trying. See Ch. 7 for more on objections to claimed exemptions.

SEE AN EXPERT

Property out of state. You'll generally choose the exemptions of the state you live in when you file as long as you've lived there for at least two years. If you want to protect your equity in a home in a state other than the one you file in, see a lawyer.

Check if debtor claims a homestead exemption that exceeds $155,675. Check this box if all of the following apply:

- The exemptions of the state you are using allow a homestead of more than $155,675.
- You have more than $155,675 equity in your home.
- You acquired your home at least 40 months prior to your bankruptcy filing date.

If you didn't acquire your home at least 40 months before filing, and you didn't purchase it from the proceeds of selling a home in the same state, your homestead exemption may be capped at $155,675,

Sample Schedule C—page 1

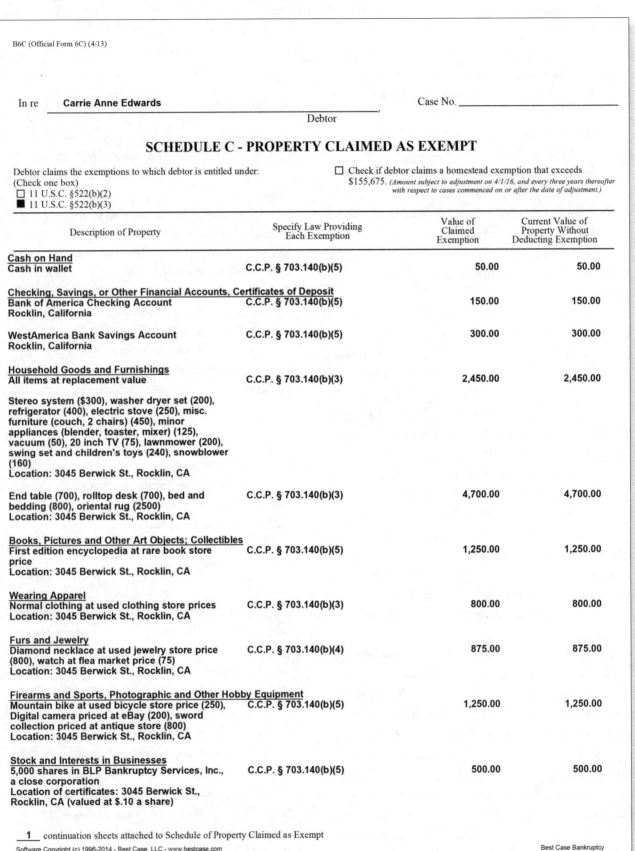

B6C (Official Form 6C) (4/13)

In re **Carrie Anne Edwards**   Case No. _____
_____,
Debtor

SCHEDULE C - PROPERTY CLAIMED AS EXEMPT

Debtor claims the exemptions to which debtor is entitled under: ☐ Check if debtor claims a homestead exemption that exceeds
(Check one box) $155,675. *(Amount subject to adjustment on 4/1/16, and every three years thereafter*
☐ 11 U.S.C. §522(b)(2)   *with respect to cases commenced on or after the date of adjustment.)*
■ 11 U.S.C. §522(b)(3)

Description of Property	Specify Law Providing Each Exemption	Value of Claimed Exemption	Current Value of Property Without Deducting Exemption
Cash on Hand Cash in wallet	C.C.P. § 703.140(b)(5)	50.00	50.00
Checking, Savings, or Other Financial Accounts, Certificates of Deposit Bank of America Checking Account Rocklin, California	C.C.P. § 703.140(b)(5)	150.00	150.00
WestAmerica Bank Savings Account Rocklin, California	C.C.P. § 703.140(b)(5)	300.00	300.00
Household Goods and Furnishings All items at replacement value	C.C.P. § 703.140(b)(3)	2,450.00	2,450.00
Stereo system ($300), washer dryer set (200), refrigerator (400), electric stove (250), misc. furniture (couch, 2 chairs) (450), minor appliances (blender, toaster, mixer) (125), vacuum (50), 20 inch TV (75), lawnmower (200), swing set and children's toys (240), snowblower (160) Location: 3045 Berwick St., Rocklin, CA			
End table (700), rolltop desk (700), bed and bedding (800), oriental rug (2500) Location: 3045 Berwick St., Rocklin, CA	C.C.P. § 703.140(b)(3)	4,700.00	4,700.00
Books, Pictures and Other Art Objects; Collectibles First edition encyclopedia at rare book store price Location: 3045 Berwick St., Rocklin, CA	C.C.P. § 703.140(b)(5)	1,250.00	1,250.00
Wearing Apparel Normal clothing at used clothing store prices Location: 3045 Berwick St., Rocklin, CA	C.C.P. § 703.140(b)(3)	800.00	800.00
Furs and Jewelry Diamond necklace at used jewelry store price (800), watch at flea market price (75) Location: 3045 Berwick St., Rocklin, CA	C.C.P. § 703.140(b)(4)	875.00	875.00
Firearms and Sports, Photographic and Other Hobby Equipment Mountain bike at used bicycle store price (250), Digital camera priced at eBay (200), sword collection priced at antique store (800) Location: 3045 Berwick St., Rocklin, CA	C.C.P. § 703.140(b)(5)	1,250.00	1,250.00
Stock and Interests in Businesses 5,000 shares in BLP Bankruptcy Services, Inc., a close corporation Location of certificates: 3045 Berwick St., Rocklin, CA (valued at $.10 a share)	C.C.P. § 703.140(b)(5)	500.00	500.00

___1___ continuation sheets attached to Schedule of Property Claimed as Exempt

Sample Schedule C—page 2

B6C (Official Form 6C) (4/13) -- Cont.

In re **Carrie Anne Edwards** , Case No. _____
Debtor

SCHEDULE C - PROPERTY CLAIMED AS EXEMPT
(Continuation Sheet)

Description of Property	Specify Law Providing Each Exemption	Value of Claimed Exemption	Current Value of Property Without Deducting Exemption
Government & Corporate Bonds, Other Negotiable & Non-negotiable Inst. Negotiable promissory note from Jonathan Edwards, Carrie's brother, dated 11/3/xx Location: 3045 Berwick St., Rocklin, CA	C.C.P. § 703.140(b)(5)	500.00	500.00
Other Liquidated Debts Owing Debtor Including Tax Refund Refund for 2015 taxes (expected but not yet received)	C.C.P. § 703.140(b)(5)	600.00	600.00
Patents, Copyrights and Other Intellectual Property Copyright in book published by Nolo Press (Independent Paralegal's Handbook)	C.C.P. § 703.140(b)(5)	1,000.00	1,000.00
Automobiles, Trucks, Trailers, and Other Vehicles 2003 23 foot Travel Trailer Location: 3045 Berwick St., Rocklin, CA	C.C.P. § 703.140(b)(5)	11,000.00	11,000.00
Office Equipment, Furnishings and Supplies Used computer valued at eBay price, used in business	C.C.P. § 703.140(b)(5)	800.00	800.00
Copier (used Xerox), used in business	C.C.P. § 703.140(b)(5)	300.00	300.00
Total:		26,525.00	26,525.00

Sheet __1__ of __1__ continuation sheets attached to the Schedule of Property Claimed as Exempt

regardless of the exemption available in the state where your home is located. See Ch. 4 for detailed information on the homestead exemption cap.

The following instructions cover one column at a time. But rather than listing all your exempt property in the first column and then completing the second column before moving on to the third column, you might find it easier to list one exempt item and complete all columns for that item before moving on to the next exempt item.

Description of Property. To describe the property you claim as exempt, take these steps:

Step 1: Turn to Ch. 3 to find out which exemptions are available to you and which property to claim as exempt (if you have already used the Property Exemption Worksheet to identify your exempt property, skip this step).

Step 2: Decide which of the real estate you listed on Schedule A, if any, you want to claim as exempt. Remember that state homestead allowances usually apply only to property you are living in when you file, but that you can use a wildcard exemption for any type of property. Use the same description you used in the Description and Location of Property column of Schedule A.

Step 3: Decide which of the personal property you listed on Schedule B you want to claim as exempt. For each item identified, list both the category of property (preprinted in the Type of Property column) and the specific item, from the Description and Location of Property column. If the exemptions you are using apply to an entire category, such as clothing, simply list "clothing" as the item you are exempting.

Specify Law Providing Each Exemption. You'll find citations to the specific laws that create exemptions in the state and federal exemption lists in Appendix A. Remember to use the rules for choosing your exemptions explained in detail in Ch. 3.

You can simplify this process by entering the name of the statutes you are using at the top of the form. The name is noted at the top of the exemption list you use. For example, you might type "All law references are to the Florida Statutes Annotated unless otherwise noted."

For each item of property you are claiming as exempt, enter the citation (number) of the specific law that creates the exemption, as set out on the exemption list. If you are combining part or all of a wildcard exemption with a regular exemption (which is commonly done in California), list both citations. If the wildcard and the regular exemption have the same citation, list the citation twice and put "wildcard" next to one of the citations. If you use any reference other than one found in the state statutes you are using, such as a federal nonbankruptcy exemption or a court case, list the entire reference for the exempt item.

Value of Claimed Exemption. Claim the full exemption amount allowed, up to the value of the item. The amount allowed is listed in Appendix A.

Bankruptcy law allows married couples to double all exemptions unless the state expressly prohibits it. That means that each of you can claim the entire amount of each exemption, if you are both filing. If your state's chart in Appendix A doesn't say your state forbids doubling, go ahead and double. You are entitled to double all federal exemptions, if you use them.

If you are using part or all of a wildcard exemption in addition to a regular exemption, list both amounts. For example, if the regular exemption for an item of furniture is $200, and you plan to exempt it to $500 using $300 from your state's wildcard exemption, list $200 across from the citation you listed for the regular exemption and $300 across from the citation you listed for the wildcard exemption (or across from the term "wildcard").

How to Exempt Property of Undetermined Value

If you have property that is expensive or impossible to value, you can simply put "undetermined" or "unknown" on Schedule A (real estate) or Schedule B (personal property) and then put the following on Schedule C where you claim the exemption: "Exempt up to its full value under [cite to exemption statute]."

If the exemption available to you for that property is not adequate to cover the property's value, the trustee can file a formal objection and prove his or her case in court. However, trustees are busy folk, and if the trustee doesn't object to your exemption claim within 30 days after your 341 hearing, you may escape with the whole enchilada.

CAUTION

Don't claim more than you need for any particular item. For instance, if you're allowed household furniture up to a total amount of $2,000, don't inflate the value of each item of furniture simply to get to $2,000. Use the values you stated on Schedule B.

Current Value of Property Without Deducting Exemption. Enter the current (replacement) value of the item you are claiming as exempt. For most items, this information is listed on Schedules A and B. However, if you listed the item as part of a group in Schedule B, list it separately here and assign it a separate replacement value.

Schedule D—Creditors Holding Secured Claims

In this schedule, you list all creditors who hold claims secured by your property. This includes:

- holders of a mortgage or deed of trust on your real estate
- creditors who have won lawsuits against you and recorded judgment liens against your property
- doctors or lawyers to whom you have granted a security interest in the outcome of a lawsuit, so that the collection of their fees would be postponed (the expected court judgment is the collateral)
- contractors who have filed mechanics' or materialmen's liens on your real estate
- taxing authorities, such as the IRS, that have obtained tax liens against your property
- creditors with either a purchase-money or non-purchase-money security agreement (see "Nature of Lien" below), and
- all parties who are trying to collect secured debts, such as collection agencies and attorneys.

Line-by-line instructions and a completed sample of Schedule D follow.

In re and **Case No.** Follow instructions for Schedule A.

☐ **Check this box if debtor has no creditors holding secured claims to report on this Schedule D.** Check the box at the bottom of the Schedule's instructions if you have no secured creditors, then skip ahead to Schedule E. Everyone else, keep reading.

Creditor's Name and Mailing Address Including Zip Code, and Account Number. List all secured creditors, preferably in alphabetical order. For each, fill in the last four digits of the account number, if you know it; the creditor's name; and the complete mailing address, including zip code. As mentioned earlier, the mailing address should be the contact address shown on at least two written communications you received from the creditor during the previous 90 days. Call the creditor to get this information if you don't have it.

Credit Card Debts

Most credit card debts, including cards issued by banks, gasoline companies, or department stores, are unsecured and should be listed on Schedule F. Some department stores, however, claim to retain a security interest in all durable goods, such as furniture, appliances, electronics equipment, and jewelry, bought using the store credit card. Also, if you were issued a bank or store credit card as part of a plan to restore your credit, you may have had to post property or cash as collateral for debts incurred on the card. If either of these exceptions apply to you, list the credit card debt on Schedule D. If you are unsure, use Schedule F.

If you have more than one secured creditor for a given debt, list the original creditor first, followed by the other creditors. For example, if you've been sued or hounded by a collection agency, list the information for the collection agency after the original creditor.

If, after typing up your final papers, you discover that you've missed a few creditors, don't retype your papers to preserve perfect alphabetical order. Simply add the creditors at the end. If your creditors don't all fit on the first page of Schedule D, make as many copies of the preprinted continuation page as you need to list them all.

If the creditor is a child, list the child's initials and the name and address of the child's parent or guardian. For example, "A.B., a minor child, by John Doe, Guardian, 111 Alabama Avenue, San Francisco, CA 94732." Don't state the child's name.

Codebtor. Someone who owes money with you probably isn't the first person you think of as your creditor. But if someone else agreed to cosign your loan, lease, or purchase, then creditors can go after your codebtor, who will then look to you to cough up the money. So, if someone else (other than a spouse with whom you are filing jointly) can be legally forced to pay your debt to a listed secured creditor, list that person in the creditor column of this Schedule and put an "X" in this column. You'll also need to list the codebtor as a creditor in Schedules F and H (explained below).

The most common codebtors are:

- cosigners
- guarantors (people who guarantee payment of a loan)
- ex-spouses with whom you jointly incurred debts before divorcing
- joint owners of real estate or other property
- coparties in a lawsuit
- nonfiling spouses in a community property state (most debts incurred by a nonfiling spouse during marriage are considered community debts, making that spouse equally liable with the filing spouse for the debts), and
- nonfiling spouses in states other than community property states, for debts incurred by the filing spouse for basic living necessities such as food, shelter, clothing, and utilities.

Husband, Wife, Joint, or Community. Follow the instructions for Schedule A.

Date Claim Was Incurred, Nature of Lien, and Description and Value of Property Subject to Lien. This column calls for a lot of information for each secured debt. If you list two or more creditors on the same secured claim (such as the lender and a collection agency), simply put ditto marks (") in this column for the second creditor. Let's take these one at a time.

Date Claim Was Incurred. For most claims, the date the claim was incurred is the date you signed the security agreement. If you didn't sign a security agreement with the creditor, the date is most likely the date a contractor or judgment creditor recorded a lien against your property or the date a taxing authority notified you of a tax liability or assessment of taxes due.

Nature of Lien. What kind of property interest does your secured creditor have? Here are the possible answers:

- **First mortgage.** You took out a loan to buy your house. (This is a specific kind of purchase-money security interest.)
- **Second mortgage and HELOC (home equity line of credit).** List these loans as well as any other debt that is secured by your home.

Sample Schedule D

B6D (Official Form 6D) (12/07)

In re   **Carrie Anne Edwards**   Case No. _____

                                   Debtor

SCHEDULE D - CREDITORS HOLDING SECURED CLAIMS

State the name, mailing address, including zip code, and last four digits of any account number of all entities holding claims secured by property of the debtor as of the date of filing of the petition. The complete account number of any account the debtor has with the creditor is useful to the trustee and the creditor and may be provided if the debtor chooses to do so. List creditors holding all types of secured interests such as judgment liens, garnishments, statutory liens, mortgages, deeds of trust, and other security interests.

List creditors in alphabetical order to the extent practicable. If a minor child is a creditor, the child's initials and the name and address of the child's parent or guardian, such as "A.B., a minor child, by John Doe, guardian." Do not disclose the child's name. See, 11 U.S.C. §112 and Fed. R. Bankr. P. 1007(m). If all secured creditors will not fit on this page, use the continuation sheet provided.

If any entity other than a spouse in a joint case may be jointly liable on a claim, place an "X" in the column labeled "Codebtor" ,include the entity on the appropriate schedule of creditors, and complete Schedule H - Codebtors. If a joint petition is filed, state whether the husband, wife, both of them, or the marital community may be liable on each claim by placing an "H", "W", "J", or "C" in the column labeled "Husband, Wife, Joint, or Community".

If the claim is contingent, place an "X" in the column labeled "Contingent". If the claim is unliquidated, place an "X" in the column labeled "Unliquidated". If the claim is disputed, place an "X" in the column labeled "Disputed". (You may need to place an "X" in more than one of these three columns.)

Total the columns labeled "Amount of Claim Without Deducting Value of Collateral" and "Unsecured Portion, if Any" in the boxes labeled "Total(s)" on the last sheet of the completed schedule. Report the total from the column labeled "Amount of Claim" also on the Summary of Schedules and, if the debtor is an individual with primarily consumer debts, report the total from the column labeled "Unsecured Portion" on the Statistical Summary of Certain Liabilities and Related Data.

☐   Check this box if debtor has no creditors holding secured claims to report on this Schedule D.

CREDITOR'S NAME AND MAILING ADDRESS INCLUDING ZIP CODE, AND ACCOUNT NUMBER (See instructions above.)	CODEBTOR	Husband, Wife, Joint, or Community	DATE CLAIM WAS INCURRED, NATURE OF LIEN, AND DESCRIPTION AND VALUE OF PROPERTY SUBJECT TO LIEN	CONTINGENT	UNLIQUIDATED	DISPUTED	AMOUNT OF CLAIM WITHOUT DEDUCTING VALUE OF COLLATERAL	UNSECURED PORTION, IF ANY
Account No. GMAC PO Box 23567 Duchesne, UT 84021	-		November 2009 **Purchase Money Security** 2009 Buick LaCrosse (45,000 miles) fully loaded, good condition (replacement value - nada.com) Location: 3045 Berwick St., Rocklin, CA					
			Value $ 8,000.00				15,000.00	7,000.00
Account No. **Grand Junction Mortgage** 3456 Eighth St Clearlake, CA 95422	-		12/xx **First Mortgage** Residence Location: 3045 Berwick St, Rocklin, CA Residence is in foreclosure. I am seeking a mortgage modification.					
			Value $ 130,000.00				135,000.00	5,000.00
Account No. **Lending Tree** PO Box 3333 Palo Alto, CA 94310	-		12/xx **Second Mortgage** Residence Location: 3045 Berwick St, Rocklin, CA Residence is in foreclosure. I am hoping to modify the mortgage.					
			Value $ 130,000.00				18,000.00	18,000.00
Account No.								
			Value $					

_0_   continuation sheets attached

	Subtotal (Total of this page)	168,000.00	30,000.00
	Total (Report on Summary of Schedules)	168,000.00	30,000.00

- **Purchase-money security interest.** You took out a loan to purchase the property that secures the loan—for example, a car note. The creditor must have perfected the security interest by filing or recording it with the appropriate agency within 20 days. (*Fidelity Financial Services, Inc. v. Fink,* 522 U.S. 211 (1998).) Otherwise, the creditor has no lien and you should list the debt on Schedule F (unsecured debt) instead.

- **Nonpossessory, non-purchase-money security interest.** You borrowed money for a purpose other than buying the collateral. This includes refinanced home loans, home equity loans, or loans from finance companies.

- **Possessory, non-purchase-money security interest.** This is what a pawnshop owner has when you pawn your property.

- **Judgment lien.** This means someone sued you, won a court judgment, and recorded a lien against your property.

- **Tax lien.** This means a federal, state, or local government agency recorded a lien against your property for unpaid taxes.

- **Child support lien.** This means that another parent or a government agency has recorded a lien against your property for unpaid child support.

- **Mechanics' or materialmen's lien.** This means someone performed work on your real property or personal property (for example, a car) but didn't get paid and recorded a lien on that property. Such liens can be an unpleasant surprise if you paid for the work, but your contractor didn't pay a subcontractor who got a lien against your property.

- **Unknown.** If you don't know what kind of lien you are dealing with, put "Don't know nature of lien" after the date. The bankruptcy trustee can help you figure it out later.

Description of Property. Describe each item of real estate and personal property that is collateral for the secured debt listed in the first column. Use the same description you used on Schedule A for real property or Schedule B for personal property. If a creditor's lien covers several items of property, list all items affected by the lien.

Value of Property. The amount you put here must agree with what you listed on Schedule A or B. If you put only the total value of a group of items on Schedule B, you must now get more specific. For instance, if a department store has a secured claim against your washing machine, and you listed your "washer/dryer set" on Schedule B, now you must provide the washer's specific replacement value. You may have already done this on the Property Exemption Worksheet. If not, see the instructions for "Current Value" on Schedule B.

Contingent, Unliquidated, Disputed. Indicate whether the creditor's secured claim is contingent, unliquidated, or disputed. Check all categories that apply. If you're uncertain of which to choose, check the one that seems closest. If none apply, leave them blank. Briefly, these terms mean:

- **Contingent.** The claim depends on some event that hasn't yet occurred and may never occur. For example, if you cosigned a secured loan, you won't be liable unless the principal debtor defaults. Your liability as cosigner is contingent upon the default.

- **Unliquidated.** This means that a debt may exist, but the exact amount hasn't been determined. For example, say you've sued someone for injuries you suffered in an auto accident, but the case isn't over. Your lawyer has taken the case under a contingency fee agreement—he'll get a third of the recovery if you win, and nothing if you lose—and has a security interest in the final recovery amount. The debt to the lawyer is unliquidated because you don't know how much, if anything, you'll win.

- **Disputed.** A claim is disputed if you and the creditor do not agree about the existence or amount of the debt. For instance, suppose the IRS says you owe $10,000 and has put a lien on your property, and you say you owe $500. List the full amount of the lien, not the amount you think you owe. As long as the debt is listed, it will be discharged. So the actual amount in dispute is not that important.

TIP
You're not admitting you owe the debt. You may think you don't really owe a contingent, unliquidated, or disputed debt, or you may not want to "admit" that you owe the debt. By listing a debt here, however, you aren't admitting anything. Instead, you are making sure that, if you owe the debt after all, it will be discharged in your bankruptcy (if it is dischargeable; see Ch. 9). To protect yourself from someone claiming that you admitted to owing a debt you're not sure you owe, check the "disputed" box.

Amount of Claim Without Deducting Value of Collateral. For each secured creditor, list the amount it would take to pay off the secured claim, regardless of what the property is worth. The lender can give you this figure. In some cases, the amount of the secured claim may be more than the property's value.

> **EXAMPLE:** Your original loan was for $13,000, plus $7,000 in interest (for $20,000 total). You've made enough payments so that $15,000 will cancel the debt. You would put $15,000 in this column.

If you have more than one creditor for a given secured claim (for example, the lender and a collection agency), list the debt only for the lender and put ditto marks (") for each subsequent creditor.

Subtotal/Total. Total the amounts in the "Amount of Claim" column for each page. Do not include the amounts represented by the ditto marks if you listed multiple creditors for a single debt. On the final page of Schedule D, which may be the first page or a preprinted continuation page, enter the total of all secured claims.

Unsecured Portion, If Any. If the replacement value of the collateral is equal to or greater than the amount of the claim, enter "0," meaning that the creditor's claim is fully secured. If the replacement value of the collateral is less than the amount of the claim(s) listed, enter the difference here.

How to List Creditors Associated With Foreclosed or Repossessed Property

Until your property is sold in a foreclosure sale and a deed has been recorded showing a transfer of ownership to the lender or new purchaser, you still own the property and any mortgages on the property are considered to be secured debts. You must list all lenders, mortgage servicers, foreclosing trustees, and attorneys listed on foreclosure papers as secured creditors on Schedule D. You should list the amounts of the mortgages only once, however. After a deed has been recorded showing that you no longer own the property, your mortgage debt is no longer secured debt, and you should list all these parties on Schedule F as unsecured creditors.

The same is true with repossessed cars. Once you no longer own the car, the car note gets listed on Schedule F.

> **EXAMPLE:** If the current value of your car is $5,000 but you still owe $6,000 on your car loan, enter $1,000 in this column ($6,000–$5,000). This is the amount of the loan that is unsecured by the collateral (your car).

If you list an amount in this column for a creditor, do not list this amount again on Schedule F (where you will list all other creditors with unsecured claims). Otherwise, this unsecured amount will be listed twice.

Schedule E—Creditors Holding Unsecured Priority Claims

Schedule E identifies certain creditors who may be entitled to be paid first—by the trustee—out of your nonexempt assets. Even if you don't have any nonexempt assets to be distributed, you still need to fill this form out if you have any unsecured priority debts.

Set out below are a sample completed Schedule E and line-by-line instructions.

In re and **Case No.** Follow the instructions for Schedule A.

☐ **Check this box if debtor has no creditors holding unsecured priority claims to report on this Schedule E.** Priority claims are claims that must be paid first in your bankruptcy case. The most common examples are unsecured income tax debts and past-due alimony or child support. There are several other categories of priority debts, however. Read further to figure out whether or not you can check this box.

Types of priority claims. These are the categories of priority debts, as listed on Schedule E. Check the appropriate box on the form if you owe a debt in that category.

☐ **Domestic support obligations.** Check this box for claims for domestic support that you owe to, or that are recoverable by, a spouse, former spouse, or child; the parent, legal guardian, or responsible relative of such a child; or a governmental unit to whom such a domestic support claim has been assigned.

☐ **Extensions of credit in an involuntary case.** Don't check this box. You are filing a voluntary, not an involuntary, bankruptcy case.

☐ **Wages, salaries, and commissions.** If you own a business and owe a current or former employee wages, vacation pay, or sick leave that was earned within 180 days before you filed your petition or within 180 days of the date you ceased your business, check this box. If you owe money to an independent contractor who did work for you, and the money was earned within 180 days before you filed your petition or within 180 days of the date you ceased your business, check this box only if, in the 12 months before you file for bankruptcy, this independent contractor earned at least 75% of his or her total independent contractor receipts from you. Only the first $12,475 owed per employee or independent contractor is a priority debt.

☐ **Contributions to employee benefit plans.** Check this box if you own a business and you owe contributions to an employee benefit fund for services rendered by an employee within 180 days before you filed your petition, or within 180 days of the date you ceased your business.

☐ **Certain farmers and fishermen.** Check this box only if you operate or operated a grain storage facility and owe a grain producer, or you operate or operated a fish produce or storage facility and owe a U.S. fisherman for fish or fish products. Only the first $6,150 owed per person is a priority debt.

☐ **Deposits by individuals.** If you took money from people who planned to purchase, lease, or rent goods or services from you that you never delivered, you may owe a priority debt. For the debt to qualify as a priority, the goods or services must have been planned for personal, family, or household use. Only the first $2,775 owed (per person) is a priority debt.

☐ **Taxes and certain other debts owed to governmental units.** Check this box if you owe unsecured back taxes or if you owe any other debts to the government, such as fines imposed for driving under the influence of drugs or alcohol. Not all tax debts are unsecured priority claims. For example, if the IRS has recorded a lien against your real property, and the equity in your property fully covers the amount of your tax debt, your debt is a secured debt. It should be on Schedule D, not on this schedule.

☐ **Commitments to maintain the capital of an insured depository institution.** Don't check this box. It is for business bankruptcies.

☐ **Claims for death or personal injury while debtor was intoxicated.** Check this box if there are claims against you for death or personal injury resulting from your operation of a motor vehicle or vessel while intoxicated from using alcohol, a drug, or another substance. This priority doesn't apply to property damage—only to personal injury or death.

If you didn't check any of the priority debt boxes, go back and check the first box, showing you have no unsecured priority claims to report. Then go on to Schedule F.

If you checked any of the priority debt boxes, make as many photocopies of the continuation page as the number of priority debt boxes you checked. Complete a separate sheet for each type of priority debt, using the following instructions:

In re and **Case No.** Follow the instructions for Schedule A.

Sample Schedule E—page 1

B6E (Official Form 6E) (4/13)

In re   **Carrie Anne Edwards** _____   Case No. _____

                                             Debtor

SCHEDULE E - CREDITORS HOLDING UNSECURED PRIORITY CLAIMS

A complete list of claims entitled to priority, listed separately by type of priority, is to be set forth on the sheets provided. Only holders of unsecured claims entitled to priority should be listed in this schedule. In the boxes provided on the attached sheets, state the name, mailing address, including zip code, and last four digits of the account number, if any, of all entities holding priority claims against the debtor or the property of the debtor, as of the date of the filing of the petition. Use a separate continuation sheet for each type of priority and label each with the type of priority.

The complete account number of any account the debtor has with the creditor is useful to the trustee and the creditor and may be provided if the debtor chooses to do so. If a minor child is a creditor, state the child's initials and the name and address of the child's parent or guardian, such as "A.B., a minor child, by John Doe, guardian." Do not disclose the child's name. See, 11 U.S.C. §112 and Fed. R. Bankr. P. 1007(m).

If any entity other than a spouse in a joint case may be jointly liable on a claim, place an "X" in the column labeled "Codebtor," include the entity on the appropriate schedule of creditors, and complete Schedule H-Codebtors. If a joint petition is filed, state whether the husband, wife, both of them, or the marital community may be liable on each claim by placing an "H," "W," "J," or "C" in the column labeled "Husband, Wife, Joint, or Community." If the claim is contingent, place an "X" in the column labeled "Contingent." If the claim is unliquidated, place an "X" in the column labeled "Unliquidated." If the claim is disputed, place an "X" in the column labeled "Disputed." (You may need to place an "X" in more than one of these three columns.)

Report the total of claims listed on each sheet in the box labeled "Subtotals" on each sheet. Report the total of all claims listed on this Schedule E in the box labeled "Total" on the last sheet of the completed schedule. Report this total also on the Summary of Schedules.

Report the total of amounts entitled to priority listed on each sheet in the box labeled "Subtotals" on each sheet. Report the total of all amounts entitled to priority listed on this Schedule E in the box labeled "Totals" on the last sheet of the completed schedule. Individual debtors with primarily consumer debts report this total also on the Statistical Summary of Certain Liabilities and Related Data.

Report the total of amounts not entitled to priority listed on each sheet in the box labeled "Subtotals" on each sheet. Report the total of all amounts not entitled to priority listed on this Schedule E in the box labeled "Totals" on the last sheet of the completed schedule. Individual debtors with primarily consumer debts report this total also on the Statistical Summary of Certain Liabilities and Related Data.

☐ Check this box if debtor has no creditors holding unsecured priority claims to report on this Schedule E.

TYPES OF PRIORITY CLAIMS (Check the appropriate box(es) below if claims in that category are listed on the attached sheets)

■ **Domestic support obligations**

Claims for domestic support that are owed to or recoverable by a spouse, former spouse, or child of the debtor, or the parent, legal guardian, or responsible relative of such a child, or a governmental unit to whom such a domestic support claim has been assigned to the extent provided in 11 U.S.C. § 507(a)(1).

☐ **Extensions of credit in an involuntary case**

Claims arising in the ordinary course of the debtor's business or financial affairs after the commencement of the case but before the earlier of the appointment of a trustee or the order for relief. 11 U.S.C. § 507(a)(3).

☐ **Wages, salaries, and commissions**

Wages, salaries, and commissions, including vacation, severance, and sick leave pay owing to employees and commissions owing to qualifying independent sales representatives up to $12,475* per person earned within 180 days immediately preceding the filing of the original petition, or the cessation of business, whichever occurred first, to the extent provided in 11 U.S.C. § 507(a)(4).

☐ **Contributions to employee benefit plans**

Money owed to employee benefit plans for services rendered within 180 days immediately preceding the filing of the original petition, or the cessation of business, whichever occurred first, to the extent provided in 11 U.S.C. § 507(a)(5).

☐ **Certain farmers and fishermen**

Claims of certain farmers and fishermen, up to $6,150* per farmer or fisherman, against the debtor, as provided in 11 U.S.C. § 507(a)(6).

☐ **Deposits by individuals**

Claims of individuals up to $2,775* for deposits for the purchase, lease, or rental of property or services for personal, family, or household use, that were not delivered or provided. 11 U.S.C. § 507(a)(7).

■ **Taxes and certain other debts owed to governmental units**

Taxes, customs duties, and penalties owing to federal, state, and local governmental units as set forth in 11 U.S.C. § 507(a)(8).

☐ **Commitments to maintain the capital of an insured depository institution**

Claims based on commitments to the FDIC, RTC, Director of the Office of Thrift Supervision, Comptroller of the Currency, or Board of Governors of the Federal Reserve System, or their predecessors or successors, to maintain the capital of an insured depository institution. 11 U.S.C. § 507 (a)(9).

☐ **Claims for death or personal injury while debtor was intoxicated**

Claims for death or personal injury resulting from the operation of a motor vehicle or vessel while the debtor was intoxicated from using alcohol, a drug, or another substance. 11 U.S.C. § 507(a)(10).

* Amount subject to adjustment on 4/01/16, and every three years thereafter with respect to cases commenced on or after the date of adjustment.

                                       2____ continuation sheets attached

Sample Schedule E—page 2

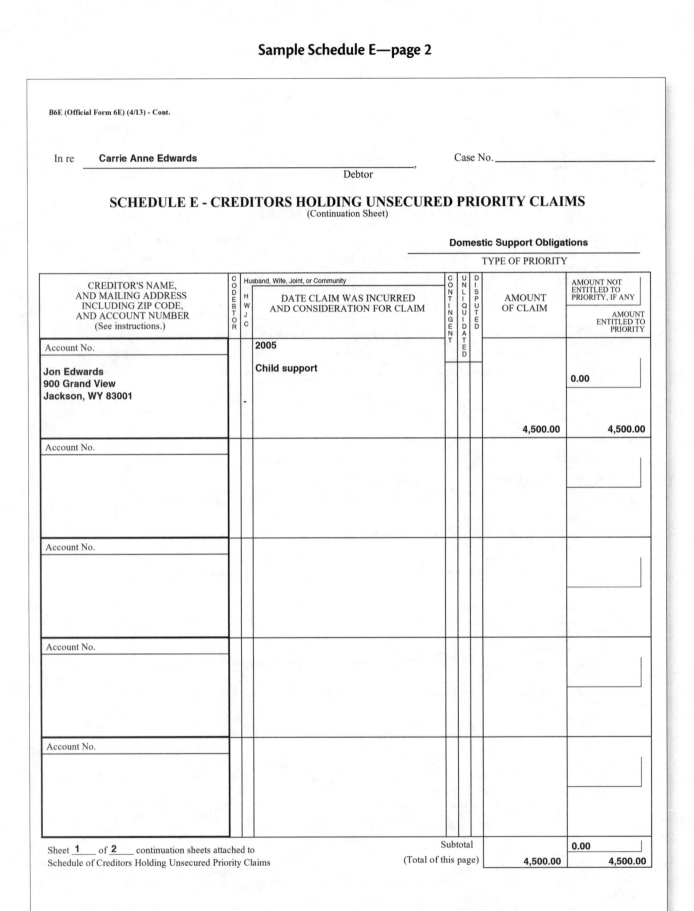

B6E (Official Form 6E) (4/13) - Cont.

In re **Carrie Anne Edwards** Case No. _____
                                      Debtor

SCHEDULE E - CREDITORS HOLDING UNSECURED PRIORITY CLAIMS
(Continuation Sheet)

Domestic Support Obligations

TYPE OF PRIORITY

CREDITOR'S NAME, AND MAILING ADDRESS INCLUDING ZIP CODE, AND ACCOUNT NUMBER (See instructions.)	CODEBTOR	Husband, Wife, Joint, or Community	DATE CLAIM WAS INCURRED AND CONSIDERATION FOR CLAIM	CONTINGENT	UNLIQUIDATED	DISPUTED	AMOUNT OF CLAIM	AMOUNT NOT ENTITLED TO PRIORITY, IF ANY / AMOUNT ENTITLED TO PRIORITY
Account No. Jon Edwards 900 Grand View Jackson, WY 83001		-	2005 Child support				4,500.00	0.00 4,500.00
Account No.								
Account No.								
Account No.								
Account No.								

Sheet **1** of **2** continuation sheets attached to
Schedule of Creditors Holding Unsecured Priority Claims

Subtotal (Total of this page) | 4,500.00 | 0.00 / 4,500.00

Sample Schedule E—page 3

B6E (Official Form 6E) (4/13) - Cont.

In re **Carrie Anne Edwards** ,   Case No. _____
Debtor

SCHEDULE E - CREDITORS HOLDING UNSECURED PRIORITY CLAIMS
(Continuation Sheet)

Taxes and Certain Other Debts
Owed to Governmental Units

TYPE OF PRIORITY

CREDITOR'S NAME, AND MAILING ADDRESS INCLUDING ZIP CODE, AND ACCOUNT NUMBER (See instructions.)	CODEBTOR	Husband, Wife, Joint, or Community (HWJC)	DATE CLAIM WAS INCURRED AND CONSIDERATION FOR CLAIM	CONTINGENT	UNLIQUIDATED	DISPUTED	AMOUNT OF CLAIM	AMOUNT NOT ENTITLED TO PRIORITY, IF ANY	AMOUNT ENTITLED TO PRIORITY
Account No. **IRS Columbus, OH 43266**		-	April 15, 20XX tax liability and interest				3,000.00	0.00	3,000.00
Account No.									
Account No.									
Account No.									
Account No.									

Sheet **2** of **2** continuation sheets attached to Schedule of Creditors Holding Unsecured Priority Claims

	Subtotal (Total of this page)	3,000.00	0.00	3,000.00
	Total (Report on Summary of Schedules)	7,500.00	0.00	7,500.00

Nondischargeable Student Loans Are Not Priority Debts

Just because a debt is not dischargeable in bankruptcy, does not make it a priority debt. This often causes confusion as some debtors want to put nondischargeable debts (like student loans) on Schedule E. For example, student loans (which are garden variety unsecured, nonpriority debts) should be listed on Schedule F (not Schedule E), even though they are usually nondischargeable. The same is true for debts arising from drunk driving and fraud, overpayments by government agencies, and traffic tickets and other criminal offenses. Only the debts that are identified on Schedule E are considered priority debts.

Type of Priority. Insert the category for one of the boxes you checked (for example, "Domestic support obligations").

Creditor's Name, Mailing Address Including Zip Code, and Account Number. List the name and complete mailing address (including zip code) of each priority creditor, as well as the account number, if you know it. The address should be the one provided in two written communications you have received from the creditor within the past 90 days, if possible. You may have more than one priority creditor for a given debt. For example, if you've been sued or hounded by a collection agency, list the collection agency in addition to the original creditor.

If the creditor is a child, list the child's initials and the name and address of the child's parent or guardian. For example, "A.B., a minor child, by John Doe, Guardian, 111 Alabama Avenue, San Francisco, CA 94732." Don't state the child's name.

Codebtor. If someone else can be legally forced to pay your debt to a priority creditor, enter an "X" in this column and list the codebtor in the creditor column of this schedule. You'll also need to list the codebtor as a creditor in Schedule F and Schedule H. Common codebtors are listed in the instructions for Schedule D.

Husband, Wife, Joint, or Community. Follow the instructions for Schedule A.

Date Claim Was Incurred and Consideration for Claim. State the date you incurred the debt—this may be a specific date or a period of time. Also briefly state what the debt is for. For example, "goods purchased," "hours worked for me," or "deposit for my services."

Contingent, Unliquidated, Disputed. Follow the instructions for Schedule D.

Amount of Claim. For each priority debt other than taxes, list the amount it would take to pay off the debt in full, even if it's more than the priority limit. For taxes, list only the amount that is unsecured (and therefore a priority). You should list the secured amount on Schedule D. If the amount isn't determined, write "not yet determined" in this column.

Amount Entitled to Priority. If the priority claim is larger than the maximum indicated on the first page of Schedule E (for example, $12,475 of wages owed to each employee), put the maximum here. If the claim is less than the maximum, put the amount you entered in the Total Amount of Claim column here.

Amount Not Entitled to Priority, If Any. List any portion of the debt that is not entitled to priority here. For example, if you owe an employee $15,000 in wages, only the first $12,475 is entitled to priority. That amount should be listed in the "Amount Entitled to Priority" column; here, you would list the remaining $2,525.

Subtotal/Total. At the bottom of each continuation page, list the subtotals of the "Amount of Claim," "Amount Entitled to Priority," and "Amount Not Entitled to Priority, If Any" columns. Enter the total amounts for each of these categories on the final page of Schedule E.

Schedule F—Creditors Holding Unsecured Nonpriority Claims

In this schedule, list all possible creditors you haven't listed in Schedules D or E. You should include debts that are or may be nondischargeable, such as a student loan. Even if you believe that you don't owe the debt or you owe only a small amount and intend to pay it off, you must include it here. It's essential that you list every creditor to whom you owe, or possibly owe, money. The only way you can legitimately leave off a creditor is if your balance owed is $0.

> **TIP**
> **You can pay creditors after you file.** You may be tempted to leave some creditors (like your doctor, favorite electrician, or a relative who loaned you money) off of your bankruptcy schedules, in order to stay in their good graces. That's not a good idea: You must list all of your creditors. However, there is nothing to prevent you from paying a discharged debt after your bankruptcy is complete. The only effect bankruptcy has on the debt is that the creditor can't pursue it through collections or place it on your credit report. If you plan to pay certain creditors after your bankruptcy, let them know before you file. This will lessen the sting of your bankruptcy filing. Although your promise is unenforceable, creditors will gladly accept your money.

Even if you plan (and want) to repay a particular creditor, list the debt and get it discharged anyway. The creditor will be legally barred from trying to collect the debt, but you can always pay the debt voluntarily out of property or income you receive after you file for bankruptcy.

> **EXAMPLE:** Peter owes his favorite aunt $8,000. Peter files for bankruptcy and lists the debt, which is discharged when Peter's bankruptcy is over. Peter can voluntarily repay the $8,000 out of wages he earns any time after he files, because the wages he earns after filing are not part of his bankruptcy estate. He cannot use property that belongs to the bankruptcy estate, however, until he receives a discharge. The important thing is, repayment is completely voluntary on Peter's part. Peter's aunt can't sue him in court to enforce payment of the debt.

Inadvertent errors or omissions on this schedule can come back to haunt you. If you don't list a debt you owe to a creditor, it might not be discharged in bankruptcy if your estate has assets that are distributed to your other creditors by the trustee, or if the creditor is otherwise prejudiced by being left out (although it is sometimes possible in these circumstances to reopen

the bankruptcy and include the creditor). Also, leaving a creditor off the schedule might raise suspicions that you deliberately concealed information, perhaps to give that creditor preferential treatment in violation of bankruptcy rules. (See Ch. 9 for more on what happens to debts not listed on your schedules.)

> **TIP**
> **Use your credit reports.** It is often a good idea to order your credit report in order to determine whether any creditors who are unknown to you claim that you owe them money. The more complete you are in listing possible creditors (even if you've never heard from them), the more powerful your bankruptcy discharge will be. You can get a free annual credit report from each of the three major credit reporting agencies at www.annualcreditreport.com. Beware of other imposter sites, like www.freecreditreport.com, that sound like www.annualcreditreport.com. Most of these sites charge you for your report or require you to sign up for monthly "memberships" in order to get your report.

It's also a good idea to get a credit report if you are having problems finding a creditor's recent address. Finally, it's not uncommon for the same debt to be listed two or more times on the same report. If there are two different addresses, list both addresses on your bankruptcy matrix but only list the one debt on your Schedule F. (For more information on credit reports and how to obtain them, see Ch. 8.) Don't rely exclusively on credit reports, however; you must disclose every debt on your bankruptcy forms, whether or not it appears in a credit report.

Below are a sample completed Schedule F and line-by-line instructions. Use as many preprinted continuation pages as you need.

In re and **Case No.** Follow the instructions for Schedule A.

☐ **Check this box if debtor has no creditors holding unsecured claims to report on this Schedule F.** Check this box if you have no unsecured nonpriority debts. This would be very rare.

Creditor's Name, Mailing Address Including Zip Code, and Last Four Digits of Account Number. List, preferably in alphabetical order, the name and complete mailing address of each unsecured creditor, as well as the last four digits of the account number (if you know it).

If you have more than one unsecured creditor for a given debt, list the original creditor first, followed by the other creditors. For example, for a particular debt, you might have the name, address, and account number for the original creditor, a collection agency run by the original creditor, an independent collection agency, an attorney debt collector, and an attorney who has sued you.

It's best to list all the creditors, because it never hurts to be thorough. But you could omit the intermediate collectors and just list the original creditor and the latest collector or attorney. Or, if you no longer have contact information for the original creditor, listing the latest collector will do.

When you are typing your final papers, if you get to the end and discover that you left a creditor off, don't start all over again in search of perfect alphabetical order. Just add the creditor to the end of the list.

Creditors That Are Often Overlooked

One debt may involve several different creditors. Remember to include:

- your ex-spouse, if you are still obligated under a divorce decree or settlement agreement to pay joint debts, turn any property over to your ex, or make payments as part of your property division
- anyone who has cosigned a promissory note or loan application you signed
- any holder of a loan or promissory note that you cosigned for someone else
- the original creditor, anybody to whom the debt has been assigned or sold, and any other person (such as a bill collector or an attorney) trying to collect the debt, and
- anyone who may sue you because of a car accident, business dispute, or the like.

Codebtor. If someone else can be legally forced to pay your debt to a listed unsecured creditor, enter an "X" in this column and list the codebtor as a creditor in this schedule. Also, list the codebtor in Schedule H. The instructions for Schedule D list common codebtors.

Husband, Wife, Joint, or Community. Follow the instructions for Schedule A.

Date Claim Was Incurred and Consideration for Claim. If Claim Is Subject to Setoff, So State. State when the debt was incurred. It may be one date or a period of time. With credit card debts, put the approximate time over which you ran up the charges, unless the unpaid charges were made on one or two specific dates. Then state what the debt was for. You can be general ("clothes" or "household furnishings") or specific ("refrigerator" or "teeth capping").

If you are entitled to a setoff against the debt—that is, the creditor owes you some money, too—list the amount and why you think you are entitled to the setoff. If there is more than one creditor for a single debt, put ditto marks (") in this column for the subsequent creditors.

Contingent, Unliquidated, Disputed. Follow the instructions for Schedule D.

Amount of Claim. List the amount of the debt claimed by the creditor even if you dispute the debt. That way you can be sure that the entire debt is discharged (assuming it is dischargeable). If you aren't sure of the amount, don't lose sleep over it. As long as you list the debt, it will be discharged (again, assuming it is dischargeable). For instance if the debt is $3,000 and you list it as $2,000, the entire debt of $3,000 will be discharged. If there's more than one creditor for a single debt, put the debt amount across from the original creditor and put ditto marks (") across from each subsequent creditor you have listed. Be as precise as possible when stating the amount. If you must approximate, write "approx." after the amount.

Sample Schedule F—page 1

B6F (Official Form 6F) (12/07)

In re   **Carrie Anne Edwards**   ,   Case No._____

                                       Debtor

SCHEDULE F - CREDITORS HOLDING UNSECURED NONPRIORITY CLAIMS

State the name, mailing address, including zip code, and last four digits of any account number, of all entities holding unsecured claims without priority against the debtor or the property of the debtor, as of the date of filing of the petition. The complete account number of any account the debtor has with the creditor is useful to the trustee and the creditor and may be provided if the debtor chooses to do so. If a minor child is a creditor, state the child's initials and the name and address of the child's parent or guardian, such as "A.B., a minor child, by John Doe, guardian." Do not disclose the child's name. See, 11 U.S.C. §112 and Fed. R. Bankr. P. 1007(m). Do not include claims listed in Schedules D and E. If all creditors will not fit on this page, use the continuation sheet provided.

If any entity other than a spouse in a joint case may be jointly liable on a claim, place an "X" in the column labeled "Codebtor," include the entity on the appropriate schedule of creditors, and complete Schedule H - Codebtors. If a joint petition is filed, state whether the husband, wife, both of them, or the marital community may be liable on each claim by placing an "H," "W," "J," or "C" in the column labeled "Husband, Wife, Joint, or Community."

If the claim is contingent, place an "X" in the column labeled "Contingent." If the claim is unliquidated, place an "X" in the column labeled "Unliquidated." If the claim is disputed, place an "X" in the column labeled "Disputed." (You may need to place an "X" in more than one of these three columns.)

Report the total of all claims listed on this schedule in the box labeled "Total" on the last sheet of the completed schedule. Report this total also on the Summary of Schedules and, if the debtor is an individual with primarily consumer debts, report this total also on the Statistical Summary of Certain Liabilities and Related Data.

☐   Check this box if debtor has no creditors holding unsecured claims to report on this Schedule F.

CREDITOR'S NAME, MAILING ADDRESS INCLUDING ZIP CODE, AND ACCOUNT NUMBER (See instructions above.)	CODEBTOR	Husband, Wife, Joint, or Community		DATE CLAIM WAS INCURRED AND CONSIDERATION FOR CLAIM. IF CLAIM IS SUBJECT TO SETOFF, SO STATE.	CONTINGENT	UNLIQUIDATED	DISPUTED	AMOUNT OF CLAIM
		H W	J C					
Account No. **Alan Accountant** **5 Green St.** **Cleveland, OH 44118**	-			**4 /XX** **Tax preparation**				**500.00**
Account No. **41 89-0000-2613-5556** **American Allowance** **PO Box 1** **New York, NY 10001**	-			**1/xx to 4/xx** **credit card charges**				**5,600.00**
Account No. **Angel of Mercy Hospital** **4444 Elevisior St.** **Belmont, CA 94003**	-			**12/xx** **uninsured surgery and medical treatment**				**34,000.00**
Account No. **Bob Jones III** **4566 Fifth Ave.** **New York, NY 10020**	-			**5/xx** **Auto accident--negligence claim**				**75,000.00**
2 continuation sheets attached					Subtotal (Total of this page)			**115,100.00**

Sample Schedule F—page 2

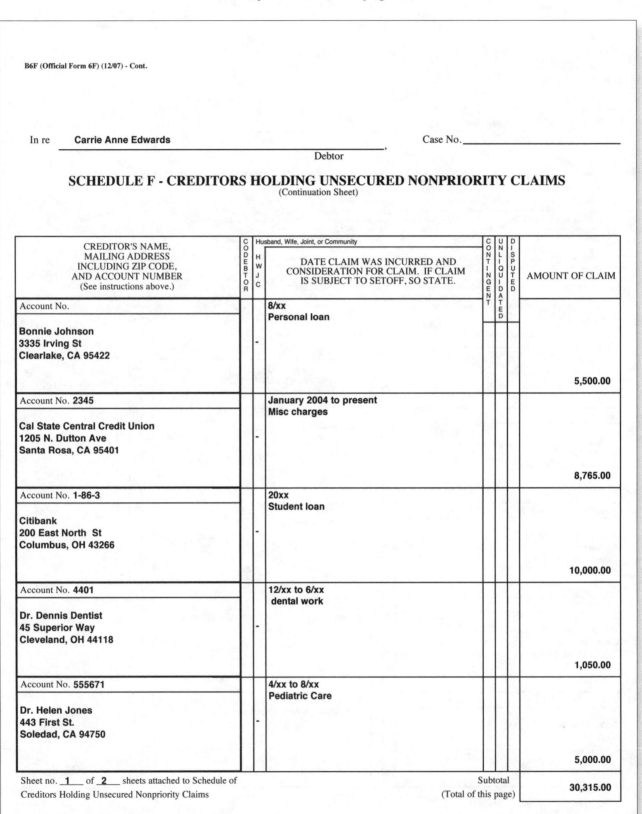

B6F (Official Form 6F) (12/07) - Cont.

In re   **Carrie Anne Edwards**   ,   Case No. _____
                                      Debtor

SCHEDULE F - CREDITORS HOLDING UNSECURED NONPRIORITY CLAIMS
(Continuation Sheet)

CREDITOR'S NAME, MAILING ADDRESS INCLUDING ZIP CODE, AND ACCOUNT NUMBER (See instructions above.)	CODEBTOR	H W J C	DATE CLAIM WAS INCURRED AND CONSIDERATION FOR CLAIM. IF CLAIM IS SUBJECT TO SETOFF, SO STATE.	CONTINGENT	UNLIQUIDATED	DISPUTED	AMOUNT OF CLAIM
Account No. **Bonnie Johnson** **3335 Irving St** **Clearlake, CA 95422**		-	**8/xx** **Personal loan**				**5,500.00**
Account No. **2345** **Cal State Central Credit Union** **1205 N. Dutton Ave** **Santa Rosa, CA 95401**		-	**January 2004 to present** **Misc charges**				**8,765.00**
Account No. **1-86-3** **Citibank** **200 East North St** **Columbus, OH 43266**		-	**20xx** **Student loan**				**10,000.00**
Account No. **4401** **Dr. Dennis Dentist** **45 Superior Way** **Cleveland, OH 44118**		-	**12/xx to 6/xx** **dental work**				**1,050.00**
Account No. **555671** **Dr. Helen Jones** **443 First St.** **Soledad, CA 94750**		-	**4/xx to 8/xx** **Pediatric Care**				**5,000.00**

Sheet no. __1__ of __2__ sheets attached to Schedule of Creditors Holding Unsecured Nonpriority Claims

Subtotal
(Total of this page)   **30,315.00**

Sample Schedule F—page 3

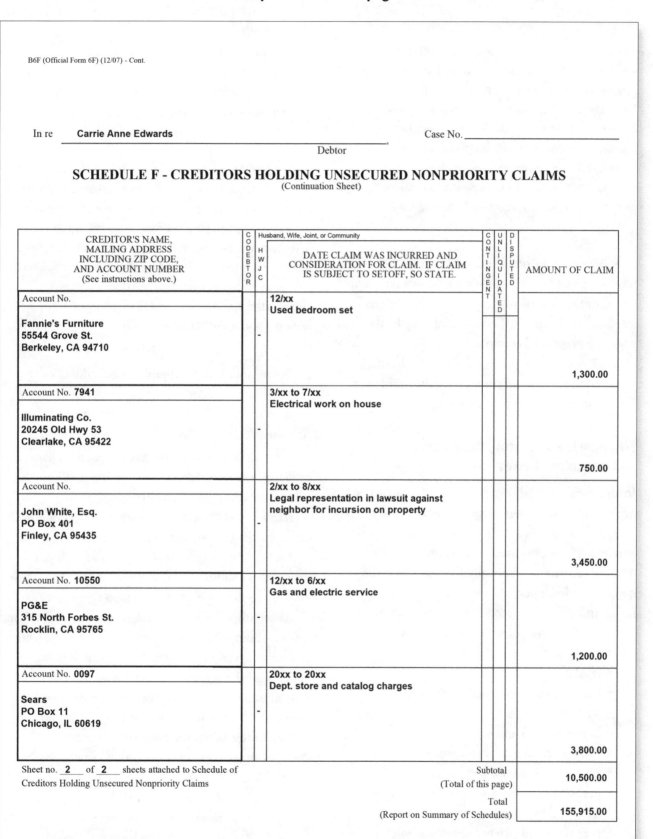

B6F (Official Form 6F) (12/07) - Cont.

In re   **Carrie Anne Edwards**   Case No. _____
                                                           ,
                                         Debtor

SCHEDULE F - CREDITORS HOLDING UNSECURED NONPRIORITY CLAIMS
(Continuation Sheet)

CREDITOR'S NAME, MAILING ADDRESS INCLUDING ZIP CODE, AND ACCOUNT NUMBER (See instructions above.)	CODEBTOR	Husband, Wife, Joint, or Community H W J C	DATE CLAIM WAS INCURRED AND CONSIDERATION FOR CLAIM. IF CLAIM IS SUBJECT TO SETOFF, SO STATE.	CONTINGENT	UNLIQUIDATED	DISPUTED	AMOUNT OF CLAIM
Account No. **Fannie's Furniture** **55544 Grove St.** **Berkeley, CA 94710**	-		**12/xx** **Used bedroom set**				**1,300.00**
Account No. **7941** **Illuminating Co.** **20245 Old Hwy 53** **Clearlake, CA 95422**	-		**3/xx to 7/xx** **Electrical work on house**				**750.00**
Account No. **John White, Esq.** **PO Box 401** **Finley, CA 95435**	-		**2/xx to 8/xx** **Legal representation in lawsuit against neighbor for incursion on property**				**3,450.00**
Account No. **10550** **PG&E** **315 North Forbes St.** **Rocklin, CA 95765**	-		**12/xx to 6/xx** **Gas and electric service**				**1,200.00**
Account No. **0097** **Sears** **PO Box 11** **Chicago, IL 60619**	-		**20xx to 20xx** **Dept. store and catalog charges**				**3,800.00**

Sheet no. **2** of **2** sheets attached to Schedule of
Creditors Holding Unsecured Nonpriority Claims

Subtotal (Total of this page)	**10,500.00**
Total (Report on Summary of Schedules)	**155,915.00**

Listing Debts on Foreclosed and Repossessed Property

Debts that were secured debts prior to a foreclosure or repossession become unsecured debts after title reverts to the secured lender, and you should list them on Schedule F as unsecured debts. If you know what the alleged deficiency was (the difference between what you owed and what the lender ultimately got in the foreclosure or repossession sale), list the deficiency. If you don't yet know—because the foreclosure or repossession was so recent—list the entire debt.

Subtotal/Total. Total the amounts in the last column for this page. Do not include the amounts represented by the ditto marks if you listed multiple creditors for a single debt. On the final page (which may be the first page or a preprinted continuation page), enter the total of all unsecured, nonpriority claims. On the first page in the bottom left-hand corner, note the number of continuation pages you are attaching.

Schedule G—Executory Contracts and Unexpired Leases

In this form, you list every executory contract or unexpired lease to which you're a party. "Executory" means the contract is still in force—that is, both parties are still obligated to perform important acts under it. Similarly, "unexpired" means that the contract or lease period hasn't run out—that is, it is still in effect. Common examples of executory contracts and unexpired leases are:

- car leases
- residential leases or rental agreements
- business leases or rental agreements
- service contracts
- business contracts
- time-share contracts or leases
- contracts of sale for real estate
- personal property leases, such as equipment used in a beauty salon
- copyright and patent license agreements

- leases of real estate (surface and underground) for the purpose of harvesting timber, minerals, or oil
- future homeowners' association fee requirements
- agreements for boat docking privileges, and
- insurance contracts.

ⓘ **CAUTION**

If you're behind in your payments. If you are not current on payments that were due under a lease or an executory contract, the delinquency should also be listed as a debt on Schedule D, E, or F. The sole purpose of Schedule G is to identify existing contractual obligations that you still owe or that someone owes you. Later, you will be given the opportunity to state whether you want the lease or contract to continue in effect.

Below are a sample completed Schedule G and line-by-line instructions.

In re and **Case No.** Follow the instructions for Schedule A.

☐ **Check this box if debtor has no executory contracts or unexpired leases.** Check this box if it applies; otherwise, complete the form.

Name and Mailing Address, Including Zip Code, of Other Parties to Lease or Contract. Provide the name and full address (including zip code) of each party—other than yourself—to each lease or contract. These parties are either people who signed agreements or the companies for whom these people work. If you're unsure about whom to list, include the person who signed an agreement, any company whose name appears on the agreement, and anybody who might have an interest in having the contract or lease enforced. If you still aren't sure, put "don't know."

Description of Contract or Lease and Nature of Debtor's Interest. For each lease or contract, give:

- a description of the basic type (for instance, residential lease, commercial lease, car lease, business obligation, or copyright license)
- the date the contract or lease was signed

Sample Schedule G

B6G (Official Form 6G) (12/07)

In re   **Carrie Anne Edwards** _____ ,   Case No._____

Debtor

SCHEDULE G - EXECUTORY CONTRACTS AND UNEXPIRED LEASES

Describe all executory contracts of any nature and all unexpired leases of real or personal property. Include any timeshare interests. State nature of debtor's interest in contract, i.e., "Purchaser", "Agent", etc. State whether debtor is the lessor or lessee of a lease. Provide the names and complete mailing addresses of all other parties to each lease or contract described. If a minor child is a party to one of the leases or contracts, state the child's initials and the name and address of the child's parent or guardian, such as "A.B., a minor child, by John Doe, guardian." Do not disclose the child's name. See, 11 U.S.C. §112 and Fed. R. Bankr. P. 1007(m).

☐ Check this box if debtor has no executory contracts or unexpired leases.

Name and Mailing Address, Including Zip Code, of Other Parties to Lease or Contract	Description of Contract or Lease and Nature of Debtor's Interest. State whether lease is for nonresidential real property. State contract number of any government contract.
Beauty Products Leasing Co. **44332 Eighth St.** **Geismar, LA 70734**	**Laser skin treatment machine. Lease for 5-year period that expires on May 2012**
Herman Jones **45543 Woodleigh Court** **Smith River, CA 95567**	**Sales contract for debtor's home entered into between debtor and Herman Jones on 2 /1/XX**

0

_____ continuation sheets attached to Schedule of Executory Contracts and Unexpired Leases

- the date the contract is to expire (if any)
- a summary of each party's rights and obligations under the lease or contract, and
- the contract number, if the contract is with any government body.

Schedule H—Codebtors

In Schedules D, E, and F, you identified those debts for which you have codebtors—usually, a cosigner, guarantor, ex-spouse, nonfiling spouse in a community property state, nonfiling spouse for a debt for necessities, nonmarital partner, or joint contractor. You must also list those codebtors here. In addition, you must list the name and address of any spouse or former spouse who lived with you in Puerto Rico or in a community property state during the eight-year period immediately preceding your bankruptcy filing. (To remind you, the community property states are Alaska, Arizona, California, Idaho, Louisiana, Nevada, New Mexico, Texas, Washington, and Wisconsin.) If you are married but filing separately, include all names used by your spouse during the eight-year period.

In Chapter 7 bankruptcy, your codebtors will be wholly responsible for your debts, unless they, too, declare bankruptcy.

Below are a sample completed Schedule H and line-by-line instructions.

In re and **Case No.** Follow instructions for Schedule A.

☐ **Check this box if debtor has no codebtors.** Check this box if it applies; otherwise, complete the form.

What Happens to Executory Contracts and Unexpired Leases in Bankruptcy

The trustee has 60 days after you file for bankruptcy to decide whether an executory contract or unexpired lease should be assumed (continued in force) as property of the estate or terminated (rejected). If the lease or contract would generate funds for your unsecured creditors, then it will be assumed; otherwise, it will be rejected. As a general matter, most leases and contracts are liabilities and are rejected by the trustee. However, you have the right to assume a lease on personal property (for instance, a car lease) on your own, as long as you give the creditor written notice and the creditor agrees. (11 U.S.C. § 365(p).) You provide this written notice in the Statement of Intention.

As a general rule, people filing Chapter 7 bankruptcies are not parties to leases or contracts that would likely add value to their bankruptcy estates. This isn't an absolute rule, however. If the trustee could sell a lease to someone else for a profit (because you're paying less than market rent, for example), the trustee might assume the lease and assign it for a lump sum that could be distributed to your creditors. But this would be highly unusual. Trustees aren't looking for ways to put you on the street or penalize you for getting a great rent deal.

It's also possible that you'll want to get out of a contract or lease, such as a residential or an auto lease or a time-share you can't afford. Be sure to state at the bankruptcy meeting or even on your papers that you would like the trustee to terminate the agreement. But remember this is up to the trustee to decide.

If the lease is assigned or terminated or the contract is terminated, you and the other parties to the agreement are cut loose from any obligations, and any money you owe the creditor will be discharged in your bankruptcy, even if the debt arose after your filing date. For example, say you are leasing a car when you file for bankruptcy. You want out of the lease. The car dealer cannot repossess the car until the trustee terminates the lease, which normally must occur within 60 days of when you file. During that 60-day period, you can use the car without paying for it. The payments you don't make during this period will be discharged as if they were incurred prior to your bankruptcy.

Bankruptcy law has special rules for executory contracts related to intellectual property (copyright, patent, trademark, or trade secret), real estate, and time-share leases. If you are involved in one of these situations, see a lawyer.

Sample Schedule H

B6H (Official Form 6H) (12/07)

In re   **Carrie Anne Edwards**   Case No. _____

                                      Debtor

SCHEDULE H - CODEBTORS

    Provide the information requested concerning any person or entity, other than a spouse in a joint case, that is also liable on any debts listed by debtor in the schedules of creditors. Include all guarantors and co-signers. If the debtor resides or resided in a community property state, commonwealth, or territory (including Alaska, Arizona, California, Idaho, Louisiana, Nevada, New Mexico, Puerto Rico, Texas, Washington, or Wisconsin) within the eight year period immediately preceding the commencement of the case, identify the name of the debtor's spouse and of any former spouse who resides or resided with the debtor in the community property state, commonwealth, or territory. Include all names used by the nondebtor spouse during the eight years immediately preceding the commencement of this case. If a minor child is a codebtor or a creditor, state the child's initials and the name and address of the child's parent or guardian, such as "A.B., a minor child, by John Doe, guardian." Do not disclose the child's name. See, 11 U.S.C. §112 and Fed. R. Bankr. P. 1007(m).

☐   Check this box if debtor has no codebtors.

NAME AND ADDRESS OF CODEBTOR	NAME AND ADDRESS OF CREDITOR
Bonnie Johnson **3335 Irving St.** **Clearlake, CA 95422**	**Fannie's Furniture** **55544 Grove St.** **Berkeley, CA 94710**

0

_____ continuation sheets attached to Schedule of Codebtors

Name and Address of Codebtor. List the name and complete address (including zip code) of each codebtor. If the codebtor is a nonfiling, current spouse, put all names by which that person was known during the previous eight years.

If the creditor is a child, list the child's initials and the name and address of the child's parent or guardian. For example, "A.B., a minor child, by John Doe, Guardian, 111 Alabama Avenue, San Francisco, CA 94732." Don't state the child's name.

Name and Address of Creditor. List the name and address of each creditor (as listed on Schedule D, E, or F) to which each codebtor is indebted.

> **EXAMPLE:** Tom Martin cosigned three different loans—with three different banks—for debtor Mabel Green, who is filing for bankruptcy. In the first column, Mabel lists Tom Martin as a codebtor. In the second, Mabel lists each of the three banks.

FOR MARRIED COUPLES
If you are married and filing alone. If you live in a community property state, your spouse may be a codebtor for most of the debts you listed in Schedules D, E, and F. This is because, in these states, most debts incurred by one spouse are owed by both spouses. In this event, don't relist all the creditors in the second column. Simply write "all creditors listed in Schedules D, E, and F, except:" and then list any creditors whom you alone owe.

If you lived with a former spouse in a community property state or Puerto Rico in the eight-year period prior to filing, list his or her name and address.

Schedule I—Your Income

In this Schedule, you calculate your actual current income (not your average monthly income for the six-month period before you file, which you'll calculate in Form 22A-1 below).

Directly below is a sample completed Schedule I and line-by-line instructions for completing it. At the top of the page, enter your name in the Debtor 1 space and, if your spouse is filing, your spouse's name in the Debtor 2 space. Next, fill in the name of the judicial district you're filing in, such as "Western District of Virginia." You won't have a case number yet so leave that line blank. Also, since you haven't filed anything yet, leave check boxes on the top right-hand side blank as well.

For the rest of the form, if you are married and filing jointly, you must fill in the information in the "Debtor 2 or nonfiling spouse" column. Both you and your spouse are equally responsible for providing accurate information on this form. You also must fill in the "Debtor 2 or nonfiling spouse" column if you are married and *not* filing jointly, unless you are separated and no longer living under the same roof. If you consider yourself to be separated but are still living under the same roof, you don't need to list your spouse's income, but it is better to do so to be on the safe side. Also, if you need additional room to fully answer a question, attach a continuation sheet to your schedule. Be sure to write your name and case number on any additional page.

Part 1: Describe Employment. Enter your employment status and provide the requested employment information. If you have more than one employer, list each additional employer on a continuation sheet. If you are retired, unemployed, or disabled, enter that in the blank for "occupation."

Part 2: Give Details About Monthly Income. Enter your estimated monthly gross income (this is how much you make before anything is taken out of your check; so don't deduct anything yet—that's coming up) by adding together all of your wages, salary, and commission from "regular employment" (this means work that you normally do on a regular basis). List this figure on Line 2. Put your estimated monthly overtime pay on Line 3. Add Lines 2 and 3 together (your total monthly income) and list this number in two places—on Line 4 of Page 1 and at the top of Page 2 where it says "Copy line 4 here."

Three Different Income Figures

The bankruptcy law that went into effect in October 2005 produces a number of strange results. One of these is that you will report three different income figures: the "current monthly income" figure in Form 22A-1, the actual income you report here, and the annual income figures you report in your Statement of Financial Affairs (see below).

Schedule I explicitly states that the income you report there will likely be different from what you report as your current monthly income on Form 22A-1. That's because the income you report on Form 22A-1 is your average gross income for the six months before you file, but the income you report here is the actual net income you expect to be receiving every month going forward. If, for example, you lost your job a couple of months ago and are now earning much less, your income will be lower than what you reported on Form 22A-1.

Line 5: List all payroll deductions. In the eight blanks, enter the deductions taken from your gross salary. The deductions listed are the most common ones, but you may have others to report, such as state disability taxes, wages withheld or garnished for child support, credit union payments, or perhaps payments on a student loan or a car. List these deductions on Line 5h.

Line 6: Add the payroll deductions. Add all of your payroll deductions together and list the total in this space.

Line 7: Calculate total monthly take-home pay. Subtract your payroll deductions (Line 6) from your income total (Line 4) and enter your total monthly take-home pay on Line 7.

Line 8: List all other income regularly received. In the following eight spaces, you'll list all other types of income you receive.

Line 8a: Net income from rental property, business, profession, or farm. Here, the bankruptcy court wants to know how much money you receive from other income-generating activities. You'll answer this question if you are self-employed, operate a sole proprietorship, are a member of a business partnership, receive money from rental property, or are a farmer.

Attach statements that list the gross receipts, ordinary and necessary business expenses, and net income for each activity. (Subtract the expenses from your gross receipts to get your net income.) Enter your total net income from your rental property, business, profession, or farm on line 8a.

Line 8b: Interest and dividends. Enter the average estimated monthly interest you receive from bank or security deposits and other investments, such as stock.

Line 8c: Family support payments that you, a non-filing spouse, or a dependent regularly receive. Enter the average monthly amount you, your non-filing spouse, or your dependent receives for support. This includes child support, alimony, spousal support, or maintenance.

Line 8d: Unemployment compensation. Enter the estimated amount you currently receive in unemployment compensation.

Line 8e: Social Security. Enter the total monthly amount you receive in retirement, disability, or survivors benefits from the Social Security Administration.

Line 8f: Other government assistance. Enter the total amount of government assistance you receive each month, such as public assistance, veterans benefits, and workers' compensation. If you receive assistance in the form of food stamps or other food programs, specify the source and include the monthly value.

Line 8g: Pension or retirement income. Enter the total monthly amount of all pension, annuity, IRA, Keogh, or other retirement benefits you currently receive.

Line 8h: Other monthly income. Specify any other income (such as royalty payments or payments from a trust) you receive on a regular basis, and enter the monthly amount here. You may have to divide by three, six, or 12 if you receive the payments quarterly, semiannually, or annually.

Line 9: Add all other income. Add together all of your entries from Lines 8a through 8h and enter the amount on Line 9.

Line 10: Calculate monthly income. Add your total monthly take-home pay in Lines 7 to 9. If you are filing jointly, combine your total from Line 10 with your spouse's total and enter your joint monthly income total in the far right space.

Sample Schedule I—page 1

Fill in this information to identify your case:

Debtor 1	Carrie Anne Edwards
Debtor 2 (Spouse, if filing)	
United States Bankruptcy Court for the:	EASTERN DISTRICT OF CALIFORNIA
Case number (If known)	

Check if this is:
☐ An amended filing
☐ A supplement showing post-petition chapter 13 income as of the following date:

_____
MM / DD/ YYYY

Official Form B 6I

Schedule I: Your Income   12/13

Be as complete and accurate as possible. If two married people are filing together (Debtor 1 and Debtor 2), both are equally responsible for supplying correct information. If you are married and not filing jointly, and your spouse is living with you, include information about your spouse. If you are separated and your spouse is not filing with you, do not include information about your spouse. If more space is needed, attach a separate sheet to this form. On the top of any additional pages, write your name and case number (if known). Answer every question.

Part 1: Describe Employment

1. **Fill in your employment information.**

   If you have more than one job, attach a separate page with information about additional employers.

   Include part-time, seasonal, or self-employed work.

   Occupation may include student or homemaker, if it applies.

		Debtor 1	Debtor 2 or non-filing spouse
	Employment status	■ Employed ☐ Not employed	☐ Employed ☐ Not employed
	Occupation	Retail	
	Employer's name	Macy's	
	Employer's address	2356 Cleveland Ave. Santa Rosa, CA 95402	
	How long employed there?	2 months	

Part 2: Give Details About Monthly Income

Estimate monthly income as of the date you file this form. If you have nothing to report for any line, write $0 in the space. Include your non-filing spouse unless you are separated.

If you or your non-filing spouse have more than one employer, combine the information for all employers for that person on the lines below. If you need more space, attach a separate sheet to this form.

		For Debtor 1	For Debtor 2 or non-filing spouse
2.	**List monthly gross wages, salary, and commissions** (before all payroll deductions). If not paid monthly, calculate what the monthly wage would be.	2. $ 4,950.67	$ N/A
3.	**Estimate and list monthly overtime pay.**	3. +$ 0.00	+$ N/A
4.	**Calculate gross Income.** Add line 2 + line 3.	4. $ 4,950.67	$ N/A

Sample Schedule I—page 2

Debtor 1 **Carrie Anne Edwards** _____ Case number (*if known*) _____

			For Debtor 1	For Debtor 2 or non-filing spouse
	Copy line 4 here	4.	$ 4,950.67	$ N/A
5.	**List all payroll deductions:**			
5a.	**Tax, Medicare, and Social Security deductions**	5a.	$ 541.67	$ N/A
5b.	**Mandatory contributions for retirement plans**	5b.	$ 0.00	$ N/A
5c.	**Voluntary contributions for retirement plans**	5c.	$ 0.00	$ N/A
5d.	**Required repayments of retirement fund loans**	5d.	$ 0.00	$ N/A
5e.	**Insurance**	5e.	$ 0.00	$ N/A
5f.	**Domestic support obligations**	5f.	$ 0.00	$ N/A
5g.	**Union dues**	5g.	$ 0.00	$ N/A
5h.	**Other deductions.** Specify: _____	5h.+	$ 0.00	+ $ N/A
6.	**Add the payroll deductions.** Add lines 5a+5b+5c+5d+5e+5f+5g+5h.	6.	$ 541.67	$ N/A
7.	**Calculate total monthly take-home pay.** Subtract line 6 from line 4.	7.	$ 4,409.00	$ N/A
8.	**List all other income regularly received:**			
8a.	**Net income from rental property and from operating a business, profession, or farm** Attach a statement for each property and business showing gross receipts, ordinary and necessary business expenses, and the total monthly net income.	8a.	$ 0.00	$ N/A
8b.	**Interest and dividends**	8b.	$ 0.00	$ N/A
8c.	**Family support payments that you, a non-filing spouse, or a dependent regularly receive** Include alimony, spousal support, child support, maintenance, divorce settlement, and property settlement.	8c.	$ 400.00	$ N/A
8d.	**Unemployment compensation**	8d.	$ 0.00	$ N/A
8e.	**Social Security**	8e.	$ 0.00	$ N/A
8f.	**Other government assistance that you regularly receive** Include cash assistance and the value (if known) of any non-cash assistance that you receive, such as food stamps (benefits under the Supplemental Nutrition Assistance Program) or housing subsidies. Specify: _____	8f.	$ 0.00	$ N/A
8g.	**Pension or retirement income**	8g.	$ 0.00	$ N/A
8h.	**Other monthly income.** Specify: _____	8h.+	$ 0.00	+ $ N/A
9.	**Add all other income.** Add lines 8a+8b+8c+8d+8e+8f+8g+8h.	9.	$ 400.00	$ N/A
10.	**Calculate monthly income.** Add line 7 + line 9. Add the entries in line 10 for Debtor 1 and Debtor 2 or non-filing spouse.	10.	$ 4,809.00 +	$ N/A =	$ 4,809.00
11.	**State all other regular contributions to the expenses that you list in Schedule J.** Include contributions from an unmarried partner, members of your household, your dependents, your roommates, and other friends or relatives. Do not include any amounts already included in lines 2-10 or amounts that are not available to pay expenses listed in *Schedule J.* Specify: _____	11.	+$ 0.00	
12.	**Add the amount in the last column of line 10 to the amount in line 11.** The result is the combined monthly income. Write that amount on the *Summary of Schedules* and *Statistical Summary of Certain Liabilities* and Related *Data*, if it applies	12.	$ 4,809.00 **Combined monthly income**	

13. **Do you expect an increase or decrease within the year after you file this form?**

■ No.

☐ Yes. Explain: _____

Line 11: State all other regular contributions to the expenses that you list in Schedule J. If you receive any help with your expenses on a regular basis, such as from a partner that lives with you (for example, a live-in girlfriend or boyfriend), another member of your household, dependent, roommate, friend or family member, list that amount on Line 11. Include only money that is available to pay expenses and specify the circumstances ("My parents give me $500 each month for rent") on the line provided.

Line 12: Add lines 10 and 11 together. Add the total on Line 10 to the number on Line 11. This is your "combined monthly income." Keep this figure handy because you'll use it on two additional forms: the Summary of Schedules and the Statistical Summary of Certain Liabilities and Related Data forms.

Line 13: Expected increase or decrease in income. If you don't expect your income to change in the next year, check the "No" box—you are done with this form. If you expect your income to increase, check "Yes" and explain why you believe so. Be aware that if you indicate that you will soon be enjoying a significantly higher income, you might face a motion from the U.S. Trustee seeking to force you into Chapter 13. But you must be accurate and complete, so regardless of the consequences you must disclose that fact here. Of course, if your income is due to decrease any time soon, you should use this part of the form to indicate that as well.

Schedule J—Your Expenses

In this form, you must list your family's total monthly expenditures, even if you're married and filing alone. Be complete and accurate. Expenditures for items the trustee considers luxuries may not be considered reasonable and may be disregarded. For instance, payments on expensive cars or investment property may be disregarded by the trustee. If this happens and you end up having enough excess income to fund a Chapter 13 plan, you may be forced into Chapter 13 if you don't want your case dismissed. Reasonable

expenditures for housing, utilities, food, medical care, clothing, education, and transportation will be counted. Be ready to support high amounts with bills, receipts, and canceled checks.

EXAMPLE 1: Joe owes $100,000 (excluding his mortgage and car), earns $4,000 a month, and spends $3,900 a month for the other items listed on Schedule J, including payments on a midpriced car and a moderately priced family home. Joe would probably be allowed to proceed with a Chapter 7 bankruptcy because his monthly disposable income ($100) wouldn't put much of a dent in his $100,000 debt load, even over a five-year period.

EXAMPLE 2: Same facts, except that Joe's Schedule J expenditures total only $2,200 a month. In this case, the court might rule that because Joe has $1,800 a month in disposable income, he could pay off most of his $100,000 debt load over a three- to five-year period, either informally or under a Chapter 13 repayment plan. The court could dismiss Joe's Chapter 7 bankruptcy petition or pressure him to convert it to Chapter 13 bankruptcy.

EXAMPLE 3: Same facts as Example 2, but Joe is incurably ill and will soon have to quit working. The court will more than likely allow him to proceed with a Chapter 7 bankruptcy.

Review the sample completed Schedule J, below, and the guidelines for completing it.

> CAUTION
> **Once again, be accurate.** Creditors sometimes try to use the information on these forms to prove that you committed fraud when you applied for credit. If a creditor can prove that you lied on a credit application, the debt may survive bankruptcy. (See Ch. 9 for more information.) If being accurate on this form will substantially contradict information you previously gave a creditor, see a bankruptcy attorney before filing.

Fill in the top of Schedule J by following the instructions for Schedule I. Just as with Schedule I, ignore the two boxes on the top, right-hand side of the form since you haven't filed your petition yet. You'll check the third box on the right-hand side in only two rare circumstances:

- you and your spouse are married but live in separate residences, or
- you and your spouse are separated, live in separate residences, and are filing jointly.

If either of the above fits your situation, check the box that says "A separate filing for Debtor 2 because Debtor 2 maintains a separate household."

TIP

Using bankruptcy to eliminate debts before divorce. If you are getting divorced, one of the best ways to handle marital debt is to discharge it in Chapter 7 bankruptcy before the divorce is final (if the type of debt is dischargeable). Many people don't realize that if a family law court orders you to pay debt that is in the name of both spouses, filing bankruptcy *after* divorce will not alleviate your responsibility to pay that debt. Resolving the debt issues through a bankruptcy *before* the divorce allows both parties to truly start fresh without the financial burden from the previous relationship.

Part 1: Describe Your Household. Here, you explain your current living situation. Enter your filing status and tell the court whether you and your spouse live in the same household. If you have dependents, don't list their names. Instead, list them according to their relationship to you, such as "son," "daughter," "granddaughter," "parent." Provide each dependent's age and check the appropriate box indicating where the dependent lives. If you pay expenses for someone other than yourself and your dependents, check "Yes" to question three.

Part 2: Estimate Your Ongoing Monthly Expenses. In this section, you tell the court how much money it takes for you to live each month, otherwise known as your monthly budget. The trustee uses this schedule to decide whether you have enough money left over

each month to pay your creditors through a Chapter 13 plan, and if so, how much. In other words, it is important to get it right. Here are some pointers:

- Use the actual cost of your bills on the date you file your bankruptcy.
- If you make some payments biweekly, quarterly, semiannually, or annually, prorate them to show your monthly payment.
- Do not list the payroll deductions you listed on Schedule I.
- Include payments for your dependents' expenses as long as they are reasonable and necessary for the dependents' support.

When Expenses on Schedule J Trigger an Audit

One of the things that triggers a bankruptcy audit is listing higher than expected expenses on Schedule J. So what is considered to be higher than expected? A good rule of thumb is that anything over and above the IRS National and Local Standards used in the means test calculation could be considered suspect. Of course, this doesn't mean that you shouldn't list the actual amount of your expenses. To the contrary, you are required by law to be accurate on your schedules (and you should be fair to yourself, as well). Just realize that the trustee may not be the only one questioning you about expenses that are higher than the "standards." If your figures trigger an audit, the U.S. Trustee's Office will contact you with a few questions as well. In both instances, be prepared to show documentation in the way of receipts.

Most of the line items listed in this form are self-explanatory, but not all. Below you'll find help for the categories that aren't clear, tips to keep you out of trouble with the trustee, and suggestions for expenses you may have forgotten about. As a reminder, make sure to retain receipts for all the expenses you list because receipts are the key to staying in the trustee's good graces.

Sample Schedule J—page 1

Fill in this information to identify your case:

Debtor 1	**Carrie Anne Edwards**
Debtor 2 (Spouse, if filing)	
United States Bankruptcy Court for the:	EASTERN DISTRICT OF CALIFORNIA
Case number (If known)	

Check if this is:

☐ An amended filing

☐ A supplement showing post-petition chapter 13 expenses as of the following date:

_____
MM / DD / YYYY

☐ A separate filing for Debtor 2 because Debtor 2 maintains a separate household

---

Official Form B 6J
Schedule J: Your Expenses

12/13

Be as complete and accurate as possible. If two married people are filing together, both are equally responsible for supplying correct information. If more space is needed, attach another sheet to this form. On the top of any additional pages, write your name and case number (if known). Answer every question.

Part 1:   Describe Your Household

1. **Is this a joint case?**

    ■ No. Go to line 2.

    ☐ Yes. **Does Debtor 2 live in a separate household?**

        ☐ No
        ☐ Yes. Debtor 2 must file a separate Schedule J.

2. **Do you have dependents?**   ☐ No

Do not list Debtor 1 and Debtor 2.	■ Yes.	Fill out this information for each dependent..............	Dependent's relationship to Debtor 1 or Debtor 2	Dependent's age	Does dependent live with you?
Do not state the dependents' names.					☐ No
			Daughter	**12**	■ Yes
					☐ No
			Son	**14**	■ Yes
					☐ No
			_____	_____	☐ Yes
					☐ No
			_____	_____	☐ Yes

3. **Do your expenses include expenses of people other than yourself and your dependents?**   ■ No   ☐ Yes

Part 2:   Estimate Your Ongoing Monthly Expenses

Estimate your expenses as of your bankruptcy filing date unless you are using this form as a supplement in a Chapter 13 case to report expenses as of a date after the bankruptcy is filed. If this is a supplemental *Schedule J*, check the box at the top of the form and fill in the applicable date.

Include expenses paid for with non-cash government assistance if you know the value of such assistance and have included it on *Schedule I: Your Income* (Official Form 6I.)

			Your expenses

4. **The rental or home ownership expenses for your residence.** Include first mortgage payments and any rent for the ground or lot.   4. $ **900.00**

    If not included in line 4:

4a.	Real estate taxes	4a. $	0.00
4b.	Property, homeowner's, or renter's insurance	4b. $	0.00
4c.	Home maintenance, repair, and upkeep expenses	4c. $	75.00
4d.	Homeowner's association or condominium dues	4d. $	0.00
5.	**Additional mortgage payments for your residence,** such as home equity loans	5. $	0.00

Sample Schedule J—page 2

Debtor 1   **Carrie Anne Edwards**   Case number (if known) _____

6.	**Utilities:**		
	6a. Electricity, heat, natural gas	6a. $	150.00
	6b. Water, sewer, garbage collection	6b. $	150.00
	6c. Telephone, cell phone, Internet, satellite, and cable services	6c. $	330.00
	6d. Other. Specify: _____	6d. $	0.00
7.	**Food and housekeeping supplies**	7. $	450.00
8.	**Childcare and children's education costs**	8. $	525.00
9.	**Clothing, laundry, and dry cleaning**	9. $	40.00
10.	**Personal care products and services**	10. $	50.00
11.	**Medical and dental expenses**	11. $	300.00
12.	**Transportation.** Include gas, maintenance, bus or train fare. Do not include car payments.	12. $	400.00
13.	**Entertainment, clubs, recreation, newspapers, magazines, and books**	13. $	100.00
14.	**Charitable contributions and religious donations**	14. $	300.00
15.	**Insurance.** Do not include insurance deducted from your pay or included in lines 4 or 20.		
	15a. Life insurance	15a. $	0.00
	15b. Health insurance	15b. $	200.00
	15c. Vehicle insurance	15c. $	200.00
	15d. Other insurance. Specify: _____	15d. $	0.00
16.	**Taxes.** Do not include taxes deducted from your pay or included in lines 4 or 20. Specify: _____	16. $	0.00
17.	**Installment or lease payments:**		
	17a. Car payments for Vehicle 1	17a. $	450.00
	17b. Car payments for Vehicle 2	17b. $	0.00
	17c. Other. Specify: _____	17c. $	0.00
	17d. Other. Specify: _____	17d. $	0.00
18.	**Your payments of alimony, maintenance, and support that you did not report as deducted from your pay on line 5,** *Schedule I, Your Income* **(Official Form 6I).**	18. $	0.00
19.	**Other payments you make to support others who do not live with you.** Specify: _____	19. $	0.00
20.	**Other real property expenses not included in lines 4 or 5 of this form or on** *Schedule I: Your Income.*		
	20a. Mortgages on other property	20a. $	0.00
	20b. Real estate taxes	20b. $	0.00
	20c. Property, homeowner's, or renter's insurance	20c. $	100.00
	20d. Maintenance, repair, and upkeep expenses	20d. $	0.00
	20e. Homeowner's association or condominium dues	20e. $	0.00
21.	**Other:** Specify: _____	21. +$	0.00
22.	**Your monthly expenses.** Add lines 4 through 21. The result is your monthly expenses.	22. $	4,720.00
23.	**Calculate your monthly net income.**		
	23a. Copy line 12 *(your combined monthly income)* from Schedule I.	23a. $	4,809.00
	23b. Copy your monthly expenses from line 22 above.	23b. -$	4,720.00
	23c. Subtract your monthly expenses from your monthly income. The result is your *monthly net income.*	23c. $	89.00

24. **Do you expect an increase or decrease in your expenses within the year after you file this form?**
For example, do you expect to finish paying for your car loan within the year or do you expect your mortgage payment to increase or decrease because of a modification to the terms of your mortgage?

■ No.
☐ Yes.
Explain: [   ]

Line 4b: Home maintenance, repair, and upkeep expenses. If your home is new, you may not have much in the way of upkeep expenses. On the other hand, older homes often need costly loving care. If you anticipate costly repairs in the near future, such as painting, plumbing, roofing, or termite repairs, consider getting an estimate and prorating the cost over a number of months. Here are examples of other common maintenance items (be prepared to explain why you can't perform some of these services yourself):

- yard and pool care
- tree trimming
- pest control
- lightbulb replacement
- heating or air conditioner servicing, and
- smoke detector maintenance.

Line 8: Childcare and children's education costs. If you pay for childcare, it is likely one of your biggest expenses. Listing enrichment activities such as karate and swimming lessons will be difficult to justify.

Line 10: Personal care products and services. Personal care products can add up fast since this category includes things such as toothpaste, soap, razors, shampoo, conditioner, lip balm, talcum powder, lotion, and cotton swabs. Services include haircuts for yourself and family. Even so, trustees look at this category with a critical eye, so you will certainly want to stay away from budgeting luxurious services like manicures and pedicures (unless, of course, you can demonstrate such services are necessary for your profession or that you need it for health reasons).

Line 14: Charitable contributions and religious donations. There is no limit to how much you can claim for charitable contributions or religious donations. As a rule of thumb, however, it is wise to consider limiting your charitable contribution budget to an amount that reflects prior contributions. Also, your tithing budget should be no more than ten percent of your income. In both cases, be prepared to show receipts of past contributions and that you have an established history of donating at that level before.

Line 17: Installment or lease payments. Since your budget reflects the expenses you anticipate paying, you should only include your car payment if you plan to keep the car. Don't include payments for credit cards and other debts you won't be responsible for once you receive your discharge.

Line 22. Your monthly expenses.
To complete Schedule J, add all of your expenses on lines 4 through 21 and enter the total amount on Line 22.

Line 23. Calculate your monthly net income. Enter your combined monthly income figure from Schedule I (Line 12) onto Line 23a. Enter your total monthly expenses (the amount you listed on Line 22) on Line 23b. To determine your monthly net income (how much you have left over each month after paying your bills), subtract your monthly expenses (Line 23b) from your monthly income (Line 23a) and enter the result on Line 23c.

Don't worry if you have a negative number as long as your math is accurate. The point of this schedule is to show at a glance whether you have significantly more income than expenses.

Do you expect an increase or decrease in expenses? To finish the form, indicate whether you expect an increase or decrease in your expenses within the next year. If so, check "Yes," and explain why in the box immediately to the right. If not, check "No." You are done with Schedule J.

CAUTION
Don't underestimate your expenses. As indicated above, a significant net income might lead the trustee to challenge your Chapter 7 filing. Sometimes people give low estimates of their expenses because they don't want to appear to be living beyond their means. Or sometimes people's expenses are low because they have been unemployed, but have increased or will increase soon because they have recently started working again. If this describes your situation, go back over your expenses and make sure they are accurate in light of your actual situation.

Dismissal for Abuse

As explained in Ch. 1, bankruptcy law has an eligibility requirement called the "means test" to determine who qualifies for Chapter 7 bankruptcy. Debtors whose "current monthly income"—their average income over the six months before they filed for bankruptcy—exceeds their state's median income must take the means test. In the means test, debtors calculate their disposable income by subtracting certain allowable expenses (in amounts set by the IRS) and deductions from their current monthly income. If they have enough disposable income to fund a Chapter 13 repayment plan, their Chapter 7 case will be a "presumed abuse" of the bankruptcy laws and will be dismissed or converted to Chapter 13.

If you either pass the means test or don't have to take it at all, your case won't be a presumed abuse. However, the court can still find that allowing you to use Chapter 7 would be an abuse of the bankruptcy process if all of the circumstances show that you could afford a repayment plan. Some courts have dismissed Chapter 7 cases or converted them to Chapter 13 under this theory if the debtor's Schedule I and Schedule J show that the debtor has significantly more income than expenses.

Because the law on abuse is unsettled, we suggest that you be very cautious claiming expenses for luxury items. If your income exceeds your expenses on these schedules by more than a small amount, you may want to talk to a lawyer before filing. Either of these situations might result in the U.S. Trustee challenging your right to use Chapter 7.

Summary of Schedules

This form helps the bankruptcy trustee and judge get a quick look at your bankruptcy filing. Below are a completed Summary of Schedules and line-by-line instructions.

Court Name. Copy this information from Form 1—Voluntary Petition.

In re and **Case No.** Follow the instructions for Schedule A.

Name of Schedule. This lists the schedules. Don't add anything.

Attached (Yes/No). You should have completed all of the schedules, so type "Yes" in this column for each schedule, even if you added no information.

No. of Sheets. Enter the number of pages you completed for each schedule. Remember to count continuation pages. Enter the total at the bottom of the column.

Assets, Liabilities, Other. For each column—Assets, Liabilities, and Other—copy the totals from Schedules A, B, D, E, F, I, and J and enter them where indicated. Add up the amounts in the Assets and Liabilities columns and enter their totals at the bottom. (Once you've completed this form, you can go back and fill in the "Statistical/Administrative Information" section on Form 1—Voluntary Petition.)

Statistical Summary of Certain Liabilities and Related Data

This form asks you to list information from your other bankruptcy paperwork. Fill in the blanks using your completed schedules. You will need to come back to this form to fill in your current monthly income after completing Form 22A-1 (instructions for this form are below).

Declaration Concerning Debtor's Schedules

In this form, you are required to swear that everything you have said on your schedules is true and correct. Deliberate lying is a major sin in bankruptcy and could cost you your bankruptcy discharge, a fine of up to $500,000, and up to five years in prison.

Below is a completed declaration and instructions.

In re and **Case No.** Follow the instructions for Schedule A.

Declaration Under Penalty of Perjury by Individual Debtor. Enter the total number of pages in your schedules (the number on the Summary of Schedules plus one). Enter the date and sign the form. Be sure that your spouse signs and dates the form if you are filing jointly.

Sample Summary of Schedules

B6 Summary (Official Form 6 - Summary) (12/14)

United States Bankruptcy Court
Eastern District of California

In re   **Carrie Anne Edwards**   ,   Case No. _____

Debtor

Chapter _____ 7 _____

SUMMARY OF SCHEDULES

Indicate as to each schedule whether that schedule is attached and state the number of pages in each. Report the totals from Schedules A, B, D, E, F, I, and J in the boxes provided. Add the amounts from Schedules A and B to determine the total amount of the debtor's assets. Add the amounts of all claims from Schedules D, E, and F to determine the total amount of the debtor's liabilities. Individual debtors must also complete the "Statistical Summary of Certain Liabilities and Related Data" if they file a case under chapter 7, 11, or 13.

NAME OF SCHEDULE	ATTACHED (YES/NO)	NO. OF SHEETS	ASSETS	LIABILITIES	OTHER
A - Real Property	Yes	1	130,000.00		
B - Personal Property	Yes	4	34,525.00		
C - Property Claimed as Exempt	Yes	2			
D - Creditors Holding Secured Claims	Yes	1		168,000.00	
E - Creditors Holding Unsecured Priority Claims (Total of Claims on Schedule E)	Yes	3		7,500.00	
F - Creditors Holding Unsecured Nonpriority Claims	Yes	3		155,915.00	
G - Executory Contracts and Unexpired Leases	Yes	1			
H - Codebtors	Yes	1			
I - Current Income of Individual Debtor(s)	Yes	2			4,809.00
J - Current Expenditures of Individual Debtor(s)	Yes	2			4,720.00
Total Number of Sheets of ALL Schedules		20			
Total Assets			164,525.00		
Total Liabilities				331,415.00	

Sample Statistical Summary of Certain Liabilities and Related Data

B 6 Summary (Official Form 6 - Summary) (12/14)

United States Bankruptcy Court
Eastern District of California

In re   **Carrie Anne Edwards**   Case No. _____

Debtor   Chapter _____ 7 _____

STATISTICAL SUMMARY OF CERTAIN LIABILITIES AND RELATED DATA (28 U.S.C. § 159)

If you are an individual debtor whose debts are primarily consumer debts, as defined in § 101(8) of the Bankruptcy Code (11 U.S.C.§ 101(8)), filing a case under chapter 7, 11 or 13, you must report all information requested below.

☐ Check this box if you are an individual debtor whose debts are NOT primarily consumer debts. You are not required to report any information here.

This information is for statistical purposes only under 28 U.S.C. § 159.

Summarize the following types of liabilities, as reported in the Schedules, and total them.

Type of Liability	Amount
Domestic Support Obligations (from Schedule E)	4,500.00
Taxes and Certain Other Debts Owed to Governmental Units (from Schedule E)	3,000.00
Claims for Death or Personal Injury While Debtor Was Intoxicated (from Schedule E) (whether disputed or undisputed)	0.00
Student Loan Obligations (from Schedule F)	0.00
Domestic Support, Separation Agreement, and Divorce Decree Obligations Not Reported on Schedule E	0.00
Obligations to Pension or Profit-Sharing, and Other Similar Obligations (from Schedule F)	0.00
TOTAL	7,500.00

State the following:

Average Income (from Schedule I, Line 12)	4,809.00
Average Expenses (from Schedule J, Line 22)	4,720.00
Current Monthly Income (from Form 22A-1 Line 11; OR, Form 22B Line 14; OR, Form 22C-1 Line 14)	5,350.67

State the following:

1. Total from Schedule D, "UNSECURED PORTION, IF ANY" column		30,000.00
2. Total from Schedule E, "AMOUNT ENTITLED TO PRIORITY" column	7,500.00	
3. Total from Schedule E, "AMOUNT NOT ENTITLED TO PRIORITY, IF ANY" column		0.00
4. Total from Schedule F		155,915.00
5. Total of non-priority unsecured debt (sum of 1, 3, and 4)		185,915.00

Sample Declaration Concerning Debtor's Schedules

B6 Declaration (Official Form 6 - Declaration). (12/07)

United States Bankruptcy Court
Eastern District of California

In re **Carrie Anne Edwards** _____   Case No. _____

Debtor(s)   Chapter **7** _____

DECLARATION CONCERNING DEBTOR'S SCHEDULES

DECLARATION UNDER PENALTY OF PERJURY BY INDIVIDUAL DEBTOR

I declare under penalty of perjury that I have read the foregoing summary and schedules, consisting of __**22**__ sheets, and that they are true and correct to the best of my knowledge, information, and belief.

Date _____   Signature   **/s/ Carrie Anne Edwards** _____
Carrie Anne Edwards
Debtor

Penalty for making a false statement or concealing property: Fine of up to $500,000 or imprisonment for up to 5 years or both. 18 U.S.C. §§ 152 and 3571.

Form 7—Statement of Financial Affairs

This form gives information about your recent financial transactions, such as payments to creditors, sales, or other transfers of property and gifts. Under certain circumstances, the trustee may be entitled to take back property that you transferred to others prior to filing for bankruptcy, and sell it for the benefit of your unsecured creditors.

The questions on the form are, for the most part, self-explanatory. Spouses filing jointly combine their answers and complete only one form.

If you have no information for a particular item, check the "None" box. If you fail to answer a question and don't check "None," you will have to amend your papers—that is, file a corrected form—after you file. Add continuation sheets if necessary.

CAUTION

Be honest and complete. Don't give in to the temptation to leave out a transfer or two, assuming that the trustee won't find out or go after the property. You must sign this form under penalty of perjury. And, if it appears to the trustee that you left information out intentionally, your bankruptcy may be dismissed and you could even be criminally prosecuted—although this is extremely rare.

On the other hand, you are entitled to take the form and its instructions quite literally. Carefully read the form's general instructions and the instructions for each separate item, and then answer according to the literal meaning of the form's words. If you do this, you won't be held to account for answers that may be wrong. Of course you may have to amend your paperwork if your interpretation is not the same as the trustee's, but at least you won't be suspected of lying or playing fast and loose with the bankruptcy forms.

A completed Statement of Financial Affairs and instructions follow.

Court Name. Copy this information from Form 1 —Voluntary Petition.

In re and **Case No.** Follow the instructions for Schedule A.

CAUTION

Be prepared to explain inconsistencies in reported income. You list income three separate times in your bankruptcy papers. On Schedule I, you report your current income. On Form 22A-1, you report your income for the previous six months. On the Statement of Financial Affairs, you report your annual gross income for the previous two to three years. None of these numbers will be the same, but if the income you report on your Statement of Financial Affairs is substantially higher than your income reported on the other forms, the trustee may want to know why. For example, if on the Statement of Financial Affairs you report your annual gross income for the previous year as $100,000 but on Form 22A-1 report your current monthly income as $4,000 a month (annualized to $48,000), the trustee may want you to explain the discrepancy.

1. Income from employment or operation of business. Enter your gross income for this year (how much you've made year-to-date) and for the previous two years. This means the total income before taxes and other payroll deductions or business expenses are subtracted.

2. Income other than from employment or operation of business. Include interest, dividends, royalties, workers' compensation, other government benefits, and all other money you have received from sources other than your job or business during the last two years. Provide the source of each amount, the dates received, and the reason you received the money so that the trustee can verify it if he or she desires.

Make sure the amounts you provide here are consistent with the income disclosed on the tax return you provided to the trustee. For example, if you claim $25,000 gross income for the previous year on this form, your tax return for that year should list the same or a similar figure.

3. Payments to creditors. Here you list payments you've recently made to creditors. There are two kinds of creditors: regular creditors and insiders. An insider— defined on the first page of the Statement of Financial Affairs—is essentially a relative or close business associate. All other creditors are regular creditors, even friends.

a. Individual or joint debtor(s) with primarily consumer debts. List payments made to a regular creditor that total more than $600, if the payments were made:

- to repay a loan, installment purchase, or other debt, and
- during the 90 days before you file your bankruptcy petition.

If you have made payments exceeding $600 during that 90-day period to satisfy a domestic support obligation (child support or alimony), identify that amount with an asterisk. Include payments made as part of a creditor repayment plan negotiated by an approved budget and credit counseling agency.

b. Debtor whose debts are not primarily consumer debts. If your debts are primarily business debts, list all payments or other transfers made to a creditor within 90 days of filing regarding property that is worth $6,225 or more.

c. All debtors. List all payments or other transfers made to an insider creditor, if the payments or transfers were made within one year before you file your bankruptcy petition. Include alimony and child support payments.

The purpose of these questions is to find out whether you have preferred any creditor over others. If you have paid a regular creditor during the 90 days before you file, or an insider during the year before you file, the trustee can demand that the creditor turn over the amount to the court so the trustee can use it to pay your other unsecured creditors. (See Ch. 3.) The trustee may ask you to produce written evidence of any payments you list here, such as copies of canceled checks, check stubs, or bank statements.

> ⚠ CAUTION
> **Don't use your tax refund to repay a debt.**
> Many people use their tax refunds to repay loans from relatives. If you repay more than $600, however, it counts as a preference that the trustee can take back. The better strategy is to hang on to the money, declare it on Schedule B, and claim it as exempt on Schedule C assuming that the exemptions you are using provide for it. Then, after your bankruptcy, it will be yours to do with what you want. If you've already repaid the loan, perhaps the relative can return the money and you can exempt it as described above. If the money is gone, your relative can reject the trustee's demand and say, in effect, "sue me." For amounts less than $1,000 or so, it's unlikely that the trustee will sue; the expense will likely outweigh whatever the trustee could recover. But you never know. If you have no way to exempt your tax refund, you are permitted to spend it on living expenses and necessities prior to filing bankruptcy, but make sure you can document your expenditures.

4. Suits and administrative proceedings, executions, garnishments and attachments.

   a. Include all court actions that you are currently involved in or that you were involved in during the year before filing. Court actions include personal injury cases, small claims actions, contract disputes, divorces, paternity actions, support or custody modification actions, and the like. Include:

- **Caption of suit and case number.** The caption is the case title (such as Carrie Edwards v. Ginny Jones). The case number is assigned by the court clerk and appears on the first page of any court-filed paper.
- **Nature of proceeding.** A phrase, or even a one-word description, is sufficient. For example, "suit by debtor for compensation for damages to debtor's car caused by accident," or "divorce."
- **Court or agency and location.** This information is on any summons you received or prepared.
- **Status or disposition.** State whether the case is awaiting trial, pending a decision, on appeal, or finished.

   b. If, at any time during the year before you file for bankruptcy, your wages, real estate, or personal property was taken from you under the authority of a court order to pay a debt, enter the requested information. If you don't know the exact date, put "on or about" and the approximate date.

5. Repossessions, foreclosures and returns. If, at any time during the year before you file for bankruptcy, a creditor repossessed or foreclosed on property you had bought and were making payments on, or had pledged as collateral for a loan, give the requested information. For instance, if your car, boat, or video equipment was repossessed because you defaulted on your payments, describe it here. Also, if you voluntarily returned property to a creditor because you couldn't keep up the payments, enter that here.

6. Assignments and receiverships.

   a. If, at any time during the 120 days (four months) before you file for bankruptcy, you assigned (legally transferred) your right to receive benefits or property to a creditor to pay a debt, list it here. Examples include assigning a percentage of your wages to a creditor for several months or assigning a portion of a personal injury award to an attorney. The assignee is the person to whom the assignment was made, such as the creditor or attorney. The terms of the assignment should be given briefly—for example, "wages assigned to Snorkle's Store to satisfy debt of $500."

   b. Identify all of your property that has been in the hands of a court-appointed receiver, custodian, or another official during the year before you file for bankruptcy. If you've made child support payments directly to a court, and the court, in turn, paid your child's other parent, list those payments here.

7. Gifts. Provide the requested information about gifts you've made in the past year. The bankruptcy court and trustee want this information to make sure you haven't improperly unloaded any property before filing for bankruptcy. List all charitable donations of more than $100 and gifts to family members of more than $200.

You don't have to list gifts to family members that are "ordinary and usual," but there is no easy way to identify such gifts. The best test is whether someone outside of the family might think the gift was unusual under the circumstances. If so, list it. Forgiving a loan is also a gift, as is charging interest substantially below the market rate. Other gifts include giving a car or prepaid trip to a business associate.

8. Losses. Provide the requested information. Include gambling losses. If the loss was for an exempt item, most states let you keep the insurance proceeds up to the limit of the exemption. (See Appendix A.) If the item was not exempt, the trustee is entitled to the proceeds. In either case, list any proceeds you've received or expect to receive. If you experience a loss after you file, you should promptly amend your papers, as this question applies to losses both before you file and afterward.

9. Payments related to debt counseling or bankruptcy. If you paid an improperly high fee to an attorney, bankruptcy petition preparer, debt consultant, or debt consolidator, the trustee may try to get some of it back to distribute to your creditors. Be sure to list all payments someone else made on your behalf, as well as payments you made directly.

10. Other transfers.

a. List all real and personal property that you've sold or given to someone else during the two years before you file for bankruptcy. Some examples are selling or abandoning (junking) a car, pledging your house as security (collateral) for a loan, granting an easement on real estate, or trading property. Also, describe any transfer within the past two years to your ex-spouse as part of a marital settlement agreement. If you are filing alone, describe gifts to your current spouse made during that same period.

Don't include any gifts you listed in Item 7. Also, don't list property you've parted with as a regular part of your business or financial affairs. For example, if you operate a mail order book business, don't list the books you sold during the past year. Similarly, don't put down payments for regular goods and services, such as your phone bill,

utilities, or rent. The idea is to disclose transfers of property that might legally belong in your bankruptcy estate.

Be accurate about the value of the transferred property. If property is transferred for roughly the same amount that it's worth, there shouldn't be a problem. Only when the property is not transferred for fair market value will the transfer raise the inference that it was unloaded to the detriment of your creditors.

> **EXAMPLE 1:** Three years before filing for bankruptcy, Jack sold some personal electronic mixing equipment to a friend for a modest sum. This sale wasn't made within the previous two years, so Jack needn't list it here.

> **EXAMPLE 2:** John has accumulated a collection of junked classic cars to resell to restoration hobbyists. Within the past year, John has sold three of the cars for a total of $20,000. Because this is part of John's regular business, he needn't report the sales here. However, as a sole proprietor, John will be completing Questions 18 through 20.

> **EXAMPLE 3:** Within the year before filing for bankruptcy, Louise, a nurse, sold a vintage Jaguar E-type for $17,000. Because this isn't part of her business, Louise should list this sale here.

b. List all transfers of your own property you have made in the previous ten years to an irrevocable trust that lists you as a beneficiary. These types of trusts—referred to as self-settled trusts—are commonly used by wealthy people to shield their assets from creditors and by disabled people to preserve their right to receive government benefits. In bankruptcy, however, assets placed in a self-settled trust will be considered nonexempt. There is an exception that applies to assets placed in certain special needs trusts. (*In re Schultz*, 368 B.R. 832 (D. Minn. 2007).) If you are the beneficiary of a self-settled trust, you should talk to a bankruptcy attorney before filing.

Sample Statement of Financial Affairs—page 1

B7 (Official Form 7) (04/13)

United States Bankruptcy Court
Eastern District of California

In re   **Carrie Anne Edwards** _____

Case No. _____

                                      Debtor(s)

Chapter   **7** _____

STATEMENT OF FINANCIAL AFFAIRS

      This statement is to be completed by every debtor. Spouses filing a joint petition may file a single statement on which the information for both spouses is combined. If the case is filed under chapter 12 or chapter 13, a married debtor must furnish information for both spouses whether or not a joint petition is filed, unless the spouses are separated and a joint petition is not filed. An individual debtor engaged in business as a sole proprietor, partner, family farmer, or self-employed professional, should provide the information requested on this statement concerning all such activities as well as the individual's personal affairs. To indicate payments, transfers and the like to minor children, state the child's initials and the name and address of the child's parent or guardian, such as "A.B., a minor child, by John Doe, guardian." Do not disclose the child's name. See, 11 U.S.C. § 112; Fed. R. Bankr. P. 1007(m).

      Questions 1 - 18 are to be completed by all debtors. Debtors that are or have been in business, as defined below, also must complete Questions 19 - 25. **If the answer to an applicable question is "None," mark the box labeled "None."** If additional space is needed for the answer to any question, use and attach a separate sheet properly identified with the case name, case number (if known), and the number of the question.

DEFINITIONS

      "In business." A debtor is "in business" for the purpose of this form if the debtor is a corporation or partnership. An individual debtor is "in business" for the purpose of this form if the debtor is or has been, within six years immediately preceding the filing of this bankruptcy case, any of the following: an officer, director, managing executive, or owner of 5 percent or more of the voting or equity securities of a corporation; a partner, other than a limited partner, of a partnership; a sole proprietor or self-employed full-time or part-time. An individual debtor also may be "in business" for the purpose of this form if the debtor engages in a trade, business, or other activity, other than as an employee, to supplement income from the debtor's primary employment.

      "Insider." The term "insider" includes but is not limited to: relatives of the debtor; general partners of the debtor and their relatives; corporations of which the debtor is an officer, director, or person in control; officers, directors, and any persons in control of a corporate debtor and their relatives; affiliates of the debtor and insiders of such affiliates; and any managing agent of the debtor. 11 U.S.C. § 101(2), (31).

---

1. Income from employment or operation of business

None
☐

State the gross amount of income the debtor has received from employment, trade, or profession, or from operation of the debtor's business, including part-time activities either as an employee or in independent trade or business, from the beginning of this calendar year to the date this case was commenced. State also the gross amounts received during the **two years** immediately preceding this calendar year. (A debtor that maintains, or has maintained, financial records on the basis of a fiscal rather than a calendar year may report fiscal year income. Identify the beginning and ending dates of the debtor's fiscal year.) If a joint petition is filed, state income for each spouse separately. (Married debtors filing under chapter 12 or chapter 13 must state income of both spouses whether or not a joint petition is filed, unless the spouses are separated and a joint petition is not filed.)

AMOUNT	SOURCE
$60,100.00	**2014 -- Employment at Microsoft as software engineer**
$54,100.00	**2015 -- Employment at Microsoft and Macy's retail**
$0.00	**2016 -- None yet earned in 2016**

---

2. Income other than from employment or operation of business

None
■

State the amount of income received by the debtor other than from employment, trade, profession, or operation of the debtor's business during the **two years** immediately preceding the commencement of this case. Give particulars. If a joint petition is filed, state income for each spouse separately. (Married debtors filing under chapter 12 or chapter 13 must state income for each spouse whether or not a joint petition is filed, unless the spouses are separated and a joint petition is not filed.)

      AMOUNT   SOURCE

Sample Statement of Financial Affairs—page 2

B7 (Official Form 7) (04/13)
2

___

3. Payments to creditors

None ☐ *Complete a. or b., as appropriate, and c.*

    a. *Individual or joint debtor(s) with primarily consumer debts:* List all payments on loans, installment purchases of goods or services, and other debts to any creditor made within **90 days** immediately preceding the commencement of this case unless the aggregate value of all property that constitutes or is affected by such transfer is less than $600. Indicate with an asterisk (*) any payments that were made to a creditor on account of a domestic support obligation or as part of an alternative repayment schedule under a plan by an approved nonprofit budgeting and credit counseling agency. (Married debtors filing under chapter 12 or chapter 13 must include payments by either or both spouses whether or not a joint petition is filed, unless the spouses are separated and a joint petition is not filed.)

NAME AND ADDRESS OF CREDITOR	DATES OF PAYMENTS	AMOUNT PAID	AMOUNT STILL OWING
Lonetree **PO Box 305** **Lucerne, CA 95458**	**12/10/xx**	**$800.00**	**$0.00**

None ■ b. *Debtor whose debts are not primarily consumer debts:* List each payment or other transfer to any creditor made within **90 days** immediately preceding the commencement of the case unless the aggregate value of all property that constitutes or is affected by such transfer is less than $6,225*. If the debtor is an individual, indicate with an asterisk (*) any payments that were made to a creditor on account of a domestic support obligation or as part of an alternative repayment schedule under a plan by an approved nonprofit budgeting and credit counseling agency. (Married debtors filing under chapter 12 or chapter 13 must include payments and other transfers by either or both spouses whether or not a joint petition is filed, unless the spouses are separated and a joint petition is not filed.)

NAME AND ADDRESS OF CREDITOR	DATES OF PAYMENTS/ TRANSFERS	AMOUNT PAID OR VALUE OF TRANSFERS	AMOUNT STILL OWING

None ■ c. *All debtors:* List all payments made within **one year** immediately preceding the commencement of this case to or for the benefit of creditors who are or were insiders. (Married debtors filing under chapter 12 or chapter 13 must include payments by either or both spouses whether or not a joint petition is filed, unless the spouses are separated and a joint petition is not filed.)

NAME AND ADDRESS OF CREDITOR AND RELATIONSHIP TO DEBTOR	DATE OF PAYMENT	AMOUNT PAID	AMOUNT STILL OWING

4. Suits and administrative proceedings, executions, garnishments and attachments

None ☐ a. List all suits and administrative proceedings to which the debtor is or was a party within **one year** immediately preceding the filing of this bankruptcy case. (Married debtors filing under chapter 12 or chapter 13 must include information concerning either or both spouses whether or not a joint petition is filed, unless the spouses are separated and a joint petition is not filed.)

CAPTION OF SUIT AND CASE NUMBER	NATURE OF PROCEEDING	COURT OR AGENCY AND LOCATION	STATUS OR DISPOSITION
Bob Jones III v. Carrie Edwards, Case No.: MCV-34457	**Negligence action for auto accident**	**Placer County Superior Court** **10820 Justice Center Dr.** **Roseville, CA 95678**	**Trial pending**

None ☐ b. Describe all property that has been attached, garnished or seized under any legal or equitable process within **one year** immediately preceding the commencement of this case. (Married debtors filing under chapter 12 or chapter 13 must include information concerning property of either or both spouses whether or not a joint petition is filed, unless the spouses are separated and a joint petition is not filed.)

NAME AND ADDRESS OF PERSON FOR WHOSE BENEFIT PROPERTY WAS SEIZED	DATE OF SEIZURE	DESCRIPTION AND VALUE OF PROPERTY
JNR Adjustment Co. **PO Box 27070** **Minneapolis, MN 55427**	**4/7/xx**	**Wage garnishment for two months totaling $510 for judgment on debt owed to DVD club.**

___

* Amount subject to adjustment on 4/01/16, and every three years thereafter with respect to cases commenced on or after the date of adjustment.

Sample Statement of Financial Affairs—page 3

B7 (Official Form 7) (04/13)

3

5. Repossessions, foreclosures and returns

None ☐   List all property that has been repossessed by a creditor, sold at a foreclosure sale, transferred through a deed in lieu of foreclosure or returned to the seller, within **one year** immediately preceding the commencement of this case. (Married debtors filing under chapter 12 or chapter 13 must include information concerning property of either or both spouses whether or not a joint petition is filed, unless the spouses are separated and a joint petition is not filed.)

NAME AND ADDRESS OF CREDITOR OR SELLER	DATE OF REPOSSESSION, FORECLOSURE SALE, TRANSFER OR RETURN	DESCRIPTION AND VALUE OF PROPERTY
Eskanos & Adler **2325 Clayton Rd.** **Concord, CA 94520**	**4/30/xx**	**Repossessed furniture worth $800**
Grand Junction Mortgage **3456 Eighth St.** **Clearlake, CA 95422**	**Notice of Default Sent** **3/20/xx**	**Home described in Schedule A. Sale is scheduled but hasn't happened yet.**

6. Assignments and receiverships

None ■   a. Describe any assignment of property for the benefit of creditors made within **120 days** immediately preceding the commencement of this case. (Married debtors filing under chapter 12 or chapter 13 must include any assignment by either or both spouses whether or not a joint petition is filed, unless the spouses are separated and a joint petition is not filed.)

NAME AND ADDRESS OF ASSIGNEE	DATE OF ASSIGNMENT	TERMS OF ASSIGNMENT OR SETTLEMENT

None ■   b. List all property which has been in the hands of a custodian, receiver, or court-appointed official within **one year** immediately preceding the commencement of this case. (Married debtors filing under chapter 12 or chapter 13 must include information concerning property of either or both spouses whether or not a joint petition is filed, unless the spouses are separated and a joint petition is not filed.)

NAME AND ADDRESS OF CUSTODIAN	NAME AND LOCATION OF COURT CASE TITLE & NUMBER	DATE OF ORDER	DESCRIPTION AND VALUE OF PROPERTY

7. Gifts

None ☐   List all gifts or charitable contributions made within **one year** immediately preceding the commencement of this case except ordinary and usual gifts to family members aggregating less than $200 in value per individual family member and charitable contributions aggregating less than $100 per recipient. (Married debtors filing under chapter 12 or chapter 13 must include gifts or contributions by either or both spouses whether or not a joint petition is filed, unless the spouses are separated and a joint petition is not filed.)

NAME AND ADDRESS OF PERSON OR ORGANIZATION	RELATIONSHIP TO DEBTOR, IF ANY	DATE OF GIFT	DESCRIPTION AND VALUE OF GIFT
Universal Life Church **43322 First St.** **Lakeport, CA 95453**	**None**	**Monthly**	**Charitable contributions of $300 per month**

8. Losses

None ■   List all losses from fire, theft, other casualty or gambling within **one year** immediately preceding the commencement of this case **or since the commencement of this case.** (Married debtors filing under chapter 12 or chapter 13 must include losses by either or both spouses whether or not a joint petition is filed, unless the spouses are separated and a joint petition is not filed.)

DESCRIPTION AND VALUE OF PROPERTY	DESCRIPTION OF CIRCUMSTANCES AND, IF LOSS WAS COVERED IN WHOLE OR IN PART BY INSURANCE, GIVE PARTICULARS	DATE OF LOSS

Sample Statement of Financial Affairs—page 4

B7 (Official Form 7) (04/13)

4

9. Payments related to debt counseling or bankruptcy

None ☐

List all payments made or property transferred by or on behalf of the debtor to any persons, including attorneys, for consultation concerning debt consolidation, relief under the bankruptcy law or preparation of the petition in bankruptcy within **one year** immediately preceding the commencement of this case.

NAME AND ADDRESS OF PAYEE	DATE OF PAYMENT, NAME OF PAYER IF OTHER THAN DEBTOR	AMOUNT OF MONEY OR DESCRIPTION AND VALUE OF PROPERTY
Jim McDonald, Esq. **444 State St.** **Ukiah, CA 95482**	**7/21/xx**	**$100 for bankrupcty advice**
ABC Bankruptcy Counseling **1731 Second St.** **Bloomfield, NJ 07003**	**2/12/xx**	**$25 for pre-filing bankruptcy counseling course**

10. Other transfers

None ☐

a. List all other property, other than property transferred in the ordinary course of the business or financial affairs of the debtor, transferred either absolutely or as security within **two years** immediately preceding the commencement of this case. (Married debtors filing under chapter 12 or chapter 13 must include transfers by either or both spouses whether or not a joint petition is filed, unless the spouses are separated and a joint petition is not filed.)

NAME AND ADDRESS OF TRANSFEREE, RELATIONSHIP TO DEBTOR	DATE	DESCRIBE PROPERTY TRANSFERRED AND VALUE RECEIVED
Robert James **5554 15th St.** **Lakeport, CA 95453** **Arm's length transaction**	**3/23/xx**	**10 Infinity XX sold for $8,000, fair market value according to www.kbb.com, money spent on house payment, car payment, and bills.**

None ■

b. List all property transferred by the debtor within **ten years** immediately preceding the commencement of this case to a self-settled trust or similar device of which the debtor is a beneficiary.

NAME OF TRUST OR OTHER DEVICE	DATE(S) OF TRANSFER(S)	AMOUNT OF MONEY OR DESCRIPTION AND VALUE OF PROPERTY OR DEBTOR'S INTEREST IN PROPERTY

11. Closed financial accounts

None ☐

List all financial accounts and instruments held in the name of the debtor or for the benefit of the debtor which were closed, sold, or otherwise transferred within **one year** immediately preceding the commencement of this case. Include checking, savings, or other financial accounts, certificates of deposit, or other instruments; shares and share accounts held in banks, credit unions, pension funds, cooperatives, associations, brokerage houses and other financial institutions. (Married debtors filing under chapter 12 or chapter 13 must include information concerning accounts or instruments held by or for either or both spouses whether or not a joint petition is filed, unless the spouses are separated and a joint petition is not filed.)

NAME AND ADDRESS OF INSTITUTION	TYPE OF ACCOUNT, LAST FOUR DIGITS OF ACCOUNT NUMBER, AND AMOUNT OF FINAL BALANCE	AMOUNT AND DATE OF SALE OR CLOSING
WestAmerica Bank **444 North Main St.** **Rocklin, CA 95677**	**Checking Acct. #4444444**	**Final balance ($50) 7/1/xx**

Sample Statement of Financial Affairs—page 5

B7 (Official Form 7) (04/13)
5

---

12. Safe deposit boxes

None
■

List each safe deposit or other box or depository in which the debtor has or had securities, cash, or other valuables within **one year** immediately preceding the commencement of this case. (Married debtors filing under chapter 12 or chapter 13 must include boxes or depositories of either or both spouses whether or not a joint petition is filed, unless the spouses are separated and a joint petition is not filed.)

NAME AND ADDRESS OF BANK OR OTHER DEPOSITORY	NAMES AND ADDRESSES OF THOSE WITH ACCESS TO BOX OR DEPOSITORY	DESCRIPTION OF CONTENTS	DATE OF TRANSFER OR SURRENDER, IF ANY

---

13. Setoffs

None
■

List all setoffs made by any creditor, including a bank, against a debt or deposit of the debtor within **90 days** preceding the commencement of this case. (Married debtors filing under chapter 12 or chapter 13 must include information concerning either or both spouses whether or not a joint petition is filed, unless the spouses are separated and a joint petition is not filed.)

NAME AND ADDRESS OF CREDITOR	DATE OF SETOFF	AMOUNT OF SETOFF

---

14. Property held for another person

None
☐

List all property owned by another person that the debtor holds or controls.

NAME AND ADDRESS OF OWNER	DESCRIPTION AND VALUE OF PROPERTY	LOCATION OF PROPERTY
Bonnie Johnson **3335 Irving St.** **Clearlake, CA 95422**	**Poodle (Binkie) $300**	**Edwards residence**
Vannie Edwards **4444 Cleveland Ave.** **Pope Valley, CA 94567**	**$50,000 savings account owned by my grandmother. I am on the account as an informal trustee to help her manage her expenses. I am operating under a fiduciary duty to only withdraw funds for my grandmother's benefit.**	**Bank of America, 5555 Cleveland Ave.** **Pope Valley, CA 94567**

---

15. Prior address of debtor

None
☐

If the debtor has moved within **three years** immediately preceding the commencement of this case, list all premises which the debtor occupied during that period and vacated prior to the commencement of this case. If a joint petition is filed, report also any separate address of either spouse.

ADDRESS	NAME USED	DATES OF OCCUPANCY
21 Scarborough Rd. South **Cleveland Heights, OH 41118**	**Carrie Edwards**	**1/1/xx - 5/1/xx**

---

16. Spouses and Former Spouses

None
☐

If the debtor resides or resided in a community property state, commonwealth, or territory (including Alaska, Arizona, California, Idaho, Louisiana, Nevada, New Mexico, Puerto Rico, Texas, Washington, or Wisconsin) within **eight years** immediately preceding the commencement of the case, identify the name of the debtor's spouse and of any former spouse who resides or resided with the debtor in the community property state.

NAME
Torrey Edwards

Sample Statement of Financial Affairs—page 6

B7 (Official Form 7) (04/13)

6

17. Environmental Information.

For the purpose of this question, the following definitions apply:

"Environmental Law" means any federal, state, or local statute or regulation regulating pollution, contamination, releases of hazardous or toxic substances, wastes or material into the air, land, soil, surface water, groundwater, or other medium, including, but not limited to, statutes or regulations regulating the cleanup of these substances, wastes, or material.

"Site" means any location, facility, or property as defined under any Environmental Law, whether or not presently or formerly owned or operated by the debtor, including, but not limited to, disposal sites.

"Hazardous Material" means anything defined as a hazardous waste, hazardous substance, toxic substance, hazardous material, pollutant, or contaminant or similar term under an Environmental Law

None
■ a. List the name and address of every site for which the debtor has received notice in writing by a governmental unit that it may be liable or potentially liable under or in violation of an Environmental Law. Indicate the governmental unit, the date of the notice, and, if known, the Environmental Law:

SITE NAME AND ADDRESS	NAME AND ADDRESS OF GOVERNMENTAL UNIT	DATE OF NOTICE	ENVIRONMENTAL LAW

None
■ b. List the name and address of every site for which the debtor provided notice to a governmental unit of a release of Hazardous Material. Indicate the governmental unit to which the notice was sent and the date of the notice.

SITE NAME AND ADDRESS	NAME AND ADDRESS OF GOVERNMENTAL UNIT	DATE OF NOTICE	ENVIRONMENTAL LAW

None
■ c. List all judicial or administrative proceedings, including settlements or orders, under any Environmental Law with respect to which the debtor is or was a party. Indicate the name and address of the governmental unit that is or was a party to the proceeding, and the docket number.

NAME AND ADDRESS OF GOVERNMENTAL UNIT	DOCKET NUMBER	STATUS OR DISPOSITION

18 . Nature, location and name of business

None
■ a. *If the debtor is an individual*, list the names, addresses, taxpayer identification numbers, nature of the businesses, and beginning and ending dates of all businesses in which the debtor was an officer, director, partner, or managing executive of a corporation, partner in a partnership, sole proprietor, or was self-employed in a trade, profession, or other activity either full- or part-time within **six years** immediately preceding the commencement of this case, or in which the debtor owned 5 percent or more of the voting or equity securities within **six years** immediately preceding the commencement of this case.

If the debtor is a partnership, list the names, addresses, taxpayer identification numbers, nature of the businesses, and beginning and ending dates of all businesses in which the debtor was a partner or owned 5 percent or more of the voting or equity securities, within **six years** immediately preceding the commencement of this case.

If the debtor is a corporation, list the names, addresses, taxpayer identification numbers, nature of the businesses, and beginning and ending dates of all businesses in which the debtor was a partner or owned 5 percent or more of the voting or equity securities within **six years** immediately preceding the commencement of this case.

NAME	LAST FOUR DIGITS OF SOCIAL-SECURITY OR OTHER INDIVIDUAL TAXPAYER-I.D. NO. (ITIN)/ COMPLETE EIN	ADDRESS	NATURE OF BUSINESS	BEGINNING AND ENDING DATES

None
■ b. Identify any business listed in response to subdivision a., above, that is "single asset real estate" as defined in 11 U.S.C. § 101.

NAME	ADDRESS

Sample Statement of Financial Affairs—page 7

B7 (Official Form 7) (04/13)
7

The following questions are to be completed by every debtor that is a corporation or partnership and by any individual debtor who is or has been, within **six years** immediately preceding the commencement of this case, any of the following: an officer, director, managing executive, or owner of more than 5 percent of the voting or equity securities of a corporation; a partner, other than a limited partner, of a partnership, a sole proprietor, or self-employed in a trade, profession, or other activity, either full- or part-time.

*(An individual or joint debtor should complete this portion of the statement **only** if the debtor is or has been in business, as defined above, within six years immediately preceding the commencement of this case. A debtor who has not been in business within those six years should go directly to the signature page.)*

---

19. Books, records and financial statements

None
■ a. List all bookkeepers and accountants who within **two years** immediately preceding the filing of this bankruptcy case kept or supervised the keeping of books of account and records of the debtor.

NAME AND ADDRESS   DATES SERVICES RENDERED

None
■ b. List all firms or individuals who within the **two years** immediately preceding the filing of this bankruptcy case have audited the books of account and records, or prepared a financial statement of the debtor.

NAME   ADDRESS   DATES SERVICES RENDERED

None
■ c. List all firms or individuals who at the time of the commencement of this case were in possession of the books of account and records of the debtor. If any of the books of account and records are not available, explain.

NAME   ADDRESS

None
■ d. List all financial institutions, creditors and other parties, including mercantile and trade agencies, to whom a financial statement was issued by the debtor within **two years** immediately preceding the commencement of this case.

NAME AND ADDRESS   DATE ISSUED

---

20. Inventories

None
■ a. List the dates of the last two inventories taken of your property, the name of the person who supervised the taking of each inventory, and the dollar amount and basis of each inventory.

DATE OF INVENTORY   INVENTORY SUPERVISOR   DOLLAR AMOUNT OF INVENTORY
                                                             (Specify cost, market or other basis)

None
■ b. List the name and address of the person having possession of the records of each of the inventories reported in a., above.

DATE OF INVENTORY   NAME AND ADDRESSES OF CUSTODIAN OF INVENTORY
                                           RECORDS

---

21 . Current Partners, Officers, Directors and Shareholders

None
■ a. If the debtor is a partnership, list the nature and percentage of partnership interest of each member of the partnership.

NAME AND ADDRESS   NATURE OF INTEREST   PERCENTAGE OF INTEREST

None
■ b. If the debtor is a corporation, list all officers and directors of the corporation, and each stockholder who directly or indirectly owns, controls, or holds 5 percent or more of the voting or equity securities of the corporation.

NAME AND ADDRESS   TITLE   NATURE AND PERCENTAGE
                                                              OF STOCK OWNERSHIP

Sample Statement of Financial Affairs—page 8

B7 (Official Form 7) (04/13)

8

---

22 . Former partners, officers, directors and shareholders

None
■   a. If the debtor is a partnership, list each member who withdrew from the partnership within **one year** immediately preceding the commencement of this case.

NAME	ADDRESS	DATE OF WITHDRAWAL

None
■   b. If the debtor is a corporation, list all officers, or directors whose relationship with the corporation terminated within **one year** immediately preceding the commencement of this case.

NAME AND ADDRESS	TITLE	DATE OF TERMINATION

---

23 . Withdrawals from a partnership or distributions by a corporation

None
■   If the debtor is a partnership or corporation, list all withdrawals or distributions credited or given to an insider, including compensation in any form, bonuses, loans, stock redemptions, options exercised and any other perquisite during **one year** immediately preceding the commencement of this case.

NAME & ADDRESS OF RECIPIENT, RELATIONSHIP TO DEBTOR	DATE AND PURPOSE OF WITHDRAWAL	AMOUNT OF MONEY OR DESCRIPTION AND VALUE OF PROPERTY

---

24. Tax Consolidation Group.

None
■   If the debtor is a corporation, list the name and federal taxpayer identification number of the parent corporation of any consolidated group for tax purposes of which the debtor has been a member at any time within **six years** immediately preceding the commencement of the case.

NAME OF PARENT CORPORATION	TAXPAYER IDENTIFICATION NUMBER (EIN)

---

25. Pension Funds.

None
■   If the debtor is not an individual, list the name and federal taxpayer-identification number of any pension fund to which the debtor, as an employer, has been responsible for contributing at any time within **six years** immediately preceding the commencement of the case.

NAME OF PENSION FUND	TAXPAYER IDENTIFICATION NUMBER (EIN)

* * * * * *

DECLARATION UNDER PENALTY OF PERJURY BY INDIVIDUAL DEBTOR

I declare under penalty of perjury that I have read the answers contained in the foregoing statement of financial affairs and any attachments thereto and that they are true and correct.

Date _____   Signature   **/s/ Carrie Anne Edwards**
                                                  Carrie Anne Edwards
                                                  Debtor

Penalty for making a false statement: Fine of up to $500,000 or imprisonment for up to 5 years, or both. 18 U.S.C. §§ 152 and 3571

11. Closed financial accounts. Provide information for each account in your name or for your benefit that was closed or transferred to someone else during the past year.

12. Safe deposit boxes. Provide information for each safe deposit box you've had within the past year.

13. Setoffs. A setoff is when a creditor, often a bank, uses money in a customer's account to pay a debt owed to the creditor by that customer. For example, many credit unions tie loans to the borrower's savings and checking accounts, so that any default on the loan can be deducted from those accounts. Here, list any setoffs that your creditors have made during the previous 90 days. The trustee may require the bank to turn over the money obtained through setoff and use it to repay your creditors. To learn how to prevent a setoff from happening to you, see "Warning: Stop Your Bank From Draining Your Account," in Ch. 2.

14. Property held for another person. Describe all the property you've borrowed from, are storing for, or hold in trust for someone else. Examples include arrangements as simple as storing your neighbor's tractor on your property to more complex things such as funds in an irrevocable trust held for someone else as beneficiary but controlled by you as trustee, and property you're holding as executor or administrator of an estate. This type of property is not part of your bankruptcy estate. However, you must disclose it so the trustee is aware of it and can ask for more details. (Some people dishonestly describe all of their property as being in trust or otherwise belonging to someone else, hoping to avoid having to give it to the trustee. Disclosures in this part of the Statement of Financial Affairs allow the trustee to explore this possibility.)

A trustee who becomes interested in property you describe here may invoke several court procedures designed to get more information. However, it is unlikely that the trustee will invade your house to seize the property. If you can establish that the property truly belongs to someone else—by producing the trust document, for example—you needn't worry about losing it in your bankruptcy case.

If You Are Listed on Someone Else's Account

In the instructions for completing Schedule B, we explained that you should list any bank accounts you have been added to for money management purposes. Here, you should describe the account and explain, as you did on Schedule B, that you are on the account only to manage it for your relative, and that the money in the account belongs to the relative, not to you.

EXAMPLE: You are renting an unfurnished apartment owned by a friend. The friend has left a valuable baby grand piano in your care. If and when you decide to move, you have agreed to place the piano in storage for your friend. Because you don't own the piano, but rather are taking care of it for your friend, you would describe it here.

15. Prior address of debtor. If you have moved within the three years before you file for bankruptcy, list all of your residences within those three years.

16. Spouses and former spouses. If you lived in a community property state (or Puerto Rico) within eight years prior to filing for bankruptcy, list the name of your spouse and of any former spouses who lived with you in the community property state. To remind you, community property states are Alaska, Arizona, California, Idaho, Louisiana, Nevada, New Mexico, Texas, Washington, and Wisconsin.

17. Environmental information. Few individuals will have much to say here. It's intended primarily for businesses that do business on polluted premises. Still, read the questions carefully and provide the requested information, if applicable.

18. Nature, location and name of business. Provide all of the information requested on Line **a** if you are in business or have been in business for the previous six years. Note that the definition of business is very broad: It includes not only sole proprietors, but anyone self-employed in a trade, or profession or another activity either full or part time or involved in a business in which the debtor owned 5% or more of the voting or equity securities within the six-year period. It is very important that you answer this question completely so that the trustee will have a good idea of how you earned your money over the past six years and what you did with your business interests (if you are no longer in business).

SKIP AHEAD

If you don't own a business. Only debtors who have been in business have to provide responses on Lines 19 through 25. If you aren't one, go on to Line 26.

If the majority of your business income for any one business comes from renting, leasing, or otherwise operating a single piece of real property (other than an apartment building with less than four units), include your business name and the address of the property on Line **b**.

19. Books, records and financial statements.

a. Identify every person other than yourself— usually a bookkeeper or an accountant—who was involved in the accounting of your business during the previous two years. If you were the only person involved in your business's accounting, check "None."

b. If your books weren't audited during the past two years, check "None." Otherwise, fill in the requested information.

c. Usually, you, your bookkeeper, your account-ant, an ex-business associate, or possibly an ex-mate will have business records. If any are missing, explain (you'll be better off if the loss of your records was beyond your control).

d. You may have prepared a financial statement if you applied to a bank for a loan or line of credit for your business or in your own name. If you're self-employed and applied for a personal loan to purchase a car or house, you probably submitted a financial statement as evidence of your ability to repay. Such statements include:

- balance sheets (these compare assets with liabilities)
- profit and loss statements (these compare income with expenses), and

- financial statements (these provide an overall financial description of a business).

20. Inventories. If your business doesn't have an inventory because it's a service business, check "None." If your business deals in products, but you are primarily the middle person or original manufacturer, put "no inventory required" or "materials purchased for each order as needed." If you have an inventory, fill in the information requested in Items **a** and **b**.

21 through 25. These items are intended for a filer who is part of a business entity, such as a partnership, corporation, or limited liability company. Our book is designed for individuals only, so you should be able to check "None" for each of these items. If you are part of a business entity, consult with a bankruptcy lawyer before filing.

Declaration Under Penalty of Perjury by Individual Debtor. Sign and date this section. If you're filing jointly, be sure your spouse dates and signs it as well.

Form 8—Chapter 7 Individual Debtor's Statement of Intention

This form is very important if you owe any secured debts (Schedule D) or are a party to any executory contracts (such as a time-share) or unexpired leases (Schedule G). This is where you inform the trustee and your secured creditors about the contract or lease and what you want to happen to the collateral for each of your secured debts. Briefly, you may:

- reaffirm the debt under a reaffirmation agree-ment that will continue your liability for all or part of the debt despite your bankruptcy
- redeem the debt by buying the collateral at its replacement value, or
- voluntarily surrender the collateral.

These options were discussed in detail in Ch. 5; you should return to that chapter now if you want more guidance on your options here.

If you are a party to a lease (for instance, a car lease or an executory contract), you may indicate on this form that you want to assume the lease or contract.

Sample Statement of Intention—page 1

B8 (Form 8) (12/08)

United States Bankruptcy Court
Eastern District of California

In re   **Carrie Anne Edwards**

Debtor(s)

Case No. _____

Chapter   **7**

CHAPTER 7 INDIVIDUAL DEBTOR'S STATEMENT OF INTENTION

PART A - Debts secured by property of the estate. (Part A must be fully completed for **EACH** debt which is secured by property of the estate. Attach additional pages if necessary.)

Property No. 1

Creditor's Name:
GMAC

Describe Property Securing Debt:
2009 Buick LaCrosse (45,000 miles) fully loaded, good condition (replacement value - nada.com)
Location: 3045 Berwick St., Rocklin, CA

Property will be (check one):
☐ Surrendered   ■ Retained

If retaining the property, I intend to (check at least one):
☐ Redeem the property
■ Reaffirm the debt
☐ Other. Explain _____ (for example, avoid lien using 11 U.S.C. § 522(f)).

Property is (check one):
☐ Claimed as Exempt   ■ Not claimed as exempt

Property No. 2

Creditor's Name:
Grand Junction Mortgage

Describe Property Securing Debt:
Residence
Location: 3045 Berwick St, Rocklin, CA
Residence is in foreclosure. I am seeking a mortgage modification.

Property will be (check one):
☐ Surrendered   ■ Retained

If retaining the property, I intend to (check at least one):
☐ Redeem the property
☐ Reaffirm the debt
■ Other. Explain **Debtor will retain collateral and continue to make regular payments.** (for example, avoid lien using 11 U.S.C. § 522(f)).

Property is (check one):
☐ Claimed as Exempt   ■ Not claimed as exempt

Sample Statement of Intention—page 2

B8 (Form 8) (12/08)   Page 2

Property No. 3	
Creditor's Name: **Lending Tree**	**Describe Property Securing Debt:** **Residence** **Location: 3045 Berwick St, Rocklin, CA** **Residence is in foreclosure. I am hoping to modify the mortgage.**

Property will be (check one):

☐ Surrendered   ■ Retained

If retaining the property, I intend to (check at least one):
☐ Redeem the property
☐ Reaffirm the debt
■ Other. Explain __Debtor will retain collateral and continue to make regular payments.__ (for example, avoid lien using 11 U.S.C. § 522(f)).

Property is (check one):
☐ Claimed as Exempt   ■ Not claimed as exempt

PART B - Personal property subject to unexpired leases. (All three columns of Part B must be completed for each unexpired lease. Attach additional pages if necessary.)

Property No. 1		
Lessor's Name: **Beauty Products Leasing Co.**	**Describe Leased Property:** **Laser skin treatment machine. Lease for 5-year period that expires on May 2018**	Lease will be Assumed pursuant to 11 U.S.C. § 365(p)(2): ■ YES ☐ NO

I declare under penalty of perjury that the above indicates my intention as to any property of my estate securing a debt and/or personal property subject to an unexpired lease.

Date _____   Signature __/s/ Carrie Anne Edwards__
                                                  Carrie Anne Edwards
                                                  Debtor

If you want to walk away from the lease or contract, you can indicate that you are rejecting it. The bankruptcy trustee can assume the lease if you decide to reject it, but this is rarely done in personal Chapter 7 cases. The trustee might do so if you had a long-term lease as part of your business and the trustee believes it can be sold to a third party for the benefit of your creditors.

Under 11 U.S.C. § 365p, you must provide the lessor with written notice that you intend to assume the lease or contract. You do this by sending the lessor or party to the executory contract a copy of the Statement of Intention. The statute gives the lessor or contract party the option to agree to the assumption and notify you of any conditions you must meet (for example, catching up on your payments, if you're behind). The lessor or contract party is very likely to let you assume the lease or contract; the alternative would be for you to walk away without any penalty.

> **CAUTION**
>
> **Check your mileage on a leased car.** Before you decide to assume your car lease, check your mileage first. If your mileage substantially exceeds the limit in your lease and you plan on turning your car in when the lease is up, think again about whether it makes sense to keep the car. You may be better off letting it go now and getting out from under the excess-mileage charges.

> **FOR MARRIED COUPLES**
>
> **If you are married.** If you're filing jointly, complete only one form, even though it says "Individual Debtor's Statement of Intention."

Below is a completed Statement of Intention and instructions.

Court Name. Copy this information from Form 1—Voluntary Petition.

In re and **Case No.** Follow the instructions for Schedule A.

Chapter. Type in "7."

Part A—Debts secured by property of the estate. Here, you list each of your secured debts and indicate what you plan to do with the property securing the debt (the collateral). The form provides space to list three secured property items; if you have more, attach extra sheets. For each piece of property, you must list the creditor's name and describe the property, as you did on Schedule D. Then, you must check the appropriate box to indicate whether you are surrendering the property (giving it back to lender) or retaining it.

If retaining the property, I intend to. The next choices are more difficult. If you plan to enter into a reaffirmation agreement with the lender, check the "Reaffirm the debt" box. If you are able to redeem the property by paying the lesser of what you owe or the replacement value of the property, check that box. Very few debtors can afford this option. If there is equity in the property and you qualify to "avoid the lien" because it impairs an exemption, check the "Other" box and write "avoid the lien" in the blank space. (All of these options are covered in detail in Ch. 5.)

Do You Have to Reaffirm Your Mortgage to Keep Your Home?

Some mortgage lenders are under the impression that you can be forced to reaffirm your mortgage debt as a condition of retaining your home. The majority of courts considering this issue disagree—ruling that the reaffirmation rule only applies to personal property. (See for example, *In re Pope*, 2011 WL 671972 (Bankr. E.D. Va. 2011).) However, one Florida bankruptcy court held that your mortgage lender can require you to reaffirm your mortgage, subject to the court's ultimate approval. (*In re Steinberg*, 447 B.R. 355 (Bankr. S.D. Fla. 2011).)

CAUTION
Think long and hard before reaffirming a mortgage. Although you can reaffirm a mortgage like any other secured debt, bankruptcy professionals often advise against it because it will leave you with a large debt after your bankruptcy case is over. If you don't reaffirm, there are some consequences. Your lender won't report your continued payments on the mortgage to the credit reporting agencies, so your payments won't help you rehabilitate your credit. Also, you may not be able to modify your mortgage unless you reaffirm, because many mortgage servicers take the position that once your bankruptcy filing wipes out the promissory note, there's nothing left to modify. Despite these benefits, reaffirming a mortgage is usually a bad idea. The better approach is to modify your mortgage before filing for bankruptcy and don't reaffirm.

☐ **Other.** In some cases, your lender will not require you to reaffirm but rather will let you keep the property as long as you remain current on the payments. If this is your lender's choice, you can check the "Other" box and put "Debtor will retain collateral and continue to make regular payments."

Property is. If you are moving to avoid a lien, check the "Claimed as Exempt" box. Also, if you have any equity in the property securing the debt (that is, the property is worth more than you owe), check the "exempt" box. If, however, you are underwater on the property (you owe more than it's worth), check the "Not claimed as exempt" box; you have no equity to protect with an exemption.

Part B—Personal property subject to unexpired leases. In the first box, list the name of the creditor (lessor). In the middle box, describe the leased property as you did on Schedule G. In the third box, indicate whether you want the lease to continue after bankruptcy the same as before (check "Yes") or whether you want to walk away from the lease (check "No").

Sign and date the form. Even if you have no secured debts or leases to include, you must file the form with your signature and the date.

The Ride-Through Option and the Statement of Intention

If yours is a jurisdiction that allows the ride-through option, and your lender agrees to its use, then check the "Other" box and write in "retain and pay." If the ride-through option is not available in your jurisdiction, or your lender does not favor this option, you may be able to get a similar result by doing the following: Check the "Reaffirm" box on the Statement of Intention, make sure the reaffirmation agreement is filed with the court, and then see what the judge does at the reaffirmation hearing. If the judge does not approve the reaffirmation, case law indicates that you will be entitled to use the ride-through option, as long as you remain current on your payments. See Ch. 5 for more on the ride-through option.

CAUTION
Save up those monthly payments. Often, secured creditors will not accept payments while your bankruptcy case is open, but will expect you to get current after the bankruptcy discharge, when the automatic stay is no longer in place. If a creditor refuses your payments during bankruptcy, be sure to save the money so you'll be able to get current on your payments for the property you intend to keep.

Credit Card Debts

If you owe money on a bank or department store credit card and want to keep the card through bankruptcy, contact the bank or store before you file. If you offer to reaffirm the debt, some banks or stores may let you keep the credit card. If you do reaffirm it, list it on the Statement of Intention, even though, technically, it isn't a secured debt. But think twice before you do this. If you don't reaffirm the debt, it will be discharged in bankruptcy—giving you the fresh start that is, after all, the purpose of the process. Also, as with any other reaffirmation agreement, the judge will have to approve it. Most judges are reluctant to approve a reaffirmation of credit card debt.

Signature. Date and sign the form. If you're married and filing jointly, your spouse must also date and sign the form.

Certification of Non-Attorney Bankruptcy Petition Preparer. If a BPP typed your forms, have that person complete this section. Otherwise, type "N/A" anywhere in the box.

Form 21—Statement of Social Security Number

This form requires you to list your full Social Security number. It will be available to your creditors and the trustee but, to protect your privacy, will not be part of your regular bankruptcy case file.

The Means Test Forms

Two forms—Forms 22A-1 and 22A-2—make up what's known as the means test, an important test that helps the U.S. Trustee decide whether your income and expenses allow you to file for Chapter 7 bankruptcy, or whether you will have to repay your creditors in a Chapter 13 bankruptcy. If you don't have to take the means test, you fill out a third form, Form 22A-1Supp. Here's what each of the forms does:

Form 22A-1. The first form determines whether your income is below the median income for your state. If it is, you qualify for a Chapter 7 bankruptcy and do not need to fill out the second form.

Form 22A-1Supp. If you don't have to take the means test, you fill out the supplement to Form 22A-1. (The circumstances that allow you to skip the means test are discussed below.)

Form 22A-2. If your income is above the state median, you fill out the second form, which is the actual means test calculation.

SKIP AHEAD

Debtors with primarily business debts, or qualifying military service, can skip ahead. Forms 22A-1 and 22A-2 are only for debtors whose debts are primarily consumer debts. If more than 50% of your debt load is attributable to the operation of a business, you are a business debtor and do not need to complete the entire form. Instead, check Box 1, "There is no presumption of abuse," in the top right corner of Form 22A-1 and then complete the Statement of Exemption from Presumption of Abuse. The same is true if you have qualifying military service. Check Box 3, "The Means Test does not apply now because of qualified military service but it could apply later," and then complete the Statement of Exemption from Presumption of Abuse. You can find a sample Statement of Exemption from Presumption of Abuse (Official Form 22A-1Supp), along with instructions for completing it, later in this chapter.

If You Fail the Means Test

If the information you provide on this form shows that your income exceeds the state median and you can pay more than $12,475 or at least 25% of the debts you listed in Schedule F over a five-year period, your Chapter 7 filing will be presumed to be abusive, and the U.S. Trustee will ask the court to either dismiss your Chapter 7 filing or, with your consent, convert your case to a Chapter 13 case. If this happens to you, we highly recommend that you obtain the services of an attorney to help you stay in Chapter 7, unless you are willing to sign up for a five-year Chapter 13 repayment plan. If you convert, you can use most of the bankruptcy papers filed in your Chapter 7 case in your Chapter 13 case. However, you'll need help coming up with a repayment plan.

What Is Income?

While it is pretty clear that the money you receive from your job is income, you may not realize that almost all other money you receive is considered income, too. In fact, the list of the funds not considered income—Social Security benefits, tax refunds, and loan proceeds—is much shorter than that of reportable income. Here's what you'll need to include:

- gross wages, salary, tips, bonuses, overtime, and commissions
- income received from operating a business
- real property income, such as rents
- pension and retirement income, including from the government
- income payments received from your 401(k) and IRA
- interest and dividends from investments
- royalties from things such as oil, music, or book rights
- spousal support and child support received for your dependent
- money received for household expenses from a family member or roommate
- unemployment compensation and private disability income
- gambling and litigation proceeds
- trust income, and
- cash gifts

Form 22A-1—Chapter 7 Statement of Your Current Monthly Income

Below is a completed Form 22A-1 with instructions for filling it out. To get started, follow the instructions for Schedules I and J to complete the top left box. For now, leave the top right box as it is. You'll complete this box after you finish filling out the form.

RESOURCE

Prefer to let your computer crunch the numbers? Rather than completing the means test form by hand, you can use an online calculator to run the numbers for you. You'll find an excellent free calculator (as well as a treasure trove of bankruptcy information and resources) at www.legalconsumer.com. Just click on the means test link, enter your zip code number, and away you go. When you finish, copy the numbers you get onto your bankruptcy form.

Part 1: Calculate Your Current Monthly Income.

Line 1 asks you to provide your filing and marital status. The boxes you check will determine whether you provide information for yourself only, or if you need to provide your spouse's information, as well. If you are not married, married and legally separated, or married and living separately, complete Column A only. If you're married and filing jointly, or married but your spouse is not filing with you, complete Columns A and B.

CAUTION

Use the right figures. The figures you provide on Lines 2 through 11 should be the *average* monthly income that you received during the six *full* months before you file your bankruptcy. For example, if you file on January 15, 2016, provide information from July 1, 2015 through December 31, 2015 (the six full months before January 15th). Be sure to state each amount as a monthly figure, regardless of how often you receive that income. Also, if your income varied during that time, add it all together and divide it by six. Don't include income you and your spouse received jointly, such as rental income, more than once. If you don't have income to report for a particular question, simply write $0.

Sample Chapter 7 Statement of Current Monthly Income—page 1

Fill in this information to identify your case:	Check one box only as directed in this form and in Form 22A-1Supp:

Fill in this information to identify your case:

Debtor 1   **Carrie Anne Edwards**

Debtor 2
(Spouse, if filing)

United States Bankruptcy Court for the: Eastern District of California

Case number
(if known)

Check one box only as directed in this form and in Form 22A-1Supp:

■ 1. There is no presumption of abuse

☐ 2. The calculation to determine if a presumption of abuse applies will be made under *Chapter 7 Means Test Calculation* (Official Form 22A-2).

☐ 3. The Means Test does not apply now because of qualified military service but it could apply later.

☐ Check if this is an amended filing

Official Form 22A - 1
Chapter 7 Statement of Your Current Monthly Income
12/14

Be as complete and accurate as possible. If two married people are filing together, both are equally responsible for being accurate. If more space is needed, attach a separate sheet to this form. Include the line number to which the additional information applies. On the top of any additional pages, write your name and case number (if known). If you believe that you are exempted from a presumption of abuse because you do not have primarily consumer debts or because of qualifying military service, complete and file *Statement of Exemption from Presumption of Abuse Under § 707(b)(2)* (Official Form 22A-1Supp) with this form.

Part 1:	Calculate Your Current Monthly Income

1. **What is your marital and filing status?** Check one only.

    ■ **Not married.** Fill out Column A, lines 2-11.

    ☐ **Married and your spouse is filing with you.** Fill out both Columns A and B, lines 2-11.

    ☐ **Married and your spouse is NOT filing with you. You and your spouse are:**

        ☐ **Living in the same household and are not legally separated.** Fill out both Columns A and B, lines 2-11.

        ☐ **Living separately or are legally separated.** fill out Column A, lines 2-11; do not fill out Column B. By checking this box, you declare under penalty of perjury that you and your spouse are legally separated under nonbankruptcy law that applies or that you and your spouse are living apart for reasons that do not include evading the Means Test requirements. 11 U.S.C § 707(b)(7)(B).

Fill in the average monthly income that you received from all sources, derived during the 6 full months before you file this bankruptcy case. 11 U.S.C. § 101(10A). For example, if you are filing on September 15, the 6-month period would be March 1 through August 31. If the amount of your monthly income varied during the 6 months, add the income for all 6 months and divide the total by 6. Fill in the result. Do not include any income amount more than once. For example, if both spouses own the same rental property, put the income from that property in one column only. If you have nothing to report for any line, write $0 in the space.

		Column A Debtor 1	Column B Debtor 2 or non-filing spouse
2.	**Your gross wages, salary, tips, bonuses, overtime, and commissions** (before all payroll deductions).	$ 4,950.67	$
3.	**Alimony and maintenance payments.** Do not include payments from a spouse if Column B is filled in.	$ 0.00	$
4.	**All amounts from any source which are regularly paid for household expenses of you or your dependents, including child support.** Include regular contributions from an unmarried partner, members of your household, your dependents, parents, and roommates. Include regular contributions from a spouse only if Column B is not filled in. Do not include payments you listed on line 3.	$ 400.00	$

5. **Net income from operating a business, profession, or farm**

Gross receipts (before all deductions)	$ 0.00		
Ordinary and necessary operating expenses	-$ 0.00		
Net monthly income from a business, profession, or farm	$ 0.00	Copy here -> $ 0.00	$

6. **Net income from rental and other real property**

Gross receipts (before all deductions)	$ 0.00		
Ordinary and necessary operating expenses	-$ 0.00		
Net monthly income from rental or other real property	$ 0.00	Copy here -> $ 0.00	$

7. **Interest, dividends, and royalties** $ 0.00 $

Sample Chapter 7 Statement of Current Monthly Income—page 2

Debtor 1   **Carrie Anne Edwards**   Case number (*if known*) _____

	Column A Debtor 1	Column B Debtor 2 or non-filing spouse
8. Unemployment compensation	$ 0.00	$

Do not enter the amount if you contend that the amount received was a benefit under the Social Security Act. Instead, list it here:

For you	$ 0.00
For your spouse	$

9. Pension or retirement income. Do not include any amount received that was a benefit under the Social Security Act. $ 0.00 $

10. Income from all other sources not listed above. Specify the source and amount. Do not include any benefits received under the Social Security Act or payments received as a victim of a war crime, a crime against humanity, or international or domestic terrorism. If necessary, list other sources on a separate page and put the total on line 10c.

10a. _____	$ 0.00	$
10b. _____	$ 0.00	$
10c. Total amounts from separate pages, if any.	+ $ 0.00	$

11. Calculate your total current monthly income. Add lines 2 through 10 for each column. Then add the total for Column A to the total for Column B.

$ **5,350.67**   + $ _____   = $ **5,350.67**

Total current monthly income

Part 2:   **Determine Whether the Means Test Applies to You**

12. Calculate your current monthly income for the year. Follow these steps:

12a. Copy your total current monthly income from line 11   Copy line 11 here=>   12a. $ **5,350.67**

Multiply by 12 (the number of months in a year)   **x 12**

12b. The result is your annual income for this part of the form   12b. $ **64,208.04**

13. Calculate the median family income that applies to you. Follow these steps:

Fill in the state in which you live.   **CA**

Fill in the number of people in your household.   **3**

Fill in the median family income for your state and size of household.   13. $ **68,917.00**

14. How do the lines compare?

14a. ■   Line 12b is less than or equal to line 13. On the top of page 1, check box 1, *There is no presumption of abuse.* Go to Part 3.

14b. ☐   Line 12b is more than line 13. On the top of page 1, check box 2, *The presumption of abuse is determined by Form 22A-2.* Go to Part 3 and fill out Form 22A-2.

Part 3:   **Sign Below**

By signing here, I declare under penalty of perjury that the information on this statement and in any attachments is true and correct.

X **/s/ Carrie Anne Edwards**
Carrie Anne Edwards
Signature of Debtor 1

Date _____
    MM / DD / YYYY

If you checked line 14a, do NOT fill out or file Form 22A-2.

If you checked line 14b, fill out Form 22A-2 and file it with this form.

What If You Receive Income During the Six-Month Period That You Earned Before That Period?

Some courts insist that you include all income you actually received during the reporting period, even if you earned it or became entitled to receive it before the six-month period began. (*In re Miller*, 519 B.R. 819 (B.A.P. 10th Cir. 2014).) Not all courts agree, however. (See, *In re Arnoux*, 442 B.R. 769 (Bankr. E.D. Wash. 2010).)

As with everything involving bankruptcy, unless you are familiar with the requirements and practices in your particular court, it is better to err on the side of being conservative. That would mean reporting all income received during the six-month period. Check with a local attorney if this would make the difference between passing or not passing the means test.

Line 2. Gross wages, salary, tips, bonuses, overtime, and commissions. Enter your average monthly earnings over the last six months from gross wages, salary, tips, bonuses, overtime, and commissions. ("Gross" means before any taxes, Social Security, or any other amounts are withheld.)

Line 3. Alimony and maintenance payments. Enter any alimony, spousal support, and maintenance payments you receive from someone other than your current spouse.

Line 4. All amounts from any source that are regularly paid for household expenses of you or your dependents, including child support. Enter the monthly average of any amounts regularly contributed by someone else to your household income. This includes regular contributions from an unmarried partner, members of your household, your dependents, parents and roommates. If you are filing separately but your spouse's income is included in Column B, don't include any contributions that your spouse makes to your household; his or her income is already being taken into account.

Line 5. Net income from operating a business, profession, or farm. In the first blank, list your monthly gross receipts before deductions (add everything up for the six-month period and then divide by six). Compute your average ordinary and necessary monthly expenses for the business for the six-month period and insert it in the second blank. Subtract your monthly expenses from your gross receipts to obtain the net monthly income. Transfer the net monthly income to Column A if it is your business or yours and your spouse's joint business. Transfer the number to Column B if the business belongs to your spouse only.

Line 6. Net income from rental and other real property. Follow the instructions for Line 5 to find the net monthly income for your rental or other real property. Transfer the net monthly income to either your income column or your spouse's income column, but not both.

Line 7. Interest, dividends, and royalties. Enter your average monthly income from interest, dividends, and royalties over the last six months.

Line 8. Unemployment compensation. Your average monthly unemployment compensation goes here. If the amount received was a Social Security benefit, do not list it in Column A or B. Instead, list it in the specific spaces provided for you or your spouse.

Line 9. Pension or retirement income. This is where you include your average monthly pension and retirement income. Don't include Social Security retirement benefits.

Line 10. Income from all other sources not listed above. If you received any income that you didn't already list, you identify it here using continuation pages if necessary. Don't include money received under the Social Security Act, payments received as a victim of a war crime, a crime against humanity, or international or domestic terrorism.

Line 11. Calculate your total current monthly income. Add together all of the entries in Column A and all of the entries in Column B (enter a zero in Column B if there is no co-debtor). Add the two income totals together and enter the result in the far right space. This is your total current monthly income.

Part 2: Determine Whether the Means Test Applies to You.

This is where the rubber meets the road. In this part, you compare the current monthly income figure you calculated in Part 1 of this form to the median family income for your state. If your income is more than the median, you'll have to fill out the next form, Form 22A-2; depending on that form's figures and calculations, you may be barred from using Chapter 7. If your income is equal to or less than the median, you can skip Form 22A-2 and file your Chapter 7 papers. Keep reading to find out where you stand.

Line 12. Calculate your current monthly income for the year. First, copy your total current monthly income from Line 11 to Line 12a. Then, convert your monthly figure to an annual one by multiplying it by 12. This is your current annual income and it goes on Line 12b.

Line 13. Calculate the median family income that applies to you. Fill in your state and family size. (If you're not sure which household members to count, see "Determine Your Household Size," in Ch. 1.) The most recent state median income figures as of the publishing date of this book are in Appendix B. You can find the current figures on the U.S. Trustee's website at www.justice.gov/ust. Click "Means Testing Information" and then scroll down to the link "State Median Family Income."

Line 14. How do the lines compare? Do the math. If your income (Line 12a) is less than your state's median income (Line 13), you pass the means test without further calculations. Check Box 14a and the first box on the top of Page 1 of this form, "There is no presumption of abuse." Because your income is low enough, you don't need to complete the next form.

If your income (Line 12a) is more than state's median income (Line 13), you must do more calculations to see if you qualify for Chapter 7 bankruptcy. Check Box 14b and the second box on the top of Page 1 of this form, "The calculation to determine if a presumption of abuse applies will be made under Chapter 7 Means Test Calculation (Official Form B 22A2)." Now you must complete Form 22A-2.

Part 3: Sign Below.

By signing Form 22A-1, you declare under penalty of perjury that all information you provided is true and correct. The instructions at the bottom of the page tell you whether you must file Form 22A-2.

> **TIP**
> **Consider postponing your filing.** If you conclude that you'll have to take the means test, think about whether your income will decrease in the current or future several months. If you recently lost a high-paying job or had a sudden decrease in commissions or royalties, for example, your average income over the past six months might look pretty substantial. But in a few months, when you average in your lower earnings, it will come down quite a bit—perhaps even to less than the state median. If so, you might want to delay your bankruptcy filing if you can.

Form 22A-2—Chapter 7 Means Test Calculation

If you're still reading then you probably make more than your state's median household income, and, as a result, you've arrived at the beginning of the means test. The purpose of the means test is to find out whether you have enough income to pay some of your unsecured, nonpriority debts over a five-year period. (Your unsecured, nonpriority debts are those you listed in Schedule F, above.)

Below is a blank Form 22A-2 with step-by-step instructions for filling it out. Getting started is simple enough—fill out the box in the top left by following the instructions for Schedules I and J. As with Form 22A-1, don't fill out the box in the top right just yet. You'll do that after you finish the form.

Part 1: Determine Your Adjusted Income.

The first part of the means test calculation allows you to subtract the portion of your spouse's income that isn't used to pay for monthly household expenses. (If you and your spouse are filing together, then you don't get to adjust your income here.)

Line 1. Start by copying Line 11 from Form 22A-1 onto Line 1. This is your current monthly income.

Line 2. Next, select the box that most accurately describes your filing status.

Line 3. If you're married but filing individually (without your spouse), you can deduct the portion of your spouse's income used to pay for things other than household debts. Be aware that the U.S. Trustee takes the position that you can deduct only the following debts:

- your spouse's student loans
- your spouse's tax debt, including tax withholdings from earnings
- repayment of a loan that benefits only the other spouse, such as the repayment of a 401(k) loan, or
- funds used to support another person, such as a child from another marriage or spousal support for an ex-spouse.

For example, if your nonfiling spouse has a monthly income of $2,000, but your spouse contributes only $400 a month to your household, you can enter $1,600 here as long as the excluded income goes to pay a debt meeting the criteria above. (Also, don't include a deduction for credit cards used for household expense.) This is commonly referred to as the marital adjustment deduction.

Line 4. Adjust your current monthly income by subtracting the amount in Line 3d from the amount on Line 1. This is your adjusted current monthly income.

Part 2. Calculate Your Deductions From Your Income.

In this part, you will figure out what expenses you can deduct from your currently monthly income. After you subtract all allowed expenses, you will be left with your monthly disposable income—the amount you would have left over, in theory, to pay into a Chapter 13 plan.

While you're allowed to deduct living expenses from your income, there's a catch. Since the bankruptcy court does not allow for lavish living, you're not allowed to deduct the actual costs for all of your expenses, only for some of them. Instead, you must calculate certain expenses according to the standards set by the IRS.

(The IRS uses these standards to decide how much a delinquent taxpayer should have to give the agency each month to repay back taxes on an installment plan.)

RESOURCE
Where to find the IRS standards. To find the IRS standards, go to the U.S. Trustee's website at www.justice.gov/ust. Choose "Means Testing Information" from the left column. Choose the correct filing date from the drop-down menu and click "Go." As you scroll down, you'll see links for the National Standards as well as Local Standards (you will have to select either your state or your region for the Local Standards, depending on the type of expense). You can also get these figures from your court clerk.

Here are some tips for filling out Lines 6 through 15.

- Deduct the expense amounts set forth by the IRS regardless of your actual expenses.
- Do not "double dip" by deducting amounts that you already subtracted from your spouse's income in Line 3 or business operating expenses you already subtracted in Lines 5 and 6 on Form 22A-1.
- If your actual expense is higher than the standard deduction, you'll get a chance later on to include the actual amount.
- "You" refers to both you and your spouse if you were required to fill in Column B on Form 22A-1.

Line 5. Number of people used in determining your deductions from income. List the number of people you claim on your federal tax return plus any other dependents you support, whether or not they live in your household.

Items Using the National Standards

Use the IRS National Standards for Lines 6 and 7. (See "Where to find the IRS standards," above.)

Line 6: Food, clothing, and other items. Enter the total IRS National Standards for Food, Clothing, and Other Items for your family size and income level. This is the amount the IRS believes you should get to spend for food, clothing, household supplies, personal care, and miscellaneous other items.

Line 7: Out of pocket health care allowance. Enter the amount you are allowed to claim for heath expenses from the IRS National Standards for Out-of-Pocket Health Care. You can claim more for household members who are at least 65 years old. The total amount you can claim is quite small; if you spend more than you're allowed to claim here, you can list the rest on Line 22. Lines 7a through 7f ask you to split the expenses into two groups—expenses for those over 65 and for those under 65. Enter your total deduction amount on Line 7g.

Local IRS Standards

Use the IRS Local Standards for Lines 8 through 15. (See "Where to find the IRS standards," above.)

Line 8. Housing and utilities—insurance and operating expenses. Enter the amount of the IRS Housing and Utilities Standards listed for your county, using the figure under the "Non-Mortgage" column.

Line 9. Housing and utilities—mortgage or rent expenses. Calculate your mortgage or rent expenses using lines 9a through 9c.

Line 9a. Enter the amount of the IRS Housing and Utilities Standards for your county for mortgage or rent expenses according to your family size. Use the figure under the "Mortgage/Rent" column, and enter it on Line 9a.

Line 9b: Here you calculate your total average monthly payment for all mortgages and debts secured by your home. On the lines provided, list each of your secured creditors and the average monthly payment to each. To get the average monthly payment, add up all payments due in the next 60 months, and then divide by 60. Total the payments for all creditors, and list that number in the "Total average monthly payment" box. Copy that number in two additional places: The line immediately to the right (there is an arrow pointing to it) and on Line 33a.

Line 9c. Subtract the amount listed on Line 9b from the amount listed on Line 9a. Enter that number twice on Line 9c (there are two blanks right next to each other for the same number). If you get a negative number, enter "0." This is your net mortgage or rent expense. (You will use this information later on in the

section on Deductions for Debt Payments. The extra steps in this section ensure that you don't end up double-counting the mortgage deduction.)

Line 10. If you think the IRS Local Standards are incorrect, explain why and list your additional expenses here. If you believe your housing expenses are higher than the IRS Local Standards because the standards are wrong, and the incorrect standards affect your monthly expense calculation, explain why on the lines provided and list any additional amount you claim on Line 10.

CAUTION
Stay away from Line 10. Seriously. After combing through the opinions of the brightest bankruptcy minds in the land, it appears no one really knows the purpose of Line 10. In fact, even the U.S. Trustee's official position fails to shed much light on this dilemma, and instead, chooses only to warn debtors—rather mysteriously at that—that claiming additional housing expenses leads to unwanted objections by trustees. Since no one can figure out what else could be listed on Line 10, and taking into account that the bankruptcy court's favorite phrase is "Pigs get fat, hogs get slaughtered," unless you think up (and list) a great justification for your adjustment, the prudent course of action is to take what you get on Lines 8 and 9 and skip Line 10 altogether.

Line 11. Local transportation expenses. Indicate the number of cars for which you pay operating expenses or for which somebody else contributes to the operating expenses. If you don't have a car, check "0" and go to Line 14 (you'll get to deduct public transportation expenses on that line). If you have one car, select the second box and proceed to Line 12. If you have two or more cars, check the third box and go to line 12.

Line 12. Vehicle operation expense. These are your expenses for operating a car (maintenance, gas, etc.). On Line 12, enter the IRS Local Transportation Standards amount for your area and the number of cars you claim expenses for (the amount differs depending upon where you live).

Line 13: Vehicle ownership or lease expense. These are your expenses for owning or leasing a car. Start by listing the year, make, model and mileage of Vehicle 1 on the lines following the instruction "Describe Vehicle 1." You'll do the same for Vehicle 2 immediately following Line 13c. You figure out your vehicle expense by completing Lines 13a through 13f.

> CAUTION
> **You must have car payments to make this deduction.** Keep in mind that you can only claim an ownership/lease expense on Line 13 for a car that you actually make loan or lease payments on. If you own your car free and clear, you are not entitled to the ownership/lease expense deduction. (*Ranson v. FIA Card Services, N.A.*, 562 U.S. 61 (2011).)

Line 13a: On Line 13a, enter the IRS Local Transportation Standards for ownership of a first car. The amount is actually a national figure; currently, it is $517. (See "Where to find the IRS standards," above. Scroll down to the Local Transportation Expense Standards drop-down menu and choose your region. The ownership figure is near the bottom of the page.)

Line 13b: On Line 13b, enter your average monthly payment (over the next five years) for all debts secured by your first car. For example, assume you have three years left to pay on the car and the monthly payment is $350. The total amount you will owe in the next five years is $12,600 (36 months times $350). If you spread that amount over the next five years—by dividing the total by 60, the number of months in five years—you'll see that you have an average monthly payment of $210. You'll enter this number three times: Under the heading "Average monthly payment"; in the "Copy 13b here," blank; and on Line 33b.

Line 13c: Subtract Line 13b from Line 13a and enter the amount on line 13c. Also copy the same number on the blank immediately to the right. This is your net vehicle ownership or lease expense for Vehicle 1.

Lines 13d through 13f. If you have another car, go through the same calculations for Vehicle 2 as you did for Vehicle 1.

Line 14. Public transportation expense. If you don't have a car and use public transportation, enter the amount listed under "Public Transportation" from the IRS Local Transportation Expense Standards. This is a national figure and is currently set at $184. (To get the most up-to-date figure, see "How to find the IRS standards," above. Scroll to the Local Transportation Expense Standards drop-down menu and choose your region. The public transportation cost is toward the middle of the page.)

Converting Taxes to a Monthly Figure

If you are paid weekly, biweekly, or twice a month, you will have to convert the tax amounts on your pay stubs to a monthly amount. And, if you pay quarterly taxes (estimated income taxes, for example), you'll need to convert that figure as well. Here's how to do it:

- Weekly taxes: Multiply by 4.3 to get a monthly amount.
- Biweekly taxes: Divide by 2 to get a weekly amount, then multiply by 4.3.
- Bimonthly taxes: Divide by 2.
- Quarterly taxes: Divide by 3.

Line 15. Additional public transportation expense. If you have a car and also use public transportation, you may claim a public transportation expense here. Find the correct amount by following the instructions for Line 14 above.

Other Necessary Expenses

While the below expenses are based on IRS expense categories, you list your actual expenditures (there isn't a standard IRS figure).

Line 16. Taxes. Enter the total average monthly expense that you actually incur for all taxes *other than real estate or sales taxes.* Examples of taxes that you enter here are income taxes, self-employment taxes, Social Security taxes, and Medicare taxes. In some cases, these taxes will show up on your wage stub. You'll need to convert the period covered by your wage stub to a monthly figure. (Use the conversion rules above to arrive at monthly figures.) Once you have figured out how much you pay each month for each type of tax, add them together and enter the total in the column on the right.

Line 17. Involuntary deductions. Enter all of your mandatory payroll deductions here. Use the conversion rules above to arrive at monthly figures. Make sure you deduct only mandatory deductions (such as mandatory retirement contributions, union dues, and uniform costs). Don't include contributions to a 401(k) because they are voluntary.

Line 18. Life insurance. Enter any monthly payments you make for term life insurance. Do not enter payments for any other type of insurance, such as credit insurance, car insurance, renter's insurance, insurance on your own life, and whole life insurance policies. (Whole life insurance is the type that allows you to borrow against the policy.)

Line 19. Court-ordered payments. Enter the amount of any payments you make pursuant to a court order. Child support and alimony are the most common examples, but you may also make payments to satisfy a court money judgment or a criminal fine. Do not include court-ordered payments toward a child support or alimony arrearage; only the payments you need to stay current should be entered here.

Line 20. Education. Enter the total monthly amount that you pay for education required by your employer to keep your job, and the total monthly amount you pay for the education of a physically or mentally challenged dependent child if there is no public education available that provides similar services. Included in this amount would be the actual costs of after-school enrichment educational services for a physically or mentally challenged child, and the actual education expenses you are paying in support of an individual educational plan.

Line 21. Childcare. Enter the average monthly expense of childcare, including babysitting, preschool, nursery school, and regular childcare. If your employment is seasonal—and therefore your need for regular childcare is seasonal—add your childcare costs up for the year and divide the total by 12. Remember that childcare and education are not the same. For instance, childcare for a child who is of public education school age should only cover the hours before and after school.

Line 22. Additional health care expenses. Enter the average monthly amount you pay for out-of-pocket health care expenses, but only to the extent it exceeds the amount you were allowed to claim on Line 7. Do not include payments for health insurance or health savings accounts; those go on Line 25.

Line 23. Optional telephones and telephone services. Enter the average monthly expenses you pay for any communication devices (other than basic home telephone and cell phone services) that are necessary for the health and welfare of you or your dependents. Examples provided by the form are pagers, call waiting, caller identification, special long distance services, or business cell phone service. Arguably virtually all of these devices are necessary for the health and welfare of your family; however, some expenses might not be allowed—for example, a cell phone you use for your business or Internet service. When in doubt, list the expense.

Line 24. Add all of the expenses allowed under the IRS expense allowances. Add together all amounts listed on Lines 6 through 23 and enter the total amount on Line 24.

Additional Expense Deductions

The means test allows you to deduct certain types of expenses not included in the IRS categories. These go on Lines 25 through 32. However, you can't list an expense twice. If you already claimed an expense elsewhere, don't list it again here.

Line 25. Health insurance, disability insurance, and health savings account expenses. Here, list your reasonably necessary monthly expenses for health insurance, disability insurance, and health savings accounts (HSAs) on the lines provided. The form allows you to list a "reasonable" expense whether you actually pay that amount each month or not. If, however, you pay less than the reasonable amount you list, you must indicate how much you actually spend each month on the additional line provided. If the U.S. Trustee or one of your creditors later wants to challenge your expense claims—for example, to argue that you really have more disposable income than the form indicates—they can use this information.

Line 26. Continued contributions to the care of household or family members. Anything you spend to care for a member of your household or immediate family because of the member's age, illness, or disability can be deducted here. If your contributions are episodic—a wheelchair here, a vacation with a companion there—estimate your average monthly expense and enter it here.

CAUTION

Your response here could affect eligibility for government benefits. Expenses you list here could render the person you are assisting ineligible for Social Security or other government benefits. For example, if you state that you are spending $500 a month for the care of a relative, and that relative is receiving SSI, your relative might receive a lower benefit amount each month, to reflect your contribution. On the other hand, if you are making such expenditures, you are required to disclose them here. If you find yourself in this predicament, talk to a lawyer.

Line 27. Protection against family violence. The average monthly expense for security systems and any other method of protecting your family should be entered here.

Line 28. Additional home energy costs. If your actual home energy costs exceed the figure you entered on Line 8, enter the extra amount you spend here. As the form indicates, you may need to prove this extra expense to the trustee. Whether you need to provide proof will depend on the results of this means test. If the amount you enter here is the deciding factor in determining that you don't have enough disposable income to fund a Chapter 13 plan, proof will definitely be required.

Line 29. Education expenses for dependent children. This item is for money you spend on your children's education. If your average monthly expense is $156.25 or more, you can claim $156.25 per child in this blank; that's the maximum you can deduct. If your average monthly expense per child is less than $156.25, enter the actual expense amount. Remember not to list an amount twice; if you already listed an expense on Line 20 or 21, for example, don't repeat it here.

Line 30. Additional food and clothing expense. Here, you can list the amount by which your actual expenses for food and clothing exceed the IRS allowance for these items as entered in Line 19. However, you cannot list more than 5% over the IRS allowance.

Line 31. Continuing charitable contributions. If you have been making charitable contributions to an organization before your bankruptcy filing date, you can enter them here as long as the group is organized and operated exclusively for religious, charitable, scientific, literary, or educational purposes; to foster national or international amateur sports competition (but only if no part of its activities involve the provision of athletic facilities or equipment); or for the prevention of cruelty to children or animals. The organization also can't be disqualified from tax exemption status because of its political activities.

Line 32. Add all of the additional expense deductions. Enter the total of Lines 25 through 31 in the column on the right.

Can You List Mortgage and Car Payments You've Stopped Making?

If you have stopped making payments on your house or car, the majority of courts that have addressed the issue would allow you to include the payments anyway (because they are contractually due). However, some courts haven't allowed deductions for payments that aren't being made. If you don't know how the courts in your area handle this issue, first take the means test without deducting anything here. If you pass anyway, then there is no problem.

However, if you need the deduction to pass the test, include it and then argue in court (if it comes to that) that the law and the form both allow deductions for debts that are contractually due, whether or not payments are actually being made. See Ch. 10 for suggestions on legal research; you can find citations to cases that address this issue at www.legalconsumer.com. This would also be an excellent time to talk to a local bankruptcy lawyer.

Deductions for Debt Payment

Here, you deduct average monthly payments you will have to make over the next five years. Once you complete this section, you can put all the numbers together to figure out whether you pass the means test.

Line 33. Secured debts. This is where you add your monthly house and car payments (which you've already calculated) together with monthly payments on other secured debts. To get the monthly figure for each secured creditor, add up the total amount that will come due within the next 60 months, and then divide the total by 60.

Line 33a. Copy the amount you listed on Line 9b (you may have already done so). This is your average monthly mortgage payment.

Line 33b. Copy the amount you listed on Line 13b. This is your average monthly payment for Vehicle 1.

Line 33c. Copy the amount you listed on Line 13c. This is your average monthly payment for Vehicle 2.

Lines 33d through 33f. For each additional secured creditor, list the creditor's name, the property securing the debt, and the average monthly payment on the debt. Also, check the box that indicates whether the payment includes taxes or insurance.

Line 33g. Add Lines 33a through 33f and enter the amount in both blank spaces on this line. This is your total average monthly payment on secured debts.

Line 34. Arrearages on property you need to support yourself. Here you'll list amounts you'd need to pay in order to catch up on past-due payments for property that you need to support yourself or your family. Property necessary for support typically includes a car, your home, and anything you need for your employment (like work tools). If you listed any property on Lines 33a through 33f that you need to support yourself and your dependents, check "Yes." Next, you list any past due amounts you owe those creditors. In the spaces provided, list the creditor, the property involved, and the total past due amount (the past due amount goes in the "Total cure amount" column. For each entry, divide the cure amount figure by 60 and enter the result in the "Monthly cure amount" column. Add up the monthly cure amounts and enter that figure on the two lines next to "Total."

Line 35. Past-due priority debts. List the average monthly amount you will have to pay for priority claims over the next five years (list past-due amounts only; don't list ongoing payments you make to stay current). Your priority claims are the ones you listed in Schedule E. They include certain tax debts, child support, and alimony. Divide by 60 to arrive at the monthly average.

Line 36. Are you eligible to file a case under Chapter 13? Here you determine whether you are eligible to file for Chapter 13 bankruptcy. You can skip this section for now. If you pass the means test (meaning that your income calculated on Line 39d is less than $7,475), you won't need to fill it out anyway. If your income is $7,475 or more after you finish the form, come back to this section and follow these steps:

1. Add Lines 33, 34, and 35.
2. Divide Line 41b by 60 (this provides the average monthly payment you would have to make to pay down 25% of your unsecured debt over five years).
3. Add this number to the total of Lines 33, 34, and 35. Put the resulting number on the space in Line 36 labeled, "Projected monthly plan payment if you were filing under Chapter 13." This is the average amount you would have to pay into a Chapter 13 plan to cover your secured debts, arrearages on those debts, priority debts, and 25% of your unsecured debts.
4. On the "Current multiplier for your district…" line, enter the multiplier percentage from the U.S. Trustee's website for your state and district. (See "Where to find the IRS standards," above. Scroll to the bottom of the page to the section called "Administrative Expenses Multipliers," and click "Schedules," then scroll down to your district to get the percentage.)
5. Multiply the two amounts. This is your average monthly administrative expense if you were filing under Chapter 13.

Line 37. Add all of the deductions for debt payment. Add Lines 33g through 36 and enter the total on Line 37.

Total Deductions From Income

Here you total up everything you can deduct from your income.

Line 38. Add all of the deductions. Copy Line 24 (your IRS expense allowances) onto the first line. Copy Line 32 (your additional expense deductions) onto the second line. Copy Line 37 (your deductions for debt payment) onto the third line. Total the three lines and enter the result twice as directed.

Part 3:   Determine Whether There Is a Presumption of Abuse.

This is where you find out whether you received a passing grade on the means test. If you have enough income left over after your allowable deductions to fund a Chapter 13 plan, the presumption of abuse arises and you probably cannot file for Chapter 7 bankruptcy. This is one of the rare moments in life that you hope you have less money after you pay all your bills rather than more, because if you don't have enough discretionary income left over to fund a Chapter 13 plan, you're good to go.

Line 39. Calculate monthly disposable income for 60 months. Follow the prompts in Lines 39a through 39d to determine your monthly disposable income.

Line 39a. Copy Line 4, your adjusted current monthly income, here.

Line 39b. Copy Line 30, your total deductions, here.

Line 39c. Subtract Line 39b from Line 39a. Enter your monthly disposable income in the two spaces provided on Line 39c.

Line 39d. Multiply Line 39c by 60 and enter the amount in the two spaces provided on Line 39d.

Line 40. Find out whether there is a presumption of abuse. Here you must check one of three boxes.

- If the amount on Line 39d is less than $7,475, check the top box. This means that you don't have enough money left over to make a Chapter 13 plan feasible so you can file for Chapter 7. If you checked the top box, go back to the first page and check the box at the top, right-hand side of the page ("There is no presumption of abuse.") Then move on to Part 5 where you sign the form.

- If the amount on Line 39d is more than $12,475, you have enough income to make a Chapter 13 plan feasible, and you probably won't be allowed to stay in Chapter 7. Go back to the first page and check the second box at the top, right-hand side of the page ("There is a presumption of abuse.") Then move on to Part 5 where you sign the form.

- If the amount on Line 39d is at least $7,475, but not more than $12,475, you will have to do a few more calculations to see where you fall. To do so, complete Lines 41(a) and (b).

Line 41a. Enter the amount listed on Line 5 of Statistical Summary of Certain Liabilities and Related Data. (This is the total amount of your unsecured nonpriority debt.)

Line 41b. Multiply line 41a by 0.25. Enter the amount in the two spaces provided.

Line 42. Determine whether your leftover income will pay at least 25% of your unsecured, nonpriority debt. Here, you determine whether the income you have left after your allowed deductions (listed on Line 39d) is sufficient to pay 25% of your total nonpriority, unsecured debt (listed on Line 41b).

If the amount on Line 39d is less than the amount on Line 41b, congratulations! You have passed the means test. Go back to the first page, check the box on the top right-hand side of the page ("There is no presumption of abuse") and move to Part 5 where you will sign the form.

If the amount on Line 39b is greater than the amount on Line 41b, then unfortunately, you did not pass the means test. The form instructs you to go back to the first page, check the bottom box at the top right-hand side of the page ("There is a presumption of abuse"), and move to Part 5 where you will sign the form.

Part 4: Give Details About Special Circumstances.
If you don't pass the means test, you might still be allowed to file for Chapter 7 if you have expenses stemming from an unusual or catastrophic situation that the trustee finds compelling. These types of expenses are listed on Part 4 of Form 22A-2 so that the trustee can evaluate your particular situation and determine whether the expenses are reasonably necessary to support you and your family.

You can list two types of expenses in Part 4—additional expenses not listed elsewhere and expenses already listed elsewhere that need explanation as to why they are reasonable and necessary. For example, in one case, both spouses in a married couple who filed jointly had jobs in rural communities that required them to drive enormous distances. By documenting the travel expenses, which were not adequately covered in the means test transportation allowance, they were able to reduce their disposable income below the means test threshold. (*In re Batzkeil*, 349 B.R. 581 (Bankr. N.D. Iowa 2006).)

Higher-than-expected expenses can also be listed here too. Say a tornado hits your town, destroys your house, and paralyzes a family member. In Part 4, you would list the increased costs involved in temporarily relocating elsewhere, buying replacement clothes and basic supplies, rebuilding the house, and healing the hurt family member.

Part 4 provides the trustee with a snapshot of your financial picture so he or she can determine whether a valid justification exists to waive the presumption of abuse.

What Happens If You Fail the Means Test?

If, after completing Form 22A-2, you check "The presumption arises" box on the top of Page 1, the court clerk will issue a notice to that effect shortly after you file your bankruptcy, and the United States Trustee will decide, upon further examination of your paperwork and within 30 days after your 341 hearing, whether to seek to have your case dismissed or converted to Chapter 13. While it's not automatic, a dismissal or conversion will most likely be sought in cases where the presumption arises.

TIP
Double-check your expenses. Before signing the form in Part 5, review the form and carefully examine the expense items that aren't mandated by the IRS. Often, people underestimate their actual expenses. If you find that you underestimated one or more expenses, or left out an expense that is provided for in the form, make the adjustments and see whether you can get a passing grade. Because this form is so complex, we recommend that you go through it at least twice before arriving at your final figures.

SEE AN EXPERT
See a lawyer if the presumption arises and you want to stay in Chapter 7. If you have to check the box stating that the presumption (of abuse) arises, your Chapter 7 filing may be in trouble. Unless you are willing to proceed under Chapter 13, or have your bankruptcy dismissed, we strongly suggest that you find a bankruptcy lawyer to help you from this point on.

Part 5: Sign Below.
Sign and date the form. You are done.

Chapter 7 Means Test Calculation—page 1

Fill in this information to identify your case:	

Debtor 1 _____ _____ _____
First Name   Middle Name   Last Name

Debtor 2
(Spouse, if filing) First Name   Middle Name   Last Name

United States Bankruptcy Court for the: _____ District of _____
(State)

Case number _____
(If known)

Check the appropriate box as directed in lines 40 or 42:

According to the calculations required by this Statement:

☐ 1. There is no presumption of abuse.

☐ 2. There is a presumption of abuse.

☐ Check if this is an amended filing

Official Form B 22A2

Chapter 7 Means Test Calculation

12/14

To fill out this form, you will need your completed copy of *Chapter 7 Statement of Your Current Monthly Income* (Official Form 22A-1).

Be as complete and accurate as possible. If two married people are filing together, both are equally responsible for being accurate. If more space is needed, attach a separate sheet to this form. Include the line number to which the additional information applies. On the top of any additional pages, write your name and case number (if known).

Part 1:   **Determine Your Adjusted Income**

1. Copy your total current monthly income. .... Copy line 11 from Official Form 22A-1 here ➔ ....1. $_____

2. Did you fill out Column B in Part 1 of Form 22A–1?

    ☐ No. Fill in $0 on line 3d.

    ☐ Yes. Is your spouse filing with you?

        ☐ No. Go to line 3.

        ☐ Yes. Fill in $0 on line 3d.

3. **Adjust your current monthly income by subtracting any part of your spouse's income not used to pay for the household expenses of you or your dependents.** Follow these steps:

    On line 11, Column B of Form 22A–1, was any amount of the income you reported for your spouse NOT regularly used for the household expenses of you or your dependents?

    ☐ No. Fill in 0 on line 3d.

    ☐ Yes. Fill in the information below:

State each purpose for which the income was used	Fill in the amount you are subtracting from
For example, the income is used to pay your spouse's tax debt or to support people other than you or your dependents	your spouse's income

3a. _____ $_____

3b. _____ $_____

3c. _____   + $_____

3d. **Total.** Add lines 3a, 3b, and 3c................................. $_____   Copy total here ➔ ....3d.   — $_____

4. **Adjust your current monthly income.** Subtract line 3d from line 1. $_____

Chapter 7 Means Test Calculation—page 2

Debtor 1 _____   Case number (*if known*)_____
        First Name   Middle Name   Last Name

Part 2:	Calculate Your Deductions from Your Income

The Internal Revenue Service (IRS) issues National and Local Standards for certain expense amounts. Use these amounts to answer the questions in lines 6-15. To find the IRS standards, go online using the link specified in the separate instructions for this form. This information may also be available at the bankruptcy clerk's office.

Deduct the expense amounts set out in lines 6-15 regardless of your actual expense. In later parts of the form, you will use some of your actual expenses if they are higher than the standards. Do not deduct any amounts that you subtracted from your spouse's income in line 3 and do not deduct any operating expenses that you subtracted from income in lines 5 and 6 of Form 22A–1.

If your expenses differ from month to month, enter the average expense.

Whenever this part of the form refers to *you*, it means both you and your spouse if Column B of Form 22A–1 is filled in.

5. **The number of people used in determining your deductions from income**

   Fill in the number of people who could be claimed as exemptions on your federal income tax return, plus the number of any additional dependents whom you support. This number may be different from the number of people in your household.

National Standards   You must use the IRS National Standards to answer the questions in lines 6-7.

6. **Food, clothing, and other items:** Using the number of people you entered in line 5 and the IRS National Standards, fill in the dollar amount for food, clothing, and other items. $_____

7. **Out-of-pocket health care allowance:** Using the number of people you entered in line 5 and the IRS National Standards, fill in the dollar amount for out-of-pocket health care. The number of people is split into two categories—people who are under 65 and people who are 65 or older—because older people have a higher IRS allowance for health care costs. If your actual expenses are higher than this IRS amount, you may deduct the additional amount on line 22.

   People who are under 65 years of age

   7a. Out-of-pocket health care allowance per person $_____

   7b. Number of people who are under 65   X _____

   7c. **Subtotal.** Multiply line 7a by line 7b. $_____ Copy line 7c here➜ ...... $_____

   People who are 65 years of age or older

   7d. Out-of-pocket health care allowance per person $_____

   7e. Number of people who are 65 or older   X _____

   7f. **Subtotal.** Multiply line 7d by line 7e. $_____ Copy line 7f here➜ ...... + $_____

   7g. **Total**. Add lines 7c and 7f... $_____ Copy total here➜ .... 7g. $_____

Chapter 7 Means Test Calculation—page 3

Debtor 1 _____   Case number *(if known)*_____
      First Name   Middle Name   Last Name

Local Standards   You must use the IRS Local Standards to answer the questions in lines 8-15.

Based on information from the IRS, the U.S. Trustee Program has divided the IRS Local Standard for housing for bankruptcy purposes into two parts:

- **Housing and utilities – Insurance and operating expenses**
- **Housing and utilities – Mortgage or rent expenses**

To answer the questions in lines 8-9, use the U.S. Trustee Program chart.

To find the chart, go online using the link specified in the separate instructions for this form. This chart may also be available at the bankruptcy clerk's office.

8. **Housing and utilities – Insurance and operating expenses:** Using the number of people you entered in line 5, fill in the dollar amount listed for your county for insurance and operating expenses. $_____

9. **Housing and utilities – Mortgage or rent expenses:**

    9a. Using the number of people you entered in line 5, fill in the dollar amount listed for your county for mortgage or rent expenses.   9a. $_____

    9b. Total average monthly payment for all mortgages and other debts secured by your home.

        To calculate the total average monthly payment, add all amounts that are contractually due to each secured creditor in the 60 months after you file for bankruptcy. Then divide by 60.

Name of the creditor	Average monthly payment
_____	$_____
_____	$_____
_____	+ $_____

        9b. Total average monthly payment $_____   Copy line 9b here ➜ – $_____   Repeat this amount on line 33a.

    9c. Net mortgage or rent expense.
        Subtract line 9b (*total average monthly payment*) from line 9a (*mortgage or rent expense*). If this amount is less than $0, enter $0.   9c. $_____   Copy line 9c here ➜ $_____

10. **If you claim that the U.S. Trustee Program's division of the IRS Local Standard for housing is incorrect and affects the calculation of your monthly expenses, fill in any additional amount you claim.** $_____

    Explain why: _____
    _____

11. **Local transportation expenses:** Check the number of vehicles for which you claim an ownership or operating expense.

    ☐ 0. Go to line 14.
    ☐ 1. Go to line 12.
    ☐ 2 or more. Go to line 12.

12. **Vehicle operation expense:** Using the IRS Local Standards and the number of vehicles for which you claim the operating expenses, fill in the *Operating Costs* that apply for your Census region or metropolitan statistical area. $_____

Chapter 7 Means Test Calculation—page 4

Debtor 1 _____   Case number *(if known)*_____
         First Name   Middle Name   Last Name

13. **Vehicle ownership or lease expense:** Using the IRS Local Standards, calculate the net ownership or lease expense for each vehicle below. You may not claim the expense if you do not make any loan or lease payments on the vehicle. In addition, you may not claim the expense for more than two vehicles.

Vehicle 1   **Describe Vehicle 1:** _____

_____

13a. Ownership or leasing costs using IRS Local Standard   13a. $_____

13b. Average monthly payment for all debts secured by Vehicle 1.
Do not include costs for leased vehicles.

To calculate the average monthly payment here and on line 13e, add all amounts that are contractually due to each secured creditor in the 60 months after you filed for bankruptcy. Then divide by 60.

Name of each creditor for Vehicle 1	Average monthly payment
_____	$_____

Copy 13b here ➜   − $_____   Repeat this amount on line 33b.

13c. Net Vehicle 1 ownership or lease expense
Subtract line 13b from line 13a. If this amount is less than $0, enter $0.   13c. $_____

Copy net Vehicle 1 expense here ..... ➜ $_____

Vehicle 2   **Describe Vehicle 2:** _____

_____

13d. Ownership or leasing costs using IRS Local Standard   13d. $_____

13e. Average monthly payment for all debts secured by Vehicle 2. Do not include costs for leased vehicles.

Name of each creditor for Vehicle 2	Average monthly payment
_____	$_____

Copy 13e here ➜   − $_____   Repeat this amount on line 33c.

13f. Net Vehicle 2 ownership or lease expense
Subtract line 13e from 13d. If this amount is less than $0, enter $0.   13f. $_____

Copy net Vehicle 2 expense here ..... ➜ $_____

14. **Public transportation expense**: If you claimed 0 vehicles in line 11, using the IRS Local Standards, fill in the *Public Transportation* expense allowance regardless of whether you use public transportation. $_____

15. **Additional public transportation expense**: If you claimed 1 or more vehicles in line 11 and if you claim that you may also deduct a public transportation expense, you may fill in what you believe is the appropriate expense, but you may not claim more than the IRS Local Standard for *Public Transportation*. $_____

Chapter 7 Means Test Calculation—page 5

Debtor 1 _____   Case number (*if known*)_____
          First Name   Middle Name   Last Name

Other Necessary Expenses   In addition to the expense deductions listed above, you are allowed your monthly expenses for the following IRS categories.

16. **Taxes:** The total monthly amount that you will actually owe for federal, state and local taxes, such as income taxes, self-employment taxes, social security taxes, and Medicare taxes. You may include the monthly amount withheld from your pay for these taxes. However, if you expect to receive a tax refund, you must divide the expected refund by 12 and subtract that number from the total monthly amount that is withheld to pay for taxes.

    Do not include real estate, sales, or use taxes. $_____

17. **Involuntary deductions:** The total monthly payroll deductions that your job requires, such as retirement contributions, union dues, and uniform costs.

    Do not include amounts that are not required by your job, such as voluntary 401(k) contributions or payroll savings. $_____

18. **Life insurance:** The total monthly premiums that you pay for your own term life insurance. If two married people are filing together, include payments that you make for your spouse's term life insurance. Do not include premiums for life insurance on your dependents, for a non-filing spouse's life insurance, or for any form of life insurance other than term. $_____

19. **Court-ordered payments:** The total monthly amount that you pay as required by the order of a court or administrative agency, such as spousal or child support payments.

    Do not include payments on past due obligations for spousal or child support. You will list these obligations in line 35. $_____

20. **Education:** The total monthly amount that you pay for education that is either required:

    ■ as a condition for your job, or

    ■ for your physically or mentally challenged dependent child if no public education is available for similar services. $_____

21. **Childcare:** The total monthly amount that you pay for childcare, such as babysitting, daycare, nursery, and preschool.

    Do not include payments for any elementary or secondary school education. $_____

22. **Additional health care expenses, excluding insurance costs:** The monthly amount that you pay for health care that is required for the health and welfare of you or your dependents and that is not reimbursed by insurance or paid by a health savings account. Include only the amount that is more than the total entered in line 7.
    Payments for health insurance or health savings accounts should be listed only in line 25. $_____

23. **Optional telephones and telephone services:** The total monthly amount that you pay for telecommunication services for you and your dependents, such as pagers, call waiting, caller identification, special long distance, or business cell phone service, to the extent necessary for your health and welfare or that of your dependents or for the production of income, if it is not reimbursed by your employer.   + $_____

    Do not include payments for basic home telephone, internet and cell phone service. Do not include self-employment expenses, such as those reported on line 5 of Official Form 22A-1, or any amount you previously deducted.

24. **Add all of the expenses allowed under the IRS expense allowances.**
    Add lines 6 through 23. $_____

Chapter 7 Means Test Calculation—page 6

Debtor 1 _____ Case number *(if known)*_____
           First Name   Middle Name   Last Name

Additional Expense Deductions	These are additional deductions allowed by the Means Test.
	Note: Do not include any expense allowances listed in lines 6-24.

25. **Health insurance, disability insurance, and health savings account expenses.** The monthly expenses for health insurance, disability insurance, and health savings accounts that are reasonably necessary for yourself, your spouse, or your dependents.

   Health insurance $_____

   Disability insurance $_____

   Health savings account   **+** $_____

   Total $_____   **Copy total here**➔ .... $_____

   Do you actually spend this total amount?

   ☐ No. How much do you actually spend? $_____
   ☐ Yes

26. **Continued contributions to the care of household or family members.** The actual monthly expenses that you will continue to pay for the reasonable and necessary care and support of an elderly, chronically ill, or disabled member of your household or member of your immediate family who is unable to pay for such expenses. $_____

27. **Protection against family violence.** The reasonably necessary monthly expenses that you incur to maintain the safety of you and your family under the Family Violence Prevention and Services Act or other federal laws that apply. $_____

   By law, the court must keep the nature of these expenses confidential.

28. **Additional home energy costs.** Your home energy costs are included in your non-mortgage housing and utilities allowance on line 8.

   If you believe that you have home energy costs that are more than the home energy costs included in the non-mortgage housing and utilities allowance, then fill in the excess amount of home energy costs. $_____

   You must give your case trustee documentation of your actual expenses, and you must show that the additional amount claimed is reasonable and necessary.

29. **Education expenses for dependent children who are younger than 18.** The monthly expenses (not more than $156.25* per child) that you pay for your dependent children who are younger than 18 years old to attend a private or public elementary or secondary school.

   You must give your case trustee documentation of your actual expenses, and you must explain why the amount claimed is reasonable and necessary and not already accounted for in lines 6-23. $_____

   * Subject to adjustment on 4/01/16, and every 3 years after that for cases begun on or after the date of adjustment.

30. **Additional food and clothing expense.** The monthly amount by which your actual food and clothing expenses are higher than the combined food and clothing allowances in the IRS National Standards. That amount cannot be more than 5% of the food and clothing allowances in the IRS National Standards. $_____

   To find a chart showing the maximum additional allowance, go online using the link specified in the separate instructions for this form. This chart may also be available at the bankruptcy clerk's office.

   You must show that the additional amount claimed is reasonable and necessary.

31. **Continuing charitable contributions.** The amount that you will continue to contribute in the form of cash or financial instruments to a religious or charitable organization. 26 U.S.C. § 170(c)(1)-(2). $_____

32. **Add all of the additional expense deductions.** $_____
   Add lines 25 through 31.

Chapter 7 Means Test Calculation—page 7

Debtor 1 _____   Case number (if known)_____
First Name   Middle Name   Last Name

Deductions for Debt Payment

33. **For debts that are secured by an interest in property that you own, including home mortgages, vehicle loans, and other secured debt, fill in lines 33a through 33g.**

    To calculate the total average monthly payment, add all amounts that are contractually due to each secured creditor in the 60 months after you file for bankruptcy. Then divide by 60.

    Average monthly payment

    Mortgages on your home:

    33a. Copy line 9b here ....➔ $_____

    Loans on your first two vehicles:

    33b. Copy line 13b here. ....➔ $_____

    33c. Copy line 13e here. ....➔ $_____

Name of each creditor for other secured debt	Identify property that secures the debt	Does payment include taxes or insurance?	
33d. _____	_____	☐ No ☐ Yes	$_____
33e. _____	_____	☐ No ☐ Yes	$_____
33f. _____	_____	☐ No ☐ Yes	+ $_____

33g. Total average monthly payment. Add lines 33a through 33f. .... $_____   Copy total here➔ $_____

34. **Are any debts that you listed in line 33 secured by your primary residence, a vehicle, or other property necessary for your support or the support of your dependents?**

    ☐ No. Go to line 35.
    ☐ Yes. State any amount that you must pay to a creditor, in addition to the payments listed in line 33, to keep possession of your property (called the *cure amount*). Next, divide by 60 and fill in the information below.

Name of the creditor	Identify property that secures the debt	Total cure amount		Monthly cure amount
_____	_____	$_____	÷ 60 =	$_____
_____	_____	$_____	÷ 60 =	$_____
_____	_____	$_____	÷ 60 =	+ $_____

    Total $_____   Copy total here➔ $_____

35. **Do you owe any priority claims such as a priority tax, child support, or alimony — that are past due as of the filing date of your bankruptcy case?** 11 U.S.C. § 507.

    ☐ No. Go to line 36.
    ☐ Yes. Fill in the total amount of all of these priority claims. Do not include current or ongoing priority claims, such as those you listed in line 19.

    Total amount of all past-due priority claims .... $_____   ÷ 60 = $_____

Chapter 7 Means Test Calculation—page 8

Debtor 1 _____   Case number *(if known)*_____
       First Name   Middle Name   Last Name

36. **Are you eligible to file a case under Chapter 13?** 11 U.S.C. § 109(e).
    For more information, go online using the link for *Bankruptcy Basics* specified in the separate
    instructions for this form. *Bankruptcy Basics* may also be available at the bankruptcy clerk's office.

    ☐ No. Go to line 37.

    ☐ Yes. Fill in the following information.

        Projected monthly plan payment if you were filing under Chapter 13 $_____

        Current multiplier for your district as stated on the list issued by the
        Administrative Office of the United States Courts (for districts in Alabama and
        North Carolina) or by the Executive Office for United States Trustees (for all
        other districts).   x _____

        To find a list of district multipliers that includes your district, go online using the
        link specified in the separate instructions for this form. This list may also be
        available at the bankruptcy clerk's office.

        Average monthly administrative expense if you were filing under Chapter 13 $_____   **Copy total here ➜** $_____

37. **Add all of the deductions for debt payment.**
    Add lines 33g through 36. $_____

Total Deductions from Income

38. **Add all of the allowed deductions.**

    Copy line 24, *All of the expenses allowed under IRS
    expense allowances* .... $_____

    Copy line 32, *All of the additional expense deductions* .... $_____

    Copy line 37, *All of the deductions for debt payment* .... + $_____

    Total deductions $_____   **Copy total here ➜** $_____

Part 3:	**Determine Whether There Is a Presumption of Abuse**

39. **Calculate monthly disposable income for 60 months**

    39a. Copy line 4, *adjusted current monthly income* ..... $_____

    39b. Copy line 38, *Total deductions* .... − $_____

    39c. Monthly disposable income. 11 U.S.C. § 707(b)(2). $_____   **Copy line 39c here ➜** $_____
        Subtract line 39b from line 39a.

        For the next 60 months (5 years)...   x 60

    39d. **Total.** Multiply line 39c by 60. ....39d. $_____   **Copy line 39d here ➜** $_____

40. **Find out whether there is a presumption of abuse.** Check the box that applies:

    ☐ **The line 39d is less than $7,475*.** On the top of page 1 of this form, check box 1, *There is no presumption of abuse.* Go
    to Part 5.

    ☐ **The line 39d is more than $12,475*.** On the top of page 1 of this form, check box 2, *There is a presumption of abuse.* You
    may fill out Part 4 if you claim special circumstances. Then go to Part 5.

    ☐ **The line 39d is at least $7,475*, but not more than $12,475*.** Go to line 41.

        * Subject to adjustment on 4/01/16, and every 3 years after that for cases filed on or after the date of adjustment.

Chapter 7 Means Test Calculation—page 9

Debtor 1 _____ Case number *(if known)*_____
First Name   Middle Name   Last Name

41. 41a. **Fill in the amount of your total nonpriority unsecured debt.** If you filled out *A Summary of Your Assets and Liabilities and Certain Statistical Information Schedules* (Official Form 6), you may refer to line 5 on that form.

41a. $_____

x   .25

41b. **25% of your total nonpriority unsecured debt.** 11 U.S.C. § 707(b)(2)(A)(i)(I)
Multiply line 41a by 0.25.

$_____   Copy here→ $_____

42. **Determine whether the income you have left over after subtracting all allowed deductions is enough to pay 25% of your unsecured, nonpriority debt.**
Check the box that applies:

☐ **Line 39d is less than line 41b.** On the top of page 1 of this form, check box 1, *There is no presumption of abuse.* Go to Part 5.

☐ **Line 39d is equal to or more than line 41b.** On the top of page 1 of this form, check box 2, *There is a presumption of abuse.* You may fill out Part 4 if you claim special circumstances. Then go to Part 5.

Part 4:	Give Details About Special Circumstances

43. **Do you have any special circumstances that justify additional expenses or adjustments of current monthly income for which there is no reasonable alternative?** 11 U.S.C. § 707(b)(2)(B).

☐ No. Go to Part 5.

☐ Yes. Fill in the following information. All figures should reflect your average monthly expense or income adjustment for each item. You may include expenses you listed in line 25.

You must give a detailed explanation of the special circumstances that make the expenses or income adjustments necessary and reasonable. You must also give your case trustee documentation of your actual expenses or income adjustments.

Give a detailed explanation of the special circumstances	Average monthly expense or income adjustment
_____	$_____
_____	$_____
_____	$_____
_____	$_____

Part 5:	Sign Below

By signing here, I declare under penalty of perjury that the information on this statement and in any attachments is true and correct.

✗ _____   ✗ _____
Signature of Debtor 1   Signature of Debtor 2

Date _____   Date _____
MM / DD   / YYYY   MM / DD   / YYYY

Form 22A-1Supp—Statement of Exemption from Presumption of Abuse

Some people automatically qualify for Chapter 7 bankruptcy even if their income is too high or they can't pass the means test. Those include:

- people whose debts are primarily business debts
- disabled veterans who incurred most of their debts while on active duty or performing a homeland defense activity, and
- certain Reservists and members of the National Guard.

You fill out this form to find out if you qualify for one of these exemptions. Below is a completed 22A-1 Supp form and step-by-step instructions to help you do so.

To get started, follow the instructions for Schedules I and J to complete the top left box. Since you haven't filed anything yet, you don't need to worry about the top right-hand side box. Leave it unchecked. If you are filing jointly, and you think your spouse qualifies for an exemption, your spouse should fill out a separate Form 22A-1Supp. You will both also fill out separate 22A-1 forms—you'll see why below.

Part 1: Identify the Kind of Debts You Have.

This part asks whether your debts are primarily consumer debts. If they are not, then they are business debts and you qualify for the exemption.

What Are Consumer Debts?

Consumer debts are those that are "incurred by an individual primarily for a personal, family, or household purpose." This includes things such as food, clothing, shelter, childcare, and entertainment; in other words, everyday living expenses and personal extravagances. For example, using your credit cards to buy clothes for yourself and your family, to purchase a television, and go the movies would be typical ways people incur consumer debts.

What Are Nonconsumer Debts?

Nonconsumer debts are any debts that don't fall into the consumer debt category. That is, in order to declare that your debts are primarily nonconsumer debts (and avoid the means test), over 50% of your debt must be for something other than personal, family, or household purposes. The purpose of your debt is determined at the time you incurred it.

Below are some of the most common types of nonconsumer debts.

Business debts. Expenses you incur to run a business are nonconsumer debts. These include expenses such as:

- rent or mortgage on your office space or storefront
- vehicles used in your business
- building and fixture expenses
- products used in or sold by your business
- utilities, such as heating and air, at your place of business
- your business phone
- personal guarantees for business debt
- business-related legal fees, and
- liabilities arising from accidents related to your business.

It is common for businesses to keep track of expenses by using a credit card to purchase supplies and needed services. If you've used a credit card exclusively in your business, it will be considered a business debt. For instance, if you ran a plumbing business and used credit to buy necessary supplies such as pipes, toilet fixtures, trucks, and plumbing tools, those debts would be considered "business debt." If those debts constituted more than 50% of your total debt, then you would qualify for the exemption.

Tax debts. Many types of tax debts are considered to be nonconsumer, even income tax debts. The reasoning is that no one intentionally incurs tax debt for personal, family, or household expenses. Check with a lawyer if you are unsure.

Statement of Exemption from Presumption of Abuse

Fill in this information to identify your case:

Debtor 1 _____
First Name   Middle Name   Last Name

Debtor 2 _____
(Spouse, if filing) First Name   Middle Name   Last Name

United States Bankruptcy Court for the: _____ District of _____

Case number _____
(If known)

☐ Check if this is an amended filing

OFFICIAL FORM B 22A1 SUPP

Statement of Exemption from Presumption of Abuse Under § 707(b)(2) 12/14

File this supplement together with *Chapter 7 Statement of Your Current Monthly Income* (Official Form 22A-1), if you believe that you are exempted from a presumption of abuse. Be as complete and accurate as possible. If two married people are filing together, and any of the exclusions in this statement applies to only one of you, the other person should complete a separate Form 22A-1 if you believe that this is required by 11 U.S.C. § 707(b)(2)(C).

Part 1: Identify the Kind of Debts You Have

1. **Are your debts primarily consumer debts?** *Consumer debts* are defined in 11 U.S.C. § 101(8) as "incurred by an individual primarily for a personal, family, or household purpose." Make sure that your answer is consistent with the "Nature of Debts" box on page 1 of the *Voluntary Petition* (Official Form 1).

   ☐ No. Go to Form 22A-1; on the top of page 1 of that form, check box 1, *There is no presumption of abuse,* and sign Part 3. Then submit this supplement with the signed Form 22A-1.

   ☐ Yes. Go to Part 2.

Part 2: Determine Whether Military Service Provisions Apply to You

2. **Are you a disabled veteran** (as defined in 38 U.S.C. § 3741(1))?

   ☐ No. Go to line 3.

   ☐ Yes. Did you incur debts mostly while you were on active duty or while you were performing a homeland defense activity? 10 U.S.C. § 101(d)(1)); 32 U.S.C. § 901(1).

   　☐ No. Go to line 3.

   　☐ Yes. Go to Form 22A-1; on the top of page 1 of that form, check box 1, *There is no presumption of abuse,* and sign Part 3. Then submit this supplement with the signed Form 22A-1.

3. **Are you or have you been a Reservist or member of the National Guard?**

   ☐ No. Complete Form 22A-1. Do not submit this supplement.

   ☐ Yes. Were you called to active duty or did you perform a homeland defense activity? 10 U.S.C. § 101(d)(1); 32 U.S.C. § 901(1)

   　☐ No. Complete Form 22A-1. Do not submit this supplement.

   　☐ Yes. Check any one of the following categories that applies:

   　　☐ **I was called to active duty after September 11, 2001,** for at least 90 days and remain on active duty.

   　　☐ **I was called to active duty after September 11, 2001,** for at least 90 days and was released from active duty on _____, which is fewer than 540 days before I file this bankruptcy case.

   　　☐ **I am performing a homeland defense activity for at least 90 days.**

   　　☐ **I performed a homeland defense activity for at least 90 days,** ending on _____, which is fewer than 540 days before I file this bankruptcy case.

   If you checked one of the categories to the left, go to Form 22A-1. On the top of page 1 of Form 22A-1, check box 3, *The Means Test does not apply now,* and sign Part 3. Then submit this supplement with the signed Form 22A-1. You are not required to fill out the rest of Official Form 22A-1 during the exclusion period. The *exclusion period* means the time you are on active duty or are performing a homeland defense activity, and for 540 days afterward. 11 U.S.C. § 707(b)(2)(D)(ii).

   If your exclusion period ends before your case is closed, you may have to file an amended form later.

Other debts. It's not always obvious which debts are consumer and which are not. For example, sometimes student loans are considered nonconsumer debts, especially if they were incurred to attend a professional school and the money went toward tuition (not housing or food). See *In re De Cunae*, 2013 WL 6389205 (Bankr. S.D. Tex. 2013).

> **TIP**
>
> **If your debts might be nonconsumer, check with a lawyer.** If you are unsure whether a certain category of debt is consumer or nonconsumer, and if it were nonconsumer, you'd be able to skip the means test, consider talking to a lawyer. Of course, if you would pass the means test anyway, don't bother.

Line 1. If more than 50% of your debts fall into the consumer category, check "Yes," and proceed to Part 2 of this form. (When we say 50%, we mean 50% of the total amount of your debt load; not the number of debts you have in each category. So for example, if you have one mortgage in the amount of $200,000 and three separate business debts that total $50,000, your debts would be primarily consumer because more than half of your total debt load ($250,000) is made up of your mortgage.)

If more than 50% of your debts are nonconsumer in nature, check "No," go to the top of Form 22A-1 and check Box 1, "There is no presumption of abuse," and then skip the rest of Form 22A-1 (other than signing it in Part 5). Attach Form 22A-1Supp to Form 22A-1.

Part 2: Determine Whether Military Service Provisions Apply to You.

This part assesses whether you are a part of a small group of military personnel who qualify for this exemption. You qualify for a military service exemption if you fall into one of the following categories:

- you are a disabled veteran and incurred most of your debts while on active duty or while performing a homeland defense activity

- you have been on active duty for at least 90 days (with your duty beginning sometime after September 11, 2001)
- you were released from active duty less than 540 days before filing bankruptcy (with your duty lasting at least 90 days and beginning sometime after September 11, 2001)
- you are performing a homeland defense activity that will last for at least 90 days, or
- you performed a homeland defense activity fewer than 540 days before filing bankruptcy and the activity lasted for at least 90 days.

If you meet one of these conditions, read and check the appropriate boxes on Form 22A-1Supp. Next, check Box 3 at the top of Form 22A-1 and skip the rest of Form 22A-1 (other than signing it in Part 5). Attach Form 22A-1Supp to Form 22A-1.

Forms 201A and 201B—Notice to Consumer Debtors Under § 342(b) and Certification

This form, required by the new bankruptcy law, gives you some information about credit counseling and the various chapters of bankruptcy available. It also warns you sternly of the consequences of lying on your bankruptcy papers, concealing assets, and failing to file the required forms on time.

After you have read Form 201A, sign and date Form 201B (which certifies that you have read the notice in Form 201A) in the section labeled "Certification of the Debtor." If a bankruptcy petition preparer assisted you with the paperwork, he or she should fill in the top portion of Form 201B.

We don't provide samples of these forms in this book because they are so straightforward. Like all of the official forms, you can find these on www.uscourts.gov/forms/bankruptcy-forms.

Creditor Mailing List

As part of your bankruptcy filing, you are required to submit a list of all of your creditors so the court can give them official notice of your bankruptcy. Depending on the jurisdiction, this might be called the "mailing matrix," master address list, creditor mailing matrix, or something else. This list must be prepared in a specific format prescribed by your local bankruptcy court. Your court may also require you to submit a declaration, or "verification," stating that your list is correct (as always, be sure to check your court's local rules). In a few courts, the form consists of boxes on a page in which you enter the names and addresses of your creditors. This is an artifact from the time when the trustee would use the form to prepare mailing labels.

Now, however, most courts ask you to submit the list on a computer disk in a particular word processing format, or at least submit a computer printout of the names so that they can be scanned. You should check with the bankruptcy court clerk or the court's local rules to learn the precise format. Then, take these steps:

Step 1: Make a list of all of your creditors, in alphabetical order. You can copy them from Schedules D, E, F, and H. Be sure to include cosigners and joint debtors. If, however, you and your spouse jointly incurred a debt and are filing jointly, don't include your spouse. Also include collection agencies, sheriffs, and attorneys who either have sued you or are trying to collect the debt. And, if you're seeking to discharge marital debts you assumed during a divorce, include both your ex-spouse and the creditors. Finally, if you have two or more debts owed to the same creditor at the same address, you can just list one.

Step 2: Compile the information gathered in Step 1 in the format required by your local court.

> ⓘ **CAUTION**
> **It is very important to be complete when preparing the creditor mailing list.** If you leave a creditor off the list and the creditor does not find out about your bankruptcy by some other means, that debt may survive your bankruptcy if there is a priority distribution in your case. However, if you have no assets to be distributed (as is typically the case), the debt will still be discharged, unless the creditor could have successfully challenged the discharge had it known of your bankruptcy. See Ch. 9 for more information about the discharge of debts not included in your bankruptcy papers.

How to File Your Papers

Gather up all of the forms you have completed, as well as the documents you gathered at the beginning of this chapter. Make sure you have everything on the Bankruptcy Forms Checklist and Bankruptcy Documents Checklist (you can find these checklists in Appendix B).

> ⓘ **CAUTION**
> **Using a bankruptcy petition preparer increases the paperwork.** If you use a petition preparer, there will be several additional forms to file.

Basic Filing Procedures

Once you've got all of your papers together, follow these filing instructions.

Step 1: Put all your bankruptcy forms in the proper order.

Step 2: Check that you, and your spouse if you're filing a joint petition, have signed and dated each form where required.

Step 3: Make the required number of copies, plus one additional copy for you to keep just in case your papers are lost in the mail (if you file by mail). In addition, make:

- one extra copy of the Statement of Intention for each person listed on that form, and
- one extra copy of the Statement of Intention for the trustee.

Step 4: Unless the court clerk will hole-punch your papers when you file them, use a standard two-hole punch (copy centers have them) to punch the top center of your original set of bankruptcy papers. Don't staple any forms together.

Step 5: If you plan to mail your documents to the court, address a 9" × 12" envelope to yourself and affix adequate postage to handle one copy of all the paperwork. Although many people prefer to file by mail, we recommend that you personally take your papers to the bankruptcy court clerk if at all possible. Going to the court will give you a chance to correct minor mistakes on the spot.

Step 6: If you can pay the filing fee, clip or staple a money order to the petition, payable to the U.S. Trustee (courts won't accept a check and sending cash in the mail is unwise). If you want to pay in installments, attach a completed Application and Order to Pay Filing Fee in Installments (Form 3A), plus any additional papers required by your court's local rules (see "Paying in Installments," below). If you don't think you can afford installment payments, you may be able to obtain a fee waiver (Form 3B) (see "Waiver of Filing Fee," below). For both installment payments and fee waivers, you might have to appear before the bankruptcy judge to justify your request.

Step 7: Take or mail the original and copies of all forms to the correct bankruptcy court.

Serving the Statement of Intention

The bankruptcy rules require you to serve (by mail) the Statement of Intention on each creditor listed on the statement. You have between 30 and 45 days to do this. We recommend you do it immediately so you don't forget. If you don't serve your Statement of Intention on time, the creditor can repossess the collateral. The trustee must also be served. The trustee's contact information will be provided either on the copy of your papers that the clerk returns to you or on the notice of filing you receive several days after you file.

Have a friend or relative (other than your spouse, if you are filing jointly) over the age of 18 mail, by first class, a copy of your Statement of Intention to the bankruptcy trustee and to all the creditors listed on that form. Be sure to keep the original.

On a Proof of Service by Mail (a copy is in Appendix C), enter the name and complete address of the trustee and all creditors to whom your friend or relative sent your Statement of Intention. Have that person sign and date the Proof of Service.

Paying in Installments

You can pay in up to four installments over 120 days. You can ask the judge to give you extra time for a particular installment, but all installments ultimately must be paid within 180 days after you file. You might have to appear at a separate hearing a couple of weeks after you file to make your case for installment payments before the bankruptcy judge. If the judge refuses your request, you will be given some time to come up with the fees (probably ten days, perhaps longer). Because of this "appearance before the judge" requirement, many debtors prefer to raise the whole fee before filing and hopefully get through their entire bankruptcy without ever meeting up with the judge.

If you are applying to pay in installments, you must file a completed Form 3A (Application and Order to Pay Filing Fee in Installments) when you file your petition. You can find this form along with all the other bankruptcy forms at www.uscourts.gov/forms/bankruptcy-forms.

The application is easy to fill out. At the top, fill in the name of the court (this is on Form 1—Voluntary Petition), your name (and your spouse's name if you're filing jointly), and "7" in the blank after "Chapter." Leave the Case No. space blank. Then enter:

- the total filing fee you must pay: $335 (Item 1)
- the amount you propose to pay when you file the petition (Item 4, first blank)
- the number of additional installments you need (the total maximum is four), and
- the amount and date you propose for each installment payment (Item 4, second, third, and fourth blanks).

You (and your spouse, if you're filing jointly) must sign and date the application. Leave the rest blank.

CAUTION
Make installment payments on time. If you pay the fee in installments, make sure you make each payment in a timely manner. If you don't, the court may dismiss your bankruptcy and you will then have to pay the entire fee to reopen your case.

Waiver of Filing Fee

You also may apply to have your fees waived altogether by filing Form 3B. This form is fairly complex and asks for a lot of the information you've provided in the schedules completed earlier in this chapter. You can find this form on the official U.S. Courts website at www.uscourts.gov/forms/bankruptcy-forms. Although some judges habitually refuse to grant fee waivers, there is no harm in trying (other than perhaps having to take time off work to appear before the judge and justify your request). If you receive a waiver and it later turns out that you could pay the fee, the court can revoke your waiver (*In re Kauffman*, 354 B.R. 682 (Bankr. D. Vt. 2006).)

If the court denies your application, you'll have to pay the full filing fee within a week to ten days. For this reason, don't ask for a waiver unless you have the means to come up with the fee if your efforts fail.

Emergency Filing

If you want to file for bankruptcy in a hurry to get an automatic stay, you can accomplish that (in most places) by filing Form 1—Voluntary Petition, the Mailing Matrix, and Form 21 (Statement of Social Security Number). Some courts also require you to file a cover sheet and an Order Dismissing Chapter 7 Case, which will be processed if you don't file the rest of your papers within 14 days. (Bankruptcy Rule 1007(c).) If the bankruptcy court for your district requires this form, you can get it from the court (possibly on its website), a local bankruptcy attorney, or a bankruptcy petition preparer.

If you don't follow up by filing the additional documents within 14 days, your bankruptcy case will be dismissed. You can file again, if necessary. You'll have to ask the court to keep the automatic stay in effect once 30 days have passed after you file. (See Ch. 2.)

For an emergency filing, follow these steps:

Step 1: Check with the court to find out exactly what forms must be submitted for an emergency filing.

Step 2: Fill in Form 1—Voluntary Petition, including Exhibit D.

Step 3: On a Mailing Matrix (or whatever other form is required by your court), list all your creditors, as well as collection agencies, sheriffs, attorneys, and others who are seeking to collect debts from you.

Step 4: Fill in the Statement of Social Security Number and any other papers the court requires.

Step 5: File the originals and the required number of copies, accompanied by your fee (or an application for payment of fee in installments) and a self-addressed envelope with the bankruptcy court. Keep copies of everything for your records.

Step 6: File all other required forms within 14 days. If you don't, your case will probably be dismissed.

After You File

Filing a bankruptcy petition has a dramatic effect on your creditors and your property.

The Automatic Stay

The instant you file for Chapter 7 bankruptcy, your creditors are subject to the automatic stay, as described in detail in Ch. 2. If you haven't read that chapter, now is the time to do it.

The Trustee Takes Ownership of Your Property

When you file your bankruptcy papers, the trustee becomes the owner of all the property in your bankruptcy estate as of that date. (See Ch. 3 for an explanation of what's in your bankruptcy estate.) However, the trustee won't actually take physical control of the property. Most, if not all, of your property will be exempt, which means the trustee will return it to your legal possession after your bankruptcy is closed. If you have any questions about dealing with property after you file, ask the trustee or the trustee's staff.

While your bankruptcy is pending, do not throw out, give away, sell, or otherwise dispose of the property you owned as of your filing date—unless and until the bankruptcy trustee says otherwise. Even if all of your property is exempt, you are expected to hold on to it, in case the trustee or a creditor challenges your exemption claims.

If some of your property is nonexempt, the trustee may ask you to turn it over. Or, the trustee may decide that the property is worth too little to bother with and abandon it. (Typically, the trustee doesn't let you know that property is abandoned, but once you receive your discharge, the property is deemed abandoned.)

You are allowed to spend cash you had when you filed (declared on Schedule B) to make day-to-day purchases for necessities such as groceries, personal effects, and clothing. Just make sure you can account for what happened to that cash: You may need to reimburse the bankruptcy estate if the money wasn't exempt and the trustee disapproves your purchases.

What Happens to Business Property

If you are operating a sole proprietorship or a solely owned corporation or limited liability company (LLC), you might have to shut down the business—at least temporarily—until the trustee can assess the nature and value of your inventory and assets, as well as any exemptions you can claim in the property. This shut-down period will last for a couple of months and perhaps even longer. If your business is service-oriented and lacks machines or inventory, you can probably continue in business without interruption.

Business entities aren't part of a personal bankruptcy. However, if you (or you and your spouse) are the sole owner of an entity like a corporation or an LLC, the trustee can step into your shoes, vote your shares to dissolve the business, and sell off whatever inventory and assets you can't personally exempt. Because it takes some time to assess the business assets and go through the necessary corporate procedures, you might have to shut down your business at least while that process is going on. And if you aren't able to exempt your business assets, you'll have to shut down for good.

TIP

If you are worried about losing property or your business, contact the trustee sooner rather than later. If you have any property that you might have to surrender, the best course of action is to contact the trustee as soon as possible. This accomplishes two things: It establishes your forthrightness (which is important in bankruptcy) and provides insight into what the trustee might do. Ask the trustee what you can expect to happen to the property and answer the trustee's questions. The trustee may give you particular instructions, such as to forward rental or trust fund payments, or may arrange to set up a time to view the property. It also isn't unheard of for a trustee to quickly decide that your dance studio or mobile glass repair business is of no value to the bankruptcy estate. This type of advance information may give you time to figure out how to buy your property back at a discounted price, afford you the relief of knowing your property is not at risk, or simply give you time to acclimate to it being sold.

In a Chapter 7 case, with a few exceptions, the trustee has no claim to property you acquire or income you earn after you file. You are free to spend it as you please. The exceptions are: property from an insurance settlement, a marital settlement agreement, or an inheritance that you become entitled to receive within 180 days after your filing date. (See Ch. 3.)

Handling Your Case in Court

For most people, the Chapter 7 bankruptcy process is fairly straightforward. In fact, it proceeds pretty much on automatic pilot. The bankruptcy trustee decides whether your papers pass muster and, if not, what amendments you need to file. Ordinarily, you have few decisions to make.

This chapter tells you how to handle the routine procedures that move your bankruptcy case along, and how to deal with complications that may arise if any of the following occur:

- You or the trustee discovers an error in your papers.
- A creditor asks the court to lift the automatic stay.
- You decide to object to a creditor's claim.
- A creditor objects to the discharge of a particular debt.
- A creditor or the trustee objects to your claim that an item of property is exempt.
- You decide to dismiss your case or convert it to another type of bankruptcy, such as a Chapter 13 bankruptcy.
- You need to reopen your case for some reason after it has been closed.
- Your case is dismissed, and you want to refile it and keep the protection of the automatic stay.

Some of these problems—fixing a simple error in your papers, for example—you can handle yourself. For more complicated problems, such as fighting a creditor in court about the discharge of a large debt, you'll probably need a lawyer's help.

RESOURCE

If you're going to court. If you face any of the special problems covered in this chapter, your first step should be to take a look at *Represent Yourself in Court*, by Paul Bergman and Sara Berman (Nolo). In addition to valuable information about handling federal court proceedings, this book has a special chapter on bankruptcy court.

Routine Bankruptcy Procedures

A routine Chapter 7 bankruptcy case takes three to six months from beginning to end and follows a series of predictable steps.

The Court Sends a Notice of Bankruptcy Filing

Shortly after you file for bankruptcy, the court sends an official notice to you and all of the creditors listed in your mailing matrix. This notice contains several crucial pieces of information.

Your Filing Date and Case Number

This information puts the creditors on notice that you have filed for bankruptcy and gives them a reference number (your case number) to use when seeking information about your case.

Whether the Case Is an Asset Case or a No-Asset Case

When you filled in the bankruptcy petition, you had to check one of the following two boxes:

- ☐ Debtor estimates that funds will be available for distribution to unsecured creditors.
- ☐ Debtor estimates that, after any exempt property is excluded and administrative expenses paid, there will be no funds available for distribution to unsecured creditors.

The box you check determines the type of notice the court sends to your creditors. If you checked the first box, your case is known as an "asset case" and your creditors will be advised to file a claim describing what you owe them. If you checked the second box, your case will be known as a "no-asset" case and your creditors will be told to not file a claim. However, they will also be informed that they will have an opportunity to file a claim later if it turns out that there are assets available after all.

The Date for the 341 hearing

The notice also sets a date for the meeting of creditors (also called the "341 hearing"), usually several weeks later. Mark this date carefully—it is very important for several reasons:

- You must attend the 341 hearing; if you don't, your case can be dismissed.
- Your creditors must file their claims (if it is an asset case) within 60 days after this meeting.

How a Routine Chapter 7 Bankruptcy Proceeds		
Step	**Description**	**When It Happens**
You begin your case by filing bankruptcy papers.	You file the petition and supporting schedules with the bankruptcy clerk, who scans them into the court records.	When you decide to do so. Once you file, your creditors are barred from taking collection actions.
The court notifies creditors that you have filed for bankruptcy.	A notice of your filing is mailed to you and your creditors, stating the date of the 341 hearing and contact information for the trustee.	A few days after you file.
The court assigns a trustee to the case.	The trustee's job is to review your paperwork and take possession of any nonexempt property.	The trustee is appointed at the same time the notice to creditors is mailed.
You provide your most recent tax return to the trustee.	You must give the trustee your most recent tax return but can black out sensitive information, such as your Social Security number and date of birth.	Seven days prior to the 341 hearing.
The 341 hearing is held.	The 341 hearing is the only personal appearance most filers make. The judge is not there and creditors seldom attend. The trustee questions you about your paperwork. Most meetings last a few minutes.	Between 20 and 40 days after the date you file.
The means test is applied in appropriate cases.	The U.S. Trustee starts a process leading to dismissal or conversion of your case to Chapter 13 if your papers show that you have adequate income to fund a Chapter 13 debt repayment plan.	The U.S. Trustee must file a statement within ten days after the 341 hearing if it appears from the paperwork or information gleaned in the 341 hearing that your income is over the state median and you can't pass the means test.
Objections to exemption claim are filed.	If the trustee or a creditor disagrees with an exemption you have claimed, a formal written objection must be filed with the court.	Within 30 days after the 341 hearing.
Secured property is dealt with.	If you owe money on property, you must either redeem or reaffirm the debt if you want to keep the property.	Within 30 days after the 341 hearing.
You attend budget counseling.	You must undergo personal financial management counseling before you can get your discharge.	Within 60 days after the 341 hearing, you must file proof that you completed counseling.
The court holds a reaffirmation hearing.	If you reaffirm a debt and aren't represented by a lawyer, you must attend a court hearing where the judge reviews your decision.	Roughly 60 days after your 341 hearing.
The court grants your discharge.	The court mails a notice of discharge that discharges all debts that can legally be discharged, unless the court has ruled otherwise in your bankruptcy case (very rare). The automatic stay is lifted at this time.	Roughly 90 days after you file, and no less than 60 days after your 341 hearing.
Your case is closed.	The trustee distributes any property collected from you to your unsecured creditors.	A few days or weeks after your discharge.

- Your creditors must file any objections they have to the discharge of their debts within 60 days after this meeting.
- The trustee and your creditors must file any objections they have to your exemption claims.

Contact Information for the Trustee

The notice of filing will also provide the name, address, and telephone number of the trustee assigned to your case. You will probably be able to find the trustee's email address on the notice since most trustees agree to allow the court to contact them by email, which is called "electronic service." If you can't find it, call the trustee's office, get the trustee's email address, and communicate in that way if possible.

Your Creditors Must Cease Most Collection Actions

When the court mails your creditors official notice of your filing, the automatic stay goes into effect. The automatic stay prohibits most creditors and government support entities from taking any action to collect the debts you owe them until the court says otherwise.

There are some notable exceptions to the automatic stay, however. Ch. 2 provides detailed information on the automatic stay, including which actions it does—and does not—prohibit.

In addition, the bankruptcy court can lift the automatic stay for a particular creditor—that is, allow the creditor to continue collection efforts. (Lifting the automatic stay is covered in "Special Problems," below.)

Creditors won't know that they have to stop their collection efforts until they receive notice of your bankruptcy filing. The notice sent by the court may take a week or more to reach your creditors. If you need quicker results, send your own notice to creditors (and bill collectors, landlords, or sheriffs about to enforce an eviction order). A sample letter notifying your creditors is shown below. You can also call your creditors. Be prepared to give your bankruptcy case number, the date you filed, and the name of the court in which you filed.

Notice to Creditor of Filing for Bankruptcy

Lynn Adams
18 Orchard Park Blvd.
East Lansing, MI 48823

June 15, 20xx

Cottons Clothing Store
745 Main Street
Lansing, MI 48915

Dear Cottons Clothing:

On June 14, 20xx, I filed a voluntary petition under Chapter 7 of the U.S. Bankruptcy Code. The case number is 43-6736-91. I filed my case *in pro per*; no attorney is assisting me. Under 11 U.S.C. § 362(a), you may not:

- take any action against me or my property to collect any debt
- enforce any lien on my real or personal property
- repossess any property in my possession
- discontinue any service or benefit currently being provided to me, or
- take any action to evict me from where I live.

A violation of these prohibitions may be considered contempt of court and punished accordingly.

Very truly yours,

Lynn Adams

Lynn Adams

If a creditor tries to collect a debt in violation of the automatic stay, you can ask the bankruptcy court to hold the creditor in contempt of court and to award you money damages. The procedures for making this request are beyond the scope of this book.

Attend the 341 Hearing (Meeting of Creditors)

At the 341 hearing, the trustee gets information from the debtor, usually by asking a few questions, and resolves any issues he or she sees in your paperwork. Some trustees question a debtor more closely about items in the bankruptcy papers than others. The trustee may want to see documentation of some of your figures, such as the value of a house or car;

if you don't have this paperwork with you, the trustee will postpone the meeting to another date to give you time to find the necessary documents. Typically, you won't have to appear at another meeting, but can submit these documents by mail or email, depending on the trustee's preference.

If You Can't Appear

Sometimes, a person who has filed for bankruptcy is unable to attend the 341 hearing for a legitimate reason, such as a serious illness. If that is true in your case, contact the trustee for information on how to proceed. Here is what the U.S. Trustee's office tells the regular trustees about how to handle people who are unable to appear:

"The trustee should consult with the United States Trustee regarding the general procedures for approving a debtor's alternative appearance when extenuating circumstances prevent the debtor from appearing in person. Extenuating circumstances may include military service, serious medical condition, or incarceration. In such instances, a debtor's appearance at a § 341(a) meeting may be secured by alternative means, such as telephonically. When the debtor(s) cannot personally appear before the trustee, arrangements should be made for an independent third party authorized to administer oaths to be present at the alternate location to administer the oath and to verify the debtor's identity and state the Social Security number on the record.... On the rare occasion when other arrangements need to be made to address a particular situation, the trustee should consult with the United States Trustee about the appropriate safeguards to follow. The trustee also may allow such debtors to provide proof of identity and Social Security numbers at the trustee's office at their convenience any time before the next scheduled meeting.

"When a trustee becomes aware of a debtor's disability, including hearing impairment, the trustee must notify the United States Trustee immediately so that reasonable accommodation can be made. The United States Trustee has procedures in place to address the special needs of debtors."

For most people, the 341 hearing is brief. Very few, if any, creditors show up, but *you* must show up. If you don't appear and haven't notified the trustee in advance, your case will very likely be scheduled for dismissal, which means you'll have to explain yourself to the judge. Some trustees will automatically give you a second chance without seeking dismissal. Especially if you have a good excuse for not attending, the trustee is likely to reschedule.

FOR MARRIED COUPLES
If you're married and filing jointly. Both you and your spouse must attend the first scheduled 341 hearing. If the meeting is continued to another date for a technical reason—to turn over certain papers to the trustee, for example—only one spouse may have to attend. Ask the trustee whether both of you have to come back, or whether one will do.

Preparing for the 341 Hearing

Before the hearing, call the regular trustee whose name and phone number appear on the notice of bankruptcy filing from the court. Explain that you're proceeding without a lawyer ("in pro se") and ask what records you're required to bring. At a minimum, you should take a copy of every paper you've filed with the bankruptcy court.

You should also bring the following:
- evidence of your current income (if the wage stubs you already had to file don't provide this information)
- statements from financial institutions for all of your deposit and investment accounts through the date you filed bankruptcy
- your most recent tax return (you are required to give this to the trustee at least seven days before the 341 hearing, but bring it with you if you haven't given it to the trustee yet), and
- if you had to take the means test, proof of your monthly expenses.

You may be asked to bring copies of all documents that describe your debts and property, such as bills, deeds, contracts, and licenses. Some trustees also require you to bring financial records, such as tax returns (in addition to the one you filed with the court), checkbooks, and records for any business you have operated in the past six years. You have a right to redact (black out) all but the last four digits of your Social Security number on any papers you submit. You can also redact the names of your minor children, full dates of birth, and full Social Security numbers.

Some people become anxious at the prospect of answering a trustee's questions and consider having an attorney accompany them. But if you were completely honest in preparing your bankruptcy papers, there's no reason to have an attorney with you at the 341 hearing. If the trustee does have tough questions, it is you, not the attorney, who will have to answer them. What's more, many trustees don't like it when a debtor huddles with an attorney before answering a particular question, which means you'll be mostly on your own even if you pay a lawyer to accompany you to the hearing.

If you think you've been dishonest on the forms or with a creditor, or have attempted to unload some of your property before filing, see a lawyer before you go to the hearing.

You can visit the hearing room where your district holds 341 hearings (typically, the nearest federal building) and watch other 341 hearings if you think that might help alleviate some anxiety. Just check with the U.S. Trustee's office in your district (see www.usdoj.gov/ust for contact information) to find out when these hearings are held.

A day or so before the 341 hearing, thoroughly review the papers you filed with the bankruptcy court. If you discover mistakes, make careful note of them. You'll probably have to correct your papers after the hearing, but that's an easy process. (Instructions are in "Amending Your Bankruptcy Papers," below.)

After reviewing your papers, go over the list of questions the trustee may ask (set out in "What Will the Trustee Ask You?" below). Despite the fact that these are "required" questions, few trustees ask all of them, and many trustees ask only one or two. Still, it's a good idea to be able to answer them all, if they relate to your situation.

At the beginning of the hearing, the trustee may ask you whether you have read the Statement of Information required by 11 U.S.C. § 342 (this is Form 201A. You filed 201A with your papers and signed a form (Form 201B)). If you read Chs. 1 and 2, you have learned all the information on this form. Review it before the hearing, so you can tell the trustee that you've read it.

> **CAUTION**
>
> **Don't forget your ID.** You'll need identification at the 341 hearing. Bring both a photo ID (such as a driver's license, a passport, or an identification card) and proof of your Social Security number. Many trustees require you to present a Social Security card, so if you can't find yours, it's a good idea to order one as soon as possible.

The Routine 341 Hearing

Most 341 hearings are quick and simple. You appear in the designated meeting place at the date and time stated on the bankruptcy notice. A number of other people who have filed for bankruptcy will be there, too, for their own 341 hearings. When your name is called, you'll be asked to sit or stand near the front of the hearing room. The trustee will swear you in and ask you for your identification. At that point, many trustees look you in the eye and sternly ask whether everything in your papers is 100% true and correct. If you are uncertain about information in your papers or you have lied, the trustee is likely to pick up on your hesitancy and follow up with more questions that may make you uncomfortable. That's why it's so important that you:

- review your papers before filing them
- file amendments before the 341 hearing if you discover any errors after you file (refer to "Amending Your Bankruptcy Papers," below)
- review your papers again shortly before the 341 hearing, and
- volunteer any additional changes at the hearing.

Then you can confidently answer "yes" to the trustee's first question.

The trustee will probably be most interested in:

- how you came up with a value for a big ticket item, such as your home or car
- anticipated tax refunds
- any possible right that you have to sue someone because of a recent accident or business loss
- reasons for inconsistencies in your paperwork or omitted information (such as answering "none" to the questions about clothing or bank accounts when it's obvious that you have either or both)
- recent large payments to creditors or relatives, and
- possible inheritances or insurance proceeds coming your way.

Hold Your Head High

No matter how well you prepare for the 341 hearing, you may feel nervous and apprehensive about coming face to face with the trustee and possibly your creditors, to whom you've disclosed the intimate details of your finances over the last several years. You may feel angry with yourself and your creditors at having to be there. You may be embarrassed. You may think you're being perceived as a failure.

Nonsense. It takes courage to face your situation and deal firmly with it. Bankruptcy, especially when you're handling your own case without a lawyer, isn't an easy out. Try to see this as a turning point at which you're taking positive steps to improve your life. Go to the 341 hearing proud that you've chosen to take control over your life and legal affairs.

TIP

Ask to continue (postpone) the 341 hearing if you need to. As explained above, you can usually change the date of your 341 hearing if you can't make the date originally set. But what if you want to leave your hearing once it has begun? For example, more than a few people have panic reactions in stressful situations. If this happens to you, you can pretty much count on the trustee to

continue the hearing for a couple of weeks. In fact, you don't have to panic to want to continue the hearing: Just ask for a continuance and there shouldn't be a problem.

If your answer to a trustee's question is different from what you said in your bankruptcy papers, the trustee will have reason to suspect your entire case—and your bankruptcy may change from a routine procedure to an uphill battle. If you know that you have made mistakes, you should call them to the trustee's attention before the trustee raises the issue. If you are caught in a contradiction, immediately explain how it happened. Even if someone else prepared your papers for you, you can't use that as an excuse. You are responsible for the information in your papers, which is why you should thoroughly review them before appearing.

When the trustee is finished questioning you, any creditors who have appeared will have an opportunity to ask you questions. Most often, no creditors show up. If any do appear, they will probably be secured creditors who want to clarify your intentions regarding the collateral securing the debt. For example, if you've taken out a car loan and the car is the collateral, the creditor may ask whether you are going to reaffirm the debt or whether you might prefer to redeem the car at its replacement value. Also, if you obtained any cash advances or ran up credit card debts shortly before filing for bankruptcy, the credit card issuers may show up to question you about the circumstances and what you did with the proceeds. And, finally, a creditor might also ask for an explanation if information in your bankruptcy papers differs from what was on your credit application. When the creditors are through asking questions, the hearing will end.

Except in highly unusual situations, the trustee and any creditors should be finished questioning you in five minutes or less. When the trustee and creditors (if any show up) are done, the hearing will be concluded and you will be told you can leave. If you have no secured debts or nonexempt property, and neither you nor your creditors will be asking the court to rule on the dischargeability of a debt or the continuing effect

What Will the Trustee Ask You?

The trustee is *required* to ask the following questions at your 341 hearing (although most don't):

- State your name and current address for the record.
- Have you read the Bankruptcy Information Sheet provided by the U.S. Trustee?
- Did you sign the petition, schedules, statements, and related documents you filed with the court? Did you read the petition, schedules, statements, and related documents before you signed them, and is the signature your own?
- Please provide your picture ID and Social Security card for review.
- Are you personally familiar with the information contained in the petition, schedules, statements, and related documents?
- To the best of your knowledge, is the information contained in the petition, schedules, statements, and related documents true and correct?
- Are there any errors or omissions to bring to my or the court's attention at this time?
- Are all of your assets identified on the schedules?
- Have you listed all of your creditors on the schedules?
- Have you previously filed for bankruptcy? (If so, the trustee must obtain the case number and the discharge information to determine your discharge eligibility.)

The trustee may also ask additional questions, such as these:

- Do you own or have any interest in any real estate?
  - Property that you own: When did you purchase the property? How much did the property cost? What are the mortgages encumbering it? What do you estimate the present value of the property to be? Is that the whole value or your share? How did you arrive at that value?
  - Property that you're renting: Have you ever owned the property in which you live? Is its owner in any way related to you?
- Have you made any transfers of any property, or given any property away, within the last year (or a longer period if applicable under state law)? If so,

what did you transfer? To whom was it transferred? What did you receive in exchange? What did you do with the funds?

- Does anyone hold property belonging to you? If so, who holds the property, and what is it? What is its value?
- Do you have a claim against anyone or any business? If there are large medical debts, are the medical bills from injury? Are you the plaintiff in any lawsuit? What is the status of each case, and who is representing you?
- Are you entitled to life insurance proceeds or an inheritance as a result of someone's death? If so, please explain the details. (If you become a beneficiary of anyone's estate within six months of the date your bankruptcy petition was filed, the trustee must be advised within ten days through your counsel of the nature and extent of the property you will receive.)
- Does anyone owe you money? If so, is the money collectible? Why haven't you collected it? Who owes the money, and where is that person?
- Have you made any large payments, over $600, to anyone in the past year?
- Were your federal income tax returns filed on a timely basis? When was the last return filed? Do you have copies of the federal income tax returns? At the time of the filing of your petition, were you entitled to a tax refund from the federal or state government?
- Do you have a bank account, either checking or savings? If so, in what banks and what were the balances as of the date you filed your petition?
- When you filed your petition, did you have:
  - any cash on hand
  - any U.S. Savings Bonds
  - any other stocks or bonds
  - any certificates of deposit, or
  - a safe deposit box in your name or in anyone else's name?
- Do you own an automobile? If so, what is the year, make, and value? Do you owe any money on it? Is it insured?

of a lien, your case will effectively be over. No one will come to your house to inventory your property. No one will call your employer to confirm the information on your papers. Your bankruptcy case turns into a waiting game until the court sends you your notice of discharge and case closure. That should happen 60 to 75 days after your 341 hearing.

Some trustees have their own questionnaires and requests for documents that they want you to complete. They will either mail these to you so you can complete them before the 341 hearing, or ask you to complete them while you are waiting for your turn to be questioned. Also, you may be asked to complete a brief form asking who assisted you in filling in your paperwork and who explained some of the choices you made (such as why you chose to file a Chapter 7 bankruptcy). The purpose of this form is to smoke out nonlawyer bankruptcy petition preparers who are providing legal advice as part of their service. (See Ch. 10 for more on bankruptcy petition preparers.)

Potential Problems at the 341 Hearing

If you or your papers give any indication that you own valuable nonexempt property, the trustee may question you vigorously about how you decided what it's worth. For instance if you have valued your real estate at $150,000, and the trustee thinks it's worth a lot more, you will be asked where you got your figures. Or, a creditor who's owed a lot of money may grill you about the circumstances of the debt, hoping

to show that you incurred the debt without intending to pay it, or by lying on a credit application, and that therefore it should survive bankruptcy. (See Ch. 8.)

You may also be closely questioned about why you claimed that certain property is exempt. For some reason, some bankruptcy trustees, who are usually attorneys, believe that claiming exemptions requires legal expertise. If this happens to you, simply describe the process you went through in selecting your exemptions from Appendix A. If you consulted an attorney about exemptions or other issues, mention this also. This questioning won't affect your case unless the trustee disagrees with your exemption claims.

Make Sure the 341 Hearing Is Closed

The 30-day period in which the trustee and creditors may file objections to exemptions starts running when the 341 hearing is finished or "closed." The hearing is officially closed—and the clock starts to run on objections—only when the trustee so notes in the court's docket. The trustee's oral statement alone at the 341 hearing isn't enough to officially close the hearing. Check the court file to make sure that the trustee closed (or adjourned) the 341 hearing, and follow up with the trustee if you don't see an entry like that. Otherwise, the 30-day period to file objections never starts to run, and the trustee and creditors will have unlimited time to file objections.

CAUTION

You're responsible for your paperwork, even if you used a bankruptcy petition preparer. You must provide the property valuation and other information in your bankruptcy papers. You cannot shift responsibility for the accuracy and thoroughness of your petition to the preparer, whose job is just to enter the information you supply. If you use a preparer, check all of your paperwork carefully before signing it and filing it with the court.

Deal With Nonexempt Property

After the 341 hearing, the trustee is supposed to collect all of your nonexempt property and have it sold to pay off your creditors. Normally, the trustee accepts the exemptions you claim on Schedule C and goes after only property you haven't claimed as exempt. If, however, the trustee or a creditor disagrees with an exemption you claimed and files a written objection with the bankruptcy court within 30 days of the 341 hearing, the court will schedule a hearing. After listening to both sides, the judge will decide the issue. (See "Special Problems," below.)

If you really want to keep certain nonexempt items and can borrow money from friends or relatives, or you've come into some cash since you filed for bankruptcy, you may be able to trade cash for the item. The trustee, whose sole responsibility at this stage is to maximize what your creditors get paid, is interested simply in how much money your property can produce, not in taking a particular item. So the trustee will probably be happy to accept cash instead of nonexempt property you want to keep.

> **EXAMPLE:** Maura files for Chapter 7 bankruptcy and claims her parlor grand piano as exempt. The trustee disagrees, and the judge rules that the piano is not exempt. To replace the piano on the open market might cost Maura $7,000. The trustee determines that the piano would probably sell for $4,500 at an auction, and is willing to let Maura keep the piano if she can come up with $3,750, to avoid the cost of moving the piano, storing it, and selling it at auction.

The trustee may also be willing to let you keep nonexempt property if you volunteer to trade exempt property of equal value. For instance, the trustee might be willing to let Maura keep her nonexempt piano if she gives up her car, even though Maura could claim the car as exempt. Again, the trustee is interested in squeezing as many dollars as possible from the estate and usually won't care whether the money comes from exempt or nonexempt assets.

Deal With Secured Property

When you filed and served your Statement of Intention, you told the trustee and your creditors whether you wanted to keep property that is security for a debt or give it to the creditor in return for cancellation of the debt.

The law contradicts itself on the time limits for carrying out your intentions. Depending on which provision you believe, you have either 30 or 45 days after the date set for your first 341 hearing to deal with your secured property. If you miss the deadline, the creditor can repossess the collateral—the automatic stay no longer applies (see Ch. 2). Because of these serious consequences, we strongly recommend that you handle your secured property within 30 days of the hearing, just in case the court follows this earlier deadline. (Ch. 5 explains how to decide what to do with your secured property and how to carry out your intentions.)

Complete an Approved Debtor Education Course

After you file for bankruptcy but before you get your discharge, you must take a two-hour course in personal financial management. Known as "debtor education," this course is typically offered by the same agencies that provide the credit counseling you must complete before you file. (You can find counseling agencies at www.usdoj.gov/ust; click "Credit Counseling & Debtor Education.") As with credit counseling, you can expect to pay about $50 for this course, and you can ask for a fee waiver if you can't afford the fee. Unlike credit counseling, which you can complete by phone, you are supposed to take your debtor education course in person or online.

Once you complete the counseling (and no later than 60 days after the first date set for your 341 hearing), you must file Form 23 with the court to certify that you've met the requirement. You must also file the certificate you get from the counseling agency. If you don't file these documents on time, the court can close your case without granting you a discharge of your debts, which means your bankruptcy case was pointless. While it's possible to reopen your case to file the required form, it's obviously much easier to get the counseling and file the form as soon after you file your bankruptcy papers as possible. Although you have 60 days from your 341 hearing to get this done, you're better off not delaying it.

You might be able to obtain a disability waiver of this counseling requirement—which means you wouldn't have to take it if the following apply:

- You have a severe physical impairment.
- You make a reasonable effort, despite the impairment, to participate in the counseling.
- You are unable, because of your impairment, to meaningfully participate in the course.

(See *In re Hall*, 347 B.R. 532 (Bankr. N.D. W.Va. 2006).)

Attend the Reaffirmation Hearing

If you have signed and filed a reaffirmation agreement, the court will hold a hearing. At the hearing, the judge will determine whether making payments under the reaffirmation agreement would impose an undue hardship on you, and whether it would be in your best interest to reaffirm the debt. You can find a complete explanation of the reaffirmation process—including what happens if the judge won't approve the agreement—in Ch. 5.

Understand Your Discharge Order

About 60 to 75 days after the 341 hearing, the court will send you a copy of your discharge order. On the back, it says that all debts you owed as of your filing date are discharged—unless they aren't. It then lists the types of debt that are not discharged. (A sample discharge order is below.) You will notice that the order does not refer to your debts or state which of your specific debts are or aren't discharged. To get a handle on this crucial information, carefully read Ch. 9.

Make several photocopies of the discharge order and keep them in a safe place. Send them to creditors who attempt to collect their debt after your case is over, or to credit reporting agencies that still list you as owing a discharged debt. Refer to Ch. 8 regarding postbankruptcy collection efforts.

Amending Your Bankruptcy Papers

One of the helpful aspects of bankruptcy procedure is that you can amend any of your papers at any time before your final discharge. This means that if you made a mistake on papers you've filed, you can correct it easily.

Despite this liberal amendment policy (as stated in Bankruptcy Rule 1009), some judges will not let you amend your exemption schedule after the deadline for creditors to object to the exemptions has passed. If you run into one of these judges, you'll need to talk to a bankruptcy attorney. (Although in light of a recent U.S. Supreme Court case, this may no longer be allowed. See *Law v. Siegel*, 134 S. Ct. 1188 (2014).)

In most courts, you will have to pay to amend your bankruptcy papers only if you are amending Schedules D, E, or F to add a new creditor or change an address, because these changes require the court to make an additional mailing. The fee for this type of amendment is currently $30.

If you become aware of debts or property that you should have included in your papers, amending your petition will avoid any suspicion that you're trying to conceal things from the trustee. If you don't amend your papers after discovering this kind of information, your bankruptcy petition may be dismissed or one or more of your debts may not be discharged if that new information comes to light.

Even if your bankruptcy case is already closed, some courts will allow you to reopen your case and amend your papers to add an omitted creditor who tries to collect the debt. (See Ch. 8.)

B18 (Official Form 18) (12/07)

United States Bankruptcy Court

_____ District Of _____

In re _____,

[Set forth here all names including married, maiden, and trade names used by debtor within last 8 years.]

                             Debtor

Address _____

_____

Last four digits of Social-Security or other Individual Taxpayer-Identification No(s)(if any).: _____

Employer Tax-Identification No(s).(EIN) [if any]:_____

)
)
)
)
)
)
)
)
)
)
)
)
)
)
)
)
)

Case No. _____

Chapter 7

DISCHARGE OF DEBTOR

    It appearing that the debtor is entitled to a discharge, **IT IS ORDERED:** The debtor is granted a discharge under section 727 of title 11, United States Code, (the Bankruptcy Code).

Dated: _____

BY THE COURT

_____
United States Bankruptcy Judge

SEE THE BACK OF THIS ORDER FOR IMPORTANT INFORMATION.

B18 (Official Form 18) (12/07) - Cont.

EXPLANATION OF BANKRUPTCY DISCHARGE
IN A CHAPTER 7 CASE

This court order grants a discharge to the person named as the debtor. It is not a dismissal of the case and it does not determine how much money, if any, the trustee will pay to creditors.

Collection of Discharged Debts Prohibited

The discharge prohibits any attempt to collect from the debtor a debt that has been discharged. For example, a creditor is not permitted to contact a debtor by mail, phone, or otherwise, to file or continue a lawsuit, to attach wages or other property, or to take any other action to collect a discharged debt from the debtor. *[In a case involving community property:* There are also special rules that protect certain community property owned by the debtor's spouse, even if that spouse did not file a bankruptcy case.] A creditor who violates this order can be required to pay damages and attorney's fees to the debtor.

However, a creditor may have the right to enforce a valid lien, such as a mortgage or security interest, against the debtor's property after the bankruptcy, if that lien was not avoided or eliminated in the bankruptcy case. Also, a debtor may voluntarily pay any debt that has been discharged.

Debts that are Discharged

The chapter 7 discharge order eliminates a debtor's legal obligation to pay a debt that is discharged. Most, but not all, types of debts are discharged if the debt existed on the date the bankruptcy case was filed. (If this case was begun under a different chapter of the Bankruptcy Code and converted to chapter 7, the discharge applies to debts owed when the bankruptcy case was converted.)

Debts that are Not Discharged.

Some of the common types of debts which are <u>not</u> discharged in a chapter 7 bankruptcy case are:

a. Debts for most taxes;

b. Debts incurred to pay nondischargeable taxes;

c. Debts that are domestic support obligations;

d. Debts for most student loans;

e. Debts for most fines, penalties, forfeitures, or criminal restitution obligations;

f. Debts for personal injuries or death caused by the debtor's operation of a motor vehicle, vessel, or aircraft while intoxicated;

g. Some debts which were not properly listed by the debtor;

h. Debts that the bankruptcy court specifically has decided or will decide in this bankruptcy case are not discharged;

i. Debts for which the debtor has given up the discharge protections by signing a reaffirmation agreement in compliance with the Bankruptcy Code requirements for reaffirmation of debts; and

j. Debts owed to certain pension, profit sharing, stock bonus, other retirement plans, or to the Thrift Savings Plan for federal employees for certain types of loans from these plans.

This information is only a general summary of the bankruptcy discharge. There are exceptions to these general rules. Because the law is complicated, you may want to consult an attorney to determine the exact effect of the discharge in this case.

> **CAUTION**
>
> **Try to get it right the first time.** Too many changes can make you look dishonest, which can get your case dismissed and (if it seems you were hiding assets) investigated. Of course, if the facts have changed since you filed your petition, or you notice mistakes, you should amend. But the more accurate your papers are at the outset, the less likely your case will run into trouble.

Common Amendments

Even a simple change in one form may require changes to several other forms. Here are some of the more common reasons for amendments and the forms that you may need to amend. Exactly which forms you'll have to change depends on your court's rules. (Instructions for making the amendments are below.)

Add or Delete Exempt Property on Schedule C

If you want to add or delete property from your list of exemptions, you must file a new Schedule C. Depending on the omission you may need to change:

- Schedule A, if the property is real estate and you didn't list it there
- Schedule B, if the property is personal property and you didn't list it there
- Schedule D and Form 8—Chapter 7 Individual Debtor's Statement of Intention, if the property is collateral for a secured debt and isn't already listed
- Form 7—Statement of Financial Affairs, if any transactions regarding the property weren't described on that form, or
- the Mailing Matrix, if the exempt item is tied to a particular creditor.

Add or Delete Property on Schedule A or B

You may have forgotten to list some of your property on your schedules. Or, you may have received property after filing for bankruptcy. The following property must be reported to the bankruptcy trustee if you receive it, or become entitled to receive it, within 180 days after filing for bankruptcy:

- property you inherit or become entitled to inherit

- property from a marital settlement agreement or divorce decree, and
- death benefits or life insurance policy proceeds. (See Ch. 3.)

If you have new property to report for any of these reasons, you may need to file amendments to:

- Schedule A, if the property is real estate
- Schedule B, if the property is personal property
- Schedule C, if the property was claimed as exempt and it's not, or you want to claim it as exempt
- Schedule D and Form 8—Chapter 7 Individual Debtor's Statement of Intention, if the property is collateral for a secured debt
- Form 7—Statement of Financial Affairs, if any transactions regarding the property haven't been described on that form, or
- the Mailing Matrix, if the item is tied to a particular creditor.

If your bankruptcy case is already closed, see Ch. 8.

Change Your Plans for Secured Property

If you've changed your plans for dealing with an item of secured property, you must file an amended Form 8—Chapter 7 Individual Debtor's Statement of Intention.

Correct Your List of Creditors

To correct your list of creditors, you may need to amend:

- Schedule C, if the debt is secured and you plan to claim the collateral as exempt
- Schedule D, if the debt is a secured debt
- Schedule E, if the debt is a priority debt (as defined in Ch. 6)
- Schedule F, if the debt is unsecured
- Form 7—Statement of Financial Affairs, if any transactions regarding the property haven't been described on that form, or
- the Mailing Matrix, which contains the names and addresses of all your creditors.

If your bankruptcy case is already closed, see Ch. 8.

Add an Omitted Payment to a Creditor

If you didn't report a payment to a creditor made within the year before you filed for bankruptcy, you must amend your Form 7—Statement of Financial Affairs.

How to File an Amendment

To make an amendment, take these steps:

Step 1: Fill out the Amendment Cover Sheet in Appendix B, if no local form is required. Otherwise, use the local form. If you use our form, here's how to fill it in:

- Put the appropriate information in the top blanks (for instance, "Western District of Tennessee").
- After "In re," enter your name, the name of your spouse if you're married and filing jointly, and all other names you have used in the last eight years.
- Enter your address, the last four digits of your Social Security number, and a taxpayer ID number (if you have one because of a business you own).
- On the right side, enter your case number.
- Check the boxes of the forms you are amending. If you are adding new creditors or changing addresses, check the box that you have enclosed the appropriate fee (currently $30).
- Sign the form.
- Continue to the declaration about the truth of the amendment.
- Enter your name (and the name of your spouse if you're filing jointly) after "I (we)."
- Enter the number of pages that will be accompanying the cover sheet.
- Enter the date you are signing the document.
- Sign (both you and your spouse, if you're filing jointly) at the bottom to swear under penalty of perjury that your amendment is true.

Step 2: Make copies of the forms affected by your amendment.

Step 3: Check your local court rules or ask the court clerk whether you must retype the whole form to make the correction, or if you can just type the new information on another blank form. If you can't find the answer, ask a local bankruptcy lawyer or nonattorney bankruptcy petition preparer. If it's acceptable to just type the new information, precede the information you're typing with "ADD," "CHANGE," or "DELETE" as appropriate. At the bottom of the form, type "AMENDED" in capital letters.

Step 4: Call or visit the court and ask what order the papers must be in and how many copies are required.

Step 5: Make the required number of copies, plus one copy for yourself, one for the trustee, and one for any creditor affected by your amendment.

Step 6: Have a friend or relative mail, first class, a copy of your amended papers to the bankruptcy trustee and to any creditor affected by your amendment.

Step 7: Enter the name and complete address of every new creditor affected by your amendment on the Proof of Service by Mail (a copy is in Appendix B). Also enter the name and address of the bankruptcy trustee. Then have the person who mailed the amendment to the trustee and new creditors sign and date the proof of service.

Step 8: Mail or take the original amendment and proof of service and copies to the bankruptcy court. Enclose a money order for the filing fee, if required. If you use the mail, enclose a prepaid self-addressed envelope so the clerk can return a file-stamped set of papers to you.

If the 341 hearing occurred before you file your amendment, the court is likely to schedule another one.

Filing a Change of Address

If you move while your bankruptcy case is still open, you must give your new address to the court, the trustee, and your creditors. Here's how to do it:

Step 1: Make one or two photocopies of the blank Notice of Change of Address and Proof of Service forms in Appendix B.

Step 2: Fill in the Change of Address form with your old address, new address, and date you moved.

Step 3: Make one photocopy for the trustee, one for your records, and one for each creditor listed in Schedules D, E, and F or the Mailing Matrix.

Step 4: Have a friend or relative mail a copy of the Notice of Change of Address to the trustee and to each creditor.

Step 5: Have the friend or relative complete and sign the Proof of Service by Mail form, listing the bankruptcy trustee and the names and addresses of all creditors to whom the notice was mailed.

Step 6: File the original notice and original Proof of Service with the bankruptcy court.

Special Problems

Sometimes, complications arise in a bankruptcy—usually when a creditor files some type of motion or objects to the discharge of a debt or the entire bankruptcy. If a creditor does this, the court will notify you by sending you a Notice of Motion or Notice of Objection. (See a copy of the blank form, below.) At that point, you may need to go to court yourself or get an attorney to help you. Here are some of the more common complications that may crop up.

You Failed the Means Test

If you didn't pass the means test (described in Ch. 6) but decided to file for Chapter 7 anyway, you may face a motion to dismiss or convert your case to a Chapter 13 bankruptcy.

Presumed Abuse

If you don't pass the means test, your Chapter 7 bankruptcy will be presumed to be abusive. This means that you won't be allowed to proceed unless you can establish that the presumption of abuse should be set aside because of special circumstances.

However, none of this is automatic. To stop your Chapter 7 bankruptcy on the grounds of abuse, someone—a creditor, the trustee, or, most likely, the U.S. Trustee—must request a court hearing to dismiss or convert your case. The U.S. Trustee must file a statement, within ten days after your 341 hearing, indicating whether your case should be considered a presumed abuse. (This statement is required only if your income is more than the state median; see Ch. 1 for more information.) Five days after the U.S. Trustee's statement is filed, the court must send it to all of your creditors, to inform them of the U.S. Trustee's decision and give them an opportunity to file a motion to dismiss or convert your case.

Within 30 days after filing this statement, the U.S. Trustee must either:

- file its own motion to dismiss or convert your case on grounds of abuse, or
- explain why a motion to convert or dismiss isn't appropriate (for example, because you passed the means test).

These duties and time limits apply only to the U.S. Trustee. If your income is more than the state median, your creditors can file a motion to dismiss or convert any time after you file, but no later than 60 days after the first date set for your 341 hearing.

Defending a Motion to Dismiss or Convert

If the U.S. Trustee (or a trustee or a creditor, in some cases) files a motion to dismiss or convert your case on the basis of presumed abuse, you are entitled to notice of the hearing at least 20 days in advance. You will receive papers in the mail explaining the grounds for the motion and what you need to do to respond. Because abuse is presumed, you will bear the burden of proving that your filing really isn't abusive, and that you should be allowed to proceed.

There are two basic defenses to this type of motion:

1. **You didn't fail the means test.** To defend on this basis, you must be able to show that you actually passed the means test and the party bringing the motion to dismiss or convert misinterpreted the information you provided in Form 22A-1 and Form 22A-2 or misinterpreted the applicable law (for example, by including Social Security benefits in your current monthly income when the law says they should be excluded).

2. **Special circumstances exist that allow you to pass the means test.** Bankruptcy law gives a serious medical condition or a call to active duty in the armed forces as examples of special circumstances, but this isn't an exhaustive list. However, it isn't enough just to show that special circumstances exist: You must also show that they justify additional expenses or adjustments to your current monthly income "for which there is no reasonable alternative."

To prove special circumstances, you must itemize each additional expense or adjustment of your income, and provide:

- documentation for the expense or adjustment, and
- a detailed explanation of the special circumstances that make the expense or adjustment necessary and reasonable.

You will win only if the additional expenses or adjustments to your income enable you to pass the means test. (Ch. 6 explains how to make this calculation.)

EXAMPLE: Maureen and Ralph have a child (Sarah) with severe autism. Sarah is making remarkable progress in her private school, for which Maureen and Ralph pay $1,000 a month. No equivalent school is available at a lower tuition. Under the means test guidelines, Maureen and Ralph are entitled to deduct only $150 a month from the income for private school expenses. If Maureen and Ralph were allowed to deduct the full $1,000 monthly tuition, they would easily pass the means test. By documenting Sarah's condition, the necessity for the extra educational expense, and the fact that moving her to a less expensive school would greatly undermine her progress, Maureen and Ralph would have a good chance of convincing the court to allow the $1,000 expense, which would, in turn, rebut the presumption of abuse.

Motions to Dismiss for Abuse Under All the Circumstances

As we've explained, it's possible to have your case dismissed if it appears that your Chapter 7 filing is an abuse of the bankruptcy code under all the circumstances. Motions to dismiss for this reason tend to focus primarily on whether the debtor's expenses are unnecessarily extravagant. For example, an Ohio bankruptcy court ruled that a mortgage expense on a $400,000 home and an expense for repayment of a 401(k) loan should not be allowed. Without those expenses, the debtors had adequate income to fund a Chapter 13 plan, which made their case an abuse under all the circumstances. (*In re Felske*, 385 B.R. 649 (Bankr. N.D. Ohio 2008).)

The grounds for dismissal don't necessarily have to exist when you file for bankruptcy. One appellate court ruled that a motion to dismiss for abuse may be brought on the basis of events occurring anytime before the discharge. (*In re Cortez*, 457 F.3d 448 (5th Cir. 2006).) So if you get a new job or win the lottery, or some other event happens while your case is pending that would enable you to proceed under Chapter 13, you may face a challenge to your Chapter 7 case. (See also *In re Henebury*, 361 B.R. 595 (Bankr. S.D. Fla. 2007).)

If you face dismissal on this ground, you will need to explain why it's unlikely you could complete a Chapter 13 bankruptcy, or why expenses that are challenged by the trustee are really necessary for you to get a fresh start. There is no clear test of what constitutes abuse under all the circumstances. As with obscenity, the judges will know it when they see it. Fortunately, the U.S. Trustee (usually the party bringing these motions) has the burden of proving the abuse. If you pass the means test, your eligibility for Chapter 7 bankruptcy is presumed and the trustee has to overcome that presumption.

Bankruptcy courts have issued written decisions on a variety of special circumstance claims. If you need to prove special circumstances to pass the means test, you will definitely want to check with a local attorney or do your own research to find out how bankruptcy courts in your state have treated the special circumstances you're claiming. (See Ch. 10.)

A frequently addressed issue is whether payments on nondischargeable student loans can be considered a special circumstance. While a few courts have held that they can be, more courts have gone the other way and ruled that student loan payments do not constitute special circumstances. (See, for example, *In re Champagne*, 389 B.R. 191 (Bankr. Kan. 2008) and *In re Pageau*, 383 B.R. 281 (Bankr. S.D. Ind. 2008).)

Here are some cases in which the court has allowed a particular special circumstances claim. But remember that courts in your area may see the issue differently:

- unusually high transportation expenses (*In re Batzkiel,* 349 B.R. 581 (Bankr. N.D. Iowa 2006); *In re Turner,* 376 B.R. 370 (Bankr. D. N.H. 2007))
- mandatory repayment of 401(k) loan (*In re Lenton,* 358 B.R. 651 (Bankr. E.D. Pa. 2006))
- reduction in income (*In re Martin,* 371 B.R. 347 (Bankr. C.D. Ill. 2007) (diminished future availability of overtime hours); *In re Tamez,* No. 07-60047 (Bankr. W.D. Tex. 2007) (reduction in income due to voluntary job changes))
- wife's pregnancy in a joint case (*In re Martin,* 371 B.R. 347 (Bankr. C.D. Ill. 2007))
- joint debtors who have two separate households (*In re Graham*, 363 B.R. 844 (Bankr. S.D. Ohio 2007); *In re Armstrong*, No. 06-31414 (Bankr. N.D. Ohio 2007))
- unusually high rent expenses (*In re Scarafiotti*, 375 B.R. 618 (Bankr. D. Colo. 2007)), and
- court-ordered child support payments (*In re Littman*, 370 B.R. 820 (Bankr. D. Idaho 2007)).

A Creditor Asks the Court to Lift the Automatic Stay

Your automatic stay lasts from the date you file your papers until the date you receive your bankruptcy discharge or the date your bankruptcy case is closed, whichever happens first. For example, assume you receive a discharge but the trustee keeps your case open because the trustee is waiting to collect your tax refund or an inheritance you are due to receive in the future. In this situation, the automatic stay would not be in effect after your discharge, even though your case would still be open.

As long as the stay is in effect, most creditors must get permission from a judge to take any action against you or your property that might affect your bankruptcy estate. (See Ch. 2 for information on which creditors are affected by the stay and which are free to proceed with collection efforts despite the stay.) To get this permission, the creditor must file a request in writing called a Motion to Lift Stay. The court will schedule a hearing on this motion and send you written notice. You will have a certain period of time to file a written response. Even if you decide not to file a response, you may still be able to appear in court to argue that the stay shouldn't be lifted. Check your local rules on this point.

If you don't show up for the hearing—even if you filed a written response—the stay will probably be lifted as requested by the creditor, unless lifting the stay would potentially harm other creditors. For instance, if the creditor is seeking permission to repossess your car, and your equity in the car would produce some income for your unsecured creditors if sold by the trustee, the court may refuse to lift the stay whether or not you show up.

After hearing the motion, the judge will either rule "from the bench" (announce a decision right then and there), or "take it under submission" and mail a decision in a few days. A creditor can ask a judge to lift the stay within a week or two after you file, but a delay of several weeks to several months is more common.

B20A (Official Form 20A) (Notice of Motion or Objection) (12/10)

United States Bankruptcy Court
_____ District of _____

In re
_[Set forth here all names including married, maiden, and
trade names used by debtor within last 8 years.]_

                      Debtor

Address   _____

                _____

Last four digits of Social Security or Individual Tax-payer Identification
(ITIN) No(s).,(if any): _____

Employer's Tax Identification (EIN) No(s).(if any): _____
_____

Case No. _____

Chapter _____

NOTICE OF [MOTION TO] [OBJECTION TO]

_____ has filed papers with the court to [relief sought in motion or objection].

    <u>**Your rights may be affected.**</u> **You should read these papers carefully and discuss them with your attorney, if you have one in this bankruptcy case. (If you do not have an attorney, you may wish to consult one.)**

    If you do not want the court to [relief sought in motion or objection], or if you want the court to consider your views on the [motion] [objection], then on or before <u>(date)</u> , you or your attorney must:

    [File with the court a written request for a hearing {_or, if the court requires a written response_, an answer, explaining your position} at:

        {address of the bankruptcy clerk's office}

    If you mail your {request}{response} to the court for filing, you must mail it early enough so the court will **receive** it on or before the date stated above.

    You must also mail a copy to:

        {movant's attorney's name and address}

        {names and addresses of others to be served}]

    [Attend the hearing scheduled to be held on <u>(date)</u> , <u>(year)</u> , at _____ a.m./p.m. in Courtroom_____, United States Bankruptcy Court, {address}.]

    [Other steps required to oppose a motion or objection under local rule or court order.]

    If you or your attorney do not take these steps, the court may decide that you do not oppose the relief sought in the motion or objection and may enter an order granting that relief.

Date: _____

Signature: _____
Name:
Address

Do You Have an Ownership Interest in the Property?

There are many kinds of ownership interests. You can own property outright. You can own the right to possess it sometime in the future. You can co-own it jointly with any number of other owners. You can own the right to possess it, while someone else actually owns legal title.

For most kinds of property, there's an easy way to tell if you have an ownership interest: If you would be entitled to receive any cash if the property were sold, you have an ownership interest.

For intangible property, however—property you can't see or touch—it may be harder to show your ownership interest. This most often arises in cases involving contracts concerning residential real estate.

For instance, if you have a lease (a type of contract) on your home when you file, most bankruptcy courts would consider it an ownership interest in the property and would not lift the stay to let a landlord go ahead with eviction, regardless of the reason. But if the lease expired by its own terms before you filed—which converted your interest from a "leasehold" to a month-to-month tenancy—most courts would rule that you have no ownership interest in the property and would lift the stay, allowing the eviction to go forward.

Another ownership interest is the contractual right to continued coverage that an insured person has under an insurance policy. This means the automatic stay prevents insurance companies from canceling insurance policies.

Grounds for Lifting the Stay

The bankruptcy court may lift the automatic stay for several reasons:

- The activity being stayed is not a legitimate concern of the bankruptcy court. For instance, the court will let a child custody hearing proceed, because its outcome won't affect your economic situation.
- The activity being stayed is going to happen no matter what the bankruptcy court does. For instance, if a lender shows the court that a mortgage foreclosure will ultimately occur, regardless of the bankruptcy filing, the court will usually lift the stay and let the foreclosure proceed. (If you want to keep your house, you may be better off filing for Chapter 13 bankruptcy. See Ch. 4.)
- The stay is harming the creditor's interest in property you own or possess. For instance, if you've stopped making payments on a car and it's losing value, the court may lift the stay. That would allow the creditor to repossess the car now, unless you're willing and able to periodically pay the creditor an amount equal to the ongoing depreciation until your case is closed.
- You have no ownership interest in the property sought by the creditor (ownership interests are explained just above). If you don't own some interest in property that a creditor wants, the court isn't interested in protecting the property—and won't hesitate to lift the stay. The most common example is when a month-to-month tenant files bankruptcy to forestall an eviction. Because the tenancy has no monetary value, it is not considered to be property of the estate, and the stay will almost always be lifted.

Opposing a Request to Lift the Stay

Generally, a court won't lift the stay if you can show that it's necessary to preserve your property for yourself (if it's exempt) or for the benefit of your creditors (if it's not), or to maintain your general economic condition. You may also need to convince the court that the creditor's investment in the property will be protected while the bankruptcy is pending.

Here are situations and some possible responses you can make if creditors try to get the stay lifted:

- **Repossession of cars or other personal property.** If the stay is preventing a creditor from repossessing personal property pledged as collateral, such as your car, furniture, or jewelry, the creditor will probably argue that the stay should be lifted because you might damage the collateral or because the property is depreciating (declining in value) while your bankruptcy case is pending. Your response should depend on the facts. If the property is still in good shape, be prepared to prove it to the judge.

If the property is worth more than you owe on it, you can argue that depreciation won't hurt the creditor, because the property could be repossessed later and sold for the amount of the debt or more. But if, as is common, you have little or no equity in the property, you'll need to propose a way to protect the creditor's interest while you keep the property—assuming you want it. One way to do this is to pay the creditor a cash security deposit that would offset the expected depreciation.

If you intend to keep secured property (see Ch. 5), you can argue that lifting the stay would deprive you of your rights under the bankruptcy laws. For example, if you intend to redeem a car by paying its replacement value, the court should deny the motion to lift the stay until you have an opportunity to do so.

- **Utility disconnections.** For 20 days after you file your bankruptcy petition, a public utility—electric, gas, telephone, or water company—may not alter, refuse, or discontinue service to you, or discriminate against you in any other way, solely on the basis of an unpaid debt or your bankruptcy filing. (11 U.S.C. § 366(a).) If your service was disconnected before you filed, the utility company must restore it within 20 days after you file for bankruptcy—without requiring a deposit—if you request it.

  Twenty days after the order to continue service, the utility is entitled to discontinue service unless you provide adequate assurance that your future bills will be paid. (11 U.S.C. § 366(b).) Usually, that means you'll have to come up with a security deposit.

  If you and the utility can't agree on the size of the deposit, the utility may cut off service, which means you'll need to get a lawyer and ask the bankruptcy court to have it reinstated. If

the utility files a motion to lift the stay, argue at the hearing that your deposit is adequate.

- **Evictions.** Filing for bankruptcy has been a favorite tactic for some eviction defense clinics, which file a bare-bones bankruptcy petition to stop evictions even if the tenant's debts don't justify bankruptcy. However, the automatic stay doesn't apply if your landlord obtained a judgment for eviction before you filed for bankruptcy, or if the eviction is based on your endangerment of the property or use of illegal controlled substances on the premises. These exceptions to the general rules (which have their own exceptions) are explained in Ch. 2.

- **Foreclosures.** If the lender cannot show proof that it owns the mortgage, you may be able to oppose a lender's motion to lift the stay on the grounds that the lender had no right to file the motion in the first place.

If the lender proves that it owns the mortgage, you may be able to oppose the motion to lift the stay if you can show that you can resume regular payments and begin to catch up on your arrears. In that case, the judge may allow you additional time to cure your default under the protection of the automatic stay instead of granting the lender's motion.

The Trustee or a Creditor Disputes a Claimed Exemption

After the 341 hearing, the trustee and creditors have 30 days to object to the exemptions you claimed. If the deadline passes and the trustee or a creditor wants to challenge an exemption, it's usually too late, even if the exemption statutes don't support the claimed exemption. (*Taylor v. Freeland and Kronz,* 503 U.S. 638 (1992).) The objections must be in writing and filed with the bankruptcy court. Copies must be served on the trustee, you, and your lawyer, if you have one.

In some cases, the trustee can object to an exemption after the 30-day period has passed. For instance, in one case, the debtor stated that the value of certain stock options was unknown and used a $4,000 or so wildcard exemption to cover the value, whatever it was. Eight months after the bankruptcy case was closed, the trustee asked the debtor what happened to the stock options. As it happened, they had been cashed out for nearly $100,000. The trustee sought to have the case reopened to recover the excess value. The debtor argued that the 30-day period prevented a reexamination of the exemption claim.

Reasons for Objecting

The most common grounds for objecting are:

- You aren't eligible to use the state exemptions you claimed. You may use a state's exemptions only if you have made that state your domicile (your true home) for at least two years before filing. If you haven't been domiciled in your current state for at least two years, you must use the exemptions for the state where you were living for the better part of the 180-day period ending two years before you filed for bankruptcy. (See Ch. 3 for more on these rules, and Ch. 4 for more on the stricter rules that apply to homestead exemptions.)

- The claimed item isn't exempt under the law. For example, a plumber who lives in New Jersey and selects his state exemptions might try to exempt his plumbing tools under the "goods and chattels" exemption. The trustee and creditors are likely to object on the ground that these are work tools rather than goods and chattels, and that New Jersey has no "tools of the trade" exemption.

- Within ten years before you filed for bankruptcy, you sold nonexempt property and purchased exempt property to hinder, delay, or cheat your creditors. (Ways to avoid this accusation are discussed in Ch. 3.)

- Property you claimed as exempt is worth more than you say it is. If the property's true replacement value is higher than the exemption limit for that item, the item can be sold and the excess over the exemption limit distributed to your creditors (assuming you don't buy the property back from the trustee at a negotiated price).

EXAMPLE: In Connie's state, clothing is exempt to a total of $2,000. Connie values her mink coat at $1,000 and her other clothes at $1,000, bringing her within the $2,000 exemption. A creditor objects to the $1,000 valuation of the coat, claiming that such mink coats routinely sell for $3,000 and up. If the creditor prevails, Connie would have to surrender the coat to the trustee. She'd get the first $1,000 (the exempt amount of the coat's sale price). Or, Connie could keep the coat if she gave the trustee a negotiated amount of cash ($2,000 or less) or other property of equivalent value.

- You and your spouse have doubled an exemption where doubling isn't permitted.

EXAMPLE: David and Marylee, a married couple, file for bankruptcy using California's System 1 exemptions. Each claims a $2,975 exemption in their family car, for a total of $5,950. California bars a married couple from doubling the System 1 automobile exemption. They can only claim $2,975.

Responding to Objections

When objection papers are filed, the court schedules a hearing. The creditor or trustee must prove to the bankruptcy court that the exemption is improper. You don't have to prove anything. In fact, you don't have to respond to the objection or show up at the hearing unless the bankruptcy court orders, or local rules require, that you do so. Of course, you can—and probably should—either file a response or show up at the hearing to defend your claim of a legitimate exemption. If you don't show up, the bankruptcy judge will decide on the basis of the paperwork filed by the objecting party and the applicable laws, which most often means you'll lose—especially if the trustee or a bankruptcy attorney is objecting.

A Creditor Objects to the Discharge of a Debt

There are a variety of reasons a creditor may object to the discharge of a debt. In consumer bankruptcies, the most common reason is that the creditor believes you made fraudulent statements to borrow the money in the first place (for example, on a credit card application). See Ch. 9 for more on this and other potential grounds for objecting to the discharge of a debt.

You Want to Get Back Exempt Property Taken by a Creditor

You may have filed for bankruptcy after a creditor:

- repossessed collateral (such as a car) under a security agreement, or
- seized some of your property as part of a judgment collection action.

If so, you should have described the event in your Statement of Financial Affairs, which you filed along with your bankruptcy petition and schedules. Repossessions are difficult to undo, because they occur under a contract that you voluntarily entered into. However, property seized to satisfy a judgment can be pulled back into your bankruptcy estate if the seizure occurred within the three months before you filed. If the property is not exempt (or at least some of it is not exempt), the trustee may go after it so that it can be sold for the benefit of your unsecured creditors. If the property is exempt (meaning you are entitled to keep it), you can go after it yourself. However, you'll have to file a formal complaint in the bankruptcy court against the creditor.

The process for getting the bankruptcy judge to order property returned to you is a complex one; you'll probably need the assistance of an attorney. Given the cost of attorneys, it's seldom worth your while to go after this type of property unless it's valuable or an irreplaceable family heirloom. Keep in mind that most property is only exempt up to a certain value—for example, a car may be exempt up to $1,200, furnishings up to $1,000. Thus, even if you get the property back, the trustee may decide to sell it, in which case you'll receive only the exempt amount from the proceeds.

You Want to Dismiss Your Case

If you change your mind after you file for bankruptcy, you can ask the court to dismiss your case.

Common reasons for wanting to dismiss a case include the following:

- You discover that a major debt you thought was dischargeable isn't. You don't have enough other debts to justify your bankruptcy case.
- You realize that an item of property you thought was exempt isn't. You don't want to lose it in bankruptcy.
- You come into a sum of money and can afford to pay your debts.
- You realize that you have more property in your estate than you thought and decide that you don't have to file for bankruptcy after all.
- Your bankruptcy case turns out to be more complex than you originally thought. You need a lawyer, but you don't have the money to hire one.
- The emotional stress of bankruptcy is too much for you.

It is within the court's discretion to dismiss your case. That means the court can grant or refuse the dismissal. How the courts make this decision varies from district to district. In some districts, dismissing a case is next to impossible if your bankruptcy estate has assets that can be sold. However, if yours is a no-asset case and no creditor objects to the dismissal, you may have better luck dismissing it.

If you want to dismiss your case, you must file a request with the court. Instructions on how to do this follow. Depending on how receptive your local bankruptcy court is to dismissal, you may need the help of a lawyer.

Step 1: Check your court's local rules for time limits, format of papers, and other requirements for voluntary dismissals. (See Ch. 10 for information on finding local rules online.) If you can't find the information you need from reading your local rules, ask the court clerk, the trustee assigned to your case, a local bankruptcy petition preparer, or a bankruptcy lawyer for help.

Step 2: Refer to the sample Petition for Voluntary Dismissal and a sample Order Granting Voluntary Dismissal provided below. Follow along with the sample as you type your caption, inserting your own information in the blanks.

Step 3: If you're using a typewriter, make a few photocopies of what you have typed so far, so you can make two different documents with that one caption.

Step 4: On one copy of your caption, center and type "PETITION FOR VOLUNTARY DISMISSAL." The text of the petition will be similar to the sample but tailored to the facts of your case. In particular, you will put your filing date in Paragraph 1; in Paragraph 3 you will explain your own reason for wanting to dismiss the case.

Step 5: Sign and date the petition. If you filed together with your spouse, both of you must sign. Otherwise, leave the spouse's signature line blank.

Step 6: On another photocopy of the caption you made, center and type: "[PROPOSED] ORDER GRANTING VOLUNTARY DISMISSAL." Then type the text of the order from the sample at the end of this chapter. Include the blanks; the judge will fill them in.

Step 7: Make at least three copies of your signed petition and your blank order.

Step 8: Take your originals and copies to the bankruptcy court clerk. When you get to the court clerk, explain that you are filing a petition to dismiss your case. The clerk will take your originals and one or more of your copies. Ask the clerk the following:

- What notice to your creditors is required?
- If there is a problem, will you be contacted? If not, how will you learn of the problem?
- If the judge signs the order, when can you expect to get it?

- Once you have a signed order, who sends copies to your creditors—you or the court? If you send the copies, do you also have to file a Proof of Service?

Step 9: Once you receive the signed order, put it away for safekeeping if you don't have to notify your creditors. If you do, make copies and send one to each.

Step 10: If you have to file a Proof of Service, follow the instructions in Ch. 5.

You Want to Reopen Your Case

At several places in this book, we've suggested that you might have to reopen your case (for example, to file a motion to avoid a lien or to file Form 23 proving that you completed budget counseling). To reopen your case, you must file what's called an "ex parte motion." This simply means that you don't have to provide formal notice to the other parties in your case. Instead, you just have to prepare and file your request and an accompanying order, and demonstrate that you have given written notice of your motion to the trustee and the U.S. Trustee. You don't have to schedule a hearing; the judge will consider your request and either grant or deny it based solely on your paperwork.

Here, we provide the forms necessary to ask the court to reopen your case to allow you to file Form 23, and to ask the court for a discharge. There are four forms in all:

- a request to reopen the case
- an order reopening the case
- a request for a discharge, and
- an order that a discharge be entered.

If you want the court to reopen your case for a different reason, you'll have to change the forms. Describe why you need the case to be reopened and tailor the additional forms to request the ultimate relief you want the court to grant (for example, to avoid a lien). If you have trouble completing these forms or figuring out what to say, talk to a bankruptcy lawyer.

Petition for Voluntary Dismissal

UNITED STATES BANKRUPTCY COURT

_____ [*name of district*] _____ DISTRICT OF _____ [*your state*] _____

In re _____)
     [*Set forth here all names including married,*)
     maiden, and trade names used by debtor)
     within last 8 years.])
                          Debtor(s)) Case No. _____
Address _____)
)
_____) Chapter 7
)
Last four digits of Social Security or Individual)
Taxpayer Identification No(s). (ITIN) (*if any*): _____)
)
Employer's Tax Identification No(s). (EIN) (*if any*): _____)
_____)

PETITION FOR VOLUNTARY DISMISSAL

The debtor in the above-mentioned case hereby moves to dismiss his/her bankruptcy case for the following reasons:

1. Debtor filed a voluntary petition under Chapter 7 of the Bankruptcy Code on _____ , 20____ .

2. No complaints objecting to discharge or to determine the dischargeability of any debts have been filed in the case.

3. Debtor realizes that filing a Chapter 7 bankruptcy petition was erroneous. Debtor now realizes that a particular debt may not be dischargeable. Debtor would have to litigate this matter, and Debtor does not feel he/she has the ability to do so on his/her own nor the resources to hire an attorney to do it for him/her. Debtor intends to pursue other means of handling his/her debts.

4. No creditor has filed a claim in this case.

5. No creditor has requested relief from the automatic stay.

WHEREFORE, Debtor prays that this bankruptcy case be dismissed without prejudice.

Dated: _____   _____
                                              Signature of Debtor

Dated: _____   _____
                                              Signature of Debtor's Spouse

Order Granting Voluntary Dismissal

UNITED STATES BANKRUPTCY COURT

_____ [*name of district*] _____ DISTRICT OF _____ [*your state*] _____

In re _____)
      [*Set forth here all names including married,*)
      maiden, and trade names used by debtor)
      within last 8 years.])
                    Debtor(s)) Case No. _____
Address _____)
)
_____) Chapter 7
)
Last four digits of Social Security or Individual)
Taxpayer Identification No(s). (ITIN) (*if any*): _____)
)
Employer's Tax Identification No(s). (EIN) (*if any*): _____)
_____)

[PROPOSED] ORDER GRANTING VOLUNTARY DISMISSAL

AND NOW, this _____ day of _____, 20____, the Court having found that the voluntary dismissal of this case is in the best interests of the debtor and does not prejudice the rights of any of his or her creditors, it is hereby ordered that the petition for voluntary dismissal is approved.

Dated: _____ _____
                                        U.S. Bankruptcy Judge

Request to Reopen Case

UNITED STATES BANKRUPTCY COURT

_____ [*name of district*] _____ DISTRICT OF _____ [*your state*] _____

In re _____)
    [*Set forth here all names including married,*)
    maiden, and trade names used by debtor)
    within last 8 years.])
                Debtor(s)) Case No. _____
Address _____)
)
_____) Chapter 7
)
Last four digits of Social Security or Individual)
Taxpayer Identification No(s). (ITIN) (*if any*): _____)
)
Employer's Tax Identification No(s). (EIN) (*if any*): _____)
_____)

EX-PARTE APPLICATION TO REOPEN CLOSED CASE UNDER 11 U.S.C. SECTION 350(b)

To the Honorable [*name of bankruptcy judge*]:

Debtor/Applicant [*your name*] herein applies to have [*his/her*] case reopened and respectfully represents:

1. On [*date you filed your petition*], Applicant filed a Petition for Relief under Chapter 7 of Title 11 of the United States Code, and on [*date your case was closed*], said case was closed without an order of discharge under 11 U.S.C. Section 727.

2 The reason given for the Court's denial of a discharge was that the Court failed to timely receive Official Form 23, proof of personal financial management counseling under 11 U.S.C. Section 111.

3. Prior to closure of [*his/her*] case, Applicant had in fact undertaken and completed personal financial management counseling pursuant to 11 U.S.C. Section 111 but inadvertently failed to file a completed Official Form 23 with the court.

4. Applicant seeks to reopen [*his/her*] case in order to file Official Form 23 and to move the court to enter a discharge under 11 U.S.C. Section 727.

5. Attached to this application is a copy of Official Form 23 that Applicant will immediately file upon reopening of this case.

6. Reopening [*his/her*] case by ex-parte application for the purpose of filing Form 23 and seeking a discharge is authorized under 11 U.S.C. Section 350(b).

7. Wherefore Applicant prays that the above-entitled case be reopened for the purpose of permitting Applicant to file Official Form 23 and move the Court for a discharge in [*his/her*] Chapter 7 bankruptcy case.

Dated: _____ Signed: _____
                                                 [*your name*]

Order Granting Request to Reopen Case

UNITED STATES BANKRUPTCY COURT

_____ [*name of district*] _____ DISTRICT OF _____ [*your state*] _____

In re _____)
    [*Set forth here all names including married,*)
    maiden, and trade names used by debtor)
    within last 8 years.])
                 Debtor(s)) Case No. _____
Address _____)
)
_____) Chapter 7
)
Last four digits of Social Security or Individual)
Taxpayer Identification No(s). (ITIN) (*if any*): _____)
)
Employer's Tax Identification No(s). (EIN) (*if any*): _____)
_____)

ORDER TO REOPEN CLOSED CASE

Based on debtor's Ex-Parte Application to Reopen Closed Case and applicable law, it is hereby ordered that Case No: [*case number*] be reopened for the purpose of permitting Applicant to file Official Form 23 and apply for an order of discharge under 11 U.S.C. Section 727.

Date: _____ Signed: _____
                               U.S. Bankruptcy Judge

Request for Discharge

UNITED STATES BANKRUPTCY COURT

_____[*name of district*]_____ DISTRICT OF _____[*your state*]_____

In re _____)
    [*Set forth here all names including married,*)
    maiden, and trade names used by debtor)
    within last 8 years.])
                  Debtor(s)) Case No. _____
Address _____)
)
_____) Chapter 7
)
Last four digits of Social Security or Individual)
Taxpayer Identification No(s). (ITIN) (*if any*): _____)
)
Employer's Tax Identification No(s). (EIN) (*if any*): _____)
_____)

EX-PARTE APPLICATION FOR THE COURT TO ENTER
AN ORDER OF DISCHARGE UNDER 11 U.S.C. SECTION 727

To the Honorable [*name of bankruptcy judge*]:

Debtor/Applicant [*your name*] herein applies to have an order of discharge entered in [*his/her*] case and respectfully represents:

1. On [*date you filed your petition*], Applicant filed a Petition for Relief under Chapter 7 of Title 11 of the United States Code, and on [*date your case was closed*], said case was closed without an order of discharge under 11 U.S.C. Section 727.

2. The reason given for the Court's denial of a discharge was that the Court failed to timely receive Official Form 23, proof of personal financial management counseling under 11 U.S.C. Section 111.

3. Applicant sought and obtained an Order to Reopen [*his/her*] case in order to refile Official Form 23 and move the court to enter a discharge under 11 U.S.C. Section 727.

4. On [*date you filed Form 23*], Applicant filed Official Form 23 with the court clerk.

5. Wherefore Applicant prays that the honorable court enter an Order of Discharge in [*his/her*] case under 11 U.S.C. Section 727.

Date: _____ Signed: _____
                                    [*your name*]

Order Granting Request for Discharge

UNITED STATES BANKRUPTCY COURT

_____ *[name of district]* _____ DISTRICT OF _____ *[your state]* _____

In re _____)
      [Set forth here all names including married,)
      maiden, and trade names used by debtor)
      within last 8 years.])
                            Debtor(s)) Case No. _____
Address _____)
)
_____) Chapter 7
)
Last four digits of Social Security or Individual)
Taxpayer Identification No(s). (ITIN) (*if any*): _____)
)
Employer's Tax Identification No(s). (EIN) (*if any*): _____)
_____)

ORDER TO GRANT REQUEST FOR DISCHARGE

Based on debtor's Ex-Parte Application for the Court to Enter an Order of Discharge, it is hereby ordered that a

discharge be entered under 11 U.S.C. Section 727 in Case No. [*case number*] .

Date: _____ Signed: _____
                                                U.S. Bankruptcy Judge

Sample Proof of Service by Mail

UNITED STATES BANKRUPTCY COURT

_____ [*name of district*] _____ DISTRICT OF _____ [*your state*] _____

In re _____)
    [*Set forth here all names including married,*)
    maiden, and trade names used by debtor)
    within last 8 years.])
                    Debtor(s)) Case No. _____
Address _____)
)
_____) Chapter 7
)
Last four digits of Social Security or Individual)
Taxpayer Identification No(s). (ITIN) (*if any*): _____)
)
Employer's Tax Identification No(s). (EIN) (*if any*): _____)
_____)

PROOF OF SERVICE BY MAIL

    I, _____ [*name of server*] _____ , declare that: I am a resident

or employed in the County of _____ [*server's county*] _____ , State of _____ [*server's state*] _____ .

My residence/business address is _____ [*server's address*] _____ .

I am over the age of eighteen years and not a party to this case.

    On _____ [*date request served*] _____ , 20 ___ , I served the enclosed _____ [*papers served*] _____

_____

on the following parties by placing true and correct copies thereof enclosed in a sealed envelope with postage

thereon fully prepaid in the United States Mail at _____ [*city and state*] _____ ,

addressed as follows:

    [*name and address of trustee*]
    [*address of U.S. Trustee*]

    I declare under penalty of perjury that the foregoing is true and correct, and that this declaration was executed on

Date: _[*date Proof of Service signed*]_ , 20 ___ at _____
                                          City and State

                         _____ [*Server's signature*] _____
                         Signature

Life After Bankruptcy

Congratulations! After you receive your final discharge, you can get on with your life and enjoy the fresh start that bankruptcy offers. There may still be a few things left to do, however. For example, you may want to rebuild your credit. You may also need to take action if any of the following occurs:

- You receive or discover new nonexempt property.
- A creditor tries to collect a nondischargeable debt.
- A creditor tries to collect a debt that has been discharged in your bankruptcy.
- A creditor or the trustee asks the court to revoke your discharge in your bankruptcy.
- A government agency or private employer discriminates against you because of your bankruptcy.

This chapter explains how these events typically unfold, and how you can respond to them. But don't worry: Very few people face these circumstances. If you were complete and honest in your paperwork, it's very unlikely that you'll run into any postbankruptcy problems. We provide the information in this chapter just in case you're one of the rare exceptions.

Newly Acquired or Discovered Property

If you omit property from your bankruptcy papers, or you acquire certain kinds of property soon after you file, the trustee may reopen your case after your discharge (if the trustee learns about the property). The trustee probably won't take action unless the property is nonexempt and is valuable enough to justify the expense of reopening the case, seizing and selling the property, and distributing the proceeds among your creditors. If the property you acquire or discover after discharge is of little value, you should still tell the trustee about it, even if you think the assets don't justify reopening the case. Whether to reopen is the trustee's decision, not yours.

Notifying the Trustee

It's your legal responsibility to notify the bankruptcy trustee if either of the following occurs:

- Within 180 days of filing for bankruptcy, you receive or become entitled to receive certain types of property.
- You discover that you failed to list some of your nonexempt property in your bankruptcy papers.

Newly Acquired Property

If you receive, or become entitled to receive, certain property within 180 days after your bankruptcy filing date, you must report it to the trustee, even if you think the property is exempt or your case is already closed. If you don't report it and the trustee learns of your acquisition, the trustee could ask the court to revoke your discharge. (See "Attempts to Revoke Your Discharge," below.) You must report:

- an inheritance (property you receive, or become entitled to receive, because of someone's death)
- property from a divorce settlement, or
- proceeds of a life insurance policy or death benefit plan. (11 U.S.C. § 541(a)(5).)

These categories of property are discussed in more detail in Ch. 3.

To report this property to the trustee, use the form called Supplemental Schedule for Property Acquired After Bankruptcy Discharge. A blank copy is in Appendix B. The form is self-explanatory. When you've filled it out, follow these steps:

Step 1: Photocopy a Proof of Service by Mail (a blank copy is in Appendix B) and fill it out, but don't sign it.

Step 2: Make three photocopies of the Supplemental Schedule and the Proof of Service forms.

Step 3: Have a friend or relative mail the original Supplemental Schedule and a copy of the Proof of Service to the trustee and the U.S. Trustee, and then sign the original Proof of Service.

Step 4: File a copy of the Supplemental Schedule and the original Proof of Service with the bankruptcy court. No additional filing fee is required.

Step 5: Keep a copy of the Supplemental Schedule and the Proof of Service for your records.

In some areas, the court may require you to file amended bankruptcy papers. If that happens, follow the instructions in Ch. 7 in "Amending Your Bankruptcy Papers."

Property Not Listed in Your Papers

If, after your bankruptcy case is closed, you discover some property that you should have listed in your bankruptcy papers, you don't need to file any documents with the court. You must, however, notify the trustee. A sample letter is shown below.

Letter to Trustee

1900 Wishbone Place
Wilkes-Barre, PA 18704
October 22, 20xx

Francine J. Chen
Trustee of the Bankruptcy Court
217 Federal Building
197 S. Main St.
Wilkes-Barre, PA 18701

Dear Ms. Chen:

I've just discovered that I own some property I didn't know of while my bankruptcy case was open. Apparently, when I was a child I inherited a bank account from my uncle, the proceeds of which were supposed to be turned over to me when I turned 21. Although I turned 21 eight years ago, for some unknown reason I never got the money.

The account, #2424-5656-08 in the Bank of New England, 1700 Minuteman Plaza, Boston, MA 02442, has a balance of $4,975.19. As you know, I opted for the federal exemptions in my case and do not own a home. I believe this property would be exempt under 11 U.S.C. § 522(d)(5). Please let me know how you intend to proceed.

Sincerely,
Ondine Wallace
Ondine Wallace

> **CAUTION**
>
> **Omitting property could put your discharge at risk.** If the trustee believes you were playing fast and loose with the bankruptcy court by intentionally omitting the property from your petition, the trustee can get your case reopened and attempt to cancel your discharge. If it would appear to a neutral person that your omission could have been deliberate, consult a bankruptcy lawyer before talking to the trustee.

Trustee's Motion to Reopen Your Bankruptcy Case

If any of the new or newly discovered property is valuable and nonexempt, the trustee may try to reopen your case, take the property, and have it sold to pay your creditors. As noted above, the trustee will probably do this if it looks like the profit from selling the property will be large enough to offset the cost of reopening your bankruptcy case and administering the sale.

To get to these new assets, the trustee files a motion to reopen the case. Judges usually grant these motions, unless they think too much time has passed or the property isn't valuable enough to justify reopening. How much time constitutes "too much time" varies with the facts of the case. Once the case is reopened, the trustee asks the court for authorization to sell the new assets and distribute the proceeds.

> **CAUTION**
>
> **Get help if you're fighting the trustee's attempt to reopen your case.** If you can bear to lose the property, consider consenting to what the trustee wants. But if your discharge or valuable property is at stake, consult a bankruptcy lawyer. You could oppose the motion to reopen on your own, but you will need to do a lot of legal research. (See Ch. 10 for tips on lawyers and research.)

Newly Discovered Creditors

Perhaps you inadvertently failed to list a particular creditor on your schedule. As we pointed out in Ch. 7, you can always amend if you discover the omission while your bankruptcy case is still open. But suppose you don't become aware of your omission until your bankruptcy is closed. Does that mean that the debt survives your bankruptcy? Not at all. If the creditor had actual knowledge of your bankruptcy, then it's the same as if the creditor were actually listed in your papers.

Suppose now that the omitted creditor didn't have actual knowledge, or, as is more common than you might think, you lost track of one or more of your creditors and had no way to identify them in your bankruptcy schedules. Even then, the chances are great that the debt will be considered discharged.

If yours was a no-asset case (that is, all your property was exempt), the debt is considered discharged unless, by being left out, your creditor lost the opportunity to contest the discharge on the ground that the debt was caused by your fraudulent or embezzling behavior, or by a willful and malicious act (such as assault or libel). It is often possible to reopen the bankruptcy and let the bankruptcy judge rule on whether the debt is, in fact, dischargeable. If the creditor sues you in state court for a judgment, you could argue the issue in that forum or have the case removed to bankruptcy court.

If yours was an asset case—that is, at some point in your case, your unsecured creditors received some property from your bankruptcy estate—your situation is more difficult. Your nonexempt assets were already distributed to your other unsecured creditors, so the omitted creditor would be unfairly discriminated against if the debt were discharged. If the debt is a large one, you might want to hire a lawyer to reopen the case and argue that the debt should be discharged due to your particular circumstances. (See Ch. 10 for advice on finding and working with a lawyer.)

Postbankruptcy Attempts to Collect Debts

After bankruptcy, creditors whose debts haven't been discharged are entitled to be paid. Creditors whose debts have been discharged cannot pursue the debt further. But it isn't always clear into which category a creditor falls. The bankruptcy court doesn't give you an itemized list of your discharged debts. Instead, your

final discharge paper merely explains the types of debts that are discharged in general terms. Because of this lack of specificity, it occasionally can be tough to figure out whether a particular debt has been wiped out.

How do you know which debts have been discharged and which debts must still be paid? Here's the general rule: All the debts you listed in your bankruptcy papers are discharged unless a creditor successfully objected to the discharge of a particular debt in the bankruptcy court, or the debt falls in one of the following categories:

- student loans (unless you obtained a court ruling that it would be an undue hardship for you to repay them)
- taxes that became due within the past three years or that were assessed within the previous 240 days
- debts you took on to pay nondischargeable taxes
- child support or alimony
- fines and penalties or court fees
- debts related to personal injury or death caused by your intoxicated driving
- debts not discharged in a previous bankruptcy because of fraud or misfeasance
- certain condominium and cooperative fees incurred after your filing date, or
- loans you took out from a retirement fund.

Ch. 9 discusses all of these categories in more detail.

In addition, if only one spouse files for bankruptcy in a community property state, the other spouse's share of the community debts (debts incurred during the marriage) is generally also discharged. The community property states are Alaska (if the spouses agree in writing), Arizona, California, Idaho, Louisiana, Nevada, New Mexico, Texas, Washington, and Wisconsin.

Finally, as noted above, even if a debt is not listed in your bankruptcy papers, it will be considered discharged if yours was a no-asset case—unless the creditor could have successfully challenged the discharge in bankruptcy court if the creditor were properly notified of your case.

Even if you think some of your debts weren't discharged in bankruptcy, the creditors may never try to collect. Many creditors believe that bankruptcy cuts off their rights, period; even attorneys often don't understand that some debts survive bankruptcy.

If a creditor does try to collect a debt after your bankruptcy discharge, write to the creditor and state that your debts were discharged. Unless you're absolutely certain that the debt wasn't discharged—for example, a student loan unless the court ordered otherwise—this is a justifiable position for you to take.

Letter to Creditor

388 Elm Street
Oakdale, WY 95439
March 18, 20xx

Bank of Wyoming
18th and "J" Streets
Cheyenne, WY 98989

To Whom It May Concern:

I've received numerous letters from your bank claiming that I owe $6,000 for charges between September 1997 and September 1999. I received a bankruptcy discharge of my debts on February 1, 20xx. I enclose a copy of the discharge for your reference.

Sincerely,

Brenda Woodruff

Brenda Woodruff

If the creditor ignores your letter and continues collection efforts, there are other ways to respond:

- **Amend your bankruptcy papers.** Remember that an unlisted debt is discharged in a no-asset case, unless the creditor was deprived of a chance to oppose the debt's discharge. You can reopen the bankruptcy, amend your papers to list the debt, and then see what the creditor does.
- **Do nothing.** The creditor knows you've just been through bankruptcy, have little or no nonexempt property, and probably have no way to pay the debt, especially all at once. Thus, if you don't

respond to collection efforts, the creditor may decide to leave you alone, at least for a while.

- **Try to get judgments wiped out.** If a creditor sued you and won before you filed for bankruptcy, the creditor may try to collect on that judgment, unless you can convince a state court that the judgment was discharged in bankruptcy. Creditors can try to enforce judgments years after they won them, so it's a good idea for you to reopen the bankruptcy case and ask the judge to rule that the judgment is discharged. (See Ch. 7 for information on reopening your case.)
- **Negotiate.** If the debt is arguably nondischargeable, you can try to negotiate for a lower balance or a payment schedule that works for you. Again, the creditor knows you've just been through bankruptcy and it may be willing to compromise.
- **Defend in court.** If the creditor sues you for a nondischargeable debt, you can raise any defenses you have to the debt itself.

EXAMPLE: The Department of Education sued Edna for failing to pay back a student loan she received. Edna refused to make the payments because the trade school she gave the money to went out of business before classes even began. Because this is a valid defense to the collection of a student loan, Edna should respond to the lawsuit and assert her defense.

- **Protest a garnishment or another judgment collection effort.** A creditor who has sued you and won a court judgment for a nondischargeable debt is likely to try to take (garnish) your wages or other property to satisfy the judgment. But the creditor can't take it all. What was exempt during bankruptcy under your state's general exemptions is still exempt. (Appendix A lists exempt property.) Nonetheless, the creditor can still request that 25% of your wages be taken out of each paycheck. If the debt was for child support or alimony, the creditor can take even more: up to 60% if you don't currently support anyone and up to 50% if you do. Those amounts may increase by 5% if you haven't paid child support in more than 12 weeks.

Soon after the garnishment—or, in some states, before—the state court must notify you of the garnishment, what's exempt under your state's laws, and how you can protest. You can protest a garnishment if it isn't justified or causes you hardship. To protest, you'll have to file a document in the state court. That document goes by different names in different states. In New York, for example, it's called a Discharge of Attachment; in California, it's a Claim of Exemption. If you do protest, the state court must hold a hearing within a reasonable time, where you can present evidence as to why the court should not enforce the garnishment. The court may not agree, but it's certainly worth a try.

Protesting a wage garnishment is usually a relatively straightforward procedure. Because states are required to tell you how to proceed, you'll probably be able to handle it without the assistance of a lawyer.

Most states also have procedures for objecting to other types of property garnishments, such as a levy of a bank account. You'll have to do a bit of research at a law library to learn the exact protest procedure, which is generally similar to the one for protesting a wage garnishment. (See Ch. 10 for tips on doing your own research.)

Dealing With Difficult Debts After Bankruptcy

For some debts, such as taxes, child support, or alimony, exempt property may be taken and a garnishment protest will do little good. Don't be surprised if the U.S. Treasury Department initially garnishes nearly 100% of your wages to pay back federal income taxes. The best strategy here is to attempt to negotiate the amount down, not to fight the creditor's right to garnish in the first place.

Attempts to Collect Clearly Discharged Debts

If a creditor tries to collect a debt that clearly was discharged in your bankruptcy, you should respond at once with a letter like the one shown below. Again, you can assume a debt was discharged if you listed it in your bankruptcy papers, the creditor didn't successfully object to its discharge, and it doesn't fall into one of the nondischargeable categories listed under "Postbankruptcy Attempts to Collect Debts," above. Also, if yours was a no-asset case, you can assume the debt was discharged even if the debt wasn't listed. If you live in a community property state and your spouse filed alone, your share of the community debts is often considered discharged.

If a debt was discharged, the law prohibits creditors from filing a lawsuit, sending you collection letters, calling you, withholding credit, and threatening to file or actually filing a criminal complaint against you.

Letter to Creditor

1905 Fifth Road
N. Miami Beach, FL 35466

March 18, 20xx

Bank of Miami
2700 Finances Hwy
Miami, FL 36678

To Whom It May Concern:

I've been contacted once by letter and once by phone by Rodney Moore of your bank. Mr. Moore claims that I owe $4,812 on Visa account number 1234 567 890 123.

As you're well aware, this debt was discharged in bankruptcy on February 1, 20xx. Thus, your collection efforts are in violation of the bankruptcy court's discharge order under federal law, 11 U.S.C. § 524. If they continue, I won't hesitate to pursue my legal rights.

Sincerely,

Dawn Schaffer

Dawn Schaffer

If the collection efforts don't immediately stop, you'll likely need the assistance of a lawyer to write the creditor again and, if that doesn't work, to sue the creditor in the bankruptcy court (after reopening your case). If the creditor sues you over the debt, you'll want to raise the discharge as a defense and sue the creditor yourself to stop the illegal collection efforts. The bankruptcy court has the power to hold the creditor in contempt. The court may also fine the creditor for the humiliation, inconvenience, and anguish you suffered, and order the creditor to pay your attorneys' fees. (See, for example, *In re Barbour*, 77 B.R. 530 (Bankr. E.D. N.C. 1987), where the court fined a creditor $900 for attempting to collect a discharged debt.)

You can bring a lawsuit to stop collection efforts in state court or in the bankruptcy court. Bankruptcy courts are often more familiar with the prohibitions against collection and may be more sympathetic to you. If the creditor sues you (almost certainly in state court), you or your attorney can file papers requesting that the case be transferred to the bankruptcy court.

A debt collector's attempt to collect a debt discharged in bankruptcy may also violate the federal Fair Debt Collection Practices Act (FDCPA). The FDCPA prohibits debt collectors from engaging in deceptive practices, including misrepresenting the legal status of a debt. Several courts have ruled that by stating that payment was due on discharged debts, debt collectors misrepresented the legal status of the debts, and therefore violated the FDCPA. Although the FDCPA applies to debt collectors only, and not creditors (with a few exceptions), some states have fair debt laws that apply to creditors. If a creditor in one of those states attempts to collect a debt discharged in bankruptcy, you may have a state fair debt claim against it.

Attempts to Revoke Your Discharge

In rare instances, a trustee or creditor may ask the bankruptcy court to revoke the discharge of *all* your debts. If the trustee or a creditor attempts to revoke your discharge, consult a bankruptcy attorney. (See Ch. 10 for tips on finding a lawyer.)

Your discharge can be revoked only if the creditor or trustee proves any of the following:

- You obtained the discharge through fraud that the trustee or creditor discovered after your discharge.
- You intentionally didn't tell the trustee that you acquired property from an inheritance, a divorce settlement, or a life insurance policy or death benefit plan within 180 days after you filed for bankruptcy.
- Before your case was closed, you refused to obey an order of the bankruptcy court or, for a reason other than the privilege against self-incrimination, you refused to answer an important question asked by the court.

For the court to revoke your discharge on the basis of fraud, the trustee or creditor must file a complaint within one year of your discharge. For the court to revoke your discharge on the basis of your fraudulent failure to report property or your refusal to obey an order or answer a question, the complaint must be filed either within one year of your discharge or before your case is closed, whichever is later. You're entitled to receive a copy of the complaint and to respond, and the court must hold a hearing on the matter before deciding whether to revoke your discharge.

If your discharge is revoked, you'll owe your debts, just as if you'd never filed for bankruptcy. Any payment your creditors received from the trustee, however, will be credited against what you owe.

Postbankruptcy Discrimination

Although declaring bankruptcy has some adverse consequences, they might not be as bad as you think. There are laws that will protect you from most types of postbankruptcy discrimination by the government and by private employers.

Government Discrimination

All federal, state, and local governmental units are prohibited from denying, revoking, suspending, or refusing to renew a license, permit, charter, franchise, or other similar grant solely because you filed for bankruptcy. (11 U.S.C. § 525(a).) This law provides important protections, but it does not insulate debtors from all adverse consequences of filing for bankruptcy. Lenders, for example, can consider your bankruptcy filing when reviewing an application for a government loan or extension of credit. (See, for example, *Watts v. Pennsylvania Housing Finance Co.,* 876 F.2d 1090 (3rd Cir. 1989) and *Toth v. Michigan State Housing Development Authority*, 136 F.3d 477 (6th Cir. 1998).) Still, under this provision of the Bankruptcy Code, the government cannot use your bankruptcy as a reason to:

- deny you a job or fire you
- deny you or terminate your public benefits
- evict you from public housing (although if you have a Section 8 voucher, you may not be protected)
- deny you or refuse to renew your state liquor license
- withhold your college transcript
- deny you a driver's license, or
- deny you a contract, such as a contract for a construction project.

In addition, lenders may not exclude you from government-guaranteed student loan programs. (11 U.S.C. § 525(c).)

In general, once any government-related debt has been discharged, all acts against you that arise out of that debt also must end. If, for example, you lost your driver's license because you didn't pay a court judgment that resulted from a car accident, you must be granted a license once the debt is discharged. If your license was also suspended because you didn't have insurance, you may not get your license back until you meet the requirements set forth in your state's financial responsibility law.

If, however, the judgment wasn't discharged, you can still be denied your license until you pay up. If you and the government disagree about whether or not the debt was discharged, see "Postbankruptcy Attempts to Collect Debts," above.

Keep in mind that only government denials based on your bankruptcy are prohibited. You may be denied a loan or job, or an apartment for reasons unrelated to the bankruptcy. This includes denials for reasons related to your future creditworthiness—for example, because the government concludes you won't be able to repay a Small Business Administration loan.

Nongovernment Discrimination

Private employers may not fire you or otherwise discriminate against you solely because you filed for bankruptcy. (11 U.S.C. § 525(b).) While the law expressly prohibits employers from firing you, employers may refuse to hire you because you went through bankruptcy.

Unfortunately, other forms of discrimination in the private sector aren't illegal. If you seek to rent an apartment and the landlord does a credit check, sees your bankruptcy, and refuses to rent to you, there's not much you can do other than try to show that you'll pay your rent and be a responsible tenant. It's often helpful if you can prepay your rent for a few months, or, if it is permitted under your state's laws, provide a bigger security deposit. (However, if you file for bankruptcy in the midst of a lease, your landlord cannot use this as grounds to evict you before the lease term is up.)

If a private employer refuses to hire you because of a poor credit history—not because you filed for bankruptcy—you may have little recourse.

If you suffer illegal discrimination because of your bankruptcy, you can sue in state court or in the bankruptcy court. You'll probably need the assistance of an attorney.

Rebuilding Credit

Although a bankruptcy filing can remain on your credit record for up to ten years after your discharge, you can probably rebuild your credit in about three years to the point that you won't be turned down for a major loan. Most creditors look for steady employment and a history, since bankruptcy, of making and paying for purchases on credit. And many creditors disregard a bankruptcy completely after about five years.

 RESOURCE
Rebuilding your credit. For more information on rebuilding your credit, see *Credit Repair*, by Robin Leonard and Margaret Reiter (Nolo).

Should You Rebuild Your Credit?

Habitual overspending can be just as hard to overcome as excessive gambling or drinking. If you think you may be a compulsive spender, one of the worst things you might do is rebuild your credit. You need to get a handle on your spending habits, not give yourself more opportunities to indulge them.

Debtors Anonymous is a 12-step support program similar to Alcoholics Anonymous. It has programs nationwide. If a Debtors Anonymous group or a therapist recommends that you stay out of the credit system for a while, follow that advice. Even if you don't feel you're a compulsive spender, paying as you go may still be the best strategy.

Debtors Anonymous meets all over the country. Take a look at its website, which is extremely informative, at www.debtorsanonymous.org. To find a meeting near you, consult the website or send a self-addressed stamped envelope to Debtors Anonymous, General Services Board, P.O. Box 920888, Needham, MA 02492-0009. Or call and speak to a volunteer or leave a message at 781-453-2743.

Create a Budget

The first step to rebuilding your credit is to create a budget. Making a budget will help you control impulses to overspend and help you start saving money—an essential part of rebuilding your credit. The budget counseling you had to get during your bankruptcy case should give you a good start.

Before you put yourself on a budget that limits how much you spend, take some time to find out exactly how much money you spend right now. Write down every cent you spend for the next 30 days: 50¢ for the paper, $2 for your morning coffee, $5 for lunch, $3 for the bridge or tunnel toll, and so on. If you omit any money spent, your picture of how much you spend, and your budget, will be inaccurate.

At the end of the 30 days, review your ledger. Are you surprised? Are you impulsively buying things, or do you tend to buy the same types of things consistently? If the latter, you'll have an easier time planning a budget than if your spending varies tremendously from day to day.

Think about the changes you need to make to put away a few dollars at the end of every week. Even if you think there's nothing to spare, try to set a small goal—even $5 a week. It will help. If you spend $2 per day on coffee, that adds up to $10 per week and at least $40 per month. Making coffee at home might save you most of that amount. If you buy the newspaper at the corner store every day, consider subscribing. A subscription doesn't involve extending credit; if you don't pay, they simply stop delivering.

Once you understand your spending habits and identify the changes you need to make, you're ready to make a budget. At the top of a sheet of paper, write down your monthly net income—that is, the amount you bring home after taxes and other mandatory deductions. At the left, list everything you spend money on in a month. Include any bank or other deposit accounts you use or plan to use for saving money and any nondischarged, reaffirmed, or other debts you make payments on. To the right

Avoiding Financial Problems

These nine rules, suggested by people who have been through bankruptcy, will help you stay out of financial trouble.

1. **Create a realistic budget and stick to it.**

2. **Don't buy on impulse.** When you see something you hadn't planned to purchase, go home and think it over. It's unlikely you'll decide to return to the store and buy it.

3. **Avoid sales.** Buying a $500 item on sale for $400 isn't a $100 savings if you didn't need the item in the first place.

4. **Get medical insurance.** Because you can't avoid medical emergencies, living without medical insurance is an invitation to financial ruin.

5. **Charge items only if you can pay for them now.** Don't charge based on future income; sometimes future income doesn't materialize.

6. **Avoid large house payments.** Obligate yourself only for what you can afford now and increase your mortgage payments only as your income increases. Again, don't obligate yourself based on future income that you might not have.

7. **Think long and hard before agreeing to cosign or guarantee a loan for someone.** Your signature obligates you as if you were the primary borrower. You can't be sure that the other person will pay.

8. **Avoid joint obligations with people who have questionable spending habits**—even your spouse or significant other. If you incur a joint debt, you're probably liable for it all if the other person defaults.

9. **Avoid high-risk investments,** such as speculative real estate, penny stocks, and junk bonds. Invest conservatively in things such as certificates of deposit, money market funds, and government bonds. And never invest more than you can afford to lose.

of each item, write down the amount of money you spend, deposit, or pay each month. Finally, total up the amount. If it exceeds your monthly income, make some changes—by eliminating or reducing unnecessary expenditures—and start over. Once your budget is final, stick to it.

Check Your Credit Report for Accuracy

Rebuilding your credit requires you to keep incorrect information out of your credit file.

Start by obtaining a copy of your file from one of the "big three" credit reporting agencies:

- Equifax
- Experian, and
- TransUnion.

To get your report, don't contact the credit reporting agency itself. Instead, request the report from the Annual Credit Report Request Service, P.O. Box 105281, Atlanta, GA 30348-5281; 877-322-8228; www.annualcreditreport.com.

You will need to provide your name and any previous names, addresses for the last two years, telephone number, year or date of birth, employer, and Social Security number.

You are entitled to a free copy of your credit report once a year, thanks to an amendment to the Fair Credit Reporting Act (FCRA). For more information, follow the links at www.ftc.gov.

You can also get a free copy of your report if you were denied credit, your credit account was terminated, you weren't granted credit in the amount you requested, a creditor made other unfavorable changes to your account, or a creditor took adverse actions related to your application for credit. You are entitled to a free copy if you are on public assistance or if you're unemployed and planning to look for work in the next 60 days. In addition, you can have a free copy if you believe that your file contains errors due to identity theft (fraudulent use of your name, Social Security number, and so on) or someone's fraud. If you are not entitled to a free copy of your report, expect to pay no more than $9 for a copy from one of the credit reporting agencies.

> ! **CAUTION**
> **Don't pay for a credit score.** The credit reporting agency might offer to tell you your credit *score*, for a fee. You don't need that now. Your goal is to check your credit *report* to make sure the information in it is accurate.

In addition to your credit history, your credit report will tell you the sources of the information it contains and the names of people or institutions that have received your file within the last year, or within the last two years if they sought your file for employment reasons.

Credit reports can contain negative information for up to seven years, except for bankruptcy filings, which can remain on your report for ten years. You will want to challenge outdated entries as well as incorrect or incomplete information. The credit reporting agency must investigate the accuracy of anything you challenge within 30 days, and either correct it or, if it can't verify the item, remove it.

If, after the investigation, the agency keeps information in your file that you still believe is wrong, you are entitled to write a statement of up to 100 words giving your version, to be included in your file. An example of such a statement is shown below. Be sure the statement is tied to a particular item in your file. When the item eventually is removed from your file, the statement will be also. If you write a general "my life was a mess and I got into debt" statement, however, it will stay for a full seven years from the date you submit it, even if the negative items come out sooner.

Your statement, or a summary of it, must be given to anyone who receives your credit report. In addition, if you request it, the agency must pass on a copy or summary of your statement to any person who received your report within the past year, or two years if your report was requested for employment-related reasons.

You also want to keep new negative information out of your file. To do this, remain current on your bills. What you owe, as well as how long it takes you to pay, will show up in that file.

Letter to Credit Reporting Agency

74 Ash Avenue
Hanover, NH 03222

March 18, 20xx

Credit Reporters of New England
4118 Main Blvd.
Manchester, NH 03101

To Whom It May Concern:

Your records show that I am unemployed. That's incorrect. I am a self-employed cabinetmaker and carpenter. I work out of my home and take orders from people who are referred to me through various sources. My work is known in the community and that's how I earn my living.

Sincerely,
Denny Porter
Denny Porter

Avoid Credit Repair Agencies

You've probably seen ads for companies that claim they can fix your credit, qualify you for a loan, and get you a credit card. Stay clear of these companies. Their practices are almost always deceptive and sometimes illegal. Some steal the credit files or Social Security numbers of people who have died or live in places like Guam or the U.S. Virgin Islands, and then replace your file with these other files. Others create new identities for debtors by applying to the IRS for taxpayer ID numbers and telling debtors to use them in place of their Social Security numbers.

But even the legitimate companies can't do anything for you that you can't do yourself. If items in your credit file are correct, these companies cannot get them removed. About the only difference between using a legitimate credit repair agency and doing it yourself is the money you will save by going it alone.

In addition to information about credit accounts, credit reports also contain information from public records, including arrests and lawsuits.

After receiving your bankruptcy discharge, be sure to modify public records to reflect what occurred in the bankruptcy, so wrong information won't appear in your credit file. For example, if a court case was pending against you at the time you filed for bankruptcy and, as part of the bankruptcy, the potential judgment against you was discharged, be sure the court case is formally dismissed. You may need the help of an attorney. (See Ch. 10 for information on finding a lawyer.)

When Discharged Debts Appear on Your Credit Report

On occasion, a creditor will continue to report a debt that has been discharged in bankruptcy. Although some courts have ruled that listing a discharged debt on a credit report is an attempt to collect the debt in violation of the federal discharge injunction, other courts have allowed the credit reporting agency to continue reporting the debt. This issue is subject to much litigation. If a clearly discharged debt shows up on your credit report, see a bankruptcy lawyer to find out whether it makes sense for you to take action against the creditor and/or the credit reporting agency.

Negotiate With Some Creditors

If you owe a debt that shows up as past due on your credit file (perhaps the debt wasn't discharged in bankruptcy, was reaffirmed in bankruptcy, or was incurred after you filed), you can take steps to make it current. Contact the creditor and ask that the item be removed in exchange for either full or partial payment. On a revolving account (such as a department store), consider asking the creditor to "re-age" the account—that is, to make the current month the first repayment month and show no late payments on the account.

> **CAUTION**
>
> **Think carefully before asking a creditor to re-age your account.** If you later fail to keep your payments current, the creditor can report your account to the credit reporting agencies as delinquent based on the later missed payment date, rather than the original missed payment date. This means the delinquent account will remain on your credit report longer—seven years from the later missed payment date. If you're sure you can keep the account current, however, then re-aging may be a good plan for you.

Stabilize Your Income and Employment

Your credit history is not the only thing lenders will consider in deciding whether to give you credit. They also look carefully at the stability of your income and employment. And, if you start getting new credit before you're back on your feet financially, you'll end up in the same mess that led you to file for bankruptcy in the first place.

Get a Credit Card

Once you have your budget and some money saved, you can begin to get some positive information in your credit file. One way to do this is by getting a secured credit card.

Some banks will give you a credit card and a line of credit if you deposit money into a savings account. These are called secured credit cards. In exchange, you cannot remove the money from your account. Because it's difficult to guarantee a hotel reservation or rent a car without presenting at least one major credit card, get such a card if you truly believe you'll control any impulses to overuse—or even use it.

Another reason to have these cards is that, in a few years, banks and other large creditors will be more apt to grant you credit if, since your bankruptcy, you've made and paid for purchases on credit. A major drawback with these cards, however, is that they often have extremely high interest rates. So use the card only to buy inexpensive items you can pay for when the bill arrives. Otherwise, you're going to pay a bundle in interest and may end up back in financial trouble.

Be sure to shop around before signing up for a secured credit card. Even though you just filed for bankruptcy, you'll probably still get offers for unsecured cards in the mail. Often, these cards have better terms than do secured cards. If you do choose a secured credit card, be sure it isn't secured by your home. And make sure the card issuer reports to the credit reporting agencies. Some don't—which means the card will do little to rebuild your credit.

> **CAUTION**
> **Avoid credit card look-alikes.** Some cards allow you to make purchases only from the issuing company's own catalogs. The items in the catalog tend to be overpriced and of mediocre quality. And your use of the card isn't reported to credit reporting agencies, so you won't be rebuilding your credit.

Work With a Local Merchant

Another step to consider in rebuilding your credit is to approach a local merchant (such as a jewelry or furniture store) about purchasing an item on credit. Many local stores will work with you in setting up a payment schedule, but be prepared to put down a deposit of up to 30%, pay a high rate of interest, or find someone to cosign the loan.

Borrow From a Bank

Bank loans provide an excellent way to rebuild credit. A few banks offer something called a passbook savings loan. But, in most cases, you'll have to apply for a standard bank loan. You probably won't qualify for such a loan unless you bring in a cosigner, offer some property as collateral, or agree to a very high rate of interest.

The amount you can borrow will depend on how much the bank requires you to deposit (in the case of a passbook loan) or its general loan term limits.

Banks that offer passbook loans typically give you one to three years to repay the loan. But don't pay the loan back too soon—give it about six to nine months to appear on your credit file. Standard bank loans are paid back on a monthly schedule.

Before you take out any loan, be sure you understand the terms:

- **Interest rate.** The interest rate on your loan will probably be between two and six percentage points more than what the bank charges its customers with the best credit.
- **Prepayment penalties.** Usually, you can pay the loan back as soon as you want without incurring any prepayment penalties. Prepayment penalties are fees banks sometimes charge if you pay back a loan early and the bank doesn't collect as much interest from you as it had expected. The penalty is usually a small percentage of the loan amount.
- **Whether the bank reports the loan to a credit reporting agency.** This is key; the whole reason you want to take out the loan is to rebuild your credit, which means you want the loan to appear in your file. You may have to make several calls to find a bank that reports loans.

Which Debts Are Discharged

Not all debts can be discharged in a Chapter 7 bankruptcy. Some debts survive the bankruptcy process—they remain valid and collectable, just as they were before you filed for bankruptcy. To understand exactly what bankruptcy will do for you, you need to know which of your debts, if any, you will still owe after your bankruptcy case is over.

When granting your final discharge, the bankruptcy court won't specify which of your debts have been discharged. Instead, you'll receive a standard form from the court stating that you have received a discharge. (A copy appears in Ch. 7.) This chapter helps you figure out exactly which of your debts are discharged and which debts may survive.

Here's the lay of the land:

- Certain kinds of debts are always discharged in bankruptcy, except in rare circumstances.
- Some types of debts are never discharged in bankruptcy.
- Student loan and income tax debts are not discharged unless you can prove that your situation is an exception to the rule.
- Some types of debts are discharged unless the creditor comes to court and successfully objects to the discharge.

Debts Your Creditors Claim Are Nondischargeable

Some of your creditors may claim that the debts you owe them cannot be wiped out in bankruptcy. For example, computer leases—for software and hardware—often contain clauses stating that if you're unable to complete the lease period, you can't eliminate the balance of the debt in bankruptcy.

Don't fall for these arguments. The only debts you can't discharge in bankruptcy are the ones specifically listed in the Bankruptcy Code as nondischargeable— and we'll describe them in this chapter. Don't let your creditors intimidate you into thinking otherwise.

Debts That Will Be Discharged in Bankruptcy

Certain types of debts will be discharged—that is, you will no longer be responsible for repaying them—when you receive your Chapter 7 discharge. The bankruptcy trustee will divide your nonexempt assets (if you have any) among your creditors, then the court will discharge any amount that remains unpaid at the end of your case.

Credit Card Debts

Without a doubt, the vast majority of those who file for bankruptcy are trying to get rid of credit card debts. Happily for these filers, most bankruptcies succeed in this mission. With a few rare exceptions for cases involving fraud or luxury purchases immediately prior to your bankruptcy (outlined in "Debts That Survive Chapter 7 Bankruptcy," below), credit card debts are wiped out in bankruptcy.

Medical Bills

Many people who file for bankruptcy got into financial trouble because of medical bills. Some 40 million Americans have no medical insurance or other access to affordable medical care and must rely on emergency rooms for their primary care. Many more millions of working Americans either have inadequate insurance from their employers or can't afford the plans that are available to them.

Luckily, bankruptcy provides an out: Your medical bills will be discharged at the end of your bankruptcy case. In fact, billions of dollars in medical bills are discharged in bankruptcy every year.

Lawsuit Judgments

Most civil court cases are about money. If someone wins one of these lawsuits against you, the court issues a judgment ordering you to pay. If you don't come up with the money voluntarily, the judgment holder is entitled to collect it by, for example, grabbing your bank account, levying your wages, or placing a lien on your home.

Money judgments are almost always dischargeable in bankruptcy, regardless of the facts that led to the lawsuit in the first place. There are a couple of exceptions (discussed in "Debts That Survive Chapter 7 Bankruptcy," below), but in the vast majority of cases, money judgments are discharged. Even liens on your home arising from a court money judgment can be cancelled if they interfere with your homestead exemption. (See Ch. 5 for more on how bankruptcy affects a judicial lien on your home.)

Debts Arising From Car Accidents

Car accidents usually result in property damage and sometimes in personal injuries. Often, the driver who was responsible for the accident is insured and doesn't have to pay personally for the damage or injury. Sometimes, however, the driver who was at fault either has no insurance or has insurance that isn't sufficient to pay for everything. In that situation, the driver is financially responsible for the harm.

If the accident was the result of the debtor's negligence—careless driving or failing to drive in a prudent manner—the debt arising from the accident can be discharged in bankruptcy. The debt might also qualify for discharge even if it resulted from reckless driving. If, however, the accident was the result of the driver's willful and malicious act (defined in "Debts Not Dischargeable in Bankruptcy If the Creditor Successfully Objects," below) or drunk driving, it will survive bankruptcy.

Obligations Under Leases and Contracts

Increasingly in our society, things are leased rather than owned. And most leases have severe penalty clauses that kick in if you are unable to make the monthly payment or do something else the lease requires you to do.

Some debtors also have obligations under a contract, such as a contract to sell real estate, buy a business, deliver merchandise, or perform in a play. The other party may want to force you to hold up your end of the deal, even if you don't want (or are unable) to, and sue you for breach of contract damages.

Obligations and liabilities under these types of agreements can also be discharged in bankruptcy. Almost always, filing for bankruptcy will convert your lease or contractual obligation into a dischargeable debt, unless the trustee believes the lease or contract will produce money to pay your unsecured creditors or the court finds that you've filed for bankruptcy precisely for the purpose of getting out of a personal services contract (such as a recording contract).

Personal Loans and Promissory Notes

Money you borrow in exchange for a promissory note (or even a handshake and an oral promise to pay the money back) is almost always dischargeable in bankruptcy. As with any debt, however, the court may refuse to discharge a loan debt if the creditor can prove that you acted fraudulently. (See "Debts That Survive Chapter 7 Bankruptcy," below.) But that almost never happens.

Other Obligations

The sections above outline the most common debts that are discharged in bankruptcy, but this isn't an exhaustive list. Any obligation or debt will be discharged unless it fits within one of the exceptions discussed in "Debts That Survive Chapter 7 Bankruptcy," below.

Debts That Survive Chapter 7 Bankruptcy

Under bankruptcy law, there are several categories of debt that are "not dischargeable" in Chapter 7 (that is, you will still owe them after your bankruptcy is final). Some debts:

- can't be discharged under any circumstances
- will not be discharged unless you convince the court that they fit within a narrow exception to the rule, and
- will be discharged, unless the creditor convinces the court that they shouldn't be.

Are Secured Debts Dischargeable?

Some types of secured debts are contractually linked to specific items of property, called collateral. If you don't pay the debt, the creditor can take the collateral. The most common secured debts include loans for cars and homes. If you have a debt secured by collateral, bankruptcy eliminates your personal liability for the underlying debt—that is, the creditor can't sue you to collect the debt itself. But bankruptcy doesn't eliminate the creditor's hold, or "lien," on the property that served as collateral under the contract. Other types of secured debts arise involuntarily, often as a result of a lawsuit judgment or an enforcement action by the IRS on taxes that are old enough to be discharged (covered below). In these cases, too, bankruptcy gets rid of the underlying debt, but may not eliminate a lien placed on your property by the IRS or a judgment creditor.

Chapter 7 bankruptcy offers several options for dealing with secured debts, such as buying the property from the creditor for its replacement value, reaffirming the contract, or surrendering the property. Secured debts and options for dealing with them are discussed in Ch. 5.

Debts Not Dischargeable Under Any Circumstances

There are certain debts that bankruptcy doesn't affect at all: You will continue to owe them just as if you had never filed.

Domestic Support Obligations

Debts defined as "domestic support obligations" are not dischargeable. Domestic support obligations are child support, alimony, and any other debt that is in the nature of alimony, maintenance, or support. For example, one spouse may have agreed to pay some of the other spouse's or the children's future living expenses (shelter, clothing, health insurance, and transportation) in exchange for a lower support obligation. The obligation to pay future living expenses may be treated as support owed to the other spouse (and considered nondischargeable), even though no court ordered it.

If one spouse is responsible for paying the other spouse's attorneys' fees, numerous courts have held that this is a debt in nature of support. However, what one spouse owes to his or her own lawyer is not in the nature of support and can be discharged. (See *In re Rios*, 901 F.2d 71 (7th Cir. Ill. 1990); see also *In re Chase*, 372 B.R. 125 (Bankr. S.D. N.Y. 2007), in which the court rejected arguments as to why expert witness fees relating to a child custody case should survive bankruptcy, despite claims of fraud and false pretenses.)

To be nondischargeable under this section, a domestic support obligation must have been established—or must be capable of becoming established—in:

- a separation agreement, divorce decree, or property settlement agreement
- an order of a court authorized by law to impose support obligations, or
- a determination by a child support enforcement agency or another government unit that is legally authorized to impose support obligations.

A support obligation that has been assigned to a private entity for reasons other than collection (for example, as collateral for a loan) is dischargeable. This exception rarely applies, however: Almost all assignments of support to government or private entities are made for the purpose of collecting the support.

Other Debts Owed to a Spouse, Former Spouse, or Child

Under the old bankruptcy law, debts owed to a spouse or child, other than support that arose from a divorce or separation, were discharged unless the spouse or child appeared in court to contest the debt. Under the 2005 bankruptcy law, this category of debt is now automatically nondischargeable. The most common of these types of debts is when one spouse agrees to assume responsibility for marital debt or promises to pay the other spouse in exchange for his or her share of the family home. These types of obligations will now be nondischargeable if they are owed to a spouse, former spouse, or child, and arose out of "a divorce or separation or in connection with a separation agreement, divorce decree, or other order of a court of record, or a determination made in accordance with State or territorial law by a governmental unit." (11 U.S.C. Section 523 (15).) (Note that these types of debts are treated differently in Chapter 13. If a court determines that an obligation arising out of a divorce is not in the nature of support, then it is treated like other general unsecured debts in the Chapter 13 plan. *In re Nelson*, 451 B.R. 918 (Bankr. D. Or. 2011).)

However, debts that are not nondischargeable as against an ex-spouse may still be dischargeable as against the actual creditor. If this is the case, debtors are unlikely to ever get called upon to pay the debt. This is because the creditor would have to go after the ex-spouse for payment of the debt, and then the ex-spouse would have to go after the debtor. For a variety of reasons, creditors usually don't seek payment of the debt from the debtor's ex-spouse.

CAUTION

The rule doesn't apply to separated domestic partners. Note that this rule doesn't apply to debts arising from a separation agreement between domestic partners. This is one example of many as to why civil unions do not provide the same benefits as marriage.

Fines, Penalties, and Restitution

You can't discharge fines, penalties, or restitution that a federal, state, or local government has imposed to punish you for violating a law. Examples include:

- fines or penalties imposed under federal election law
- charges imposed for time spent in a court jail (*In re Donohue*, No. 05-01651 (Bankr. N.D. Iowa 2006))
- fines for infractions, misdemeanors, or felonies
- fines imposed by a judge for contempt of court
- fines imposed by a government agency for violating agency regulations
- surcharges imposed by a court or an agency for enforcement of a law
- restitution you are ordered to pay to victims in federal criminal cases, and
- debts owed to a bail bond company as a result of bond forfeiture.

However, one court has held that a restitution obligation imposed on a minor in a juvenile court proceeding can be discharged, because it isn't punitive in nature. (*In re Sweeney*, 492 F.3d 1189 (10th Cir. 2007).)

Overpayments by a government entity are not by themselves nondischargeable. Often the overpayment is due to a clerical error by the agency and not attributable to the recipient's wrongdoing. In such cases, the debt is dischargeable unless one of the following applies:

- The agency makes a finding, after a hearing was held or offered, that the overpayment was fraudulent.
- The overpayment is in the nature of a fine or penalty.

Otherwise, the debt will be discharged unless the agency comes into bankruptcy court and proves fraud.

Certain Tax Debts

While regular income tax debts are dischargeable if they are old enough and meet some other requirements (discussed in "Debts Not Dischargeable Unless You Can Prove That an Exception Applies," below), other types of taxes are frequently not dischargeable. The specific rules depend on the type of tax.

Fraudulent income taxes. You cannot discharge debts for income taxes if you didn't file a return or you were intentionally avoiding your tax obligations. Returns filed on your behalf by the IRS are not considered filed by you, and therefore don't make you eligible for a discharge of income tax debt.

Property taxes. Property taxes aren't dischargeable unless they became due more than a year before you file for bankruptcy. Even if your personal liability to pay the property tax is discharged, however, the tax lien on your property will remain. From a practical standpoint, this discharge won't help you much, because you'll have to pay off the lien before you can transfer the property with clear title. In fact, you may even face a foreclosure action by the tax creditor if you take too long to come up with the money.

Other taxes. Other types of taxes that aren't dischargeable are mostly business related: payroll taxes, excise taxes, and customs duties. Sales, use, and poll taxes are also probably not dischargeable.

> **SEE AN EXPERT**
>
> **Get help for business tax debts.** If you owe any of these nondischargeable tax debts, see a bankruptcy attorney before you file.

Court Fees

If you are a prisoner, you can't discharge a fee imposed by a court for filing a case, motion, or complaint, an appeal, or for other costs and expenses assessed for that court filing, even if you claimed that you were unable to afford the fees. (You can discharge these types of fees in Chapter 13, however.)

Intoxicated Driving Debts

If you kill or injure someone while you are driving and are illegally intoxicated by alcohol or drugs, any debts resulting from the incident aren't dischargeable. Even if a judge or jury finds you liable but doesn't specifically find that you were intoxicated, the debt may still be nondischargeable. The judgment against you won't be discharged if the bankruptcy court (or a state court in a judgment collection action) determines that you were, in fact, intoxicated.

Note that this rule applies only to personal injuries: Debts for property damage resulting from your intoxicated driving are dischargeable.

> **EXAMPLE:** Christopher was in a car accident in which he injured Ellen and damaged her car. He was convicted of driving under the influence. Several months later, Christopher filed for bankruptcy and listed Ellen as a creditor. After the bankruptcy case was over, Ellen sued Christopher, claiming that the debt wasn't discharged because Christopher was driving while intoxicated. (She didn't have to file anything in the bankruptcy proceeding.) If Ellen shows that Christopher was illegally intoxicated under his state's laws, she will be able to pursue her personal injury claim against him. She is barred, however, from trying to collect for the damage to her car.

Condominium, Cooperative, and Homeowners' Association Fees

You cannot discharge fees assessed after your bankruptcy filing date by a membership association for a condominium, housing cooperative, or lot in a homeownership association if you or the trustee have an ownership interest in the condominium, cooperative, or lot. As a practical matter, this means that any fees that become due after you file for Chapter 7 bankruptcy will survive the bankruptcy, but fees you owed prior to filing will be discharged.

It's not uncommon for condominium ownership to continue after the bankruptcy is filed—until such time as ownership is transferred to a third party. This may be the case even though the debtor has moved out long before filing for bankruptcy. In this situation, condo fees will continue to mount after the bankruptcy filing and must be paid—or a lawsuit will be filed.

Debts for Loans From a Retirement Plan

If you've borrowed from your 401(k) or another retirement plan that is qualified under IRS rules for tax-deferred status, you'll be stuck with that debt. Bankruptcy does not discharge 401(k) loans. Why not? Because only debts you owe to another person or entity can be discharged in bankruptcy. A 401(k) loan is money you borrowed from yourself. (You can, however, discharge a loan from a retirement plan in Chapter 13.)

Debts You Couldn't Discharge in a Previous Bankruptcy

If a bankruptcy court dismissed a previous bankruptcy case because of your fraud or other bad acts (for instance, misfeasance or failure to cooperate with the trustee), you cannot discharge any debts that you tried to discharge in that earlier bankruptcy. (This rule doesn't affect debts you incurred after filing the earlier bankruptcy case.)

Debts Not Dischargeable Unless You Can Prove That an Exception Applies

Some debts cannot be discharged in Chapter 7 unless you show the bankruptcy court that the debt really is dischargeable because it falls within an exception. To get this type of debt discharged, you can take one of two courses of action:

- While your case is open, ask the bankruptcy court to rule that the debt should be discharged. To do this, you have to file and serve a Complaint to Determine Dischargeability of a Debt and then show, in court, that your debt isn't covered by the general rule. (The grounds and procedures for getting such debts discharged are discussed in "Disputes Over Dischargeability," below.) If you succeed, the court will rule that the debt is discharged, and the creditor won't be allowed to collect it after bankruptcy.

- In the alternative, you may decide not to take any action during your bankruptcy. If the creditor attempts to collect after your case is closed, you can try to reopen your bankruptcy and raise the issue then (by bringing a contempt motion or by filing a Complaint to Determine Dischargeability). Or, you can wait until the creditor sues you over the debt (or, if you've already lost a lawsuit, until the creditor tries to collect on the judgment), then argue in state court that the debt has been discharged.

The advantage of not raising the issue in the bankruptcy court is that you avoid the hassle of litigating the issue. And the problem may never come up again if the creditor doesn't pursue the debt. The down side to this strategy is that questions about whether the debt has been discharged will be left hanging over your head after the bankruptcy case is over.

As a general rule, you are better off litigating issues of dischargeability in the bankruptcy court—either during or after your bankruptcy—because bankruptcy courts tend to tilt in the interest of giving the debtor a fresh start, and may be more willing to give you the benefit of the doubt.

If your creditor is a federal or state taxing agency or a student loan creditor, you are probably better off raising the issue during your bankruptcy. On the other hand, you might be better off not raising the issue in your bankruptcy case if you're up against an individual creditor whose claim is not big enough to justify hiring a lawyer. These creditors are probably less likely to pursue you—or even know that they can—after your bankruptcy is over.

Student Loans

Virtually all student loans, whether made by the government, a nonprofit, or a private lender, are not dischargeable unless the debtor shows undue hardship.

To discharge your student loan on the basis of undue hardship, you must file a separate action in the bankruptcy court (a Complaint to Determine Dischargeability of Student Loan) and obtain a court ruling in your favor on this issue. Succeeding in an action to discharge a student loan debt typically requires the services of an attorney, although it's possible to do it yourself if you're willing to put in the time and deal with skeptical judges. (See "Disputes Over Dischargeability," below.)

When determining whether undue hardship exists, courts use several tests (depending on where the court is located). In two of the more commonly used tests, courts look at either:

- the three factors listed below (these come from a case called *Brunner v. New York State Higher Education Services, Inc.*, 46 B.R. 752 (S.D. N.Y. 1985), aff'd, 831 F.2d 395 (2nd Cir. 1987)), or

- the totality of the circumstances, which essentially means the court will consider all of the facts it deems relevant in deciding whether undue hardship exists.

The majority of courts use the *Brunner* three-factor test. You must show that all three factors tilt in your favor in order to demonstrate undue hardship. The factors are:

- **Poverty.** Based on your current income and expenses, you cannot maintain a minimal standard of living and repay the loan. The court must consider your current and future employment and income (or your employment and income potential), education, and skills; how marketable your skills are; your health; and your family support obligations.

- **Persistence.** It's not enough that you can't repay your loan right now. You must also show that your current financial condition is likely to continue for a significant part of the repayment period. In one recent case, for example, a debtor with bipolar disorder lost her job as a result of stopping her medication. Because her history demonstrated that she could remain employed as long as she took her medication, however, the court found that her economic condition would not necessarily persist—and it rejected her undue hardship claim. (*In re Kelly*, 351 B.R. 45 (Bankr. E.D. N.Y. 2006).)

- **Good faith.** You must prove that you've made a good-faith effort to repay the debt. Someone who files for bankruptcy immediately after getting out of school or after the period for paying back the loan begins will not fare well in court. Nor will someone who hasn't tried hard to find work. And if you haven't made payments, it helps to show that you've applied for a deferment or forbearance. (See *In re Kitterman*, 349 B.R. 775 (Bankr. W.D. Ky. 2006), in which the court found that the debtor lacked a good faith effort to repay his student loans because he didn't reapply for a deferment after his first request for a deferment was denied). In the past, many courts also found that the debtor's failure to apply for one of the federal flexible repayment programs was grounds to deny a request to discharge student loans. But that is changing somewhat. Some courts have discharged student loans even when the debtor did not apply for a reduced payment plan under one of the federal student loan repayment programs, a forbearance, or deferment. (See *In re Roth*, 490 B.R. 908, 919 (B.A.P. 9th Cir. 2013).) Those courts insist that it's important to look at each debtor's particular situation.

In the past it was extremely difficult to discharge student loans under most circumstances and that is still the case in some jurisdictions. This doesn't mean that the factors cannot be met, however—they can. (See *In re Lamento*, 520 B.R. 667 (Bankr. N.D. Ohio 2014).) Fortunately, other courts are beginning to discharge loans that they might not have ten years ago. For example, a Nebraska court discharged the student loans of a 28-year-old woman who was unable to secure higher paying employment after diligently trying for several years. (*In Matter of DeLaet*, 2015 WL 850629 (Bankr. D. Neb. 2015).) As well, in Illinois, the court did not require proof that the debtor made actual student loan payments in the past when the overall circumstances evidenced a lack of ability to pay. (*Krieger v. Educ. Credit Mgmt. Corp.*, 713 F.3d 882 (7th Cir. 2013).)

The bottom line is that while it is still difficult to meet the standard necessary to discharge student loans, courts will do it in the right circumstances, and, as the new student loan crisis unfolds, it appears some courts may even soften the traditionally harsh application of *Brunner*.

SEE AN EXPERT

Consult with a lawyer about discharging your loan. There are dozens of court cases that interpret the three factors from the *Brunner* case or explain what the "totality of the circumstances" include. If you are filing for bankruptcy and you have substantial student loan debt, you should talk to an attorney who is knowledgeable on these issues.

If the cost of an attorney seems impossibly high, do a quick cost–benefit analysis. If you have an excellent chance of getting your loan discharged, paying an attorney $3,000 to help you discharge a $30,000 loan is not a bad deal. On the other hand, if your loan is $5,000, the deal doesn't look as good.

Because no lawyer can guarantee a successful outcome no matter how good your case is, to some extent you are gambling $3,000 to win $30,000 (win in the sense that you wouldn't have to pay back the loan). To minimize the risk, you might consider paying one or two attorneys a few hundred dollars each for opinions on your likelihood of success. If they agree that you would probably get the loan discharged, you might feel better paying $3,000 (or more) for help in getting the student loan discharged. Of course, if you don't have the money to pay the lawyer, all of this is pie in the sky.

Complaint to Determine Dischargeability of Student Loan

UNITED STATES BANKRUPTCY COURT

_____ [*name of district*] _____ DISTRICT OF _____ [*your state*] _____

In re _____)
    [*Set forth here all names including married,*)
    maiden, and trade names used by debtor)
    within last 8 years.])
                 Debtor(s)) Case No. _____
Address _____)
)
_____) Chapter 7
)
)
Last four digits of Social Security or Individual)
Taxpayer Identification No(s). (ITIN) (*if any*): _____)
)
Employer's Tax Identification No(s). (EIN) (*if any*): _____)
_____)

COMPLAINT TO DETERMINE
DISCHARGEABILITY OF STUDENT LOAN

1. Debtor(s) filed this case under Chapter 7 of the Bankruptcy Code on __[*insert the date you filed your petition*]__ . This Court thus has jurisdiction over this action under 28 U.S.C. § 1334. This proceeding is a core proceeding.

2. One of the unsecured debts owing by the Debtor(s) and listed on Schedule F—Creditors Holding Unsecured Nonpriority Claims, is a student loan owing to __[*insert the name of the holder of your loan*]__ .

3. This loan was incurred to pay expenses at __[*insert the name of the school(s) you attended*]__ .

4. Based on the Debtor(s)' current income and expenses, the Debtor(s) cannot maintain a minimal living standard and repay the loan. [*Insert information about your current and future employment, your income and income potential, education, skills and the marketability of your skills, health, and family support obligations.*]

5. The Debtor(s)' current financial condition is likely to continue for a significant portion of the repayment period of the loan. [*Insert information about your health including any life-threatening, debilitating, or chronic conditions you have.*]

6. The Debtor(s) has/have made a good-faith effort to repay his or her debt.

7. The Debtor(s) has/have filed for bankruptcy for reasons other than just to discharge his or her student loan.

Date: _____ Signed: _____
                                Debtor in Propria Persona

Date: _____ Signed: _____
                                Debtor in Propria Persona

Special Rules for HEAL and PLUS Loans

The federal Health Education Assistance Loans (HEAL) Act, not bankruptcy law, governs HEAL loans. Under the HEAL Act, to discharge a loan, you must show that the loan became due more than seven years ago, and that repaying it would not merely be a hardship, but would impose an "unconscionable burden" on your life.

Parents can get Parental Loans for Students (PLUS loans) to finance a child's education. Even though the parent does not receive the education, the loan is treated like any other student loan if the parent files for bankruptcy. The parent must meet the undue hardship test to discharge the loan.

Getting Your Transcript

If you don't pay back loans obtained directly from your college, the school can withhold your transcript. But if you file for bankruptcy and receive a discharge of the loan, the school can no longer withhold your records. (*In re Gustafson*, 111 B.R. 282 (9th Cir. B.A.P. 1990).) In addition, while your bankruptcy case is pending, the school cannot withhold your transcript, even if the court eventually rules your school loan nondischargeable. (*Loyola University v. McClarty*, 234 B.R. 386 (E.D. La. 1999).)

Regular Income Taxes

People who are considering bankruptcy because of tax problems are almost always concerned about income taxes they owe to the IRS or the state equivalent. There is a myth afoot that income tax debts can never be discharged in bankruptcy. This is not true, however, if the debt is relatively old and you can meet several other conditions. Tax debts that qualify under these rules are technically discharged; however, you may have to file a complaint in the bankruptcy court to determine dischargeability of the debt and have the judge order the IRS to honor the discharge.

Income tax debts are dischargeable if you meet all of these conditions:

- You filed a legitimate (nonfraudulent) tax return for the tax year or years in question. If the IRS completes a Substitute for Return on your behalf that you neither sign nor consent to, your return is not considered filed. (See *In re Bergstrom*, 949 F.2d 341 (10th Cir. 1991).)
- The liability you wish to discharge is for a tax return (not a Substitute for Return) that you actually filed at least two years before you filed for bankruptcy.
- The tax return for the liability you wish to discharge was first due at least three years before you filed for bankruptcy. (If you filed for an extension, the three-year period begins on the extended due date, not the original due date.)
- The IRS has not assessed your liability for the taxes within the 240 days before you filed for bankruptcy. You're probably safe if you do not receive a formal notice of assessment of federal taxes from the IRS within that 240-day period. If you're unsure of the assessment date, consider seeing a tax lawyer—but don't rely on the IRS for the date. If the IRS gives you the wrong date—telling you that the 240 days have elapsed—the IRS won't be held to it if it turns out to be wrong. (See, for example, *In re Howell*, 120 B.R. 137 (B.A.P. 9th Cir. 1990).) Under the 2005 bankruptcy law, the 240-day period is extended by the period of time collections were suspended because you were negotiating with the IRS for an offer in compromise or because of a previous bankruptcy.

> **EXAMPLE:** Fred filed a tax return in August 2011 for the 2010 tax year. In March 2013, the IRS audited Fred's 2010 return and assessed a tax due of $8,000. In May 2014, Fred files for bankruptcy. The taxes that Fred wishes to discharge were for tax year 2010. The return for those taxes was due on April 15, 2011, more than three years prior to Fred's filing date. The tax return was filed in August 2011, more than two years before Fred's bankruptcy filing date, and the assessment date of March 2013 was more than 240 days before the filing date. Fred can discharge those taxes.

• You didn't willfully evade payment of a tax. What constitutes willful tax evasion is a subjective matter, depending on the view of the IRS personnel making the judgment. See "Willful Evasion of Tax," below, for a list of factors that may cause the IRS to suspect willful tax evasion. Recently, the Sixth Circuit Court of Appeals ruled that the mere fact that a debtor did not pay income tax, without other evidence, is not enough for the IRS to prove that the nonpayment was willful or intentional. (*U.S. v. Storey*, 640 F.3d 739 (6th Cir. 2011).)

TIP
Get an account transcript to make sure you've got the dates right. If you want to make sure you have met all the requirements to get a tax debt discharged, you can obtain an account transcript from the IRS. To find out how, visit www.irs.gov and type "account transcript" in the search box.

If you meet each of these five requirements, your personal liability for the taxes should be discharged. However, any lien placed on your property by the taxing authority will remain after your bankruptcy.

Different Rules Apply Out West

If you try to discharge your student loans in one of the federal courts that make up the 9th Circuit Court of Appeals (which includes Alaska, Arizona, California, Hawaii, Idaho, Montana, Nevada, Oregon, Utah, and Washington), a much wider variety of factors might be considered. Circumstances that could potentially allow a discharge include:

• The debtor or debtor's dependent has a serious mental or physical disability, which prevents employment or advancement.
• The debtor has an obligation to care for dependents.
• The debtor has a lack of, severely limited, or poor quality education.
• The debtor has a lack of usable or marketable job skills.
• The debtor is underemployed.
• The debtor's income potential in his or her chosen field has maxed out, and the debtor has no more lucrative job skills.
• The debtor has limited work years remaining in which to pay back the loan.
• The debtor's age or other factors prevent retraining or relocation as a means of earning more to repay the loan.
• The debtor lacks assets that could be used to repay the loan.

• The debtor's potentially increasing expenses outweigh any potential appreciation in the debtor's assets or increases in the debtor's income.
The debtor lacks better financial options elsewhere.
(See *Educational Credit Management Corp. v. Nys*, 446 F.3d 938 (9th Cir. 2006).)

Some western courts have used the Nys factors in discharging student loans of relatively young, able-bodied, working debtors. For example, in *Scott v. U.S. Dept. of Ed.*, 417 B.R. 623 (Bankr. W.D. Wash. 2009), the court discharged the student loans of a young couple with children who had no realistic prospects of earning more income in the future and could not maintain a minimum standard of living while making loan payments. And in *Hedlund v. Educational Resources Institute*, 718 F.3d 848 (9th Cir. 2013), the 9th Circuit discharged a portion of a 30-something man's law school loans because he never passed the bar exam, did not have a realistic possibility of earning more than his $40,000 per year salary as a probation officer, repeatedly tried to work out a payment plan, and could not maintain a minimum standard of living for himself and his family while paying back $85,000 in student loans. Despite these rulings, however, the bar is still high for discharging student loans, so be sure to consult with an experienced bankruptcy lawyer (or two) to get an opinion in your case.

The result is that the taxing authority can't go after your bank account or wages, but you'll have to pay off the lien before you can sell your real estate (or other property to which the lien is attached) with a clear title.

Penalties and interest on taxes that are dischargeable are also dischargeable. If the underlying tax debt is nondischargeable, courts are split as to whether you can discharge the penalties or not.

> **EXAMPLE:** Jill failed to file a tax return for 2007. In 2011, the IRS discovers Jill's failure and in January 2013 assesses taxes of $5,000 and penalties and interest of $12,000. Jill files for bankruptcy in January 2014. Because Jill didn't file a return for 2007, she can't discharge the tax, even though it became due more than three years past (and more than 240 days have elapsed since the taxes were assessed). Jill may be able

to discharge the IRS penalties for failure to file a tax return and failure to pay the tax. Or course, the IRS is likely to argue that she cannot discharge the penalties, and some courts will agree.

CAUTION

Debts incurred to pay nondischargeable taxes will also be nondischargeable. If you borrowed money or used your credit card to pay taxes that would otherwise not be discharged, you can't eliminate that loan or credit card debt in a Chapter 7 bankruptcy. In other words, you can't turn a nondischargeable tax debt into a dischargeable tax debt by paying it on your credit card. This is true for any type of nondischargeable tax owed to a governmental agency. You might consider using Chapter 13 instead, which allows you to discharge this type of debt.

Willful Evasion of Tax

The IRS views certain facts as red flags of possible willful tax evasion. They include:

- membership in a tax protest organization
- a pattern of unfiled returns
- filing a fraudulent, frivolous, blank, or incomplete return
- repeatedly understating income or overstating deductions on returns
- serial failure to pay taxes
- concealing, giving away, or trading away valuable assets or transferring title
- selling assets way below fair value (especially to insiders)
- setting up an abusive trust or sham tax shelter and transferring assets to it
- creating a corporation and transferring assets to it
- changing banks or bank accounts frequently
- closing bank accounts and conducting business in cash only
- adding another person's name to a bank account
- depositing income in another's bank account

- using a foreign bank account
- changing your name or the spelling of your name
- changing your Social Security number
- an altercation with a revenue officer
- engaging in money laundering
- withdrawing cash from a bank and hiding it
- claiming an incorrect number of exemptions on your tax return
- purchasing property in someone else's name
- refusing to cooperate with a revenue officer or deliberately obstructing an audit or investigation
- losing, concealing, or destroying financial documents
- maintaining inadequate records
- concealing your actual residence address or business address
- trading valuable assets for less valuable assets
- devising clever schemes such as divorcing your spouse, directing all income to him or her, and renting a room in his or her house, and
- living a lavish lifestyle knowing that delinquent taxes have not been paid.

Debts Not Dischargeable in Bankruptcy If the Creditor Successfully Objects

Four types of debts may survive Chapter 7 bankruptcy if, and only if, the creditor both:

- files a formal objection—called a Complaint to Determine Dischargeability—during the bankruptcy proceedings, and
- proves that the debt fits into one of the categories discussed below.

> **TIP**
> **Creditors might not bother to object.** Even though bankruptcy rules give creditors the right to object to the discharge of certain debts, many creditors—and their attorneys—don't fully understand this right. Even a creditor who knows the score might sensibly decide to write off the debt rather than contest it. It can cost a lot to bring a dischargeability action (as this type of case is known). If the debt isn't huge, a cost–benefit analysis might show that it will be cheaper to forgo collecting the debt than to fight about it in court.

Debts Arising From Fraud

In order for a creditor to prove that one of your debts should survive bankruptcy because you incurred it through fraud, the debt must fit one of the categories below.

Debts from intentionally fraudulent behavior. If a creditor can show that a debt arose because of your dishonest act, and that the debt wouldn't have arisen had you been honest, the court probably will not let you discharge the debt. Here are some common examples:

- You wrote a check for something and stopped payment on it, even though you kept the item.
- You wrote a check against insufficient funds but assured the merchant that the check was good.
- You rented or borrowed an expensive item and claimed it was yours, in order to use it as collateral to get a loan.
- You got a loan by telling the lender you'd pay it back, when you had no intention of doing so.

For this type of debt to be nondischargeable, your deceit must be intentional, and the creditor must have relied on your deceit in extending credit. Again, these are facts that the creditor has to prove before the debt will be ruled nondischargeable by the court.

Debts from a false written statement about your financial condition. If a creditor proves that you incurred a debt by making a false written statement, the debt isn't dischargeable. Here are the rules:

- The false statement must be written—for instance, made in a credit application, rental application, or résumé.
- The false statement must have been "material"— that is, it was a potentially significant factor in the creditor's decision to extend you credit. The two most common materially false statements are omitting debts and overstating income.
- The false statement must relate to your financial condition or the financial condition of an "insider"—a person close to you or a business entity with which you're associated.
- The creditor must have relied on the false statement, and the reliance must have been reasonable.
- You must have intended to deceive the creditor. This is extremely hard for the creditor to prove based simply on your behavior. The creditor would have to show outrageous behavior on your part, such as adding a "0" to your income (claiming you make $180,000 rather than $18,000) on a credit application.

Recent debts for luxuries. If you run up more than $650 in debt to any one creditor for luxury goods or services within the 90 days before you file for bankruptcy, the law presumes that your intent was fraudulent regarding those charges. If the creditor presents these facts to the bankruptcy court, all the charges will survive your bankruptcy unless you prove that your intent wasn't fraudulent. "Luxury goods and services" do not include things that are reasonably necessary for the support and maintenance of you and your dependents (what that means is decided on a case-by-case basis).

Recent cash advances. If you get cash advances from any one creditor totaling more than $925 under an open-ended consumer credit plan within the 70 days before you file for bankruptcy, the debt is nondischargeable if the creditor presents these facts to the court. "Open-ended" means there's no date when the debt must be repaid, but rather, as with most credit cards, you may take forever to repay the debt as long as you pay a minimum amount each month.

Debts Arising From Debtor's Willful and Malicious Acts

If the act that caused the debt was willful *and* malicious (that is, you intended to inflict a specific injury to person or property), the debt isn't dischargeable if the creditor successfully objects. However, for reasons probably related to ignorance of their rights, creditors don't often object in this situation.

Generally, crimes involving intentional injury to people or damage to property are considered willful and malicious acts. Examples are assaults, rape, intentionally setting fire to a house (arson), or vandalism.

Your liability for personal injury or property damage the victim sustained in these types of cases will almost always be ruled nondischargeable—but (once again) only if the victim-creditor objects during your bankruptcy case. Other acts that would typically be considered to be willful and malicious include:

- kidnapping
- deliberately causing extreme anxiety, fear, or shock
- libel or slander, and
- illegal acts by a landlord to evict a tenant, such as removing a door or changing the locks.

Debts From Embezzlement, Larceny, or Breach of Fiduciary Duty

A debt incurred as a result of embezzlement, larceny, or breach of fiduciary duty is not dischargeable if the creditor successfully objects to its discharge.

"Embezzlement" means taking property entrusted to you for another and using it for yourself. "Larceny" is another word for theft. "Breach of fiduciary duty" is the failure to live up to a duty of trust you owe someone, based on a relationship where you're required to manage property or money for another, or where your relationship is a close and confidential one. Common fiduciary relationships include those between:

- spouses
- business partners
- attorney and client
- estate executor and beneficiary
- in-home caregiver and recipient of services, and
- guardian and ward.

Debts or Creditors You Don't List

Bankruptcy requires you to list all of your creditors on your bankruptcy papers and provide their most current addresses. This gives the court some assurance that everyone who needs to know about your bankruptcy will receive notice. As long as you do your part, the debt will be discharged (as long as it's otherwise dischargeable under the rules), even if the official notice fails to reach the creditor for some reason beyond your control—for example, because the post office errs or the creditor moves without leaving a forwarding address.

Suppose, however, that you forget to list a creditor on your bankruptcy papers or carelessly misstate a creditor's identity or address. In that situation, the court's notice may not reach the creditor and the debt may not be discharged. Here are the rules:

- If the creditor knew or should have known of your bankruptcy through other means, such as a letter or phone call from you, the debt will be discharged even though the creditor wasn't listed. In this situation, the creditor should have taken steps to protect its interests, even though it didn't receive formal notice from the court.
- If all of your assets are exempt—that is, you have a no-asset case—the debt will be discharged unless the debt is nondischargeable in any circumstances. In this situation, the creditor wouldn't have benefited from receiving notice because there is no property to distribute. However, if the lack of notice deprives a creditor of the opportunity to successfully object to the discharge by filing a complaint in the bankruptcy court (such as for a fraudulent debt), the debt may survive your bankruptcy.

If an Unknown Creditor Pops Up After Bankruptcy

If a creditor comes out of the woodwork after your bankruptcy case is closed, you can always reopen your case, name the creditor, and then seek an amended discharge. (See Ch. 7 for more on reopening a case.) If it's the kind of debt that will be discharged anyway, many courts won't let you reopen because there is no need to. The debt is discharged by law and most creditors know this. However, if the creditor continues to try to collect the debt, you can haul the creditor into the bankruptcy court on a contempt charge.

Disputes Over Dischargeability

If your debt is not one that's automatically discharged, there may be a dispute over whether the debt should survive your bankruptcy. For example, if the debt is one that you have to prove should be discharged, you may have to file a Complaint to Determine Dischargeability. Or, if the creditor must prove that the debt should not be discharged, you might have to defend yourself in court against the creditor's claims.

Complaints to Determine Dischargeability

If you want to have a student loan or tax debt wiped out, you will have to prove to the court that you meet all of the requirements for discharge. To do this, you must file a formal complaint with the bankruptcy court along with a summons that the court generates when you file the complaint. Generally, you can file your complaint any time after you file for bankruptcy. Some courts may impose their own deadlines, however, so check your court's local rules.

Suppose, for example, that you want to have a student loan discharged. As discussed above, you will have to prove that it would be an undue hardship to repay the loan. You will file at least two forms: a Complaint to Determine Dischargeability (we provide a sample form above), stating the facts that make repayment an undue hardship, and a Proof of Service (see example in Appendix B), showing that you served the complaint on the affected creditor and the trustee.

Can You Litigate the Dischargeability of a Debt Without a Lawyer?

It's not uncommon for a bankruptcy filer to qualify for a student loan discharge or a discharge of a tax debt, but not be able to afford a lawyer to handle the case. In such a situation, it may make sense for you to handle your own case without a lawyer. But, you must be prepared to receive a fair amount of flack from the judge and from the opposing lawyers. They, after all, are familiar with the proper forms and procedures whereas you are a first-timer.

Remember, though, that neither the judge nor the lawyers can do you harm if you make honest mistakes. If you file the wrong paperwork or make the wrong arguments, you will almost always be given an opportunity to correct your mistakes. It happens to lawyers all the time.

If you plan to go it alone, get a copy of *Represent Yourself in Court*, by Paul Bergman and Sara Berman (Nolo), and use the Internet to do some research (for example, search for "discharging student loans in Chapter 7 bankruptcy" and "bankruptcy adversary actions"). Ch. 10 has more on doing legal research. If you are shot down at some point in the process, simply ask the court what you need to do to correct the problem. After all, you have a right to represent yourself and it is wrong of the judge to put you down simply because you are unfamiliar with the process.

If the judge tells you to "get a lawyer," and that helping you would impinge on his or her impartiality, explain that you really can't afford a lawyer and all you are asking for is a clear explanation of what you did wrong and what, in the judge's opinion, you need to do to get on the right track. It is the rare judge who will continue to stonewall your attempts to get your day in court.

You also may want to consider consulting with a bankruptcy lawyer from time to time to get your bearings, or hire a lawyer to handle this proceeding alone (but not to represent you in your entire bankruptcy case). See "Unbundled Services," in Ch.10, for more on this.

These forms are intended only to give you an idea of what a complaint to determine dischargeability of a student loan looks like. Your court may require more or different forms. If you plan to file a complaint yourself, you must familiarize yourself with the rules of bankruptcy procedure regarding pleadings and service of process. For example, Bankruptcy Rule 7004 provides the basic rules for how you must serve different defendants in an adversary process such as this one.

> CAUTION
> **Get help from a lawyer if you need it.** Before you charge off into court, here is a heartfelt warning: Embarking upon federal litigation in the bankruptcy court can be quite a challenge if you don't have substantial coaching from someone who has experience in the field.

Creditor Objections to Discharges

To object formally to the discharge of a debt, the creditor must file a document called a Complaint to Determine Dischargeability of a Debt. The creditor must give you and the trustee a copy of the complaint. To defend against the objection, you must file a written response within a specified time limit and be prepared to argue your case in court.

If the debt is one of the types that will be discharged unless the creditor objects, the creditor has the burden of proving that the debt fits within the specified category. For instance, if the creditor claims that the debt arose from a "willful and malicious injury" you caused, the creditor will have to prove that your actions were willful and malicious. Similarly, if the creditor is arguing that a particular debt arose from your fraudulent acts, the creditor will have to prove that all the required elements of fraud were present. Absent this proof, the bankruptcy court will reject the creditor's lawsuit and maybe even award you attorneys' fees (if you use an attorney).

Keep in mind, however, that if you plead guilty to a criminal charge involving fraud, a document from the court showing your conviction may be all that's necessary to convince the judge to rule the debt nondischargeable. A no-contest plea, on the other hand, would not have the same effect, because that type of plea can't be used as evidence in a later civil case (such as a bankruptcy case).

The fact that the creditor has the burden of proof doesn't mean that you should sit back and do nothing. You should be prepared with proof of your own to show that the creditor's allegations in the complaint are not true (unless, of course, you already admitted your guilt in a prior case by pleading guilty or being convicted after trial).

Objections on the Basis of Credit Card Fraud

Increasingly, the creditors most likely to object to the discharge of a debt are credit card issuers. Except for charges made shortly before filing for bankruptcy, there are few specific rules about what constitutes credit card fraud in bankruptcy. But courts are looking to the following factors to determine fraud:

- **Timing.** A short time between incurring the charges and filing for bankruptcy may suggest fraudulent intent.
- **Manipulation of the system.** Incurring more debt after consulting an attorney may lead a judge to conclude that you ran up your debts in anticipation of your bankruptcy filing.
- **Amount.** As mentioned earlier, recent charges over $650 for luxuries will be presumed to be fraudulent.
- **Crafty use of the card.** Multiple charges under $50 (to avoid preclearance of the charge by the credit card issuer) when you've reached your credit limit will start to look a lot like fraud.
- **Deliberate misuse.** Charges after the card issuer has ordered you to return the card or sent several "past due" notices don't look good.
- **Last-minute sprees.** Changes in your pattern of use of the card (for instance, much travel after a sedentary life), charges for luxuries, and multiple charges on the same day could lead to problems.

- **Bad-faith use.** Charges made when you were clearly insolvent and unable to make the required minimum payment (for instance, you had lost your job and had no other income or savings) are a no-no.

  Banks claim that insolvency is evidenced by any of the following:

  - A notation in the customer's file that the customer has met with an attorney (perhaps because the customer told the creditor he or she was considering bankruptcy and had talked to an attorney about it).

  - A rapid increase in spending, followed by 60–90 days without activity.

  - The date noted on any attorney's fee statement, if the customer consults a lawyer for help with a bankruptcy.

Of course, the mere fact that a creditor challenges your discharge of a credit card debt doesn't mean the creditor will win in court. In most of these cases, the creditor files a standard 15- to 20-paragraph form complaint, which states conclusions without supporting facts. The creditor rarely attaches your account statements, but only a printout of the charges to which it is objecting.

Research Tips

If you want to read cases supporting the debtor's position when a credit card issuer claims fraud, visit a law library or search the Internet for some of these cases:

- *In re Hearn,* 211 B.R. 774 (N.D. Ga. 1997)
- *In re Etto,* 210 B.R. 734 (N.D. Ohio 1997)
- *In re Hunter,* 210 B.R. 212 (M.D. Fla. 1997)
- *In re Davis,* 176 B.R. 118 (W.D. N.Y. 1994)
- *In re Kitzmiller,* 206 B.R. 424 (N.D. W.Va. 1997)
- *In re Christensen,* 193 B.R. 863 (N.D. Ill. 1996)
- *In re Chinchilla,* 202 B.R. 1010 (S.D. Fla. 1996)
- *In re Grayson,* 199 B.R. 397 (W.D. Mo. 1996), and
- *In re Vianese,* 195 B.R. 572 (N.D. N.Y. 1995).

For tips on doing your own legal research, see "Legal Research" in Ch. 10.

Questions for Credit Card Companies

If you find yourself facing a dischargeability action over a credit card debt, you'll have an opportunity to send questions (called interrogatories) to the company, to be answered under oath. Here are some you might consider asking:

- You (the card issuer) have alleged that I obtained funds from you by false pretenses and false representations. Please state with particularity the nature of the false pretenses and false representations.
- State all steps taken by you, the card issuer, to determine my creditworthiness.
- Identify all means that you, the card issuer, used to verify my income, expenses, assets, or liabilities. Identify any documents obtained in the verification process.
- Identify your general policies concerning the decision to grant credit and how those policies were applied to me.
- You have alleged that at the time I obtained credit from you, I did not intend to repay it. State all facts in your possession to support this allegation.
- Identify all credit policies you allege were violated by me. State how such policies were communicated to me, and identify all documents that contained those policies.
- Identify the dates on which you claim any of the following events occurred:
  - I consulted a bankruptcy attorney.
  - I had a reduction in income.
  - I formed the intent not to repay this debt.
  - I violated the terms of the credit agreement.
- State whether you believe that every user of a credit card who does not later repay the debt has committed fraud.
- If the answer to the preceding question is no, state all facts that give rise to allegations of fraud in this debtor's use of the card.

After receiving a list of questions like these, the credit card issuer is likely to conclude that you are serious about defending yourself. It might even withdraw its complaint.

Some very sophisticated debtors may be able to represent themselves in this type of case. If you decide to do this, you'll need lots of time to familiarize yourself with general litigation procedures and strategies, as well as the bankruptcy cases in your district that deal with this issue. Start by getting a copy of *Represent Yourself in Court*, by Paul Bergman and Sara Berman (Nolo).

CAUTION

Consider getting help from a lawyer. Allegations of fraud should make you seriously consider consulting an attorney. If a creditor challenges discharge of a debt by claiming you engaged in fraud, but the judge finds in your favor, the judge may order the creditor to reimburse you for the money you spent on attorneys' fees.

Help Beyond the Book

Although this book covers routine bankruptcy procedures in some detail, it doesn't come close to covering everything. That would require thousands of pages, most of them irrelevant for nearly all readers. That said, here are some suggestions if you need more information or advice than this book provides.

The major places to go for follow-up help are:

- **bankruptcy petition preparers,** when you're ready to file for bankruptcy, but need assistance in typing the forms and organizing them for filing in your district
- **lawyers,** when you want information, advice, or legal representation, and
- **law libraries and the Internet,** when you want to do your own research on issues raised in the course of your bankruptcy.

Before we discuss each of these resources in more detail, here's a general piece of advice: Maintain control of your case whenever possible. By getting this book, you've taken responsibility for your own legal affairs. If you decide to get help from others, shop around until you find someone who respects your efforts as a self-helper and recognizes your right to participate in the case as a valuable partner.

Information and Advice From an Author

You can find more bankruptcy information—and updates for this book—at Nolo's website, www.nolo.com. In addition, author Albin Renauer has created an information-rich website at www.legalconsumer.com. This site provides valuable resources, includes up-to-date, state-by-state exemption laws, a means-test calculator, help finding bankruptcy forms online, and much more.

Debt Relief Agencies

Under the new bankruptcy law, any person, business, or organization that you pay or otherwise compensate for help with your bankruptcy is considered a debt relief agency—and must identify itself as such. The two main types of debt relief agencies are lawyers and bankruptcy petition preparers (BPPs). Credit counseling agencies and budget counseling agencies are not debt relief agencies. Nor are any of the following:

- employers or employees of debt relief agencies (for instance, legal secretaries)
- nonprofit organizations that have federal 501(c)(3) tax-exempt status
- any creditor who works with you to restructure your debt
- banks, credit unions, and other deposit institutions, or
- an author, publisher, distributor, or seller of works subject to copyright protection when acting in that capacity (in other words, Nolo and the stores that sell its books aren't debt relief agencies).

This section explains what the bankruptcy law requires of debt relief agencies generally, so you'll know what you can expect for your money.

Mandatory Contract

Within five days after a debt relief agency assists you, it (or he or she) must enter into a contract with you that explains, clearly and conspicuously:

- what services the agency will provide
- what the agency will charge for the services, and
- the terms of payment.

The agency must give you a copy of the completed, signed contract.

Mandatory Disclosures and Notices

Debt relief agencies must inform you, in writing, that:

- All information you are required to provide in your bankruptcy papers must be complete, accurate, and truthful.
- You must completely and accurately disclose your assets and liabilities in the documents you file to begin your case.
- You must undertake a reasonable inquiry to establish the replacement value of any item you plan to keep, before you provide that value on your forms.

Sample Notice From Debt Relief Agency

IMPORTANT INFORMATION ABOUT BANKRUPTCY ASSISTANCE SERVICES FROM AN ATTORNEY OR A BANKRUPTCY PETITION PREPARER

If you decide to seek bankruptcy relief, you can represent yourself, you can hire an attorney to represent you, or you can get help in some localities from a bankruptcy petition preparer who is not an attorney. THE LAW REQUIRES AN ATTORNEY OR A BANKRUPTCY PETITION PREPARER TO GIVE YOU A WRITTEN CONTRACT SPECIFYING WHAT THE ATTORNEY OR A BANKRUPTCY PETITION PREPARER WILL DO FOR YOU AND HOW MUCH IT WILL COST. Ask to see the contract before you hire anyone.

The following information helps you understand what must be done in a routine bankruptcy case to help you evaluate how much service you need. Although bankruptcy can be complex, many cases are routine. Before filing a bankruptcy case, either you or your attorney should analyze your eligibility for different forms of debt relief available under the Bankruptcy Code and which form of relief is most likely to be beneficial for you. Be sure you understand the relief you can obtain and its limitations.

To file a bankruptcy case, documents called a petition, schedules and Statement of Financial Affairs, as well as in some cases a Statement of Intention need to be prepared correctly and filed with the bankruptcy court. You will have to pay a filing fee to the bankruptcy court. Once your case starts, you will have to attend the required first meeting of creditors where you may be questioned by your creditors.

If you choose to file a Chapter 7 case, you may be asked by a creditor to reaffirm a debt. You may want help deciding whether to do so. A creditor is not permitted to coerce you into reaffirming your debts.

If you choose to file a Chapter 13 case in which you repay your creditors what you can afford over three to five years, you may also want help with preparing your Chapter 13 plan and with the confirmation hearing on your plan which will be before a bankruptcy judge.

If you select another type of relief under the Bankruptcy Code other than Chapter 7 or Chapter 13, you will want to find out what should be done from someone familiar with that type of relief.

Your bankruptcy case may also involve litigation. You are generally permitted to represent yourself in litigation in bankruptcy court, but only attorneys, not bankruptcy petition preparers, can give you legal advice.

- Your current monthly income, the amounts you provide in the means test, and your computation of projected disposable income (in a Chapter 13 case), as stated in your bankruptcy papers, must be based on a reasonable inquiry into their accuracy.
- Your case may be audited, and your failure to cooperate in the audit may result in dismissal of your case or some other sanction, including a possible criminal penalty.

In addition to these stark warnings—which most debt relief agencies would rather not have to give—a debt relief agency must also give you a general notice regarding some basic bankruptcy requirements and your options for help in filing and pursuing your case. Above is the notice that you can expect to receive from any debt relief agency within three business days after the agency first offers to provide you with services. Failure to give you this notice—in a timely manner—can land the agency in big trouble.

Finally, every debt relief agency has to give you some plain-English written information about the basic tasks associated with most bankruptcies, such as how to deal with secured debts and choose exemptions. Ideally, debt relief agencies would freely distribute this book, which has all of the information required (and much more, of course).

Restrictions on Debt Relief Agencies

A debt relief agency may not:
- fail to perform any service that the agency told you it would perform in connection with your bankruptcy case
- counsel you to make any statement in a document that is untrue and misleading or that the agency should have known was untrue or misleading, or
- advise you to incur more debt in order to pay for the agency's services (for instance, accepting a credit card or steering you to a cash advance business).

Any contract that doesn't comply with the requirements on debt relief agencies may not be enforced against you. A debt relief agency is liable to you for costs and fees, including legal fees, if the agency negligently or intentionally:
- fails to comply with the law's restrictions on debt relief agencies, or
- fails to file a document that results in dismissal of your case or conversion to another bankruptcy chapter.

In sum, debt relief agencies are on the hook if they are negligent in performing the services required by the bankruptcy law or other services they have agreed to provide.

Bankruptcy Petition Preparers

Even though you should be able to handle routine bankruptcy procedures yourself, you may want someone familiar with the bankruptcy forms and courts in your area to use a computer to enter your data in the official forms and print them out for filing with the court. For this level of assistance—routine form preparation and organization—consider using a bankruptcy petition preparer (BPP).

What a Bankruptcy Petition Preparer Can Do for You

BPPs are very different from lawyers. BPPs are prohibited from giving you legal advice, which includes information such as:
- whether to file a bankruptcy petition or which chapter (7, 11, 12, or 13) is appropriate
- whether your debts will be discharged under a particular chapter
- whether you will be able to hang on to your home or other property if you file under a particular chapter (that is, which exemptions you should choose)
- information about the tax consequences of a case brought under a particular chapter or whether tax claims in your case can be discharged
- whether you should offer to repay or agree to reaffirm a debt
- how to characterize the nature of your interest in property or debts, and
- information about bankruptcy procedures and rights.

Fees

All fees charged by debt relief agencies are reviewed by the U.S. Trustee for reasonableness. However, unlike lawyers' fees, which can vary widely according to the circumstances, a BPP's fees are subject to a strict cap of $200. The rationale offered by the U.S. Trustee for this cap—and by the courts that have upheld it—is that BPP fees can be set according to what general typists charge per page in the community. Because BPPs aren't supposed to be doing anything other than "typing" the forms, the argument goes, they shouldn't be able to charge rates for professional services.

Rates allowed for BPPs are far less than lawyers charge. For that reason, BPPs are a good choice for people who want some help getting their forms typed and organized in a way that will sail past the court clerk and satisfy the trustee.

How Bankruptcy Petition Preparers Are Regulated

Anyone can be a BPP. Yes, anyone. There is nothing in the bankruptcy code that requires BPPs to have any particular level of education, training, or experience. Unlike most other jobs, a prison record is no handicap to becoming a BPP. How, then, are BPPs regulated? Regulation is provided by the U.S. Trustee's office, which reviews all bankruptcy petitions prepared by a BPP. BPPs must provide their name, address, telephone number, and Social Security number on the bankruptcy petition, as well as on every other bankruptcy document they prepare. The U.S. Trustee uses this information to keep tabs on BPPs.

BPPs are also regulated at the 341 hearing, where the bankruptcy trustee can ask you about the manner in which the BPP conducts his or her business. For instance, if you are representing yourself, the trustee might ask how you got the information necessary to choose your exemptions (see Ch. 3) or how you decided which bankruptcy chapter to use.

If the BPP provided you with this information, the trustee may refer the case to the U.S. Trustee's office and the BPP will be hauled into court to explain why

he or she violated the rules against giving legal advice. The BPP may be forced to return the fee you paid and may even be banned from practicing as a BPP, if it's not the first offense. None of this will have any effect on your case, however, other than the inconvenience of being dragged into court.

Can BPPs Give You Written Information?

Under the Bankruptcy Code, BPPs are supposed to prepare your bankruptcy forms under your direction. This means you are supposed to tell the BPP what exemptions to choose, whether to file under Chapter 7 or Chapter 13, what approach to take in respect to your secured debts (car note, mortgage, and so on), and what values to place on your property. That's fine in theory, but unless you have the benefit of this book or another source of legal information, there is no way you would have adequate bankruptcy expertise to tell the BPP how to proceed. In an attempt to bridge this gap, many BPPs hand their customers written materials that contain all the information their customers need to direct the case. Unfortunately, providing a customer with written legal information about bankruptcy has itself been held to be the unauthorized practice of law in many states (California is an important exception). Whether these holdings will continue remains to be seen.

BPPs can be fined for certain actions and inactions spelled out in the bankruptcy code (11 U.S.C. § 110). These are:

- failing to put their name, address, and Social Security number on your bankruptcy petition
- failing to give you a copy of your bankruptcy documents when you sign them
- using the word "legal" or any similar term in advertisements, or advertising under a category that includes such terms, and
- accepting court filing fees from you. You must pay the filing fee to the court yourself or, in some districts, give the BPP a cashier's check made out to the court.

Finally, under the law, a BPP must submit a statement under oath with each petition prepared stating how much you paid the BPP in the previous 12 months and any fees that you owe but haven't yet paid. If the charges are more than are permitted, the BPP will be ordered to return the excess fees to you.

A BPP who engages in any fraudulent act in regard to your case or fails to comply with the rules governing behavior listed above may be required to return your entire fee as well as pay a $500 fine for each transgression. By engaging in serious fraud, the BBP may be fined up to $2,000 and three times your fee, and even be ordered to cease providing BPP services. Simply put, fraudulent BPPs (those who would take your money without providing promised services or counsel you to play fast and loose with the bankruptcy system) are likely to be weeded out in a hurry.

How to Find Bankruptcy Petition Preparers

You're more likely to find a BPP if you live on the West Coast. The best way to find a reputable BPP in your area is to get a recommendation from someone who has used a particular BPP and has been satisfied with his or her work.

BPPs sometimes advertise in classified sections of local newspapers and in the yellow pages. You may have to look hard to spot their ads, however, because they go by different names in different states. In California, your best bet is to find a legal document assistant (the official name given to independent paralegals in California) who also provides BPP services. Check the website maintained by the California Association of Legal Document Assistants (www.calda.org). In Arizona, hunt for a legal document preparer. In other states, especially Florida, search for paralegals who directly serve the public (often termed independent paralegals or legal technicians).

CAUTION

A bankruptcy petition preparer cannot represent you. If you decide to use a BPP, remember that you are representing yourself and are responsible for the outcome of your case. This means not only learning about your rights under the bankruptcy law and understanding the proper procedures to be followed, but also accepting responsibility for correctly and accurately filling in the bankruptcy petition and schedules. If, for example, you lose your home because it turned out to be worth much more than you thought, and the homestead exemption available to you didn't cover your equity, you can't blame the BPP. Nor can you blame the BPP if other property is taken from you because you didn't get the necessary information— from a lawyer or from this book—to properly claim your exemptions. The point is, unless you hire a lawyer to represent you, you are solely responsible for acquiring the information necessary to competently pursue your case.

Bankruptcy Lawyers

Bankruptcy lawyers (a type of debt relief agency under the new law) are regular lawyers who handle bankruptcy cases. Under the pre-2005 law, it was usually possible to find an affordable bankruptcy lawyer who would provide at least a minimal level of representation throughout your case. However, for the reasons discussed below, lawyers are now charging a lot more to represent clients in bankruptcies.

When You May Need a Lawyer

Most Chapter 7 bankruptcies sail through without a hitch. However, there are some situations in which you may need some help from a bankruptcy lawyer:

- Your average gross income during the six months before you file is more than your state's median income, and it looks like you won't be able to pass the means test. (See Ch. 1 and Ch. 6 for more information on these calculations.)
- You want to hold onto a house or motor vehicle and the information we provide on these subjects doesn't adequately address your situation or answer all of your questions.
- You want to get rid of a student loan or income tax debt that won't be wiped out in bankruptcy unless you convince a court in a separate proceeding that it should be discharged.
- A creditor files a lawsuit in the bankruptcy court claiming that one of your debts should

survive your bankruptcy because you incurred it through fraud or other misconduct.

- The bankruptcy trustee (the court official in charge of your case) seeks to have your whole bankruptcy dismissed because you didn't give honest and complete answers to questions about your assets, liabilities, and economic transactions.

- The U.S. Trustee asks the court to dismiss your case—or force you into Chapter 13— because your income is high enough to fund a Chapter 13 repayment plan, or because the trustee believes that your filing is an abuse of the Chapter 7 bankruptcy process for other reasons.

- You have given away or sold valuable property for less than it is worth within the last two years.

- You went on a recent buying spree with your credit card (especially if you charged more than $650 on luxury goods within the past 90 days).

- You want help negotiating with a creditor or the bankruptcy court, and the amount involved justifies hiring a bankruptcy lawyer to assist you.

- You have a large lien on your property because of a court judgment against you, and you want to remove the lien in your bankruptcy case.

- A creditor is asking the court to allow it to proceed with its collection action despite your bankruptcy filing (for instance, a creditor wants to foreclose on your house because you are behind on your mortgage payments) and you want to oppose the request.

- You are being evicted by your landlord because you have fallen behind on your rent.

Even if you aren't facing one of these complications, you may still want a lawyer's help. If you find the thought of going through the bankruptcy process overwhelming, a lawyer can take charge of your case and relieve you of the responsibility to get everything done. The lawyer can accompany you to the 341 hearing, work with you to make sure that your documents are complete and accurate, get all your paperwork filed on time, and generally handle all of the little details that go into a successful bankruptcy case. Although representation comes at a price— which can be considerable—you will have the peace of mind of knowing that someone is watching your back. While we obviously believe that many people can handle their own Chapter 7 bankruptcies, it isn't right for everyone, especially if you have other significant sources of stress in your life or simply don't feel up to handling it all by yourself.

Full-Service Lawyer Representation

In a general sense, you are represented by a lawyer if you contract with the lawyer to handle some or all of your bankruptcy case for you. More specifically, there are two types of representation—the type where you hire a lawyer to assume complete responsibility for your bankruptcy, and the type where you represent yourself but hire a lawyer to handle one particular aspect of your bankruptcy case. We refer to the first type of representation as "full-service representation" and the second type of representation as unbundled services (discussed below).

When providing full-service representation, a bankruptcy lawyer is responsible for making sure that all of your paperwork is filed on time and that the information in your paperwork is accurate. These duties require the lawyer to review various documents—for instance, your credit report, tax returns, and home value appraisal—both to ensure the accuracy of your paperwork and to make sure that you are filing for bankruptcy under the appropriate chapter. If your paperwork is inaccurate or you filed under Chapter 7 when you should have filed under Chapter 13, the lawyer can be fined a hefty amount and be required to return your fees.

In exchange for their basic fee, full-service bankruptcy lawyers typically are also responsible for appearing on your behalf at the 341 hearing (see Ch. 7), representing you if a creditor opposes the discharge of a debt (see Ch. 9), and eliminating any liens that the bankruptcy laws allow to be stripped from your property (see Ch. 5).

Sometimes, a case appears to be simple at the beginning but starts looking more complicated later on. In that event, you might start out representing yourself but later decide to hire an attorney to handle a tricky issue that arises.

Unbundled Services

As mentioned earlier, changes in bankruptcy law mean that many people who would have hired a full-service lawyer in the past will now have to represent themselves. However, this doesn't mean that they can't get a lawyer to help out with some aspect of the case. Since the 1990s, lawyers have been increasingly willing to offer their services on a piecemeal basis and provide legal advice over the telephone and Internet to help people who are representing themselves. In bankruptcy cases, lawyers are increasingly willing to step in and handle a particular matter, such as having liens removed from your property or handling a dischargeability action brought by you or a creditor.

When lawyers do specific jobs at a client's request but don't contract for full-service representation in the underlying case, they are said to be providing an unbundled service. For example, you may be able to hire an attorney to handle a specific procedure—such as to defend against a motion for relief from stay—while you handle the main part of the bankruptcy yourself.

Few court cases discuss the boundaries of unbundled services. Some courts have held that attorneys can't "ghostwrite" legal documents for nonlawyers—because that would be a type of fraud on the court—but the issue has not been decided by most courts. Also, nothing prevents a lawyer from appearing for you in a limited capacity and putting his or her own name on associated documents.

Lawyers providing unbundled services usually charge an hourly fee. As a general rule, you should bring an attorney into the case for an unbundled service only if a dispute involves something valuable enough to justify the attorney's fees. If a creditor objects to the discharge of a $500 debt, and it will cost you $400 to hire an attorney, you may be better off

trying to handle the matter yourself, even though this increases the risk that the creditor will win. If, however, the dispute is worth $1,000 and the attorney will cost you $200, hiring the attorney makes better sense.

Unfortunately, many bankruptcy attorneys do not like to appear or do paperwork on a piecemeal basis. Justified or not, these attorneys believe that by doing a little work for you, they might be on the hook if something goes wrong in another part of your case—that is, if they are in for a penny, they are in for a pound. Also, the bar associations of some states frown on unbundled services on ethical grounds. On the other hand, a number of other state bar associations are starting to encourage their attorneys to offer unbundled services simply because so many people—even middle-income people—are unable to afford full representation.

Consulting With a Bankruptcy Lawyer

Under the pre-2005 bankruptcy law, many people were able to represent themselves with a Nolo book as their main source of information. Bankruptcy law is now more complex, but in many cases, it's still just a matter of knowing what to put in the forms and what forms to file. For many people, however, a book just won't do the trick, no matter how well written and complete—they want to talk to a human being. Because of unauthorized practice laws and restrictions in the bankruptcy law, however, there is only one kind of human being who is authorized to answer your questions about bankruptcy law and procedure: a lawyer.

Even if you use a BPP to prepare your paperwork, and are using this book, you may wish to talk to a lawyer to get the information you need to make your own choices and tell the BPP what you want in your papers. For instance, a BPP can't choose your exemptions for you, because that would be considered the practice of law—something only lawyers can do. However, a lawyer can help you decide which exemptions to pick so you can tell the BPP what to put in the form that lists your exemptions.

How to Find a Bankruptcy Lawyer

Where there's a bankruptcy court, there are bankruptcy lawyers. They're listed in the yellow pages under "Attorneys," and often advertise online. You should use an experienced bankruptcy lawyer, not a general practitioner, to advise you on or handle matters associated with bankruptcy.

There are several ways to find the best bankruptcy lawyer for your job:

- **Personal referrals.** This is your best approach. If you know someone who was pleased with the services of a bankruptcy lawyer, call that lawyer first.

- **Bankruptcy petition preparers.** If there's a BPP in your area, he or she may know some bankruptcy attorneys who are both competent and sympathetic to self-helpers. It is here that you are most likely to find a good referral to attorneys who are willing to deliver unbundled services, including advice over the telephone.

- **Legal Aid.** Legal Aid offices are partially funded by the federal Legal Services Corporation and offer legal assistance in many areas. A few offices may do bankruptcies, although most do not. To qualify for Legal Aid, you must have a very low income.

- **Legal clinic.** Many law schools sponsor legal clinics and provide free legal advice to consumers. Some legal clinics have the same income requirements as Legal Aid; others offer free services to low- and moderate-income people.

- **Group legal plans.** If you're a member of a plan that provides free or low-cost legal assistance and the plan covers bankruptcies, make that your first stop in looking for a lawyer.

- **Lawyer referral panels.** Most county bar associations will give you the names of bankruptcy attorneys who practice in your area. But bar associations may not provide much screening. Take the time to check out the credentials and experience of the person to whom you're referred.

- **Internet lawyer directories.** In response to reader inquiries about finding a good lawyer, Nolo created a first-class lawyer directory (at www.nolo.com). If you need a bankruptcy lawyer, Nolo's lawyer directory can help you find one who's right for you. All participating attorneys promise respectful service, and Nolo's profiles provide more in-depth information than any other lawyer directory about each attorney's experience. Another excellent source is the membership directory of The National Association of Consumer Bankruptcy Attorneys (NACBA at www.nacba.org). NACBA provides members with excellent education and training on all aspects of bankruptcy and foreclosure.

- **ABI pro bono resources.** The American Bankruptcy Institute maintains a list, by state, of Legal Aid or other organizations that provide free bankruptcy services. Often these services consist of bankruptcy clinics where you can get help completing forms or ask questions about bankruptcy in general or your case in particular. A few organizations will prepare forms for or represent you in bankruptcy. Go to the ABI's website at www.bankruptcyresources.org, choose "Find Help," choose your state, and then click on "Pro Bono Resources."

Fees

For a routine Chapter 7 bankruptcy, a full-service lawyer will likely charge you somewhere between $1,000 and $2,000 (plus the $335 filing fee). You'll also have to pay additional fees for credit counseling. In most situations, you will have to pay the attorney in full before the attorney will file your case. Once you file your Chapter 7 bankruptcy, any money you owe the attorney is discharged along with your other dischargeable unsecured debts.

For some people needing bankruptcy, coming up with a few thousand dollars to pay an attorney and cover the filing fee can be a struggle. One option is to stop making payments on credit cards and sock that money away for your bankruptcy lawyer fees. Don't do this until you first consult with a lawyer, though. If bankruptcy ends up not working for you, it'll be tough to get back on track with your credit card payments. Another option is to ask for help from a relative. A relative can use a credit card to pay your attorney.

On your bankruptcy papers, you must state the amount you are paying your bankruptcy lawyer. Because every penny you pay to a bankruptcy lawyer is a penny not available to your creditors (at least in theory), the court has the legal authority to make the attorney justify his or her fee. This rarely happens, however, because attorneys know the range of fees generally allowed by local bankruptcy judges and set their fees accordingly. This means that you probably won't find much variation in the amounts charged by lawyers in your area (although it never hurts to shop around).

The scope and range of services that the attorney promises you in return for your initial fee will be listed in what's called a "Rule 2016 Attorney Fee Disclosure Form." This form is filed as part of your bankruptcy papers. In the typical Chapter 7 case, the attorney's fee will include the routine tasks associated with a bankruptcy filing: counseling, preparing bankruptcy and reaffirmation forms, and attendance at the 341 hearing. Any task not included in the Rule 2016 disclosure form is subject to a separate fee.

If your case will likely require more attorney time, you may—and probably will—be charged extra, according to the attorney's hourly fee or other criteria he or she uses. A typical bankruptcy attorney charges between $200 and $300 an hour (rural and urban) and would charge a minimum of roughly $400 to $600 for a court appearance. Some attorneys will add these fees to their standard fee and require you to pay it all in advance. For instance, if the attorney's standard fee is $1,000, but the attorney sees extra work down the line, you may be charged $2,000 or more in anticipation of the extra work.

Other attorneys will happily just charge you their standard fee up front and wait until after you file to charge you for the extra work. Because these fees are earned after your bankruptcy filing, they won't be discharged in your bankruptcy and the attorney need not collect them up front. However the attorney charges you, you are protected against fee gouging. An attorney must file a supplemental Rule 2016 form to obtain the court's permission for any postfiling fees.

What to Look for in a Lawyer

No matter how you find a lawyer, these three suggestions will help you make sure you have the best possible working relationship.

First, fight any urge you may have to surrender to, or be intimidated by, the lawyer. You should be the one who decides what you feel comfortable doing about your legal and financial affairs. Keep in mind that you're hiring the lawyer to perform a service for you, so shop around if the price or personality isn't right.

Second, make sure you have good "chemistry" with any lawyer you hire. When making an appointment, ask to talk directly to the lawyer. If you can't, this may give you a hint as to how accessible he or she is. Of course, if you're told that a paralegal will be handling the routine aspects of your case under the supervision of a lawyer, you may be satisfied with that arrangement. If you do talk directly, ask some specific questions. Do you get clear, concise answers? If not, try someone else. Also, pay attention to how the lawyer responds to your knowledge. If you've read this book, you're already better informed than most clients and some lawyers are threatened by clients who have done their homework.

Finally, once you find a lawyer you like, make an hour-long appointment to discuss your situation fully. The lawyer or a paralegal in the lawyer's office will tell you what, if anything, to bring to the meeting (if not, be sure to ask ahead of time). Some lawyers will want to see a recent credit report and tax return, while others will send you a questionnaire to complete prior to your visit. Depending on the circumstances, you may also be asked to bring your bills and documents pertaining to your home and other real estate you own. Some lawyers prefer not to deal with details during the first visit, and will simply ask you to come as you are.

Your main goal at the initial conference is to find out what the lawyer recommends in your particular case and how much it will cost. Go home and think about the lawyer's suggestions. If they don't make sense or you have other reservations, call someone else.

Legal Research

Legal research can vary from the very simple to the hopelessly complex. In this section, we are staying on the simple side. If you would like to learn more about legal research or if you find that our suggestions come up a bit short in your particular case, we recommend that you obtain a copy of *Legal Research*, by Stephen Elias and the Editors of Nolo (Nolo), which provides a plain-English tutorial on legal research in the law library and on the Internet.

Sources of Bankruptcy Law

Bankruptcy law comes from a variety of sources:

- federal bankruptcy statutes passed by Congress
- federal rules about bankruptcy procedure issued by a federal judicial agency
- local rules issued by individual bankruptcy courts
- federal and bankruptcy court cases applying bankruptcy laws to specific disputes
- laws (statutes) passed by state legislatures that define the property you can keep in bankruptcy, and
- state court cases interpreting state exemption statutes.

Not so long ago, you would have had to visit a law library to find these resources. Now you can find most of them on the Internet. However, if you are able to visit a decent-sized law library, your research will be the better for it. Using actual books allows you to more easily find and read relevant court interpretations of the underlying statutes and rules—which are crucial to getting a clear picture of what the laws and rules really mean.

There is another important reason to visit the law library, if possible. While you can find superficial discussions and overviews of various aspects of bankruptcy on the Internet, you'll find in-depth encyclopedias and treatises in the law library that delve into every aspect of bankruptcy. In other words, you can find not only the law itself, but also what the experts have to say about all the picky little issues that have arisen over the years. Also, books in a law library are almost always subjected to a rigorous quality

control process—as is this book—whereas you never know what you're getting on the Internet. To avoid getting lost in cyberspace, follow our suggestions below for researching bankruptcy law online and avoid the temptation to settle for the first hit in a Google search.

Below, we show you how to get to the resources you'll most likely be using, whether you are doing your research on the Internet or in the law library.

Bankruptcy Background Materials: Overviews, Encyclopedias, and Treatises

Before digging into the primary law sources (statutes, rules, cases, and so on that we discuss below), you may want to do some background reading to get a firm grasp of your issue or question.

The Internet

A number of Internet sites contain large collections of articles written by experts about various aspects of bankruptcy. Good starting places are Nolo's website, www.nolo.com, and www.legalconsumer.com, which offer lots of information and resources.

Another approach to searching for bankruptcy-related materials is Google. Both the basic Google search and Google Scholar (http://scholar.google.com) are amazingly responsive to plain-language queries. For example, if you want to know more about discharging student loans, you would use Google Scholar, click the "Articles" radio button and enter "discharging student loans in bankruptcy" in the search box and pull up a bevy of links to related articles. Similarly, if you want to read court opinions about discharging debts in bankruptcy you would do the same search but use the "Case law" button.

The Law Library

Providing you with a good treatise or encyclopedia discussion of bankruptcy is where the law library shines. This type of resource is not typically available online unless you find a way to access the expensive legal databases—Westlaw and Lexis—marketed almost exclusively to lawyers.

How to Use Law Libraries

Law libraries that are open to the public are most often found in and around courthouses. Law schools also frequently admit the public at least some of the time (not, typically, during exam time, over the summer, or during other breaks in the academic year).

Almost without exception, law libraries come with law librarians. The law librarians will be helpful as long as you ask them the right questions. For example, the law librarians will help you find specific library resources (such as, where to find the federal bankruptcy statutes or rules), but they normally won't teach you the ins and outs of legal research. Nor will they give an opinion about what a law means, how you should deal with the court, or how your particular question should be answered. For instance, if you want to find a state case interpreting a particular exemption, the law librarian will show you where your state code is located on the shelves and may even point out the volumes that contain the exemptions. The librarian won't, however, help you interpret the exemption, apply the exemption to your specific facts, or tell you how to raise the exemption in your bankruptcy case. Nor is the librarian likely to tell you what additional research steps you can or should take. When it comes to legal research in the law library, self help is the order of the day.

Collier on Bankruptcy

It's a good idea to get an overview of your subject before trying to find a precise answer to a precise question. The best way to do this is to find a general commentary on your subject by a bankruptcy expert. For example, if you want to find out whether a particular debt is nondischargeable, you should start by reading a general discussion about the type of debt you're dealing with. Or, if you don't know whether you're entitled to claim certain property as exempt, a good overview of your state's exemptions would get you started on the right track.

The most complete source of this type of background information is a set of books known as *Collier on Bankruptcy*, by Lawrence P. King, et al. (Matthew Bender). It's available in virtually all law libraries. *Collier* is both incredibly thorough and meticulously up to date; semiannual supplements, with all the latest developments, are in the front of each volume. In addition to comments on every aspect of bankruptcy law, *Collier* contains the bankruptcy statutes, rules, and exemption lists for every state.

Collier is organized according to the bankruptcy statutes. This means that the quickest way to find information in it is to know what statute you're looking for. (See the Bankruptcy Code sections set out below.) If you still can't figure out the governing statute, start with the *Collier* subject-matter index. Be warned, however, that the index can be difficult to use because it contains a lot of bankruptcy jargon you may be unfamiliar with. A legal dictionary will be available in the library.

Bankruptcy (National Edition) published by The Rutter Group

This four-volume set authored by Kathleen P. March, Esq., and Judge Alan M. Ahart provides nice crisp treatments of all the pesky little issues that can arise in a bankruptcy case. Because of its relatively low cost (at least from a library's standpoint; it goes for $696), you are more likely to be able to find it in small county and court law libraries.

Foreclosure Resources

If you are facing foreclosure, you'll definitely want to look at *The Foreclosure Survival Guide,* by Stephen Elias (Nolo). This book explains the options available to you, then walks you through the necessary steps for handling your particular situation. The National Consumer Law Center (NCLC) offers a helpful resource titled Foreclosure Prevention Counseling, available through the NCLC Foreclosure Prevention Resource Center at www.consumerlaw.org/fprc.

Other Background Resources

For general discussions of bankruptcy issues, there are several other good places to start. An excellent all-around resource is called Consumer Bankruptcy Law and Practice. This volume, published by the National Consumer Law Center, is updated every year. It contains a complete discussion of Chapter 7 bankruptcy procedures, the official bankruptcy forms, and a marvelous bibliography.

Another good treatise is a legal encyclopedia called American Jurisprudence, 2nd Series. Almost all law libraries carry it. The article on bankruptcy has an extensive table of contents, and the entire encyclopedia has an index. Between these two tools, you should be able to zero in on helpful material. Finally, some large and well-stocked law libraries carry a looseleaf publication known as the Commerce Clearing House (CCH) Bankruptcy Law Reporter (BLR). In this publication, you can find all three primary source materials relating to bankruptcy: statutes, rules, and cases.

If you are looking for information on adversary proceedings (such as how to defend against a creditor's challenge to the dischargeability of a debt), turn to *Represent Yourself in Court*, by Paul Bergman and Sara J. Berman (Nolo). It has an entire chapter on representing yourself in adversary proceedings in bankruptcy court. If you need information on court procedures or the local rules of a specific court, consult the Collier Bankruptcy Practice Manual.

Finding Federal Bankruptcy Statutes

Title 11 of the United States Code contains all the statutes that govern your bankruptcy.

The Internet

If you are using the Internet, go to the Legal Information Institute of Cornell University Law School, www.law.cornell.edu. Cornell lets you browse laws by subject matter and also offers a keyword search. To help you in your browsing, below is a table setting out the various subject matter sections of the U.S. Code that apply to bankruptcy.

The Law Library

Virtually every law library has at least one complete set of the annotated United States Code ("annotated" means that each statute is followed by citations and summaries of cases interpreting that provision). If you already have a citation to the statute you are seeking, you can use the citation to find the statute. However, if you have no citation—which is frequently the case—you can use either the index to Title 11 (the part of the Code that applies to bankruptcy) or the table we set out just below, which matches various issues that are likely to interest you with specific sections of Title 11.

Once you have found and read the statute, you can browse the one-paragraph summaries of written opinions issued by courts that have interpreted that particular statute. You will be looking to see whether a court has addressed your particular issue. If so, you can find and read the entire case in the law library. Reading what a judge has had to say about the statute regarding facts similar to yours is an invaluable guide to understanding how a judge is likely to handle the issue in your case, although when and where the case was decided may be important.

Finding the Federal Rules of Bankruptcy Procedure (FRBP)

The Federal Rules of Bankruptcy Procedure govern what happens if an issue is contested in the bankruptcy court. They also apply to certain routine bankruptcy procedures, such as deadlines for filing paperwork. Because most cases sail through the court without any need for the bankruptcy judge's intervention, you may not need to be familiar with these rules. However, certain types of creditor actions in the bankruptcy court must proceed by way of a regular lawsuit conducted under both these rules and the Federal Rules of Civil Procedure—for example, complaints to determine dischargeability of a debt. If you are representing yourself in such a lawsuit, you'll want to know these rules and look at the cases interpreting them. Any law library will have these rules. Your bankruptcy court's website will also have a link to the rules, as does www.law.cornell.edu.

Bankruptcy Code Sections (11 U.S.C.)

§ 101 Definitions

§ 109 Who May File for Which Type of Bankruptcy; Credit Counseling Requirements

§ 110 Rules for Bankruptcy Petition Preparers

§ 111 Budget and Credit Counseling Agencies

§ 302 Who Can File Joint Cases

§ 326 How Trustees Are Compensated

§ 332 Consumer Privacy Ombudsmen

§ 341 Meeting of Creditors

§ 342 Notice of Creditors' Meeting; Informational Notice to Debtors; Requirements for Notice by Debtors

§ 343 Examination of Debtor at Creditors' Meeting

§ 348 Converting From One Type of Bankruptcy to Another

§ 349 Dismissing a Case

§ 350 Closing and Reopening a Case

§ 362 The Automatic Stay

§ 365 How Leases and Executory Contracts Are Treated in Bankruptcy

§ 366 Continuing or Reconnecting Utility Service

§ 501 Filing of Creditors' Claims

§ 506 Allowed Secured Claims and Lien Avoidance

§ 507 Priority Claims

§ 521 Paperwork Requirements and Deadlines

§ 522 Exemptions; Residency Requirements for Homestead Exemption; Stripping Liens From Property

§ 523 Nondischargeable Debts

§ 524 Effect of Discharge and Reaffirmation of Debts

§ 525 Prohibited Postbankruptcy Discrimination

§ 526 Restrictions on Debt Relief Agencies

§ 527 Required Disclosures by Debt Relief Agencies

§ 528 Requirements for Debt Relief Agencies

§ 541 What Property Is Part of the Bankruptcy Estate

§ 547 Preferences

§ 548 Fraudulent Transfers

§ 554 Trustee's Abandonment of Property in the Bankruptcy Estate

§ 707 The Means Test; Dismissal for Abuse; Conversion From Chapter 7 to Chapter 13

§ 722 Redemption of Liens on Personal Property

§ 727 Chapter 7 Discharge; Financial Management Counseling Requirements

Finding Local Court Rules

Every bankruptcy court operates under a set of local rules that govern how it does business and what is expected of the parties who use it. Throughout this book, we have cautioned you to read the rules for your particular court so that your dealings with the court will go smoothly—and so you won't end up getting tossed out of court if you become involved in litigation, such as an action to determine the dischargeability of a debt or a creditor's motion to lift the automatic stay.

Your bankruptcy court clerk's office will have the local rules available for you. Most courts also post their local rules on their own websites. To find the website for your court, take these steps:

Step 1: Go to www.uscourts.gov

Step 2: Use the Court Locator to find the bankruptcy court near you.

Step 3: Browse the list until you find your bankruptcy court and click on "Details" for it.

Step 4: Click on the link to your court's website.

Court websites usually contain other helpful information as well, including case information, official and local bankruptcy forms, court guidelines (in addition to the local rules), information for lawyers and BPPs, information about the court and its judges, and the court calendar.

At the law library, the *Collier Bankruptcy Practice Manual* has the local rules for most (if not all) of the nation's bankruptcy courts.

Finding Federal Court Bankruptcy Cases

Court opinions are vital to understanding how a particular law might apply to your individual case. The following levels of federal courts issue bankruptcy-related opinions:

- the U.S. Supreme Court
- the U.S. Courts of Appeals
- the Bankruptcy Appellate Panels
- the U.S. District Courts, and
- the bankruptcy courts.

Most bankruptcy-related opinions are, not surprisingly, issued by the bankruptcy courts. By comparison, very few bankruptcy opinions come out of the U.S. Supreme Court. The other courts are somewhere in the middle.

The Internet

Depending on the date the case was decided, U.S. Supreme Court decisions and U.S. Court of Appeals decisions are available for free on the Internet. For $18.95 a month you can also subscribe to VersusLaw (at www.versuslaw.com), which provides U.S. Court of Appeals cases for an earlier period than you can get for free—often back to 1950. VersusLaw doesn't require you to sign a long-term contract. So, one payment of $18.95 gets you a month's worth of research. Not too shabby. VersusLaw also publishes many U.S. District Court cases on its website. Opinions by the bankruptcy courts are generally not yet available over the Internet, unless you subscribe to Lexis or Westlaw, both of which are extremely pricey.

U.S. Supreme Court. To find a Supreme Court case, go to http://supreme.nolo.com. Use one of the search options to locate a particular case. If you don't know the case name and you don't have a citation, enter some relevant words relating to your issue and see what you pull up. You can search cases all the way back to 1893.

U.S. Court of Appeals. If you know the case name, you can find a U.S. Court of Appeals case back to 1924. Follow these steps:

Step 1: Go to http://law.justia.com/cases/federal/appellate-courts.

Step 2: You can narrow your search by Circuit Court, state, or year. Whether you narrow the search or not, enter the case name or part of the case name in the search box at the top of the page.

You can also find many cases through a Google search. If you don't know the case name and instead want to search by keyword, you'll have to use VersusLaw or sign up for one of the pricier services that lawyers use, like Westlaw, Lexis, or FastCase (www.fastcase.com).

U.S. District Courts and Bankruptcy Courts. If you know the case name, you can find U.S. District Court cases back to 1924 and bankruptcy court cases back to 1980. Follow these steps:

Step 1: Go to http://law.justia.com/cases/federal/appellate-courts.

Step 2: You can narrow your search by state. Whether you narrow the search or not, enter the case name or part of the case name in the search box at the top of the page.

You can also find some cases through a Google search. For U.S. District Court cases, if you don't know the case name and instead want to search by keyword, you'll have to use VersusLaw. For bankruptcy cases, you'll need to head to the nearest law library or use a pricier service like Westlaw, Lexis, or FastCase.

The Law Library

U.S. Supreme Court cases are published in three different book series:

- *Supreme Court Reports*
- *Supreme Court Reporter*, and
- *Supreme Court Lawyer's Edition.*

Some law libraries carry all three of these publications; others have only one. The cases are the same, but each series has different editorial enhancements.

U.S. Court of Appeals cases are published in the *Federal Reporter* (abbreviated simply as "F."). Most law libraries, large and small, carry this series.

Many U.S. District Court cases are published in the *Federal Supplement* (F.Supp), a series available in most law libraries.

Written opinions of bankruptcy judges, and related appeals, are published in the *Bankruptcy Reporter* (B.R.), available in most mid- to large-sized libraries.

To accurately understand how your bankruptcy court is likely to interpret the laws in your particular case, sooner or later you will need access to the *Bankruptcy Reporter*.

State Statutes

The secret to understanding what property you can keep frequently lies in the exemptions that your state allows you to claim. These exemptions are found in your state's statutes.

The Internet

Every state has its statutes online, including its exemption statutes. This means that you can read your state's exemption statutes for yourself. Follow these steps:

Step 1: Go to Appendix A. At the top of your state's exemption table, you'll see a general reference to the collection of laws for your state that contain the exemption statutes.

Step 2: Go to www.nolo.com/legal-research. Click on "State Law Resources."

Step 3: Find your state and click on it.

Step 4: This will bring you to a page for your state. Look for the link to the state's official code. Click on the link and then look for the collection of statutes mentioned in Appendix A. Use the citation on the far right of your state's exemption table in Appendix A to find exactly what you need.

The Law Library

Your law library will have your state's statutes in book form, usually referred to as your state's code, annotated statutes, or compiled laws. Use Appendix A in this book to find a reference to the exemption statute you want to read, then use that reference to locate the exemption statute in the code. Once you find and read the statute, you can browse the summaries of court opinions interpreting the statute and, if you wish, read the cases in their entirety.

Alternatively, if your library has a copy of *Collier on Bankruptcy* (see above) or *Bankruptcy* by the Rutter Group, you can find the exemptions for your state, accompanied by annotations summarizing state court interpretations.

State Court Cases

State courts are sometimes called on to interpret exemption statutes. If a court has interpreted the statute in which you are interested, you'll definitely want to chase down the relevant case and read it for yourself.

The Internet

All states make their more recent cases available free on the Internet—usually back to about 1996. To find these cases for your state:

Step 1: Go to www.law.cornell.edu/opinions. html#state.

Step 2: Click on your state.

Step 3: Locate the link to the court opinions for your state. This may be one link, or there may be separate links for your state's supreme court and your state's courts of appeal (the lower trial courts seldom publish their opinions, so you probably won't be able to find them).

If you want to go back to an earlier case, consider subscribing to VersusLaw at www.versuslaw.com. As mentioned earlier, you don't have to sign a long-term contract.

The Law Library

Your law library will have a collection of books that contain opinions issued by your state's courts. If you have a citation, you can go right to the case. If you don't have a citation, you'll need to use a digest to find relevant bankruptcy cases. Finding cases by subject matter is a little too advanced for this brief summary. See *Legal Research,* by Stephen Elias and the Editors of Nolo (Nolo), for more help.

Other Helpful Resources

Probably the most helpful bankruptcy website is maintained by the Office of the United States Trustee, at www.usdoj.gov/ust. This site provides lists of approved credit and financial management counseling agencies, median income figures for every state, and the IRS national, regional, and local expenses you will need to complete the means test. You can download official bankruptcy forms from www.uscourts.gov/ federalcourts/bankruptcy.aspx. However, this site doesn't include required local forms; for those, you'll have to visit your court or its website.

As part of the bankruptcy process, you are required to give the replacement (retail) value for all of the property you list in Schedule A (real property) and Schedule B (personal property). These figures are also the key to figuring out which of your property is exempt. Here are some tips on finding these values:

- Cars: Use the *Kelley Blue Book*, at www.kbb. com, or the website of the National Auto Dealers Association, www.nada.com.
- Other personal property: Check prices on eBay, www.ebay.com.
- Homes: Check the prices for which comparable homes have sold in the recent past. You can get details on comparable homes, including sales history, number of bedrooms and baths, and square footage at www.zillow.com/homes/ recently-sold. Or try sites like www.home-values. com, and http://list.realestate.yahoo.com/re/ homevalues.

Glossary

341 hearing. A hearing that the debtor is required to attend in a bankruptcy case, at which the trustee and creditors may ask the debtor questions about his or her property, information in the documents and forms he or she filed, and his or her debts.

341 notice. A notice sent to the debtor and the debtor's creditors announcing the date, time, and place for the first meeting of creditors. The 341 notice is sent along with the notice of bankruptcy filing and information about important deadlines by which creditors have to take certain actions, such as filing objections.

342 notice. A notice that the court clerk is required to give to debtors pursuant to Section 342 of the bankruptcy code, to inform them of their obligations as bankruptcy debtors and the consequences of not being completely honest in their bankruptcy cases.

707(b) action. An action taken by the U.S. Trustee, the regular trustee, or any creditor, under authority of Section 707(b) of the bankruptcy code, to dismiss a debtor's Chapter 7 filing on the ground of abuse.

Abuse. Misuse of the Chapter 7 bankruptcy remedy. This term is typically applied to a Chapter 7 bankruptcy filing that should have been filed under Chapter 13 because the debtor appears to have enough disposable income to fund a Chapter 13 repayment plan.

Accounts receivable. Money or other property that one person or business owes to another for goods or services. Accounts receivable most often refer to the debts owed to a business by its customers.

Administrative expenses. The trustee's fee, the debtor's attorneys' fee, and other costs of bringing a bankruptcy case that a debtor must pay in full in a Chapter 13 repayment plan. Administrative costs are typically 10% of the debtor's total payments under the plan.

Administrative Office of the United States Courts. The federal government agency that issues court rules and forms to be used by the federal courts, including bankruptcy courts.

Adversary action. Any lawsuit that begins with the filing of a formal complaint and formal service of process on the parties being sued. In a bankruptcy case, adversary actions are often brought to determine the dischargeability of a debt or to recover property transferred by the debtor shortly before filing for bankruptcy.

Affidavit. A written statement of facts, signed under oath in front of a notary public.

Allowed secured claim. A debt that is secured by collateral or a lien against the debtor's property, for which the creditor has filed a proof of claim with the bankruptcy court. The claim is secured only to the extent of the value of the property— for example, if a debtor owes $5,000 on a note for a car that is worth only $3,000, the remaining $2,000 is an unsecured claim.

Amendment. A document filed by the debtor that changes one or more documents previously filed with the court. A debtor often files an amendment because the trustee requires changes to the debtor's paperwork based on the testimony at the meeting of creditors.

Animals. An exemption category in many states. Some states specifically exempt pets or livestock and poultry. If your state simply allows you to exempt "animals," you may include livestock, poultry, or pets. Some states exempt only domestic animals, which are usually considered to be all animals except pets.

Annuity. A type of insurance policy that pays out during the life of the insured, unlike life insurance, which pays out at the insured's death. Once the insured reaches the age specified in the policy, he or she receives monthly payments until death.

Appliance. A household apparatus or machine, usually operated by electricity, gas, or propane. Examples include refrigerators, stoves, washing machines, dishwashers, vacuum cleaners, air conditioners, and toasters.

Arms and accoutrements. Arms are weapons (such as pistols, rifles, and swords); accoutrements are the furnishings of a soldier's outfit, such as a belt or pack, but not clothes or weapons.

Arms-length creditor. A creditor with whom the debtor deals in the normal course of business, as opposed to an insider (a friend, relative, or business partner).

Articles of adornment. See "jewelry."

Assessment benefits. See "stipulated insurance."

Assisted person. Any person contemplating or filing for bankruptcy who receives bankruptcy assistance, whose debts are primarily consumer debts, and whose nonexempt property is valued at less than $150,000. A person or an entity that offers help to an assisted person is called a "debt relief agency."

Automatic stay. An injunction automatically issued by the bankruptcy court when a debtor files for bankruptcy. The automatic stay prohibits most creditor collection activities, such as filing or continuing lawsuits, making written requests for payment, or notifying credit reporting bureaus of an unpaid debt.

Avails. Any amount available to the owner of an insurance policy other than the actual proceeds of the policy. Avails include dividend payments, interest, cash or surrender value (the money you'd get if you sold your policy back to the insurance company), and loan value (the amount of cash you can borrow against the policy).

Bankruptcy Abuse Prevention and Consumer Protection Act of 2005. The formal name of the new bankruptcy law that took effect on October 17, 2005.

Bankruptcy administrator. The official responsible for supervising the administration of bankruptcy cases, estates, and trustees in Alabama and North Carolina, where there is no U.S. Trustee.

Bankruptcy Appellate Panel. A specialized court that hears appeals of bankruptcy court decisions (available only in some regions).

Bankruptcy assistance. Goods or services provided to an "assisted person" for the purpose of providing information, advice, counsel, document preparation or filing, or attendance at a creditors' meeting; appearing in a case or proceeding on behalf of another person; or providing legal representation.

Bankruptcy Code. The federal law that governs the creation and operation of the bankruptcy courts and establishes bankruptcy procedures. (You can find the bankruptcy code in Title 11 of the United States Code.)

Bankruptcy estate. All of the property you own when you file for bankruptcy, except for most pensions and educational trusts. The trustee technically takes control of your bankruptcy estate for the duration of your case.

Bankruptcy lawyer. A lawyer who specializes in bankruptcy and is licensed to practice law in the federal courts.

Bankruptcy petition preparer. Any nonlawyer who helps someone with his or her bankruptcy. Bankruptcy petition preparers (BPPs) are a special type of debt relief agency, regulated by the U.S. Trustee. Because they are not lawyers, BPPs can't represent anyone in bankruptcy court or provide legal advice.

Bankruptcy Petition Preparer Fee Declaration. An official form bankruptcy petition preparers must file with the bankruptcy court to disclose their fees.

Bankruptcy Petition Preparer Notice to Debtor. A written notice that bankruptcy petition preparers must provide to debtors who use their services. The notice explains that bankruptcy petition preparers aren't attorneys and that they are permitted to perform only certain acts, such as entering information in the bankruptcy petition and schedules under the direction of their clients.

Benefit or benevolent society benefits. See "fraternal benefit society benefits."

Building materials. Items, such as lumber, brick, stone, iron, paint, and varnish, that are used to build or improve a structure.

Burial plot. A cemetery plot.

Business bankruptcy. A bankruptcy in which the debts arise primarily from the operation of a business, including bankruptcies filed by corporations, limited liability companies, and partnerships.

Certification. The act of signing a document under penalty of perjury. (The document that is signed is also called a certification.)

Chapter 7 bankruptcy. A liquidation bankruptcy, in which the trustee sells the debtor's nonexempt property and distributes the proceeds to the debtor's creditors. At the end of the case, the debtor receives a discharge of all remaining debts, except those that cannot legally be discharged.

Chapter 9 bankruptcy. A type of bankruptcy restricted to governmental units.

Chapter 11 bankruptcy. A type of bankruptcy intended to help a business reorganize its debt load in order to remain in business. A Chapter 11 bankruptcy is typically much more expensive than a Chapter 7 or 13 bankruptcy because all of the lawyers must be paid out of the bankruptcy estate.

Chapter 12 bankruptcy. A type of bankruptcy designed to help small farmers reorganize their debts.

Chapter 13 bankruptcy. A type of consumer bankruptcy designed to help individuals reorganize their debts and pay all or a portion of them over three to five years.

Chapter 13 plan. A document filed in a Chapter 13 bankruptcy in which the debtor shows how all of his or her projected disposable income will be used over a three- to five-year period to pay all mandatory debts—for example, back child support, taxes, and mortgage arrearages—as well as some or all unsecured, nonpriority debts, such as medical and credit card bills.

Claim. A creditor's assertion that the bankruptcy filer owes it a debt or an obligation.

Clothing. As an exemption category, the everyday clothes you and your family need for work, school, household use, and protection from the elements. In many states, luxury items and furs are not included in the clothing exemption category.

Codebtor. A person who assumes an equal responsibility, along with the debtor, to repay a debt or loan.

Collateral. Property pledged by a borrower as security for a loan.

Common law property states. States that don't use a community property system to classify marital property.

Community property. Certain property owned by married couples in Arizona, California, Idaho, Louisiana, New Mexico, Nevada, Texas, Washington, Wisconsin, and, if both spouses agree, Alaska. Very generally, all property acquired during the marriage is considered community property, belonging equally to both spouses, except for gifts and inheritances by one spouse. Similarly, all debts incurred during the marriage are considered community debts, owed equally by both spouses, with limited exceptions.

Complaint. A formal document that initiates a lawsuit.

Complaint to determine dischargeablity. A complaint initiating an adversary action in bankruptcy court that asks the court to decide whether a particular debt should be discharged at the end of the debtor's bankruptcy case.

Condominium. A building or complex in which separate units, such as townhouses or apartments, are owned by individuals, and the common areas (lobby, hallways, stairways, and so on) are jointly owned by the unit owners.

Confirmation. The bankruptcy judge's ruling approving a Chapter 13 plan.

Confirmation hearing. A court hearing conducted by a bankruptcy judge in which the judge decides whether a debtor's proposed Chapter 13 plan appears to be feasible and meets all applicable legal requirements.

Consumer bankruptcy. A bankruptcy in which a preponderance of the debt was incurred for personal, family, or household purposes.

Consumer debt. A debt incurred by an individual for personal, family, or household purposes.

Contingent debts. Debts that may be owed if certain events happen or conditions are satisfied.

Contingent interests in the estate of a decedent. The right to inherit property if one or more conditions to the inheritance are satisfied (for example, a debtor who will inherit property only if he survives his brother has a contingent interest).

Conversion. When a debtor who has filed one type of bankruptcy switches to another type—as when a Chapter 7 debtor converts to a Chapter 13 bankruptcy, or vice versa.

Cooperative housing. A building or another residential structure that is owned by a corporation formed by the residents. In exchange for purchasing stock in the corporation, the residents have the right to live in particular units.

Cooperative insurance. Compulsory employment benefits provided by a state or federal government, such as old age, survivors, disability, and health insurance, to assure a minimum standard of living for lower- and middle-income people. Also called social insurance.

Court clerk. The court employee who is responsible for accepting filings and other documents, and generally maintaining an accurate and efficient flow of paper and information in the court.

Cramdown. In a Chapter 13 bankruptcy, the act of reducing a secured debt to the replacement value of the collateral securing the debt.

Credit and debt counseling. Counseling that explores the possibility of repaying debts outside of bankruptcy and educates the debtor about credit, budgeting, and financial management. Under the new bankruptcy law, a debtor must undergo credit counseling with an approved provider before filing for bankruptcy.

Credit insurance. An insurance policy that covers a borrower for an outstanding loan. If the borrower dies or becomes disabled before paying off the loan, the policy will pay off the balance due.

Creditor. A person or an institution to which money is owed.

Creditor committee. In a Chapter 11 bankruptcy, a committee that represents the unsecured debtors in reorganization proceedings.

Creditor matrix. A specially formatted list of creditors that a debtor must file with the bankruptcy petition. The matrix helps the court notify creditors of the bankruptcy filing and the date and time set for the first meeting of creditors.

Creditors' meeting. See "341 hearing."

Crops. Products of the soil or earth that are grown and raised annually and gathered in a single season. Thus, oranges (on the tree or harvested) are crops; an orange tree isn't.

Current market value. What property could be sold for. This is how a debtor's property was previously valued for purposes of determining whether the property is protected by an applicable exemption. Under the new bankruptcy law, property must be valued at its "replacement cost."

Current monthly income. As defined by the new bankruptcy law, a bankruptcy filer's total gross income (whether taxable or not), averaged over the six-month period immediately preceding the month in which the bankruptcy is filed. The current monthly income is used to determine whether the debtor can file for Chapter 7 bankruptcy, among other things.

Debt. An obligation of any type, including a loan, credit, or promise to perform a contract or lease.

Debt relief agency. An umbrella term for any person or agency—including lawyers and bankruptcy petition preparers, but excluding banks, non-profit and government agencies, and employees of debt relief agencies—that provides bankruptcy assistance to a debtor. See "bankruptcy assistance" and "assisted person."

Debtor. Someone who owes money to another person or business. Also, the generic term used to refer to anyone who files for bankruptcy.

Declaration. A written statement that is made under oath but not witnessed by a notary public.

Declaration of homestead. A form filed with the county recorder's office to put on record your right to a homestead exemption. In most states, the homestead exemption is automatic—that is, you are not required to record a homestead declaration in order to claim the homestead exemption. A few states do require such a recording, however.

Disability benefits. Payments made under a disability insurance or retirement plan when the insured is unable to work (or retires early) because of disability, accident, or sickness.

Discharge. A court order, issued at the conclusion of a Chapter 7 or Chapter 13 bankruptcy case, which legally relieves the debtor of personal liability for debts that can be discharged in that type of bankruptcy.

Discharge exceptions. Debts that are not discharged in a bankruptcy case. The debtor continues to owe these debts even after the bankruptcy is concluded.

Discharge hearing. A hearing conducted by a bankruptcy court to explain the discharge, urge the debtor to stay out of debt, and review reaffirmation agreements to make sure they are feasible and fair.

Dischargeability action. An adversary action brought by a party who asks the court to determine whether a particular debt qualifies for discharge.

Dischargeable debt. A debt that is wiped out at the conclusion of a bankruptcy case, unless the judge decides that it should not be.

Dismissal. When the court orders a case to be closed without providing the relief available under the bankruptcy laws. For example, a Chapter 13 case might be dismissed because the debtor fails to propose a feasible plan; a Chapter 7 case might be dismissed for abuse.

Disposable income. The difference between a debtor's "current monthly income" and allowable expenses. This is the amount that the bankruptcy law deems available to pay into a Chapter 13 plan.

Domestic animals. See "animals."

Domestic support obligation. An obligation to pay alimony or child support to a spouse, child, or government entity pursuant to an order by a court or other governmental unit.

Doubling. The ability of married couples to double the amount of certain property exemptions when filing for bankruptcy together. The federal bankruptcy exemptions allow doubling. State laws vary—some permit doubling and some do not.

Education Individual Retirement Account. A type of account to which a person can contribute a certain amount of tax-deferred funds every year for the educational benefit of the debtor or certain relatives. Such an account is not part of the debtor's bankruptcy estate.

Emergency bankruptcy filing. An initial bankruptcy filing that includes only the petition and the creditor matrix, filed right away because the debtor needs the protection of the automatic stay to prevent a creditor from taking a certain action, such as a foreclosure. An emergency filing case will be dismissed if the other required documents and forms are not filed in a timely manner.

Endowment insurance. An insurance policy that gives an insured who lives for a specified time (the endowment period) the right to receive the face value of the policy (the amount paid at death). If the insured dies sooner, the beneficiary named in the policy receives the proceeds.

Equity. The amount you get to keep if you sell property—typically the property's market value, less the costs of sale and the value of any liens on the property.

ERISA-qualified benefits. Pensions that meet the requirements of the Employee Retirement Income Security Act (ERISA), a federal law that sets minimum standards for such plans and requires beneficiaries to receive certain notices.

Executory contract. A contract in which one or both parties still have a duty to carry out one or more of the contract's terms.

Exempt property. Property described by state and federal laws (exemptions) that a debtor is entitled to keep in a Chapter 7 bankruptcy. Exempt property cannot be taken and sold by the trustee for the benefit of the debtor's unsecured creditors.

Exemptions. State and federal laws specifying the types of property creditors are not entitled to take to satisfy a debt, and the bankruptcy trustee is not entitled to take and sell for the benefit of the debtor's unsecured creditors.

Farm tools. Tools used by a person whose primary occupation is farming. Some states limit farm tools of the trade to items that can be held in the hand, such as hoes, axes, pitchforks, shovels, scythes, and the like. In other states, farm tools also include plows, harnesses, mowers, reapers, and so on.

Federal exemptions. A list of exemptions contained in the federal bankruptcy code. Some states give debtors the option of using the federal exemptions rather than the state exemptions.

Federal Rules of Bankruptcy Procedure. A set of rules issued by the Administrative Office of the United States Courts, which govern bankruptcy court procedures.

Filing date. The date a bankruptcy petition in a particular case is filed. With few exceptions, debts incurred after the filing date are not discharged. Similarly, property owned before the filing date is part of the bankruptcy estate, while property acquired after the filing date is not.

Fines, penalties, and restitution. Debts owed to a court or a victim as a result of a sentence in a criminal matter. These debts are generally not dischargeable in bankruptcy.

Foreclosure. The process by which a creditor with a lien on real estate forces a sale of the property in order to collect on the lien. Foreclosure typically occurs when a homeowner defaults on a mortgage.

Fraternal benefit society benefits. Benefits, often group life insurance, paid for by fraternal societies, such as the Elks, Masons, Knights of Columbus, or the Knights of Maccabees, for their members. Also called benefit society, benevolent society, or mutual aid association benefits.

Fraud. Generally, an act that is intended to mislead another for the purpose of financial gain. In a bankruptcy case, fraud is any writing or representation intended to mislead creditors for the purpose of obtaining a loan or credit, or any act intended to mislead the bankruptcy court or the trustee.

Fraudulent transfer. In a bankruptcy case, a transfer of property to another for less than the property's value for the purpose of hiding the property from the bankruptcy trustee—for instance, when a debtor signs a car over to a relative to keep it out of the bankruptcy estate. Fraudulently transferred property can be recovered and sold by the trustee for the benefit of the creditors.

Fraudulently concealed assets. Property that a bankruptcy debtor deliberately fails to disclose as required by the bankruptcy rules.

Furnishings. An exemption category recognized in many states, which includes furniture, fixtures in your home (such as a heating unit, furnace, or built-in lighting), and other items with which a home is furnished, such as carpets and drapes.

Good faith. In a Chapter 13 case, when a debtor files for bankruptcy with the sincere purpose of paying off debts over the period of time required by law rather than for manipulative purposes—such as to prevent a foreclosure that by all rights should be allowed to proceed.

Goods and chattels. See "personal property."

Group life or group health insurance. A single insurance policy covering individuals in a group (for example, employees) and their dependents.

Head of household. A person who supports and maintains, in one household, one or more people who are closely related to the person by blood, marriage, or adoption. Also referred to as "head of family."

Health aids. Items needed to maintain their owner's health, such as a wheelchair, crutches, a prosthesis, or a hearing aid. Many states require that health aids be prescribed by a physician.

Health benefits. Benefits paid under health insurance plans, such as Blue Cross/Blue Shield, to cover the costs of health care.

Heirloom. An item with special monetary or sentimental value, which is passed down from generation to generation.

Home equity loan. A loan made to a homeowner on the basis of the equity in the home—and secured by the home in the same manner as a mortgage.

Homestead declaration. See "declaration of homestead."

Homestead exemption. A state or federal exemption applicable to property where the debtor lives when he or she files for bankruptcy—usually including boats and mobile homes.

Household good. As an exemption category, an item of permanent nature (as opposed to items consumed, like food or cosmetics) used in or about the house. This includes linens, dinnerware, utensils, pots and pans, and small electronic equipment like radios. Many state laws specifically list the types of household goods that fall within this exemption, as do the federal bankruptcy laws.

Householder. A person who supports and maintains a household, with or without other people. Also called a "housekeeper."

Impairs an exemption. When a lien, in combination with any other liens on the property and the amount the debtor is entitled to claim as exempt, exceeds the value of the property the debtor could claim in the absence of any liens. For example, if property is worth $15,000, there are $5,000 worth of liens on the property, and the debtor is entitled to a $5,000 exemption in the property, a lien that exceeded $5,000 would impair the debtor's exemption. Certain types of liens that impair an exemption may be removed (avoided) by the debtor if the court so orders.

Implement. As an exemption category, an instrument, tool, or utensil used by a person to accomplish his or her job.

In lieu of homestead (or burial) exemption. Designates an exemption that is available only if you don't claim the homestead (or burial) exemption.

Individual Debtor's Statement of Intention. An official bankruptcy form that debtors with secured debts must file to indicate what they want to do with the property that secures the debt. For instance, a debtor with a car note must indicate whether he or she wants to keep the car and continue the debt (reaffirmation), pay off the car note at a reduced price (redemption), or give the car back to the creditor and cancel the debt.

Injunction. A court order prohibiting a person or an entity from taking specified actions—for example, the automatic stay (in reality an automatic injunction), which prevents most creditors from trying to collect their debts.

Insider creditor. A creditor with whom the debtor has a personal relationship, such as a relative, friend, or business partner.

Intangible property. Property that cannot be physically touched, such as an ownership share in a corporation or a copyright. Documents—such as a stock certificate—may provide evidence of intangible property.

Involuntary dismissal. When a bankruptcy judge dismisses a case because the debtor fails to carry out his or her duties—such as filing papers in a timely manner and cooperating with the trustee—or because the debtor files the bankruptcy in bad faith or engages in abuse by wrongfully filing for Chapter 7 when he or she should have filed for Chapter 13.

Involuntary lien. A lien that is placed on the debtor's property without the debtor's consent—for instance, when the IRS places a lien on property for back taxes.

IRS expenses. A table of national and regional expense estimates published by the IRS. Debtors whose "current monthly income" is more than their state's "median family income" must use the IRS expenses to calculate their average net income in a Chapter 7 case, or their disposable income in a Chapter 13 case.

Jewelry. Items created for personal adornment; usually includes watches. Also called "articles of adornment."

Joint debtors. Married people who file for bankruptcy together and pay a single filing fee.

Judgment proof. A description of a person whose income and property are such that a creditor can't (or won't) seize them to enforce a money judgment—for example, a dwelling protected by a homestead exemption or a bank account containing only a few dollars.

Judicial lien. A lien created by the recording of a court money judgment against the debtor's property—usually real estate.

Lease. A contract that governs the relationship between an owner of property and a person who wishes to use the property for a specific period of time—as in car and real estate leases.

Lien. A legal claim against property that must be paid before title to the property can be transferred. Liens can also often be collected through repossession (personal property) or foreclosure (real estate), depending on the type of lien.

Lien avoidance. A bankruptcy procedure in which certain types of liens can be removed from certain types of property. Liens that are not avoided survive the bankruptcy even though the underlying debt may be cancelled—for instance, a lien remains on a car even if the debt evidenced by the car note is discharged in the bankruptcy.

Life estate. The right to live in, but not own, a specific home until your death.

Life insurance. A policy that provides for the payment of money to an individual (called the beneficiary) in the event of the death of another (called the insured). The policy matures (becomes payable) only when the insured dies.

Lifting the stay. When a bankruptcy court allows a creditor to continue with debt collection or other activities that are otherwise banned by the automatic stay. For instance, the court might allow a landlord to proceed with an eviction or a lender to repossess a car because the debtor has defaulted on the note.

Liquid assets. Cash or items that are easily convertible into cash, such as a money market account, stock, U.S. Treasury bill, or bank deposit.

Liquidated debt. An existing debt for a specified amount arising out of a contract or court judgment. In contrast, an unliquidated debt is a claim for an as-yet uncertain amount, such as for injuries suffered in a car accident before the case goes to court.

Lost future earnings. The portion of a lawsuit judgment intended to compensate an injured person for the money he or she won't be able to earn in the future because of the injury. Also called lost earnings payments or recoveries.

Luxuries. In bankruptcy, goods or services purchased by the debtor that a court decides were not appropriate in light of the debtor's insolvency. This might include vacations, jewelry, costly cars, or frequent meals at expensive restaurants.

Mailing matrix. See "creditor matrix."

Marital debts. Debts owed jointly by a married couple.

Marital property. Property owned jointly by a married couple.

Marital settlement agreement. An agreement between a divorcing couple that sets out who gets what percentage (or what specific items) of the marital property, who pays what marital debts, and who gets custody and pays child support if there are children of the marriage.

Materialmen's and mechanics' liens. Liens imposed by statute on real estate when suppliers of materials, labor, and contracting services used to improve the real estate are not properly compensated.

Matured life insurance benefits. Insurance benefits that are currently payable because the insured person has died.

Means test. A formula that uses predefined income and expense categories to determine whether a debtor whose income is more than the median family income for his or her state should be allowed to file a Chapter 7 bankruptcy.

Median family income. An annual income figure for which there are as many families with incomes below that level as there are above that level. The U.S. Census Bureau publishes median family income figures for each state and for different family sizes. In bankruptcy, the median family income is used as a basis for determining whether a debtor must pass the means test to file Chapter 7 bankruptcy, and whether a debtor filing a Chapter 13 bankruptcy must commit all his or her projected disposable income to a five-year repayment plan.

Meeting of creditors. See "341 hearing."

Mortgage. A contract in which a loan to purchase real estate is secured by the real estate as collateral. If the borrower defaults on loan payments, the lender can foreclose on the property.

Motion. A formal legal procedure in which the bankruptcy judge is asked to rule on a dispute in the bankruptcy case. To bring a motion, a party must file a document explaining what relief is requested, the facts of the dispute, and the legal reasons why the court should grant the relief. The party bringing the motion must mail these documents to all affected parties and let them know when the court will hear argument on the motion.

Motion to avoid judicial lien on real estate. A motion brought by a bankruptcy debtor that asks the bankruptcy court to remove a judicial lien on real estate because the lien impairs the debtor's homestead exemption.

Motion to lift stay. A motion in which a creditor asks the court for permission to continue a court action or collection activities in spite of the automatic stay.

Motor vehicle. A self-propelled vehicle suitable for use on a street or road. This includes a car, truck, motorcycle, van, and moped. See also "tools of the trade."

Musical instrument. An instrument having the capacity, when properly operated, to produce a musical sound. Pianos, guitars, drums, drum machines, synthesizers, and harmonicas are all musical instruments.

Mutual aid association benefits. See "fraternal benefit society benefits."

Mutual assessment or mutual life. See "stipulated insurance."

Necessities. Articles needed to sustain life, such as food, clothing, medical care, and shelter.

Newly discovered creditors. Creditors whom the debtor discovers after the bankruptcy is filed. If the case is still open, the debtor can amend the list to include the creditors; if the case is closed, it usually can be reopened to accommodate the amendment.

Nonbankruptcy federal exemptions. Federal laws that allow a debtor who has not filed for bankruptcy to keep creditors away from certain property. The debtor can also use these exemptions in bankruptcy if the debtor is using a state exemption system.

Nondischargeable debt. Debt that survives bankruptcy, such as back child support and most student loans.

Nonexempt property. Property in the bankruptcy estate that is unprotected by the exemption system available to the debtor (this is typically—but not always—the exemption system in the state where the debtor files bankruptcy). In a Chapter 7 bankruptcy, the trustee may sell it for the benefit of the debtor's unsecured creditors. In a Chapter 13 bankruptcy, debtors must propose a plan that pays their unsecured creditors at least the value of their unsecured property.

Nonpossessory non-purchase-money lien. A lien placed on property that is already owned by the debtor and is used as collateral for the loan without being possessed by the lender. In contrast, a non-purchase-money, possessory lien exists on collateral that is held by a pawnshop.

Nonpriority debt. A type of debt that is not entitled to be paid first in bankruptcy, as priority debts are. Nonpriority debts do not have to be paid in full in a Chapter 13 case.

Nonpriority, unsecured claim. A claim that is not for a priority debt (such as child support) and is not secured by collateral or other property. Typical examples include credit card debt, medical bills, and student loans. In a Chapter 13 repayment plan, nonpriority, unsecured claims are paid only after all other debts are paid.

Notice of appeal. A form that must be filed with a court when a party wishes to appeal a judgment or an order issued by the court. Often, the notice of appeal must be filed within ten days of the date the order or judgment is entered in the court's records.

Objection. A document one party files to oppose a proposed action by another party—for instance, when a creditor or trustee files an objection to a bankruptcy debtor's claim of exemption.

Order for relief. The court's automatic injunction against certain collection and other activities that might negatively affect the bankruptcy estate. Another name for the "automatic stay."

Oversecured debt. A debt that is secured by collateral that is worth more than the amount of the debt.

PACER. An online, fee-based database containing bankruptcy court dockets (records of proceedings in bankruptcy cases) and federal court documents, such as court rules and recent appellate court decisions.

Pain and suffering damages. The portion of a court judgment intended to compensate for past, present, and future mental and physical pain, suffering, impairment of ability to work, and mental distress caused by an injury.

Partially secured debt. A debt secured by collateral that is worth less than the debt itself—for instance, when a person owes $15,000 on a car that is worth only $10,000.

Party in interest. Any person or entity that has a financial interest in the outcome of a bankruptcy case, including the trustee, the debtor, and all creditors.

Pension. A fund into which payments are made to provide an employee with income after retirement. Typically, the beneficiary can't access the account before retirement without incurring a significant penalty, usually a tax. There are many types of pensions, including defined benefit pensions, provided by many large corporations, and individual pensions (such as 401(k) and IRA accounts). In bankruptcy, most pensions are not considered part of the bankruptcy estate and are therefore not affected by a bankruptcy filing.

Personal financial responsibility counseling. A two-hour class intended to teach good budget management. Every consumer bankruptcy filer must attend such a class in order to obtain a discharge in Chapter 7, Chapter 12, or Chapter 13 bankruptcy.

Personal injury cause of action. The right to seek compensation for physical and mental suffering, including injury to body, reputation, or both. For example, someone who is hit and injured by a car might have a personal injury cause of action against the driver.

Personal injury recovery. The portion of a lawsuit judgment or insurance settlement that is intended to compensate someone for physical and mental suffering, including physical injury, injury to

reputation, or both. Bankruptcy exemptions usually do not apply to compensation for pain or suffering or punitive damages—in other words, that part of the recovery can be taken by the trustee in a Chapter 7 case.

Personal property. All property not classified as real property, including tangible items, such as cars and jewelry, and intangible property, such as stocks and pensions.

Petition. The document a debtor files to officially begin a bankruptcy case and ask for relief. Other documents and schedules must be filed to support the petition at the time it is filed, or shortly afterwards.

Pets. See "animals."

Preference. A payment made by a debtor to a creditor within a defined period prior to filing for bankruptcy—within three months for arms-length creditors (regular commercial creditors) and one year for insider creditors (friends, family, or business associates). Because a preference gives that debtor an edge over other debtors in the bankruptcy case, the trustee can recover the preference and distribute it among all of the creditors.

Prepetition. Any time prior to the moment the bankruptcy petition is filed.

Prepetition counseling. Debt or credit counseling that occurs before the bankruptcy petition is filed—as opposed to personal financial management counseling, which occurs after the petition is filed.

Presumed abuse. In a Chapter 7 bankruptcy, when the debtor has a current monthly income in excess of the family median income for the state where the debtor lives, and has sufficient income to propose a Chapter 13 plan under the "means test." If abuse is presumed, the debtor has to prove that his or her Chapter 7 filing is not abusive in order to proceed further.

Primarily business debts. When the majority of debt owed by a bankruptcy debtor—in dollar terms—arises from debts incurred to operate a business.

Primarily consumer debts. When the majority of debt owed by a bankruptcy debtor—in dollar terms—arises from debts incurred for personal or family purposes.

Priority claim. See "priority debt."

Priority creditor. A creditor who has filed a Proof of Claim showing that the debtor owes it a priority debt.

Priority debt. A type of debt that is paid first if there are distributions to be made from the bankruptcy estate. Priority debts include alimony and child support, fees owed to the trustee and attorneys in the case, and wages owed to employees. With one exception (back child support obligations assigned to government entities), priority claims must be paid in full in a Chapter 13 bankruptcy.

Proceeds for damaged exempt property. Money received through insurance coverage, arbitration, mediation, settlement, or a lawsuit to pay for exempt property that has been damaged or destroyed. For example, if a debtor had the right to use a $30,000 homestead exemption, but his or her home was destroyed by fire, the debtor can instead exempt $30,000 of the insurance proceeds.

Projected disposable income. The amount of income a debtor will have left over each month, after deducting allowable expenses, payments on mandatory debts, and administrative expenses from his or her current monthly income. This is the amount the debtor must pay toward his or her unsecured nonpriority debts in a Chapter 13 plan.

Proof of Claim. A formal document filed by bankruptcy creditors in a bankruptcy case to assert their right to payments from the bankruptcy estate, if any payments are made.

Proof of Service. A document signed under penalty of perjury by the person serving a document showing how the service was made, who made it, and when.

Property of the estate. See "bankruptcy estate."

Purchase-money loans. Loans that are made to purchase specific property items, and that use the property as collateral to assure repayment, such as car loans and mortgages.

Purchase-money security interest. A claim on property owned by the holder of a loan that was used to purchase the property and that is secured by the property (as collateral).

Reaffirmation. An agreement entered into after a bankruptcy filing (postpetition) between the debtor and a creditor in which the debtor agrees to repay all or part of a prepetition debt after the bankruptcy is over. For instance, a debtor makes an agreement with the holder of a car note that the debtor can keep the car and will continue to pay the debt after bankruptcy.

Real property. Real estate (land and buildings on the land, usually including mobile homes attached to a foundation).

Reasonable investigation. A bankruptcy attorney's obligation, under the new bankruptcy law, to look into the information provided to them by their clients.

Redemption. In a Chapter 7 bankruptcy, when the debtor obtains legal title to collateral for a secured debt by paying the secured creditor the replacement value of the collateral in a lump sum. For example, a debtor may redeem a car note by paying the lender the replacement value of the car (what a retail vendor would charge for the car, considering its age and condition).

Reopen a case. To open a closed bankruptcy case—usually for the purpose of adding an overlooked creditor or filing a motion to avoid an overlooked lien. A debtor must request that the court reopen the case.

Repayment plan. An informal plan to repay creditors most or all of what they are owed outside of bankruptcy. Also refers to the plan proposed by a debtor in a Chapter 13 case.

Replacement cost. What it would cost to replace a particular item by buying it from a retail vendor, considering its age and condition—for instance, when buying a car from a used car dealer, furniture from a used furniture shop, or electronic equipment on eBay.

Repossession. When a secured creditor takes property used as collateral because the debtor has defaulted on the loan secured by the collateral.

Request to lift the stay. A written request filed in bankruptcy court by a creditor, which seeks permission to engage in debt collection activity otherwise prohibited by the automatic stay.

Schedule A. The official bankruptcy form a debtor must file to describe all of his or her real property.

Schedule B. The official bankruptcy form a debtor must file to describe all personal property owned by the debtor, including tangible property, such as jewelry and vehicles, and intangible property, such as investments and accounts receivable.

Schedule C. The official bankruptcy form a debtor must file to describe the property the debtor is claiming as exempt and the legal basis for the claims of exemption.

Schedule D. The official bankruptcy form a debtor must file to describe all secured debts owed by the debtor, such as car notes and mortgages.

Schedule E. The official bankruptcy form a debtor must file to describe all priority debts owed by the debtor, such as back child support and taxes.

Schedule F. The official bankruptcy form a debtor must file to describe all nonpriority, unsecured debts owed by the debtor, such as most credit card and medical bills.

Schedule G. The official bankruptcy form a debtor must file to describe any leases and executory contracts (contracts under which one or both parties still have obligations) to which the debtor is a party.

Schedule H. The official bankruptcy form a debtor must file to describe all codebtors that might be affected by the bankruptcy.

Schedule I. The official bankruptcy form a debtor must file to describe the debtor's income.

Schedule J. The official bankruptcy form a debtor must file to describe the debtor's actual monthly expenses.

Schedules. Official bankruptcy forms a debtor must file, detailing the debtor's property, debts, income, and expenses.

Second deed of trust. A loan against real estate made after the original mortgage (or first deed of trust). Most home equity loans are second deeds of trust.

Secured claim. A debt secured by collateral under a written agreement (for instance, a mortgage or car note) or by operation of law—such as a tax lien.

Secured creditor. The owner of a secured claim.

Secured debt. A debt secured by collateral.

Secured property. Property that is collateral for a secured debt.

Security interest. A claim to property used as collateral. For instance, a lender on a car note retains legal title to the car until the loan is paid off.

Serial bankruptcy filing. A practice used by some debtors to file and dismiss one bankruptcy after another to obtain the protection of the automatic stay, even though the bankruptcies themselves offer no debt relief—for instance, when a debtor files successive Chapter 13 cases to prevent foreclosure of his or her home even though there are no debts to repay.

Sickness benefits. See "disability benefits."

State exemptions. State laws that specify the types of property creditors are not entitled to take to satisfy a debt, and the bankruptcy trustee is not entitled to take and sell for the benefit of the debtor's unsecured creditors.

Statement of Affairs. The official bankruptcy form a debtor must file to describe the debtor's legal, economic, and business transactions for the several years prior to filing, including gifts, preferences, income, closing of deposit accounts, lawsuits, and other information that the trustee needs to assess the legitimacy of the bankruptcy and the true extent of the bankruptcy estate.

Statement of Current Monthly Income and Disposable Income Calculation. The official bankruptcy form a debtor must file in a Chapter 13 case, setting out the debtor's current monthly income and calculating the debtor's projected disposable income that will determine how much will be paid to the debtor's unsecured creditors.

Statement of Current Monthly Income and Means Test Calculation. The official bankruptcy form a debtor must file in a Chapter 7 filing that shows the debtor's current monthly income, calculates whether the debtor's income is higher than the state's median family income, and, if so, uses the means test to determine whether a Chapter 7 bankruptcy would constitute abuse.

Statement of Intention. The official bankruptcy form a debtor must file in a Chapter 7 case to tell the court and secured creditors how the debtor plans to treat his or her secured debts—that is, reaffirm the debt, redeem the debt, or surrender the property and discharge the debt.

Statement of Social Security Number. The official bankruptcy form a debtor must file to disclose the debtor's complete Social Security number.

Statutory lien. A lien imposed on property by law, such as tax liens and mechanics' liens, as opposed to voluntary liens (such as mortgages) and liens arising from court judgments (judicial liens).

Stay. See "automatic stay."

Stipulated insurance. An insurance policy that allows the insurance company to assess an amount on the insured, above the standard premium payments, if the company experiences losses worse than had been calculated into the standard premium. Also called assessment, mutual assessment, or mutual life insurance.

Stock options. A contract between a corporation and an employee that gives the employee the right to purchase corporate stock at a specific price mentioned in the contract (the strike price).

Strip down of lien. In a Chapter 13 bankruptcy, when the amount of a lien on collateral is reduced to the collateral's replacement value. See "cramdown."

Student loan. A type of loan made for educational purposes by nonprofit or commercial lenders with repayment and interest terms dictated by federal law. Student loans are not dischargeable in bankruptcy unless the debtor can show that repaying the loan would impose an "undue hardship."

Substantial abuse. Under the old bankruptcy law, filing a Chapter 7 bankruptcy when a Chapter 13 bankruptcy was feasible.

Suits, executions, garnishments, and attachments. Activities engaged in by creditors to enforce money judgments, typically involving the seizure of wages and bank accounts.

Summary of Schedules. The official bankruptcy form a debtor must file to summarize the property and debt information contained in a debtor's schedules.

Surrender value. See "avails."

Surrendering collateral. In Chapter 7 bankruptcy, the act of returning collateral to a secured lender in order to discharge the underlying debt—for example, returning a car to discharge the car note.

Tangible personal property. See "tangible property" and "personal property."

Tangible property. Property that may be physically touched. Examples include money, furniture, cars, jewelry, artwork, and houses. Compare "intangible property."

Tax lien. A statutory lien imposed on property to secure payment of back taxes—typically income and property taxes.

Tenancy by the entirety. A way that married couples can hold title to property in about half of the states. When one spouse dies, the surviving spouse automatically owns 100% of the property. In most cases, this type of property is not part of the bankruptcy estate if only one spouse files.

To ___ acres. A limitation on the size of a homestead that may be exempted.

Tools of the trade. Items needed to perform a line of work that a debtor is currently doing and relying on for support. For a mechanic, plumber, or carpenter, for example, tools of trade are the implements used to repair, build, and install. Traditionally, tools of the trade were limited to items that could be held in the hand. Most states, however, now embrace a broader definition, and a debtor may be able to fit many items under a tool of the trade exemption.

Transcript of tax return. A summary of a debtor's tax return provided by the IRS upon the debtor's request, usually acceptable as a substitute for the return in the instances when a return must be filed under the new bankruptcy law.

Trustee. An official appointed by the bankruptcy court to carry out the administrative tasks associated with a bankruptcy and to seize and sell nonexempt property in the bankruptcy estate for the benefit of the debtor's unsecured creditors.

U.S. Trustee. An official employed by the Office of the U.S. Trustee (a division of the U.S. Department of Justice) who is responsible for overseeing the bankruptcy trustees, regulating credit and personal financial management counselors, regulating bankruptcy petition preparers, auditing bankruptcy cases, ferreting out fraud, and generally making sure that the bankruptcy laws are obeyed.

Undersecured debt. A debt secured by collateral that is worth less than the debt.

Undue hardship. The conditions under which a debtor may discharge a student loan—for example, when the debtor has no income and little chance of earning enough to repay the loan in the future.

Unexpired lease. A lease that is still in effect.

Unmatured life insurance. A policy that is not yet payable because the insured is still alive.

Unscheduled debt. A debt that is not included in the schedules accompanying a bankruptcy filing, perhaps because it was overlooked or intentionally left out.

Unsecured priority claims. Priority claims that aren't secured by collateral, such as back child support or taxes for which no lien has been placed on the debtor's property.

Valuation of property. The act of determining the replacement value of property for the purpose of describing it in the bankruptcy schedules, determining whether it is protected by an applicable exemption, redeeming secured property, or cramming down a lien in Chapter 13 bankruptcy.

Voluntary dismissal. When a bankruptcy debtor dismisses his or her Chapter 7 or Chapter 13 case on his or her own, without coercion by the court.

Voluntary lien. A lien agreed to by the debtor, as when the debtor signs a mortgage, car note, or second deed of trust.

Weekly net earnings. The earnings a debtor has left after mandatory deductions, such as income tax, mandatory union dues, and Social Security contributions, have been subtracted from the debtor's gross income.

Wildcard exemption. A dollar value that the debtor can apply to any type of property to make it—or more of it—exempt. In some states, filers may use the unused portion of a homestead exemption as a wildcard exemption.

Willful and malicious act. An act done with the intent to cause harm. In a Chapter 7 bankruptcy, a debt arising from the debtor's willful and malicious act is not discharged if the victim proves to the bankruptcy court's satisfaction that the act occurred.

Willful or malicious act resulting in a civil judgment. A bad act that was careless or reckless, but was not necessarily intended to cause harm. In a Chapter 13 case, a debt arising from the debtor's act that was either willful or malicious is not discharged if it is part of a civil judgment.

Wrongful death cause of action. The right to seek compensation for having to live without a deceased person. Usually only the spouse and children of the deceased have a wrongful death cause of action.

Wrongful death recoveries. The portion of a lawsuit judgment intended to compensate a plaintiff for having to live without a deceased person. The compensation is intended to cover the earnings and the emotional comfort and support the deceased would have provided.

State and Federal Exemption Charts

The charts in this appendix summarize the laws that determine how much property a debtor can keep when filing for Chapter 7 bankruptcy. The charts are divided into categories of property, such as insurance, personal property, and wages. Following each exemption, we list the numerical citation to the state statute that includes the exemption. You'll need this information to complete your bankruptcy forms, as explained in Ch. 6.

The states are listed alphabetically, followed by the federal exemptions. (We also note the states that allow you to choose between the federal and state bankruptcy exemptions—see Ch. 3 for more information.)

> **RELATED TOPIC**
> **Need help understanding a term?** Many of the categories, types of property, and other terms used in these charts are defined in the Glossary, which you'll find right before this appendix.

Doubling

When a married couple files for bankruptcy jointly, federal law and the laws of many states allow them each to claim the full amount of an exemption. (11 U.S.C. § 522.) Because a couple gets to claim twice the amount available to those who file alone, this practice is informally known as "doubling."

Not all states allow doubling, however. And some states allow married couples to double only certain exemptions (for example, they might be able to double personal property exemptions but not the homestead exemption). In the charts that follow, we indicate exemptions that cannot be doubled (and states that don't allow doubling at all). Unless you see a note stating that you cannot double, assume that you can.

Residency Requirements for Claiming State Exemptions

Usually a bankruptcy filer uses the bankruptcy exemptions in the state where he or she resides (or the federal exemptions if allowed by that state.) However, some filers will have to use the exemptions of the state where they *used* to live. See Ch. 3 for detailed information.

Wage Garnishment Laws and Exemptions in Bankruptcy

Almost every state has a wage garnishment law that applies to judgment creditors, limiting how much they can take from your paycheck. In most states, you can use the wage garnishment law as an exemption in bankruptcy. Some states, however, don't allow this. If your state doesn't let bankruptcy filers use the wage garnishment law as an exemption, we indicate that on the chart. Some states have a specific statute that exempts a certain portion of wages in bankruptcy—obviously, you can use this in bankruptcy.

The federal bankruptcy exemptions do not have a separate exemption for wages. If you use the federal exemptions (assuming your state gives you the choice), the only way you can protect wages is by using the wildcard exemption.

What Income Is Exempt?

In most states, you can use the wage garnishment law to protect income that was already earned but not yet received on the day you filed for bankruptcy—called "earned but unpaid wages."

In some states, the wage garnishment exemption also protects wages you received before you filed for bankruptcy (it's easiest to claim the exemption if these wages are not mixed with other funds). In other states, the wage garnishment exemption does not protect wages that you received prior to filing for bankruptcy.

Some state exemptions protect all kinds of "earnings," regardless of type, while others protect only wages for the "performance of services," and exclude other kinds of income.

Checking the Law in Your State

Before relying on a wage garnishment statute to protect your wages, make sure that the judge in your jurisdiction agrees that the garnishment statute creates an exemption that can be used in bankruptcy. Often, the best way to do this is to ask a local bankruptcy attorney. (Many provide free initial consultations.)

You can also find information about this issue on www.legalconsumer.com. It tracks a dozen or so collected cases on wage garnishment and bankruptcy (search for "Do wage garnishment laws create an exemption in bankruptcy?").

Retirement Accounts

Virtually all types of tax-exempt retirement accounts are exempt in bankruptcy, whether you use the state or federal exemptions. You can exempt 401(k)s, 403(b)s, profit-sharing and money purchase plans, IRAs (including Roth, SEP, and SIMPLE IRAs), and defined-benefit plans.

These exemptions are unlimited—that is, the entire account is exempt, regardless of how much money is in it—except in the case of traditional and Roth IRAs. For these types of IRAs only, the exemption is limited to a total value of $1,245,475 per person (this figure will be adjusted every three years for inflation). If you have more than one traditional or Roth IRA, you don't get to exempt $1,245,475 per account; your total exemption, no matter how many accounts you have, is $1,245,475.

If you are using the federal bankruptcy exemptions, you can find this new retirement account provision at 11 U.S.C. § 522(d)(12). If you are using state exemptions, cite 11 U.S.C. § 522(b)(3)(C) as the applicable exemption when you complete your bankruptcy papers.

Confirm Exemptions Before Relying on Them

The exemptions in the following charts were current when this book went to press, but your state may have changed the law since then. In addition, states often carve out exceptions to the exemptions, which are far too detailed to list here. For instance, even if an item is listed as exempt in one of these charts, you might have to give it up to pay child support or a tax debt.

Before relying on any particular exemption, consider:

- reading the exemption statute yourself, using the research information in Ch. 10, and
- cross-checking the chart's information against the exemptions for your state listed on www. legalconsumer.com.

Last, but certainly not least, consult with a bankruptcy lawyer.

CAUTION
These charts provide general information only. There are exceptions to state exemption laws that are much too detailed to include here. Consider doing further legal research or consulting with an attorney about the exemptions you plan to claim, particularly if you anticipate— or are facing—a challenge to your exemption claim.

Alabama

Federal bankruptcy exemptions not available. All law references are to Alabama Code unless otherwise noted.

ASSET	EXEMPTION	LAW
homestead	Real property or mobile home to $5,000; property cannot exceed 160 acres	6-10-2
	Must record homestead declaration before attempted sale of home	6-10-20
insurance	Annuity proceeds or avails to $250 per month	27-14-32
	Disability proceeds or avails to an average of $250 per month	27-14-31
	Fraternal benefit society benefits	27-34-27
	Life insurance proceeds or avails	6-10-8; 27-14-29
	Life insurance proceeds or avails if clause prohibits proceeds from being used to pay beneficiary's creditors	27-15-26
	Mutual aid association benefits	27-30-25
pensions	Tax-exempt retirement accounts, including 401(k)s, 403(b)s, profit-sharing and money purchase plans, SEP and SIMPLE IRAs, and defined-benefit plans	11 U.S.C. § 522(b)(3)(C)
	Traditional and Roth IRAs to $1,245,475 per person	11 U.S.C. § 522(b)(3)(C); (n)
	IRAs, Roth IRAs & other retirement accounts	19-3B-508
	Judges (only payments being received)	12-18-10(a),(b)
	Law enforcement officers	36-21-77
	Spendthrift trusts (with exceptions)	19-3B-501 to 503
	State employees	36-27-28
	Teachers	16-25-23
personal property	Books of debtor & family	6-10-6
	Burial place for self & family	6-10-5
	Church pew for self & family	6-10-5
	Clothing of debtor & family	6-10-6
	Family portraits or pictures	6-10-6
public benefits	Aid to blind, aged, disabled & other public assistance, including earned income tax credit(*In re James*, 406 F. 3d 1340 (11th Cir 2005))	38-4-8; 38-5-5
	Crime victims' compensation	15-23-15(e)
	Southeast Asian War POWs' benefits	31-7-1; 31-7-2
	Unemployment compensation	25-4-140
	Workers' compensation	25-5-86
tools of trade	Arms, uniforms, equipment that state military personnel are required to keep	31-2-78
wages	With respect to consumer loans, consumer credit sales & consumer leases, 75% of weekly net earnings or 30 times the federal minimum hourly wage; all other cases, 75% of earned but unpaid wages; bankruptcy judge may authorize more for low-income debtors	5-19-15; 6-10-7
wildcard	$3,000 of any personal property, except wages	6-10-6; 6-10-126

Alaska

Alaska exemption amounts are adjusted regularly by administrative order. Current amounts are found at 8 Alaska Admin. Code tit. 8, § 95.030. Amounts reflect adjustment as of 10/1/2012.

ASSET	EXEMPTION	LAW
homestead	$72,900 (joint owners may each claim a portion, but total can't exceed $72,900)	09.38.010(a)
insurance	Disability benefits	09.38.015(b); 09.38.030(e)(1),(5)
	Fraternal benefit society benefits	21.84.240
	Life insurance or annuity contracts, total avails to $500,000	09.38.025
	Medical, surgical, or hospital benefits	09.38.015(a)(3)
miscellaneous	Alimony, to extent wages exempt	09.38.030(e)(2)
	Child support payments made by collection agency	09.38.015(b)
	Liquor licenses	09.38.015(a)(7)
	Property of business partnership	09.38.100(b)
pensions	Tax-exempt retirement accounts, including 401(k)s, 403(b)s, profit-sharing and money purchase plans, SEP and SIMPLE IRAs, and defined-benefit plans	11 U.S.C. § 522(b)(3)(C)
	Traditional and Roth IRAs to $1,245,475 per person	11 U.S.C. § 522(b)(3)(C); (n)
	Elected public officers (only benefits building up)	09.38.015(b)
	ERISA-qualified benefits deposited more than 120 days before filing bankruptcy	09.38.017
	Judicial employees (only benefits building up)	09.38.015(b)
	Public employees (only benefits building up)	09.38.015(b); 39.35.505
	Roth & traditional IRAs, medical savings accounts	09.38.017(e)(3)
	Teachers (only benefits building up)	09.38.015(b)
	Other pensions, to extent wages exempt (only payments being received)	09.38.030(e)(5)
personal property	Books, musical instruments, clothing, family portraits, household goods & heirlooms to $4,050 total	09.38.020(a)
	Building materials	34.35.105
	Burial plot	09.38.015(a)(1)
	Cash or other liquid assets to $1,890; for sole wage earner in household, $2,970 (restrictions apply—see *wages*)	09.38.030(b)
	Deposit in apartment or condo owners' association	09.38.010(e)
	Health aids needed	09.38.015(a)(2)
	Jewelry to $1,350	09.38.020(b)
	Money held in mortgage escrow accounts after July 1, 2008	09.38.015(e)
	Motor vehicle to $4,050; vehicle's market value can't exceed $27,000	09.38.020(e)
	Personal injury recoveries, to extent wages exempt	09.38.030(e)(3)
	Pets to $1,350	09.38.020(d)
	Proceeds for lost, damaged, or destroyed exempt property	09.38.060
	Tuition credits under an advance college tuition payment contract	09.38.015(a)(8)
	Wrongful death recoveries, to extent wages exempt	09.38.030(e)(3)

public benefits	Adult assistance to elderly, blind, disabled	47.25.550
	Alaska benefits for low-income seniors	09.38.015(a)(11)
	Alaska longevity bonus	09.38.015(a)(5)
	Crime victims' compensation	09.38.015(a)(4)
	Federally exempt public benefits paid or due	09.38.015(a)(6)
	General relief assistance	47.25.210
	Senior care (prescription drug) benefits	09.38.015(a)(10)
	20% of permanent fund dividends	43.23.065
	Unemployment compensation	09.38.015(b); 23.20.405
	Workers' compensation	23.30.160
tools of trade	Implements, books & tools of trade to $3,780	09.38.020(c)
wages	Weekly net earnings to $473; for sole wage earner in a household, $743; if you don't receive weekly or semimonthly pay, you can claim $1,890 in cash or liquid assets paid any month; for sole wage earner in household, $2,970	9.38.030(a),(b); 9.38.050(b)
wildcard	None	

Arizona

Federal bankruptcy exemptions not available. All law references are to Arizona Revised Statutes unless otherwise noted.

ASSET	EXEMPTION	LAW
homestead	Real property, an apartment, or mobile home you occupy to $150,000; sale proceeds exempt 18 months after sale or until new home purchased, whichever occurs first (spouses may not double)	33-1101(A)
	May record homestead declaration to clarify which one of multiple eligible parcels is being claimed as homestead	33-1102
insurance	Fraternal benefit society benefits	20-877
	Group life insurance policy or proceeds	20-1132
	Health, accident, or disability benefits	33-1126(A)(4)
	Life insurance cash value or proceeds, or annuity contract if owned at least two years and beneficiary is dependent family member	33-1126(A)(6); 20-1131(D)
	Life insurance proceeds to $20,000 if beneficiary is spouse or child	33-1126(A)(1)
miscellaneous	Alimony, child support needed for support	33-1126(A)(3)
	Minor child's earnings, unless debt is for child	33-1126(A)(2)
pensions see also wages	Tax-exempt retirement accounts, including 401(k)s, 403(b)s, profit-sharing and money purchase plans, SEP and SIMPLE IRAs, and defined-benefit plans	11 U.S.C. § 522(b)(3)(C)
	Traditional and Roth IRAs to $1,245,475 per person	11 U.S.C. § 522(b)(3)(C); (n)
	Board of regents members, faculty, & administrative officers under board's jurisdiction	15-1628(I)
	District employees	48-227

pensions (continued)	ERISA-qualified benefits deposited over 120 days before filing	33-1126(B)
	IRAs & Roth IRAs (*In re Herrscher*, 121 B.R. 29 (D. Ariz. 1989))	33-1126(B)
	Firefighters	9-968
	Police officers	9-931
	Public Safety Personnel Retirement System	38-850(c)
	Rangers	41-955
	State employees' retirement & disability	38-792; 38-797.11
personal property *spouses may double all personal property*	Household furniture & appliances not covered by other exemptions to $6,000 total	33-1123
	Bank deposit to $300 in one account	33-1126(A)(9)
	Bible; bicycle; sewing machine; typewriter; computer; burial plot; rifle, pistol, or shotgun to $1,000 total	33-1125
	Books to $250; clothing to $500; wedding & engagement rings to $2,000; watch to $150; pets, horses, milk cows & poultry to $800; musical instruments to $400	33-1125
	Food & fuel to last 6 months	33-1124
	Funeral deposits to $5,000	32-1391.05(4)
	Health aids	33-1125(9)
	Motor vehicle to $6,000 ($12,000, if debtor is physically disabled)	33-1125(8)
	Prepaid rent or security deposit to $2,000 or 1½ times your rent, whichever is less, in lieu of homestead	33-1126(C)
	Proceeds for sold or damaged exempt property	33-1126(A)(5),(8)
	Wrongful death awards	12-592
public benefits	Unemployment compensation	23-783(A)
	Welfare benefits	46-208
	Workers' compensation	23-1068(B)
tools of trade *husband & wife may double*	Arms, uniforms, & accoutrements of profession or office required by law	33-1130(3)
	Farm machinery, utensils, seed, instruments of husbandry, feed, grain, & animals to $5,000 total	33-1130(2)
	Library & teaching aids of teacher	33-1127
	Tools, equipment, instruments, & books to $2,500	33-1130(1)
wages	75% of earned but unpaid weekly net earnings or 30 times the federal minimum hourly wage; 50% of wages for support orders; bankruptcy judge may authorize more for low-income debtors	33-1131
wildcard	None	

Arkansas

Federal bankruptcy exemptions available. All law references are to Arkansas Code Annotated unless otherwise noted.

Note: In 1990, the 8th Circuit Court of Appeals declared Arkansas' bankruptcy exemption statute (found at Ark. Code Ann. § 16-66-218) unconstitutional for bankruptcy purposes as it relates to personal property. (*In re Holt*, 894 F.2d 1005 (8th Cir. 1990).) The court said that the Arkansas Constitution's provision of a $200 exemption for any personal property ($500 if married) acted as a cap and overrode the more generous exemption amounts in the statute. The personal property exemptions may be used in a nonbankruptcy context, however.

ASSET	EXEMPTION	LAW
homestead *choose Option 1 or 2*	1. For married person or head of family: unlimited exemption on real or personal property used as residence to ¼ acre in city, town, or village, or 80 acres elsewhere; if property is between ¼ and 1 acre in city, town, or village, or 80 to 160 acres elsewhere, additional limit is $2,500; homestead may not exceed 1 acre in city, town, or village, or 160 acres elsewhere (spouses may not double)	Constitution 9-3; 9-4, 9-5; 16-66-210;16-66-218(b)(3), (4); *In re Stevens*, 829 F.2d 693 (8th Cir. 1987)
	2. Real or personal property used as residence to $800 if single; $1,250 if married	16-66-218(a)(1)
insurance	Annuity contract	23-79-134
	Disability benefits	23-79-133
	Fraternal benefit society benefits	23-74-403
	Group life insurance	23-79-132
	Life, health, accident, or disability cash value or proceeds paid or due to $500	16-66-209; Constitution 9-1, 9-2; *In re Holt*, 894 F.2d 1005 (8th Cir. 1990)
	Life insurance proceeds if clause prohibits proceeds from being used to pay beneficiary's creditors	23-79-131
	Life insurance proceeds or avails if beneficiary isn't the insured	23-79-131
	Mutual assessment life or disability benefits to $1,000	23-72-114
	Stipulated insurance premiums	23-71-112
pensions	Tax-exempt retirement accounts, including 401(k)s, 403(b)s, profit-sharing and money purchase plans, SEP and SIMPLE IRAs, and defined-benefit plans	11 U.S.C. § 522(b)(3)(C)
	Traditional and Roth IRAs to $1,245,475 per person	11 U.S.C. § 522(b)(3)(C); (n)
	Disabled firefighters	24-11-814
	Disabled police officers	24-11-417
	Firefighters	24-10-616
	IRA deposits to $20,000 if deposited over 1 year before filing for bankruptcy	16-66-218(b)(16)
	Police officers	24-10-616
	School employees	24-7-715
	State police officers	24-6-205; 24-6-223

ASSET	EXEMPTION	LAW
personal property	Burial plot to 5 acres, if choosing federal homestead exemption (Option 2)	16-66-207; 16-66-218(a)(1)
	Clothing	Constitution 9-1, 9-2
	Prepaid funeral trusts	23-40-117
public benefits	Crime victims' compensation	16-90-716(e)
	Unemployment compensation	11-10-109
	Workers' compensation	11-9-110
tools of trade	Implements, books & tools of trade to $750	16-66-218(a)(4)
wages	Earned but unpaid wages due for 60 days; in no event less than $25 per week	16-66-208; 16-66-218(b)(6)
wildcard	$500 of any personal property if married or head of family; $200 if not married	Constitution 9-1, 9-2

California—System 1

Federal bankruptcy exemptions not available. California has two systems; you must select one or the other. All law references are to California Code of Civil Procedure unless otherwise noted. Many exemptions do not apply to claims for child support.

Note: California's exemption amounts are no longer updated in the statutes themselves. California Code of Civil Procedure Section 740.150 deputized the California Judicial Council to update the exemption amounts every three years. (The next revision will be in 2016.) As a result, the amounts listed in this chart will not match the amounts that appear in the cited statutes. The current exemption amounts can be found on the California Judicial Council website, www.courts.ca.gov/forms.htm.

ASSET	EXEMPTION	LAW
homestead	Real or personal property you occupy including mobile home, boat, stock cooperative, community apartment, planned development, or condo to $75,000 if single & not disabled; $100,000 for families if no other member has a homestead (if only one spouse files, may exempt one-half of amount if home held as community property & all of amount if home held as tenants in common); $175,000 if 65 or older, or physically or mentally disabled; $175,000 if 55 or older, single & earn gross annual income under $25,000 or married & earn gross annual income under $35,000 & creditors seek to force the sale of your home; forced sale proceeds received exempt for 6 months after (spouses may not double); separated married debtor may claim homestead in community property homestead occupied by other spouse	704.710; 704.720; 704.730; *In re McFall*, 112 B.R. 336 (9th Cir. B.A.P. 1990)
	May file homestead declaration to protect exemption amount from attachment of judicial liens and to protect proceeds of voluntary sale for 6 months	704.920
insurance	Disability or health benefits	704.130
	Fidelity bonds	Labor 404
	Fraternal benefit society benefits	704.170
	Fraternal unemployment benefits	704.120
	Homeowners' insurance proceeds for 6 months after received, to homestead exemption amount	704.720(b)
	Life insurance proceeds if clause prohibits proceeds from being used to pay beneficiary's creditors	Ins. 10132; Ins. 10170; Ins. 10171

insurance (continued)	Matured life insurance benefits needed for support	704.100(c)
	Unmatured life insurance policy cash surrender value completely exempt; loan value exempt to $12,200	704.100(b)
miscellaneous	Business or professional licenses	695.060
	Inmates' trust funds to $1,525 (spouses may not double)	704.090
	Property of business partnership	Corp. 16501-04
pensions	Tax-exempt retirement accounts, including 401(k)s, 403(b)s, profit-sharing and money purchase plans, SEP and SIMPLE IRAs, and defined-benefit plans	11 U.S.C. § 522(b)(3)(C)
	Traditional and Roth IRAs to $1,245,475 per person	11 U.S.C. § 522(b)(3)(C); (n)
	County employees	Gov't 31452
	County firefighters	Gov't 32210
	County peace officers	Gov't 31913
	Private retirement benefits, including IRAs & Keoghs	704.115
	Public employees	Gov't 21255
	Public retirement benefits	704.110
personal property	Appliances, furnishings, clothing, & food	704.020
	Bank deposits from Social Security Administration to $3,050 ($4,575 for husband & wife); unlimited if SS funds are not commingled with other funds	704.080
	Bank deposits of other public benefits to $1,525 ($2,275 for husband & wife)	
	Building materials to repair or improve home to $3,050 (spouses may not double)	704.030
	Burial plot	704.200
	Funds held in escrow	Fin. 17410
	Health aids	704.050
	Jewelry, heirlooms, & art to $7,625 total (spouses may not double)	704.040
	Motor vehicles to $2,900, or $2,900 in auto insurance for loss or damages (spouses may not double)	704.010
	Personal injury & wrongful death causes of action	704.140(a); 704.150(a)
	Personal injury & wrongful death recoveries needed for support; if receiving installments, at least 75%	704.140(b), (c), (d); 704.150(b), (c)
public benefits	Aid to blind, aged, disabled; public assistance	704.170
	Financial aid to students	704.190
	Relocation benefits	704.180
	Unemployment benefits	704.120
	Union benefits due to labor dispute	704.120(b)(5)
	Workers' compensation	704.160
tools of trade	Tools, implements, materials, instruments, uniforms, one commercial vehicle, books, furnishings, & equipment to $7,625 total ($15,250 total if used by both spouses in same occupation)	704.060
	Commercial vehicle (Vehicle Code § 260) to $4,850 ($9,700 total if used by both spouses in same occupation) (this counts toward total tools of trade exemption)	704.060

wages	Minimum 75% of wages paid within 30 days prior to filing	704.070
	Public employees' vacation credits; if receiving installments, at least 75%	704.113
wildcard	None	

California—System 2

Refer to the notes for California—System 1, above.

Note: Married couples may not double any exemptions. (*In re Talmadge*, 832 F.2d 1120 (9th Cir. 1987); *In re Baldwin*, 70 B.R. 612 (9th Cir. B.A.P 1987).)

ASSET	EXEMPTION	LAW
homestead	Real or personal property, including co-op, used as residence to $25,575; unused portion of homestead may be applied to any property	703.140(b)(1)
insurance	Disability benefits	703.140(b)(10)(C)
	Life insurance proceeds needed for support of family	703.140(b)(11)(C)
	Unmatured life insurance contract accrued avails to $13,675	703.140(b)(8)
	Unmatured life insurance policy other than credit	703.140(b)(7)
miscellaneous	Alimony, child support needed for support	703.140(b)(10)(D)
pensions	Tax-exempt retirement accounts, including 401(k)s, 403(b)s, profit-sharing and money purchase plans, SEP and SIMPLE IRAs, and defined-benefit plans	11 U.S.C. § 522(b)(3)(C)
	Traditional and Roth IRAs to $1,245,475 per person	11 U.S.C. § 522(b)(3)(C); (n)
	ERISA-qualified benefits needed for support	703.140(b)(10)(E)
personal property	Animals, crops, appliances, furnishings, household goods, books, musical instruments, & clothing to $650 per item	703.140(b)(3)
	Burial plot to $25,575, in lieu of homestead	703.140(b)(1)
	Health aids	703.140(b)(9)
	Jewelry to $1,525	703.140(b)(4)
	Motor vehicles to $5,100	703.140(b)(2)
	Personal injury recoveries to $25,075	703.140(b)(11)(D), (E)
	Wrongful death recoveries needed for support	703.140(b)(11)(B)
public benefits	Crime victims' compensation	703.140(b)(11)(A)
	Public assistance	703.140(b)(10)(A)
	Social Security	703.140(b)(10)(A)
	Unemployment compensation	703.140(b)(10)(A)
	Veterans benefits	703.140(b)(10)(B)
tools of trade	Implements, books & tools of trade to $7,625	703.140(b)(6)
wages	None	
wildcard	$1,350 of any property	703.140(b)(5)
	Unused portion of homestead or burial exemption of any property	703.140(b)(5)

Colorado

Federal bankruptcy exemptions not available. All law references are to Colorado Revised Statutes unless otherwise noted.

ASSET	EXEMPTION	LAW
homestead	Real property, mobile home, manufactured home, or house trailer you occupy to $60,000; $90,000 if owner, spouse, or dependent is disabled or at least 60 years old; sale proceeds exempt 2 years after received	38-41-201; 38-41-201.6; 38-41-203; 38-41-207; *In re Pastrana*, 216 B.R. 948 (D. Colo., 1998)
	Spouse or child of deceased owner may claim homestead exemption	38-41-204
insurance	Disability benefits to $200 per month; if lump sum, entire amount exempt	10-16-212
	Fraternal benefit society benefits	10-14-403
	Group life insurance policy or proceeds	10-7-205
	Homeowners' insurance proceeds for 1 year after received, to homestead exemption amount	38-41-209
	Life insurance cash surrender value to $100,000, except contributions to policy within past 48 months	13-54-102(1)(l)
	Life insurance proceeds if clause prohibits proceeds from being used to pay beneficiary's creditors	10-7-106
miscellaneous	Child support or domestic support obligation	13-54-102(u); 13-54-102.5
	Property of business partnership	7-60-125
pensions *see also wages*	Tax-exempt retirement accounts, including 401(k)s, 403(b)s, profit-sharing and money purchase plans, SEP and SIMPLE IRAs, and defined-benefit plans	11 U.S.C. § 522(b)(3)(C)
	Traditional and Roth IRAs to $1,245,475 per person	11 U.S.C. § 522(b)(3)(C); (n)
	ERISA-qualified benefits, including IRAs & Roth IRAs	13-54-102(1)(s)
	Firefighters & police officers	31-30.5-208; 31-31-203
	Public employees' pensions, deferred compensation & defined contribution plans	24-51-212
	Veterans pension for veteran, spouse, or dependents if veteran served in war or armed conflict	13-54-102(1)(h); 13-54-104
personal property	1 burial plot per family member	13-54-102(1)(d)
	Clothing to $1,500	13-54-102(1)(a)
	Food & fuel to $600	13-54-102(1)(f)
	Health aids	13-54-102(1)(p)
	Household goods to $3,000	13-54-102(1)(e)
	Jewelry & articles of adornment to $2,000	13-54-102(1)(b)
	Motor vehicles or bicycles used for work to $5,000; $10,000 if used by a debtor or by a dependent who is disabled or 60 or over	13-54-102(j) (I), (II)
	Personal injury recoveries	13-54-102(1)(n)
	Family pictures & books to $1,500	13-54-102(1)(c)
	Proceeds for damaged exempt property	13-54-102(1)(m)
	Security deposits	13-54-102(1)(r)

ASSET	EXEMPTION	LAW
public benefits	Aid to blind, aged, disabled; public assistance	26-2-131
	Crime victims' compensation	13-54-102(1)(q); 24-4.1-114
	Disability benefits to $3,000	13-54-102(v)
	Earned income tax credit or refund	13-54-102(1)(o)
	Unemployment compensation	8-80-103
	Veterans benefits for veteran, spouse, or child if veteran served in war or armed conflict	13-54-102(1)(h)
	Workers' compensation	8-42-124
tools of trade	Livestock or other animals, machinery, tools, equipment, & seed of person engaged in agriculture, to $50,000 total	13-54-102(1)(g)
	Professional's library to $3,000 (if not claimed under other tools of trade exemption)	13-54-102(1)(k)
	Stock in trade, supplies, fixtures, tools, machines, electronics, equipment, books & other business materials, to $20,000 total	13-54-102(1)(i)
	Military equipment personally owned by members of the National Guard	13-54-102(1) (h.5)
wages	Minimum 75% of weekly net earnings or 30 times the federal or state minimum wage, whichever is greater, including pension & insurance payments. *In re Nye*, 210 B.R. 857 (D. Colo. 1997); *In re Kobemusz*, 160 B.R. 844 (D. Colo. 1993)	13-54-104
wildcard	None	

Connecticut

Federal bankruptcy exemptions available. All law references are to Connecticut General Statutes Annotated unless otherwise noted.

ASSET	EXEMPTION	LAW
homestead	Owner-occupied real property, including co-op or mobile manufactured home, to $75,000; applies only to claims arising after 1993, but to $125,000 in the case of a money judgment arising out of services provided at a hospital	52-352a(e); 52-352b(t)
insurance	Disability benefits paid by association for its members	52-352b(p)
	Fraternal benefit society benefits	38a-637
	Health or disability benefits	52-352b(e)
	Life insurance proceeds if clause prohibits proceeds from being used to pay beneficiary's creditors	38a-454
	Life insurance proceeds or avails	38a-453
	Unmatured life insurance policy avails to $4,000 if beneficiary is dependent	52-352b(s)
miscellaneous	Alimony, to extent wages exempt	52-352b(n)
	Child support	52-352b(h)
	Farm partnership animals & livestock feed reasonably required to run farm where at least 50% of partners are members of same family	52-352d
pensions	Tax-exempt retirement accounts, including 401(k)s, 403(b)s, profit-sharing and money purchase plans, SEP and SIMPLE IRAs, and defined-benefit plans	11 U.S.C. § 522(b)(3)(C)

pensions (continued)	Traditional and Roth IRAs to $1,245,475 per person	11 U.S.C. § 522(b)(3)(C); (n)
	ERISA-qualified benefits, including IRAs, Roth IRAs & Keoghs, to extent wages exempt	52-321a; 52-352b(m)
	Medical savings account	52-321a
	Municipal employees	7-446
	State employees	5-171; 5-192w
	Teachers	10-183q
personal property	Appliances, food, clothing, furniture, bedding	52-352b(a)
	Burial plot	52-352b(c)
	Health aids needed	52-352b(f)
	Motor vehicle to $3,500	52-352b(j)
	Proceeds for damaged exempt property	52-352b(q)
	Residential utility & security deposits for 1 residence	52-352b(l)
	Spendthrift trust funds required for support of debtor & family	52-321(d)
	Transfers to a licensed debt adjuster	52-352b(u)
	Tuition savings accounts	52-321a(E)
	Wedding & engagement rings	52-352b(k)
public benefits	Crime victims' compensation	52-352b(o); 54-213
	Public assistance	52-352b(d)
	Social Security	52-352b(g)
	Unemployment compensation	31-272(c); 52-352b(g)
	Veterans benefits	52-352b(g)
	Workers' compensation	52-352b(g)
tools of trade	Arms, military equipment, uniforms, musical instruments of military personnel	52-352b(i)
	Tools, books, instruments, & farm animals needed	52-352b(b)
wages	Minimum 75% of earned but unpaid weekly disposable earnings, or 40 times the state or federal hourly minimum wage, whichever is greater	52-361a(f)
wildcard	$1,000 of any property	52-352b(r)

Delaware

Federal bankruptcy exemptions not available. All law references are to Delaware Code Annotated (in the form "title number-section number") unless otherwise noted.

Note: A single person may exempt no more than $25,000 total in all exemptions (not including retirement plans and principal residence); a husband and wife may exempt no more than $50,000 total (10-4914).

ASSET	EXEMPTION	LAW
homestead	Real property or manufactured home used as principal residence to $125,000 in 2012; $125,000 for working or married persons where one spouse is 65 or older (spouses may not double)	10-4914(c)
	Property held as tenancy by the entirety may be exempt against debts owed by only one spouse	*In re Kelley*, 289 B.R. 38 (Bankr. D. Del. 2003)
insurance	Annuity contract proceeds to $350 per month	18-2728
	Fraternal benefit society benefits	18-6218
	Group life insurance policy or proceeds	18-2727
	Health or disability benefits	18-2726

insurance (continued)	Life insurance proceeds if clause prohibits proceeds from being used to pay beneficiary's creditors	18-2729
	Life insurance proceeds or avails	18-2725
pensions	Tax-exempt retirement accounts, including 401(k)s, 403(b)s, profit-sharing and money purchase plans, SEP and SIMPLE IRAs, and defined-benefit plans	11 U.S.C. § 522(b)(3)(C)
	Traditional and Roth IRAs to $1,245,475 per person	11 U.S.C. § 522(b)(3)(C); (n)
	IRAs, Roth IRAs & any other retirement plans	10-4915
	Kent County employees	9-4316
	Police officers	11-8803
	State employees	29-5503
	Volunteer firefighters	16-6653
personal property	Bible, books, & family pictures	10-4902(a)
	Burial plot	10-4902(a)
	Church pew or any seat in public place of worship	10-4902(a)
	Clothing, includes jewelry	10-4902(a)
	College investment plan account (limit for year before filing is $5,000 or average of past two years' contribution, whichever is more)	10-4916
	Principal and income from spendthrift trusts	12-3536
	Pianos & leased organs	10-4902(d)
	Sewing machines	10-4902(c)
public benefits	Aid to blind	31-2309
	Aid to aged, disabled; general assistance	31-513
	Crime victims' compensation	11-9011
	Unemployment compensation	19-3374
	Workers' compensation	19-2355
tools of trade	Tools of trade and/or vehicle necessary for employment to $15,000 each	10-4914(c)
	Tools, implements & fixtures to $75 in New Castle & Sussex Counties; to $50 in Kent County	10-4902(b)
wages	85% of earned but unpaid wages	10-4913
wildcard	$500 of any personal property, except tools of trade, if head of family	10-4903

District of Columbia

Federal bankruptcy exemptions available. All law references are to District of Columbia Code unless otherwise noted.

ASSET	EXEMPTION	LAW
homestead	Any property used as a residence or co-op that debtor or debtor's dependent uses as a residence	15-501(a)(14)
	Property held as tenancy by the entirety may be exempt against debts owed by only one spouse	*Estate of Wall*, 440 F.2d 215 (D.C. Cir. 1971)
insurance	Disability benefits	15-501(a)(7); 31-4716.01
	Fraternal benefit society benefits	31-5315
	Group life insurance policy or proceeds	31-4717
	Life insurance payments	15-501(a)(11)
	Life insurance proceeds if clause prohibits proceeds from being used to pay beneficiary's creditors	31-4719
	Life insurance proceeds or avails	31-4716

insurance (continued)	Other insurance proceeds to $200 per month, maximum 2 months, for head of family; else $60 per month	15-503
	Unmatured life insurance contract other than credit life insurance	15-501(a)(5)
miscellaneous	Alimony or child support	15-501(a)(7)
pensions *see also wages*	Tax-exempt retirement accounts, including 401(k)s, 403(b)s, profit-sharing and money purchase plans, SEP and SIMPLE IRAs, and defined-benefit plans	11 U.S.C. § 522(b)(3)(C)
	Traditional and Roth IRAs to $1,245,475 per person	11 U.S.C. § 522(b)(3)(C); (n)
	ERISA-qualified benefits, IRAs, Keoghs, etc. to maximum deductible contribution	15-501(b)(9)
	Any stock bonus, annuity, pension, or profit-sharing plan	15-501(a)(7)
	Judges	11-1570(f)
	Public school teachers	38-2001.17; 38-2021.17
personal property	Appliances, books, clothing, household furnishings, goods, musical instruments, pets to $425 per item or $8,625 total	15-501(a)(2)
	Cemetery & burial funds	43-111
	Cooperative association holdings to $500	29-928
	Food for 3 months	15-501(a)(12)
	Health aids	15-501(a)(6)
	Higher education tuition savings account	47-4510
	Residential condominium deposit	42-1904.09
	All family pictures; all the family library to $400	15-501(a)(8)
	Motor vehicle to $2,575	15-501(a)(1)
	Payment, including pain & suffering, for loss of debtor or person depended on	15-501(a)(11)
	Uninsured motorist benefits	31-2408.01(h)
	Wrongful death damages	15-501(a)(11); 16-2703
public benefits	Aid to blind, aged, disabled; general assistance	4-215.01
	Crime victims' compensation	4-507(e); 15-501(a)(11)
	Social Security	15-501(a)(7)
	Unemployment compensation	51-118
	Veterans benefits	15-501(a)(7)
	Workers' compensation	32-1517
tools of trade	Library, furniture, tools of professional or artist to $300	15-501(a)(13)
	Tools of trade or business to $1,625	15-501(a)(5)
	Mechanic's tools to $200	15-503(b)
	Seal & documents of notary public	1-1206
wages	Minimum 75% of earned but unpaid wages, pension payments; bankruptcy judge may authorize more for low-income debtors	16-572
	Nonwage (including pension & retirement) earnings to $200 per month for head of family; else $60 per month for a maximum of two months	15-503
	Payment for loss of future earnings	15-501(e)(11)
wildcard	Up to $850 in any property, plus up to $8,075 if you don't use the homestead exemption	15-501(a)(3)

Florida

Federal bankruptcy exemptions not available. All law references are to Florida Statutes Annotated unless otherwise noted.

ASSET	EXEMPTION	LAW
homestead	Real or personal property including mobile or modular home to unlimited value; cannot exceed half acre in municipality or 160 acres elsewhere; spouse or child of deceased owner may claim homestead exemption	222.01; 222.02; 222.03; 222.05; Constitution 10-4; *In re Colwell*, 196 F.3d 1225 (11th Cir. 1999)
	May file homestead declaration	222.01
	Property held as tenancy by the entirety may be exempt against debts owed by only one spouse	*Havoco of America, Ltd. v. Hill*, 197 F.3d 1135 (11th Cir. 1999)
insurance	Annuity contract proceeds; does not include lottery winnings	222.14; *In re Pizzi*, 153 B.R. 357 (S.D. Fla. 1993)
	Death benefits payable to a specific beneficiary, not the deceased's estate	222.13
	Disability or illness benefits	222.18
	Fraternal benefit society benefits	632.619
	Life insurance cash surrender value	222.14
miscellaneous	Alimony, child support needed for support	222.201
	Damages to employees for injuries in hazardous occupations	769.05
pensions *see also wages*	Tax-exempt retirement accounts, including 401(k)s, 403(b)s, profit-sharing and money purchase plans, SEP and SIMPLE IRAs, and defined-benefit plans	11 U.S.C. § 522(b)(3)(C)
	Traditional and Roth IRAs to $1,245,475 per person	11 U.S.C. § 522(b)(3)(C); (n)
	County officers, employees	122.15
	ERISA-qualified benefits, including IRAs & Roth IRAs	222.21(2)
	Firefighters	175.241
	Police officers	185.25
	State officers, employees	121.131
	Teachers	238.15
personal property	Any personal property to $1,000 (husband & wife may double); to $4,000 if no homestead claimed	222.25(4) Const. Art. X. § 4(a)(2)
	Health aids	222.25(2)
	Motor vehicle to $1,000	222.25(1)
	Preneed funeral contract deposits	497.56(8)
	Prepaid college education trust deposits	222.22(1)
	Prepaid hurricane savings accounts	222.22(4)
	Prepaid medical savings account & health savings account deposits	222.22(2)
public benefits	Crime victims' compensation, unless seeking to discharge debt for treatment of injury incurred during the crime	960.14
	Earned income tax credit	222.25(3)
	Public assistance	222.201
	Social Security	222.201
	Reemployment assistance	222.201; 443.051(2), (3)

public benefits (continued)	Veterans benefits	222.201; 744.626
	Workers' compensation	440.22
tools of trade	None	
wages	100% of wages for heads of family up to $750 per week either unpaid or paid & deposited into bank account for up to 6 months	222.11
	Federal government employees' pension payments needed for support & received 3 months prior	222.21
wildcard	See personal property	

Georgia

Federal bankruptcy exemptions not available. All law references are to the Official Code of Georgia Annotated unless otherwise noted.

ASSET	EXEMPTION	LAW
homestead	Real or personal property, including co-op, used as residence to $21,500 (to $43,000 if married and debtor spouse is sole owner); up to $5,000 of unused portion of homestead may be applied to any property	44-13-100(a)(1); 44-13-100(a)(6); *In re Burnett*, 303 B.R. 684 (M.D. Ga. 2003)
insurance	Annuity & endowment contract benefits	33-28-7
	Disability or health benefits to $250 per month	33-29-15
	Fraternal benefit society benefits	33-15-62
	Group insurance	33-30-10
	Proceeds & avails of life insurance	33-26-5; 33-25-11
	Life insurance proceeds if policy owned by someone you depended on, needed for support	44-13-100(a)(11)(C)
	Unmatured life insurance contract	44-13-100(a)(8)
	Unmatured life insurance dividends, interest, loan value, or cash value to $2,000 if beneficiary is you or someone you depend on	44-13-100(a)(9)
miscellaneous	Alimony, child support needed for support	44-13-100(a)(2)(D)
pensions	Tax-exempt retirement accounts, including 401(k)s, 403(b)s, profit-sharing and money purchase plans, SEP and SIMPLE IRAs, and defined-benefit plans	11 U.S.C. § 522(b)(3)(C)
	Traditional and Roth IRAs to $1,245,475 per person	11 U.S.C. § 522(b)(3)(C); (n)
	Employees of nonprofit corporations	44-13-100(a)(2.1)(B)
	ERISA-qualified benefits & IRAs	18-4-22
	Public employees	44-13-100(a)(2.1)(A); 47-2-332
	Payments from IRA necessary for support	44-13-100(a)(2)(F)
	Other pensions needed for support	18-4-22; 44-13-100(a)(2)(E); 44-13-100(a)(2.1)(C)

personal property	Animals, crops, clothing, appliances, books, furnishings, household goods, musical instruments to $300 per item, $5,000 total	44-13-100(a)(4)
	Burial plot, in lieu of homestead	44-13-100(a)(1)
	Compensation for lost future earnings needed for support to $7,500	44-13-100(a)(11)(E)
	Health aids	44-13-100(a)(10)
	Jewelry to $500	44-13-100(a)(5)
	Motor vehicles to $5,000	44-13-100(a)(3)
	Personal injury recoveries to $10,000	44-13-100(a)(11)(D)
	Wrongful death recoveries needed for support	44-13-100(a)(11)(B)
public benefits	Aid to blind	49-4-58
	Aid to disabled	49-4-84
	Crime victims' compensation	44-13-100(a)(11)(A)
	Local public assistance	44-13-100(a)(2)(A)
	Old age assistance	49-4-35
	Social Security	44-13-100(a)(2)(A)
	Unemployment compensation	44-13-100(a)(2)(A)
	Veterans benefits	44-13-100(a)(2)(B)
	Workers' compensation	34-9-84
tools of trade	Implements, books & tools of trade to $1,500	44-13-100(a)(7)
wages	Minimum 75% of earned but unpaid weekly disposable earnings, or 30 times the state or federal hourly minimum wage, whichever is greater, for private & federal workers; bankruptcy judge may authorize more for low-income debtors	18-4-20; 18-4-21
wildcard	$600 of any property	44-13-100(a)(6)
	Unused portion of homestead exemption to $5,000	44-13-100(a)(6)

Hawaii

Federal bankruptcy exemptions available. All law references are to Hawaii Revised Statutes unless otherwise noted.

ASSET	EXEMPTION	LAW
homestead	Head of family or over 65 to $30,000; all others to $20,000; property cannot exceed 1 acre; sale proceeds exempt for 6 months after sale (spouses may not double)	651-91; 651-92; 651-96
	Property held as tenancy by the entirety may be exempt against debts owed by only one spouse or reciprocal beneficiary	509-2; *Security Pacific Bank v. Chang*, 818 F.Supp. 1343 (D. Haw. 1993)
insurance	Annuity contract or endowment policy proceeds if beneficiary is insured's spouse, child, or parent	431:10-232(b)
	Accident, health, or sickness benefits	431:10-231
	Fraternal benefit society benefits	432:2-403
	Group life insurance policy or proceeds	431:10-233

insurance (continued)	Life insurance proceeds if clause prohibits proceeds from being used to pay beneficiary's creditors	431:10D-112
	Life or health insurance policy for spouse or child	431:10-234
miscellaneous	Property of business partnership	425-125
pensions	Tax-exempt retirement accounts, including 401(k)s, 403(b)s, profit-sharing and money purchase plans, SEP and SIMPLE IRAs, and defined-benefit plans	11 U.S.C. § 522(b)(3)(C)
	Traditional and Roth IRAs to $1,245,475 per person	11 U.S.C. § 522(b)(3)(C); (n)
	IRAs, Roth IRAs, and ERISA-qualified benefits deposited over 3 years before filing bankruptcy	651-124
	Firefighters	88-169
	Police officers	88-169
	Public officers & employees	88-91; 653-3
personal property	Appliances & furnishings	651-121(1)
	Books	651-121(1)
	Burial plot to 250 sq. ft. plus tombstones, monuments, & fencing	651-121(4)
	Clothing	651-121(1)
	Jewelry, watches, & articles of adornment to $1,000	651-121(1)
	Motor vehicle to wholesale value of $2,575	651-121(2)
	Proceeds for sold or damaged exempt property; sale proceeds exempt for 6 months after sale	651-121(5)
public benefits	Crime victims' compensation & special accounts created to limit commercial exploitation of crimes	351-66; 351-86
	Public assistance paid by Department of Health Services for work done in home or workshop	346-33
	Temporary disability benefits	392-29
	Unemployment compensation	383-163
	Unemployment work relief funds to $60 per month	653-4
	Workers' compensation	386-57
tools of trade	Tools, implements, books, instruments, uniforms, furnishings, fishing boat, nets, motor vehicle, & other property needed for livelihood	651-121(3)
wages	Prisoner's wages held by Department of Public Safety (except for restitution, child support, & other claims)	353-22.5
	Unpaid wages due for services of past 31 days	651-121(6)
wildcard	None	

Idaho

Federal bankruptcy exemptions not available. All law references are to Idaho Code unless otherwise noted.

ASSET	EXEMPTION	LAW
homestead	Real property or mobile home to $100,000; sale proceeds exempt for 6 months (spouses may not double)	55-1003; 55-1113
	Must record homestead exemption for property that is not yet occupied	55-1004

insurance	Annuity contract proceeds to $1,250 per month; if not yet receiving payments from the annuity, cash surrender value to amount of premiums paid during 6 months before bankruptcy petition	41-1836
	Death or disability benefits	11-604(1)(a); 41-1834
	Fraternal benefit society benefits	41-3218
	Group life insurance benefits	41-1835
	Homeowners' insurance proceeds to amount of homestead exemption	55-1008
	Life insurance proceeds if clause prohibits proceeds from being used to pay beneficiary's creditors	41-1930
	Life insurance proceeds or avails for beneficiary other than the insured	11-604(d); 41-1833
	Medical, surgical, or hospital care benefits & amount in medical savings account	11-603(5)
	Unmatured life insurance contract, other than credit life insurance, owned by debtor	11-605(9)
	Unmatured life insurance contract interest or dividends to $5,000 owned by debtor or person debtor depends on	11-605(10)
miscellaneous	Alimony, child support	11-604(1)(b)
	Liquor licenses	23-514
pension *see also wages*	Tax-exempt retirement accounts, including 401(k)s, 403(b)s, profit-sharing and money purchase plans, SEP and SIMPLE IRAs, and defined-benefit plans	11 U.S.C. § 522(b)(3)(C)
	Traditional and Roth IRAs to $1,245,475 per person	11 U.S.C. § 522(b)(3)(C); (n)
	ERISA-qualified benefits	55-1011
	Firefighters	72-1422
	Government & private pensions, retirement plans, IRAs, Roth IRAs, Keoghs, etc.	11-604A
	Police officers	50-1517
	Public employees	59-1317
personal property	Appliances, furnishings, books, clothing, pets, musical instruments, family portraits, & sentimental heirlooms to $750 per item, $7,500 total	11-605(1)
	Building materials	45-514
	Burial plot	11-603(1)
	College savings program account	11-604A(4)(b)
	Crops cultivated on maximum of 50 acres, to $1,000; water rights to 160 inches	11-605(6) and (7)
	Firearm (1) to $750	11-605(8)
	Health aids	11-603(2)
	Jewelry to $1,000	11-605(2)
	Motor vehicle to $7,000	11-605(3)
	Personal injury recoveries	11-604(1)(c)
	Proceeds for damaged exempt property for 3 months after proceeds received	11-606
	Provisions (food, water, and storage equipment) sufficient for up to 12 months	11-605(4)
	Wrongful death recoveries	11-604(1)(c)

public benefits	Aid to blind, aged, disabled	56-223
	Federal, state & local public assistance, including earned income tax credit (but not child or education tax credit) (*In re Jones*, 107 B.R. 751 (Bankr. D. Idaho 1989; *In re Steinmetz*, 261 B.R. 32 (Bankr. D. Idaho 2001); *In re Crampton*, 249 B.R. 215 (Bankr.D. Idaho 2000))	11-603(4)
	General assistance	56-223
	Social Security	11-603(3)
	Unemployment compensation	11-603(6)
	Veterans benefits	11-603(3)
	Workers' compensation	72-802
tools of trade	Arms, uniforms & accoutrements that peace officer, National Guard, or military personnel is required to keep	11-605(6)
	Implements, books & tools of trade to $2,500	11-605(3)
wages	Minimum 75% of earned but unpaid weekly disposable earnings, or 30 times the federal hourly minimum wage, whichever is greater but not more than $1,500 in a calendar year; pension payments; bankruptcy judge may authorize more for low-income debtors	11-207; 11-605-12; 11-206
wildcard	$800 in any tangible personal property	11-605(11)

Illinois

Federal bankruptcy exemptions not available. All law references are to Illinois Compiled Statutes Annotated unless otherwise noted.

Note: Although one court has held that the Illinois Wage Deduction Act creates a bankruptcy exemption, *In re Mayer*, 288 B.R. 869 (Bankr. N.D. Ill. 2008) (Wedoff, J.), most other Illinois courts addressing the issue have found that it does not. (*In re Radzilowsky*, 448 B.R. 767 (Bankr. N.D. Ill. May 6, 2011); *In re Kapusta*, 2011 WL 2173675 (C.D. Ill. June 2, 2011); *In re Koeneman*, 410 B.R. 820 (C.D. Ill. 2009); *In re Thum*, 329 B.R. 848 (Bankr. C.D. Ill. 2005).)

ASSET	EXEMPTION	LAW
homestead	Real or personal property including a farm, lot & buildings, condo, co-op, or mobile home to $15,000; sale proceeds exempt for 1 year	735-5/12-901; 735-5/12-906
	Spouse or child of deceased owner may claim homestead exemption	735-5/12-902
	Illinois recognizes tenancy by the entirety, with limitations	750-65/22; 765-1005/1c; *In re Gillissie*, 215 B.R. 370 (Bankr. N.D. Ill. 1998); *Great Southern Co. v. Allard*, 202 B.R. 938 (N.D. Ill. 1996)
insurance	Fraternal benefit society benefits	215-5/299.1a
	Health or disability benefits	735-5/12-1001(g)(3)
	Homeowners' proceeds if home destroyed, to $15,000	735-5/12-907
	Life insurance, annuity proceeds, or cash value if beneficiary is insured's child, parent, spouse, or other dependent	215-5/238; 735-5/12-1001(f)
	Life insurance proceeds to a spouse or dependent of debtor to extent needed for support	735-5/12-1001(f), (g)(3)

miscellaneous	Alimony, child support	735-5/12-1001(g)(4)
	Property of business partnership	805-205/25
pensions	Tax-exempt retirement accounts, including 401(k)s, 403(b)s, profit-sharing and money purchase plans, SEP and SIMPLE IRAs, and defined-benefit plans	11 U.S.C. § 522(b)(3)(C)
	Traditional and Roth IRAs to $1,245,475 per person	11 U.S.C. § 522(b)(3)(C); (n)
	Civil service employees	40-5/11-223
	County employees	40-5/9-228
	Disabled firefighters; widows & children of firefighters	40-5/22-230
	IRAs and ERISA-qualified benefits	735-5/12-1006
	Firefighters	40-5/4-135; 40-5/6-213
	General Assembly members	40-5/2-154
	House of correction employees	40-5/19-117
	Judges	40-5/18-161
	Municipal employees	40-5/7-217(a); 40-5/8-244
	Park employees	40-5/12-190
	Police officers	40-5/3-144.1; 40-5/5-218
	Public employees	735-5/12-1006
	Public library employees	40-5/19-218
	Sanitation district employees	40-5/13-805
	State employees	40-5/14-147
	State university employees	40-5/15-185
	Teachers	40-5/16-190; 40-5/17-151
personal property	Bible, family pictures, schoolbooks & clothing	735-5/12-1001(a)
	Health aids	735-5/12-1001(e)
	Illinois College Savings Pool accounts invested more than 1 year before filing if below federal gift tax limit, or 2 years before filing if above	735-5/12-1001(j)
	Motor vehicle to $2,400	735-5/12-1001(c)
	Personal injury recoveries to $15,000	735-5/12-1001(h)(4)
	Preneed cemetery sales funds, care funds & trust funds	235-5/6-1; 760-100/4; 815-390/16
	Prepaid tuition trust fund	110-979/45(g)
	Proceeds of sold exempt property	735-5/12-1001
	Wrongful death recoveries	735-5/12-1001(h)(2)
public benefits	Aid to aged, blind, disabled; public assistance, including earned income tax credit and child tax credit (applies to future payments but not funds already received) (*In re Fish*, 224 B.R. 82 (Bankr. S.D. Ill 1998); *In re Vazquez*, No. 13-32174 (Bankr. N.D. Ill 2014); *In re Frueh*, No. 14-B-81029 (Bankr. W.D. Ill 2014))	305-5/11-3; 735-5/12-1001(g)(1)
	Crime victims' compensation	735-5/12-1001(h)(1)

public benefits (continued)	Restitution payments on account of WWII relocation of Aleuts & Japanese Americans	735-5/12-1001(12)(h)(5)
	Social Security	735-5/12-1001(g)(1)
	Unemployment compensation	735-5/12-1001(g)(1), (3)
	Veterans benefits	735-5/12-1001(g)(2)
	Workers' compensation	820-305/21
	Workers' occupational disease compensation	820-310/21
tools of trade	Implements, books, & tools of trade to $1,500	735-5/12-1001(d)
wages	Minimum 85% of earned but unpaid weekly wages or 45 times the federal minimum hourly wage (or state minimum hourly wage, if higher); bankruptcy judge may authorize more for low-income debtors (some judges may not allow this exemption). See note at beginning of Illinois chart.	735-5/12-803
wildcard	$4,000 of any personal property (does not include wages)	735-5/12-1001(b)

Indiana

Federal bankruptcy exemptions not available. All law references are to Indiana Statutes Annotated unless otherwise noted.

ASSET	EXEMPTION	LAW
homestead *see also* *wildcard*	Real or personal property used as residence to $17,600	34-55-10-2(c)(1)
	Property held as tenancy by the entirety may be exempt against debts incurred by only one spouse	34-55-10-2(c)(5); 32-17-3-1
insurance	Employer's life insurance policy on employee	27-1-12-17.1
	Fraternal benefit society benefits	27-11-6-3
	Group life insurance policy	27-1-12-29
	Life insurance policy, proceeds, cash value, or avails if beneficiary is insured's spouse or dependent	27-1-12-14
	Life insurance proceeds if clause prohibits proceeds to be used to pay beneficiary's creditors	27-2-5-1
	Mutual life or accident proceeds needed for support	27-8-3-23; *In re Stinnet*, 321 B.R. 477 (S.D. Ind. 2005)
miscellaneous	Property of business partnership	23-4-1-25
pensions	Tax-exempt retirement accounts, including 401(k)s, 403(b)s, profit-sharing and money purchase plans, SEP and SIMPLE IRAs, and defined-benefit plans	11 U.S.C. § 522(b)(3)(C)
	Traditional and Roth IRAs to $1,245,475 per person	11 U.S.C. § 522(b)(3)(C); (n)
	Firefighters	36-8-7-22; 36-8-8-17
	Police officers	36-8-8-17; 10-12-2-10
	Public employees	5-10.3-8-9
	Public or private retirement benefits & contributions	34-55-10-2(c)(6)
	Sheriffs	36-8-10-19
	State teachers	5-10.4-5-14

personal property	Education savings account (529 and Coverdell) contributions made more than 2 years prior to filing; contributions made more than 1 but less than 2 years prior to filing to $5,000; no exemption for contributions made less than 1 year prior to filing	34-55-10-2(c)(9), (10)
	Health aids	34-55-10-2(c)(4)
	Money in medical care savings account or health savings account	34-55-10-2(c)(7), (8)
	Spendthrift trusts	30-4-3-2
	$350 of any intangible personal property, except money owed to you	34-55-10-2(c)(3)
public benefits	Crime victims' compensation, unless seeking to discharge the debts for which the victim was compensated	5-2-6.1-38
	Earned income tax credit (but not child tax credit) (*In re King*, 508 B.R. 71 (Bankr. N.D. Ind. 2014); *In re Jackson*, No. 12–9635–RLM–7A (Bankr. S.D. In. 2013))	34-55-10-2(c)(11)
	Supplemental state fair relief fund	34-13-8; 34-55-102(c)(13)
	Unemployment compensation	22-4-33-3
	Veterans disability benefits	34-55-10-2(c)(12)
	Workers' compensation	22-3-2-17
tools of trade	National Guard uniforms, arms & equipment	10-16-10-3
wages	Minimum 75% of earned but unpaid weekly disposable earnings, or 30 times the federal hourly minimum wage; bankruptcy judge may authorize more for low-income debtors. (*In re Haraughty*, 403 B.R. 607 (Bankr. S.D. Indiana 2009).)	24-4.5-5-105
wildcard	$9,350 of any real estate or tangible personal property	34-55-10-2(c)(2)

Iowa

Federal bankruptcy exemptions not available. All law references are to Iowa Code Annotated unless otherwise noted.

ASSET	EXEMPTION	LAW
homestead	May record homestead declaration	561.4
	Real property or an apartment to an unlimited value; property cannot exceed ½ acre in town or city, 40 acres elsewhere (spouses may not double)	499A.18; 561.2; 561.16
insurance	Accident, disability, health, illness, or life proceeds or avails	627.6(6)
	Disability or illness benefit	627.6(8)(c)
	Employee group insurance policy or proceeds	509.12
	Fraternal benefit society benefits	512B.18
	Life insurance proceeds if clause prohibits proceeds from being used to pay beneficiary's creditors	508.32
	Life insurance proceeds paid to spouse, child, or other dependent (limited to $10,000 if acquired within 2 years of filing for bankruptcy)	627.6(6)
	Upon death of insured, up to $15,000 total proceeds from all matured life, accident, health, or disability policies exempt from beneficiary's debts contracted before insured's death	627.6(6)(c)

miscellaneous	Alimony, child support needed for support	627.6(8)(d)
	Liquor licenses	123.38
pensions *see also wages*	Tax-exempt retirement accounts, including 401(k)s, 403(b)s, profit-sharing and money purchase plans, SEP and SIMPLE IRAs, and defined-benefit plans	11 U.S.C. § 522(b)(3)(C)
	Traditional and Roth IRAs to $1,245,475 per person	11 U.S.C. § 522(b)(3) (C); (n)
	Disabled firefighters, police officers (only payments being received)	410.11
	Federal government pension	627.8
	Firefighters	411.13
	Other pensions, annuities & contracts fully exempt; however, contributions made within 1 year prior to filing for bankruptcy not exempt to the extent they exceed normal & customary amounts	627.6(8)(e)
	Peace officers	97A.12
	Police officers	411.13
	Public employees	97B.39
	Retirement plans, Keoghs, IRAs, Roth IRAs, ERISA-qualified benefits	627.6(8)(f)
personal property	Bibles, books, portraits, pictures & paintings to $1,000 total	627.6(3)
	Burial plot to 1 acre	627.6(4)
	Clothing & its storage containers, household furnishings, appliances, musical instruments, and other personal property to $7,000	627.6(5)
	Health aids	627.6(7)
	Jewelry to $2,000	627.6(1)(6)
	Residential security or utility deposit, or advance rent, to $500	627.6(14)
	Rifle or musket; shotgun	627.6(2)
	One motor vehicle to $7,000	627.6(9)
	Wedding or engagement rings, limited to $7,000 (minus any amounts used under the jewelry exemption) if purchased after marriage and within last two years	627.6(1)(a)
	Wrongful death proceeds and awards needed for support of debtor and dependents	627.6(15)
public benefits	Adopted child assistance	627.19
	Aid to dependent children	239B.6
	Any public assistance benefit, including earned income tax credit and child tax credit (*In re Hatch*, 13-03342-als7 (Bankr. N.D. Iowa 2014); *In re Longstreet*, 246 B.R. 611 (Bankr. S.D. Iowa 2000))	627.6(8)(a)
	Social Security	627.6(8)(a)
	Unemployment compensation	627.6(8)(a)
	Veterans benefits	627.6(8)(b)
	Workers' compensation	627.13
tools of trade	Farming equipment; includes livestock, feed to $10,000	627.6(11)
	National Guard articles of equipment	29A.41
	Nonfarming equipment to $10,000	627.6(10)

wages	Expected annual earnings	Amount NOT exempt per year	642.21

Expected annual earnings	Amount NOT exempt per year
$0 to $11,999	$250
$12,000 to $15,999	$400
$16,000 to $23,999	$800
$24,000 to $34,999	$1,000
$35,000 to $49,999	$2,000
More than $50,000	10%

In re Irish, 311 B.R. 63 (8th Cir. B.A.P. 2004)

	Not exempt from spousal or child support	
	Wages or salary of a prisoner	356.29
wildcard	$1,000 of any personal property, including cash	627.6(14)

Kansas

Federal bankruptcy exemptions not available. Although Kansas has opted out of the federal exemptions, it does allow debtors to use exemptions in 11 U.S.C.A. § 522(d)(10). See K.S.A. 60-2312(b). All law references are to Kansas Statutes Annotated unless otherwise noted.

ASSET	EXEMPTION	LAW
homestead	Real property or mobile home you occupy or intend to occupy to unlimited value; property cannot exceed 1 acre in town or city, 160 acres on farm	60-2301; Constitution 15-9
insurance	Cash value of life insurance; not exempt if obtained within 1 year prior to bankruptcy with fraudulent intent	60-2313(a)(7); 40-414(b)
	Disability & illness benefits	60-2313(a)(1)
	Fraternal life insurance benefits	60-2313(a)(8)
	Life insurance proceeds	40-414(a)
miscellaneous	Alimony, maintenance & support	60-2312(b)
	Liquor licenses	60-2313(a)(6); 41-326
pensions	Tax-exempt retirement accounts, including 401(k)s, 403(b)s, profit-sharing and money purchase plans, SEP and SIMPLE IRAs, and defined-benefit plans	11 U.S.C. § 522(b)(3)(C)
	Traditional and Roth IRAs to $1,245,475 per person	11 U.S.C. § 522(b)(3) (C); (n)
	Elected & appointed officials in cities with populations between 120,000 & 200,000	13-14a10
	ERISA-qualified benefits	60-2308(b)
	Federal government pension needed for support & paid within 3 months of filing for bankruptcy (only payments being received)	60-2308(a)
	Firefighters	12-5005(e); 14-10a10
	Judges	20-2618
	Police officers	12-5005(e); 13-14a10
	Public employees	74-4923; 74-49,105
	State highway patrol officers	74-4978g
	State school employees	72-5526
	Payment under a stock bonus, pension, profit-sharing, annuity, or similar plan or contract on account of illness, disability, death, age, or length of service, to the extent reasonably necessary for support	60-2312(b)

personal property	Burial plot or crypt	60-2304(d)
	Clothing to last 1 year	60-2304(a)
	Earned income tax credit	60-2315
	Food & fuel to last 1 year	60-2304(a)
	Funeral plan prepayments	60-2313(a)(10); 16-310(d)
	Furnishings & household equipment	60-2304(a)
	Jewelry & articles of adornment to $1,000	60-2304(b)
	Motor vehicle to $20,000; if designed or equipped for disabled person, no limit	60-2304(c)
public benefits	Crime victims' compensation	60-2313(a)(7); 74-7313(d)
	Earned income tax credit	60-2315
	General assistance	39-717(c)
	Social Security	60-2312(b)
	Unemployment compensation	60-2313(a)(4); 44-718(c)
	Veterans benefits	60-2312(b)
	Workers' compensation	60-2313(a)(3); 44-514
tools of trade	Books, documents, furniture, instruments, equipment, breeding stock, seed, grain & stock to $7,500 total	60-2304(e)
	National Guard uniforms, arms & equipment	48-245
wages	Minimum 75% of disposable weekly wages or 30 times the federal minimum hourly wage per week, whichever is greater; bankruptcy judge may authorize more for low-income debtors; *In re Urban* 262 B.R. 865 (Bankr. D. Kan. 2001)	60-2310
wildcard	None	

Kentucky

Federal bankruptcy exemptions available. All law references are to Kentucky Revised Statutes unless otherwise noted.

ASSET	EXEMPTION	LAW
homestead	Real or personal property used as residence to $5,000; sale proceeds exempt	427.060; 427.090
insurance	Annuity contract proceeds to $350 per month	304.14-330
	Cooperative life or casualty insurance benefits	427.110(1)
	Fraternal benefit society benefits	427.110(2)
	Group life insurance proceeds	304.14-320
	Health or disability benefits	304.14-310
	Life insurance policy if beneficiary is a married woman	304.14-340
	Life insurance proceeds if clause prohibits proceeds from being used to pay beneficiary's creditors	304.14-350
	Life insurance proceeds or cash value if beneficiary is someone other than insured	304.14-300
miscellaneous	Alimony, child support needed for support	427.150(1)

pensions	Tax-exempt retirement accounts, including 401(k)s, 403(b)s, profit-sharing and money purchase plans, SEP and SIMPLE IRAs, and defined-benefit plans	11 U.S.C. § 522(b)(3)(C)
	Traditional and Roth IRAs to $1,245,475 per person	11 U.S.C. § 522(b)(3) (C); (n)
	ERISA-qualified benefits, including IRAs, SEPs & Keoghs deposited more than 120 days before filing	427.150
	Firefighters	67A.620; 95.878
	Police officers	427.120; 427.125
	State employees	61.690
	Teachers	161.700
	Urban county government employees	67A.350
personal property	Burial plot to $5,000, in lieu of homestead	427.060
	Clothing, jewelry, articles of adornment & furnishings to $3,000 total	427.010(1)
	Health aids	427.010(1)
	Lost earnings payments needed for support	427.150(2)(d)
	Medical expenses paid & reparation benefits received under motor vehicle reparation law	304.39-260
	Motor vehicle to $2,500	427.010(1)
	Personal injury recoveries to $7,500 (not to include pain & suffering or pecuniary loss)	427.150(2)(c)
	Prepaid tuition payment fund account	164A.707(3)
	Wrongful death recoveries for person you depended on, needed for support	427.150(2)(b)
public benefits	Aid to blind, aged, disabled; public assistance, includes earned income tax credit if eligible for Kentucky benefits (*In re Beltz*, 263 B.R. 525 (Bankr. W.D. Ky. 2001))	205.220(c)
	Crime victims' compensation	427.150(2)(a)
	Unemployment compensation	341.470(4)
	Workers' compensation	342.180
tools of trade	Library, office equipment, instruments & furnishings of minister, attorney, physician, surgeon, chiropractor, veterinarian, or dentist to $1,000	427.040
	Motor vehicle of auto mechanic, mechanical, or electrical equipment servicer, minister, attorney, physician, surgeon, chiropractor, veterinarian, or dentist to $2,500	427.030
	Tools, equipment, livestock & poultry of farmer to $3,000	427.010(1)
	Tools of nonfarmer to $300	427.030
wages	Minimum 75% of disposable weekly earnings or 30 times the federal minimum hourly wage per week, whichever is greater; bankruptcy judge may authorize more for low-income debtors	427.010(2), (3)
wildcard	$1,000 of any property	427.160

Louisiana

Federal bankruptcy exemptions not available. All law references are to Louisiana Revised Statutes Annotated unless otherwise noted.

ASSET	EXEMPTION	LAW
homestead	Property you occupy to $35,000 (if debt is result of catastrophic or terminal illness or injury, limit is full value of property as of 1 year before filing); cannot exceed 5 acres in city or town, 200 acres elsewhere (spouses may not double)	20:1(A)(1),(2),(3)
	Spouse or child of deceased owner may claim homestead exemption; spouse given home in divorce gets homestead	20:1(B)
insurance	Annuity contract proceeds & avails	22:912
	Fraternal benefit society benefits	22:298
	Group insurance policies or proceeds	22:944
	Health, accident, or disability proceeds or avails	22:1015
	Life insurance proceeds or avails; if policy issued within 9 months of filing, exempt only to $35,000	22:912
miscellaneous	Property of minor child	13:3881(A)(3); Civil Code Art. 223
pensions	Tax-exempt retirement accounts, including 401(k)s, 403(b)s, profit-sharing and money purchase plans, SEP and SIMPLE IRAs, and defined-benefit plans	11 U.S.C. § 522(b)(3)(C)
	Traditional and Roth IRAs to $1,245,475 per person	11 U.S.C. § 522(b)(3)(C); (n)
	Assessors	11:1403
	Court clerks	11:1526
	District attorneys	11:1583
	ERISA-qualified benefits, including IRAs, Roth IRAs & Keoghs, if contributions made over 1 year before filing for bankruptcy	13:3881; 20:33(1)
	Firefighters	11:2263
	Gift or bonus payments from employer to employee or heirs whenever paid	20:33(2)
	Judges	11:1378
	Louisiana University employees	11:952.3
	Municipal employees	11:1735
	Parochial employees	11:1905
	Police officers	11:3513
	School employees	11:1003
	Sheriffs	11:2182
	State employees	11:405
	Teachers	11:704
	Voting registrars	11:2033
personal property	Arms, military accoutrements; bedding; dishes, glassware, utensils, silverware (nonsterling); clothing, family portraits, musical instruments; bedroom, living room & dining room furniture; poultry, 1 cow, household pets; heating & cooling equipment, refrigerator, freezer, stove, washer & dryer, iron, sewing machine	13:3881(A)(4)
	Cemetery plot, monuments	8:313

ASSET	EXEMPTION	LAW
personal property (continued)	Disaster relief insurance proceeds	13:3881(A)(7)
	Engagement & wedding rings to $5,000	13:3881(A)(5)
	Motor vehicle to $7,500	13:3881(A)(7)
	Motor vehicle modified for disability to $7,500	13:3881(A)(8)
	Spendthrift trusts	9:2004
public benefits	Aid to blind, aged, disabled; public assistance	46:111
	Crime victims' compensation	46:1811
	Earned income tax credit	13:3881(A)(6)
	Unemployment compensation	23:1693
	Workers' compensation	23:1205
tools of trade	Tools, instruments, books, $7,500 of equity in a motor vehicle, one firearm to $500, needed to work	13:3881(A)(2)
wages	Minimum 75% of disposable weekly earnings or 30 times the federal minimum hourly wage per week, whichever is greater; bankruptcy judge may authorize more for low-income debtors	13:3881(A)(1)
wildcard	None	

Maine

Federal bankruptcy exemptions not available. All law references are to Maine Revised Statutes Annotated, in the form "title number-section number," unless otherwise noted.

ASSET	EXEMPTION	LAW
homestead	Real or personal property (including cooperative) used as residence to $47,500; if debtor has minor dependents in residence, to $95,000; if debtor over age 60 or physically or mentally disabled, $95,000; proceeds of sale exempt for six months	14-4422(1)
insurance	Annuity proceeds to $450 per month	24-A-2431
	Death benefit for police, fire, or emergency medical personnel who die in the line of duty	25-1612
	Disability or health proceeds, benefits, or avails	14-4422(13)(A), (C); 24-A-2429
	Fraternal benefit society benefits	24-A-4118
	Group health or life policy or proceeds	24-A-2430
	Life, endowment, annuity, or accident policy, proceeds or avails	14-4422(14)(C); 24-A-2428
	Life insurance policy, interest, loan value, or accrued dividends for policy from person you depended on, to $4,000	14-4422(11)
	Unmatured life insurance policy, except credit insurance policy	14-4422(10)
miscellaneous	Alimony & child support needed for support	14-4422(13)(D)
pensions	Tax-exempt retirement accounts, including 401(k)s, 403(b)s, profit-sharing and money purchase plans, SEP and SIMPLE IRAs, and defined-benefit plans	11 U.S.C. § 522(b)(3)(C)
	Traditional and Roth IRAs to $1,245,475 per person	11 U.S.C. § 522(b)(3)(C); (n)
	ERISA-qualified benefits needed for support	14-4422(13)(E)
	Judges	4-1203
	Legislators	3-703
	State employees	5-17054

personal property	Animals, crops, musical instruments, books, clothing, furnishings, household goods, appliances to $200 per item	14-4422(3)
	Balance due on repossessed goods; total amount financed can't exceed $2,000	9-A-5-103
	Burial plot in lieu of homestead exemption	14-4422(1)
	Cooking stove; furnaces & stoves for heat	14-4422(6)(A), (B)
	Food to last 6 months	14-4422(7)(A)
	Fuel not to exceed 10 cords of wood, 5 tons of coal, or 1,000 gal. of heating oil	14-4422(6)(C)
	Health aids	14-4422(12)
	Jewelry to $750	14-4422(4)
	Lost earnings payments needed for support	14-4422(14)(E)
	Military clothes, arms & equipment	37-B-262
	Motor vehicle to $5,000	14-4422(2)
	Personal injury recoveries to $12,500	14-4422(14)(D)
	Seeds, fertilizers & feed to raise & harvest food for 1 season	14-4422(7)(B)
	Tools & equipment to raise & harvest food	14-4422(7)(C)
	Wrongful death recoveries needed for support	14-4422(14)(B)
public benefits	Maintenance under the Rehabilitation Act	26-1411-H
	Crime victims' compensation	14-4422(14)(A)
	Federal, state, or local public assistance benefits; earned income and child tax credits (but see *In re Tetrault*, No. 12-21373 (Bankr. D. Maine 2013) (child tax credit not exempt if no refund))	14-4422(13)(A); 22-3180, 22-3766
	Social Security	14-4422(13)(A)
	Unemployment compensation	14-4422(13)(A), (C)
	Veterans benefits	14-4422(13)(B)
	Workers' compensation	39-A-106
tools of trade	Books, materials & stock to $5,000	14-4422(5)
	Commercial fishing boat, 5-ton limit	14-4422(9)
	One of each farm implement (& its maintenance equipment needed to harvest & raise crops)	14-4422(8)
wages	None	
wildcard	Unused portion of exemption in homestead to $6,000; to be used for animals, crops, musical instruments, books, clothing, furnishings, household goods, appliances, jewelry, tools of the trade & personal injury recoveries	14-4422(16)
	$400 of any property	14-4422(15)

Maryland

Federal bankruptcy exemptions not available. All law references are to Maryland Code of Courts & Judicial Proceedings unless otherwise noted. New Maryland homestead exemption is indexed for inflation by matching the federal homestead amount.

ASSET	EXEMPTION	LAW
homestead	Owner-occupied residential property or co-op or condo to $22,975 (spouses may double). Includes manufactured home that has been converted to real property pursuant to Real Property Art. 8B-201. Property held as tenancy by the entirety is exempt against debts owed by only one spouse	11-504(f); *In re Birney*, 200 F.3d 225 (4th Cir. 1999)
insurance	Disability or health benefits, including court awards, arbitrations & settlements	11-504(b)(2)
	Fraternal benefit society benefits	Ins. 8-431; Estates & Trusts 8-115
	Life insurance or annuity contract proceeds or avails if beneficiary is insured's dependent, child, or spouse	Ins. 16-111(a); Estates & Trusts 8-115
	Medical insurance benefits deducted from wages plus medical insurance payments to $145 per week or 75% of disposable wages	Commercial Law 15-601.1(3)
miscellaneous	Child support	11-504(b)(6)
	Alimony to same extent wages are exempt	11-504(b)(7)
pensions	Tax-exempt retirement accounts, including 401(k)s, 403(b)s, profit-sharing and money purchase plans, SEP and SIMPLE IRAs, and defined-benefit plans	11 U.S.C. § 522(b)(3)(C)
	Traditional and Roth IRAs to $1,245,475 per person	11 U.S.C. § 522(b)(3)(C); (n)
	ERISA-qualified benefits, including IRAs, Roth IRAs & Keoghs	11-504(h)(1), (4)
	State employees	State Pers. & Pen. 21-502
personal property	Appliances, furnishings, household goods, books, pets & clothing to $1,000 total	11-504(b)(4)
	Burial plot	Bus. Reg. 5-503
	Health aids	11-504(b)(3)
	Perpetual care trust funds	Bus. Reg. 5-603
	Prepaid college trust funds	Educ. 18-1913
	Lost future earnings recoveries	11-504(b)(2)
public benefits	Baltimore Police death benefits	Code of 1957 art. 24, 16-103
	Crime victims' compensation	Crim. Proc. 11-816(b)
	Public assistance benefits	Human Services § 5-407(a)(1), (2)
	Unemployment compensation	Labor & Employment 8-106
	Workers' compensation	Labor & Employment 9-732
tools of trade	Clothing, books, tools, instruments & appliances to $5,000	11-504(b)(1)

ASSET	EXEMPTION	LAW
wages	Earned but unpaid wages, the greater of 75% or $145 per week; in Kent, Caroline, Queen Anne's & Worcester Counties, the greater of 75% or 30 times federal minimum hourly wage. *In re Stine*, 360 F.3d 455 (4th Cir. 2004); *Bank of America v. Stine*, 379 Md. 76, 839 A.2d 727, 729 (2003)	Commercial Law 15-601.1
wildcard	$6,000 in cash or any property	11-504(b)(5)
	An additional $5,000 personal property	11-504(f)

Massachusetts

Federal bankruptcy exemptions available. All law references are to Massachusetts General Laws Annotated, in the form "title number-section number," unless otherwise noted.

ASSET	EXEMPTION	LAW
homestead	Property held as tenancy by the entirety may be exempt against debt for nonnecessity owed by only one spouse	209-1
	Automatic homestead for principal residence (including mobile home) to $125,000; to $500,000 if homestead declaration is recorded and complies with Massachusetts law; spouses may not double; trust beneficiaries are eligible for exemption; owners with a disability or 62 or older may each exempt up to $500,000, but aggregate cannot be more than $1,000,000. *In re Peirce*, 467 B.R. 260 (Bankr. D. Mass.)	188-1, 2, 5
	Spouse or children of deceased owner may claim homestead exemption	188-2
insurance	Disability benefits to $400 per week	175-110A, 175-36B
	Fraternal benefit society benefits	176-22
	Group annuity policy or proceeds	175-132C
	Group life insurance policy	175-135; 175-36
	Life insurance or annuity contract proceeds if clause prohibits proceeds from being used to pay beneficiary's creditors. *In re Sloss*, 279 B.R. 6 (Bankr. D. Mass. 2002)	175-119A
	Life insurance policy if beneficiary is a married woman. *In re Sloss*, 279 B.R. 6 (Bankr. D. Mass. 2002)	175-126
	Life or endowment policy, proceeds, or cash value. *In re Sloss*, 279 B.R. 6 (Bankr. D. Mass. 2002)	175-125
	Medical malpractice self-insurance	175F-15
miscellaneous	Property of business partnership	108A-25
pensions *see also wages*	Tax-exempt retirement accounts, including 401(k)s, 403(b)s, profit-sharing and money purchase plans, SEP and SIMPLE IRAs, and defined-benefit plans	11 U.S.C. § 522(b)(3)(C)
	Traditional and Roth IRAs to $1,245,475 per person	11 U.S.C. § 522(b)(3)(C); (n)
	Credit union employees	171-84
	ERISA-qualified benefits, including IRAs & Keoghs to specified limits	235-34A; 246-28
	Private retirement benefits	32-41
	Public employees	32-19
	Savings bank employees	168-41; 168-44

ASSET	EXEMPTION	LAW
personal property	2 cows, 12 sheep, 2 swine, 4 tons of hay	235-34(4)
	Beds & bedding; heating unit, stove, refrigerator, freezer & hot water heater; clothing	235-34(1)
	Bibles & books to $500 total	235-34(3)
	Burial plots, tombs & church pew	235-34(11),(8)
	Cash for fuel, heat, water, or light to $500 per month	235-34(1)
	Cash to $2,500/month for rent, in lieu of homestead	235-34(14)
	Cooperative association shares to $100	235-34(13)
	Food or cash for food to $600	235-34(7)
	Household furnishings to $15,000	235-34(2)
	Jewelry to $1,225	235-34(18)
	Motor vehicle to $7,500; to $15,000 if used by elderly or disabled debtor	235-34(16)
	Moving expenses for eminent domain	79-6A
	Sewing machine, computer, TV to $300	235-34(12)
	Trust company, bank, or credit union deposits to $2,500	235-34(15); 235-28A
public benefits	Public assistance	235-34(15)
	Temporary assistance for needy families	118-10
	Unemployment compensation	151A-36
	Veterans benefits	115-5
	Workers' compensation	152-47
tools of trade	Arms, accoutrements & uniforms required	235-34(10)
	Fishing boats, tackle & nets to $1,500	235-34(9)
	Materials you designed & procured to $5,000	235-34(6)
	Tools, implements & fixtures to $5,000 total	235-34(5)
wages	Earned but unpaid wages to 85% or 50x minimum wage per week	235-34(15)
wildcard	$1,000 plus up to $5,000 of unused autombile, tools of the trade, and household furniture exemptions	235-34(17)

Michigan

Federal bankruptcy exemptions available. All law references are to Michigan Compiled Laws Annotated unless otherwise noted.

Under Michigan law, bankruptcy exemption amounts are adjusted for inflation every three years (starting in 2005) by the Michigan Department of Treasury. You can find the current amounts at www.michigan.gov/documents/BankruptcyExemptions2005_141050_7.pdf or by searching Google for "Property Debtor in Bankruptcy May Exempt, Inflation Adjusted Amounts."

ASSET	EXEMPTION	LAW
homestead	Property held as tenancy by the entirety may be exempt against debts owed by only one spouse	600.5451(1)(n)
	Real property including condo to $37,775 ($56,650 if over 65 or disabled); property cannot exceed 1 lot in town, village, city, or 40 acres elsewhere; spouse or children of deceased owner may claim homestead exemption; spouses or unmarried co-owners may not double	600.5451(1) (m); *Vinson v. Dakmak*, 347 B.R. 620 (E.D. Mich. 2006)
insurance	Disability, mutual life, or health benefits	600.5451(1)(j)
	Employer-sponsored life insurance policy or trust fund	500.2210
	Fraternal benefit society benefits	500.8181

insurance (continued)	Life, endowment, or annuity proceeds if clause prohibits proceeds from being used to pay beneficiary's creditors	500.4054
	Life insurance	500.2207
miscellaneous	Property of business partnership	449.25
pensions	Tax-exempt retirement accounts, including 401(k)s, 403(b)s, profit-sharing and money purchase plans, SEP and SIMPLE IRAs, and defined-benefit plans	11 U.S.C. § 522(b)(3)(C)
	Traditional and Roth IRAs to $1,245,475 per person	11 U.S.C. § 522(b)(3)(C); (n)
	ERISA-qualified benefits, except contributions within last 120 days	600.5451(1)(l)
	Firefighters, police officers	38.559(6); 38.1683
	IRAs & Roth IRAs, except contributions within last 120 days	600.5451(1)(k)
	Judges and probate judges	38.2308; 38.1683
	Legislators	38.1057; 38.1683
	Public school employees	38.1346; 38.1683
	State employees	38.40; 38.1683
personal property	Appliances, utensils, books, furniture, jewelry & household goods to $550 each, $3,775 total	600.5451(1)(c)
	Burial plots, cemeteries	600.5451(1)(a)(vii)
	Church pew, slip, seat for entire family to $650	600.5451(1)(d)
	Clothing; family pictures	600.5451(1)(a)
	Food & fuel to last family for 6 months	600.5451(1)(b)
	Crops, animals, and feed to $2,525	600.5451(1)(e)
	1 motor vehicle to $3,475	600.5451(1)(g)
	Computer & accessories to $650	600.5451(1)(h)
	Household pets to $650	600.5451(1)(f)
	Professionally prescribed health aids	600.5451(a)
public benefits	Crime victims' compensation	18.362
	Social welfare benefits	400.63
	Unemployment compensation	421.30
	Veterans benefits for Korean War veterans	35.977
	Veterans benefits for Vietnam veterans	35.1027
	Veterans benefits for WWII veterans	35.926
	Workers' compensation	418.821
tools of trade	Arms & accoutrements required	600.6023(1)(a)
	Tools, implements, materials, stock, apparatus, or other things needed to carry on occupation to $2,525 total	600.5451(1)(i)
wages	Head of household may keep 60% of earned but unpaid wages (no less than $15/week), plus $2/week per nonspouse dependent; if not head of household may keep 40% (no less than $10/week)	600.5311
wildcard	None	

Minnesota

Federal bankruptcy exemptions available. All law references are to Minnesota Statutes Annotated, unless otherwise noted.

Note: Section 550.37(4)(a) requires certain exemptions to be adjusted for inflation on July 1 of even-numbered years; this table includes all changes made through July 1, 2014. Exemptions are published on or before the May 1 issue of the Minnesota State Register. Go to http://mn.gov. In the search box, type "dollar amount adjustments."

Note: In cases of suspected fraud, the Minnesota constitution permits courts to cap exemptions that would otherwise be unlimited. (*In re Tveten*, 402 N.W.2d 551 (Minn. 1987); *In re Medill*, 119 B.R. 685 (Bankr. D. Minn. 1990); *In re Sholdan*, 217 F.3d 1006 (8th Cir. 2000).)

ASSET	EXEMPTION	LAW
homestead	Home & land on which it is situated to $390,000; if homestead is used for agricultural purposes, $975,000; cannot exceed ½ acre in city, 160 acres elsewhere (spouses may not double)	510.01; 510.02
	Manufactured home to an unlimited value	550.37 subd. 12
insurance	Accident or disability proceeds	550.39
	Fraternal benefit society benefits	64B.18
	Life insurance proceeds to $46,000 if beneficiary is spouse or child of insured, plus $11,500 per dependent	550.37 subd. 10
	Police, fire, or beneficiary association benefits	550.37 subd. 11
	Unmatured life insurance contract dividends, interest, or loan value to $9,200 if insured is debtor or person debtor depends on	550.37 subd. 23
miscellaneous	Earnings of minor child	550.37 subd. 15
pensions	Tax-exempt retirement accounts, including 401(k)s, 403(b)s, profit-sharing and money purchase plans, SEP and SIMPLE IRAs, and defined-benefit plans	11 U.S.C. § 522(b)(3)(C)
	Traditional and Roth IRAs to $1,245,475 per person	11 U.S.C. § 522(b)(3)(C); (n)
	ERISA-qualified benefits if needed for support, up to $69,000 in present value	550.37 subd. 24
	IRAs or Roth IRAs needed for support, up to $69,000 in present value	550.37 subd. 24
	Public employees	353.15; 356.401
	State employees	352.965 subd. 8; 356.401
	State troopers	352B.071; 356.401
personal property	Appliances, furniture, radio, phonographs & TV to $10,350 total	550.37 subd. 4(b)
	Bible & books	550.37 subd. 2
	Burial plot; church pew or seat	550.37 subd. 3
	Clothing, one watch, food & utensils for family	550.37 subd. 4(a)
	Motor vehicle to $4,600 (up to $46,000 if vehicle has been modified for disability)	550.37 subd. 12(a)
	Personal injury recoveries	550.37 subd. 22
	Proceeds for damaged exempt property	550.37 subds. 9, 16
	Wedding rings to $2,817.50	550.37 subd. 4(c)
	Wrongful death recoveries	550.37 subd. 22

public benefits	Crime victims' compensation	611A.60
	Public benefits, including earned income tax credit, child tax credit, education tax credit (*In re Tomczyk*, 295 B.R. 894 (Bankr. D. Minn. 2003); *In re Dmitruk*, 517 B.R. 921 (Bankr. 8th Cir. 2014))	550.37 subd. 14
	Unemployment compensation	268.192 subd. 2
	Veterans benefits	550.38
	Workers' compensation	176.175
tools of trade *total (except teaching materials) can't exceed $13,000*	Farm machines, implements, livestock, produce & crops	550.37 subd. 5
	Teaching materials of college, university, public school, or public institution teacher	550.37 subd. 8
	Tools, machines, instruments, stock in trade, furniture & library to $11,500 total	550.37 subd. 6
wages	Minimum 75% of weekly disposable earnings or 40 times federal minimum hourly wage, whichever is greater	571.922
	Wages deposited into bank accounts for 20 days after depositing	550.37 subd. 13
	Wages paid within 6 months of returning to work after receiving welfare or after incarceration; includes earnings deposited in a financial institution in the last 60 days	550.37 subd. 14
wildcard	None	

Mississippi

Federal bankruptcy exemptions not available. All law references are to Mississippi Code unless otherwise noted.

ASSET	EXEMPTION	LAW
homestead	May file homestead declaration	85-3-27; 85-3-31
	Mobile home does not qualify as homestead unless you own land on which it is located (see *personal property*)	*In re Cobbins*, 234 B.R. 882 (S.D. Miss. 1999)
	Property you own & occupy to $75,000; if over 60 & married or widowed may claim a former residence; property cannot exceed 160 acres; sale proceeds exempt	85-3-1(b)(i); 85-3-21; 85-3-23
insurance	Disability benefits	85-3-1(b)(ii)
	Fraternal benefit society benefits	83-29-39
	Homeowners' insurance proceeds to $75,000	85-3-23
	Life insurance proceeds if clause prohibits proceeds from being used to pay beneficiary's creditors	83-7-5; 85-3-11; 85-3-13, 85-3-15
pensions	Tax-exempt retirement accounts, including 401(k)s, 403(b)s, profit-sharing and money purchase plans, SEP and SIMPLE IRAs, and defined-benefit plans	11 U.S.C. § 522(b)(3)(C)
	Traditional and Roth IRAs to $1,245,475 per person	11 U.S.C. § 522(b)(3) (C); (n)
	ERISA-qualified benefits, IRAs, Keoghs deposited over 1 year before filing bankruptcy	85-3-1(e)
	Firefighters (includes death benefits)	21-29-257; 45-2-1

pensions (continued)	Highway patrol officers	25-13-31
	Law enforcement officers' death benefits	45-2-1
	Police officers (includes death benefits)	21-29-257; 45-2-1
	Private retirement benefits to extent tax deferred	71-1-43
	Public employees retirement & disability benefits	25-11-129
	State employees	25-14-5
	Teachers	25-11-201(1)(d)
	Volunteer firefighters' death benefits	45-2-1
personal property	Mobile home to $30,000	85-3-1(d)
	Personal injury judgments to $10,000	85-3-17
	Sale or insurance proceeds for exempt property	85-3-1(b)(i)
	State health savings accounts	85-3-1(g)
	Tangible personal property to $10,000: any items worth less than $200 each; furniture, dishes, kitchenware, household goods, appliances, 1 radio, 1 TV, 1 firearm, 1 lawnmower, clothing, wedding rings, motor vehicles, tools of the trade, books, crops, health aids, domestic animals, cash on hand (does not include works of art, antiques, jewelry, or electronic entertainment equipment)	85-3-1(a)
	Tax-qualified § 529 education savings plans, including those under the Mississippi Prepaid Affordable College Tuition Program	85-3-1(f)
public benefits	Assistance to aged	43-9-19
	Assistance to blind	43-3-71
	Assistance to disabled	43-29-15
	Crime victims' compensation	99-41-23(7)
	Federal income tax refund to $5,000; earned income tax credit to $5,000; state tax refunds to $5,000	85-3-1(h); (i); (j); (k)
	Social Security	25-11-129
	Unemployment compensation	71-5-539
	Workers' compensation	71-3-43
tools of trade	*See personal property*	
wages	Earned but unpaid wages owed for 30 days; after 30 days, minimum 75% of earned but unpaid weekly disposable earnings or 30 times the federal hourly minimum wage, whichever is greater; bankruptcy judge may authorize more for low-income debtors	85-3-4
wildcard	$50,000 of any property, including deposits of money, available to Mississippi resident who is at least 70 years old; *also see personal property*	85-3-1(h)

Missouri

Federal bankruptcy exemptions not available. All law references are to Annotated Missouri Statutes unless otherwise noted.

Note: Federal bankruptcy courts have held that under *Benn v. Cole* (*In re Benn*), 491 F.3d 811, 814 (8th Cir. 2007) exemption statutes in Missouri must use the word "exempt" for property to be exempt in bankruptcy. Lower courts have interpreted this to mean that the words "not subject to execution or attachment" do *not* create an exemption for bankruptcy purposes.

Many pension exemption statutes in Missouri do not have the words required to create an exemption in bankruptcy. However, Missouri courts, interpreting the same law, point out that Missouri has long held otherwise—that such Missouri statutes do create an exemption in bankruptcy. See *Russell v. Healthmont of Missouri, LLC*, 348 S.W. 3d 784 (Missouri Court of Appeals, Western District 2011).

The Missouri wage garnishment statute may not be a valid bankruptcy exemption under *In re Benn*, because the word "exempt" does not appear in the wage garnishment statute. See *In re Parsons*, 437 B.R. 854 (Bankr. E.D. Mo. 2010).

ASSET	EXEMPTION	LAW
homestead	Property held as tenancy by the entirety may be exempt against debts owed by only one spouse	*In re Eads*, 271 B.R. 371 (Bankr. W.D. Mo. 2002)
	Real property to $15,000 or mobile home to $5,000 (joint owners may not double)	513.430(6); 513.475; *In re Smith*, 254 B.R. 751 (Bankr. W.D. Mo. 2000)
insurance	Assessment plan or life insurance proceeds	377.090
	Disability or illness benefits	513.430(10)(c)
	Fraternal benefit society benefits to $5,000, bought over 6 months before filing	513.430(8)
	Life insurance dividends, loan value, or interest to $150,000, bought over 6 months before filing	513.430(8)
	Stipulated insurance premiums	377.330
	Unmatured life insurance policy	513.430(7)
miscellaneous	Alimony, child support to $750 per month	513.430(10)(d)
	Property of business partnership	358.250
pensions	Tax-exempt retirement accounts, including 401(k)s, 403(b)s, profit-sharing and money purchase plans, SEP and SIMPLE IRAs, and defined-benefit plans	11 U.S.C. § 522(b)(3)(C)
	Traditional and Roth IRAs to $1,245,475 per person	11 U.S.C. § 522(b)(3)(C); (n)
	Employee benefit spendthrift trust	456.014
	Employees of cities with 100,000 or more people	71.207
	ERISA-qualified benefits, IRAs, Roth IRAs & other retirement accounts needed for support	513.430(10)(e), (f)
	Firefighters	87.090; 87.365; 87.485
	Highway & transportation employees	104.250
	Inherited retirement accounts	513.040(f)
	Police department employees	86.190; 86.353; 86.1430
	Public officers & employees	70.695; 70.755
	State employees	104.540
	Teachers. But see *In re Smith*, 10-60388 (W.D. Mo. 2010). See note at beginning of Missouri chart	169.090
personal property	Appliances, household goods, furnishings, clothing, books, crops, animals & musical instruments to $3,000 total	513.430(1)
	Burial grounds to 1 acre or $100	214.190
	Health aids	513.430(9)
	Health savings accounts	513.040(10)(f)
	Motor vehicles to $3,000 in aggregate	513.430(5)
	Wedding or engagement ring to $1,500 & other jewelry to $500. *In re Urie*, 2006 WL 533514 (Bankr. W.D. Mo. 2006)	513.430(2)
	Wrongful death recoveries for person you depended on	513.430(11)
public benefits	Crime victims' compensation	595.025
	Public assistance, including earned income tax credit, but not child tax credit (*In re Corbett*, No. 13–60042 (Bankr. W.D. Mo. 2013); *In re Hardy*, 495 BR 440 (Bankr. W.D. Mo. 2013))	513.430(10)(a)
	Social Security	513.430(10)(a)
	Unemployment compensation	288.380(10)(l); 513.430(10)(c)
	Veterans benefits	513.430(10)b
	Workers' compensation	287.260
tools of trade	Implements, books & tools of trade to $3,000	513.430(4)
wages	Minimum 75% of weekly earnings (90% of weekly earnings for head of family), or 30 times the federal minimum hourly wage, whichever is more; bankruptcy judge may authorize more for low-income debtors. See note at beginning of Missouri chart.	525.030
	See note at beginning of Missouri chart. Wages of servant or common laborer to $90	513.470
wildcard	$600 of any property; an additional $1,250 if head of family, plus another $350 per child under age 21	513.430(3); 513.440

Montana

Federal bankruptcy exemptions not available. All law references are to Montana Code Annotated unless otherwise noted.

ASSET	EXEMPTION	LAW
homestead	Must record homestead declaration before filing for bankruptcy	70-32-105
	Real property or mobile home you occupy to $250,000; sale, condemnation, or insurance proceeds exempt for 18 months	70-32-104; 70-32-201; 70-32-213
insurance	Annuity contract proceeds to $350 per month	33-15-514
	Disability or illness proceeds, avails, or benefits	25-13-608(1)(d); 33-15-513
	Fraternal benefit society benefits	33-7-522
	Group life insurance policy or proceeds	33-15-512
	Hail insurance benefits	80-2-245
	Life insurance proceeds if clause prohibits proceeds from being used to pay beneficiary's creditors	33-20-120
	Medical, surgical, or hospital care benefits	25-13-608(1)(f)
	Unmatured life insurance contracts	25-13-608(1)(k)
miscellaneous	Alimony, child support	25-13-608(1)(g)

pensions	Tax-exempt retirement accounts, including 401(k)s, 403(b)s, profit-sharing and money purchase plans, SEP and SIMPLE IRAs, and defined-benefit plans	11 U.S.C. § 522(b)(3)(C)
	Traditional and Roth IRAs to $1,245,475 per person	11 U.S.C. § 522(b)(3)(C); (n)
	IRAs & ERISA-qualified benefits deposited over 1 year before filing bankruptcy or up to 15% of debtor's gross annual income	31-2-106
	Firefighters	19-18-612(1)
	IRA & Roth IRA contributions & earnings made before judgment filed	25-13-608(1)(e)
	Police officers	19-19-504(1)
	Public employees	19-2-1004; 25-13-608(i)
	Teachers	19-20-706(2); 25-13-608(j)
	University system employees	19-21-212
personal property	Appliances, household furnishings, goods, animals with feed, crops, musical instruments, books, firearms, sporting goods, clothing & jewelry to $600 per item, $4,500 total	25-13-609(1)
	Burial plot	25-13-608(1)(h)
	Cooperative association shares to $500 value	35-15-404
	Health aids	25-13-608(1)(a)
	Motor vehicle to $2,500	25-13-609(2)
	Proceeds from sale or for damage or loss of exempt property for 6 months after received	25-13-610
public benefits	Aid to aged, disabled needy persons	53-2-607
	Crime victims' compensation	53-9-129
	Local public assistance	25-13-608(1)(b)
	Silicosis benefits	39-73-110
	Social Security	25-13-608(1)(b)
	Subsidized adoption payments to needy persons	53-2-607
	Unemployment compensation	31-2-106(2); 39-51-3105
	Veterans benefits	25-13-608(1)(c)
	Vocational rehabilitation to blind needy persons	53-2-607
	Workers' compensation	39-71-743
tools of trade	Implements, books & tools of trade to $3,000	25-13-609(3)
	Uniforms, arms & accoutrements needed to carry out government functions	25-13-613(b)
wages	Minimum 75% of earned but unpaid weekly disposable earnings, or 30 times the federal hourly minimum wage, whichever is greater; bankruptcy judge may authorize more for low-income debtors	25-13-614
wildcard	None	

Nebraska

Federal bankruptcy exemptions not available. All law references are to Revised Statutes of Nebraska unless otherwise noted.

ASSET	EXEMPTION	LAW
homestead	$60,000 for head of family or an unmarried person age 65 or older; cannot exceed 2 lots in city or village, 160 acres elsewhere; sale proceeds exempt 6 months after sale (spouses may not double)	40-101; 40-111; 40-113
	May record homestead declaration	40-105
insurance	Fraternal benefit society benefits to $100,000 loan value unless beneficiary convicted of a crime related to benefits	44-1089
	Life insurance proceeds and avails to $100,000	44-371
pensions *see also wages*	Tax-exempt retirement accounts, including 401(k)s, 403(b)s, profit-sharing and money purchase plans, SEP and SIMPLE IRAs, and defined-benefit plans	11 U.S.C. § 522(b)(3)(C)
	Traditional and Roth IRAs to $1,245,475 per person	11 U.S.C. § 522(b)(3)(C); (n)
	County employees	23-2322
	Deferred compensation of public employees	48-1401
	ERISA-qualified benefits including IRAs & Roth IRAs needed for support	25-1563.01
	Military disability benefits	25-1559
	School employees	79-948
	State employees	84-1324
personal property	Burial plot	12-517
	Clothing	25-1556(2)
	Crypts, lots, tombs, niches, vaults	12-605
	Furniture, household goods & appliances, household electronics, personal computers, books & musical instruments to $1,500	25-1556(3)
	Health aids	25-1556(5)
	Medical or health savings accounts to $25,000	8-1, 131(2)(b)
	Perpetual care funds	12-511
	Personal injury recoveries	25-1563.02
	Personal possessions	25-1556
public benefits	Aid to disabled, blind, aged; public assistance	68-1013
	Earned income tax credit	25-1553
	General assistance to poor persons	68-148
	Unemployment compensation	48-647
	Workers' compensation	48-149
tools of trade	Equipment or tools including a vehicle used in or for commuting to principal place of business to $2,400 (husband & wife may double)	25-1556(4); *In re Keller*, 50 B.R. 23 (D. Neb. 1985)
wages	Minimum 85% of earned but unpaid weekly disposable earnings or pension payments for head of family; minimum 75% of earned but unpaid weekly disposable earnings or 30 times the federal hourly minimum wage, whichever is greater, for all others; bankruptcy judge may authorize more for low-income debtors	25-1558
wildcard	$2,500 of any personal property except wages	25-1552

Nevada

Federal bankruptcy exemptions not available. All law references are to Nevada Revised Statutes Annotated unless otherwise noted.

ASSET	EXEMPTION	LAW
homestead	Must record homestead declaration before filing for bankruptcy	115.020
	Real property or mobile home to $550,000. Spouses may not double	115.010; 21.090(1)(m)
insurance	Annuity contract proceeds	687B.290
	Fraternal benefit society benefits	695A.220
	Group life or health policy or proceeds	687B.280
	Health proceeds or avails	687B.270
	Life insurance policy or proceeds	21.090(1)(k); *In re Bower*, 234 B.R. 109 (Nev. 1999)
	Life insurance proceeds if you're not the insured	687B.260
	Private disability insurance proceeds	21.090(1)(ee)
miscellaneous	Alimony & child support	21.090(1)(s)
	Property of some business partnerships	87.250
	Security deposits for a rental residence, except landlord may enforce terms of lease or rental agreement	21.090(1)(n)
pensions	Tax-exempt retirement accounts, including 401(k)s, 403(b)s, profit-sharing and money purchase plans, SEP and SIMPLE IRAs, and defined-benefit plans	11 U.S.C. § 522(b)(3)(C)
	Traditional and Roth IRAs to $1,245,475 per person	11 U.S.C. § 522(b)(3)(C); (n)
	ERISA-qualified benefits, deferred compensation, SEP IRA, Roth IRA, or IRA to $500,000	21.090(1)(r)
	Public employees	286.670; 21.090(1)(ii)
personal property	Appliances, household goods, furniture, wearing apparel, home & yard equipment to $12,000 total	21.090(1)(b)
	Books, works of art, musical instruments & jewelry to $5,000	21.090(1)(a)
	Burial plot purchase money held in trust	689.700; 21.090(1)(ff)
	Funeral service contract money held in trust	689.700
	Health aids	21.090(1)(q)
	Interests in qualifying trusts	21.090(1)(cc)
	Keepsakes & pictures	21.090(1)(a)
	Metal-bearing ores, geological specimens, art curiosities, or paleontological remains; must be arranged, classified, cataloged & numbered in reference books	21.100
	Mortgage impound accounts	645B.180
	Motor vehicle to $15,000; no limit on vehicle equipped for disabled person	21.090(1)(f), (o)
	1 gun	21.090(1)(i)
	Personal injury compensation to $16,500	21.090(1)(u)
	Restitution received for criminal act	21.090(1)(x)
	Stock in certain closely held corporations	21.090(1)(bb); 78.764
	Tax refunds derived from the state or federal earned income credit	21.090(1)(aa)
	Wrongful death awards to survivors	21.090(1)(v)
public benefits	Aid to blind, aged, disabled; public assistance	422.291; 21.090(1)(kk); 422A.325
	Crime victims' compensation	21.090
	Earned income tax credit (state or federal)	21.090(1)(bb)
	Industrial insurance (workers' compensation)	616C.205; 21.090(1)(gg)
	Public assistance for children	432.036; 21.090(1)(ll)
	Social Security retirement, disability, SSI, survivor benefits	21.090(1)(y)
	Unemployment compensation	612.710; 21.090(1)(hh)
	Vocational rehabilitation benefits	615.270; 21.090(1)(jj)
tools of trade	Arms, uniforms & accoutrements you're required to keep	21.090(1)(j)
	Cabin or dwelling of miner or prospector; mining claim, cars, implements & appliances to $4,500 total (for working claim only)	21.090(1)(e)
	Farm trucks, stock, tools, equipment & seed to $4,500	21.090(1)(c)
	Library, equipment, supplies, tools, inventory & materials to $10,000	21.090(1)(d)
wages	Minimum 75% of disposable weekly earnings or 50 times the federal minimum hourly wage per week, whichever is more; bankruptcy judge may authorize more for low-income debtors. *In re Christensen*, 149 P.3d 40 (2006)	21.090(1)(g)
wildcard	$1,000 of any personal property	21.090(1)(z)

New Hampshire

Federal bankruptcy exemptions available. All law references are to New Hampshire Revised Statutes Annotated unless otherwise noted.

ASSET	EXEMPTION	LAW
homestead	Real property or manufactured housing (& the land it's on if you own it) to $100,000	480:1
insurance	Firefighters' aid insurance	402:69
	Fraternal benefit society benefits	418:17
	Homeowners' insurance proceeds to $5,000	512:21(VIII)
miscellaneous	Jury, witness fees	512:21(VI)
	Property of business partnership	304-A:25
	Wages of minor child	512:21(III)
pensions	Tax-exempt retirement accounts, including 401(k)s, 403(b)s, profit-sharing and money purchase plans, SEP and SIMPLE IRAs, and defined-benefit plans	11 U.S.C. § 522(b)(3)(C)
	Traditional and Roth IRAs to $1,245,475 per person	11 U.S.C. § 522(b)(3)(C); (n)
	ERISA-qualified retirement accounts including IRAs & Roth IRAs	512:2 (XIX)
	Federally created pension (only benefits building up)	512:21(IV)
	Firefighters	102:23
	Police officers	103:18
	Public employees	100-A:26

personal property	Beds, bedding & cooking utensils	511:2(II)
	Bibles & books to $800	511:2(VIII)
	Burial plot, lot	511:2(XIV)
	Church pew	511:2(XV)
	Clothing	511:2(I)
	Cooking & heating stoves, refrigerator	511:2(IV)
	Domestic fowl to $300	511:2(XIII)
	Food & fuel to $400	511:2(VI)
	Furniture to $3,500	511:2(III)
	Jewelry to $500	511:2(XVII)
	Motor vehicle to $4,000	511:2(XVI)
	Proceeds for lost or destroyed exempt property	512:21(VIII)
	Sewing machine	511:2(V)
	1 cow, 6 sheep & their fleece, 4 tons of hay	511:2(XI); (XII)
	1 hog or pig or its meat (if slaughtered)	511:2(X)
public benefits	Aid to blind, aged, disabled; public assistance	167:25
	Unemployment compensation	282-A:159
	Workers' compensation	281-A:52
tools of trade	Tools of your occupation to $5,000	511:2(IX)
	Uniforms, arms & equipment of military member	511:2(VII)
	Yoke of oxen or horse needed for farming or teaming	511:2(XII)
wages	50 times the federal minimum hourly wage per week	512:21(II)
	Deposits in any account designated a payroll account	512:21(XI)
	Earned but unpaid wages of spouse	512:21(III)
	Note: Wage exemptions cannot be used in bankruptcy. See *In re Damast*, 136 B.R. 11 (Bankr. D. N.H. 1991)	
wildcard	$1,000 of any property	511:2(XVIII)
	Unused portion of bibles & books, food & fuel, furniture, jewelry, motor vehicle & tools of trade exemptions to $7,000	511:2(XVIII)

New Jersey

Federal bankruptcy exemptions available. All law references are to New Jersey Statutes Annotated unless otherwise noted.

ASSET	EXEMPTION	LAW
homestead	None, but survivorship interest of a spouse in property held as tenancy by the entirety is exempt from creditors of a single spouse	*Freda v. Commercial Trust Co. of New Jersey*, 570 A.2d 409 (N.J. 1990)
insurance	Annuity contract proceeds to $500 per month	17B:24-7
	Disability benefits	17:18-12
	Disability, death, medical, or hospital benefits for civil defense workers	App. A:9-57.6
	Disability or death benefits for military member	38A:4-8
	Group life or health policy or proceeds	17B:24-9
	Health or disability benefits	17:18-12; 17B:24-8
	Life insurance proceeds if clause prohibits proceeds from being used to pay beneficiary's creditors	17B:24-10
	Life insurance proceeds or avails if you're not the insured	17B:24-6b

pensions	Tax-exempt retirement accounts, including 401(k)s, 403(b)s, profit-sharing and money purchase plans, SEP and SIMPLE IRAs, and defined-benefit plans	11 U.S.C. § 522(b)(3)(C)
	Traditional and Roth IRAs to $1,245,475 per person	11 U.S.C. § 522(b)(3)(C); (n)
	Alcohol beverage control officers	43:8A-20
	City boards of health employees	43:18-12
	Civil defense workers	App. A:9-57.6
	County employees	43:10-57; 43:10-105
	ERISA-qualified benefits for city employees	43:13-9
	Firefighters, police officers, traffic officers	43:16-7; 43:16A-17
	IRAs	*In re Yuhas*, 104 F.3d 612 (3d Cir. 1997)
	Judges	43:6A-41
	Municipal employees	43:13-44
	Prison employees	43:7-13
	Public employees	43:15A-53
	School district employees	18A:66-116
	State police	53:5A-45
	Street & water department employees	43:19-17
	Teachers	18A:66-51
	Trust containing personal property created pursuant to federal tax law, including 401(k) plans, IRAs, Roth IRAs & higher education (529) savings plans	25:2-1; *In re Yuhas*, 104 F.3d 612 (3d Cir. 1997)
personal property	Burial plots	45:27-21
	Clothing	2A:17-19
	Furniture & household goods to $1,000	2A:26-4
	Personal property & possessions of any kind, stock or interest in corporations to $1,000 total	2A:17-19
public benefits	Old age, permanent disability assistance	44:7-35
	Unemployment compensation	43:21-53
	Workers' compensation	34:15-29
tools of trade	None	
wages	90% of earned but unpaid wages if annual income is less than 250% of federal poverty level; 75% if annual income is higher	2A:17-56
	Wages or allowances received by military personnel	38A:4-8
wildcard	None	

New Mexico

Federal bankruptcy exemptions available. All law references are to New Mexico Statutes Annotated unless otherwise noted.

ASSET	EXEMPTION	LAW
homestead	$60,000	42-10-9
insurance	Benevolent association benefits to $5,000	42-10-4
	Fraternal benefit society benefits	59A-44-18
	Life, accident, health, or annuity benefits, withdrawal or cash value, if beneficiary is a New Mexico resident	42-10-3
	Life insurance proceeds	42-10-5
miscellaneous	Ownership interest in unincorporated association	53-10-2
	Property of business partnership	54-1A-501

pensions	Tax-exempt retirement accounts, including 401(k)s, 403(b)s, profit-sharing and money purchase plans, SEP and SIMPLE IRAs, and defined-benefit plans	11 U.S.C. § 522(b)(3)(C)
	Traditional and Roth IRAs to $1,245,475 per person	11 U.S.C. § 522(b)(3) (C); (n)
	Pension or retirement benefits	42-10-1; 42-10-2
	Public school employees	22-11-42A
personal property	Books & furniture	42-10-1; 42-10-2
	Building materials	48-2-15
	Clothing	42-10-1; 42-10-2
	Cooperative association shares, minimum amount needed to be member	53-4-28
	Health aids	42-10-1; 42-10-2
	Jewelry to $2,500	42-10-1; 42-10-2
	Materials, tools & machinery to dig, drill, complete, operate, or repair oil line, gas well, or pipeline	70-4-12
	Motor vehicle to $4,000	42-10-1; 42-10-2
public benefits	Crime victims' compensation	31-22-15
	General assistance	27-2-21
	Occupational disease disablement benefits	52-3-37
	Unemployment compensation	51-1-37
	Workers' compensation	52-1-52
tools of trade	$1,500	42-10-1; 42-10-2
wages	Minimum 75% of disposable earnings or 40 times the federal hourly minimum wage, whichever is more; bankruptcy judge may authorize more for low-income debtors	35-12-7
wildcard	$500 of any personal property	42-10-1
	$5,000 of any real or personal property, in lieu of homestead	42-10-10

New York

Federal bankruptcy exemptions are available. All references are to Consolidated Laws of New York unless otherwise noted; Civil Practice Law & Rules are abbreviated C.P.L.R.

ASSET	EXEMPTION	LAW
homestead	Real property including co-op, condo, or mobile home, to $75,000, $125,000, or $150,000, depending on the county	C.P.L.R. 5206(a); *In re Pearl*, 723 F.2d 193 (2nd Cir. 1983)
insurance	Annuity contract benefits due the debtor, if debtor paid for the contract; $5,000 limit if purchased within 6 months prior to filing & not tax deferred	Ins. 3212(d); Debt. & Cred. 283(1)
	Disability or illness benefits to $400 per month	Ins. 3212(c)
	Life insurance proceeds & avails if the beneficiary is not the debtor, or if debtor's spouse has taken out policy	Ins. 3212(b)
	Life insurance proceeds left at death with the insurance company, if clause prohibits proceeds from being used to pay beneficiary's creditors	Est. Powers & Trusts 7-1.5(a)(2)
miscellaneous	Alimony, child support	C.P.L.R. 5205 (d)(3); Debt. & Cred. 282(2)(d)
	Property of business partnership	Partnership 51

pensions	Tax-exempt retirement accounts, including 401(k)s, 403(b)s, profit-sharing and money purchase plans, SEP and SIMPLE IRAs, and defined-benefit plans	11 U.S.C. § 522(b)(3)(C)
	Traditional and Roth IRAs to $1,245,475 per person	11 U.S.C. § 522(b)(3) (C); (n)
	ERISA-qualified benefits, IRAs, Roth IRAs & Keoghs & income needed for support	C.P.L.R. 5205(c); Debt. & Cred. 282(2)(e)
	Public retirement benefits	Ins. 4607
	State employees	Ret. & Soc. Sec. 10
	Teachers	Educ. 524
	Village police officers	Unconsolidated 5711-o
	Volunteer ambulance workers' benefits	Vol. Amb. Wkr. Ben. 23
	Volunteer firefighters' benefits	Vol. Firefighter Ben. 23
personal property	Religious texts, schoolbooks, other books to $500; pictures; clothing; church pew or seat; sewing machine, refrigerator, TV, radio; furniture, cooking utensils & tableware, dishes; food to last 120 days; stoves with fuel to last 120 days; domestic animal with food to last 120 days, to $1,000; wedding ring; watch, jewelry, art to $1,000; exemptions may not exceed $10,000 total (including tools of trade & limited annuity)	C.P.L.R. 5205(a) (1)-(6); Debt. & Cred. 283(1)
	Burial plot without structure to ¼ acre	C.P.L.R. 5206(f)
	Cash (including savings bonds, tax refunds, bank & credit union deposits) to $5,000, or to $10,000 after exemptions for personal property taken, whichever amount is less (for debtors who do not claim homestead)	Debt. & Cred. 283(2)
	College tuition savings program trust fund	C.P.L.R. 5205(j)
	Electronic deposits of exempt property into bank account in last 45 days	C.P.L.R. 5205(l)(1)
	Health aids, including service animals with food	C.P.L.R. 5205(h)
	Lost future earnings recoveries needed for support	Debt. & Cred. 282(3)(iv)
	Motor vehicle to $4,000; $10,000 if equipped for disabled person (except if municipality is creditor)	Debt. & Cred. 282(1); *In re Miller*, 167 B.R. 782 (S.D. N.Y. 1994)
	Personal injury recoveries up to 1 year after receiving	Debt. & Cred. 282(3)(iii)
	Recovery for injury to exempt property up to 1 year after receiving	C.P.L.R. 5205(b)
	Savings & loan savings to $600	Banking 407
	Security deposit to landlord, utility company	C.P.L.R. 5205(g)
	Spendthrift trust fund principal, 90% of income if not created by debtor	C.P.L.R. 5205(c), (d)
	Wrongful death recoveries for person you depended on	Debt. & Cred. 282(3)(ii)

public benefits	Aid to blind, aged, disabled	Debt. & Cred. 282(2)(c)
	Crime victims' compensation	Debt. & Cred. 282(3)(i)
	Home relief, local public assistance	Debt. & Cred. 282(2)(a)
	Public assistance, does not include earned income tax credit (*In re Fasarakis*, 423 B.R. 34 (E.D.N.Y. 2010)) but might include rent-controlled lease (*In re Santiago-Monteverde*, 2014 N.Y. Slip Op. 08051 (Ct. App. N.Y. 2014))	Soc. Serv. 137
	Social Security	Debt. & Cred. 282(2)(a)
	Unemployment compensation	Debt. & Cred. 282(2)(a)
	Veterans benefits	Debt. & Cred. 282(2)(b)
	Workers' compensation	Debt. & Cred. 282(2)(c); Work. Comp. 33, 218
tools of trade	Farm machinery, team & food for 60 days; professional furniture, books & instruments to $3,000 total	C.P.L.R. 5205(a),(b)
	Uniforms, medal, emblem, equipment, horse, arms & sword of member of military	C.P.L.R. 5205(e)
wages	90% of earned but unpaid wages received within 60 days before & anytime after filing	C.P.L.R. 5205(d); 5231
	90% of earnings from dairy farmer's sales to milk dealers	C.P.L.R. 5205(f)
	100% of pay of noncommissioned officer, private, or musician in U.S. or N.Y. state armed forces. *In re Wiltsie*, 443 B.R. 223 (Bankr. N.D. N.Y. 2011)	C.P.L.R. 5205(e)
wildcard	$1,000 of personal property, bank account, or cash in lieu of homestead	C.P.L.R. 5205(a)(9)

North Carolina

Federal bankruptcy exemptions not available. All law references are to General Statutes of North Carolina unless otherwise noted.

ASSET	EXEMPTION	LAW
homestead	Property held as tenancy by the entirety may be exempt against debts owed by only one spouse	*In re Chandler*, 148 B.R. 13 (E.D. N.C. 1992)
	Real or personal property, including co-op, used as residence to $35,000; $60,000 if 65 or older; property owned with spouse as tenants by the entirety or joint tenants with right of survivorship, and spouse has died; up to $5,000 of unused portion of homestead may be applied to any property	1C-1601(a) (1),(2)
insurance	Employee group life policy or proceeds	58-58-165
	Fraternal benefit society benefits	58-24-85
	Life insurance on spouse or children	1C-1601(a)(6); Const. Art. X § 5
miscellaneous	Alimony, support, separate maintenance, and child support necessary for support of debtor and dependents	1C-1601(a)(12)
	Property of business partnership	59-55
	Support received by a surviving spouse for 1 year, up to $10,000	30-15

pensions	Tax-exempt retirement accounts, including 401(k)s, 403(b)s, profit-sharing and money purchase plans, SEP and SIMPLE IRAs, and defined-benefit plans	11 U.S.C. § 522(b)(3)(C)
	Traditional and Roth IRAs to $1,245,475 per person	11 U.S.C. § 522(b) (3)(C); (n)
	Firefighters & rescue squad workers	58-86-90
	IRAs & Roth IRAs	1C-1601(a)(9)
	Law enforcement officers	143-166.30(g)
	Legislators	120-4.29
	Municipal, city & county employees	128-31
	Retirement benefits from another state to extent exempt in that state	1C-1601(a)(11)
	Teachers & state employees	135-9; 135-95
personal property	Animals, crops, musical instruments, books, wearing apparel, appliances, household goods & furnishings to $5,000 total; may add $1,000 per dependent, up to $4,000 total additional (all property must have been purchased at least 90 days before filing)	1C-1601(a)(4)
	Burial plot to $18,500, in lieu of homestead	1C-1601(a)(1)
	College savings account established under 26 U.S.C. § 529 to $25,000, excluding certain contributions within prior year	1C-1601(a)(10)
	Health aids	1C-1601(a)(7)
	Motor vehicle to $3,500	1C-1601(a)(3)
	Personal injury & wrongful death recoveries for person you depended on	1C-1601(a)(8)
public benefits	Aid to blind	111-18
	Crime victims' compensation	15B-17
	Public adult assistance under work first program	108A-36
	Unemployment compensation	96-17
	Workers' compensation	97-21
tools of trade	Implements, books & tools of trade to $2,000	1C-1601(a)(5)
wages	Earned but unpaid wages received 60 days before filing for bankruptcy, needed for support	1-362
wildcard	$5,000 of unused homestead or burial exemption	1C-1601(a)(2)
	$500 of any personal property	Constitution Art. X § 1

North Dakota

Federal bankruptcy exemptions not available. All law references are to North Dakota Century Code unless otherwise noted.

ASSET	EXEMPTION	LAW
homestead	Real property, house trailer, or mobile home to $100,000 (spouses may not double)	28-22-02(10); 47-18-01
insurance	Fraternal benefit society benefits	26.1-15.1-18;
	Any unmatured life insurance contract, other than credit life insurance	26.1-33-40; 28-22-03.1(4)
	Life insurance proceeds payable to deceased's estate, not to a specific beneficiary	26.1-33-40
	Life insurance surrender value to $8,000 per policy, if beneficiary is insured's dependent & policy was owned over 1 year before filing for bankruptcy; limit does not apply if more needed for support	28-22-03.1(5)

miscellaneous	Child support payments	14-09-09.31; 28-22-03.1(8)(d)
pensions	Tax-exempt retirement accounts, including 401(k)s, 403(b)s, profit-sharing and money purchase plans, SEP and SIMPLE IRAs, and defined-benefit plans	11 U.S.C. § 522(b)(3)(C)
	Traditional and Roth IRAs to $1,245,475 per person	11 U.S.C. § 522(b)(3)(C); (n)
	Disabled veterans' benefits, except military retirement pay	28-22-03.1(4)(d)
	ERISA-qualified benefits, IRAs, Roth IRAs & Keoghs to $100,000 per plan; no limit if more needed for support; total of all accounts cannot exceed $200,000	28-22-03.1(7)
	Public employees' deferred compensation	54-52.2-06
	Public employees' pensions	28-22-19(1)
personal property	One Bible or other religious text; schoolbooks; other books	28-22-02(4)
	Burial plots, church pew	28-22-02(2), (3)
	Wearing apparel to $5,000 and all clothing & family pictures	28-22-02(1), (5)
	Crops or grain raised by debtor on 160 acres where debtor resides	28-22-02(8)
	Food & fuel to last 1 year	28-22-02(6)
	Health aids	28-22-03.1(6)
	Insurance proceeds for exempt property	28-22-02(9)
	One motor vehicle to $2,950 (or $32,000 for vehicle that has been modified to accommodate owner's disability)	28-22-03.1(2)
	Personal injury recoveries to $15,000	28-22-03.1(4)(b)
	Wrongful death recoveries to $15,000	28-22-03.1(4)(a)
public benefits	Crime victims' compensation	28-22-03.1(4); 28-22-19(2)
	Old age & survivor insurance program benefits	52-09-22
	Public assistance	28-22-19(3)
	Social Security	28-22-03.1(8)(a)
	Unemployment compensation	52-06-30
	Veterans disability benefits	28-22-03.1(8)(b)
	Workers' compensation	65-05-29
tools of trade	Books, tools & implements of trade to $1,500	28-22-03.1(3)
wages	Minimum 75% of disposable weekly earnings or 40 times the federal minimum wage, whichever is more; bankruptcy judge may authorize more for low-income debtors. Note: Wage exemption cannot be used in bankruptcy.	32-09.1-03
wildcard	$7,500 of any property in lieu of homestead	28-22-03.1(1)
	Head of household not claiming crops or grain may claim $7,500 of any personal property	28-22-03
	Unmarried with no dependents not claiming crops or grain may claim $3,750 of any personal property	28-22-05

Ohio

Federal bankruptcy exemptions not available. All law references are to Ohio Revised Code unless otherwise noted. Amounts are adjusted for inflation by tracking federal exemption amounts.

ASSET	EXEMPTION	LAW
homestead	Property held as tenancy by the entirety may be exempt against debts owed by only one spouse	*In re Pernus*, 143 B.R. 856 (N.D. Ohio 1992)
	Real or personal property used as residence to $132,900	2329.66(A)(1)(b)
insurance	Benevolent society benefits to $5,000	2329.63; 2329.66(A)(6)(a)
	Disability benefits needed for support	2329.66(A)(6)(e); 3923.19
	Fraternal benefit society benefits	2329.66(A)(6)(d); 3921.18
	Group life insurance policy or proceeds	2329.66(A)(6)(c); 3917.05
	Life, endowment, or annuity contract avails for your spouse, child, or dependent	2329.66(A)(6)(b); 3911.10
	Life insurance proceeds for a spouse	3911.12
	Life insurance proceeds if clause prohibits proceeds from being used to pay beneficiary's creditors	3911.14
miscellaneous	Alimony, child support needed for support	2329.66(A)(11)
	Property of business partnership	1775.24; 2329.66(A)(14)
pensions	Tax-exempt retirement accounts, including 401(k)s, 403(b)s, profit-sharing and money purchase plans, SEP and SIMPLE IRAs, and defined-benefit plans	11 U.S.C. § 522(b)(3)(C)
	Traditional and Roth IRAs to $1,245,475 per person	11 U.S.C. § 522(b)(3)(C); (n)
	ERISA-qualified benefits needed for support	2329.66(A)(10)(b)
	Firefighters, police officers	742.47
	IRAs, Roth IRAs & Keoghs needed for support	2329.66(A)(10)(c), (a)
	Public employees	145.56
	Public safety officers' death benefit	2329.66(A)(10)(a)
	Public school employees	3309.66
	State highway patrol employees	5505.22
	Volunteer firefighters' dependents	146.13
personal property	Animals, crops, books, musical instruments, appliances, household goods, furnishings, wearing apparel, firearms, hunting & fishing equipment to $575 per item; jewelry to $1,550 in the aggregate; $12,250 total	2329.66(A)(4)(b), (c), (d); *In re Szydlowski*, 186 B.R. 907 (N.D. Ohio 1995)
	Burial plot	517.09; 2329.66(A)(8)
	Cash, money due within 90 days, tax refund, bank, security & utility deposits to $450	2329.66(A)(3); *In re Szydlowski*, 186 B.R. 907 (N.D. Ohio 1995)
	Compensation for lost future earnings needed for support, received during 12 months before filing	2329.66(A)(12)(d)

personal property (continued)	Health aids (professionally prescribed)	2329.66(A)(7)
	Motor vehicle to $3,675	2329.66(A) (2)(b)
	Personal injury recoveries to $23,000, received during 12 months before filing	2329.66(A) (12)(c)
	Tuition credit or payment	2329.66(A)(16)
	Wrongful death recoveries for person debtor depended on, needed for support, received during 12 months before filing	2329.66(A) (12)(b)
public benefits	Crime victims' compensation, received during 12 months before filing	2329.66(A)(12) (a); 2743.66(D)
	Disability assistance payments	2329.66(A)(9)(f); 5115.07
	Child tax credit and earned income tax credit	2329.66(A) (9)(g)
	Public assistance	2329.66(A)(9) (d), (e); 5107.75; 5108.08
	Unemployment compensation	2329.66(A)(9) (c); 4141.32
	Vocational rehabilitation benefits	2329.66(A)(9) (a); 3304.19
	Workers' compensation	2329.66(A)(9) (b); 4123.67
tools of trade	Implements, books & tools of trade to $2,325	2329.66(A)(5)
wages	Minimum 75% of disposable weekly earnings or 30 times the federal hourly minimum wage, whichever is higher; bankruptcy judge may authorize more for low-income debtors. *In re Jones*, 318 B.R. 841 (Bankr. S.D. Ohio 2005)	2329.66(A)(13)
wildcard	$1,225 of any property	2329.66(A)(18)

Oklahoma

Federal bankruptcy exemptions not available. All law references are to Oklahoma Statutes Annotated (in the form "title number-section number"), unless otherwise noted.

ASSET	EXEMPTION	LAW
homestead	Real property or manufactured home to unlimited value; property cannot exceed 1 acre in city, town, or village, or 160 acres elsewhere; $5,000 limit if more than 25% of total sq. ft. area used for business purposes; okay to rent homestead as long as no other residence is acquired	31-1(A)(1); 31-1(A)(2); 31-2
insurance	Annuity benefits & cash value	36-3631.1
	Assessment or mutual benefits	36-2410
	Fraternal benefit society benefits	36-2718.1
	Funeral benefits prepaid & placed in trust	36-6125
	Group life policy or proceeds	36-3632
	Life, health, accident & mutual benefit insurance proceeds & cash value, if clause prohibits proceeds from being used to pay beneficiary's creditors	36-3631.1
	Limited stock insurance benefits	36-2510
miscellaneous	Alimony, child support	31-1(A)(19)
	Beneficiary's interest in a statutory support trust	6-3010
	Liquor license	37-532
	Property of business partnership	54-1-504

pensions	Tax-exempt retirement accounts, including 401(k)s, 403(b)s, profit-sharing and money purchase plans, SEP and SIMPLE IRAs, and defined-benefit plans	11 U.S.C. § 522(b)(3)(C)
	Traditional and Roth IRAs to $1,245,475 per person	11 U.S.C. § 522(b)(3) (C); (n)
	County employees	19-959
	Disabled veterans	31-7
	ERISA-qualified benefits, IRAs, Roth IRAs, Education IRAs & Keoghs	31-1(A)(20), (24)
	Firefighters	11-49-126
	Judges	20-1111
	Law enforcement employees	47-2-303.3
	Police officers	11-50-124
	Public employees	74-923
	Tax-exempt benefits	60-328
	Teachers	70-17-109
personal property	Books, portraits & pictures	31-1(A)(6)
	Burial plots	31-1(A)(4); 8-7
	Clothing to $4,000	31-1(A)(7)
	College savings plan interest	31-1A(24)
	Deposits in an IDA (Individual Development Account)	31-1A(22)
	Food & seed for growing to last 1 year	31-1(A)(17)
	Guns for household use to $2,000	31-1A(14)
	Health aids (professionally prescribed)	31-1(A)(9)
	Household & kitchen furniture; personal computer and related equipment	31-1(A)(3)
	Livestock for personal or family use: 5 dairy cows & calves under 6 months; 100 chickens; 20 sheep; 10 hogs; 2 horses, bridles & saddles; forage & feed to last 1 year	31-1(A)(10), (11), (12), (15), (16), (17)
	Motor vehicle to $7,500	31-1(A)(13)
	Personal injury & wrongful death recoveries to $50,000	31-1(A)(21)
	Prepaid funeral benefits	36-6125(H)
	War bond payroll savings account	51-42
	Wedding and anniversary rings to $3,000	31-1(A)(8)
public benefits	Crime victims' compensation	21-142.13
	Public assistance	56-173
	Federal earned income tax credit	31-1(A)(23)
	Social Security	56-173
	Unemployment compensation	40-2-303
	Workers' compensation	85-48
tools of trade	Implements needed to farm homestead; tools, books & apparatus to $10,000 total	31-1(A)(5); 31-1(C)
wages	75% of wages earned in 90 days before filing bankruptcy; bankruptcy judge may allow more if you show hardship	12-1171.1; 31-1(A)(18); 31-1.1
wildcard	None	

Oregon

Federal bankruptcy exemptions available. All law references are to Oregon Revised Statutes unless otherwise noted.

ASSET	EXEMPTION	LAW
homestead	Prepaid rent & security deposit for renter's dwelling	*In re Casserino*, 379 F.3d 1069 (9th Cir. 2004)
	Real property of a soldier or sailor during time of war	408.440
	Real property you occupy or intend to occupy to $40,000 ($50,000 for joint owners); property cannot exceed 1 block in town or city or 160 acres elsewhere; sale proceeds exempt 1 year from sale if you intend to purchase another home or use sale proceeds for rent	18.395; 18.402; *In re Wynn*, 369 B.R. 605 (D. Or. 2007)
	Tenancy by entirety not exempt, but subject to survivorship rights of nondebtor spouse	*In re Pletz*, 225 B.R. 206 (D. Or. 1997)
insurance	Annuity contract benefits to $500 per month	743.049
	Fraternal benefit society benefits to $7,500	748.207; 18.348
	Group life policy or proceeds not payable to insured	743.047
	Health or disability proceeds or avails	743.050
	Life insurance proceeds or cash value if you are not the insured	743.046; 743.047
miscellaneous	Alimony, child support needed for support	18.345(1)(i)
	Liquor licenses	471.292 (1)
pensions	Tax-exempt retirement accounts, including 401(k)s, 403(b)s, profit-sharing and money purchase plans, SEP and SIMPLE IRAs, and defined-benefit plans	11 U.S.C. § 522(b)(3)(C)
	Traditional and Roth IRAs to $1,245,475 per person	11 U.S.C. § 522(b)(3)(C); (n)
	ERISA-qualified benefits, including IRAs & SEPs & payments to $7,500	18.358; 18.348
	Public officers', employees' pension payments to $7,500	237.980; 238.445; 18.348(2)
personal property	Books, pictures & musical instruments to $600 total	18.345(1)(a)
	Building materials for construction of an improvement	87.075
	Burial plot	65.870
	Clothing, jewelry & other personal items to $1,800 total	18.345(1)(b)
	Compensation for lost earnings payments for debtor or someone debtor depended on, to extent needed	18.345(1)(L),(3)
	Domestic animals, poultry & pets to $1,000 plus food to last 60 days (no doubling)	18.345(1)(e)
	Food & fuel to last 60 days if debtor is householder	18.345(1)(f)
	Furniture, household items, utensils, radios & TVs to $3,000 total (no doubling)	18.345(1)(f)
	Health aids	18.345(1)(h)
	Health savings accounts & medical savings accounts	18.345(1)(o)
	Higher education savings account to $7,500	348.863; 18.348(1)
personal property (continued)	Motor vehicle to $3,000	18.345(1)(d),(3)
	Personal injury recoveries to $10,000	18.345(1)(k),(3)
	Pistol, rifle or shotgun (owned by person over 16) to $1,000	18.362
	Wages deposited into a bank account to $7,500; cash for sold exempt property	18.348; 18.385
public benefits	Aid to blind to $7,500	411.706; 411.760; 18.348
	Aid to disabled to $7,500	411.706; 411.760; 18.348
	Civil defense & disaster relief to $7,500	18.348
	Crime victims' compensation	18.345(1)(j),(3); 147.325
	Federal earned income tax credit	18.345(1)(n)
	General assistance to $7,500	411.760; 18.348
	Injured inmates' benefits to $7,500	655.530; 18.348
	Medical assistance to $7,500	414.095; 18.348
	Old-age assistance to $7,500	411.706; 411.760; 18.348
	Unemployment compensation to $7,500	657.855; 18.348
	Veterans benefits & proceeds of Veterans loans	407.125; 407.595; 18.348(m)
	Vocational rehabilitation to $7,500	344.580; 18.348
	Workers' compensation to $7,500	656.234; 18.348
tools of trade	Tools, library, team with food to last 60 days, to $5,000	18.345(1)(c), (3)
wages	75% of disposable wages or $170 per week, whichever is greater; bankruptcy judge may authorize more for low-income debtors	18.385
	Wages withheld in state employee's bond savings accounts. *In re Robinson*, 241 B.R. 447 (9th Cir. B.A.P. 1999)	292.070
wildcard	$400 of any personal property not already covered by existing exemption	18.345(1)(p)

Pennsylvania

Federal bankruptcy exemptions available. All law references are to Pennsylvania Consolidated Statutes Annotated unless otherwise noted.

ASSET	EXEMPTION	LAW
homestead	None; however, property held as tenancy by the entirety may be exempt against debts owed by only one spouse	*In re Martin*, 269 B.R. 119 (M.D. Pa. 2001)
insurance	Accident or disability benefits	42-8124(c)(7)
	Fraternal benefit society benefits	42-8124(c)(1), (8)
	Group life policy or proceeds	42-8124(c)(5)
	Insurance policy or annuity contract payments where insured is the beneficiary, cash value or proceeds to $100 per month	42-8124(c)(3)
	Life insurance & annuity proceeds if clause prohibits proceeds from being used to pay beneficiary's creditors	42-8214(c)(4)
	Life insurance annuity policy cash value or proceeds if beneficiary is insured's dependent, child or spouse	42-8124(c)(6)
	No-fault automobile insurance proceeds	42-8124(c)(9)
miscellaneous	Property of business partnership	15-8342

pensions	Tax-exempt retirement accounts, including 401(k)s, 403(b)s, profit-sharing and money purchase plans, SEP and SIMPLE IRAs, and defined-benefit plans	11 U.S.C. § 522(b)(3)(C)
	Traditional and Roth IRAs to $1,245,475 per person	11 U.S.C. § 522(b)(3)(C); (n)
	City employees	53-13445; 53-23572; 53-39383; 42-8124(b)(1)(iv)
	County employees	16-4716
	Municipal employees	53-881.115; 42-8124(b)(1)(vi)
	Police officers	53-764; 53-776; 53-23666; 42-8124(b)(1)(iii)
	Private retirement benefits to extent tax-deferred, if clause prohibits proceeds from being used to pay beneficiary's creditors; exemption limited to deposits of $15,000 per year made at least 1 year before filing (limit does not apply to rollovers from other exempt funds or accounts)	42-8124(b)(1)(vii), (viii), (ix)
	Public school employees	24-8533; 42-8124(b)(1)(i)
	State employees	71-5953; 42-8124(b)(1)(ii)
personal property	Bibles & schoolbooks	42-8124(a)(2)
	Clothing	42-8124(a)(1)
	Military uniforms & accoutrements	42-8124(a)(4); 51-4103
	Sewing machines	42-8124(a)(3)
public benefits	Crime victims' compensation	18-11.708
	Korean conflict veterans benefits	51-20098
	Unemployment compensation	42-8124(a)(10); 43-863
	Veterans benefits	51-20012; 20048; 20098; 20127
	Workers' compensation	42-8124(c)(2)
tools of trade	Seamstress's sewing machine	42-8124(a)(3)
wages	Earned but unpaid wages	42-8127
	Wages of victims of abuse	42-8127(f)
wildcard	$300 of any property, including cash, real property, securities, or proceeds from sale of exempt property	42-8123

Rhode Island

Federal bankruptcy exemptions available. All law references are to General Laws of Rhode Island unless otherwise noted.

ASSET	EXEMPTION	LAW
homestead	$500,000 in land & buildings you occupy or intend to occupy as a principal residence (spouse may not double)	9-26-4.1
insurance	Accident or sickness proceeds, avails, or benefits	27-18-24
	Fraternal benefit society benefits	27-25-18
	Life insurance proceeds if clause prohibits proceeds from being used to pay beneficiary's creditors	27-4-12
	Temporary disability insurance	28-41-32

miscellaneous	Earnings of a minor child	9-26-4(9)
	Property of business partnership	7-12-36
pensions	Tax-exempt retirement accounts, including 401(k)s, 403(b)s, profit-sharing and money purchase plans, SEP and SIMPLE IRAs, and defined-benefit plans	11 U.S.C. § 522(b)(3)(C)
	Traditional and Roth IRAs to $1,245,475 per person	11 U.S.C. § 522(b)(3)(C); (n)
	ERISA-qualified benefits	9-26-4(12)
	Firefighters	9-26-5
	IRAs & Roth IRAs	9-26-4(11)
	Police officers	9-26-5
	Private employees	28-17-4
	State & municipal employees	36-10-34
personal property	Beds, bedding, furniture, household goods & supplies, to $9,600 total (spouses may not double)	9-26-4(3); In re Petrozella, 247 B.R. 591 (R.I. 2000)
	Bibles & books to $300	9-26-4(4)
	Burial plot	9-26-4(5)
	Clothing	9-26-4(1)
	Consumer cooperative association holdings to $50	7-8-25
	Debt secured by promissory note or bill of exchange	9-26-4(7)
	Jewelry to $2,000	9-26-4 (14)
	Motor vehicles to $12,000	9-26-4 (13)
	Prepaid tuition program or tuition savings account	9-26-4 (15)
public benefits	Aid to blind, aged, disabled; general assistance	40-6-14
	Crime victims' compensation	12-25.1-3(b)(2)
	State disability benefits	28-41-32
	Unemployment compensation	28-44-58
	Veterans disability or survivors death benefits	30-7-9
	Workers' compensation	28-33-27
tools of trade	Library of practicing professional	9-26-4(2)
	Working tools to $2,000	9-26-4(2)
wages	Earned but unpaid wages due military member on active duty	30-7-9
	Earned but unpaid wages due seaman	9-26-4(6)
	Earned but unpaid wages to $50	9-26-4(8)(iii)
	Wages of any person who had been receiving public assistance are exempt for 1 year after going off of relief	9-26-4(8)(ii)
	Wages of spouse & minor children	9-26-4(9)
	Wages paid by charitable organization or fund providing relief to the poor	9-26-4(8)(i)
wildcard	$6,500 in any assets	9-26-4(16)

South Carolina

Federal bankruptcy exemptions not available. All law references are to Code of Laws of South Carolina unless otherwise noted. (Amounts adjusted for inflation in 2014 (15-41-30(B).)

ASSET	EXEMPTION	LAW
homestead	Real property, including co-op, to $58,255 (single owner); $116,510 (multiple owners)	15-41-30(A)(1)
insurance	Accident & disability benefits	38-63-40(D)
	Benefits accruing under life insurance policy after death of insured, where proceeds left with insurance company pursuant to agreement; benefits not exempt from action to recover necessaries if parties agree	38-63-50
	Disability or illness benefits	15-41-30(A)(11)(C)
	Dividend, interest/loan value of unmatured life insurance contract to $4,500	15-41-30(A)(9)
	Fraternal benefit society benefits	38-38-330
	Group life insurance proceeds; cash value to $50,000	38-63-40(C); 38-65-90
	Life insurance avails from policy for person you depended on to $4,650	15-41-30(A)(9)
	Life insurance proceeds from policy for person you depended on, needed for support	15-41-30(A)(12)(c)
	Proceeds & cash surrender value of life insurance payable to beneficiary other than insured's estate & for the express benefit of insured's spouse, children, or dependents (must be purchased 2 years before filing)	38-63-40(A)
	Proceeds of life insurance or annuity contract	38-63-40(B)
	Unmatured life insurance contract, except credit insurance policy	15-41-30(A)(8)
miscellaneous	Alimony, child support	15-41-30(A)(11)(d)
	Property of business partnership	33-41-720
pensions	Tax-exempt retirement accounts, including 401(k)s, 403(b)s, profit-sharing and money purchase plans, SEP and SIMPLE IRAs, and defined-benefit plans	11 U.S.C. § 522(b)(3)(C)
	Traditional and Roth IRAs to $1,245,475 per person	11 U.S.C. § 522(b)(3)(C); (n)
	ERISA-qualified benefits; your share of the pension plan fund	15-41-30(10)(E), (14)
	Firefighters	9-13-230
	General assembly members	9-9-180
	IRAs & Roth IRAs	15-41-30(A)(13)
	Judges, solicitors	9-8-190
	Police officers	9-11-270
	Public employees	9-1-1680
personal property	Animals, crops, appliances, books, clothing, household goods, furnishings, musical instruments to $4,650 total	15-41-30(A)(3)
	Burial plot to $50,000, in lieu of homestead	15-41-30(1)
	Cash & other liquid assets to $5,825, in lieu of burial or homestead exemption	15-41-30(A)(5)
	College investment program trust fund	59-2-140
	Health aids	15-41-30(A)(10)
	Jewelry to $1,175	15-41-30(A)(4)

ASSET	EXEMPTION	LAW
personal property (continued)	Motor vehicle to $5,825	15-41-30(A)(2)
	Personal injury & wrongful death recoveries for person you depended on for support	15-41-30(A)(12)
public benefits	Crime victims' compensation	15-41-30(A)(12); 16-3-1300
	General relief; aid to aged, blind, disabled	43-5-190
	Local public assistance	15-41-30(A)(11)
	Social Security	15-41-30(A)(11)
	Unemployment compensation	15-41-30(A)(11)
	Veterans benefits	15-41-30(A)(11)
	Workers' compensation	42-9-360
tools of trade	Implements, books & tools of trade to $1,750	15-41-30(A)(6)
wages	None (use federal nonbankruptcy wage exemption)	15-41-30(A)(7)
wildcard	Up to $5,825 for any property from unused exemption amounts	15-41-30(A)(7)

South Dakota

Federal bankruptcy exemptions not available. All law references are to South Dakota Codified Law unless otherwise noted.

ASSET	EXEMPTION	LAW
homestead	Gold or silver mine, mill, or smelter not exempt	43-31-5
	May file homestead declaration	43-31-6
	Real property to unlimited value or mobile home (larger than 240 sq. ft. at its base & registered in state at least 6 months before filing) to unlimited value; property cannot exceed 1 acre in town or 160 acres elsewhere; sale proceeds to $30,000 ($170,000 if over age 70 or widow or widower who hasn't remarried) exempt for 1 year after sale (spouses may not double)	43-31-1; 43-31-2; 43-31-3; 43-31-4; 43-45-3
	Spouse or child of deceased owner may claim homestead exemption	43-31-13
insurance	Annuity contract proceeds to $250 per month	58-12-6; 58-12-8
	Endowment, life insurance, policy proceeds to $20,000; if policy issued by mutual aid or benevolent society, cash value to $20,000	58-12-4
	Fraternal benefit society benefits	58-37A-18
	Health benefits to $20,000	58-12-4
	Life insurance proceeds, if clause prohibits proceeds from being used to pay beneficiary's creditors	58-15-70
	Life insurance proceeds to $10,000, if beneficiary is surviving spouse or child	43-45-6
miscellaneous	Court-ordered alimony or support if not lump sum, up to $750 per month	43-45-2(9)
pensions	Tax-exempt retirement accounts, including 401(k)s, 403(b)s, profit-sharing and money purchase plans, SEP and SIMPLE IRAs, and defined-benefit plans	11 U.S.C. § 522(b)(3)(C)
	Traditional and Roth IRAs to $1,245,475 per person	11 U.S.C. § 522(b)(3)(C); (n)
	City employees	9-16-47
	ERISA-qualified benefits, limited to income & distribution on $1,000,000	43-45-16
	Public employees	3-12-115

personal property	Bible, schoolbooks; other books to $200	43-45-2(4)
	Burial plots, church pew	43-45-2(2), (3)
	Cemetery association property	47-29-25
	Clothing	43-45-2(5)
	Family pictures	43-45-2(1)
	Food & fuel to last 1 year	43-45-2(6)
	Health aids professionally prescribed	43-45-2(8)
public benefits	Crime victims' compensation	23A-28B-24
	Public assistance	28-7A-18
	Unemployment compensation	61-6-28
	Workers' compensation	62-4-42
tools of trade	None	
wages	Earned wages owed 60 days before filing bankruptcy, needed for support of family	15-20-12
	Wages of prisoners in work programs	24-8-10
wildcard	Head of family may claim $7,000, or nonhead of family may claim $5,000 of any personal property	43-45-4

Tennessee

Federal bankruptcy exemptions not available. All law references are to Tennessee Code Annotated unless otherwise noted.

ASSET	EXEMPTION	LAW
homestead	$5,000; $7,500 for joint owners; $25,000 if at least one dependent is a minor child (if 62 or older, $12,500 if single; $20,000 if married; $25,000 if spouse is also 62 or older)	26-2-301
	2–15-year lease	26-2-303
	Life estate	26-2-302
	Property held as tenancy by the entirety may be exempt against debts owed by only one spouse, but survivorship right is not exempt	In re Arango, 136 B.R. 740 aff'd, 992 F.2d 611 (6th Cir. 1993); In re Arwood, 289 B.R. 889 (Bankr. E.D. Tenn. 2003)
	Spouse or child of deceased owner may claim homestead exemption	26-2-301
insurance	Accident, health, or disability benefits for resident & citizen of Tennessee	26-2-110
	Disability or illness benefits	26-2-111(1)(C)
	Fraternal benefit society benefits	56-25-1403
	Life insurance or annuity	56-7-203
miscellaneous	Alimony, child support owed for 30 days before filing for bankruptcy	26-2-111(1)(E)
	Educational scholarship trust funds & prepayment plans	49-4-108; 49-7-822
pensions	Tax-exempt retirement accounts, including 401(k)s, 403(b)s, profit-sharing and money purchase plans, SEP and SIMPLE IRAs, and defined-benefit plans	11 U.S.C. § 522(b)(3)(C)
	Traditional and Roth IRAs to $1,245,475 per person	11 U.S.C. § 522(b)(3)(C); (n)
	ERISA-qualified benefits, IRAs & Roth IRAs	26-2-111(1)(D)
	Public employees	8-36-111
	State & local government employees	26-2-105
	Teachers	49-5-909

personal property	Bible, schoolbooks, family pictures & portraits	26-2-104
	Burial plot to 1 acre	26-2-305; 46-2-102
	Clothing & storage containers	26-2-104
	Health aids	26-2-111(5)
	Health savings accounts	26-2-105
	Lost future earnings payments for you or person you depended on	26-2-111(3)
	Personal injury recoveries to $7,500; wrongful death recoveries to $10,000 ($15,000 total for personal injury, wrongful death & crime victims' compensation)	26-2-111(2)(B), (C)
	Wages of debtor deserting family, in hands of family	26-2-109
public benefits	Aid to blind	71-4-117
	Aid to disabled	71-4-1112
	Crime victims' compensation to $5,000 (see personal property)	26-2-111(2)(A); 29-13-111
	Local public assistance	26-2-111(1)(A)
	Old-age assistance	71-2-216
	Relocation assistance payments	13-11-115
	Social Security	26-2-111(1)(A)
	Unemployment compensation	26-2-111(1)(A)
	Veterans benefits	26-2-111(1)(B)
	Workers' compensation	50-6-223
tools of trade	Implements, books & tools of trade to $1,900	26-2-111(4)
wages	Minimum 75% of disposable weekly earnings or 30 times the federal minimum hourly wage, whichever is more, plus $2.50 per week per child; bankruptcy judge may authorize more for low-income debtors. Note: In re Lawrence, 219 B.R. 786 (E.D. Tenn. 1998) ruled that wage garnishment is not an exemption in bankruptcy.	26-2-106, 107
wildcard	$10,000 of any personal property including deposits on account with any bank or financial institution	26-2-103

Texas

Federal bankruptcy exemptions available. All law references are to Texas Revised Civil Statutes Annotated unless otherwise noted.

ASSET	EXEMPTION	LAW
homestead	Unlimited; property cannot exceed 10 acres in town, village, city or 100 acres (200 for families) elsewhere; sale proceeds exempt for 6 months after sale (renting okay if another home not acquired, Prop. 41.003)	Prop. 41.001; 41.002; Const. Art. 16 §§ 50, 51
	If property acreage is larger than what is covered by homestead exemption, may have to file homestead declaration	Prop. 41.005; 41.021 to 41.023
insurance	Fraternal benefit society benefits	Ins. 885.316
	Life, health, accident, or annuity benefits, monies, policy proceeds & cash values due or paid to beneficiary or insured	Ins. 1108.051
	Texas employee uniform group insurance	Ins. 1551.011
	Texas public school employees group insurance	Ins. 1575.006
	Texas state college or university employee benefits	Ins. 1601.008

miscellaneous	Alimony & child support	Prop. 42.001(b) (3)
	Higher education savings plan trust account	Educ. 54.709(e)
	Liquor licenses & permits	Alco. Bev. Code 11.03
	Prepaid tuition plans	Educ. 54.639
pensions	Tax-exempt retirement accounts, including 401(k)s, 403(b)s, profit-sharing and money purchase plans, SEP and SIMPLE IRAs, and defined-benefit plans	11 U.S.C. § 522(b)(3)(C)
	Traditional and Roth IRAs to $1,245,475 per person	11 U.S.C. § 522(b)(3) (C); (n)
	County & district employees	Gov't. 811.006
	ERISA-qualified government or church benefits, including Keoghs, IRAs, & Roth IRAs	Prop. 42.0021
	Firefighters	6243e(5); 6243a-1(8.03); 6243b(15); 6243e(5); 6243e.1(1.04)
	Judges	Gov't. 831.004
	Law enforcement officers, firefighters, emergency medical personnel survivors	Gov't. 615.005
	Municipal employees & elected officials, state employees	6243h(22); Gov't. 811.005
	Police officers	6243d-1(17); 6243j(20); 6243a-1(8.03); 6243b(15); 6243d-1(17)
	Retirement benefits to extent tax-deferred	Prop. 42.0021
	Teachers	Gov't. 821.005
personal property *to $60,000 total for family, $30,000 for single adult (include tools of trade in these aggregate limits)*	Athletic & sporting equipment, including bicycles	Prop. 42.002(a) (8)
	Bible or other book containing sacred writings of a religion (doesn't count toward $30,000 or $60,000 total)	Prop. 42.001(b) (4)
	Burial plots (exempt from total)	Prop. 41.001
	Clothing & food	Prop. 42.002(a) (2), (5)
	Health aids (exempt from total)	Prop. 42.001(b) (2)
	Health savings accounts	Prop. 42.0021
	Home furnishings including family heirlooms	Prop. 42.002(a) (1)
	Jewelry (limited to 25% of total exemption)	Prop. 42.002(a) (6)
	Pets & domestic animals plus their food: 2 horses, mules, or donkeys & tack; 12 head of cattle; 60 head of other livestock; 120 fowl	Prop. 42.002(a) (10), (11)
	1 two-, three- or four-wheeled motor vehicle per family member or per single adult who holds a driver's license; or, if not licensed, who relies on someone else to operate vehicle	Prop. 42.002(a) (9)
	2 firearms	Prop. 42.002(a) (7)

public benefits	Crime victims' compensation	Crim. Proc. 56.49
	Medical assistance	Hum. Res. 32.036
	Public assistance	Hum. Res. 31.040
	Unemployment compensation	Labor 207.075
	Workers' compensation	Labor 408.201
tools of trade *included in aggregate dollar limits for personal property*	Farming or ranching vehicles & implements	Prop. 42.002(a) (3)
	Tools, equipment (includes boat & motor vehicles used in trade) & books	Prop. 42.002(a) (4)
wages	Earned but unpaid wages	Prop. 42.001(b) (1)
	Unpaid commissions not to exceed 25% of total personal property exemptions	Prop. 42.001(d)
wildcard	None	

Utah

Federal bankruptcy exemptions not available. All law references are to Utah Code unless otherwise noted.

ASSET	EXEMPTION	LAW
homestead	Must file homestead declaration before attempted sale of home	78B-5-504
	Real property, mobile home, or water rights to $30,000 if primary residence; $5,000 if not primary residence	78B-5-504
	Sale proceeds exempt for 1 year	78B-5-503(5)(b)
insurance	Disability, illness, medical, or hospital benefits	78B-5-505(1) (a)(iii)
	Fraternal benefit society benefits	31A-9-603
	Life insurance policy cash surrender value, excluding payments made on the contract within the prior year	78B-5-505(i)(a) (xiii)
	Life insurance proceeds if beneficiary is insured's spouse or dependent, as needed for support	78B-5-505(i) (a)(xi)
	Medical, surgical & hospital benefits	78B-5-505(1) (a)(iv)
miscellaneous	Alimony needed for support	78B-5-505(a) (vi), (vii)
	Child support	78B-5-505(1) (f), (k)
pensions	Tax-exempt retirement accounts, including 401(k)s, 403(b)s, profit-sharing and money purchase plans, SEP and SIMPLE IRAs, and defined-benefit plans	11 U.S.C. § 522(b)(3)(C)
	Traditional and Roth IRAs to $1,245,475 per person	11 U.S.C. § 522(b)(3) (C); (n)
	ERISA-qualified benefits, IRAs, Roth IRAs & Keoghs (benefits that have accrued & contributions that have been made at least 1 year prior to filing)	78B-5-505(1)(a) (xiv)
	Other pensions & annuities needed for support	78-23-6(3)
	Public employees	49-11-612

personal property	Animals, books & musical instruments to $1,000	78B-5-506(1)(c)
	Artwork depicting, or done by, a family member	78B-5-505(1)(a)(ix)
	Bed, bedding, carpets	78B-5-505(1)(a)(viii)
	Burial plot	78B-5-505(1)(a)(i)
	Clothing (cannot claim furs or jewelry)	78B-5-505(1)(a)(viii)
	Dining & kitchen tables & chairs to $1,000	78B-5-505(1)(b)
	Firearms to $250	78B-5-506(1)(e)
	Food to last 12 months	78B-5-505(1)(a)(viii)
	Health aids	78B-5-505(1)(a)(ii)
	Heirlooms to $1,000	78B-5-506(1)(d)
	Motor vehicle to $5,000	78B-5-506(3)
	Personal injury, wrongful death recoveries for you or person you depended on	78B-5-505(1)(a)(x)
	Proceeds for sold, lost, or damaged exempt property	78B-5-507
	Refrigerator, freezer, microwave, stove, sewing machine, washer & dryer	78B-5-505(1)(a)(viii)
	Sofas, chairs & related furnishings to $1,000	78B-5-506(1)(a)
public benefits	Crime victims' compensation	63-25a-421(4)
	General assistance	35A-3-112
	Occupational disease disability benefits	34A-3-107
	Unemployment compensation	35A-4-103(4)(b)
	Veterans benefits	78B-5-505(1)(a)(v)
	Workers' compensation	34A-2-422
tools of trade	Implements, books & tools of trade to $5,000	78B-5-506(2)
	Military property of National Guard member	39-1-47
wages	Unpaid earnings due as of the bankruptcy filing date in an amount equal to $^1/_{24}$ of the median Utah annual income if paid more than once per month and $^1/_{12}$ if paid monthly	78B-5-505(1)(a)(xvi)
wildcard	None	

Vermont

Federal bankruptcy exemptions available. All law references are to Vermont Statutes Annotated unless otherwise noted.

ASSET	EXEMPTION	LAW
homestead	Property held as tenancy by the entirety may be exempt against debts owed by only one spouse	*In re McQueen*, 21 B.R. 736 (D. Ver. 1982)
	Real property or mobile home to $125,000; may also claim rents, issues, profits & outbuildings (spouses may not double); *D'Avignon v. Palmisano*, 34 B.R. 796 (D.Vt. 1982)	27-101
	Spouse of deceased owner may claim homestead exemption	27-105
insurance	Annuity contract benefits to $350 per month	8-3709
	Disability benefits that supplement life insurance or annuity contract	8-3707

insurance (continued)	Disability or illness benefits needed for support	12-2740(19)(C)
	Fraternal benefit society benefits	8-4478
	Group life or health benefits	8-3708
	Health benefits to $200 per month	8-4086
	Life insurance proceeds for person you depended on	12-2740(19)(H)
	Life insurance proceeds if clause prohibits proceeds from being used to pay beneficiary's creditors	8-3705
	Life insurance proceeds if beneficiary is not the insured	8-3706
	Unmatured life insurance contract other than credit	12-2740(18)
miscellaneous	Alimony, child support	12-2740(19)(D)
pensions	Tax-exempt retirement accounts, including 401(k)s, 403(b)s, profit-sharing and money purchase plans, SEP and SIMPLE IRAs, and defined-benefit plans	11 U.S.C. § 522(b)(3)(C)
	Traditional and Roth IRAs to $1,245,475 per person	11 U.S.C. § 522(b)(3)(C); (n)
	Municipal employees	24-5066
	Other pensions	12-2740(19)(J)
	Self-directed accounts (IRAs, Roth IRAs, Keoghs); contributions must be made 1 year before filing	12-2740(16)
	State employees	3-476
	Teachers	16-1946
personal property	Appliances, furnishings, goods, clothing, books, crops, animals, musical instruments to $2,500 total	12-2740(5)
	Bank deposits to $700	12-2740(15)
	Cow, 2 goats, 10 sheep, 10 chickens & feed to last 1 winter; 3 swarms of bees plus honey; 5 tons coal or 500 gal. heating oil; 10 cords of firewood; 500 gal. bottled gas; growing crops to $5,000; yoke of oxen or steers, plow & ox yoke; 2 horses with harnesses, halters & chains	12-2740(6), (9)–(14)
	Health aids	12-2740(17)
	Jewelry to $500; wedding ring unlimited	12-2740(3), (4)
	Motor vehicles to $2,500	12-2740(1)
	Personal injury, lost future earnings, wrongful death recoveries for you or person you depended on	12-2740(19)(F), (G), (I)
	Stove, heating unit, refrigerator, freezer, water heater & sewing machines	12-2740(8)
public benefits	Aid to blind, aged, disabled; general assistance	33-124
	Crime victims' compensation needed for support	12-2740(19)(E)
	Social Security needed for support	12-2740(19)(A)
	Unemployment compensation	21-1367
	Veterans benefits needed for support	12-2740(19)(B)
	Workers' compensation	21-681
tools of trade	Books & tools of trade to $5,000	12-2740(2)
wages	Entire wages, if you received welfare during 2 months before filing	12-3170

wages (continued)	Minimum 75% of weekly disposable earnings or 30 times the federal minimum hourly wage, whichever is greater; bankruptcy judge may authorize more for low-income debtors. Note: The court in *In re Riendeau*, 293 B.R. 832 (D. Vt. 2002) held that Vermont's wage garnishment law does not create an exemption that can be used in bankruptcy.	12-3170
wildcard	Unused exemptions for motor vehicle, tools of trade, jewelry, household furniture, appliances, clothing & crops to $7,000	12-2740(7)
	$400 of any property	12-2740(7)

Virginia

Federal bankruptcy exemptions not available. All law references are to Code of Virginia unless otherwise noted.

ASSET	EXEMPTION	LAW
homestead	$5,000 plus $500 per dependent; rents & profits; sale proceeds exempt to $5,000 (unused portion of homestead may be applied to any personal property); exemption is $10,000 if over 65	*Cheeseman v. Nachman*, 656 F.2d 60 (4th Cir. 1981); 34-4; 34-18; 34-20
	May include mobile home	*In re Goad*, 161 B.R. 161 (W.D. Va. 1993)
	Must file homestead declaration before filing for bankruptcy	34-6
	Property held as tenancy by the entirety may be exempt against debts owed by only one spouse	*In re Bunker*, 312 F.3d 145 (4th Cir. 2002)
	Surviving spouse may claim $15,000; if no surviving spouse, minor children may claim exemption	64.2-311
insurance	Accident or sickness benefits	38.2-3406
	Burial society benefits	38.2-4021
	Cooperative life insurance benefits	38.2-3811
	Fraternal benefit society benefits	38.2-4118
	Group life or accident insurance for government officials	51.1-510
	Group life insurance policy or proceeds	38.2-3339
	Industrial sick benefits	38.2-3549
	Life insurance proceeds	38.2-3122
miscellaneous	Property of business partnership	50-73.108
	Unpaid spousal or child support	34-26(10)
pensions *see also wages*	Tax-exempt retirement accounts, including 401(k)s, 403(b)s, profit-sharing and money purchase plans, SEP and SIMPLE IRAs, and defined-benefit plans	11 U.S.C. § 522(b)(3)(C)
	Traditional and Roth IRAs to $1,245,475 per person	11 U.S.C. § 522(b)(3)(C); (n)
	City, town & county employees	51.1-802
	ERISA-qualified benefits to same extent permitted by federal bankruptcy law	34-34
	Judges	51.1-300
	State employees	51.1-124.4(A)
	State police officers	51.1-200

personal property	Bible	34-26(1)
	Burial plot	34-26(3)
	Clothing to $1,000	34-26(4)
	Family portraits & heirlooms to $5,000 total	34-26(2)
	Firearms to $3,000	34-26(4b)
	Health aids	34-26(6)
	Health savings accounts & medical savings accounts	38.2-5604
	Household furnishings to $5,000	34-26(4a)
	Motor vehicles to $6,000	34-26(8)
	Personal injury causes of action & recoveries	34-28.1
	Pets	34-26(5)
	Prepaid tuition contracts	23-38.81(E)
	Wedding & engagement rings	34-26(1a)
public benefits	Aid to blind, aged, disabled; general relief	63.2-506
	Crime victims' compensation unless seeking to discharge debt for treatment of injury incurred during crime	19.2-368.12
	Earned income tax credit or child tax credit	34-26(9)
	Payments to tobacco farmers	3.1-1111.1
	Unemployment compensation	60.2-600
	Workers' compensation	65.2-531
tools of trade	For farmer, pair of horses, or mules with gear; one wagon or cart, one tractor to $3,000; 2 plows & wedges; one drag, harvest cradle, pitchfork, rake; fertilizer to $1,000	34-27
	Tools, books & instruments of trade, including motor vehicles, to $10,000, needed in your occupation or education	34-26(7)
	Uniforms, arms, equipment of military member	44-96
wages	Minimum 75% of weekly disposable earnings or 40 times the federal minimum hourly wage, whichever is greater; bankruptcy judge may authorize more for low-income debtors	34-29
wildcard	Unused portion of homestead exemption	34-13
	$10,000 of any property for disabled veterans	34-4.1

Washington

Federal bankruptcy exemptions available. All law references are to Revised Code of Washington Annotated unless otherwise noted.

ASSET	EXEMPTION	LAW
homestead	Must record homestead declaration before sale of home if property unimproved or home unoccupied	6.15.040
	Real property or manufactured home to $125,000; unimproved property intended for residence to $15,000 (spouses may not double)	6.13.010; 6.13.030
insurance	Annuity contract proceeds to $2,500 per month	48.18.430
	Disability proceeds, avails, or benefits	48.36A.180
	Fraternal benefit society benefits	48.18.400
	Group life insurance policy or proceeds	48.18.420
	Life insurance proceeds or avails if beneficiary is not the insured	48.18.410
miscellaneous	Child support payments	6.15.010(1)(c)(iv)

pensions	Tax-exempt retirement accounts, including 401(k)s, 403(b)s, profit-sharing and money purchase plans, SEP and SIMPLE IRAs, and defined-benefit plans	11 U.S.C. § 522(b)(3)(C)
	Traditional and Roth IRAs to $1,245,475 per person	11 U.S.C. § 522(b)(3) (C); (n)
	City employees	41.28.200; 41.44.240
	ERISA-qualified benefits, IRAs, Roth IRAs & Keoghs	6.15.020
	Judges	2.10.180; 2.12.090
	Law enforcement officials & firefighters	41.26.053
	Police officers	41.20.180
	Public & state employees	41.40.052
	State patrol officers	43.43.310
	Teachers	41.32.052
	Volunteer firefighters	41.24.240
personal property	Appliances, furniture, household goods, home & yard equipment to $6,500 total for individual ($13,000 for community)	6.15.010(1)(c)(i)
	Books and electronic media to $3,500	6.15.010(1)(b)
	Burial ground	68.24.220
	Burial plots sold by nonprofit cemetery association	68.20.120
	Clothing, but no more than $3,500 in furs, jewelry, ornaments	6.15.010(1)(a)
	Fire insurance proceeds for lost, stolen, or destroyed exempt property	6.15.030
	Food & fuel for comfortable maintenance	6.15.010(1)(c)(i)
	Health aids prescribed	6.15.010(1)(c)(v)
	Health savings account & medical savings account deposits	6.15.020
	Keepsakes & family pictures	6.15.010(1)(b)
	Motor vehicle to $3,250 total for individual (two vehicles to $6,500 for community)	6.15.010(1)(c) (iii)
	Personal injury recoveries to $20,000	6.15.010(1)(c) (vi)
	Tuition units purchased more than 2 years before	6.15.010(1)(e)
public benefits	Child welfare	74.13.070
	Crime victims' compensation	7.68.070(10)
	General assistance	74.04.280
	Industrial insurance (workers' compensation)	51.32.040
	Old-age assistance	74.08.210
	Unemployment compensation	50.40.020
tools of trade	Farmer's trucks, stock, tools, seed, equipment & supplies to $10,000 total	6.15.010(1)(d)(i)
	Library, office furniture, office equipment & supplies of physician, surgeon, attorney, clergy, or other professional to $10,000 total	6.15.010(1) (d)(ii)
	Tools & materials used in any other trade to $10,000	6.15.010(1)(d) (iii)
wages	Minimum 75% of weekly disposable earnings or 30 times the federal minimum hourly wage, whichever is greater; bankruptcy judge may authorize more for low-income debtors	6.27.150
wildcard	$3,000 of any personal property (no more than $1,500 in cash, bank deposits, bonds, stocks & securities)	6.15.010(1)(c)(ii)

West Virginia

Federal bankruptcy exemptions not available. All law references are to West Virginia Code unless otherwise noted.

ASSET	EXEMPTION	LAW
homestead	Real or personal property used as residence to $25,000; unused portion of homestead may be applied to any property	38-10-4(a)
insurance	Fraternal benefit society benefits	33-23-21
	Group life insurance policy or proceeds	33-6-28
	Health or disability benefits	38-10-4(j)(3)
	Life insurance payments from policy for person you depended on, needed for support	38-10-4(k)(3)
	Unmatured life insurance contract, except credit insurance policy	38-10-4(g)
	Unmatured life insurance contract's accrued dividend, interest, or loan value to $8,000, if debtor owns contract & insured is either debtor or a person on whom debtor is dependent	38-10-4(h)
miscellaneous	Alimony, child support needed for support	38-10-4(j)(4)
pensions	Tax-exempt retirement accounts, including 401(k)s, 403(b)s, profit-sharing and money purchase plans, SEP and SIMPLE IRAs, and defined-benefit plans	11 U.S.C. § 522(b)(3)(C)
	Traditional and Roth IRAs to $1,245,475 per person	11 U.S.C. § 522(b)(3) (C); (n)
	ERISA-qualified benefits, IRAs needed for support	38-10-4(j)(5)
	Public employees	5-10-46
	Teachers	18-7A-30
personal property	Animals, crops, clothing, appliances, books, household goods, furnishings, musical instruments to $400 per item, $8,000 total	38-10-4(c)
	Burial plot to $25,000, in lieu of homestead	38-10-4(a)
	Health aids	38-10-4(i)
	Jewelry to $1,000	38-10-4(d)
	Lost earnings payments needed for support	38-10-4(k)(5)
	Motor vehicle to $2,400	38-10-4(b)
	Personal injury recoveries to $15,000	38-10-4(k)(4)
	Prepaid higher education tuition trust fund & savings plan payments	38-10-4(k)(6)
	Wrongful death recoveries for person you depended on, needed for support	38-10-4(k)(2)
public benefits	Aid to blind, aged, disabled; general assistance	9-5-1
	Crime victims' compensation	38-10-4(k)(1)
	Social Security	38-10-4(j)(1)
	Unemployment compensation	38-10-4(j)(1)
	Veterans benefits	38-10-4(j)(2)
	Workers' compensation	23-4-18
tools of trade	Implements, books & tools of trade to $1,500	38-10-4(f)
wages	Minimum 30 times the federal minimum hourly wage per week; bankruptcy judge may authorize more for low-income debtors	38-5A-3
wildcard	$800 plus unused portion of homestead or burial exemption, of any property	38-10-4(e)

Wisconsin

Federal bankruptcy exemptions available. All law references are to Wisconsin Statutes Annotated unless otherwise noted.

ASSET	EXEMPTION	LAW
homestead	Property you occupy or intend to occupy to $75,000; $150,000 for married couples filing jointly; sale proceeds exempt for 2 years if you intend to purchase another home (spouses may not double)	815.20
insurance	Federal disability insurance benefits	815.18(3)(ds)
	Fire and casualty insurance (2 years from receipt)	815.18(e)
	Fraternal benefit society benefits	614.96
	Life insurance proceeds for someone debtor depended on, needed for support	815.18(3)(i)(a)
	Life insurance proceeds held in trust by insurer, if clause prohibits proceeds from being used to pay beneficiary's creditors	632.42
	Unmatured life insurance contract (except credit insurance contract) if debtor owns contract & insured is debtor or dependents, or someone debtor is dependent on	815.18(3)(f)
	Unmatured life insurance contract's accrued dividends, interest, or loan value to $150,000 total, if debtor owns contract & insured is debtor or dependents, or someone debtor is dependent on (to $4,000 if issued less than 2 years prior)	815.18(3)(f)
miscellaneous	Alimony, child support needed for support	815.18(3)(c)
	Property of business partnership	178.21(3)(c)
pensions	Tax-exempt retirement accounts, including 401(k)s, 403(b)s, profit-sharing and money purchase plans, SEP and SIMPLE IRAs, and defined-benefit plans	11 U.S.C. § 522(b)(3)(C)
	Traditional and Roth IRAs to $1,245,475 per person	11 U.S.C. § 522(b)(3)(C); (n)
	Certain municipal employees	62.63(4)
	Firefighters, police officers who worked in city with population over 100,000	815.18(3)(ef)
	Military pensions	815.18(3)(n)
	Private or public retirement benefits	815.18(3)(j)
	Public employees	40.08(1)
personal property	Burial plot, tombstone, coffin	815.18(3)(a)
	College savings account or tuition trust fund	14.64(7); 14.63(8)
	Deposit accounts to $5,000	815.18(3)(k)
	Fire & casualty proceeds for destroyed exempt property for 2 years from receiving	815.18(3)(e)
	Household goods & furnishings, clothing, keepsakes, jewelry, appliances, books, musical instruments, firearms, sporting goods, animals & other tangible personal property to $12,000 total	815.18(3)(d)
	Lost future earnings recoveries, needed for support	815.18(3)(i)(d)
	Motor vehicles to $4,000; unused portion of $12,000 personal property exemption may be added	815.18(3)(g)
	Personal injury recoveries to $50,000	815.18(3)(i)(c)
personal property (continued)	Tenant's lease or stock interest in housing co-op, to homestead amount	182.004(6)
	Wages used to purchase savings bonds	20.921(1)(e)
	Wrongful death recoveries, needed for support	815.18(3)(i)(b)
public benefits	Crime victims' compensation	949.07
	Social services payments	49.96
	Unemployment compensation	108.13
	Veterans benefits	45.03(8)(b)
	Workers' compensation	102.27
tools of trade	Equipment, inventory, farm products, books & tools of trade to $15,000 total	815.18(3)(b)
wages	75% of weekly net income or 30 times the greater of the federal or state minimum hourly wage; bankruptcy judge may authorize more for low-income debtors	815.18(3)(h)
	Wages of county jail prisoners	303.08(3)
	Wages of county work camp prisoners	303.10(7)
	Wages of inmates under work-release plan	303.065(4)(b)
wildcard	None	

Wyoming

Federal bankruptcy exemptions not available. All law references are to Wyoming Statutes Annotated unless otherwise noted.

ASSET	EXEMPTION	LAW
homestead	Property held as tenancy by the entirety may be exempt against debts owed by only one spouse	*In re Anselmi,* 52 B.R. 479 (D. Wy. 1985)
	Real property or a house trailer you occupy to $20,000	1-20-101; 102; 104
	Spouse or child of deceased owner may claim homestead exemption	1-20-103
insurance	Annuity contract proceeds to $350 per month	26-15-132
	Disability benefits if clause prohibits proceeds from being used to pay beneficiary's creditors	26-15-130
	Fraternal benefit society benefits	26-29-218
	Group life or disability policy or proceeds, cash surrender & loan values, premiums waived & dividends	26-15-131
	Individual life insurance policy proceeds, cash surrender & loan values, premiums waived & dividends	26-15-129
	Life insurance proceeds held by insurer, if clause prohibits proceeds from being used to pay beneficiary's creditors	26-15-133
miscellaneous	Liquor licenses & malt beverage permits	12-4-604
pensions	Tax-exempt retirement accounts, including 401(k)s, 403(b)s, profit-sharing and money purchase plans, SEP and SIMPLE IRAs, and defined-benefit plans	11 U.S.C. § 522(b)(3)(C)
	Traditional and Roth IRAs to $1,245,475 per person	11 U.S.C. § 522(b)(3)(C); (n)
	Criminal investigators, highway officers	9-3-620
	Firefighters' death benefits	15-5-209
	Game & fish wardens	9-3-620
	Police officers	15-5-313(c)
	Private or public retirement funds & accounts including IRAs, Roth IRAs and SEP IRAs	1-20-110
	Public employees	9-3-426

personal property	Bedding, furniture, household articles & food to $4,000 per person in the home	1-20-106(a)(iii)
	Bible, schoolbooks & pictures	1-20-106(a)(i)
	Burial plot	1-20-106(a)(ii)
	Clothing & wedding rings to $2,000	1-20-105
	Medical savings account contributions	1-20-111
	Motor vehicle to $5,000	1-20-106(a)(iv)
	Prepaid funeral contracts	26-32-102
public benefits	Crime victims' compensation	1-40-113
	General assistance	42-2-113(b)
	Unemployment compensation	27-3-319
	Workers' compensation	27-14-702
tools of trade	Library & implements of profession to $4,000 or tools, motor vehicle, implements, team & stock in trade to $4,000	1-20-106(b)
wages	Earnings of National Guard members	19-9-401
	Minimum 75% of disposable weekly earnings or 30 times the federal hourly minimum wage, whichever is more	1-15-511; 1-15-408; 40-14-505
	Wages of inmates in adult community corrections program	7-18-114
	Wages of inmates in correctional industries program	25-13-107
	Wages of inmates on work release	7-16-308
wildcard	None	

Federal Bankruptcy Exemptions

Spouses filing jointly may double all exemptions. All references are to 11 U.S.C. § 522. These exemptions were last adjusted in 2013. Every three years ending on April 1, these amounts will be adjusted to reflect changes in the Consumer Price Index. Debtors in the following states may select the federal bankruptcy exemptions:

Alaska	Kentucky	New Jersey	Rhode Island
Arkansas	Massachusetts	New Mexico	Texas
Connecticut	Michigan	New York	Vermont
District of Columbia	Minnesota	Oregon	Washington
Hawaii	New Hampshire	Pennsylvania	Wisconsin

ASSET	EXEMPTION	SUBSECTION
homestead	Real property, including co-op or mobile home, or burial plot to $22,975; unused portion of homestead to $11,500 may be applied to any property	(d)(1); (d)(5)
insurance	Disability, illness, or unemployment benefits	(d)(10)(C)
	Life insurance payments from policy for person you depended on, needed for support	(d)(11)(C)
	Life insurance policy with loan value, in accrued dividends or interest, to $12,250	(d)(8)
	Unmatured life insurance contract, except credit insurance policy	(d)(7)
miscellaneous	Alimony, child support needed for support	(d)(10)(D)
pensions	Tax exempt retirement accounts (including 401(k)s, 403(b)s, profit-sharing and money purchase plans, SEP and SIMPLE IRAs, and defined-benefit plans)	(b)(3)(C)
	IRAs and Roth IRAs to $1,245,475 per person	(b)(3)(C)(n)

personal property	Animals, crops, clothing, appliances, books, furnishings, household goods, musical instruments to $575 per item, $12,250 total	(d)(3)
	Health aids	(d)(9)
	Jewelry to $1,550	(d)(4)
	Lost earnings payments	(d)(11)(E)
	Motor vehicle to $3,675	(d)(2)
	Personal injury recoveries to $22,975 (not to include pain & suffering or pecuniary loss)	(d)(11)(D)
	Wrongful death recoveries for person you depended on	(d)(11)(B)
public benefits	Crime victims' compensation	(d)(11)(A)
	Public assistance	(d)(10)(A)
	Social Security	(d)(10)(A)
	Unemployment compensation	(d)(10)(A)
	Veterans benefits	(d)(10)(A)
tools of trade	Implements, books & tools of trade to $2,300	(d)(6)
wages	None	
wildcard	$1,225 of any property	(d)(5)
	Up to $11,500 of unused homestead exemption amount, for any property	(d)(5)

Federal Nonbankruptcy Exemptions

These exemptions are available only if you select your state exemptions. You may use them for any exemptions in addition to those allowed by your state, but they cannot be claimed if you file using federal bankruptcy exemptions. All law references are to the United States Code.

ASSET	EXEMPTION	LAW
death & disability benefits	Government employees	5 § 8130
	Longshoremen & harbor workers	33 § 916
	War risk, hazard, death, or injury compensation	42 § 1717
miscellaneous	Debts of seaman incurred while on a voyage	46 § 11111
	Indian lands or homestead sales or lease proceeds	25 § 410; 412a
	Klamath Indian tribe benefits for Indians residing in Oregon; agricultural or grazing lands to $5,000	25 §§ 543; 545
	Life insurance benefits for serviceman's Group Life Ins. or Veteran's Group Life Ins.	38 § 1970(g)
	Military deposits in savings accounts while on permanent duty outside U.S.	10 § 1035
	Military group life insurance	38 § 1970(g)
	Railroad workers' unemployment insurance	45 § 352(e)
	Seamen's clothing	46 § 11110
	Seamen's wages (except for spousal and child support)	46 § 11109
	Minimum 75% of disposable weekly earnings or 30 times the federal minimum hourly wage, whichever is more; bankruptcy judge may authorize more for low-income debtors	15 § 1673
retirement	CIA employees	50 § 403
	Civil service employees	5 § 8346

retirement (continued)	Foreign Service employees	22 § 4060
	Military Medal of Honor roll pensions	38 § 1562(c)
	Military service employees	10 § 1440
	Railroad workers	45 § 231m
	Social Security	42 § 407
	Veterans benefits	38 § 5301
survivors benefits	Judges, U.S. court & judicial center directors, administrative assistants to U.S. Supreme Court Chief Justice	28 § 376
	Lighthouse workers	33 § 775
	Military service	10 § 1450

Worksheets, Charts, and Forms

Current Monthly Income Worksheet*

Personal Property Checklist*

Property Exemption Worksheet*

Homeowners' Worksheet*

Judicial Lien Worksheet*

Bankruptcy Forms Checklist*

Bankruptcy Documents Checklist*

Median Family Income Chart*

Amendment Cover Sheet

Notice of Change of Address

Supplemental Schedule for Property Acquired After Bankruptcy Discharge

Proof of Service by Mail

Pleading Paper

*These worksheets and checklists are also available for download on this book's companion page at: **www.nolo.com/back-of-book/HFB.html**

Current Monthly Income Worksheet

Use this worksheet to calculate your current monthly income; use figures for you and your spouse if you plan to file jointly.

Line 1. Calculate your total income over the last six months from wages, salary, tips, bonuses, overtime, and so on.

    A. Month 1 $ _____

    B. Month 2   _____

    C. Month 3   _____

    D. Month 4   _____

    E. Month 5   _____

    F. Month 6   _____

    G. TOTAL WAGES (add lines A–F) $ _____

Line 2. Add up all other income for the last six months.

    A. Business, profession, or farm income   _____

    B. Interest, dividends, and royalties   _____

    C. Rents and real property income   _____

    D. Pension and retirement income   _____

    E. Alimony or family support   _____

    F. Spousal contributions (if not filing jointly)   _____

    G. Unemployment compensation   _____

    H. Workers' compensation   _____

    I. State disability insurance   _____

    J. Annuity payments   _____

    K. Lump-sum payments   _____

    L. Other   _____

    M. TOTAL OTHER INCOME (add lines A–L) $ _____

Line 3. Calculate total income over the six months prior to filing. _____

    A. Enter total wages (Line 1G).   _____

    B. Enter total other income (Line 2M).   _____

    C. TOTAL INCOME OVER THE SIX MONTHS PRIOR TO FILING (add Lines A and B together) $ _____

Line 4. Average monthly income over the six months prior to filing. This is called your current monthly income.

    A. Enter total six-month income (Line 3C).   _____

    B. CURRENT MONTHLY INCOME (divide Line A by six) $ _____

Personal Property Checklist

Cash on hand (include sources)

- [ ] In your home
- [ ] In your wallet
- [ ] Under your mattress

Deposits of money (include sources)

- [ ] Bank account
- [ ] Brokerage account (with stockbroker)
- [ ] Certificates of deposit (CDs)
- [ ] Credit union deposit
- [ ] Escrow account
- [ ] Money market account
- [ ] Money in a safe deposit box
- [ ] Savings and loan deposit

Security deposits

- [ ] Electric
- [ ] Gas
- [ ] Heating oil
- [ ] Rental unit
- [ ] Prepaid rent
- [ ] Rented furniture or equipment
- [ ] Telephone
- [ ] Water

Household goods, supplies, and furnishings

- [ ] Antiques
- [ ] Appliances
- [ ] Carpentry tools
- [ ] Cell phones
- [ ] China and crystal
- [ ] Clocks
- [ ] Dishes
- [ ] Electronics (MP3 player, DVR, Kindle, video games)
- [ ] Food (total value)
- [ ] Furniture (list every item; go from room to room so you don't miss anything)
- [ ] Gardening tools
- [ ] Home computer (for personal use)
- [ ] Iron and ironing board
- [ ] Lamps

- [ ] Lawn mower or tractor
- [ ] Microwave oven
- [ ] Patio or outdoor furniture
- [ ] Radios
- [ ] Rugs
- [ ] Sewing machine
- [ ] Silverware and utensils
- [ ] Small appliances
- [ ] Snow blower
- [ ] Stereo system
- [ ] Telephone and answering machines
- [ ] Televisions
- [ ] Vacuum cleaner
- [ ] Video equipment (VCR, camcorder)

Books, pictures, and other art objects; stamp, coin, and other collections

- [ ] Art prints
- [ ] Bibles
- [ ] Books
- [ ] Coins
- [ ] Collectibles (such as political buttons, baseball cards)
- [ ] Family portraits
- [ ] Figurines
- [ ] Original artworks
- [ ] Photographs
- [ ] Records, CDs, audiotapes
- [ ] Stamps
- [ ] Videotapes

Apparel

- [ ] Clothing
- [ ] Furs

Jewelry

- [ ] Engagement and wedding rings
- [ ] Gems
- [ ] Precious metals
- [ ] Watches

Firearms, sports equipment, and other hobby equipment

- ☐ Board games
- ☐ Bicycle
- ☐ Camera equipment
- ☐ Electronic musical equipment
- ☐ Exercise machine
- ☐ Fishing gear
- ☐ Guns (rifles, pistols, shotguns, muskets)
- ☐ Model or remote-controlled cars or planes
- ☐ Musical instruments
- ☐ Scuba diving equipment
- ☐ Ski equipment
- ☐ Other sports equipment
- ☐ Other weapons (swords and knives)

Interests in insurance policies

- ☐ Credit insurance
- ☐ Disability insurance
- ☐ Health insurance
- ☐ Homeowners' or renters' insurance
- ☐ Term life insurance
- ☐ Whole life insurance

Annuities

Pension or profit-sharing plans

- ☐ IRA
- ☐ Keogh
- ☐ Pension or retirement plan
- ☐ 401(k) plan

Stock and interests in incorporated and unincorporated companies

Interests in partnerships

- ☐ Limited partnership interest
- ☐ General partnership interest

Government and corporate bonds and other investment instruments

- ☐ Corporate bonds
- ☐ Municipal bonds
- ☐ Promissory notes
- ☐ U.S. savings bonds

Accounts receivable

- ☐ Accounts receivable from business
- ☐ Commissions already earned

Family support

- ☐ Alimony (spousal support, maintenance) due under court order
- ☐ Child support payments due under court order
- ☐ Payments due under divorce property settlement

Other debts for which the amount owed you is known and definite

- ☐ Disability benefits due
- ☐ Disability insurance due
- ☐ Judgments obtained against third parties you haven't yet collected
- ☐ Sick pay earned
- ☐ Social Security benefits due
- ☐ Tax refund due under returns already filed
- ☐ Vacation pay earned
- ☐ Wages due
- ☐ Workers' compensation due

Any special powers that you or another person can exercise for your benefit (not related to real estate)

- ☐ A right to receive, at some future time, cash, stock, or other personal property placed in an irrevocable trust
- ☐ Current payments of interest or principal from a trust
- ☐ General power of appointment over personal property

An interest in property due to another person's death

- ☐ Any interest as the beneficiary of a living trust, if the trustor has died
- ☐ Expected proceeds from a life insurance policy where the insured has died
- ☐ Inheritance from an existing estate in probate (the owner has died and the court is overseeing the distribution of the property), even if the final amount is not yet known
- ☐ Inheritance under a will that is contingent on one or more events occurring, but only if the owner has died

All other contingent claims and claims where the amount owed you is not known, including tax refunds, counter-claims, and rights to setoff claims (claims you think you have against a person, government, or corporation, but you haven't yet sued on)

- ☐ Claims against a corporation, government entity, or an individual
- ☐ Potential tax refund on a return that is not yet filed

Patents, copyrights, and other intellectual property

- ☐ Copyrights
- ☐ Patents
- ☐ Trade secrets
- ☐ Trademarks
- ☐ Trade names

Licenses, franchises, and other general intangibles

- ☐ Building permits
- ☐ Cooperative association holdings
- ☐ Exclusive licenses
- ☐ Liquor licenses
- ☐ Nonexclusive licenses
- ☐ Patent licenses
- ☐ Professional licenses

Automobiles and other vehicles

- ☐ Car
- ☐ Minibike or motor scooter
- ☐ Mobile or motor home if on wheels
- ☐ Motorcycle
- ☐ Recreational vehicle (RV)
- ☐ Trailer
- ☐ Truck
- ☐ Van

Boats, motors, and accessories

- ☐ Boat (canoe, kayak, rowboat, shell, sailboat, pontoon, yacht)
- ☐ Boat radar, radio, or telephone
- ☐ Outboard motor

Aircraft and accessories

- ☐ Aircraft
- ☐ Aircraft radar, radio, and other accessories

Office equipment, furnishings, and supplies

- ☐ Artwork in your office
- ☐ Computers, software, modems, printers
- ☐ Copier
- ☐ Fax machine
- ☐ Furniture
- ☐ Rugs
- ☐ Supplies
- ☐ Telephones
- ☐ Typewriters

Machinery, fixtures, equipment, and supplies used in business

- ☐ Military uniforms and accoutrements
- ☐ Tools of your trade

Business inventory

Livestock, poultry, and other animals

- ☐ Birds
- ☐ Cats
- ☐ Dogs
- ☐ Fish and aquarium equipment
- ☐ Horses
- ☐ Other pets
- ☐ Livestock and poultry

Crops—growing or harvested

Farming equipment and implements

Farm supplies, chemicals, and feed

Other personal property of any kind not already listed

- ☐ Church pew
- ☐ Health aids (such as a wheelchair or crutches)
- ☐ Hot tub or portable spa
- ☐ Season tickets

Property Exemption Worksheet

1 Property	2 Replacement Value	3 Exemption	4 Statute No.
1. Cash on hand			
2. Checking, savings account, certificate of deposit, other bank accounts			
3. Security deposits held by utility companies, landlord			
4. Household goods, furniture, audio, video, and computer equipment			

1 Property	2 Replacement Value	3 Exemption	4 Statute No.

5. Books, pictures, art objects, records, compact discs, collectibles

6. Clothing

7. Furs and jewelry

1 Property	2 Replacement Value	3 Exemption	4 Statute No.
8. Sports, photographic, and hobby equipment; firearms			
9. Interest in insurance policies—specify refund or cancellation value			
10. Annuities			
11. Interests in pension or profit-sharing plans			
12. Stock and interests in incorporated/unincorporated business			
13. Interests in partnerships/joint ventures			

1 Property	2 Replacement Value	3 Exemption	4 Statute No.
14. Bonds			
15. Accounts receivable			
16. Alimony/family support to which you are entitled			
17. Other liquidated debts owed to you, including tax refunds			
18. Equitable or future interests or life estates			
19. Interests in estate of decedent or life insurance plan or trust			
20. Other contingent/unliquidated claims, including tax refunds, counterclaims			
21. Patents, copyrights, other intellectual property			

1 Property	2 Replacement Value	3 Exemption	4 Statute No.
22. Licenses, franchises			
_____	_____	_____	_____
_____	_____	_____	_____
_____	_____	_____	_____
23. Automobiles, trucks, trailers, and accessories			
_____	_____	_____	_____
_____	_____	_____	_____
_____	_____	_____	_____
_____	_____	_____	_____
24. Boats, motors, accessories			
_____	_____	_____	_____
_____	_____	_____	_____
_____	_____	_____	_____
25. Aircraft, accessories			
_____	_____	_____	_____
_____	_____	_____	_____
26. Office equipment, supplies			
_____	_____	_____	_____
_____	_____	_____	_____
_____	_____	_____	_____
_____	_____	_____	_____
_____	_____	_____	_____
_____	_____	_____	_____
_____	_____	_____	_____
27. Machinery, fixtures, etc., for business			
_____	_____	_____	_____
_____	_____	_____	_____
_____	_____	_____	_____
_____	_____	_____	_____
_____	_____	_____	_____
_____	_____	_____	_____
_____	_____	_____	_____
_____	_____	_____	_____

1 Property	2 Replacement Value	3 Exemption	4 Statute No.
28. Inventory			
29. Animals			
30. Crops—growing or harvested			
31. Farming equipment, implements			
32. Farm supplies, chemicals, feed			
33. Other personal property of any kind not listed			

Homeowners' Worksheet

Part I. Do you have any equity in your home?

1. Market value of your home ....$_____

2. Costs of sale (if unsure, put 5% of market value)...$_____

3. Amount owed on all mortgages ....$_____

4. Amount of all liens on the property ....$_____

5. Total of Lines 2, 3, and 4..$_____

6. Your equity (Line 1 minus Line 5)...$_____

   If Line 6 is zero or less, skip the rest of the worksheet. The trustee will have no interest in selling your home.

Part II. Is your property protected by an exemption?

7. Does the available homestead exemption protect your kind of dwelling?

   ☐ Yes. Go on to Line 8.

   ☐ No. Enter $0 on Line 11, then continue on to Line 12.

8. Do you have to file a "declaration of homestead" to claim the homestead exemption?

   ☐ Yes, but I have not filed it yet.

   ☐ Yes, and I have already filed it.

   ☐ No.

9. Is the homestead exemption based on lot size?

   ☐ No, it is based on equity alone. Go to Line 10.

   ☐ No, it is unlimited (true only of the exemptions for Washington, DC).

   If you are using the D.C. exemptions, you can stop here. Your home is protected.

   ☐ Yes. The exemption is limited to property of _____ acres.

   If your property is smaller than this limit, you can stop here. Your home is protected. If your property exceeds this limit, see the instructions.

   ☐ Yes, but there is an equity limit as well. The exemption is limited to property of _____ acres.

   If your property is smaller than this limit, go on to Line 10. If your property exceeds this limit, see the instructions.

10. Do you own the property with your spouse in "tenancy by the entirety"?

   ☐ Yes. *See the instructions and talk to a bankruptcy attorney to find out whether your house is fully protected.*

   ☐ No. *Go on to Line 11.*

11. Is the dollar amount of the homestead exemption limited?

   ☐ Yes. *Enter the dollar limit here:* $_____

   ☐ No dollar limit. *You can stop here. Your home is protected.*

12. Can you protect more equity with a wildcard exemption?

    ☐ Yes. *Enter the dollar amount here:* $_____

    ☐ No.

13. How much of your equity is protected?
Total of Lines 11 and 12: $_____

If the total exceeds $155,675 and you are subject to the cap on homestead exemptions, write "$155,675" on this line. See the instructions for more information.

14. Is your home fully protected?
Subtract Line 13 from Line 6: $_____

If this total is a negative number, your home is protected. If this total is a positive number, you have unprotected equity in your home, and the trustee might choose to sell (or allow you to keep it in exchange for cash or exempt property roughly equal in value to your unprotected equity).

Judicial Lien Worksheet

1. Value of your home.. $_____

2. Amount of first mortgage .... $_____

3. Amount of other mortgages and home equity loans......................... $_____

4. Amount of tax liens.. $_____

5. Amount of mechanics' liens .... $_____

6. Total of Lines 2 through 5... $_____
   (Total of all liens that are not judicial liens)

   If Line 6 is greater than Line 1, you can stop here; you can eliminate all judicial liens. Otherwise, go on to Line 7.

7. Line 1 minus Line 6.. $_____
   This is the amount of equity you can protect with an exemption.

8. Exemption amount .... $_____

   If Line 8 is greater than Line 7 you can stop here; you can eliminate all judicial liens. Otherwise, go on to Line 9.

9. Line 7 minus Line 8.. $_____
   This is the amount of the judicial liens that you can't eliminate.

10. Amount of judicial liens... $_____

    If Line 9 is greater than Line 10, you can stop here; you cannot eliminate judicial liens from this property. Otherwise go on to Line 11.

11. Line 10 minus Line 9... $_____

    This is the portion of the judicial lien that you can eliminate. (Line 9 is the portion of judicial lien you cannot eliminate.)

Bankruptcy Forms Checklist

☐ Form 1—Voluntary Petition

☐ Form 3A (if you want to pay your filing fee in installments)

☐ Form 3B (if you apply for a fee waiver)

☐ Form 6A—Schedule A—Real Property

☐ Form 6B—Schedule B—Personal Property

☐ Form 6C—Schedule C—Property Claimed as Exempt

☐ Form 6D—Schedule D—Creditors Holding Secured Claims

☐ Form 6E—Schedule E—Creditors Holding Unsecured Priority Claims

☐ Form 6F—Schedule F—Creditors Holding Unsecured Nonpriority Claims

☐ Form 6G—Schedule G—Executory Contracts and Unexpired Leases

☐ Form 6H—Schedule H—Codebtors

☐ Form 6I—Schedule I—Current Income

☐ Form 6J—Schedule J—Current Expenditures

☐ Form 6—Summary—Summary of Schedules A through J and Statistical Summary of Certain Liabilities

☐ Form 6—Declaration—Declaration Concerning Debtor's Schedules

☐ Form 7—Statement of Financial Affairs

☐ Form 8—Chapter 7 Individual Debtor's Statement of Intention

☐ Form 21—Full Social Security Number Disclosure

☐ Form 22A-1—Statement of Current Monthly Income

☐ Form 22A-1Supp—Statement of Exemption from Presumption of Abuse Under § 707(b)(2)

☐ Form 22A–2—Chapter 7 Means Test Calculation

☐ Form 23—Certification of Instructional Course on Financial Management

☐ Form 201A—Notice to Individual Consumer Debtors

☐ Creditor mailing list

Bankruptcy Documents Checklist

☐ Required local forms, if any

☐ Your most recent federal tax return (or a transcript of the return obtained from the IRS)

☐ Your credit counseling certificate

☐ Any repayment plan that was developed during your credit counseling session

☐ Your pay stubs for the previous 60 days (along with any accompanying form your local court requires)

☐ A certificate of completion for a course in personal financial management

☐ Other documents required by the trustee, if any (for example, bank statements, retirement account statements, deed of trust or mortgage payoff information, car loan statement, car registration, proof of home and car insurance, and documents showing property valuations)

Median Family Income Chart (as of May 15, 2015)

State	Family Size				State	Family Size			
	1 Earner	2 People	3 People	4 People *		1 Earner	2 People	3 People	4 People *
Alabama	$42,041	$50,614	$56,186	$66,442	Montana	$44,789	$55,729	$62,033	$68,711
Alaska	$61,054	$83,489	$87,260	$96,551	Nebraska	$43,135	$61,369	$66,871	$79,634
Arizona	$44,459	$55,116	$58,867	$68,900	Nevada	$43,685	$56,367	$59,346	$69,672
Arkansas	$39,155	$47,780	$52,613	$59,092	New Hampshire	$56,709	$68,757	$83,034	$95,964
California	$49,983	$64,779	$68,917	$79,418	New Jersey	$61,243	$71,994	$90,863	$107,452
Colorado	$52,388	$68,218	$71,976	$86,377	New Mexico	$41,383	$54,251	$54,251	$62,840
Connecticut	$60,549	$73,526	$88,483	$109,102	New York	$49,632	$61,728	$72,869	$89,586
Delaware	$52,524	$62,852	$75,505	$85,545	North Carolina	$41,068	$52,698	$57,703	$70,495
District of Columbia	$49,427	$78,368	$78,368	$78,368	North Dakota	$48,402	$68,111	$77,863	$90,329
Florida	$42,718	$52,421	$57,977	$67,539	Ohio	$43,978	$54,420	$63,142	$78,622
Georgia	$41,650	$53,684	$58,797	$69,170	Oklahoma	$42,218	$53,855	$58,013	$64,448
Hawaii	$62,098	$68,557	$81,990	$89,648	Oregon	$47,055	$58,110	$65,147	$72,668
Idaho	$43,614	$52,631	$56,857	$62,348	Pennsylvania	$48,982	$57,870	$72,866	$85,765
Illinois	$48,239	$62,440	$73,516	$84,901	Rhode Island	$48,516	$63,199	$73,145	$89,823
Indiana	$43,409	$53,935	$62,046	$74,205	South Carolina	$40,632	$51,501	$54,904	$67,641
Iowa	$44,502	$62,095	$68,150	$82,537	South Dakota	$41,083	$58,314	$58,314	$74,275
Kansas	$45,980	$60,577	$66,065	$76,017	Tennessee	$41,642	$50,983	$57,001	$67,930
Kentucky	$42,000	$49,139	$58,552	$69,794	Texas	$42,908	$58,666	$61,502	$71,973
Louisiana	$41,681	$50,078	$58,218	$74,009	Utah	$52,865	$59,546	$67,632	$73,446
Maine	$42,588	$55,147	$62,525	$76,511	Vermont	$47,248	$62,671	$73,735	$83,378
Maryland	$60,440	$77,730	$89,652	$107,091	Virginia	$53,287	$68,108	$76,261	$93,349
Massachusetts	$56,254	$70,803	$87,026	$108,545	Washington	$53,234	$66,869	$75,635	$86,161
Michigan	$45,226	$54,510	$63,995	$77,865	West Virginia	$44,261	$47,415	$54,975	$67,080
Minnesota	$50,934	$66,566	$81,044	$94,807	Wisconsin	$43,666	$59,740	$69,600	$83,686
Mississippi	$35,784	$44,832	$47,339	$59,126	Wyoming	$50,528	$65,126	$76,680	$81,782
Missouri	$42,376	$52,783	$62,110	$72,711	* Add $8,100 for each individual in excess of 4.				

UNITED STATES BANKRUPTCY COURT

_____ DISTRICT OF _____

In re _____)
　　[*Set forth here all names including married,*)
　　maiden, and trade names used by debtor)
　　within last 8 years.])
　　　　　　　　　　　　　Debtor) Case No. _____
　　　　　　　　　　　　　　　　　　)
Address _____)
　　　　　　　　　　　　　　　　　　)
_____) Chapter 7
　　　　　　　　　　　　　　　　　　)
Last four digits of Social Security or Individual)
Taxpayer Identification No(s). (ITIN) (if any): _____)
　　　　　　　　　　　　　　　　　　)
Employer's Tax Identification No(s). (EIN) (if any): _____)
_____)

AMENDMENT COVER SHEET

Presented herewith are the original and one copy of the following:

☐ Voluntary Petition (Note: Spouse may not be added or deleted subsequent to initial filing.)

☐ Schedule A—Real Property

☐ Schedule B—Personal Property

☐ Schedule C—Property Claimed as Exempt

☐ Schedule D—Creditors Holding Secured Claims

☐ Schedule E—Creditors Holding Unsecured Priority Claims

☐ Schedule F—Creditors Holding Unsecured Nonpriority Claims

☐ Schedule G—Executory Contracts and Unexpired Leases

☐ Schedule H—Codebtors

☐ Schedule I—Current Income of Individual Debtor(s)

☐ Schedule J—Current Expenditures of Individual Debtor(s)

☐ Summary of Schedules

☐ Statement of Financial Affairs

☐ I have enclosed a $30 fee because I am adding new creditors or changing addresses after the original Meeting of
　　Creditors Notice has been sent.

_____　　　　　_____
Signature of Debtor　　　　　　　　　　　　Signature of Debtor's Spouse

I (we) _____ and _____ ,

the debtor(s) in this case, declare under penalty of perjury that the information set forth in the amendment attached

hereto consisting of ____ pages is true and correct to the best of my (our) information and belief.

Dated: _____ , 20 _____

_____　　　　　_____
Signature of Debtor　　　　　　　　　　　　Signature of Debtor's Spouse

UNITED STATES BANKRUPTCY COURT

_____ DISTRICT OF _____

In re _____)
      [Set forth here all names including married,)
      maiden, and trade names used by debtor)
      within last 8 years.])
                          Debtor) Case No. _____
)
Address _____)
)
_____) Chapter 7
)
Last four digits of Social Security or Individual)
Taxpayer Identification No(s). (ITIN) (if any): _____)
)
Employer's Tax Identification No(s). (EIN) (if any): _____)
_____)

NOTICE OF CHANGE OF ADDRESS

MY (OUR) FORMER MAILING ADDRESS AND PHONE NUMBER WAS:

Name: _____

Street: _____

City: _____

State/Zip: _____

Phone: (_____) _____

PLEASE BE ADVISED THAT AS OF _____ , 20_____ , MY (OUR) NEW MAILING
ADDRESS AND PHONE NUMBER IS:

Name: _____

Street: _____

City: _____

State/Zip: _____

Phone: (_____) _____

_____
Signature of Debtor

_____
Signature of Debtor's Spouse

UNITED STATES BANKRUPTCY COURT

DISTRICT OF _____

In re _____)
    [Set forth here all names including married,)
    maiden, and trade names used by debtor)
    within last 8 years.])
                        Debtor) Case No. _____

Address _____)

_____) Chapter 7

)

Last four digits of Social Security or Individual)
Taxpayer Identification No(s). (ITIN) (if any): _____)

Employer's Tax Identification No(s). (EIN) (if any): _____)
_____)

SUPPLEMENTAL SCHEDULE FOR PROPERTY
ACQUIRED AFTER BANKRUPTCY DISCHARGE

TO: _____ , Trustee

This is to inform you that I (we) have received the following item of property since my (our) discharge but within the 180-day period after filing my (our) Bankruptcy Petition under Bankruptcy Rule 1007(h):

_____

_____

This property was obtained through an inheritance, marital settlement agreement or divorce decree, death benefits or life insurance proceeds, or other (specify):

_____

_____

☐ I (we) claim this property exempt under the following law:

_____

_____

I (we) _____ and
_____ , the debtor(s) in
this case, declare under penalty of perjury that the foregoing is true and correct.

Dated: _____ , 20 ____   _____
                                                Signature of Debtor

                                                _____
                                                Signature of Debtor's Spouse

UNITED STATES BANKRUPTCY COURT

_____ DISTRICT OF _____

In re _____)
    [*Set forth here all names including married,*)
    maiden, and trade names used by debtor)
    within last 8 years.])
                        Debtor) Case No. _____
)

Address _____)
_____) Chapter 7
)

Last four digits of Social Security or Individual)
Taxpayer Identification No(s). (ITIN) (if any): _____)
)
Employer's Tax Identification No(s). (EIN) (if any): _____)
_____)

PROOF OF SERVICE BY MAIL

I, _____ , declare that: I am a

resident or employed in the County of _____ , State of _____ .

My residence/business address is_____

_____ . I am over the age of eighteen years and not a party to this case.

On _____ , 20____ , I served the enclosed _____

_____

on the following parties by placing true and correct copies thereof enclosed in a sealed envelope with postage thereon fully

prepaid in the United States Mail at _____ , addressed as follows:

I declare under penalty of perjury that the foregoing is true and correct, and that this declaration was executed on

Date: _____ , 20 ____ at _____
                                                      City and State

_____
               Signature

1
2
3
4
5
6
7
8
9
10
11
12
13
14
15
16
17
18
19
20
21
22
23
24
25
26
27
28

Index

W

⚖ NOLO   *Online Legal Forms*

Nolo offers a large library of legal solutions and forms, created by Nolo's in-house legal staff. These reliable documents can be prepared in minutes.

Create a Document

- **Incorporation.** Incorporate your business in any state.
- **LLC Formations.** Gain asset protection and pass-through tax status in any state.
- **Wills.** Nolo has helped people make over 2 million wills. Is it time to make or revise yours?
- **Living Trust (avoid probate).** Plan now to save your family the cost, delays, and hassle of probate.
- **Trademark.** Protect the name of your business or product.
- **Provisional Patent.** Preserve your rights under patent law and claim "patent pending" status.

Download a Legal Form

Nolo.com has hundreds of top quality legal forms available for download—bills of sale, promissory notes, nondisclosure agreements, LLC operating agreements, corporate minutes, commercial lease and sublease, motor vehicle bill of sale, consignment agreements and many, many more.

Review Your Documents

Many lawyers in Nolo's consumer-friendly lawyer directory will review Nolo documents for a very reasonable fee. Check their detailed profiles at **Nolo.com/lawyers**.

NOLO *Save 15%* *off your next order*

Register your Nolo purchase, and we'll send you a **coupon for 15% off** your next Nolo.com order!

Nolo.com/customer-support/productregistration

On Nolo.com you'll also find:

Books & Software
Nolo publishes hundreds of great books and software programs for consumers and business owners. Order a copy, or download an ebook version instantly, at Nolo.com.

Online Legal Documents
You can quickly and easily make a will or living trust, form an LLC or corporation, apply for a trademark or provisional patent, or make hundreds of other forms—online.

Free Legal Information
Thousands of articles answer common questions about everyday legal issues including wills, bankruptcy, small business formation, divorce, patents, employment, and much more.

Plain-English Legal Dictionary
Stumped by jargon? Look it up in America's most up-to-date source for definitions of legal terms, free at nolo.com.

Lawyer Directory
Nolo's consumer-friendly lawyer directory provides in-depth profiles of lawyers all over America. You'll find all the information you need to choose the right lawyer.

HFB19